Relax.

You've opened the right book.

Once upon a time, people were wrong. They thought the automobile was an electric death-trap that would never replace the buggy, the Internet was only for academic shut-ins, and people who used study guides were simply *cheaters*. Then cars stopped exploding every time you started the engine, people realized you could use computers for more than just calculating the digits of *pi*, and the "cheaters" with the study guides... well, they started getting it. They got better grades, got into better schools, and just plain ol' got better. Times change. Rules change. *You snooze, you lose, buggy-drivers.*

SparkNotes is different. We've always been thinking ahead. We were the first study guides on the Internet back in 1999— you've been to SparkNotes.com haven't you? If not... Why!? This book might be posted online for free! You'll also find busy message boards, diagnostic test-prep, and all kinds of the tools you'll need to get your act together and your grades up. And if your act's already together, SparkNotes will help you brutalize the competition. Or work for peace. Your call.

We're inexpensive, not cheap. Not only are our books the best bang for the buck, they're the best bang, period. Our reputation is based on staying smart and trustworthy—one step ahead, making tough topics understandable. We explain, we strategize, we translate. We get you where you want to go: smarter, better, faster than anyone else.

If you've got something to say, tell us. Your input makes us better. Found a mistake? Check www.sparknotes.com/errors. Have a comment? Go to www.sparknotes.com/comments. Did you read all the way to the bottom? Awesome. We love you. You're gonna do just fine.

the new SAT

& PSAT

by Justin Kestler and Ben Florman
CREATORS OF SPARKNOTES

A Division of Barnes & Noble Publishing

Spark Educational Publishing
A Division of Barnes & Noble Publishing
120 Fifth Avenue
New York, NY 10011

Please submit all comments and questions or report errors to www.sparknotes.com/errors.

Printed and bound in Canada.

ISBN 1-4114-0150-6

CONTENTS

The Writing Section 33

The Critical Reading Section . 129

The Math Section. 209

ACKNOWLEDGMENTS

We would like to thank everyone at SparkNotes for their support and dedication throughout this project. We especially want to thank Laurie Barnett for her editorial wisdom and guidance and Dan Visel for making the production of this book possible.

THE UNIVERSAL LAW OF THE SAT

EVERY YEAR DEBATES CONTINUE TO RAGE ABOUT THE SAT. Is it fair? Is it biased? Is it an achievement or an aptitude test? Is it good? Is it evil? Does it measure intelligence? Does it measure anything? Does it predict how well you'll do in college, or in life?

These questions come up every year for one good reason: Nobody can answer them. (If you can answer them once and for all, you get to skip college entirely.) But there is *one* thing, and one thing only, that the SAT does predict accurately. We call this the Universal Law of the SAT:

Anyone who mentions SAT scores after graduating high school is a loser.

Once you're in college, you're never going to talk about the SAT again. It's that simple. It won't determine where you live, whom you marry, or whether or not people think you're smart. The people you meet and how well you do in college will have much more of an impact on the rest of your life than a test you take one Saturday in high school.

But you haven't made it to college yet. That's why we wrote this book: to help you face the SAT without fear, get into the college of your choice, and never have to talk about the SAT again.

—Ben and Justin

HOW TO USE THIS BOOK

THE BEST WAY TO BEAT THE NEW SAT IS TO READ THIS book from beginning to end, and then to take and study practice tests right up until a few days before the test.

But many of you may not have the time for such extensive SAT preparation, or you just may not want to work so rigorously. Fear not! This book is still for you, and you can still use it to raise your scores.

For those of you who want to fast-track your prep time, we've come up with a three-step process and a Hit List of essential SAT strategies that will make your study time as focused and efficient as possible. Here are the three steps, followed by the Hit List:

1. **Read the Hit List.** The pages we specify in each chapter teach you the strategies you need to know for the SAT in general and each question type in particular.
2. **Take the Practice Tests at the back of this book.** Use our specially coded headings on each answer explanation to pinpoint your weaknesses.
3. **Review and overcome your weaknesses.** Use the review sections of this book to learn the material with which you need help.

THE HIT LIST

Beat the New SAT

- SAT Strategies, page 21
- The SAT Personal Trainer, page 27

The Writing Section

- Beat the Essay, page 39
- Beat Identifying Sentence Errors, page 79
- Beat Improving Sentences, page 63
- Beat Improving Paragraphs, page 101

The Critical Reading Section

- Beat Sentence Completions, page 135
- Reading Passages: The Long and Short of It, page 157
- Reading Passages: The Long of It, page 161
- Reading Passages: The Short of It, page 175
- New SAT Vocabulary, page 181

The Math Section

MEET THE NEW SAT

THE SAT RELOADED

IN 1926, WHEN A SMALL GROUP OF STUDENTS SAT DOWN to take the first SAT, the letters S-A-T stood for Scholastic Aptitude Test. Back then, everybody thought the SAT could accurately predict each person's innate intelligence. The test was supposedly uncoachable, making preparation of any kind unnecessary. In 1994, the people who write the SAT backed off of the claim that the test measures aptitude and began to call it the Standardized Assessment Test. Slowly, quietly, even the words *Standardized Assessment Test* fell out of use. In 1996, the SAT people sought to clear up the confusion in a press release that declared, once and for all, "SAT is not an initialism; it does not stand for anything." So there you have it, straight from the source:

The SAT stands for nothing.

But that hasn't stopped the test. Now the SAT has undergone the most extensive changes in its 75-year history. A whole new Writing section has been added to the test, analogies have been cut, tougher math concepts have been added, quantitative comparisons are gone, and the entire test is now scored on a scale of 2400 instead of the infamous 1600.

How do you prepare for this radically new test disguised under a familiar old meaningless name? Read this book. All the facts, strategies, and study methods you need to meet and beat the new SAT lie between these two covers.

the new SAT

THE NEW SAT

Like many people in America's image-obsessed culture, the old SAT didn't think it was up to snuff. So it went under the knife, Michael Jackson–style. A nip here, a tuck there—and wham!—you've got a whole new test. The SAT doctors performed four major surgeries to make the old test new:

The SAT Extreme Makeover

PROCEDURE	STUFF ADDED	STUFF CUT	STUFF KEPT
The Verbal Face Lift	Short Reading Comp; name changed to "Critical Reading"	Analogies	Everything else
The Math Nose Job	Algebra II content	Quantitative Comparisons	Everything else
The Writing Transplant	All new section, with an essay and multiple-choice questions on grammar	All new section	All new section
SAT Enlargement Surgery: Length and Score	45 minutes longer; perfect score now 2400	1600 no longer a perfect score	A better shot at 1600

That's the summary of the changes to the test. Here's a little more detail about what the test looks like now that the bandages are off.

Just the Facts

The new SAT is 3 hours and 45 minutes long. It covers three major topics—Critical Reading, Math, and Writing—divided into seven timed sections. Each section is graded on a scale from 200–800, and a perfect score is a 2400.

The New Critical Reading Section

The former SAT Verbal section has been replaced and renamed "Critical Reading."

- **70 minutes in three timed sections.** The new SAT tests Critical Reading for 70 minutes divided across three timed sections: two 25-minute sections and one 20-minute section.
- **67 Questions that come in three types.** The Critical Reading section contains a total of 67 questions broken into three question types. It has 19 Sentence Completions, 8 Reading Comprehension questions about short paragraphs (100 words), and 40 Reading Comprehension questions about longer passages (500–800 words).
- **Critical Reading Skills.** Unlike the old Verbal section, which was basically a glorified vocabulary test, the Critical Reading section really does test reading skills.

We provide much more detail about the three Critical Reading sections and the questions they contain in the chapter devoted to Critical Reading later in this book.

The New Math Section

Here are the basic facts of the new SAT Math section.

- **70 minutes in three timed sections**. Math on the new SAT is tested for 70 minutes in three timed sections: two 25-minute sections and one 20-minute section.
- **54 questions that come in two types**. The Math section contains 54 total questions. Those questions are divided into two types: 44 multiple-choice questions and 10 grid-in questions. Quantitative Comparisons have been cut.
- **New math topics**. Math questions cover topics in basic numbers and operations, algebra, geometry, and data analysis. The algebra in the new SAT now includes a bunch of topics from Algebra II.

We'll give you more detail about the three Math sections and all the topics and types of questions they contain in the chapter devoted to Math later in this book.

The New Writing Section

The Writing section is the one everybody's talking about. An essay! Grammar! Aaargh! But, actually, it's just as beatable as every other part of the new SAT.

- **60 minutes in three timed sections**. Writing on the new SAT will be tested in three timed sections. In one section, you will be given 25 minutes to write an essay. The other two sections contain only multiple choice questions. One is 25 minutes, and the other is 10 minutes long.
- **One essay topic**. For the essay, you'll have to take and justify a stance on a broad topic. You won't have a choice of topics.
- **49 Multiple-choice questions**. The Writing section contains three types of multiple-choice questions that make up a total of 49 questions: 25 Improving Sentences, 18 Identifying Sentence Errors, and 6 Improving Paragraphs.
- **Writing skills**. The essay and the multiple-choice questions test both your writing skills and your understanding of grammar and language usage.

We'll teach you everything you need to know about the three timed Writing sections and the essay and questions they contain in the chapter devoted to Writing later in this book.

The "Variable" Section

In addition to the three Writing, three Critical Reading, and three Math sections, the new SAT also contains a tenth section. This section is a 25-minute "Variable" section. The Variable section doesn't actually count toward your final score on the new SAT. In fact, it's in the test just so that the test-makers can try out some of their new questions on you.

We know what you're thinking: It would be nice if you could figure out exactly which section was the Variable section and, since it doesn't count toward your score, just blow it off during the test. You can't do that. The Variable section will look exactly like one of the other 25-minute sections on the test, so don't go guessing which section is the Variable section. You could very easily guess wrong. You need to treat every single section of the test as if it counts.

1.2   KNOW THE SCORE

This heading sounds like the title of a lame test-prep book. But you do need to know how the questions you get right and wrong impact your overall SAT score. Let's say you take the new SAT. You get some questions right and some questions wrong, and then you end up with some odd-looking score like 2150. How did you get from there to here? Through a two-step process. First, the SAT calculates what's called the *raw score*. Then, based on everyone's results, the scorers work out a curve, feed your raw score into a computer, and out pops your *scaled score*. Here's some more detail on what each score means and how the raw and scaled scores relate to each other.

The Raw Score

There are only three ways to answer every multiple-choice question on the SAT. Your raw score is affected differently depending on which of the following three things you do on each question:

- **Get it right**: You get 1 raw point.
- **Get it wrong**: You lose .25 of a point.
- **Leave it blank**: You get 0 points.

That means your raw score for each section of the test equals the number of questions you answer correctly minus the one quarter of the questions you answer incorrectly.

$$\text{Raw Score } = \text{ Number Correct} - \frac{\text{Number Incorrect}}{4}$$

These are the fundamentals of the raw score. There are, however, a few quirks and exceptions to the raw score calculation for each of the three major sections on the new SAT. We cover those quirks in the chapters dedicated to each major section: Writing, Critical Reading, and Math.

The Scaled Score

The scaled score takes your raw score and converts it into 200 to 800 points for each section. Since the new SAT has three sections of equal weight, 2400 is the perfect scaled score on the new SAT.

The scaled score follows a curve like the standard bell curve, but it is shifted a little so that more students get 800s than get 200s. The average score on the three sections of the test is a little over 500. So the average score on the new SAT is about 1520.

The practice tests at the end of this book come with a chart that shows you how to translate your raw score into a scaled score.

SAT Scores and College Admissions

Time for a little perspective. Your SAT scores *are* important, but they're not the *only* part of your application that a college considers. Colleges also look at high school grades, course load, extracurricular activities, application essays, letters of recommendation, SAT II tests, and Advanced Placement tests. If you've got stellar grades, excellent extracurriculars, and letters of recommendation that compare your leadership abilities to George Washington's, mediocre SAT scores won't destroy your chances of acceptance. Similarly, excellent SAT scores won't secure you a spot in a top-ranked school if you took easy classes, wrote lame application essays, and didn't participate in any extracurricular activities. A college is more likely to admit an exciting, vibrant, well-rounded student with lots of extracurriculars than a kid who scored 50 points higher on the SAT but did no extracurriculars and shows no leadership skills.

To sum up, there's no question that an SAT score above a college's average will help your chances, while below-average scores will hurt. This is especially true at larger schools, where admissions committees have less time to devote to each individual application. Big schools are more likely to use SAT scores as a cutoff to whittle down their applicant pool before taking a good hard look at entire applications.

1.3 THE NEW PSAT

Like the SAT, the PSAT has been made new. In fact, the changes to the PSAT have already come into effect: the first new PSAT was given in October 2004. Yet while some of the changes made to the new PSAT are identical to those for the new SAT, some are not. Here's a summary:

- The Verbal section has been renamed "Critical Reading." It's the same length in time as the Verbal in the old PSAT (50 minutes divided into two 25-minute sections). Analogies have been eliminated and short reading comprehension questions added.
- The length of the Math section is unchanged—50 minutes divided into two 25-minute sections. Quantitative Comparison questions have been cut, and two additional grid-in questions have been added. (Don't worry if you don't know what a "grid-in" is; we cover that later.) The Math section includes some new and more difficult material.
- The PSAT already had a Writing section, so there isn't such a big change there. The new PSAT contains one 30-minute section that features multiple-choice questions, just like the old PSAT did. The new PSAT does *not* contain a scored essay, though it gives high schools the option of letting students write an essay for practice.

The long and short of it is that you can definitely use this book to prepare for the PSAT. Just ignore the part of our chapter on the Writing Section that covers the essay.

Many important scholarships, including the National Merit Scholarships, use PSAT scores as a way to evaluate students. That means the PSAT can be a very important part of your college application. If you're interested in finding out more about possible scholarships in general, or the National Merit Scholarship in particular, you should talk to your high school counselor.

1.4 THE NEW SAT AND SAT IIS

The SAT IIs are not affected by the change in the SAT, with one exception. The current SAT II Writing test will be eliminated in March 2005, when students take the new SAT for the first time. This makes sense. The new SAT Writing section is based closely on the SAT II Writing test, so why should you have to take the same test twice?

Otherwise, every other SAT II test will remain the same, and many colleges will still require you to take three different SAT IIs.

1.5 THE NEW SAT FAQ

Over the years at SparkNotes, we've read thousands of questions from students about the SAT. In the last few months, a flood of questions about the new SAT has overwhelmed us and threatened to drown the entire staff. To put a stop to this madness, we've compiled the answers to some of the most frequently asked questions students have about the new SAT.

Why do I have to take the SAT at all?

Admit it. You've asked yourself this question. Everyone has. Well, there's a quick and easy answer to that one:

Colleges make you.

If you want to go to college, you pretty much have to take the SAT (or the ACT; we cover that in this FAQ too).

But *why* do colleges put you through this ordeal? Why do they require you to take the SAT? Two reasons:

1. **Colleges consider the SAT a standard by which they can evaluate students from high schools across the country.** Imagine you're a university admissions officer considering the applications of two students, Justin and Ben. Both of these students have A averages, but Justin goes to Grade-Inflation High, whereas Ben goes to Impossible Polytechnic. How are you, the admissions officer, supposed to know that Ben's A is so much better than Justin's? That's where the SAT comes in. Ben and Justin may go to different high schools, but when they take the SAT, they're taking the same standardized test. So colleges can use the SAT as a tool to measure *all* students against each other without worrying about differences in their schools.

2. **Colleges have considered SAT scores valuable in predicting how students will perform in the first semester of college.** This reason is much more controversial. A ton of data has been thrown back and forth over the years about whether the SAT can effectively predict first semester grades, but the truth is, nobody knows. What we can't understand is why anyone cares so much about predicting first-semester grades. Sure, they're important, but shouldn't the focus be on grades throughout all four years of college? And nobody claimed that the old SAT could (or that the new SAT will) predict college grades over all four years.

Why did they change the SAT?

The official line is that the College Board, the organization behind the SAT, made the change to the new SAT for three reasons:

1. To better align the SAT to the curricula of high schools.
2. To provide a third measure—writing skills—that will help colleges make better admissions decisions.
3. To reinforce the importance of writing in education.

Okay, beautiful. Now, there's a fourth reason why the College Board switched from the old SAT to the new SAT:

4. They had to.

Here's what happened: the University of California system of schools began to criticize the old SAT because it focused more on memorization of vocabulary than on actual writing or reading skills. The University of California is the biggest client of the College Board. If the University of California had switched to another test, say the ACT, the SAT and all the money it brings in to the College Board might have slowly disappeared. Well, you know what happened next. The old SAT became the new SAT, which does indeed focus much more on reading and writing skills.

What's the ACT?

We've mentioned the ACT a couple of times now, but haven't discussed it in detail. Here's the detail. The ACT is a competitor of the SAT. Many people have argued that the ACT is actually a better test than the SAT, and, in fact, most of the changes made to create the new SAT actually made the SAT more like the ACT.

While the SAT dominates the national discussion of standardized tests for college admission, only slightly fewer students take the ACT each year than take the SAT. An increasing number of colleges around the country have begun to accept ACT scores from applicants, either in addition to SAT scores or instead of them. In general, colleges on the east and west coasts accept the SAT, while colleges in the middle of the country accept just the ACT, or both tests. But don't just assume the colleges you're applying to fit the general mold. Be certain which schools you're considering applying to require (or prefer) the SAT or the ACT.

To decide which test is right for you, you should do two things:

1. Find out whether the colleges to which you're applying require one test rather than the other test. Confirm this by speaking to representatives from the college.

2. If it doesn't matter which test you take, decide which test is better suited to your skills and will likely result in a better score. To do this, take one SAT practice test and one ACT practice test, and compare the results both in terms of how well you score and how suited you feel to the skills that the test tests.

If you'd like more information on the ACT, check out *SparkNotes: The New ACT*.

What's a good score on the new SAT?

There's no one "good" score on the SAT. A good score is different for different people. Think back to why you take the SAT. Because colleges make you. So a good score is a score that gets you into the college of your choice. Want to go to Yale? You have to shoot for at least a 2100. Interested in UCLA? You're probably looking for a 1900 or higher. Only concerned about athletic eligibility? You're looking to score more in the 1200 to 1300 range. An average score on the new SAT is somewhere around a 1520.

Having score goals and sticking to them is crucial for the new SAT. Why? Because your strategy for taking the test will differ depending on what score you need. So do some research. Check out the projected average new SAT scores of the schools you want to attend. Talk to a guidance counselor at your school. Get a clear sense of what your goals are, and then use this book to go after them.

Will the new SAT give some students an unfair advantage?

This one's tough to answer. The new SAT's changes are so significant that it's difficult for anyone to map out all of the new test's ramifications. The changes may have unintended consequences, and people won't even agree on what they are for years, if ever. That we guarantee.

For now, here's a stab at what we think might happen and who might benefit:

- **Math Whizzes vs. Literary Stars**: Since the new SAT includes a new Writing section, it's likely that students with stronger verbal skills will score proportionally higher than they would have on the old SAT. Meet Kid Math. She's the fastest number-slinger this side of the Mississippi but a bit of a bumbler when it comes to words. She got a 400 Verbal, 800 Math on the old

the new SAT

SAT. On the new SAT, she will likely get roughly a 400 Critical Reading, 400 Writing, and 800 Math, for a total score of 1600. (We're assuming Verbal scores will translate similarly to Writing and Critical Reading scores.) Now imagine Kid Verbal, who got an 800 Verbal and 400 Math on the old SAT. He could anticipate an 800 Critical Reading, 800 Writing, and 400 Math on the new SAT, for a total of 2000. A huge difference in total score, right? True, but these big differences look much bigger than they really are. Most college admission officers look at your individual scores on each test section. If they're looking for a math whiz, Kid Math still has the advantage. To sum it all up: If anyone gains an advantage from the new SAT, it'll be the literary stars, but we don't think that advantage will have much impact on actual college admissions. The lit stars might have higher SAT scores to brag about at college, but that'll just make them bigger losers.

- **Guys vs. Girls**: The SAT has almost always failed to predict accurately how women will do in college. Girls generally perform better than guys in their first year at college, but guys generally outperform girls on the SAT. The new SAT may begin to turn the tables. Girls have generally outperformed boys on the SAT II Writing test, so the inclusion of a Writing section on the new SAT may balance out overall scores. This may have some very slight effect on college admissions. It's possible that evening out the gender gap will help a few more girls get into colleges, but once again, we don't think this is going to change the admissions landscape very much.

- **Socioeconomic and Racial Issues**: The SAT was purely meant to test aptitude, or at least that was the intention from the start. It was intended to be unbiased with regard to background or education. Then they started using words like *regatta*, which nobody in the world knew except a bunch of rich kids in yacht clubs. Test-takers from poorer families and from African-American and Latino families have generally underperformed on the SAT. We just can't see how the new SAT could possibly resolve this problem. Its two most significant changes—the addition of the Writing section and tougher math—look like they'll only exacerbate the scoring gap. The SAT II Writing test has the second largest score gap between whites and Asians, and African-Americans and Latinos. And many schools in underprivileged communities in which African-Americans and Latinos make up the majority may not have the funding or the resources to teach high school juniors the algebra II math material that the new SAT covers.

These are just our predictions. We've thought long and hard about these issues, but we'll be the first to admit that we can't imagine all of the consequences of the new SAT. And since all of these predictions are so speculative, there's no use worrying too much about any of this. Why? Two reasons:

- There's not much you can do about it.
- You can definitely still prepare for the test and boost your score.

When should I take the new SAT?

Most students take the SAT for the first time in the spring of their junior year—that means either in March or in May. Depending on their scores, many students then decide to take the test again in the first semester of their senior year. If you're planning to take the test a second time, *make sure* you take it early enough so that your scores will reach colleges before the application deadline passes. If you're taking the test senior year, you should take it in either October or November to be certain nothing goes awry. The December date is often too late. So check with the schools to which you are applying and make sure that you're on track to take the test by the correct date.

Will the new SAT cost more?

As much as it pains us to say it, yes. It cost $28.50 to register for the old SAT. For the new SAT, it'll cost about 12 bucks more. Why the rise in cost? To cover the expenses of hiring all those teachers to grade all the new SAT essays.

The SAT does offer a fee waiver program to help students who might have difficulty meeting the fee requirements for the SAT. To find out if you're eligible for the fee waiver program, talk to your high school counselor.

How do I register?

There are two ways to register for the test: online or by mail. To register online, go to the website www.collegeboard.com and follow the directions there. Just know that you can't register online if you're under 13 years old, if you want to take the test on a Sunday (as opposed to a Saturday), or if you're planning on taking the test in Kenya. We're not making this up.

To register by mail, you'll first have to pick up an SAT *Registration Bulletin* from your school counselor's office. In this packet you'll find a registration form and a return envelope. Complete the form and send it in the return envelope along with the proper payment (in check or money order).

How can I raise my score on the new SAT?

Now that's a helluva question. Here's a helluva answer: Use this book.

BEAT THE NEW SAT

THE DISCIPLINE OF DISCIPLINE

BACK IN THE DAY, THE SAT CLAIMED TO BE IMPERVIOUS to studying, coaching, or preparation of any sort. Now the same people who write the test offer their own test-prep books. How times have changed.

The message is clear. You *can* prepare for the SAT. And the more you prepare, the more you'll boost your score. That's good news because it means your score and your future are in your own hands. But it's going to be tough to sit down and train for the SAT when you've got countless diversions tempting you at all times. And studying for the SAT isn't like studying for school: There's no teacher to scold you or give you a D. Getting yourself to do the work is up to you. But there *are* ways to make yourself more disciplined.

SET A TARGET SCORE

Concrete goals are better than vague hopes. Here's a vague hope: "I want to do really well on the SAT." Okay. Go study everything. In contrast, here's a concrete goal: "I want to raise my score on the SAT Math section by 40 points." If you want to raise your score on the SAT Math section by 40 points, you have to take the following three steps:

- Study the particular math concepts that give you trouble.
- Leave fewer questions blank.
- Pick up your pace.

Concrete goals allow you to come up with a specific plan. This will make the time you spend preparing for the SAT much more efficient, leaving you more time to enjoy your life.

When setting a target score, be honest and realistic. Base your target score on the range the schools you want to go to will expect. A good target score should be 50 to 100 points above the average for those schools. You can also gauge your target score by your first practice test. If you score a 500 on the Math section of the first practice test, don't set your target score at 750. You'll just get frustrated and you won't know where to focus your preparation time. Instead, your target should be about 50 points higher on each section than your score on your first practice test. That may not seem like much, but 50 points on each section of the test will raise your total score by 150 points!

The target score you choose plays a major role in your test-taking strategy. We explain how target scores affect strategy in "SAT Strategies" (on page 21).

If You Reach Your Target Score . . .

Give yourself a cookie or, if you're a health freak, a carrot. But just because you've hit your target score doesn't mean you should stop working. In fact, you should view reaching your target score as proof that you can do better than that score: Set a new target 50 to 100 points above your original, pick up your pace a little bit, and skip fewer questions.

Slow and steady wins the race and beats the test. By working to improve bit by bit, you'll integrate your knowledge of how to take the test and the subjects the test covers without burning out. If you can handle working just a little faster without becoming careless and losing points, your score will certainly go up. If you meet your new target score again, rinse and repeat.

SCHEDULE YOUR SAT STUDY TIME

You should treat your SAT prep time like you would every other set-in-stone extra-curricular activity you pursue. We know studying for the SAT will never be as thrilling as soccer practice, the school newspaper, student government, or actually, anything else at all. That's precisely *why* you need to schedule a set time for SAT studying.

Once you've scheduled your SAT time, studying won't seem like an evil intruder robbing you of an otherwise happy life. You can schedule your life around the time you've set aside to study. It's also a good idea to set up a place to study. This means somewhere quiet and out of the way, where televisions, computers, friends, siblings, and other distractors do not thrive. You may even drag yourself into the nearest public library. Point is, do whatever it takes to find a time and place to fit the SAT into your life.

2.3 USE YOUR PARENTS

The SAT gives you the chance to use your parents' nagging to your own advantage. If you really don't think you can force yourself to study on your own, make your study schedule public and ask your parents to enforce it. It may sound like a brutal last resort, but desperate times call for desperate measures.

2.4 STUDY WITH YOUR FRIENDS

Studying for the SAT with friends will make studying more bearable, so you're more likely to do it. And with a friend, you can work on tough concepts together, compare strategies, and occasionally gossip. Working with another person can help your memory too, since you're less likely to space out without realizing it.

2.5 STUDY NOW OR PERISH LATER

If you don't study for the SAT now, you won't get the score you want on the test. Then you'll have to take it again, and then you'll have to study and panic at the same time.

Back before we got involved with SparkNotes, we were both professional boxers.[*] Our coach used to tell us, "Son(s), you gotta get in, get hit, and get out." That's just what you want to do to the SAT. Get in the habit of studying furiously, hit the SAT hard on test day, and get out of there with the score you want. Then you won't have to think about the SAT ever again. No rematch. NEVER.

2.6 SPARKNOTES ONLINE TEST PREP

You didn't think SparkNotes would forget about the Web, did you? The internet access card that's bound into this book comes with a code that grants you access to SparkNotes' Online Test Prep for the SAT. SparkNotes' SAT website provides the following features:

- An **essay grading service** that offers a grade and analysis for the essay questions contained in this book. SparkNotes will grade your first essay for free.
- The three practice tests in this book, backed by **diagnostic software** that immediately analyzes your results and directs your study for efficiency and effectiveness.
- The **entire book, fully searchable**, with all the latest **updates** to keep you up to speed.

In addition to the SAT, SparkNotes Online Test Prep also covers the ACT and the most popular SAT II tests. And once you've bought this book, you can get access to the test prep for any of those other tests for $4.95, about ten dollars less than it would cost you to buy the book.

---

[*]   A total lie.

the new SAT

THE TEN SAT COMMANDMENTS

Our ten SAT commandments may seem obvious, but breaking any of them can undermine an otherwise perfect preparation and testing strategy. The Commandments are about the basics, the simple fundamental SAT laws that you need to get right before you learn all the test-preparation and strategy stuff that fills up the rest of this book. Here they are:

1. Thou shalt go to the correct test center.
2. Thou shalt bring lots of no. 2 pencils.
3. Thou shalt check your calculator batteries.
4. Thou shalt be careful filling in your answers.
5. Thou shalt know the instructions for each section.
6. Thou shalt use your test booklet as scratch paper.
7. Thou shalt answer easy questions first.
8. Thou shalt avoid carelessness.
9. Thou shalt bring bread and water.
10. Thou shalt relax!

1. Thou shalt go to the correct test center.

When you register for the SAT, you'll register to take the test at a particular test center. Make sure you go to the correct center on test day. If you go to the wrong one, you'll be put on a standby list, just like at the airport. If any free seats remain, you'll be able to take the test. But if not, you won't. (Yes, people really do make this kind of error: Ben, co-author of this fine book, actually managed to go to the wrong test center for his SAT. There were two test centers in his hometown, and he went to the wrong one. He got lucky and got a standby seat.)

2. Thou shalt bring lots of no. 2 pencils.

Zero pencils is not enough. One pencil is not enough. Two pencils is not enough because pencils break easily, and you don't want to waste time sharpening. Three pencils, minimum, is enough. But why stop there? Bring five. Bring ten! You could always share them with your desperate, broken-penciled friends.

3. Thou shalt check your calculator batteries.

True, the chances are low that your calculator will give out on you during the test. But do you really want to take that chance? Think of the embarrassment. Think of your brutally lower math scores. Think of Justin's cousin Jeff, whose calculator died mid-SAT, forcing him to abandon his score sheet and to retake the test on the day of his sister's college graduation. This particular type of SAT tragedy can be avoided. Get a new calculator, or get new batteries.

4. Thou shalt be careful filling in your answers.

The SAT scoring computer is an unintelligent, merciless machine. It has no soul. If you answered a question correctly, but somehow made a mistake in marking your answer grid, the computer will mark that question wrong. If you manage to skip question 5, but put the answer to question 6 in row 5, and the answer to question 7 in row 6, and so on, thereby throwing off your answers for an entire section . . . well, that's why humans invented the word *catastrophe*.

It's amazing how often this happens under the time pressures of the SAT. But there's a foolproof method to ensure it doesn't happen to you: Talk to yourself. As you fill in the answer sheet, say to yourself: "number 23, B; number 24, E; number 25, A." But do it quietly. You don't want to give your answers to the entire room.

5. Thou shalt know the instructions for each section.

The SAT is a timed test, and every second counts. Why waste time reading the instructions when you can know them inside out before the test? Just know what they say and what you have to do for each type of question on the test. Then you can skip right over them on the real test.

6. Thou shalt use your test booklet as scratch paper.

For some reason, certain students seem to think they have to keep their test booklets clean and pretty. You don't. When you finish taking the SAT, your test booklet is thrown away, recycled, and used to make egg cartons. So write all over that thing. Cross out answer choices. Mark questions you want to skip and come back to. Underline important statements. Draw sketches. Write equations. Thinking through problems, especially math problems, is easier when you have something to look at.

But, because the SAT is a timed test, and since your work doesn't matter, there's no reason to do *more* work than necessary to solve a problem. Speed matters on the SAT, so don't try to impress the test with excellent work. Do only what you have to do to ensure that you get the right answer.

7. Thou shalt answer easy questions first.

You're allowed to skip around within any timed section on the test. So if you're in the first Critical Reading section of the test, you could skip between Sentence Completions, short Reading Comps, and long Reading Comps. And since all questions, easy or hard, are worth the same number of points regardless of difficulty, it makes sense to answer the questions you find easier first and save the more time-consuming, difficult questions for later. This way you'll be sure to accumulate as many points as possible. You'll also make sure that you've at least glanced at every question on the test and aren't giving away points.

While taking seven minutes to solve a particularly nasty Sentence Completion may feel like a moral victory, it's quite possible that you could have used that same time to answer three other short Reading Comp questions. Do not be scared to skip a question that's giving you a lot of trouble—just remember to mark it so you can come back to it if you have time at the end.

8. Thou shalt avoid carelessness.

There are actually two kinds of carelessness: The Fast and the Faithless. Both can cost you precious points on the SAT. Here's a bit more detail about each.

The Fast

The first type of carelessness comes from moving too fast. In speeding through the test, you make yourself vulnerable to misinterpreting the question, overlooking one of the answer choices, or simply making a mathematical or logical mistake. The SAT is filled with traps that prey on the speedy.

the new SAT

The Faithless

The second type of carelessness results from lack of confidence. Lots of students are so nervous about the SAT that they lose faith in themselves as soon as they encounter a tough question. They just assume they won't be able to get the correct answer. Never assume you won't be able to answer a question without looking at it and giving it a moment's thought.

9. Thou shalt bring bread and water.

The old SAT was a long, exhausting test, and the new SAT is even longer and probably more exhausting. You'll feel like a prisoner, stripped of your freedom for almost half a day, but that doesn't mean you can't bring something along to eat and drink. You definitely can't be swigging back Gatorade during the test itself, but you will have a few breaks in between sections so you can do stuff like go to the bathroom, eat an apple, and chug down some high-octane SAT protein powder or whatever concoction you create to give yourself energy. Just be sure to bring some fuel to power you throughout the test.

10. Thou shalt relax!

The SAT is almost always portrayed as a harrowing, life-ruining stressfest. Countless magazine articles depict helpless teenagers holding their heads in panic, sweat pouring down their foreheads as they take the test. That does not have to be you. That shouldn't be you.

One of the best things you can do to chill out before the test is take the night before it off completely. That might sound crazy, but if you've spent weeks or even months in advance preparing for the test, you don't have to cram or panic. You've done all that you can do to ready yourself for the SAT and nothing you do the night before will likely make any difference. So take it easy. Go see a movie or get together with friends. Clearing your head before the test will put you in a strong position to take it on with confidence early the next morning.

SAT STRATEGIES

IMAGINE TWO CHILDREN PLAYING TAG IN A DEEP, DARK forest. Who's gonna win, a speed demon from the big city who doesn't know his way around and keeps tripping and falling? Or a slower-footed tyke who grew up in the forest and knows every root, twist, and cranny of the forest?

Here's the point: Knowing the landscape can be very helpful. If the SAT's the forest, you'll have to know the nooks and crannies of the test. That's why we wrote this chapter.

3.1 TO GUESS OR NOT TO GUESS?

Should you guess on the SAT? The answer lies deep within this fake SAT question:

> You are taking a test. On a particular question, though, there has been a printing error. The question wasn't printed at all! But the five answers have been printed. One of the five answers is right, but you don't know which one. If you randomly guess and pick an answer, what's the probability you'll choose the "right" answer?

This question describes what happens when you guess blindly on any SAT question. If you have five possible answer choices and choose one at random, you have a 20-percent chance of choosing the right one. In other words, if you were to randomly pick an answer on five of these multiple-choice questions without even looking at the answer choices, you'd probably get one question right for every five guesses you made.

Now think back to the .25 of a point taken from your raw score for each wrong answer. This "penalty" isn't some random number. It's strategically designed to eliminate any gain you might get from guessing randomly. If you guess randomly on five questions, getting one right and four wrong (as probability states you will), your raw points for those five questions will work out to

- 1 right answer = 1 raw point
- 4 wrong answers × (−.25 points per wrong answer) = −1 raw point

This adds up to a grand total of 0 raw points. So guessing's a waste of time, right? WRONG. Read on.

The Grand Rule of Guessing

Guessing's a waste of time if you're guessing among five answer choices. But there's no rule saying you have to guess among five answer choices. If you know how to guess wisely, how to eliminate answer choices before guessing, the game changes. Take the following Sentence Completion question:

> In Greek mythology, Hades, the realm of the dead, is guarded by ---- dog.
>
> (A)   an anthropomorphic
> (B)   a sanguinary
> (C)   a sesquipedalian
> (D)   a delicious
> (E)   a sententious

We used this example because we thought you may not know the meanings of the words *anthropomorphic*, *sanguinary*, *sesquipedalian*, or *sententious*. All four of these words are more obscure than the vocabulary that usually appears on the SAT. But you probably do know the meaning of *delicious* and can tell immediately that it does not fit correctly into the sentence (a delicious dog?).

True, you still don't know the right answer. All you've done is eliminate one answer choice. But once you've eliminated *delicious* as a possible answer, you only have to guess between four rather than five choices. If you guess among these four choices, you'll get one question right for every three you get wrong.

- 1 right answer = 1 raw point
- 3 wrong answers × (−.25 points per wrong answer) = −.75 raw points

This adds up to a grand total of .25 raw points. In other words, if you can eliminate just *one* answer as definitely wrong, the odds of guessing shift to your favor. And every point or fraction of a point you can jam into your raw score is worthwhile.

All this explanation adds up to The Grand Rule of Guessing:

If you can eliminate even one answer choice on a question, always guess.

Guessing Wisely Is Partial Credit

Some students out there have a thing against guessing. They have this feeling that guessing is cheating. They think guessing rewards people who don't know the answer and are just playing games with the SAT.

If you're one of those students, get over it. First, by not guessing you're hurting your own test scores. Second, guessing intelligently is just a form of partial credit. We'll use the example of the Sentence Completion question about the dog guarding Hades to make this point.

Most people taking the test will only know the word *delicious* and will only be able to throw out that word as a possible answer, leaving them with a one in four chance of guessing correctly. But let's say that you knew that *sententious* means "given to pompous moralizing" and that no hound spouting pompous moral axioms would be guarding the gateway to the Greek underworld. Now, when you look at this question, you can throw out both *delicious* and *sententious* as answer choices, leaving you with a one in three chance of getting the question right if you guess.

Your extra knowledge gives you better odds of getting this question right, just as extra knowledge should.

Grid-Ins and Guessing

There's no penalty on grid-in Math questions. If you guess and get one wrong, you won't lose any points. But, and this is a big "but," the odds of randomly guessing the right answer on a grid-in is around $1/14400$. Even without the guessing penalty, these low odds mean that if you have no idea what the answer to a grid-in question is, there's not much value in taking a wild guess.

If you have worked out a grid-in problem, and have an answer, grid it in. Even if you're unsure of the answer, gridding it in can't hurt.

3.2 ELIMINATING ANSWERS

The SAT is almost entirely a multiple-choice test.* And multiple-choice questions are particularly vulnerable to good strategy. Why? On every SAT question, the answer is always right there in front of you. It's just hidden among a bunch of wrong answers. Your job is to select the right answer.

Taking the SAT is often just that simple: You'll read a question, come up with an answer, look at the answer choices, and bingo—you'll find the answer.

But sometimes you'll read a question and just not know how to proceed. Maybe the problem is that you don't understand the vocabulary words or got stuck on the math or can't spot the grammar error. Whenever that happens, you should *not* just assume the question is impossible and skip it. Instead, first try to eliminate answer choices until you've either found the right answer or put yourself in a good position to guess by cutting at least one choice.

The strategies for eliminating answers vary by question type. The specific strategies that we explain for each question type later in this book are designed to tailor and sharpen your answer-eliminating skills to every kind of question you face on the new SAT. For now, remember that just because you don't know how to answer a question right away doesn't mean you won't be able to figure it out.

3.3 SAT TRAPS

SAT traps are those tricky answer choices that seem right but are actually wrong. The SAT knows you're going to be a little nervous when you take the test. Here's how nervous people take tests like the SAT:

- They cruise through the test until they encounter a question that they can't answer immediately.
- They think, "Oh, I'll just peek down at the answers to see if I'm on the right track. . . ."
- Bang! An SAT trap lures them into an answer that seems right at a quick glance but is actually incorrect.

---

* The essay and the math grid-ins are exceptions.

To detect SAT traps, the first step is to know they're out there. The second is to understand that unless you approach the answer choices with a plan, you will fall prey to their nasty tricks. This means that unless you've made a conscious decision to eliminate answers, you shouldn't even look at the answers until you've got your own answer. And if you are eliminating answers, recognize that traps are probably hiding in several of the answer choices, trying to trick you. Once you can spot the traps in a question, you can eliminate them, which tips the guessing odds in your favor.

An SAT trap can be many things, but it will never be the right answer. What makes SAT traps feel correct even though they're wrong? That depends on which section of the test you're taking.

Math Traps: The Right Wrong Answers

Math traps look right because they're the answers you're most likely to get if you make a simple mistake. The SAT writers have been working on math tests for a long time, and they know exactly how students will flub a question. So the SAT puts the most common wrong answers in the answer choices. Then, when students make a mistake and see their wrong answer sitting there like a great big friendly affirmation, they're likely to choose that answer rather than check their work and look for another. Here's an example SAT math question:

If $q = 4$, what is $3d(4 - 3q)$ in terms of d?

(A) $-24d$
(B) $-5d$
(C) 0
(D) $12d - 12$
(E) $24d$

The right answer to this question is **A**. But, as is often the case on SAT math questions, each of the wrong answers is a trap. Here's why:

- If you substituted in the 4 to get $3d(4 - 12) = 3d(-8)$ and then did some gnarly thing where you thought you could subtract 8 from $3d$, you'd get an answer of $-5d$, answer **B**.
- If you substituted in the 4 and forgot to multiply it by 3, you'd get $3d(4 - 4) = 3d(0) = 0$, answer **C**.
- If you forgot about the 4 in $(4 - 3q)$, you'd get $12d - 12$, answer **D**.
- If you did all the math correctly, but then forgot about the minus sign, you'd get $24d$, answer **E**.

And if you were confused from the beginning, desperate to answer something, anything, and you peeked at the answer choices to get a clue, it wouldn't be very hard to convince yourself (in your state of panicked desperation) that *any* of the answers could be correct.

Critical Reading Traps: Spurious Associations

SAT traps thrive on Sentence Completion and Reading Comprehension questions. These traps carry out their trickery through spurious association. (*Spurious* means false; it just sounds cooler.) Spurious association traps make it seem as if they fit into the question by associating themselves with a feeling or idea in the question. But they're really just fakes. An example will make this easier to grasp:

> On Halloween night, five-year old Dilbert was ---- to discover that he had received more candy than ever before.
>
> (A)   terrified
> (B)   delighted
> (C)   nonplussed
> (D)   distraught
> (E)   famished

The answer is **B**. But if you were speeding through the test and saw that the sentence was about Halloween, you may have just figured it'd be natural for five-year-old Dilbert to end up *terrified*, **A**. Or, if you saw the reference to candy, you might think of hunger, which would lead you to *famished*, **E**. The words in the answer choices seem to make sense because they have some association with incidental facts in the question. To a nervous test-taker grasping for right answers fast, these can look mighty sweet.

You may also have noticed that while it's likely that on a Math question all the wrong answers are traps of some sort or another, on Critical Reading questions only one or two of the answer choices will be traps.

Writing Traps: Don't Exist

And now for some good news: The Writing section doesn't have any SAT traps. The multiple-choice questions and the essay section don't accommodate the kind of misleading answer choices on which SAT traps thrive. Take this example, from an Improving Paragraphs SAT Writing section question:

> Which of the following is the best way to revise the underlined portion of sentence 2, reprinted below?
>
> Sixty-one percent of adults suffer from obesity, but around 3,000 people die every year from diseases directly related to it.
>
> (A)   suffer from obesity, but around
> (B)   suffer, from obesity but around
> (C)   suffer from obesity, and
> (D)   suffer from obesity, although
> (E)   suffer from obesity since

Writing section multiple-choice questions test grammar. In grammar there's only right and wrong. In other words, no traps.

3.4 YOUR TARGET SCORE AND PACING STRATEGY

Your target score greatly impacts your overall strategy on the new SAT. A student looking to score a 700 or higher on a section of the SAT needs to work very differently from someone who's hoping for a 500. The student targeting a 700 has to answer almost every question on the test—he or she must work quickly and make very few careless mistakes. But students shooting for a 500 don't have to answer every question on the test. In fact, those students shouldn't even *try* to answer every question. Because students looking for a 500 can afford to leave a bunch of questions blank, they can pick and choose which questions to answer, and they can spend more time on the questions they do answer and make sure they get those questions right.

The chart below shows approximately how many questions you can afford to leave blank in a section of the test—Writing, Critical Reading, or Math—based on your target score.

Target Score	Number You Should Leave Blank
750–800	0
700–750	0–1
650–700	1–3
600–650	2–5
550–600	4–8
500–550	7–12
450–500	10–16
400–450	14–20

This chart is just a guideline. Why? Because we don't know all your quirky test-taking traits—how careless you can be, how nervous you get, how fast you work, and so on.

But *you* do know your own particular pitfalls, and you can figure out how to overcome them. We don't just mean that you can say, "Well, I don't think I'm great at Improving Sentences questions" or "I think I sometimes get confused by geometry." We mean you can specifically identify each and every one of your weaknesses: "I really seem to have trouble with Sentence Completions in which the two blanks are supposed to be filled by words that disagree" or "Wow, circles and triangles are giving me tons of trouble." And once you've pinpointed a weakness, then you can fire up the most powerful SAT preparation technique of them all: turning practice tests into the ultimate SAT personal trainer.

THE SAT PERSONAL TRAINER

THE NEW SAT, LIKE THE OLD SAT, IS A CONFORMIST. From the first administration of the new SAT until the end of time (or the next SAT overhaul), each version of the test will ask the same number of questions about the same topics. The Math questions will cover the same concepts. The Critical Reading questions will test the same comprehension skills in the same ways. The Writing multiple choice will cover the same few rules of grammar, and the essays will always ask very broad questions.

Obviously, no two SATs are *exactly* the same. Individual questions will never repeat from test to test. But the subjects that the questions test, and the way in which the questions test those subjects, *will* stay constant.

Now here's the twist. Tons of people go to the gym, but to get the best results, you need a personal trainer. A trainer tells you what you're doing wrong and what you need to do to *target* certain areas of your body that need the most work. Using practice tests to diagnose your weaknesses turns each practice test you take into your SAT personal trainer. Sound too simple? That's probably because everyone takes practice tests. But very few students actually *study* their practice test results, and it's studying the tests that's crucial.

To prove our point, we've got a case study: Meet Molly Bloom.

THE PRACTICE TEST AS PERSONAL TRAINER

One day, an eleventh-grader named Molly Bloom sits down at the desk in her room and takes a new SAT practice test. Let's say she takes the entire test and gets only one question wrong. Molly checks her answers and then jumps up from her chair and does a little dance, shimmying to the tune of her own triumph. But after her euphoria passes, she begins to wonder which question she got wrong and returns to her chair. She discovers that it was a math question about parabolas.

Molly looks over the question and realizes that she had misidentified the vertex of the parabola. Since she got the question wrong, she studies up on her coordinate geometry. She rereads all the material she needs to know on parabolas, including what causes a parabola's vertex to shift from the origin. All this takes her about ten minutes, after which she vows never to make another mistake on an SAT question involving parabolas.

Analyzing Molly Bloom

All Molly did was study a question she got wrong until she understood why she got it wrong and what she should have done to get it right. So what's the big deal? This: Molly answered the question incorrectly because she didn't understand the topic—parabolas—that it was testing. The practice test pointed out her weakness in the clearest way possible. She got the question wrong.

Molly wasn't content just to see the correct answer and get on with her life. She wanted to understand *how* and *why* she got the question wrong and what she should have done or needed to know to get it right. So she stopped her dance party, spent some time studying the question, improved her understanding of parabola graphs, and nailed down the concepts she needed to know. If Molly were to take that same test again, she definitely would not get that question wrong.

True, Molly never will see that *exact* question again. But remember, the SAT is a standardized test, a conformist. When Molly taught herself about parabolas and their graphs, she learned how to answer not just the question she got wrong but all the similar parabola questions that are bound to show up on the real SAT she eventually takes.

Every practice test precisely targets your weaknesses. You only get questions wrong when your knowledge of whatever that question tests is weak. By studying the results of her practice test and then figuring out why she got her one question wrong, Molly used the practice test to identify her weakness and overcome it.

Molly and You

Molly has it easy. She took a practice test and got only one question wrong. Fewer than 1 percent of all people who take the new SAT will be so lucky.

So, what if you take a practice test and get fifteen questions wrong, and your errors span a number of different topics in Math, Critical Reading, and Writing? You should do exactly what Molly did. Take your test and *study* it. Identify every question you got wrong, figure out why you got it wrong, and then teach yourself what you should have done to get the question right.

If you got fifteen questions wrong, it'll take a bit of time to study your mistakes. But if you invest that time and study your practice test properly, you will avoid future mistakes and guarantee yourself better scores. So to make this method work, set aside two blocks of time when you take a practice test: the first to take the test, the second to *study your results*.

SparkNotes Practice Tests Make It Easy

The practice tests in our books were specifically designed to help you study your practice tests. Every explanation of every question in our practice tests has a heading that gives you all the information you need to help you pinpoint your weaknesses. Each question is categorized by its major subject, such as geometry, by specific subject, such as circles, and by difficulty level.

22. **D** Misplaced Modifiers	*Difficult*

Misplaced modifiers abound in Improving Sentence questions, so you should always

Instead of just showing you how to solve one question, our explanations help you focus on your broader testing tendencies and adjust your strategies accordingly.

THE PRACTICE OF TAKING A PRACTICE TEST

Our Molly Bloom example shows why studying practice tests is such a powerful SAT prep tool. Now we explain, step by step, exactly how to do it yourself.

Control Your Environment

You should do everything in your power to make every practice test you take feel like the real SAT. The more your practice resembles the real thing, the more helpful it is.

- **Take a timed test.** Don't give yourself any extra time. Be more strict with yourself than the meanest proctor you can imagine. Don't even give yourself time off for bathroom breaks. If you have to go to the bathroom, let the clock keep running. That's what'll happen on the real SAT.
- **Take the test in a single sitting.** Training yourself to endure hours of test-taking is part of your preparation.
- **Take the test without distractions.** Don't take the practice test in a room with lots of people walking through it. Go to a library, your bedroom, an empty classroom—anywhere quiet.

You'll probably find these rules annoying and restrictive, and you'll be tempted to break them. Maybe you could take the practice test in front of the TV? Or just with music playing? Sure, you could do that. No one will ever know. But we promise you that your results won't be as accurate as they will be if you simulate the real SAT experience as closely as possible.

Scoring Your Practice Test

After you take your practice test, score it and see how you did. However, when you do your scoring, don't just tally up your raw score. As part of your scoring, you should also keep a list of every question you got wrong and every question you skipped. This list will be your guide when you study your test.

HOW TO STUDY YOUR PRACTICE TEST

After grading your test, you should have a list of the questions you answered incorrectly or skipped. Studying your test involves using this list and examining each

the new SAT

question you answered incorrectly, figuring out why you got the question wrong and understanding what you could have done to get the question right.

Why'd You Get It Wrong?

There are four reasons why you might have gotten an individual question wrong:

1. You thought you solved the answer correctly, but you actually didn't.
2. You managed to eliminate some answer choices and then guessed among the remaining answers. Sadly, you guessed wrong.
3. You knew the answer but made a careless error.
4. You left it blank.

You should know which of these reasons applies to each question you got wrong. Once you figure out why you got a question wrong, you need to figure out what you could have done to get the question right.

Reason 1: Lack of Knowledge

A question answered incorrectly for reason 1 pinpoints a weakness in your knowledge. Discovering this kind of error gives you an opportunity to fill the void in your knowledge and eliminate future errors on the same question type.

For example, if the question you got wrong refers to factoring quadratics, don't just work out how to factor that one quadratic. Take the time to go over the fundamental techniques that allow you to factor *all* quadratics. Additionally, this enables you to see when a quadratic exists in an equation (those suckers can be hard to find sometimes when the SAT tries to disguise them).

Remember, you will *not* see a question exactly like the question you got wrong. But you probably *will* see a question that covers the same topic as the practice question. For that reason, when you get a question wrong, don't just figure out the right answer to the question. Study the broader topic that the question tests.

Reason 2: Guessing Wrong

If you guessed wrong, review your guessing strategy. Did you guess smartly? Could you have eliminated more answers? If yes, why didn't you? By thinking in a critical way about the decisions you made while taking the practice test, you can train yourself to make quicker, more confident, and better decisions.

If you took a guess and chose the incorrect answer, don't let that discourage you from guessing. If you eliminated at least one answer, you followed the right strategy by guessing even if you got the question wrong.

Reason 3: Carelessness

Here it might be tempting to say to yourself, "Oh, I made a careless error," and assure yourself you won't do that again. Unacceptable! You made that careless mistake for a reason, and you should figure out why. Getting a question wrong because you didn't know the answer reveals a weakness in your knowledge about the test. Making a careless mistake represents a weakness in your test-taking *method*.

To overcome this weakness, you need to approach it in the same critical way you would approach a lack of knowledge. Study your mistake. Retrace your thought process on the problem and pinpoint the origin of your carelessness. Were you rushing? Did you fall for an SAT trap? If you pin down your mistake, you are much less likely to repeat it.

Reason 4: Leaving the Question Blank

It's also a good idea to study the questions you left blank on the test, since those questions constitute a reservoir of lost points. A blank answer results from either

1. A total inability to answer a question, or
2. A lack of time.

If you were totally unable to answer a question, learn the material or at least try to identify a way you could have eliminated an answer choice in order to turn the guessing odds in your favor. If you left an answer blank because of time constraints, look over the question and see whether you think you could have answered it correctly. If you could have, then you know you need to speed up as much as possible without making more careless errors. If you couldn't have answered it correctly, then you've just identified a weakness waiting to be overcome.

Ready to overcome your new SAT weaknesses? We'll start with the Writing section.

the new SAT

THE
WRITING
SECTION

MEET THE WRITING SECTION

WE'RE NOT GOING TO DEBATE WHETHER OR NOT THE SAT should include an essay, or why some people may think it's unfair. We're just going to accept it as a fact of standardized testing life and get on with helping you meet and beat it.

Here's what we do in this chapter:

- Review what the SAT Writing section covers and how it's scored.
- Explain the specific test-taking strategies you'll need to beat the Writing section's essay and multiple-choice questions.
- Take a very close look at the SAT essay, complete with our Universal SAT Essay Template and sample essays.

Got it? Good. Let's go.

5.1 THE PSAT AND SAT II CONNECTION

The fear and mystery surrounding the SAT Writing section is overblown. It's new, they say. But actually, it isn't. It's just an old test put in a new place. All of the multiple-choice question types are derived from the PSAT, which nearly everyone studying for the SAT has already taken. And the entire section, including the essay, is really just a slightly shorter version of the SAT II Writing test that many students have had to take for years. Most colleges require students to take the SAT II Writing test in order to apply, but once the new SAT launches, the SAT II Writing test will be discontinued forever. So the big scary *new* Writing section is really just a recycled rehash of other standardized tests. That should help put your panic in check.

5.2 WHAT THE WRITING SECTION TESTS

Just like the SAT II Writing test, the new SAT Writing section tests your writing skills in two different ways:

1. An Essay Question
2. Multiple-Choice Questions

The essay gives you 25 minutes to take a position on a broad topic and back it up with examples. One question. One answer. In contrast, the new SAT contains 49 multiple choice questions, and these 49 questions are broken into three types:

- 25 Improving Sentences
- 18 Identifying Sentence Errors
- 6 Improving Paragraphs

The entire "Writing Section" of the new SAT is actually made up three smaller timed sections. Two of the timed sections are 25-minutes long, and one is 10 minutes long. Here's what each of the timed sections will contain:

- 25-minute section: The essay
- 25-minute section: 11 Improving Sentences, 18 Identifying Sentence Errors, and 6 Improving Paragraphs
- 10-minute section: 14 Improving Sentences

The 25-minute section that contains the essay will always be the first timed section of the entire new SAT. The other two sections might appear in various places in the test, but in general the multiple-choice 25-minute section will appear somewhere in the middle, and the 10-minute section will appear near the end.

5.3 WHAT THE WRITING SECTION *ACTUALLY* TESTS

Writing skills and grammar? While that may sound pretty broad and frightening, the truth about what the Writing section tests is not so extreme. First, remember that the essay section is only 25 minutes long. Nobody expects you to write a perfect and inspired piece of work in less than half an hour. In fact, the essay-graders mostly want to see that you can understand a topic and take a position. And that's pretty much it. This chapter tells you the ingredients you'll need for every SAT essay and provides a Universal SAT Essay Template that gives you a model essay pattern to follow.

The multiple-choice questions all test grammar. This chapter contains a crash course in the grammar that the SAT Writing section tests. As you'll soon learn, you definitely don't need to be a trained grammarian to do well on the Writing section. You don't have to know any technical grammar terms at all. You simply need to know the basic rules of grammar that the SAT tends to test again and again. By learning the rules, you'll train your ear to recognize where errors lurk in sentences and paragraphs, and how to fix them. The multiple-choice section does *not* test stuff like spelling or vocabulary. However, using proper spelling and appropriate vocabulary is very important on the SAT essay, since the SAT essay-graders consider your overall command of language when scoring your work.

The multiple-choice questions, combined with the essay, make up the entire new SAT Writing section. We explain each multiple-choice question type and the essay in great detail later on in the chapter.

5.4 HOW TO SCORE . . . THE WRITING SECTION

The best score you can get on the Writing section is a scaled score of 800. As with the Math and Critical Reading sections, this scaled score is derived by taking a raw score and placing it into a scoring curve. But that's where the similarities end.

In addition to the scaled 200–800 score, you'll receive two subscores: one for the multiple choice that is graded on a scale of 20 to 80, and another for the essay that is graded on a scale of 2 to 12.

The Multiple-Choice Raw Score and Subscore

The multiple-choice raw score is calculated just as you would expect. You get one point for each right answer, zero points for each answer left blank, and there's the $-\frac{1}{4}$ point "guessing penalty" for each wrong answer. The guessing penalty really should be called a "wrong-answer penalty." The SAT does *not* penalize you for making educated guesses. An educated guess is a guess you make after eliminating at least one wrong answer choice. The SAT *does* penalize you for totally random guessing. Your multiple-choice raw score in equation form looks like this:

$$\text{multiple-choice raw score} = \text{\# of correct answers} - \frac{\text{\# of wrong answers}}{4}$$

This raw score is then used in two ways: (1) It's combined with your essay raw score to calculate your overall scaled score for the Writing section; and (2) it's used to calculate your scaled subscore for the multiple-choice section. Since there are 49 total multiple-choice Writing questions, the highest possible multiple-choice raw score is 49.

The Essay Raw Score and Subscore

The raw score and subscore for the Essay are the same thing. That makes it simple. Here's how it works. Two human graders grade your essay. Each one gives your essay a grade between 1–6 (with 1 being the worst). They then combine the two grades so your essay as a whole receives a score anywhere between 2 and 12.

The Overall Scaled Writing Score

The overall Writing score, which ranges between 200 and 800, is determined by taking your raw scores for the multiple-choice section and the essay and combining them so that the essay counts for about 30 percent of your total and the multiple-choice questions account for 70 percent. To be perfectly honest, it's not worth anyone's time to get into the complicated calculations used to combine the multiple-choice writing raw score and the essay score into an overall raw score. Instead, at the end of every practice test, we provide a conversion table that will allow you to easily see your Writing scaled score. If you'd like to take a peek at one of these pages right now, turn to page 386.

Indisputable Fact: 30% Is Not 100%

Despite all the panic and pandemonium about it, the new SAT essay counts for only 30 percent of your Writing score. That means it's worth a bit less than *10 percent of the entire SAT*. A lot of people (and test-prep courses) will probably spend all their time fixated on the Essay section. But the cold, hard, factual stats prove that spending a disproportionate amount of time fixated on the essay is not the best way to structure your SAT studying time. Since the multiple-choice questions count toward more than half your writing score, *and* since they're easier to practice and predict, you should spend at least as much time preparing for those as you do for the essay.

BEAT THE ESSAY

A "GREAT SAT ESSAY" AND A "GREAT ESSAY" ARE *not* the same thing. Truly great essays take hours or even days to plan, research, and write. The SAT essay can't take more than 25 minutes. That means you've got to write an essay that convinces your grader of your genius in less time than it takes to watch *The Simpsons*, right? Wrong.

The SAT knows that 25 minutes isn't enough time for anyone, anywhere, to write a genius essay. Forget genius. Forget about trying to write an essay that changes the world. When the SAT says to you, "Here's 25 minutes, write an essay," what they're saying between the lines is: "Write a *standard* essay that does exactly what we want."

To give the SAT what it wants, you need to have a very firm essay-writing strategy in place before you sit down to take the test. You then need to apply that strategy to whatever question the SAT essay poses. In this chapter, we teach you a strategy for writing a great SAT essay that works every time, on any topic. It all starts with fast food.

6.1 THE FAST FOOD ESSAY

One of the best things about fast food is not just that it's quick, but that it's *consistent*. Walk into a McDonald's in Tosserdorf, Germany, and a Big Mac is still a robust, comforting Big Mac, just like at home. What makes fast food so consistent? Restaurants like McDonald's use the same ingredients and preparation methods at every location.

In this chapter, we show you how to apply the concept behind fast food to the process of writing the SAT essay. That way you can write a top-notch SAT essay every time. To make it happen, you need to know three key things, just like all the fast food chains:

- Know your customers.
- Know your ingredients.
- Know how to put the ingredients together.

6.2 KNOW YOUR CUSTOMERS

After you finish taking the SAT, your essay is scanned into a computer, uploaded to a secure website, and graded on computer screens at remote locations by "essay-graders." These essay-graders are either English teachers or writing teachers who have been hired and trained to grade SAT essays by the company that makes the SAT. Every essay is actually read by two graders. Each grader is instructed to spend no more than *three minutes* reading an essay before giving it a score on a scale of 1 to 6. The two grades are then added together to make up your entire essay subscore, which ranges from 2–12. (If two graders come to wildly different scores for an essay, like a 2 and a 5, a third grader is brought in.)

So the essay graders are your *customers*. You want to give them an essay that tastes just like what they're expecting. How are *you* supposed to know what *they're* expecting? You can learn exactly what SAT essay-graders expect by looking at two very important guidelines: the actual SAT essay directions and the grading criteria that the SAT gives the graders.

The SAT Essay Directions

The first thing you should *not* do when writing your SAT essay is read the directions. Don't waste your time on the real test. Instead, read the directions now and make sure you understand them.

> The essay gives you an opportunity to show how effectively you can develop and express ideas. You should, therefore, take care to develop your point of view, present your ideas logically and clearly, and use language precisely.
>
> Your essay must be written on the lines provided on your answer sheet—you will receive no other paper on which to write. You will have enough space if you write on every line, avoid wide margins, and keep your handwriting to a reasonable size. Remember that people who are not familiar with your handwriting will read what you write. Try to write or print so that what you are writing is legible to those readers.
>
> You have twenty-five minutes to write an essay on the topic assigned below. DO NOT WRITE ON ANOTHER TOPIC. AN OFF-TOPIC ESSAY WILL RECEIVE A SCORE OF ZERO.

We've translated these directions into a list of Dos and Don'ts to make all the rules easier to grasp:

DO	DON'T
Write only on the given topic as directed.	Write on a topic that relates vaguely to the one given.
Take a clear position on the topic.	Take a wishy-washy position or try to argue two sides.

DO	DON'T
Write persuasively to convince the grader.	Write creatively or ornately just to show off.
Include reasons and examples that support your position.	Include examples not directly related to your position.
Write with correct grammar and spelling.	Forget to proof your work for spelling and grammar mistakes.
Write as clearly as possible.	Use too many fancy vocabulary words or overly long sentences.
Write specifically and concretely.	Be vague or use generalizations.
Write more than one paragraph.	Put more importance on length than on quality.
Write only on the given lined paper.	Make your handwriting too large or you'll sacrifice space.
Write as neatly as possible in print or cursive.	Write in cursive if you can print. Print is much easier to read.

The Grader's Instructions

The graders must refer to a set-in-stone list of criteria when evaluating each essay and deciding what grade (1 through 6) it deserves. The following chart is our explanation of the grading criteria that the SAT gives the graders.

Score	Description of Essay
6	A 6 essay is *superior* and demonstrates a *strong and consistent* command of the language throughout the entire essay, with at most a few small errors. A 6 essay: • shows a firm grasp of critical thinking and takes a powerful and interesting position on the topic • supports and develops its position with appropriate and insightful examples, arguments, and evidence • is tightly organized and focused, with a smooth and coherent progression of ideas • demonstrates a facility with language through the use of descriptive and appropriate vocabulary • uses intelligent variation in sentence structure • contains, at most, a few errors in grammar, spelling, and punctuation.
5	A 5 essay is *strong* and demonstrates a *generally consistent* command of language throughout the entire essay, with no more than a few significant flaws and errors. A 5 essay: • shows well-developed critical thinking skills by taking a solid position on the topic • supports and develops its position on the topic with appropriate examples, arguments, and evidence • is organized and focused and features a coherent progression of ideas • demonstrates competence with language throughout by using appropriate vocabulary • uses varied sentence structure • contains few errors in grammar, spelling, and punctuation.

Score	Description of Essay
4	A 4 essay is *competent* and demonstrates a basic *command* of the language throughout the entire essay. A 4 essay: • shows adequate critical thinking skill by taking a position on the topic and supporting that position with generally appropriate examples, arguments, and evidence • is mostly organized and focused, with a progression of ideas that is mostly coherent • demonstrates inconsistent facility with language and uses mostly appropriate vocabulary • uses some variation in sentence structure • contains some errors in grammar, spelling, and punctuation.
3	A 3 essay shows *developing competence* and contains *one or more* of the following: • some critical thinking skills, as demonstrated by its position on the topic • inadequate support or development of its position based on deficiencies in examples, arguments, or evidence presented • lapses in organization and focus, including ideas that are not always coherent • a capacity for competent use of language, with occasional use of vague or inappropriate vocabulary • only minor variation in sentence structure • a variety of errors in grammar, spelling, and punctuation.
2	A 2 essay is *seriously flawed* and demonstrates a *poor command* of the language throughout the entire essay. A 2 essay contains *one or more* of the following: • poor critical thinking skills as shown by an inconsistent or unclear position on the topic • insufficient support for the position on the topic as a result of faulty or nonexistent examples, arguments, and evidence • weak organization and focus, including ideas that are frequently incoherent • poor language skills through use of limited or wrong vocabulary • errors in sentence structure • errors in grammar, spelling, punctuation, and other rules of writing that make the meaning hard to understand
1	A 1 essay is *profoundly flawed* and demonstrates a *very poor command* of the language throughout the entire essay. A 1 essay contains *one or more* of the following: • no position on the topic, or almost no support or development of the position • poor organization and focus that makes the essay incoherent • numerous vocabulary errors • fundamental errors in sentence structure • errors in grammar, spelling, and punctuation that make parts of the essay unintelligible.
0	Essays written on a topic other than the one assigned will receive a score of zero.

KNOW YOUR INGREDIENTS

To write a tasty SAT essay, you've got to know the necessary ingredients: The different grades of 1 to 6 are based on the quality of your essay in four fundamental categories.

1. **Positioning**: The strength and clarity of your stance on the given topic.
2. **Examples**: The relevance and development of the examples you use to support your argument.
3. **Organization**: The organization of each of your paragraphs and of your essay overall.
4. **Command of Language**: Sentence construction, grammar, and word choice.

Now you know your customers, and you know what they want. We'll spend the rest of this chapter teaching you precisely how to give it to them.

1. Positioning

SAT essay topics are always broad. Really, really, really broad. We're talking "the big questions of life" broad. A typical SAT essay topic gives you a statement that addresses ideas like *the concept of justice*, *the definition of success*, *the importance of learning from mistakes*.

The broad nature of SAT topics means you'll never be forced to write about topical or controversial issues of politics, culture, or society (unless you want to; we'll talk about whether you *should* want to a little later). But the broadness of the topics also means that with a little thought you can come up with plenty of examples to support your position on the topic.

Philosophers take years to write tomes on the topics of *justice* or *success*. On the SAT, you get 25 minutes. Given these time constraints, the key to writing a great SAT essay is taking a strong position on an extremely broad topic. You need to select your position strategically. To do this, follow a two-step strategy:

- Rephrase the prompt.
- Choose your position.

It's time to learn how to take a stand. Here's a sample essay topic for the new SAT:

Think carefully about the issue presented in the following excerpt and the assignment below.

"It is a mistake to suppose that men succeed through success; they much oftener succeed through failures. Precept, study, advice, and example could never have taught them so well as failure has done."
—Samuel Smiles, Scottish author (1812-1904)

Assignment:
Is there truly no success like failure? Plan and write an essay in which you develop your point of view on this issue. Support your position with reasoning and examples taken from your reading, studies, experience, or observations.

Rephrase the Prompt

Rephrase the prompt in your own words and make it more specific. If you rephrase the statement "Is there truly no success like failure?" you might come up with a sentence like "Can failure can lead to success by teaching important lessons that help us avoid repeating mistakes in the future?"

In addition to narrowing down the focus of the broad original topic, putting the SAT essay question in your own words makes it easier for you to take a position confidently, since you'll be proving your own statement rather than the more obscure version put forth by the SAT.

Choose Your Position

Agree or disagree. When you choose an argument for a paper in school, you often have to strain yourself to look for something original, something subtle. Not here. Not on the 25-minute fast food essay. Once you've rephrased the topic, agree with it or disagree. It's that simple.

You may have qualms or otherwise "sophisticated" thoughts at this point. You may be thinking, "I could argue the 'agree' side pretty well, but I'm not sure that I 100 percent believe in the agree side because. . . ." Drop those thoughts. Remember, you're not going to have a week to write this essay. You need to keep it simple. Agree or disagree, then come up with the examples that support your simple stand.

2. Examples

To make an SAT essay really shine, you've got to load it up with excellent examples. Just coming up with any three examples that fit a basic position on a broad topic is not gonna cut it. But there are two things that *do* make excellent SAT examples stand out from the crowd:

- Specific examples
- Variety of examples

Specific Examples

Good examples discuss specific events, dates, or measurable changes over time. Another way to put this is, you have to be able to talk about things that have happened in detail.

Let's say you're trying to think of examples to support the position that "learning the lessons taught by failure is a sure route to success." Perhaps you come up with the example of the American army during the Revolutionary War, which learned from its failures in the early years of the war how it needed to fight the British. Awesome! That's a *potentially* great example. To make it *actually* great, though, you have to be able to say more than just, "The American army learned from its mistakes and then defeated the British Redcoats." You need to be specific: Give dates, mention people, battles, tactics. If you use the experience of the American Army in the Revolutionary War as an example, you might mention the signing of the Treaty of Paris in 1783, which officially granted the Americans independence and gave the United States all lands east of the Mississippi River.

Just as bricks hold up a building, such detailed facts support an argument. There are literally millions of good, potential examples for every position you might choose. You need to choose examples that you know a lot about in order to be specific. Knowing a lot about an example means you know more than just the basic facts. You need to be able to use all the detailed facts about your example, such as dates and events, to show how your example proves your argument.

Knowing that the Americans defeated the British in 1783 is the start of a great example, but you must show specifically how the American victory proves the argument that "there's no success like failure." What failures on the part of the British government and army led to the Americans' success? (Morale issues, leadership differences, inadequate soldiers and supplies, the Battle of Yorktown, and so on.) The

one-two punch of a solid example and details that use the example to prove your argument make the difference between a good SAT essay example and a great one.

Variety of Examples

The other crucial thing about SAT essay examples is how much ground they cover. Sure, you could come up with three examples from your personal life about how you learned from failure. But you're much more likely to impress the grader and write a better essay if you use a broad range of examples from different areas: history, art, politics, literature, science, and so on. That means when you're thinking up examples, you should consider as wide a variety as possible, as long as all of your examples remain closely tied to proving your argument.

To prove the position that "there's no success like failure," you might choose one example from history, literature, and business or current events. Here are three examples that you might choose from those three areas:

- **History**: The Americans' victory over the British in the Revolutionary War.
- **Literature**: Dickens's success in writing about the working class based on his years spent in poverty as a child laborer.
- **Business or Current Events**: The JetBlue airline succeeding by learning from the mistakes of its competitors.

A broad array of examples like those will provide a more solid and defensible position than three examples drawn from personal experience or from just one or two areas.

A Note on Truthfulness in Examples

The SAT essay tests *how well you write*. The examples you choose to support your argument and your development of those examples is a big part of how well you write. But there's no SAT rule or law that says that the examples you use to support your arguments have to be true.

That does *not* mean you should make up examples from history or bend facts into falsehoods. Instead, it means you can take examples drawn from your personal experience or your own knowledge and present them as examples from current events, art, literature, business, or almost any other topic. For instance, let's say your Aunt Edna started a business selling chocolate-covered pretzels on the street in New York City. She started the business because she noticed that her friends and neighbors were sick and tired of the dull, flavorless New York City pretzels offered at other stands, many of which had gone out of business due to lack of demand. Her chocolate-covered pretzel business became a success based on her competitors' failures. Turn that example into an article you recently read in your local newspaper, and you've transformed your personal knowledge into a much more credible and impressive example about success and failure in business. It's certainly better to use universal examples based on facts and events that your grader might recognize. If you're in a bind, however, remember that you can bend the truth a bit and use your personal knowledge and experience to generate examples that prove your argument.

3. Organization

No matter what topic you end up writing about, the organization of your essay should be the same. That's right, the same. If you're asked to write about whether "there's no success like failure" or about the merits of the phrase "progress always comes at a cost," the *structure* of your essay should be almost identical. The SAT is looking for those standard ingredients, and the structure we're about to explain will make sure those ingredients stand out in your essay.

So what's this magical essay structure? Well, it's back to the trusty fast food analogy: A good SAT essay is a lot like a triple-decker burger.

Paragraph 1: Introduction (The Top Bun)

Paragraph 2: Example 1 (The Meat)

Paragraph 3: Example 2 (The Meat)

Paragraph 4: Example 3 (The Meat)

Paragraph 5: Conclusion (The Bottom Bun)

No matter what the topic is, what you feel about it, or which examples you choose, you should always follow this five-paragraph structure on your SAT essay. The first and last paragraphs are your essay's introduction and conclusion; each of the middle three paragraphs discusses an example that supports and illustrates your argument. That's it.

Just as important as the organization of your entire essay is the organization within each of the five paragraphs. Let's take a closer look at each paragraph next.

The Top Bun: Introduction

The introduction to an SAT essay has to do three things:

- Grab the grader's attention.
- Explain your position on the topic clearly and concisely.
- Transition the grader smoothly into your three examples.

To accomplish these three goals, you need three to four sentences in your introduction. These three to four sentences will convey your thesis statement and the overall map of your essay to the grader.

The Thesis Statement: The thesis statement is the first sentence of your essay. It identifies where you stand on the topic and should pull the grader into the essay. A good thesis statement is strong, clear, and definitive. A good thesis statement for the essay topic, "Is there truly no success like failure?" is

Learning from the lessons taught by failure is a sure route to success.

This thesis statement conveys the writer's position on the topic boldly and clearly. In only a few words, it carves out the position that the essay will take on the very broad, vague topic: learning from failure yields success.

The Essay Summary: After the thesis statement, the rest of the first paragraph should serve as a kind of summary of the examples you will use to support your position on the topic. Explain and describe your three examples to make it clear how they fit into your argument. It's usually best to give each example its own sentence. Here's an example:

> The United States of America can be seen as a success that emerged from failure: by learning from the weaknesses of the *Articles of Confederation*, the founding fathers were able to create the *Constitution*, the document on which America is built. Google Inc., the popular Internet search engine, is another example of a success that arose from learning from failure, though in this case Google learned from the failures of its competitors. Another example that shows how success can arise from failure is the story of Rod Johnson, who started a recruiting firm that rose out of the ashes of Johnson's personal experience of being laid off.

Three sentences, three examples. The grader knows exactly what to expect from your essay now and is ready to dive in.

The Meat: Three-Example Paragraphs

Each of your three-example paragraphs should follow this basic format:

- Four to five sentences long.
- The first sentence should be the **topic sentence**, which serves as the thesis statement of the paragraph. It explains what your example is and places it within the context of your argument.
- The next three to four sentences are for **developing your example**. In these sentences you show through specific, concrete discussion of facts and situations just how your example supports your essay thesis statement.

For now we're just going to show you one "meat" paragraph. As we continue through the chapter, you'll see several more, some that are good, some that are bad. This one is good:

> The United States, the first great democracy of the modern world, is also one of the best examples of a success achieved by studying and learning from earlier failures. After just five years of living under the *Articles of Confederation*, which established the United States of America as a single country for the first time, the states realized that they needed a new document and a new, more powerful government. In 1786, the Annapolis convention was convened. The result, three years later, was the *Constitution*, which created a more powerful central government while also maintaining the integrity of the states. By learning from the failure of the *Articles*, the founding fathers created the founding document of a country that has become both the most powerful country in the world and a beacon of democracy.

The best meat paragraphs on the SAT essay are specific. The SAT's essay directions say it loud and clear: "Be specific." In its topic sentence, this paragraph states that the United States is one of the great examples of "a success achieved by studying and learning from failures." It then uses the specific example of the Articles of Confederation, the Annapolis convention, and the Constitution to prove its position. It's specific throughout and even includes a few dates.

Transitions Between Meat Paragraphs: Your first meat paragraph dives right into its thesis statement, but the second and third meat paragraphs need transitions. The simplest way to build these transitions is to use words like *another* and *finally*. That means your second meat paragraph should start with a transitional phrase such as, "Another example . . ."

A slightly more sophisticated way to build transitions is to choose examples from different sources, such as from history and business. If the first paragraph is about a political instance of learning from failure and the second is from business, make that fact your transition: "As in politics, learning from failure is a means to gaining success in business as well. Take the case of. . . ."

The Bottom Bun: Conclusion

The conclusion of your essay should accomplish two main goals:

- Recap your argument while broadening it a bit.
- Expand your position. Look to the future.

To accomplish these two goals, your conclusion should contain three to four sentences.

Recap Your Argument: The recap is a one-sentence summary of what you've already argued. As in the thesis statement, the recap should be straightforward, bold, and declarative. By "broadening" your argument, we mean that you should attempt to link your specific examples to wider fields, such as politics, business, and art. Here's a recap example:

> The examples of the *Constitution*, Rod Johnson, and Google make it clear that in the realms of politics and business, the greatest successes arise from careful considerations of the lessons of failure.

Expand on Your Position: The last two or three sentences of the essay should take the argument you just recapped and push it a little further. One of the best ways to push your argument further is to look to the future and think about what would happen if the position that you've taken in your essay could be applied on a broader scale. Here's an example:

> Failure is often seen as embarrassing, something to be denied and hidden. But as the examples of the *U.S. Constitution*, Google, and Rod Johnson prove, if an individual, organization, or even a nation is strong enough to face and study its failure, then that failure can become a powerful teacher. As the examples of history and business demonstrate, if everyone had the courage and insight to view failure as a surefire way to learn from mistakes, success would be easier to achieve.

The bottom bun wraps up the entire SAT essay. And there you have it! If you follow the template we just provided, and break down the essay into its core ingredients, your SAT essay will be strong, clear, and easy to write.

The Universal SAT Essay Template

To make sure you really get the essay organization, the following chart sums it all up. Here's the SAT essay outline you should use, no matter what topic you get or what position you take:

	Length	Purpose
The Introduction		
Thesis Statement	1 sentence	Describe your argument clearly and concisely.
Essay Summary	3 sentences	Lay out the three examples you will use to support your thesis statement.
Example Paragraph 1		
Topic Sentence	1 sentence	Describe your example and fit it into the context of your overall thesis statement.
Example Development	3–4 sentences	Use specific facts to show how your example supports your argument. Be as specific as possible.

	Length	Purpose
Example Paragraph 2		
Topic Sentence	1 sentence	Describe your example and fit it into the context of your overall thesis. Provide a transition from the previous example paragraph.
Example Development	3–4 sentences	Use specific facts to show how your example supports your argument. Be as specific as possible.
Example Paragraph 3		
Topic Sentence	1 sentence	Describe your example and fit it into the context of your overall thesis. Provide a transition from the previous paragraph.
Example Development	3–4 sentences	Use specific facts to show how your example supports your argument. Be as specific as possible.
The Conclusion		
Recap	1 sentence	Summarize your argument and examples, and link the examples to broader things like politics, history, art, or business.
Broaden Your Argument	2–3 sentences	Expand your position by contemplating what would happen in the world if people (or nations, or businesses) followed the argument you make in your essay.

4. Command of Language

Taking a clear position and defending it with solid, detailed examples is a strong start to a successful SAT essay. But the SAT-graders also care about the mechanics of your writing, which we call your "command of language." Think of your command of language as your fast food essay's Special Sauce—it's the sprinkling of perfect word choice, grammar, sentence structure, and spelling that must ooze through your entire essay. An SAT essay with a clear position and strong examples won't get a perfect score without the Special Sauce, so pay close attention to these three facets of your essay (the actual SAT essay-grading guidelines mention them specifically):

- Variation in sentence structure
- Word choice
- Grammar and spelling

A Variation in Sentence Structure

> Sentence structure is very important. Sentence structure, if done well, can keep your readers engaged and help make your essay exciting and easier to read. Sentence structure, if it is monotonous and unchanging, can make your essay sound boring and unsophisticated. Sentence structure is important on the SAT essay. Sentence structure is also important in essays you write for school.

Did you notice how dull that entire last paragraph became after the first two sentences? That's because every one of those sentences not only started in the same way but also all had the same straight-ahead plodding rhythm.

Now go back and look at the earlier sample meat paragraph on the *Constitution*. Notice how the various sentences start differently and also have different internal rhythms. These variations in sentence structure keep the writing vibrant and interesting. Focus on changing the structure of your sentences as you write the essay. You don't have to invert every clause, but you should be careful not to let a few sentences in a row follow the same exact structure. You've got to mix it up. Here's the boring first paragraph of this section rewritten with varied sentence structure:

> Sentence structure is very important. Varying the structure of your sentences keeps your reader engaged and makes your writing easier to read and more exciting. Monotonous and repetitive sentence structure can make your essay sound boring and unsophisticated. Mixing up your sentence structure is crucial on the SAT essay—it's also important to consider when writing essays for school.

Much easier to read and far less repetitive, right?

Transition Between Sentences

One great way to vary your sentence structure while increasing the logical flow of your essay is to use transitions. Transitions are the words that provide the context necessary to help readers understand the flow of your argument. They're words, phrases, or sentences that take readers gently by the hand, leading them through your essay. Here are some different kinds of transitions you can use to spice up your sentence structure:

- **Showing Contrast:** *Katie likes pink nail polish.* In contrast, *she thinks red nail polish looks trashy.*
- **Elaborating:** *I love sneaking into movies.* Even more than that, *I love trying to steal candy while I'm there.*
- **Providing an Example:** *If you save up your money, you can afford pricey items.* For example, *Patrick saved up his allowance and eventually purchased a sports car.*
- **Showing Results:** *Manuel ingested nothing but soda and burgers every day for a month.* As a result, *he gained ten pounds.*
- **Showing Sequence:** *The police arrested Bob at the party.* Soon after, *his college applications were all rejected, and* eventually *Bob drifted into a life of crime.*

Overly Complex Sentences

Sometimes students think writing long complicated sentences will impress teachers. Maybe, but it won't impress SAT essay-graders. Keep your sentences short and simple. Complex sentences are difficult to understand, and your SAT essays should be as clear and easy to read as possible.

We could fill an entire book with rules about creating simple and succinct prose. Instead, we give you two handy rules to simplify the sentences that you write on the SAT essay:

1. Never write a sentence that contains more than three commas. Try to avoid sentences with more than two commas. (Unless you need to include a list.)
2. Never write a sentence that takes up more than three lines of SAT-essay paper.

Those rules are certainly not foolproof, but abiding by them will keep you from filling your SAT essay with overly complex sentences and will ultimately make your essay easier to understand.

Word Choice

When students see that "word choice" plays a part in their essay score, they think it means that they have to use tons of sophisticated vocabulary words in order to score well. That belief is wrong and potentially damaging to your SAT essay score. If you strain to put big fancy words into your essay, you're bound to end up misusing those words. And misusing a sophisticated word is a worse offense than not using one at all.

Word choice doesn't mean that you have to go for the big word every time. It means you should go for the *proper* word, the best word, the word that makes your essay as clear as possible. Let's look at part of the paragraph about the *Constitution*:

> The United States, the first great democracy of the modern world, is also one of the best examples of a success achieved by studying and learning from earlier failures. After just five years of living under the *Articles of Confederation*, which established the United States of America as a single country for the first time, the states realized that they needed a new document and a new, more powerful government. In 1786, the Annapolis convention was convened. The result, three years later, was the *Constitution*, which created a more powerful central government while also maintaining the integrity of the states. By learning from the failure of the *Articles*, the founding fathers created the founding document of a country that has become both the most powerful country in the world and a beacon of democracy.

This is 6-level writing, but it isn't teeming with five-syllable words. What the passage does is use every single word correctly. When it does reach for an uncommon word, like *beacon*, it uses the word appropriately and effectively. Now *that's* good word choice.

So don't try to use a word unless you know what it means. Don't go throwing around tough words in the hope that you're going to use it correctly and impress your reader. The likelihood is that you're going to use the word incorrectly and give the grader a bad impression. Instead, keep it simple and stick to words you know well.

Grammar and Spelling

A few grammar or spelling mistakes sprinkled throughout your essay will not destroy your score. The SAT understands that you're bound to make minor mistakes in a rushed 25-minute essay.

Graders are instructed to look out for *patterns* of errors. If a grader sees that your punctuation is consistently wrong, that your spelling of familiar words is often incorrect, or that you write run-on sentences again and again, that's when your score will suffer.

You need to be able to write solid grammatical sentences to score well on the essay. As for learning the grammar, well, you're in luck. We cover all the important grammar you need to know in "Beat Identifying Sentence Errors" and "Beat Improving Sentences."

6.4 KNOW HOW TO PUT THE INGREDIENTS TOGETHER

By now you know all of the ingredients you should use and the template you should follow to write a great SAT essay. Next you need to learn the writing process that will empower you to put it all together into a top-score-worthy essay every time. Follow the five steps we describe next and you'll be on your way to a 6.

Five Steps to a 6

Step 1	Understand the topic and take a position.	1 minute
Step 2	Brainstorm examples.	2–3 minutes
Step 3	Create an outline.	3–4 minutes

Step 4	Write the essay.	15 minutes
Step 5	Proof the essay.	2 minutes

Step 1: Understand the topic and take a position. (1 minute)

The first thing you must do before you can even think about your essay is read the topic very carefully. Here's the sample topic we use throughout this section:

> Consider the following statement and assignment. Then write an essay as directed.
>
> "There's no success like failure."
>
> Assignment:
> Write an essay in which you agree or disagree with the statement above. Remember to back up your position with specific examples from personal experience, current events, history, literature, or any other discipline. Your essay should be specific.

Make sure you understand the topic thoroughly by making it your own. To do that, use the two strategies we discussed in the Ingredients section:

- **Rephrase the Prompt.** "Failure can lead to success by teaching important lessons that help us avoid repeating mistakes in the future."
- **Choose Your Position.** (In our example, we agree with the topic.)

That's it. One step down, four more to go.

Step 2: Brainstorm examples. (2–3 minutes)

Your position is that you agree with the statement that "failure can lead to success by teaching important lessons that help us avoid repeating mistakes in the future." Terrific.

Brainstorming, or thinking up examples to support your position, is the crucial next step. Plenty of SAT-takers will succumb to the temptation to plunge straight from Step 1 into writing the essay (Step 4). Skipping the brainstorming session will leave you with an opinion on the topic but with no clearly thought-out examples to prove your point. You'll write the first thing that comes to mind, and your essay will probably derail. So even though you feel the time pressure, don't skip brainstorming.

Brainstorming seems simple. You just close your eyes and scrunch up your face and THINK REALLY HARD until you come up with some examples. But, in practice, brainstorming while staring at a blank page under time pressure can be intimidating and frustrating. To make brainstorming less daunting and more productive, we've got two strategies to suggest:

Brainstorm by Category

The best examples you can generate to support your SAT essay topic will come from a variety of sources such as science, history, politics, art, literature, business, and personal experience. So, brainstorm a list split up by category. Here's the list we brainstormed for the topic, "There's no success like failure."

Current Events	Failure of 9/11 security led to the creation of Homeland Security.
Science	Babies learn to walk only after trying and failing time and again.
History	Can't think of one.
Politics	The *US Constitution* was written only after the failure of the *Articles of Confederation*.

Art	Can't think of one.
Literature	James Joyce became a writer only after failing as a singer.
Personal Experience	Rod Johnson (your uncle) realized the need for a placement agency in South Carolina after getting laid off.
Business	Google watched the failures of its competitors and learned to improve its Internet business model and technology.

Let's say you took three minutes and came up with a list of eight categories like ours, and you got examples for five of them. That's still great. That means your next step is to choose the top three of your five potential examples.

Prepare Ahead of Time

If you want to put in the time, you could also do some brainstorming ahead of time. Brainstorming ahead of time can be a great method, because it gives you time to do more than just brainstorm. You can actually prepare examples for each of the seven categories we've brainstormed above in our chart. You could, for instance, read up about various scientists, learning about their successes, their failures, the impact of their discoveries (positive and negative), and memorize dates, events, and other facts.

The risk inherent in planning ahead is that you can get stuck with a topic on the SAT in which all your knowledge about scientists just isn't applicable. But while this is somewhat of a risk, since the SAT essay topics are so broad, you can often massage your examples to fit. Preparing ahead of time will pay off if you develop a few examples that you know a lot about for the essay. But it could backfire if it winds up that you absolutely cannot use the examples you prepared. Then you'll have to resort to thinking up examples on the spot. If you don't want to risk wasting time preparing ahead of time, don't. It's up to you.

Choose Your Top Three

When you go through your brainstormed and pre-prepared examples to decide which three you should actually use, you need to keep three things in mind:

1. Which examples can you be most specific about?
2. Which examples will give your essay the broadest range?
3. Which examples are not controversial?

The first two reasons are pretty straightforward: Specificity and variety in your examples will help you write the strongest essay. The point about controversy is a bit more subtle. Staying away from very controversial examples ensures that you won't accidentally offend or annoy your grader, who might then be more inclined to lower your grade. For instance, the 9/11 example from our brainstormed list should be cut. The event just is too full of unresolved issues to serve as a suitable essay topic, and the last thing you want to do is upset or offend your grader.

Here's another example. Let's say that you're not so certain if that story about James Joyce being a singer is even really true, and that you think lots of people might go for the babies walking example. That would mean you decide to keep the examples about the *Constitution*, Google, and the story of Rod Johnson. What if instead of referring to Rod Johnson as your enterprising uncle, you portray him as a businessman you read about in an esteemed publication recently? Transform your personal experience and make it seem like an actual example from current events. The SAT essay graders care much more about how well you write and how intelligently you can use examples to back up your position than they care about the truth of what you say in examples drawn from personal experience.

That means you've narrowed down your brainstormed topics to the top three. Next up: Outlining.

Step 3: Create an outline. (3–4 minutes)

After brainstorming comes the essay writing step that students tend to dread most—writing an outline. So we're here to encourage you to embrace the outline. Love the outline! Live the outline! At the very least, *write* the outline. On fast food essays like the SAT essay, which rewards standard conformity much more than it does creativity, organizing your ideas in outline form and then sticking to that outline is crucial. Though you may feel that you're wasting your time, we guarantee that the four or five minutes that you invest in writing an outline will *definitely* be paid back when you write the essay.

Writing the Outline

Since your outline is a kind of bare-bones "map" of your essay, the outline should follow our Universal SAT Essay Template. Here's a summary of the template:

PARAGRAPH	PURPOSE	WHAT IT SHOULD CONTAIN
1	Introduction	Thesis statement; state examples
2	Example 1	Topic sentence for example 1; explain example 1
3	Example 2	Topic sentence for example 2; explain example 2
4	Example 3	Topic sentence for example 3; explain example 3
5	Conclusion	Thesis rephrased in a broader way; a look into the future

As you write the outline, remember that conveying your ideas clearly matters at this stage. Your outline need not be articulate or even comprehensible to anyone other than you. Your outline must contain all the essential raw material that will become your thesis statement, topic sentences, and concluding statement when you write your essay.

As you sketch out your outline, consider where you want each example to go. We suggest that you put what you consider to be your strongest example first, followed by the second strongest, and then the least strong. We suggest this because the essay is a timed section, and if for some reason you run out of time and can only fit two example paragraphs between your intro and conclusion, they might as well be your best two examples. Here's a sample outline we've written based on the topic and examples we have already discussed. Notice that we've placed our examples in strongest to weakest order starting in paragraph 2.

PARAGRAPH 1: INTRODUCTION	Failure can lead to success teaching lessons, learning mistakes. Three examples: (1) US Constitution and Articles failure, (2) failed dot-coms lead to more successful online businesses, (3) guy who started successful recruiting business after getting laid off.
PARAGRAPH 2: EXAMPLE 1 (BEST)	US Constitution developed by studying the failures of previous document, Articles of Confederation. By studying failures US became true revolutionary democracy.
PARAGRAPH 3: EXAMPLE 2 (NEXT BEST)	Google studied competitors' struggles, came up with better technological solution and better business model. Since failure is good teacher, intelligent companies look for failure everywhere, even in rivals, to learn and evolve.

the new SAT

PARAGRAPH 4: **EXAMPLE 3** **(NEXT BEST)**	Johnson founded job placement agency based on difficulties finding a new job after getting laid off. Studied his failure, found problems lay with system, not with him.
PARAGRAPH 5: **CONCLUSION**	Failure often seen as embarrassing. People try to hide it. But if you or society take responsibility for it, study it, history shows failure leads to success for everyone.

Your outline does not have to be written in complete sentences. Notice how in the example above we drop verbs and write in a note-taking style. Feel free to write just enough to convey to yourself what you need to be able to follow during the actual writing of your essay. Once you have the outline down on paper, writing the essay becomes more a job of polishing language and ideas than creating them from scratch.

Step 4: Write the essay. (15 minutes)

Writing the essay consists of filling out your ideas by following your outline and plugging in what's missing. That adds up to only about ten more sentences than what you've jotted down in your outline, which should already contain a basic version of your thesis statement, one topic sentence for each of your three examples, and a conclusion statement that ties everything together. All together your essay should be about fifteen to twenty sentences long.

As you write, keep these three facets of your essay in mind:

- Organization
- Development
- Clarity

Following your outline will make sure you stick to the Universal SAT Essay Template. That means *organization* shouldn't be a problem.

As far as *development* goes, you should make sure that every sentence in the essay serves the greater goal of proving your thesis statement as well as the more immediate purpose of building on the supporting examples you present in the intro and in each example paragraph's topic sentence. You should also make sure that you are *specific* with your examples: give dates, describe events in detail, and so on.

By *clarity*, we mean the simplicity of the language that you use. That involves spelling and grammar, but it also means focusing on varying sentence length and structure as well as including a few well-placed vocabulary words that you definitely know how to use correctly.

Do not break from your outline. Never pause for a digression or drop in a fact or detail that's not entirely relevant to your essay's thesis statement. You're serving fast food, and fast food always sticks to the core ingredients and the universal recipe.

If You Run Out of Time

If you're running out of time before finishing the intro, all three example paragraphs, and the conclusion, there's still hope. Here's what you should do: Drop one of your example paragraphs. You can still get a decent score, possibly a 4 or 5, with just two. Three examples is definitely the strongest and safest way to go, but if you just can't get through three, take your two best examples and go with them. Just be sure to include an introduction and a conclusion in every SAT essay.

The Finished Essay: Our Example

Here is an example of a complete SAT essay. It's based strictly on the outline we built in step 3 of our Five Steps to a 6, with a focus on clear simple language and the occasional drop of special sauce.

Learning the lessons taught by failure is a sure route to success. The United States of America can be seen as a success that emerged from failure: by learning from the weaknesses of the *Articles of Confederation*, the founding fathers were able to create the *Constitution*, the document on which America is built. Google Inc., the popular Internet search engine, is another example of a success that arose from learning from failure, though in this case Google learned from the failures of its competitors. Another example that shows how success can arise from failure is the story of Rod Johnson, who started a recruiting firm that arose from Johnson's personal experience of being laid off.

The United States, the first great democracy of the modern world, is also one of the best examples of a success achieved by studying and learning from earlier failures. After just five years of living under the *Articles of Confederation*, which established the United States of America as a single country for the first time, the states realized that they needed a new document and a new, more powerful government. In 1786, the Annapolis convention was convened. The result, three years later, was the *Constitution*, which created a more powerful central government while also maintaining the integrity of the states. By learning from the failure of the *Articles*, the founding fathers created the founding document of a country that has become both the most powerful country in the world and a beacon of democracy.

Unlike the United States, which had its fair share of ups and downs over the years, the Internet search engine company, Google, has suffered few setbacks since it went into business in the late 1990s. Google has succeeded by studying the failures of other companies in order to help it innovate its technology and business model. Google identified and solved the problem of assessing the quality of search results by using the number of links pointing to a page as an indicator of the number of people who find the page valuable. Suddenly, Google's search results became far more accurate and reliable than those from other companies, and now Google's dominance in the field of Internet search is almost absolute.

The example of Rod Johnson's success also shows how effective learning from mistakes and failure can be. Rather than accept his failure after being laid off, Johnson decided to study it. After a month of research, Johnson realized that his failure to find a new job resulted primarily from the inefficiency of the local job placement agencies, not from his own deficiencies. A month later, Johnson created Johnson Staffing to correct this weakness in the job placement sector. Today Johnson Staffing is the largest job placement agency in South Carolina and is in the process of expanding into a national corporation.

Failure is often seen as embarrassing, something to be denied and hidden. But as the examples of the *U.S. Constitution*, Google, and Rod Johnson prove, if an individual, organization, or even a nation is strong enough to face and study its failure, then that failure can become a powerful teacher. The examples of history and business demonstrate that failure can be the best catalyst of success, but only if people have the courage to face it head on.

In the Practice Essay section at the end of this chapter, we provide analysis to explain more fully why we think this essay deserves a 6. For now, it's time to move on to the final step of our Five Steps to a 6—proofing your essay.

Step 5: Proof the essay. (2 minutes)

Proofing your essay means reading through your finished essay to correct mistakes or to clear up words that are difficult to read. If you don't have two minutes after you've finished writing the essay (step 4), spend whatever time you do have left proofing. Read over your essay and search for rough writing, bad transitions, grammatical errors, repetitive sentence structure, and all that special sauce stuff. The SAT explicitly says that handwriting will not affect your grade, but you should also be on the lookout for instances in which bad handwriting makes it look as if you've made a grammatical or spelling mistake.

If you're running out of time and you have to skip a step, proofing is the step to drop. Proofing is important, but it's the only one of the Five Steps to a 6 that isn't absolutely crucial.

TWO SAMPLE SAT ESSAYS—UP CLOSE

Below is our sample essay question, which is designed to be as close as possible to an essay question that might appear on the SAT. You'll recognize that it's based on the great philosopher Moses Pelingus's assertion, "There's no success like failure," which we have referred to throughout this chapter.

This particular essay topic presents you with a very broad idea and then asks you to explain your view and back it up with concrete examples. Not every SAT essay topic will take this form, but every SAT essay question will require you to take a position and defend it with examples.

Here's the sample prompt again:

> Consider carefully the following quotation and the assignment below it. Then plan and write an essay that explains your ideas as persuasively as possible. Keep in mind that the support you provide—both reasons and examples—will help make your view convincing to the reader.
>
> "There's no success like failure."
>
> What is your view on the idea that success can begin with failure? In an essay, support your position using an example (or examples) from literature, the arts, history, current events, politics, science and technology, or from your personal experience or observation.

Below are two different versions of responses to our sample essay question. We provide examples of a 6 essay and a 4 essay, complete with a brief analysis of each essay and how they differ from each other. We evaluate both essays according to three sets of criteria:

- Our four essential essay ingredients
- The SAT grader's checklist
- A checklist based on our Universal SAT Essay Template

As you read both examples, note that we have marked certain sentences and paragraphs to illustrate where and how the essay does or does not abide by our Universal SAT Essay Template.

A 6 Essay

Learning the lessons taught by failure is a sure route to success. (THESIS STATEMENT) The United States of America can be seen as a success that emerged from failure: by learning from the weaknesses of the *Articles of Confederation*, the founding fathers were able to create the *Constitution*, the document on which America is built. (BEST SUPPORTING EXAMPLE [1]) Google Inc., the popular Internet search engine, is another example of a success that arose from learning from failure, though in this case Google learned from the failures of its competitors. (NEXT BEST SUPPORTING EXAMPLE [2]) Another example that shows how success can arise from failure is the story of Rod Johnson, who started a recruiting firm that arose from Johnson's personal experience of being laid off. (NEXT BEST SUPPORTING EXAMPLE [3])

The United States, the first great democracy of the modern world, is also one of the best examples of a success achieved by studying and learning from earlier failures. (TOPIC SENTENCE FOR EXAMPLE 1) After just five years of living under the *Articles of Confederation*, which established the United States of America as a single country for the first time, the states realized that they needed a new document and a new more powerful government. In 1786, the Annapolis convention was convened. The result, three years later, was the *Constitution*, which created a more powerful central government while also maintaining the integrity of the states. By learning from the failure of the *Articles*, the founding fathers created the founding document of a country that has become both the most powerful country in the world and a beacon of democracy. (FOUR DEVELOPMENT SENTENCES TO SUPPORT EXAMPLE 1)

Unlike the United States, which had its fair share of ups and downs over the years, the Internet search engine company, Google Inc., has suffered few setbacks since it went into business in the late 1990s. (TOPIC SENTENCE FOR EXAMPLE 2) Google has succeeded by studying the failures of other companies in order to help it innovate its technology and business model. Google identified and solved the problem of assessing the quality of search results by using the number of links pointing to a page as an indicator of the number of people who find the page valuable. Suddenly, Google's search results became far more accurate and reliable than those from other companies, and now Google's dominance in the field of Internet search is almost absolute. (THREE DEVELOPMENT SENTENCES TO SUPPORT EXAMPLE 2)

The example of Rod Johnson's success as an entrepreneur in the recruiting field also shows how effective learning from mistakes and failure can be. (TOPIC SENTENCE FOR EXAMPLE 3) Rather than accept his failure after being laid off, Johnson decided to study it. After a month of research, Johnson realized that his failure to find a new job resulted primarily from the inefficiency of the local job placement agencies, not from his own deficiencies. A month later, Johnson created Johnson Staffing to correct this weakness in the job placement sector. Today Johnson Staffing is the largest job placement agency in South Carolina, and is in the process of expanding into a national corporation. (FOUR DEVELOPMENT SENTENCES TO SUPPORT EXAMPLE 3)

Failure is often seen as embarrassing, something to be denied and hidden. But as the examples of the *U.S. Constitution* , Google, and Rod Johnson prove, if an individual, organization, or even a nation is strong enough to face and study its failure, then that failure can become a powerful teacher. (THESIS STATEMENT REPHRASED IN BROADER WAY THAT PUSHES IT FURTHER) The examples of history and business demonstrate that failure can be the best catalyst of success, but only if people have the courage to face it head on.

Why This Essay Deserves a 6

First, we need to assess whether this essay contains the four essential ingredients of a great SAT essay. Here they are, just to refresh your memory:

1. **Positioning:** The strength and clarity of the position on the given topic.
2. **Examples:** The relevance and development of the examples used to support your argument.

3. **Organization:** The organization of each paragraph and of the essay overall.
4. **Command of Language:** Sentence construction, grammar, and word choice.

This essay serves up all four SAT essay ingredients. It takes a very strong and clear stance on the topic in the first sentence and sticks to it from start to finish. It uses three examples from a very diverse array of disciplines—from Internet technology to history and politics to a profile of an entrepreneur—and it never veers from using these examples to support the thesis statement's position. The organization of the essay follows our Universal SAT Essay Template perfectly, both at the paragraph level (topic sentences and development sentences) and at the overall essay level (intro, three meaty example paragraphs, a strong conclusion). The command of language remains solid throughout. The writer does not take risks with unfamiliar vocabulary but instead chooses a few out of the ordinary words like *beacon*, *deficiencies*, and *innovate* that sprinkle just the right amount of special sauce throughout the essay. Sentence structure varies often, making the entire essay more interesting and engaging to the grader. Finally, no significant grammar errors disrupt the overall excellence of this SAT essay.

Here's a quick-reference chart that takes a closer look at this 6 essay based on the actual SAT's evaluation criteria for graders and based on our Universal SAT Essay Template.

SAT CRITERIA FOR 6 ESSAYS	YES OR NO?
Consistently excellent, with at most a few minor errors.	YES
Takes a clear position on the topic and uses insightful relevant examples to back it up.	YES
Shows strong overall organization and paragraph development.	YES
Demonstrates a superior command of language, as shown by varied sentence structure and word choice.	YES
OUR UNIVERSAL SAT ESSAY TEMPLATE CRITERIA	**YES OR NO?**
Thesis statement in first sentence of paragraph 1.	YES
Three examples listed in paragraph 1 in order from best to worst.	YES
Topic sentence for example in paragraph 2.	YES
3–4 development sentences to support paragraph 2's example.	YES
Topic sentence for example in paragraph 3.	YES
3–4 development sentences to support paragraph 3's example.	YES
Topic sentence for example in paragraph 4.	YES
3–4 development sentences to support paragraph 4's example.	YES
Conclusion paragraph contains rephrased thesis statement.	YES
About 15 sentences total.	YES

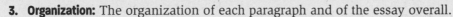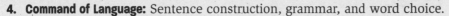

A 4 Essay

Failure can sometimes lead to success. (THESIS STATEMENT) Many Internet commerce businesses have learned from the terrible failures of the dot-com boom and bust, and today are in much stronger more successful positions than they were just a few years ago. (SUPPORTING EXAMPLE [1]). Another example proving that failure sometimes leads to success is that of Arnold "Arnie" Wagner, a heavy metal drummer who learned to play the drums in a better different style after a crippling car accident almost killed him and his band. (SUPPORTING EXAMPLE [2])

Not all Internet businesses vanished when the dot-com boom went bust—some picked up the pieces, learned from their mistakes, and moved on. The Internet boom was good to online shoppers but not so great to online businesses. Shoppers reaped the benefits of all kinds of great deals and online promotions, while e-commerce businesses did themselves in. Some Internet companies realized the mistakes others were making, such as offering too deep discounts and not charging for shipping, and they now have benefited by not suffering the same pitfalls. Only the failure of other business made this happen. (FOUR DEVELOPMENT SENTENCES TO SUPPORT EXAMPLE 1)

Arnold "Arnie" Wagner is one of the best drummers alive today. (NO TOPIC SENTENCE TO SUPPORT EXAMPLE 2) He's sure lucky to be alive! Arnie lost his right arm in a car crash just as his band Darkness Falls was beginning to establish success. Rather than give up and fail with his one arm, Wagner took the problem on courageously and decides to view it as an opportunity to change his drumming style. He has a special drum kit designed for him, complete with electronic pedals controlled by foot, which leads him to a new style and his band to even greater heights of success. (FIVE DEVELOPMENT SENTENCES TO SUPPORT EXAMPLE 2)

Failure doesn't have to end there. Often people and businesses use other's failures or even their own to learn from mistakes and try not to repeat them. Proof? Today Arnie Wagner is still on top of the drumming world, and many online businesses continue to thrive. (THESIS STATEMENT TOUCHED ON, BUT NOT REPHRASED IN BROADER WAY THAT PUSHES IT FURTHER) The examples of history and business demonstrate that failure can be the best catalyst of success, but only if people have the courage to face it head on.

Why This Essay Deserves a 4

This essay does an adequate job serving up all four SAT essay ingredients. It's competent overall but not exceptional. That's the key difference between 4 essays and 6 essays. The 4s are like average students: They do the work the night before, turn it in, and get back a passing grade that keeps their parents off their back. The 6s are above excellent students: They do their homework days in advance, turn it in early, and impress teachers with the superior quality of their work.

More specifically, this 4 essay takes a stance on the topic in the first sentence and sticks to it, but the stance is not resoundingly clear from the start: "Failure can sometimes lead to success." The thesis statement is vague and makes the essay's positioning wishy-washy, which makes it weaker overall than the 6 essay's unwavering stance. It does use examples to support its position, but its examples are not as sophisticated or as varied as the examples in the 6 essay. They're also not linked together with transitions and occasionally veer slightly off topic. The organization of the essay follows our Universal SAT Essay Template closely, but not perfectly. For starters, it contains only two examples. Though not disastrous, including only two examples limits the breadth of your support. It also makes the strength and quality of your examples all the more crucial, since having only two will make the grader scrutinize them more closely than if your support were spread over three examples.

At the sentence level, this essay does include a thesis statement and a topic sentence in the first example paragraph, but the structure begins to derail at the beginning of the second example paragraph. The writer introduces the drummer Arnie

Wagner, but not in a way that is directly related to proving the thesis statement. The paragraph meanders toward a topic sentence, but never regains a sure footing. The conclusion refers back to the thesis statement in broad terms ("Failure doesn't have to end there"), but it does not tie the essay together as well as the broadening conclusion found in the 6 essay. The command of language remains acceptable throughout. Compared to the 6 essay, this 4 essay contains significantly more spelling and grammar errors, most notably the jarring tense shift in paragraph 3. The entire passage is written in the past tense, but suddenly shifts into the present tense with the sentence that begins, "He has a special drum kit. . . ." This essay also features repetitive sentence structure that makes it a much duller read than the 6. The 4 contains no special sauce whatsoever, another contributing factor to its average quality overall.

Here's a closer look at this 4 essay based on the SAT's evaluation criteria for graders and based on our Universal SAT Essay Template. Pay special attention to the difference in criteria for 4 essays and 6 essays, and to the deficiencies in the 4 essay as compared to the 6 (the NOs in the YES/NO column). The 4 essay's NOs pinpoint its weaknesses, which we just discussed.

SAT CRITERIA FOR 4 ESSAYS	YES OR NO?
Consistently solid, with at least several minor errors and a few more serious weaknesses or mistakes.	YES
Addresses the topic presented adequately.	YES
Uses examples to support a position on the topic.	YES
Shows acceptable organization and development throughout.	YES
Competent but not consistent command of language, with several errors in grammar and usage and only slight sentence variation.	YES
OUR UNIVERSAL SAT ESSAY TEMPLATE CRITERIA	YES OR NO?
Thesis statement in first sentence of paragraph 1.	YES
Three examples listed in paragraph 1 in order from best to worst.	NO
Topic sentence for example in paragraph 2.	YES
3–4 development sentences to support paragraph 2's example.	YES
Topic sentence for example in paragraph 3.	NO
3–4 development sentences to support paragraph 3's example.	NO
Topic sentence for example in paragraph 4.	NO
3–4 development sentences to support paragraph 4's example.	NO
Conclusion paragraph contains rephrased thesis statement.	YES
About 15 sentences total.	YES

the new SAT

BEAT IMPROVING SENTENCES

CARE TO GUESS WHAT YOU HAVE TO DO for Improving Sentences Questions? That's right: You have to improve sentences. Improving Sentences questions consist of a single sentence with one underlined word or phrase. Your mission with that underlined portion of the sentence is twofold. First, you have to figure out if there's a problem with the underlined part. Then, if there is a problem, you have to decide which answer choice fixes the problem. Sometimes—one-fifth of the time, in fact—no error will exist.

The new SAT contains 25 Improving Sentences. A group of 11 of the Sentence Improvements appear in the 25-minute Writing timed section (they appear first in that section). A group of 14 Sentence Improvements makes up the entirety of the 10-minute Writing timed section. Groups of Sentence Improvements generally increase in difficulty from the first question in a group to the last question in the group.

the new SAT

THE DIRECTIONS

You know the drill. Learn the directions now so you don't have to waste time reading them when you take the actual SAT.

> Directions: The following sentences test correctness and effectiveness of expression.
>
> In choosing answers, follow the requirements of standard written English; that is, pay attention to grammar, choice of words, sentence construction, and punctuation.
> Part of the sentence or the entire sentence is underlined; beneath each sentence are five ways of phrasing the underlined material. Choice A repeats the original phrasing; the other four choices are different. If you think the original phrasing produces a better sentence than any of the alternatives, select choice A; if not, select one of the other choices.
>
> In making your selection, follow the requirements of standard written English; that is, pay attention to grammar, choice of words, sentence construction, and punctuation. Your selection should result in the most effective sentence—clear and precise, without awkwardness or ambiguity.

Notice that once again, the SAT wants you to follow the rules of standard written English when you're answering these questions. The rules of standard *spoken* English aren't accepted here, so a lot of English that's passable in speech is considered incorrect on Improving Sentences questions.

Also notice that because answer choice **A** is *always* the same as the original sentence, *you never need to waste time reading answer choice A*. So, unless you think the sentence contains no error, skip directly to **B**.

AN EXAMPLE TO SAMPLE

Here's what an Improving Sentences question looks like:

> Jenna was awarded the medal not for her academic success or her skill on the soccer field, <u>but for her being a participant in gym class</u>.
>
> (A)   but for her being a participant in gym class
> (B)   the reason being for her participation in gym class
> (C)   the reason was her participating in gym class
> (D)   but for her being participation-willing in gym class
> (E)   but for her participation in gym class

THE GOOD NEWS . . . AND THE GOOD NEWS

On this section, as on the other sections, grammar terminology is not tested. Neither is spelling. Mastering this section does not require you to memorize a huge amount of material or learn a ton of new concepts. You'll see questions on the passive voice, run-on sentences, and misplaced modifiers. You'll probably also encounter a few questions on parallelism, conjunctions, fragments, and gerunds. Although some of the material in this chapter is new, you'll notice that the SAT tests many of the same grammar rules in this section that we cover in the Identifying Sentence Errors chapter

AN EIGHT-STEP STRATEGY

All the self-help books these days have a twelve-step process to kick the habit. Improving Sentences are four steps easier to handle. Here are the eight steps:

Step 1. Read the sentence and try to hear the problem.

Step 2. If you find an error, eliminate **A**.

Step 3. Before you look at the answer choices, figure out how to fix the error.

Step 4. Find the correction that most closely matches yours.

Step 5. If no correction matches, eliminate answers that repeat the error or contain new errors.

Step 6. If you're still stumped, reach into your bag of tricks (more on those soon).

Step 7. Plug your answer back into the sentence to check it.

Step 8. If you're still stumped—cut, guess, and run.

Alright, now it's time to put that exciting eight-step process into action. Below you'll see a sample problem that we solve with the eight-step method, explaining each of the steps along the way:

> Jenna was awarded the medal not for her academic success or her skill on the soccer field, <u>but for her being a participant in gym class</u>.
>
> (A)   but for her being a participant in gym class
> (B)   the reason being for her participation in gym class
> (C)   the reason was her participating in gym class
> (D)   but for her being participation-willing in gym class
> (E)   but for her participation in gym class

Step 1: Read the sentence and try to hear the problem.

As we have discussed, relying on your ear exclusively is risky on the SAT Writing section. The writers of the SAT know most students will listen for what *sounds* right to them, but often what sounds right is actually wrong. That's because using just your ear most often means you're using spoken English as your guide. Remember that this section of the SAT tests your knowledge of standard *written* English.

In this chapter, we reinforce your understanding of the rules of standard written English. Knowing the rules gives you a strong foundation against which to check the signals your ear gives you that something in the sentence is wrong. In the sample sentence above, you might immediately notice the combined problem of wordiness and faulty parallelism—the phrase *but for her being a participant* should be rewritten in a more compact form in which all the different components of the sentence align, or flow together, correctly (more on parallelism below).

Even if you don't come up with the specific term *wordiness*, you might have the sense that something about the underlined part is vague and a bit convoluted. It's fine if you can't think of the exact term that describes the problem. A general sense that something is wrong will go a long way. Just detecting the presence of an error allows you to cut answer choice **A**, which tips the guessing odds in your favor. More on that in step 2.

Step 2: If you find an error, eliminate A.

If you're certain that there's an error somewhere in the underlined part of the sentence, you can eliminate **A** since **A** *always repeats the underlined part word for word*. Again, you won't need to know the exact term for the error in order to eliminate **A**.

The fine art of **A** elimination gives you a great advantage on Improving Sentences questions. Here's why: Cutting **A** means something more than just "one down, four to go." Even if the other four answers look like gibberish to you, cutting **A** gives you the green light to *guess*. As we explain in the introduction to this book, the SAT does not contain a guessing "penalty." The test is set up to discourage totally random guessing, but to reward educated guessing. If you can eliminate even one answer choice, the answer you choose becomes an educated guess—tipping the odds in your favor.

Step 3: Before you look at the answer choices, figure out how to fix the error.

Once you've figured out the problem in the underlined part of the sentence, say to yourself (silently—you don't want to reveal your genius to other test-takers in the room): "This would be a better sentence if it read something like *Jenna was awarded the medal not for her academic success or her skill on the soccer field, but for participating in gym class*." That version conveys the right information, but doesn't take up unnecessary space.

Have you ever noticed that if you repeat a normal, everyday word like *house* over and over it starts to seem odd? That's exactly what the answer choices of Improving Sentences questions will do to you. If you go right to the answer choices and read through them one by one, by the time you get to **C**, the answers will all sound equally confusing and wrong. Always approach the answer choices with a plan, which is what you think sounds correct. If you start looking at the answer choices with no idea of what you're looking for, it's possible all the answers will sound funny and incorrect.

Step 4: Find the correction that most closely matches yours.

Let's say your correction reads, *Jenna was awarded the medal not for her academic success or her skill on the soccer field, but for participating in gym class*. Now look at the remaining answer choices and see which one most closely matches your correction:

(A)   but for her being a participant in gym class
(B)   the reason being for her participation in gym class
(C)   the reason was her participating in gym class
(D)   but for her being participation-willing in gym class
(E)   but for her participation in gym class

E looks most like the answer you came up with before looking. It's not exactly like your prepared answer—it uses *her participation* instead of *for participating*—but it's very close. Rarely will an answer choice *exactly* match the one you generated on your own, which is fine. The purpose of preparing your own answer first is not to find an *exact* match in the answer choices but to have an idea of what is correct before you start reading the choices.

If you find an answer that matches yours, awesome. Onward to the next question. Sometimes, though, you may not be totally sure whether any of the answer choices matches yours closely enough. In that case, move to step 5.

Step 5: If no correction matches, eliminate answers that repeat the error or contain new errors.

You'll usually see a few answer choices that actually repeat the mistake. Others might fix the original mistake, but in the process add a new error to the mix.

Suppose you weren't certain that **E** matched your prepared answer closely enough. In that case, you would read through the answer choices and try to determine if they repeated the first mistake or contained a new one. Answer choice **B** has a problem similar to that of the original sentence. It says, *the reason being*, which is a wordy phrase. Meanwhile, **C** creates a new problem: the word *participating* is a gerund but should be a noun. **D** repeats the original mistake, repeating the phrase *but for her being*; it *also* introduces a new problem by using the strange phrase *participation-willing*. Only **E** neither repeats the original problem nor contains a new one.

Step 6: If still stumped, reach into your bag of tricks.

Since you've already got **E** as a pretty solid answer from step 5, there's no need to delve into the bag of Improving Sentences tricks just yet. So we're going to skip step 6 for now and go right to step 7. At the end of the chapter is a section on which tricks to use to beat Improving Sentences questions when you're in a pinch.

Step 7: Plug your answer back into the sentence to check it.

Plug the answer back into the sentence to check how well it works.

> Jenna was awarded the medal not for her academic success or her skill on the soccer field, but for her participation in gym class.

Sounds good. Sounds *right*.

Step 8: If you're *still* stumped—cut, guess, and run.

If you can't decide on an answer choice to improve the sentence's error, you've got two choices. First, if you're able to cut at least one answer choice, you should always guess. If you've got a strong hunch that the sentence contains an error but you just can't pinpoint it, cut **A** and guess. The guess odds tip in your favor if you can eliminate at least one choice, so don't worry about choosing randomly from among the four remaining choices: **B**, **C**, **D**, or **E**. If you don't know for sure if the sentence contains an error *and* you've got no clue which answer choice might solve the error, you should leave the question blank and move on to another question you can answer confidently and quickly. Every minute counts. Don't beat yourself up over an extra tough question. Use either of the strategies described in step 7 and move on pronto.

COMMON GRAMMAR ERRORS

Just like Identifying Sentence Errors questions, Improving Sentences questions cover the same grammar over and over. In fact, there are five recurring errors on Improving Sentences questions. We call them the Big Five.

The Big Five

1. Passive voice
2. Run-on sentences
3. Misplaced modifiers
4. Parallelism
5. Wordiness

We cover all of the Big Five below in more detail. Learn to spot all five and you'll be well on your way to beating Improving Sentences with ease.

1. Passive Voice

In sentences that use the active voice, the subject does the action. For example, in the sentence *My dog ate a bunch of grass*, you immediately know who ate a bunch of grass: the dog. The passive voice, in contrast, identifies the performer of the action late, or even never. For example, the sentence *A bunch of grass was eaten* leaves the reader unsure of who or what did the eating. Writers tend to avoid using the passive voice because it creates weak, wordy sentences.

So, how do you know if you are dealing with a case of "the passives"? Usually, you'll spot these words: *is, was, were, are* (or any other version of the verb *to be*) and the word *by*. If you see these words, ask yourself, What's the action and who's doing it? If the person (or entity) committing the action appears only at the end of the sentence, or doesn't appear at all, you've got a passive voice whispering bland nothings in your ear.

> After Timmy dropped his filthy socks in the hamper, <u>the offensive garment was washed by his long-suffering father</u>.
>
> (A)   the offensive garment was washed by his long-suffering father
> (B)   his long-suffering father washed the offensive garment
> (C)   the washing of the offensive garment took place by his long-suffering father
> (D)   long-suffering, the offensive garment was washed by his father
> (E)   he left the offensive garment for his long-suffering father who washed it

Here we see passive voice rearing its horrendous head. There's a *was*, a *by*, and the fact that you don't know until the last word of this sentence who washed Timmy's socks. The phrase *was washed* suggests that someone or something did the cleaning—a parent, a washing machine, a river in Egypt. The point is, you don't know how the socks got washed.

In order to fix the passive voice, the performer of the action must get a place of prominence in the sentence and clear up what they're doing. In the example above, the correct answer must make clear that Timmy's father did the load of laundry. Both answers **B** and **E** fix the passive voice problem, but **E** is wordy and redundant, so **B** is the right answer.

2. Run-On Sentences

A run-on sentence results when two complete sentences get jammed together. Run-ons usually sound breathless, as if an excited child is telling a story. Here's an example of a run-on sentence:

> I walked into the pet store and asked the clerk if she had any talking parrots, this made her roll her eyes.

The best way to test if a sentence is a run-on is to split the sentence in two and see if both halves of the sentence could function alone:

> I walked into the pet store and asked the clerk if she had any talking parrots. This made her roll her eyes.

Because each half of this sentence is complete on its own, the two halves cannot be joined together with a comma.

Here are three ways to fix run-on sentences in Improving Sentences questions:

- Method 1: Use a semicolon.
- Method 2: Add a conjunction.
- Method 3: Make the clauses relate clearly.

Method 1: Use a Semicolon

One of the most common remedies you'll find on the SAT is a semicolon. A semicolon (;) signals that both sides of the sentence are grammatically separate but closely related to one another.

> I walked into the pet store and asked the clerk if she had any talking parrots; this made her roll her eyes.

Method 2: Add a Conjunction

Another method for correcting run-on sentences is adding conjunctions. Suppose you see this run-on sentence:

> In her incredible eagerness to cheer her team to victory, Amy the cheerleader has lost her voice, therefore her performance at the games is a silent one.

If you add the conjunction *and*:

> In her incredible eagerness to cheer her team to victory, Amy the cheerleader has lost her voice and therefore her performance at the games is a silent one.

The run-on disappears.

Method 3: Make the Clauses Relate Clearly

Sometimes sentences contain strange relationships among clauses that can obscure the meaning of the sentence. (A *clause* is just a bunch of words with a subject and a predicate). Here's an example:

> The student council attempted to lure people to the dance with free food, most people attended the field hockey game.

This sentence suggests that despite the student council's efforts, people didn't go to the dance because they went to the field hockey game. You can correct this run-on sentence by adding a word that makes this relationship clear:

> Although the student council attempted to lure people to the dance with free food, most people attended the field hockey game.

Okay, time for a real example:

> The police reprimanded everyone <u>at the graduation party, they didn't seem very sympathetic to the fact that it was our senior year</u>.
>
> (A)   at the graduation party, they didn't seem very sympathetic to the fact that it was our senior year
>
> (B)   at the graduation party, seemingly the fact that it was our senior year did not make them sympathetic
>
> (C)   at the graduation party without being sympathetic to the fact that it was our senior year
>
> (D)   at the graduation party they didn't, despite the fact that it was our senior year, seem very sympathetic
>
> (E)   at the graduation party; they didn't seem very sympathetic to the fact that it was our senior year

A classic run-on. The two parts could easily stand alone:

> The police reprimanded everyone at the graduation party. They didn't seem very sympathetic to the fact that it was our senior year.

Remember, the SAT usually fixes run-ons by exchanging the comma for a semicolon. In this case, **E**, which uses the semicolon method, is the correct answer.

Notice that you could have corrected the question above by turning the second half into a subordinate clause:

> Since they reprimanded everyone at the graduation party, the police didn't seem very sympathetic to the fact that it was our senior year.

Alternatively, you could have inserted the word *and* between the two clauses:

> The police reprimanded everyone at the party, and they didn't seem very sympathetic to the fact that it was our senior year.

The majority of Improving Sentence questions dealing with run-ons will require you to use one of the three methods we've discussed to fix the sentence.

3. Misplaced Modifiers

A modifying phrase is a phrase that explains or describes a word. In standard written English, modifiers usually appear right next to the word they explain or describe. When modifiers are placed far away from the word they describe, the sentence becomes confusing because it's often unclear which word the modifying phrase is referring to, as in the following sentence:

> Eating six cheeseburgers, nausea overwhelmed Jane.

This sentence is problematic. We can logically infer that Jane was doing the eating, but because the modifying phrase (*Eating six cheeseburgers*) is so far from the word it's intended to modify (*Jane*), figuring out the meaning of the sentence takes a lot of work. It could very well seem as if "nausea" rather than "Jane" is being described.

Therefore, the meaning of the sentence could be that "nausea" ate six cheeseburger fries. The sentence as-is does not convey the meaning the writer intended.

When you see a modifier followed by a comma, make sure the word that the modifier describes comes right after the comma. A corrected version of this sentence could read:

> After eating six cheeseburgers, Jane was overwhelmed with nausea.

The phrase *eating six cheeseburgers* describes what Jane is doing, so Jane's name should come right after the phrase.

Another way to correct the sentence:

> Nausea overwhelmed Jane after she ate six cheeseburgers.

Now take a look at this sample question:

> Having a bargain price, Marcel snatched up the designer jeans right away.
>
> (A)   Having a bargain price, Marcel snatched up the designer jeans.
> (B)   Marcel who has a bargain price, snatched up the designer jeans.
> (C)   The jeans' bargain price led to Marcel's snatching them up.
> (D)   Due to their bargain price, Marcel snatched up the designer jeans.
> (E)   Based on their bargain price, the jeans were snatched up right away by Marcel.

The misplaced modifier in this sentence confuses the meaning of sentence. As it is, it sounds like Marcel has a bargain price, but he certainly isn't for sale. That means you can cut **A** right away, since it just preserves the underlined portion of the sentence. Cut **B** since it also identifies Marcel as the object with the bargain price. **C** uses the possessive awkwardly and uses *them* incorrectly to refer to the bargain price. **E** looks better, but the phrase *the jeans were snatched up* uses the passive voice.

D is the correct answer. In **D**, the phrase *bargain price* modifies *designer jeans* rather than *Marcel*. The correct answer solves another problem with the original sentence, which is the phrase *having a bargain price. Having* does not clearly express the relationship between the jeans and Marcel's purchase. In the correct answer, the phrase *due to* suggests that Marcel bought the designer jeans because they had a bargain price.

4. Parallelism

We covered parallelism in the Identifying Sentence Errors chapter, but we give it another brief review, since it's also likely to show up in Improving Sentences questions.

In every sentence, all of the different components must start, continue, and end in the same, or parallel, way. It's especially common to find errors of parallelism in sentences that list actions or items. In the example below, the pool rules are not presented in the same format, which means there is a parallelism error.

> In the pool area, there is no spitting, no running, and don't toss your half-eaten candy bars in the water.

The first two forbidden pool activities end in *–ing* (*-ing* words are called gerunds), and because of that, the third forbidden thing must also end in *–ing*. If you start with gerunds, you must continue with gerunds all the way through a list.

> In the pool area, there is no spitting, no running, and no tossing your half-eaten candy bars in the water.

the new SAT

Here's a sample Improving Sentences parallelism question:

> The unlimited shopping spree allowed Rachel to raid the department store <u>and she could eat</u> everything in the cafe.
>
> (A) and she could eat
> (B) as well as eating
> (C) so she could eat
> (D) and a meal
> (E) and to eat

The description of the shopping spree's powers begins with an infinitive, *to raid*. Therefore, on the other side of that *and*, we should find another infinitive. Instead, the original sentence contains the phrase *she could eat*, which is not parallel. **E**, the correct answer, balances both sides of the equation by substituting *to eat*. In its corrected form, the sentence is made nicely parallel and balanced by the two infinitives:

> The unlimited shopping spree allowed Rachel to raid the department store and to eat everything in the cafe.

5. Wordiness

Wordiness means using more words than you absolutely need. It's the crime you commit when you've only gotten four pages written of a six-page paper and it's 1 a.m. the night before the paper's due. It's all that meaningless redundant junk you write in a desperate attempt to fill up space. Here's an example from a paper Justin wrote senior year:

"The history of nineteenth-century France is one marked by great periods of continuity and change."

Here's what Justin's got: Wordy meaninglessness with only the vague sheen of insight. Wordiness often comes hand in hand with the passive voice, as in Justin's weak example ("is one marked by"). Other times wordiness shows up on its own. Here's an example:

> Pierre observed the diners and motels of middle America, and <u>these are sights that are depicted</u> in his trendy paintings.
>
> (A) these are sights that are depicted
> (B) the depiction of these sights is
> (C) these sights having been depicted
> (D) his depiction of these sights
> (E) he depicted these sights

This sentence is both wordy and passive. The underlined part could be said in half the space, and you could remove a few words without changing the meaning of the sentence at all. For example: *Pierre observed the diners and motels of middle America, and these sights are depicted in his trendy paintings*. But even in that succinct version, the passive voice remains: The underlined phrase does not make it clear that Pierre depicted the sights. The phrase *sights that are depicted* makes it sound like a disembodied hand put paint on canvas.

If you encountered this question on the test, you could immediately eliminate **A** if you realized there was a problem to begin with. Both **B** and **C** repeat the original mistakes. They are wordy and they avoid identifying Pierre as the performer of the action. Answer choice **D** looks much better; it's short and there are no red-flag phrases or words, such as *having been* or *is*, that suggest the passive voice. Suppose you suspect that **D** is the right answer; if you plug it back into the sentence, as you should always do, you get, *Pierre observed the diners and motels of middle America,* *and his depiction of these sights in his trendy paintings*. This newly created sentence is actually a fragment, and therefore grammatically unacceptable.

So you come to **E**: brief, clear, to the point, and entirely devoid of the passive voice. Does it check out? *Pierre observed the diners and motels of middle America, and he depicted these sights in his trendy paintings*. Yes. **E** avoids wordiness, names Pierre as the performer of the action, and is a grammatically correct sentence.

The Little Four

In addition to the Big Five, you'll likely see a question once in a while that deals with one of these four concepts:

1. Conjunctions
2. Fragments
3. Coordination and subordination
4. Pronouns

1. Conjunctions

Conjunctions are connecting words such as *and*, *but*, *that*, and *or*. They help link two parts of a sentence together. Suppose you have two sentences:

> Abigail jumped off her horse. She then dove into a pool of deep water.

A conjunction such as *and* enables you to connect the two halves of the sentence:

> Abigail jumped off her horse and into a pool of deep water.

Improving Sentences questions test you on conjunctions by including sentences in which the conjunction makes the sentence illogical or clunky.

> Nick wrote a novel <u>and it depicts</u> the life of a somewhat inspiring record store clerk.
>
> (A)   and it depicts
> (B)   being the depiction of
> (C)   it depicts
> (D)   that depicts
> (E)   and depicting in it

The right answer is **D**. In this sentence, the conjunction *that* expresses the function of the novel more smoothly than the clunky phrase *and it* does.

2. Fragments

Fragments are almost the opposite of run-on sentences. Run-on sentences have clauses squashed together and joined incorrectly. Fragments have no independent clause and therefore are incomplete sentences.

> <u>The hunchback vice principal growling</u> at students in the main office.
>
> (A)   The hunchback vice principal growling
> (B)   The hunchback vice principal having growled
> (C)   Growling, the hunchback vice principal
> (D)   It is the hunchback vice-principal
> (E)   The hunchback vice principal growls

In this sentence, the clause lacks a proper verb for the subject (*the hunchback vice principal*). The sentence would be complete if it read, *The hunchback vice principal growling at terrified students was notorious for his brutal tactics*. Notice though that

the
new
SAT

the answer choices don't fix the fragment that way. Instead, the correct answer, **E**, takes away the problem of expectation altogether. When you read *The hunchback vice principal growls at terrified students*, you don't expect the sentence to continue. He growls and that's the end of the story.

3. Coordination and Subordination

Bad coordination happens in gym class when you trip over your own feet or crash into someone else on the field. Bad coordination in a sentence happens when two clauses are joined together with a word that makes their relationship confusing.

> John made T-shirts for the swim team, <u>but he designed the logos himself</u>.
>
> (A)   but he designed the logos himself
> (B)   however, he designed the logos himself
> (C)   and he designed the logos himself
> (D)   since he designed the logos himself
> (E)   and yet, he designed the logos himself

The sentence makes it clear that John creates his own T-shirts. He also designs logos for the T-shirts. So should the word *but* express the relationship between these two activities? No, because the two activities are closely related. The word *but* would make sense only if the sentence said something like *John made T-shirts, but other than that he sat around playing video games all day*. The word *but* suggests a contrast, a change in the direction of the sentence. If you get to the middle of a sentence and it takes an unexpected turn, look for a coordination error.

In this question, you can eliminate **B** because the word *however* is also a bad choice when joining these two clauses. It expresses the same kind of contrasting relationship as does the word *but*. You can eliminate **E** for the same reason. Answer **D** isn't quite as bad as **B** and **E**, but *John made T-shirts for the swim team, since he designed the logos himself* doesn't make that much sense. John doesn't make T-shirts *because* he designs the logos, he makes T-shirts *and* designs the logos, which is exactly what **C** says. Bingo.

We thought it would be helpful to put together a list of conjunctions and split them up based on whether they suggest contrast or no contrast. Contrast conjunction words like *but* require the meaning of the sentence to change direction. For example, "I would go to school, *but* I don't feel well." Noncontrast conjunction words like *and* keep the sentence flowing in the same direction. For example, "After school I will practice piano *and* eat a snack."

Here's a chart to help you learn the most important contrast and noncontrast conjunction words.

Noncontrast Conjunctions	Contrast Conjunctions
and	but
because	though
since	although
so	while
thus	rather
therefore	instead
	unless
	despite
	however
	nevertheless
	notwithstanding

Subordination problems happen when there are two subordinate clauses and no main clause. You don't need to know what that jargon means. Instead, you just need to know subordination problems tend to occur when sentences contain more than one of the conjunction words listed above. If you see one clause that starts with *although, because, if, since,* or *so that,* and then another clause that starts with one of these words, you'll hear the subordination problem loud and clear:

> Because Teddy thought his first date with Maria went well, <u>so that he called her every day for the next week</u>.
>
> (A)   so that he called her every day for the next week
> (B)   although he called her every day for the next week
> (C)   because he called her every day for the next week
> (D)   he called her every day for the next week
> (E)   and he called her every day for the next week

You don't need to know that this sentence is an example of bad subordination. Just notice that the two parts of the sentence don't go together. Why don't they fit together? Because there's something strange about the middle of the sentence. You hit the comma, and then the sentence takes an unexpected turn.

The first part of the sentence sets you up: Since Teddy thought his first date with Maria went well, you expect something along the lines of *he invited her out again* or *he kissed her on her front porch,* right? Instead, you get the phrase *so that.* That just sounds incorrect and doesn't make a lot of sense.

Knowing the sentence contains an error allows you to eliminate **A**. In **B**, the word *although* gives you exactly the same sort of problem that plagues the original sentence. Same with **C**, *because.* He thought the date went well because he called her every day the next week? No. That doesn't make sense. In **E**, the word *and* doesn't go with the *although* that starts the sentence. Plug **D** back into the sentence to make sure it fits: *Because Teddy thought his first date with Maria went well, he called her every day for the next week.* Lookin' good.

As we emphasized a few times already, relying on your ear and on what "sounds right" is dangerous on the SAT. The SAT wants you to trust your ear and go with what you think might sound right in conversation or casual English. Remember that the SAT is anything but casual and that Improving Sentences questions test standard *written* English, not the same English you speak with friends or family. That makes learning the rules and familiarizing yourself with these words all the more important.

4. Pronouns

Pronouns are words that take the place of nouns (words for people, places, and things)—words like *she, her, hers, he, him, his, they, their, it, its, that,* and *which.* There are a number of ways that pronouns can be used incorrectly (and we cover those in our Identifying Sentence Errors chapter), but in Sentence Improvement questions one type of pronoun error generally appears: ambiguous pronouns.

An ambiguous pronoun occurs when it isn't clear to which noun the pronoun is referring. Take a look at the following sentence:

> Arnold and Ebenezer went to the store, where he bought a pair of polyester pants.

Wait a minute. Who bought the pants? Arnold or Ebenezer? You can't know, because that pronoun *he* is ambiguous. Now most Sentence Improvement questions dealing with ambiguous pronouns won't be quite as obvious as that last example. Check this out:

> Clay, Nina, and Melissa were crossing the street when, looking to the right, she saw a sign advertising a yard sale.

This sentence tries to hide the ambiguous pronoun *she* by separating it from the nouns *Clay, Nina,* and *Melissa* at the beginning of the sentence. You have to be able to see through such trickery, and notice that because there were two girls crossing the street, it's unclear which of them saw the sign.

7.6 CHEAP TRICKS

We put the Cheap Tricks at the end of this chapter because you should use them only in Cases of Desperation. Only two Cases of Desperation on Improving Sentences questions merit resorting to Cheap Tricks:

- You can't eliminate even one answer choice.
- You've eliminated all but two answer choices and find yourself wasting time agonizing over which answer choice is correct.

Before we discuss each Cheap Trick, we must add a further warning: *Do not apply the Cheap Tricks blindly.* Cheap Tricks can improve your odds of correctly answering a question on which you're stumped, but they aren't foolproof. Cheap Tricks *will* help you get a higher percentage of questions right. They won't help you get every question right.

That said, let's break open our bag of Cheap Tricks and get started.

Cheap Trick 1. Go with the shortest answer.
Cheap Trick 2. Cut answer choices that change the meaning of the sentence.
Cheap Trick 3. Cut answer choices that begin with words ending in *-ing*.
Cheap Trick 4. Get your *A* in gear.

Here's an example to show you how and when to use Cheap Tricks:

> Brent's cowboy hat looks pretty silly, <u>seeing as how he lives in New York City</u>.
>
> (A) seeing as how he lives in New York City
> (B) since he lives in New York City
> (C) considering him living in New York City
> (D) seeing that he lives in New York City
> (E) after all he doesn't live in the West

Start off by applying our eight-step strategy (see page 65) for Improving Sentences questions to this example. So, let's say you give step 1 a whirl ("Read the sentence and try to hear the problem") and you hear something funny about the phrase *seeing as how*. You can't immediately think of a solution, but step 2 tells you that if you find an error, you can eliminate **A**. Steps 3 and 4 require you to have some hunch about how to fix the error, but in this example you're hunchless. That means you should skip to step 5 and eliminate any answer choices that repeat the error. In this case, that means eliminating answer choice **D**, which repeats the awkward word *seeing*.

Let's say you now find yourself stuck. **B**, **C**, and **E** look equally good to you. It's time to bring on the cheap tricks.

Cheap Trick 1: Go with the shortest answer.

We'll make this quick. When you find yourself staring blankly at two or three answer choices, go with the shorter answer choice. The SAT likes to keep the right answers concise. In the example about Brent's goofy cowboy hat, **B** is not only the right answer, it's nice and short: *since he lives in New York City*.

Cheap Trick 2: Cut answer choices that change the meaning of the sentence.

Be suspicious of answer choices that tweak the meaning of the sentence. **E** is the obvious suspect in the sample question: *after all he doesn't live in the West*. Sure, there's a better reason than the Cheap Trick to eliminate **E**: If you substitute **E** into the original sentence, you get *Brent's cowboy hat looks pretty silly, after all he doesn't live in the West*, which is a run-on sentence. But if you didn't spot the run-on, and were in a panic, you could have eliminated **E** anyway, thanks to Cheap Trick 2. The sentence initially had to do with New York, and how ridiculous one looks sporting a cowboy hat there. **E** brings up the West—new territory. Remember, the directions explicitly instruct you to *choose the answer that best expresses the meaning of the original sentence*, so an answer choice that messes with the original meaning should be eliminated.

Cheap Trick 3: Cut answer choices that begin with words ending in –*ing*.

More often than not, gerunds (words ending in –*ing*) do not appear in correct answer choices. If you apply this trick to the goofy hat example, you can eliminate answer **C** *considering him living in New York CIty*. In cases like this one, -*ing* words are often awkward. If you read the sentence and have no idea which answer choice is right, get rid of the one with a word like *considering*.

Cheap Trick 4: Get your *A* in gear.

It's worth reiterating that about one-fifth of the answers on this section will be **A**— "no error." Students tend to freak out when they can't find errors, and they pick some random **B**, **C**, **D**, or **E** rather than go with **A**. **A** is not your enemy. In fact, **A** can be very helpful when you're in a bind on Improving Sentences questions. Here's why: Cutting **A** tips the guessing odds in your favor. That means if you're unsure how to fix the error in a sentence, but you're certain it contains some error, you can always cut **A** and guess with confidence.

BEAT

IDENTIFYING

SENTENCE ERRORS

IDENTIFYING SENTENCE ERRORS ARE TRUE TO THEIR name: On these questions, you simply find the errors in the sentences. You don't have to fix the error, name the error, or love the error. You just have to find it. Simple.

The new SAT contains 18 Identifying Sentence Error questions. They all appear in the 25-minute Writing timed section (just after the group of Sentence Improvements), and generally get harder as they move from question 1 to question 18.

8.1 THE DIRECTIONS

Here are the SAT's directions for Identifying Sentence Errors. Memorize them now to avoid having to read them and waste time when you take the actual test.

> The following sentences test your ability to recognize grammar and usage errors. Each sentence contains either a single error or no error at all. No sentence contains more than one error. The error, if there is one, is underlined and lettered. If the sentence contains an error, select the one underlined part that must be changed to make the sentence correct. If the sentence is correct, select choice E. In choosing answers, follow the requirements of standard written English.

These directions are models of clarity. But there are two subtle points that are important to understand. First, the phrase *follow the requirements of standard written English* means you must use the rules that govern formal writing rather than the

rules that govern the way you talk. That means, "Hello, how are you?" instead of "What's up?" Second, the directions tell you that some of the actual questions are completely correct. That's what answer choice **E** is all about. Students tend to find these questions especially tough. When they can't find any errors, they're not sure if they're missing something or if the sentence really is perfect. Well, we did a little snooping around through the SAT II Writing and discovered that about one-fifth of the Identifying Sentence Errors questions on the test will be answer **E**. We expect that ratio to more or less carry over to the new SAT Writing section. That means you don't need to be alarmed if you can't find an error. That will happen in about one out of every five questions.

8.2 FOUR STEPS AND SEVEN SCREW-UPS

Here's a sample Identifying Sentence Error question:

> The crowd, <u>which</u> clamored for the players to appear, <u>were</u> unusually <u>rowdy for</u> a typically
>   A   B   C
> reserved <u>audience</u>. <u>No error</u>.
>   D   E

That's all it is: A sentence with a bunch of scattered lines. Above one of those lines is an error that you've got to pick out and then identify as **A**, **B**, **C**, **D**, or **E**. Nearly every error on Identifying Sentence Errors questions will be traceable to one of seven major grammatical mistakes. We call these the Seven Deadly Screw-Ups:

1. Pronouns
2. Subject-Verb Agreement
3. Tenses
4. Parallelism
5. Adverbs and Adjectives
6. Gerunds
7. Idioms, Wrong Words, and Double Negatives

In the next section, we take a much closer look at each of the seven grammar pitfalls, complete with examples of each. First we want to show you the four-step method we've developed to help you pick out where the Seven Deadly Screw-Ups lie in every Identifying Sentence Errors question you face. Here's a chart of the four steps. An explanation of each step follows.

Step 1   Read the sentence and try to hear the screw-up.

Step 2   Eliminate underlined choices that you know are correct.

Step 3   Check for screw-ups among the remaining choices.

Step 4   If all else fails, go with **E.**

Step 1: Read the sentence and try to hear the screw-up.

Sometimes all you'll has to do is read the sentence, and immediately you'll just hear the problem.[*] It'll scream off the page and into your ear. If that happens, great. But don't expect that to happen all the time, since using your ear only works if it's well trained. Having a good ear for bad grammar is not something everybody has natu-

---

[*]   Did you hear that one? *Has* should have been *have*.

rally. It's kind of like having a good ear for music. Some people magically have perfect pitch from birth, but most people must work at developing their sense of musical pitch over time.

We're going to assume that, like us, you've not been born with the gift of an ear for perfect grammar. Even if you feel like you've got grammar safely under control, we suggest that you don't just go with your ear. Plenty of grammar that sounds right to us based on everyday speech is actually wrong.

So don't trust your untrained ear. Instead, we'll help you train your ear to become more sensitive to the Seven Deadly Screw-Ups. The key to sharpening your sensitivity to formal grammatical errors is learning what the mistakes are in detail and then simply picking them out whenever you hear and see them. Step 1 may therefore be tough for you at first, but once you've studied this entire chapter and trained your ear, you'll be more attuned to scanning for screw-ups right away. If you can't pick out the screw-up immediately after reading the sentence, always move on to step 2.

Step 2: Eliminate underlined choices that you know are correct.

Just because you can't see or hear an error doesn't mean it isn't there. That's the tricky part of Identifying Sentence Errors questions. Before deciding that **E** is the choice for you, go through a process of elimination. Take a look at each underlined part and eliminate those that you *know* are correct. For example, say you read the example sentence on page 80 once and didn't hear a problem. You would then go through the sentence again, crossing off the error-free underlined parts. *Which*—that might be wrong. You're not sure, so keep the answer choice for now. *Were*—also could be wrong. There might be a subject-verb agreement problem. Keep it. *Rowdy for*—you feel sure there's nothing wrong with that. Eliminate answer choice **C** by crossing it out in your test booklet. *A typically reserved audience* is a grammatically flawless phrase. Cross out **D** in your test booklet. Now you're down to **A** and **B**, and it's time to move to step 3. Keep **E** for the moment, since you're not yet sure whether the sentence is truly error-free.

Step 3: Check for screw-ups among the remaining answer choices.

Look at your two remaining choices, **A** and **B**. Answer choice **A** is *which*. Sometimes *which* is mistakenly used instead of *that*, but here, *which* is the correct choice.* You can eliminate **A**. What about **B**? *Were* is a verb. Subject-verb agreement problems are commonly tested on this section of the test. What is the subject of *were*? *The crowd*. Standing between the subject and the verb is the clause, *which clamored for the players to appear*. Ignore that clause for the moment to test whether the subject matches up with the verb. When you eliminate the phrase, you get *the crowd were*. That doesn't match. *The crowd* is a singular subject, and *were* is a plural verb. So **B** is the correct answer.

Step 4: If all else fails, go with E.

Again, remember that about one-fifth of answers to Identifying Sentence Errors questions are **E**, no error. Sometimes you'll read the sentence, eliminate the error-free underlined parts, and find that you've crossed out every single underlined part.

---

* *Quick tip:* When text follows a comma, choose *which*; when there is no comma, use *that*.

If this happens, don't second-guess yourself. Don't force yourself to find an error where none exists. Mark it **E**.

8.3 THE SEVEN DEADLY SCREW-UPS

The same types of grammar errors pop up again and again on Identifying Sentence Errors questions. Our list of Seven Deadly Screw-Ups tells you what kinds of errors to look and listen for, but you also need to know precisely what each one means. Below we provide a bit more background and plenty of examples to help make sure you've got each screw-up squared away in your head.

A word of advice: When going through the examples below, read them out loud to yourself. Hearing what sounds right and what sounds wrong can help burn these grammar rules into your brain. Also, we know from experience that it's easy to space out while studying grammar. Talking out loud will help keep you focused. Ready to get familiar?

Screw-Up 1: Pronouns

Pronoun errors are the most common type of screw-up found on Identifying Sentence Errors questions. To reiterate what we covered in Improving Sentences: pronouns are words that take the place of nouns (words for people, places, and things)—words like *she, her, hers, he, him, his, they, their, it, its, that,* and *which.* Let's look at this sentence:

> Ernie felt better after playing air guitar.

A pronoun is a word you would use to replace the noun *Ernie*:

> *He* felt better after playing air guitar.

"Hearing" pronoun problems might take a little practice, because people often use pronouns incorrectly in casual speech. So even if a particular pronoun sounds correct, double-check it to make sure it follows all the rules governing pronoun use. Here are those rules:

Pronoun Agreement

Pronoun agreement is by far the most frequently tested pronoun rule in Identifying Sentence Errors questions. Here's what it's all about.

Pronouns must agree in number with the noun. If the noun is plural, the pronoun must be plural; if the noun is singular, the pronoun must be singular. This sounds straightforward enough, but spotting errors in pronoun agreement on the test can be tricky because we make errors of pronoun agreement so frequently in speech. We tend to say things like *"Yo, somebody lost their shoe!"* instead of *"Yo, somebody lost his shoe!"* You might avoid saying *somebody lost his shoe* because you don't want to exclude women by saying *his*, and it's cumbersome to write *somebody lost his or her shoe.* People attempt to solve these problems with the gender-neutral *their.* So if you see it on the test, you'll know it's an error. *Their* might be gender-neutral, but it's plural, and plural pronouns cannot ever replace singular nouns.

Since this error is so common in everyday speech and therefore *sounds* correct to many people's ears, you can be sure you'll see a few questions on it on the test. The deceptively correct sound of many pronoun agreement errors serves as a good reminder of how dangerous it is to just trust your ear. Often what sounds right is dead wrong.

The sentence below is incorrect because the pronoun and the noun don't agree in number:

> Every student <u>at the party</u> tried <u>to look</u> <u>their</u> <u>best</u>. <u>No error</u>.
>   A   B   C   D   E

This sentence begins with the singular noun *student*, so the pronoun must be singular too. *Their* is plural and therefore wrong in this sentence.

The pronoun and noun also won't agree if the noun is plural and the pronoun is singular:

> <u>Even though</u> some possess the flexibility to put their legs over their heads, most people <u>vary</u> in
>   A   B
>
> <u>his or her</u> ability to achieve <u>this feat</u>. <u>No error</u>.
>   C   D   E

In this sentence, the problem is with **C**, the phrase *his or her*. Those pronouns refer to the plural noun *people*, but *his or her* is singular, because that pesky *or* makes it one or the other. This is a case in which *their* is correct, and *his or her* is incorrect.

Another kind of pronoun agreement question just tests to see if you're paying attention. On questions like the one below, you'll get into trouble if you're reading quickly and fail to make sure that the pronoun matches up with the noun it replaces:

> <u>For</u> the robber trying to decide between potential getaway cars, every car <u>up for</u> consideration
> A   B
>
> has <u>their</u> <u>own</u> set of advantages. <u>No error</u>
>   C   D   E

In this sentence, the pronoun *their* replaces the noun *car*. This is incorrect, because *car* is singular, and *their* is plural. If you were reading carelessly, however, you might assume that since the first part of the sentence contains the plural noun *cars*, the plural pronoun *their* is correct. Always be sure you're inspecting each pronoun carefully.

Pronoun Case

We're about to get on your case. **The "case" of a word refers to the function that a word performs in a sentence**. The most important thing for you to understand in reference to pronoun case is the subjective and objective case. "Huh?" Exactly. Let us explain.

A word is the subject of a sentence if it is the main noun that performs the verb. The object of a sentence is the noun toward which, or upon which, the verb is being directed. Look at this sentence:

> Sam kissed Jess.

Sam is the subject, since he performed the kiss, and Jess is the object, since she received the kiss.

When a pronoun replaces a noun, that pronoun must match the noun's case. This is important because pronouns actually have different forms, depending on their cases.

Subjective Case Pronouns	Objective Case Pronouns
I	me
you	you
he, she, it	him, her, it
we	us
they	them
who	whom

In the example sentence, *you* would replace the subject, *Sam*, with the subject pronoun, *he*, and the object, *Jess*, with the object pronoun, *her*. *He* kissed *her*.

The SAT Writing section often tests your knowledge of pronoun case in a tricky way. You'll get phrases like *her and her cats* or *him and his friends*. They try to confuse you with these phrases by including two pronouns, each of which is doing separate things. They want you to reason that if one pronoun is in a certain case, then the other pronoun should be in the same case, right? Noooo. For example:

> <u>Her</u> and <u>her friend</u> like to stay in their hotel room and <u>drink root beer</u> whenever <u>they take a trip</u>.
> A   B   C   D
> <u>No error</u>.
> E

This sample has a plural subject: *Her and her friend*. You know *her and her friend* is the subject since they are the ones who do the liking in the sentence—they perform the verb (*drink*). In this sentence, the first *her* is a pronoun and should be in the subjective case, not the objective case.

Don't worry if this all feels too technical for you. If you can grasp this kind of grammatical complexity after a few tries, then you're in great shape. But whether you know the grammar or not, there is a strategy that can help you decide if a pronoun is in the proper case. When you have a compound subject like *her and her friend*, throw out each side of the phrase and try it out in the sentence—just remember to make the verb singular, since it stops being plural when you throw out one half of the subject. If you follow this method, you'll get two sentences, which would begin in the following ways:

> Her likes to stay . . .
>
> Her friend likes to stay . . .

You should immediately be able to hear that the first sentence is wrong and the second one is right. Suddenly it seems obvious that the first part of the original sentence should read:

> She and her friend like to stay . . .

The Curious "Cases" of Me and I

The SAT particularly likes to test you on phrases such as *John and me* or *the ghost in the graveyard and I*, because many people don't know when to use *me* and when to use *I*.

Here's a quick True/False question for you: It's always more proper to use *I*—true or false? FALSE. Often *me* is the right word to use. Read the following example:

> There is usually <u>a haze of</u> blue smoke surrounding <u>Jesse and I</u> in Chem lab, especially when we
> A   B
> <u>mix</u> together chemicals of <u>unknown origin</u>. <u>No error</u>.
> C   D   E

In this example, **B** is incorrect, since it should read *Jesse and me*. So how can you tell when to use *I* and when to use *me*? It's got nothing to do with formality or propriety. *Me* is used as an object of a preposition. *I* is used as the subject (or part of the subject) of a sentence. "Give that ball to *me*." "The dog and *I* sped down the lane."

It's often hard to tell when to use *I* and when to use *me*. One of the best ways to tell is to cut out some of the surrounding words. For example, in the sentence above, if you cut out *Jesse and* from the sentence, you get the phrase *smoke surrounding I*. Though we told you not to rely on your ear exclusively, examples like this one don't require a trained ear to detect the error. You'd *never* say or write *the smoke surrounding I*. It should leap off the page and shout out its incorrectness to you.

It's always a good idea to double-check your ear. On I/me questions like this example, substitute *me* for *I* (or vice versa if the case may be). Here you'd get *smoke*

surrounding Jesse and me, which sounds better and checks out correctly if you drop *Jesse and* to get *smoke surrounding me*.

The Strange "Cases" of Me and My

It can also be tough to depend solely on your ear to try to figure out whether to use *me* or *my*. Look at this sentence:

> When it comes to me studying for the math tests, "concentration" is my middle name. No error.
> A   B   C   D   E

Although it may sound right, *me* is actually incorrect in this sentence. The *me/my* refers to studying. You need a possessive word to indicate that the sentence refers to *your* study habits. If you use *me*, the phrase means *when it comes to me*. The subject of the sentence is not *you*, it's *your study habits*. Using *my* gives the sentence the possessive meaning it needs to convey.

Pronoun Shift

This is a bad thing. A sentence should start, continue, and end with the same kind of pronouns. Pronoun shift occurs when the pronoun type changes over the course of the sentence.

> When one first begins to arm wrestle, it's important to work on your endurance and to make
> A   B
>
> your biceps appear formidable. No error.
> C   D   E

If you start talking about *one*, you have to keep talking about *one* for the duration of the sentence. Therefore, the sentence could read, *When one first begins to arm wrestle, it's important to work on one's endurance*, or, *When you first begin to arm wrestle, it's important to work on your endurance.* But the sentence cannot combine *one* and *you*. So **C** is the correct answer.

Ambiguous Pronouns

A pronoun is called "ambiguous" when it's not absolutely clear what the pronoun refers to. People use ambiguous pronouns all the time when they're talking. This works out fine in speech, as you can usually make it clear, from context or gestures, what the pronoun refers to. But in writing, you often can't provide that sort of context. Even if the result sounds awkward, you must make sure it's absolutely clear what the pronoun refers to. See if you can spot the ambiguous pronoun in the following sentence:

> Sarah told Emma that she had a serious foot odor problem, and that medicated spray might
> A   B   C   D
>
> help. No error.
> E

The pronoun *she* poses a problem in this sentence. Who has a problem with foot odor, Sarah or Emma? No one knows, because *she* is ambiguous. Grammatically and logically, *she* could refer either to Sarah or Emma. Therefore, **A** is the correct answer.

Comparisons Using Pronouns

Take special notice whenever you see a comparison made using pronouns. When a pronoun is involved in a comparison, it must match the case of the other pronoun involved:

> I'm much stronger than her, which is good, because it means I'll dominate this wrestling
> A   B   C   D
>
> match. No error.
> E

In this sentence, *I* is being compared to *her*. These two pronouns are in different cases, so one of them must be wrong. Since only *her* is underlined, it must be wrong, and therefore it's the right answer.

Another way to approach pronouns in comparisons is to realize that comparisons usually omit words. For example, it's grammatically correct to say, *Johanna is stronger than Tom*, but that phrase is actually an abbreviated version of what you're really saying. The long version is, *Johanna is stronger than Tom is*. That last *is* is invisible in the abbreviated version, but you must remember that it's there.

Let's go back to the wrestling sentence for a sec. As in the Johanna and Tom example, the word *is* is invisible, but it's implied. If you see a comparison using a pronoun and you're not sure if the pronoun is correct, add the implied *is*. In this case, adding *is* leaves you with *I'm much stronger than her is*. That sounds wrong, so you know that *she* is the correct pronoun in this case.

Take a look at this similar sentence:

> Brock Lesner <u>is</u> a <u>better</u> professional wrestler <u>than</u> <u>them</u>. <u>No error</u>.
>   A   B   C   D   E

In this comparison the word *are* is implied, since in this sentence the pronoun *them* is plural. Adding *are* leaves you with *Brock Lesner is a better professional wrestler than them are*. That sounds dead wrong, so you know that the sentence should read *Brock Lesner is a better professional wrestler than they*, and that **D** is the right answer.

Screw-Up 2: Subject-Verb Agreement

The fundamental rule about the grammatical relationships between subjects and verbs is this:

- If you have a singular subject, you must use a singular verb. If you have a plural subject, you must use a plural verb.

It sounds simple, and usually it is. For example, you know that it's incorrect to say *candy are good* or *concerts is fun*.

However, in a few instances, subject-verb agreement can get hairy. There are four varieties of subject-verb problems the SAT Writing section loves to test:

- When the subject comes after the verb
- When the subject and verb are separated
- When you have an *either/or* or *neither/nor* construction
- When the subject *seems* plural but isn't

Remember, it's not necessary to remember the *name* of the problem—you certainly don't have to memorize this list. It's only necessary to check subjects and verbs carefully to see if they match up. Knowing the different ways subjects and verbs can go astray will help you check more efficiently.

Subject After the Verb

In most sentences, the subject comes before the verb. The SAT tries to throw you off by giving you a sentence or two in which the subject comes *after* the verb and the subject-verb match-up is incorrect.

> <u>Even though</u> Esther created a petition to protest the <u>crowning</u> of a Prom Queen, <u>there is</u> many
>   A   B   C
> people who refused to sign, saying they support the <u>1950s-era</u> tradition. <u>No error</u>.
>   D   E

The SAT frequently uses this exact formulation, so be wary if you see a comma followed by the word *there*. In this kind of sentence, it's tempting to assume that just because the word *there* comes before the verb *is, there* is the subject—but it's not. *People* is the subject. And since *people* is plural, the matching verb also must be plural. *Is* is a singular verb, and therefore incorrect in this sentence.

Even when you don't see the red flag of *there is,* don't just assume that the subject always comes before the verb. Look at the following sentence:

> <u>Atop</u> my sundae, a colossal <u>mass</u> of ice cream, <u>whipped cream</u>, and sprinkles, <u>sits</u> two
> A   B   C   D
>
> maraschino cherries. <u>No error</u>.
>   E

Tricky! The answer is **D**, *sits*. Because the things doing the sitting are two maraschino cherries (plural subject), you need to use *sit* (plural verb). The sentence should read *Atop my sundae, a colossal mass of ice cream, whipped cream, and sprinkles, sit two maraschino cherries.* Why is this so sneaky? The subject, *maraschino cherries,* comes after the verb, *sits*. With all the singular stuff floating around—one sundae, one mass of ice cream and whipped cream—it's easy to assume that the verb should be singular, too. Look out for that kind of backwards construction.

Subject and Verb Are Separated

One of the SAT's most diabolical tricks is to put the subject here and the verb *waaaaay* over yonder. The test-writers hope that by the time you get to the verb, you'll forget the subject and end up baffled.

> Sundaes with whipped cream and cherries, <u>while</u> good <u>if consumed</u> in moderation, <u>is heinous</u> if
>   A   B   C
>
> eaten <u>for breakfast,</u> lunch, and dinner. <u>No error</u>.
>   D   E

In this sentence, the subject (*sundaes*) is at the beginning of the sentence, while the verb (*is*) is miles away. When this happens, it's helpful to bracket clauses that separate the subject and the verb so you can still see how the subject and verb should relate. If you ignore the phrase here (*while good if consumed in moderation*), you're left with *sundaes is heinous*. That's grammatically heinous. So **C** is the right answer.

Neither/Nor and Either/Or

In *neither/nor* and *either/or* constructions, you're always talking about two things, so it's tempting to assume that you always need a plural verb.

But if the two things being discussed are singular, you need a singular verb. For example, it's correct to say, *Neither Jason nor Sandra acts well*, because if you broke the components of the sentence in two, you would get *Jason acts well* and *Sandra acts well*. It's incorrect to say, *Neither Jason or Sandra act well*, because if you break that sentence into its components, you get *Jason act well* and *Sandra act well*.

It can be hard to hear this error, so be sure to check subject-verb match-ups carefully when you see a sentence like this one:

> <u>Neither</u> Kylie <u>nor</u> Jason <u>measure</u> up to <u>Carrie</u>. <u>No error</u>.
> A   B   C   D   E

Even though the sentence mentions two people (Jason and Kylie) who don't measure up to Carrie, both of those people are singular nouns. Therefore, the verb must be singular. *Measure* is a plural verb, when it should be a singular one, so **C** is the answer.

Tricky Singular Subjects that *Seem* Plural

There are a bunch of confusing subjects out there that are singular but masquerade as plural. It's easy to get tripped up by these singular subjects and mistakenly match them with plural verbs. Here are the leading culprits:

anybody	either	audience	nobody
anyone	group	each	none
America	number	everybody	no one
amount	neither	everyone	

In this sentence, for example, *nobody* seems plural:

> Of all of the <u>students</u> in my class, nobody, not <u>even me</u>, <u>are</u> excited about
>   A   B   C
>
> <u>the new teacher</u>. <u>No error</u>.
>   D   E

Nobody is always a singular noun, so it needs to be matched with a singular verb. The answer is **C**. The sentence should read, *Of all the students in my class, nobody, not even me, is excited about the new teacher.* Look carefully at all seemingly plural subjects to make sure they're not singular subjects masquerading as plural ones.

Be particularly careful with phrases like *as well as*, *along with*, and *in addition to*. Like the *neither/nor* construction, these phrases can trick you into thinking they require a plural verb.

> The leadoff hitter, <u>as well as</u> the cleanup hitter, <u>are</u> getting some <u>good</u> hits <u>tonight</u>. <u>No error</u>.
>   A   B   C   D   E

The actual subject here is *leadoff hitter*. Since *leadoff hitter* is a singular subject, the verb must be singular, too. The presence of the phrase *as well as* does *not* make the subject plural. Even though there are two hitters doing well, the leadoff hitter is the only subject of this sentence. **B** is the answer; the sentence should read, *The leadoff hitter, as well as the cleanup hitter, is getting some good hits tonight.* If the sentence used an *and* instead of an *as well as*, so that it read, *The leadoff hitter and the cleanup hitter are getting some good hits tonight*, then *are* would be correct. It's that *as well as* construction that changes things.

Screw-Up 3: Tenses

Identifying Sentence Errors questions test your knowledge of three common causes of tense errors. We explain each type in detail below.

- Annoying verbs
- Illogical tense switches
- The conditional

Very Annoying Verbs

Very annoying verbs never sound quite right in any tense—like *to lie, to swim,* or *to drink*. When do you lay and when do you lie? When do you swim and when have you swum? When did you drank and why are you drunk? Forget that last one.

> You LIE down for a nap.
> You LAY something down on the table.
> You LAY down yesterday.
> You SWIM across the English Channel.
> You SWAM across the Atlantic Ocean last year.
> You had SWUM across the bathtub as a child.
> You DRINK a glass of water every morning.
> You DRANK a glass of water yesterday.
> You have DRUNK three gallons of water this week.

You'll probably see one question that will test your knowledge of a confusing verb like *to lie*. Look at this sentence, for example:

> <u>On</u> Saturday afternoon, I <u>laid</u> in the sun <u>for an hour</u>, working on my <u>tan</u>. <u>No error</u>.
> A   B   C   D   E

B is the correct answer here, because *laid* is not the correct tense in the context of this sentence. The past tense of *to lie* is *lay,* so the sentence should read *I lay in the sun.*

Unfortunately, there's no easy memory trick to help you remember when to use which verb form. The only solution is to learn and memorize. To simplify that task, we're providing a table of difficult verbs in infinitive, simple past, and past participle forms. You don't have to know those technical terms, but it's well worth your time to look at the list below and learn as many of these as you can:

Infinitive	Simple Past	Past Participle
arise	arose	arisen
become	became	become
begin	began	begun
blow	blew	blown
break	broke	broken
choose	chose	chosen
come	came	come
dive	dived/dove	dived
do	did	done
draw	drew	drawn
drink	drank	drunk
drive	drove	driven
drown	drowned	drowned
dwell	dwelt/dwelled	dwelt/dwelled
eat	ate	eaten
fall	fell	fallen
fight	fought	fought
flee	fled	fled
fling	flung	flung
fly	flew	flown

Infinitive	Simple Past	Past Participle
forget	forgot	forgotten
freeze	froze	frozen
get	got	gotten
give	gave	given
go	went	gone
grow	grew	grown
hang (a thing)	hung	hung
hang (a person)	hanged	hanged
know	knew	known
lay	laid	laid
lead	led	led
lie (to recline)	lay	lain
lie (tell fibs)	lied	lied
put	put	put
ride	rode	ridden
ring	rang	rung
rise	rose	risen
run	ran	run
see	saw	seen
set	set	set
shine	shone/shined	shone
shake	shook	shaken
shrink	shrank	shrunk
shut	shut	shut
sing	sang	sung
sink	sank	sunk
sit	sat	sat
speak	spoke	spoken
spring	sprang	sprung
sting	stung	stung
strive	strove/strived	striven/strived
swear	swore	swore
swim	swam	swum
swing	swung	swung
take	took	taken
tear	tore	torn
throw	threw	thrown
wake	woke/waken	waked/woken
wear	wore	worn
write	wrote	written

Tense Switch

You don't always need to use the same tense throughout a sentence. For example, you can say:

> I used to eat chocolate bars exclusively, but after going through a conversion experience last year, I have broadened my range and now eat gummy candy, too.

This sentence has several tense switches, but they're logical and correct: The sentence uses past tense when it refers to the past and present tense when it talks about the present, and the progression from past to present makes sense.

The SAT gives you a sentence or two with incorrect tense switches. Here's an example:

> At swimming pools last summer, the heat will have brought hundreds and even
> A$$B
> thousands of people to bathe in chlorine-infested waters. No error.
> C$$D$$E

This sentence begins by talking about the past (*last summer*), but then uses the phrase *will have brought*, which refers to the future. The phrase *will have brought* doesn't fit because it suggests something continuing from the present to the future, whereas the sentence should be rooted entirely in the past. Therefore, **B** is the correct answer. Always be sure that the sentence's tenses match the time frame (past, present, or future) in which the subject is discussed.

The Conditional

Your parents are supposed to give you *un*conditional love, meaning they love you even though you refuse to be seen in public with them. So it stands to reason that the conditional is a verb form used to describe something uncertain, or dependent on something else. Conditional sentences are often characterized by the presence of the word *if*. The conditional requires a different conjugation of some verb forms, most notably the verb *to be*. For example, in the past tense, you'd write, "I *was* a good student and got good grades." In the present tense, you'd write, "I am a good student and get good grades." That's all fine and familiar so far, right? The conditional is different, however. In the conditional, you'd write, "If I *were* a good student, I would get good grades."

To conquer conditionals on the SAT, look out for the word *if* and memorize this simple formula to use the correct conjugation: "If . . . were . . . would." Here's an example:

> If I was to see a movie with Mom and Dad, I would risk my reputation. No error.
> A$$BCDE

Was may sound right to you on first reading this sentence, but when in doubt, remember the formula. *Was* violates the formula and therefore is incorrect. The sentence should read, *If I were to see a movie with Mom and Dad, I would risk my reputation.* **A** is the right answer.

Screw-Up 4: Parallelism

Parallel lines line up neatly with each other, right? Parallelism in writing means that the different components of a sentence start, continue, and end in the same way. It's especially common to find errors of parallelism in sentences that list actions or items. When you see a list of any sort, be on the alert for an error in parallelism. In the question below, for example, the activities are not presented in the same format, which means there is a parallelism error.

> Jack never liked <u>bathing the dog</u>, <u>feeding</u> the llamas, or <u>to ride</u> his personal <u>roller coaster</u>.
>   A   B   C   D
>
> <u>No error</u>.
> E

A *gerund* is a funny word for something you already know well: A verb in its *-ing* form. *Biking, parking, walking, talking*—all gerunds. The list of verbs in the example above starts out with two gerunds (*bathing, feeding*) and then switches to an infinitive (*to ride*). An *infinitive* is the *to* form of the verb. "To run" and "to hide" are two infinitive verb forms. The sentence above begins with gerund verb forms and must continue with gerunds all the way through for it to have proper parallel structure. **C** is the correct answer.

Some parallelism errors occur at the end of phrases. The sentence below is incorrect because its two halves don't end in a similar way:

> The steak <u>is definitely</u> the best entrée <u>on the menu</u>, and <u>the clam chowder</u> is the <u>best appetizer</u>.
>   A   B   C   D
>
> <u>No error</u>.
> E

The best appetizer where? In the nation? In the world? Because the first part of the sentence specifies *on the menu*, the second part of the sentence must also be specific. In corrected form, this sentence would read: "The steak is definitely the best entrée on the menu, and the clam chowder is the best appetizer in the world."

Screw-Up 5: Adverbs and Adjectives

Adverbs are often confused with adjectives, especially when used in comparisons. Below we've broken down the key adverb pitfalls you should look out for.

Confusing Adverbs with Adjectives

Adverbs are words used to describe verbs or other adverbs. Adverbs often end in *–ly* (*breathlessly, angrily*). For example, if you're describing how you ate your spaghetti dinner, you're describing a verb (eating), so you need to use an adverb. You could say something like:

> I ate my spaghetti *quickly*.

Adjectives are words used to describe nouns. Again, take the spaghetti example— but this time, suppose that instead of describing the process of eating, you're describing the actual dinner. Since you're describing a noun (dinner), you need to use an adjective. You could say something like, "I ate my *delicious* spaghetti."

People often confuse adverbs with adjectives, especially in speech. We say things like, "I ate my dinner quick." Wrong! Because you're describing an action, you must use an adverb like *quickly*. One very frequently confused adjective/adverb pair is *well* and *good*. *Well* is an adverb, and *good* is an adjective, so one can't be substituted for the other.

> This <u>paper's</u> going pretty <u>good</u>, although I'm not sure <u>I'll</u> be done <u>on time</u>. <u>No error</u>.
>   A   B   C   D   E

A paper can't go pretty good; it can only go pretty well. In order to describe the verb *going*, you have to use an adverb like *well* instead of the adjective *good*.

The SAT usually tests adverb/adjective confusion by giving you a sentence that uses an adjective when it should use an adverb.

> <u>No matter</u> how <u>careful</u> kites are flown, they <u>often</u> <u>get tangled</u> in trees. <u>No error</u>.
>   A   B   C   D   E

In this sentence, the adjective *careful* is used improperly to describe the verb *flown*. Because a verb is being described, *careful* should be *carefully*. The following sentence has a similar problem:

> The fascinating TV <u>special shows</u> how <u>quick</u> the hungry tiger <u>can devour</u> <u>its</u> prey. <u>No error</u>.
>   A   B   C   D   E

This sentence uses the adjective *quick* to describe the verb *devour*; the adverb *quickly* is the right word to use, so **B** contains the error in this sentence. Notice that in this sentence, the adjective, *quick*, is separated from the verb, *devour*, by three words. Sniffing out the improper use of an adjective can be difficult when the verb being described is not directly next to the adjective. If you see an adjective you're not sure about, don't be fooled by distracting phrases like *the hungry tiger*. Just check to see what the adjective is describing. If it's describing a verb, you'll know it's an error.

Adverb or Adjective Misuse in Comparisons

When you see a comparison or an implied comparison, check to make sure all of the adverbs and adjectives are used correctly. If you're comparing two things, you need to use what's known as a comparative modifier. Forget that term. Just remember that when comparing two items, use a word that ends in *-er*, like *smarter, better, faster*. Only when comparing three or more things can you use a superlative modifier like *smartest, best, fastest*.

The SAT will probably test your knowledge of this rule by giving you a question in which a superlative modifier is used incorrectly. Look at the following example:

> <u>Of</u> the two cars <u>I drive</u>, <u>I like</u> the Lamborghini Diablo <u>best</u>. <u>No error</u>.
>   A   B   C   D   E

This sentence contains a comparison between two cars. Because only two things are being compared, *best* is the wrong word. Only when comparing three or more things can you use words like *best*. You could figure this out by phrasing the comparison in a different way. You wouldn't say, *I like my Lamborghini Diablo best than my Civic*; you'd say, *I like my Lamborghini Diablo better than my Civic*. This rephrasing also works if you're puzzling over a sentence that compares three or more items. You wouldn't say, *After trying skydiving, hula-dancing, and pineapple-eating, I decided that I liked hula-dancing less*, because that sentence does not explain if you liked hula-dancing less than you liked skydiving, or less than you liked pineapple-eating, or less than you liked both. What you would say is, *After trying skydiving, hula-dancing, and pineapple-eating, I decided that I liked hula-dancing least*. The superlative modifier *least* makes it clear that hula-dancing was the most disagreeable of all three activities.

Here's a chart of some adjectives with their common comparative and superlative modifier forms.

Adjective	Comparative Modifier	Superlative Modifier
fast	faster	fastest
big	bigger	biggest
healthy	healthier	healthiest
tough	tougher	toughest

the new SAT

Adjective	Comparative Modifier	Superlative Modifier
smart	smarter	smartest
good	better	best
few	fewer	fewest
different	more different	most different
luxurious	more luxurious	most luxurious

Screw-Up 6: Gerunds

As we said in screw-up 4 a gerund is a verb form that ends in *–ing*, such as *prancing, divulging, stuffing,* and so on. Your understanding of gerunds will usually be tested by questions that use the infinitive "to ___" form, such as *to prance, to divulge,* and *to stuff.*

In my family, Thanksgiving dinner usually causes two or more family members to engage in a
    A   B
screaming match, thus preventing the meal to be completed. No error.
                 C   D   E

In this example, the problematic phrase is *preventing the meal to be completed.* This phrase should read *thus preventing the meal from being completed,* changing the infinitive *to be* to the conjugated form, *being.* That change preserves the parallel structure with the gerund *preventing* in the last clause. Here's another example:

To keep your engine running in the freezing cold is a good way to keep the car's interior warm
A   B   C   D
and cozy. No error.
       E

In this sentence, the infinitive verb *to keep* should be switched to the gerund *keeping* to match the gerund verb *running* in the same clause.

Screw-Up 7: Idioms, Wrong Words, and Double Negatives

Here's a twist that should make you happy: Idiom errors are easy to spot because they sound dead wrong. Oh yeah, you should know what an idiom is before we get in too deep here. Actually "in too deep" is an idiom—a form of speech that is unique to itself, has its own grammatical construction, and is usually pretty hard to understand just on its own. That makes it pretty easy to see why there's no set rule at all about idiom errors. You have to be able to read a sentence and think, "That sounds wrong," based on your familiarity with idiomatic expressions in American English. Usually it's a prepositional phrase that's off. For example:

Joan Rivers recently moved to a brand-new apartment in 108th street. No error.
               A   B   C   D   E

Here, the answer is **C**, because in American English we say, "She lives *on* this street" rather than "She lives *in* this street." There is no specific rule that explains why we use the word *on*; it's just something you probably know from years of English-speaking. The following is a list of *proper* usage of idioms that often appear on the SAT Writing:

- He can't *abide by* the no-spitting rule.
- Winona *accused me of* stealing.
- I *agreed to* eat the rotten broccoli.
- I *apologized for* losing the hamsters in the heating vent.
- She *applied for* another credit card.

- My mother pretends to *approve of* my boyfriend.
- She *argued with* the bouncer.
- I *arrived at* work at noon.
- You *believe in* ghosts.
- I can't be *blamed for* your problems.
- Do you *care about* me and my problems?
- He's in *charge of* grocery shopping.
- Nothing *compares to* you.
- What is there to *complain about*?
- He can always *count on* his mommy.
- Ice cream *consists of* milk, fat, and sugar.
- I *depend on* no one.
- That's where cats *differ from* dogs.
- It's terrible to *discriminate against* chimpanzees.
- I have a plan to *escape from* high school.
- There's no *excuse for* your awful behavior.
- You can't *hide from* your past.
- It was all he'd *hoped for*.
- I must *insist upon* it.
- It's impossible to *object to* her intelligent arguments.
- I refuse to *participate in* this discussion.
- *Pray for* me.
- *Protect me from* evil.
- *Provide me with* plenty of food, shelter, and Skittles.
- She stayed home to *recover from* the flu.
- I *rely on* myself.
- She *stared at* his ridiculous haircut.
- He *subscribes to* several trashy magazines.
- I *succeeded in* seducing him.
- *Wait for* me!
- *Work with me*, people!

Occasionally, the idiomatic association between words can affect the entire sentence in a sort of cascade of idioms. Take the following example:

> While the <u>principal</u> of the high school <u>is</u> relatively laid back, the vice principal <u>is often</u> accused
> A   B   C
>
> <u>to be</u> too harsh with the students. <u>No error</u>.
> D   E

The answer to this question is **D** because the word *accused* must take the preposition *of* rather than *to*. Idiomatically, the preposition *of* must be followed by a gerund rather than an infinitive, so the verb *to be* is incorrect. The sentence should read:

> While the principal of the high school is relatively laid back, the vice principal is often accused
> of being too harsh with the students.

Wrong Words

There are tons of frequently confused words in the English language, and while it's impossible to predict which ones the SAT will throw at you, it *is* possible to learn the difference between these pairs of words.

We've broken down wrong words into categories: words that sound the same but mean different things (like *allusion* and *illusion*), made-up words and phrases (like

should of), tricky contractions (like *its* and *it's*), and words commonly and incorrectly used as synonyms (like *disinterested* and *uninterested*).

Words That Sound the Same but Mean Different Things

In the following list, you'll find *homonyms,* such as *dying* and *dyeing.* Homonyms are words that sound the same or similar when spoken aloud but are spelled differently and have different meaning. Since the word *die* sounds exactly the same as the word *dye*, it can be hard to remember which spelling means *expire* and which means *color.* The words in this list sound pretty much the same and are therefore often set as traps to confuse you on the SAT. They're not all full-on homonyms, but they all sound alike enough to make certain questions on the SAT Writing section extra tough:

allusion/illusion An *allusion* is a reference to something.

> Johnno's essay was littered with conspicuous *allusions* to Shakespeare and Spenser.

An *illusion* is a deception or unreal image.

> By clever use of his napkin, Jason created the *illusion* that he'd eaten his rotten broccoli.

alternate/alternative An *alternate* is a substitute.

> When Evie was ousted after the voting scandal, the *alternate* took her place on the student council.

An *alternative* is a choice between two or more things.

> *The Simpsons* provides an *alternative* to mindless, poorly written sitcoms.

appraise/apprise To *appraise* is to figure out the value of something.

> After *appraising* the drawing, Richard informed Cynthia that her house was worthless.

To *apprise* is to give someone information.

> In an urgent undertone, Donald *apprised* me of the worrisome situation.

breath/breathe *Breath* and *breathe* cannot be used interchangeably. *Breath* is a noun, and *breathe* is a verb. That little *e* on the end makes all the difference. A *breath* (noun) is the lungful of air you inhale every few seconds.

> Elena took a deep *breath* and jumped off the diving board.

To *breathe* (verb) is the act of taking in that lungful of air.

> "I can't *breathe*!" gasped Mario, clutching at his throat.

conscience/conscious/conscientious A *conscience* is a sense of right and wrong.

> After he robbed the store, Pinocchio's *conscience* started to bother him.

To be *conscious* is to be awake and alert.

> Suddenly, Marie became *conscious* that she was not alone in the room.

To be *conscientious* is to be dutiful and hardworking.

> *Conscientious* Cedric completed his chores and then did his homework.

desert/dessert A *desert* is a place with sand and camels.

> The cartoon figure pulled himself across the *desert*, calling out for water.

A *dessert* is something sweet that you eat after dinner.

> My favorite *dessert* is cookie dough ice cream.

effect/affect There's a good chance you'll see this pair on the test, because the SAT knows that differentiating between *effect* and *affect* drives students crazy. *Effect* is usually a noun. The *effect* is the result of something.

> Studying had a very positive *effect* on my score.

Affect is usually a verb. To *affect* something is to change it or influence it.

> My high SAT score positively *affected* the outcome of my college applications.

The extra tricky part is that *effect* can also be a verb, and *affect* can also be a noun. In those instances, *effect* means "to cause" and *affect* means a "sense of being alive or vital." Here are two examples.

> The students marching outside the Supreme Court are hoping to *effect* change.
>
> The mummy standing silently against the wall appears to have no *affect*.

eminent/imminent An *eminent* person is one who is well known and highly regarded.

> The *eminent* author disguised himself with a beret and dark glasses.

An *imminent* event is one that is just about to happen.

> When the paparazzi's arrival seemed *imminent*, the celebrities ducked out the back entrance.

lose/loose To *lose* something is to misplace it or shake it off.

> Michel tried to *lose* the hideous shirt his girlfriend had given him for Christmas.

Loose means movable, unfastened, or promiscuous.

> The *loose* chair leg snapped off, and Doug fell to the floor.

principal/principle The *principal* is the person who calls the shots in your high school.

> *Principal* Skinner rules Springfield Elementary School with an iron fist, yet he still lives with his mother.

A *principle* is a value, or standard.

> Edward, a boy of *principle*, refused to cheat on the test.

stationary/stationery *Stationary* means immobile.

> The scarecrow remained *stationary* in the field.

Stationery is the paper you get for Christmas from your aunt.

> Nathaniel wrote thank-you notes on custom *stationery*.

Imaginary Words and Phrases

Here is a list of some words and phrases that don't actually exist but still tend to be used in writing. These mistakes happen mainly because they are the phonetic, or sounded out, spellings of words and phrases we use in speech. For example, the phrase *should of* (a grammatically incorrect phrase) sounds like the way we pronounce *should have* or *should've*, which is why it creeps into people's writing.

a lot/alot Despite widespread usage, the word *alot* does not exist. It is never grammatically correct. Always use the phrase *a lot* instead.

> Henri ate *a lot* of brie with his bread.

could've/could of *Could've* is the contraction of *could have*. People sometimes write *could of* when they mean *could've* or *could have*. Unfortunately, like *alot, could of* is not a real phrase. Never use it.

> Britney *could have* gone on the date, but she claimed to have a prior engagement.

regardless/irregardless This is an easy one because the "word" *irregardless* does not exist. Always use *regardless*.

> *Regardless* of whether your physics teacher uses fake words like *irregardless*, you should not.

should've/should of *Should of* does not exist.

> Arnold *should have* done his Spanish homework.

supposed to/suppose to *Suppose to* falls in the category of made-up phrases. It's often used in place of *supposed to* because when we're talking, we say *suppose to* instead of the grammatically correct *supposed to*.

> According to the vet, Christina is *supposed to* brush her pit bull's teeth once a month.

used to/use to *Use to* (you guessed it) is made-up. The correct spelling is *used to*.

> Alex *used to* play checkers with Anthony.

Contraction Confusion

Look deep within your soul. Do you write *its* sometimes and *it's* at other times, with little regard for which *its/it's* is which? If you do, stop it.

its/it's *Its* and *it's* are very different. *Its* is a possessive pronoun. *It's* is a contraction of *it is*.

　　It's understandable why people confuse the two words. The most common way to show possession is to add an apostrophe and an *s* (*Dorothy's braids, the tornado's wrath, Toto's bark*), which is perhaps the reason people frequently write *it's* when they should write *its*—they know they want to show possession, so they pick the word with the apostrophe and the *s*.

　　To avoid making a mistake, when you see the word *it's*, check to make sure that if you substituted *it is* for the *it's*, the sentence would still make sense. To sum up: *its* signals possession, while *it's* is a contraction of *it is*.

> This day-old soda has lost *its* fizz.

> *It's* a shame that this glass of soda was left out overnight.

their/they're/there Another bunch of very confusing words. It's too bad, but *their*, *they're*, and *there* are not interchangeable. Here's how to distinguish them:

- *Their* is a possessive pronoun.

> They lost *their* hearts in Massachusetts.

- *They're* is the contraction of *they are*.

> *They're* the ugliest couple in all of Boston.

- *There* means over yonder.

> Look! *There* they go!

whose/who's *Whose* is possessive, while *who's* is a contraction of *who is*.

> Anna-Nicole, *whose* California roll I just ate, is looking at me with hatred.
>
> *Who's* responsible for the theft and ingestion of my California roll?

your/you're *Your* is possessive. *You're* is a contraction of *you are*.

> *Your* fly is unzipped.
>
> *You're* getting sleepy.

Which Word When?

Below is a list of words people often—but incorrectly—use interchangeably.

number/amount Use *number* when referring to a group of things that can be counted.

> Faith concealed a *number* of gummy bears in various pockets of her jeans.

Use *amount* when referring to something that cannot be counted.

> Faith drank a certain *amount* of soda every day.

fewer/less Use *fewer* when referring to items that can be counted.

> Yanni complained that he had received *fewer* presents than his sister did.

Use *less* when referring to items that cannot be counted.

> Yanni's parents explained that because they loved him *less* than they loved his sister, they gave him fewer presents.

aggravate/irritate When screaming in frustration, we often say things like, "That's so aggravating!" However, this is incorrect usage. *Aggravate* is not synonymous with *irritate*. *To aggravate* is to make a condition worse.

> Betty's skin condition was *aggravated* by her constant sunbathing.

To *irritate* is to annoy.

> Aeisha enjoys *irritating* her sister by jabbing her in the leg during long car rides.

famous/infamous As you probably know, a *famous* person is someone like Julia Roberts or Tom Cruise.

> The *famous* young actor made his way up the red carpet.

An *infamous* person or thing, however, is something different. *Infamous* means notorious—famous, yes, but famous in a bad way.

> The *infamous* pirate was known the world over for his cruel escapades.

disinterested/uninterested Even reputable daily newspapers occasionally confuse *disinterested* with *uninterested*. *Disinterest* suggests impartiality.

> Nadine and Nora need a *disinterested* third party to referee their argument.

In contrast, an *uninterested* person is one who is bored.

> Nora is completely *uninterested* in hearing Nadine's opinions.

Double Negatives

A double negative is a phrase that uses two negative words instead of one. Double negatives are used very effectively by people like Tony Soprano—"I don't take nothin' from nobody"—but your score on the Writing section will get whacked if you fall prey to their tough-guy allure. You'll probably be adept at spotting double negatives such as "I don't take nothin' from nobody," but the SAT may try to trick you into missing a double negative by using words that count as negatives but don't sound like it, such as *hardly, barely,* or *scarcely.* If you see any of these kinds of words paired with another negative (don't, can't, won't), it's an error.

> Katie <u>can't scarcely</u> stand to wear her <u>gymnastics</u> leotard <u>without</u> underwear <u>underneath</u>.
>   A   B   C   D
> <u>No error</u>.
>   E

In this example, *can't* is obviously a negative word, but *scarcely* is also negative, so the two cannot be used together. **A** is the correct answer.

BEAT

IMPROVING

PARAGRAPHS

IMPROVING PARAGRAPHS QUESTIONS ARE THE toughest and most time-consuming multiple-choice questions you'll face on the new SAT Writing section. They require you to read a series of paragraphs, determine their weaknesses, and then pick the answer choice that solves the problems best.

The new SAT contains one Improving Paragraph passage followed by 6 questions. The paragraph and accompanying questions appear at the end of the 25-minute timed Writing section (just after the group of 18 Identifying Sentence Errors questions). The difficulty of Improving Paragraphs questions raises two important points: pacing and training

the new SAT

9.1 PACING

Students tend to think they have to spend the most time on the toughest questions. That's definitely *not* the best strategy, since you get the same credit for easy and difficult questions. On the PSAT and the SAT II Writing test, for example, you can skip ALL of the Improving Paragraphs questions and still score a 670. We're definitely not suggesting you skip the entire Improving Paragraphs section. We're suggesting that you not dedicate a *disproportionate* amount of time and energy to these especially tough questions, since they'll likely not amount to more than 15 or 20 percent of your score on the SAT Writing section, which is less than 10 percent of your entire score. Just as you should not spend much more time on difficult SAT questions than you do on easier ones, you should avoid spending more time than necessary preparing for Improving Paragraphs.

9.2 TRAINING

The time you do devote to preparing for Improving Paragraphs questions is certainly not a waste. Think of it as a tough training routine for the rest of the Writing section. By the time you can identify a problem with a series of paragraphs, you will have mastered the skills you need to beat each of the other question types: Identifying Sentence Errors, Improving Sentences, and even the Essay. It might be helpful to think of all four parts of the new SAT Writing section as building blocks that teach you the skills you need to beat each successive question type. Even though the questions don't come in this order, thinking about how they relate can help make your preparation more cohesive and effective. Understanding how the parts fit together will give you a greater mastery of the entire section. To sum up:

- Identifying Sentence Errors teaches you how to improve sentences.
- Improving Sentences teaches you how to improve paragraphs.
- Improving Paragraphs shows you how to write an essay.

9.3 DIRECTIONS

Here are the official directions for Improving Paragraphs:

> The following passage is an early draft of an essay. Some parts of the passage need to be rewritten.
>
> Read the passage and select the best answers for the questions that follow. Some questions are about particular sentences or parts of sentences and ask you to improve sentence structure or word choice. Other questions ask you to consider organization and development. In making your decisions, follow the conventions of standard written English. In choosing answers, follow the requirements of standard written English.

Here's a quick translation of what these directions mean: Improving Paragraphs questions present you with a rough draft of an essay. Some questions will ask you to fix or combine individual sentences, and some will address the essay as a whole. Note again the new SAT's emphasis on standard written English.

9.4 THE PARAGRAPHS

The SAT describes the passages in Improving Paragraphs questions as rough drafts of essays. Each passage usually contains three paragraphs of about five sentences each. So all together you're dealing with about 15 sentences per Improving Paragraphs passage.

The SAT's description of the passages as "first drafts" means that the passages contain simple sentence construction and a straightforward writing style. It also means that the essays are filled with errors of style, clarity, wordiness, and poor organization. It's your job to find and fix those errors. Our section on the SAT Essay tells you just what you need to know to write great SAT paragraphs and to avoid the errors you'll have to fix in Improving Paragraphs questions (see Chapter 6.0).

9.5 THE QUESTIONS

You'll come across four different types of Improving Paragraphs questions. Though the specifics of each question are crucial to understand, it's just as important to know that all four types of question share one general rule: Unlike Identifying Sentence Errors and Improving Sentences, Improving Paragraphs questions *do not focus on grammar*. Here's what they *do* focus on:

- Style
- Organization
- Syntax
- Clarity
- No Grammar!

This makes sense because Improving Paragraphs questions take a *broader* view on writing. These questions also focus on an entire passage of writing, not just on one sentence. Therefore, Improving Paragraphs questions usually approach problems at the paragraph or sentence level, which means the big picture tends to matter most. They definitely cover sentence improvement, but they do that within the context of the overall thrust or purpose of the paragraph.

Here are the four different types of Improving Paragraphs questions plus a quick explanation of each. We go over them all up close, including examples, later in the chapter.

1. Sentence Revision Questions

Sentence Revision questions, the most common question type in this section, require you to change and improve an entire sentence or a portion of one. Revision questions ask you to pick a word that should be added to clarify the meaning of a particular sentence or to choose a multiple-choice answer that would most effectively revise a flawed phrase.

2. Sentence Addition Questions

Sentence Addition questions ask you which sentences or phrases should be added to the passage in order create a smoother transition or to clarify meaning. These questions require you to take into account the meaning of the overall passage and how the paragraphs transition into or relate to one another.

3. Sentence Combination Questions

Sentence Combination questions present you with two sentences and ask you to pick the best way to join them. A semicolon? A conjunction? Which conjunction? The skills you picked up in our section on Conjunctions, Coordination and Subordination and the chart of conjunction words will be particularly useful on Sentence Combination questions.

4. Essay Analysis Questions

Essay Analysis questions require you to take a deeper, more critical look at the essay. They ask you to pick the sentence that best sums up the essay or to identify how a particular sentence functions within the essay as a whole. These questions test your understanding of the mechanics of essays, which means how essays are built from the ground up. We cover everything you need to know about essays for the SAT in our chapter on the new SAT essay (see page 39).

(see page 39)

9.6 IMPROVING PARAGRAPHS IN FIVE STEPS

There are five standard steps for dealing with all four of the Improving Paragraphs question types. Each type has its own particular quirks. First we give you the standard steps, then we go over each individual question type to explain the quirks.

Step 1: Read and outline the entire passage quickly.

This first step never varies, and you only have to do it once for every passage: *Before* looking at the questions, read and outline the entire passage very quickly. When we say quickly, we mean *quickly*. It shouldn't take you more than two minutes to read the passage and write down a quick sketch of what the paragraphs contain. The "outline" we advise you to write is really just a very sketchy road map of the passage. As you read each paragraph, sum up its purpose in a few words and write that summation next to the actual paragraph in your test booklet. Here's a quick sample of a paragraph and how we would outline it:

> Dolphins can communicate by using a series of clicking and shrieking sounds. Researchers off the coast of Florida have undertaken research to try to decode these sounds and come up with a comprehensive dolphin language. So far they've managed to translate over 100 "phrases" dolphins use to communicate.

This paragraph is all about dolphins, but more specifically about research on dolphin communication. Our outline entry for this paragraph would read something like, "Florida dolphin research—100 phrases." Just enough to cover the key facts and purpose of the passage.

As you read and outline, you're going to blaze by a lot of errors. Don't waste your time trying to fix them or even marking them. Since the passage has more sentences than the questions can possibly cover, it's a waste of time to examine each sentence carefully. You won't be asked about every single sentence, so let the questions guide you to the sentences you need to examine for problems. On this first quick read-through, your main goal is to understand the purpose of the passage and to see how its paragraphs relate. The outline sketch you build along the way will make navigating back through the passage a breeze.

Step 2: Read the question.

Read the first question, but remember not to look at the answer choices yet.

Step 3: Reread the context sentences.

Context sentences are the sentences before and after the sentence mentioned in the question. Your quick read-through of the passage will give you a general understanding of its subject. But to answer most Improving Paragraphs questions, you need to go back to the relevant part of the passage and reread the sentence mentioned in the question more carefully. It's also crucial to read the context sentences. In fact, sometimes the context can help you rewrite the sentence. For example, read the two sentences around this problematic sentence:

> Her mother told Emily to make the bed. <u>Another chore her mother told her to do was to take out the garbage</u>. Emily reluctantly complied.

Here, the first and second sentences convey similar information. The second sentence is wordy and awkward, however, while the first sentence is clean and concise. You can use the first sentence as a model for the revision of the second sentence.

Step 4: Make your own revision.

As in the other multiple-choice sections, it's important to generate your own answer before you read the answer choices. The wrong answers are SAT traps placed there to confuse you, so don't fall blindly into their clutches. Generate your own answer in your head before reading the actual answers.

If you read the example about Emily and her chores, and modeled your revision on that successful first sentence, you might come up with

> Her mother also told Emily to take out the garbage.

Step 5: Read every answer and pick the one that comes closest to your answer.

Here are the answer choices:

> (A) Another chore her mother told her to do was to take out the garbage.
> (B) Her mother additionally asked her to do the chore of taking out the garbage.
> (C) Also, take out the garbage, her mother asked.
> (D) Then, her mother told Emily to take out the garbage.
> (E) She also asked Emily to take out the garbage.

D comes closest to the revision you prepared before you looked at the answer choices, so that should be your choice.

Let's sum up all five steps:

1. Read and outline the entire passage.
2. Read the question.
3. Reread the context sentences.
4. Make up your own answer first.
5. Read every answer and pick the one that comes closest to your answer.

These fives steps apply to all four question types: Sentence Revision, Sentence Addition, Sentence Combination, and Essay Analysis. Each question type does have its own particular quirks, including one important exception, so next we take you through each type up close.

SENTENCE REVISION—UP CLOSE

The SAT asks you to revise sentences for a bunch of reasons. Most often the problem is awkward language that obscures the meaning of the sentence. The SAT poses these questions in a variety of ways. Here are some examples:

> Which of the following is the clearest version of the underlined portion of sentence 2?
>
> In the context of the third paragraph, sentence 9 could be made more precise by adding which of the following words after "*That*"?
>
> The phrase "*this thing*" in sentence 5 is made most specific in which of the following revisions?
>
> Which is the best word or phrase to add after "*The movie theater*" in order to connect sentence 3 (reprinted below) to the rest of the first paragraph?

On Improving Paragraphs questions like these, *clarity* is key. The SAT hates sentence structure that lacks specificity or could be interpreted in more than one way. Your goal on Sentence Revision questions is always to suggest alternatives that make problematic sentences clearer, simpler, and more specific.

Finally, on some Sentence Revision questions, you may be able to skip step 3 (reread the context sentences). While we think it's always a good idea to look at the context sentences, if you're pressed for time, you could just revise the sentences blindly.

Here's an example of a paragraph with a Sentence Revision question that follows. Read the paragraph and the question, and then we'll explain how to get the correct answer using our five-step method:

> (1) *Obesity is a big problem in the United States.* (2) *Sixty-one percent of adults suffer from it, but around 300,000 people die every year from diseases directly related to obesity.* (3) *Obesity is related to diabetes, high blood pressure, and getting heart disease.*
>
> 1. Which of the following is the best way to revise the underlined portion of sentence 2, reprinted below?
>
>   Sixty-one percent of adults <u>suffer from it, but around</u> 300,000 people die every year from diseases directly related to obesity.
>
> (A) suffer from it, but around
> (B) suffer, from it but around
> (C) suffer from it, and
> (D) suffer from it, although
> (E) suffer because of it, but around

Follow our five-step method:

- Read the passage and mark down something like "obesity, 61% adults, 300,000 dead per year" (step 1).
- Read the question (step 2).
- Go back and read the context sentences quickly (step 3).
- Now come up with your own answer (step 4).

At this point you may have spotted the conjunction error in the sentence. Since there's no contrast between the first half of the sentence and the second half, the conjunction word after the comma should be a noncontrast word like *and, so,* or *therefore*. Once you have an idea of the possible answer worked out on your own, read the answers and try to find a match (step 5). Happily, you've struck gold with choice **C**, which uses the conjunction to improve the sentence.

SENTENCE ADDITION—UP CLOSE

The purpose of adding a sentence is usually to smooth over a rough transition from paragraph to paragraph. Transitions are words, phrases, or entire sentences that give the reader the context necessary to understand the flow of your ideas in an essay. They're like training wheels for readers. Transitions take readers gently by the hand, leading them through a piece of writing.

When you see a Sentence Addition question and are preparing your own answer, think how best to improve the transition between the paragraphs or sentences. Here are two examples of the ways the SAT phrases Sentence Addition questions:

> Which of the following sentences should be added after sentence 7 in order to link the second paragraph to the rest of the essay?

> Which of the following sentences should be inserted at the beginning of the third paragraph, before sentence 10?

Be especially careful with questions like the second example above, which ask you to insert a sentence at the beginning of a paragraph. Sentences that begin paragraphs are usually topic sentences. A topic sentence tells the reader the subject or purpose of the paragraph. Topic sentences are crucial parts of the essay as a whole because they determine how each paragraph functions and fits in the context of the entire essay.

To understand the context for these sentences, you have to do more than just read the sentence before and the sentence after. You have to understand how the paragraph relates to the previous entire paragraph. If you've followed step 1, you'll have at your fingertips an outline of what each paragraph does. You can follow your outline to assess how one paragraph relates to another. Then you can write a possible topic sentence and examine how your sentence contradicts, modifies, or agrees with the main idea of the previous paragraph.

Here's a Sentence Addition question based on the sample obesity essay:

> (1) *Sixty-one percent of adults suffer from it, but around 300,000 people die every year from diseases directly related to obesity. (2) Obesity is related to diabetes, high blood pressure, and getting heart disease.*

> 1. Which of the following sentences should be inserted at the beginning of the next paragraph, before sentence 2?

> (A)   obesity is only a problem for the elderly
> (B)   obesity is a serious problem that affects hundreds of thousands of people.
> (C)   obesity can cause cancer
> (D)   obesity has no known cure
> (E)   obesity is not necessarily an inherited condition

Follow our five-step method:

- You've already read and outlined this passage, so you can skip straight to step 2.
- Read the question but *not* the answer choices (step 2). The paragraph in this example lacks a topic sentence, so the question is asking you to supply one.
- Go back and read the context sentences quickly (step 3). A quick glance back at the passage and your outline reveals that the paragraph is about obesity, the huge numbers of people who suffer from it, and the diseases that result from it.
- Now come up with your own answer (step 4). You might generate a topic sentence that says something like, "Obesity is a very serious condition," or some similar broad phrase that presents obesity as serious business.

- Step 5 tells you to check the answer choices. **B** does exactly what your topic sentence did—it presents obesity as a grave problem that affects many people. So **B** is the correct answer.

SENTENCE COMBINATION—UP CLOSE

Some questions ask you to combine two or three sentences. Context often doesn't play a role in answering this type of question, so you can skip step 3, which tells you to go back and read the context sentences. You should still read and outline the passage (step 1) and read the question without looking at the answer choices (step 2). Just skip ahead to steps 4 and 5, which tell you to generate your own answer (step 4) and then check it against the answer choices (step 5).

There are two ways the SAT tends to ask Sentence Combination questions:

> Which of the following is the best way to combine and revise sentences 5 and 6?

> How should the underlined portions of sentences 4 and 5, which are reprinted below, be revised so that the two sentences combine into one?

Only rarely will Sentence Combination questions require you to consider a sentences's context. Here's one example that does:

> In order to vary the repetitive sentence structure of the sentences in the first paragraph, how should sentences 8 and 9 be combined?

On questions like this one, you must look back at the relevant paragraph to familiarize yourself with the repetitive sentence structure that the question addresses. All of this adds up to a lot of time invested in one question, so you may consider leaving questions like this blank or skipping them and returning after spending your precious time on easier questions that don't require context analysis.

How to Combine Sentences

Most often you'll combine sentences by using a comma and a conjunction (a conjunction is a connecting word like *and*, *but*, or *so*). You can also combine sentences using semicolons and colons. We explain all of the different combination methods below.

Comma and Conjunction

Say the question asks you to combine these two sentences:

> She flushed her engagement ring down the toilet. The plumber got it back for her.

If you combine these two sentences through the power of a comma and a conjunction, you get

> She flushed her engagement ring down the toilet, but the plumber got it back for her.

Just be careful that the conjunction you choose makes sense. The revision below is grammatically correct, but logically flawed:

> She flushed her engagement ring down the toilet, because the plumber got it back for her.

The word *because* does not make sense, since it suggests that the woman in question flushed her ring down the toilet a second time as a result of the plumber initially retrieving it. Words like *because*, *despite*, and *therefore* indicate whether one-half of the sentence goes with the flow of the other half of the sentence. We call these words contrast words and noncontrast words, and we include a complete chart of the ones you need to know in our Beat Improving Sentences section on page 74.

Semicolon

If two sentences are closely related, you can combine them with a semicolon. Say you begin with these two sentences:

> Margaret recently met her future mother-in-law. Problems ensued immediately.

The combination with a semicolon looks like this:

> Margaret recently met her future mother-in-law; problems ensued immediately.

Expressing a Logical Relationship (Use the Answers!)

Remember how we said one type of Improving Paragraphs question requires an exception to the five-step strategy? This is it. Some Sentence Combination questions ask you to combine two sentences in a way that makes their *logical relationship* clearer. By logical relationship we mean the way the two sentences interact. On logical relationship questions, the answer choices can do a lot of the tough work for you, so you *should* read the answers first, before coming up with your own. That just means you should do step 4 by reading the answers first and then creating your own answer. A quick scan of the answers will make it clear what kind of possible logical relationship the test-writers see between the two sentences. Your job is then to pick the answer choice with the most perfect grammar *and* the most sensible logical relationship. Here's an example:

> To vary the pattern of sentences in the first paragraph, which of the following is the best way to combine sentences 2 and 3 (reprinted below)?
>
> > *My sister eats nasty cottage cheese and grapes for lunch. I eat fresh tacos.*
>
> (A) While my sister eats nasty cottage cheese and grapes for lunch, fresh tacos are what I'm eating.
> (B) In contrast to my sister eating nasty cottage cheese and grapes for lunch, I will be eating fresh tacos.
> (C) My sister was eating nasty cottage cheese and grapes for lunch, I was eating fresh tacos.
> (D) My sister eats nasty cottage cheese and grapes for lunch and I am not the same because I eat fresh tacos.
> (E) Unlike my sister, who eats nasty cottage cheese and grapes for lunch, I eat fresh tacos.

To find your answer look for two things:

- Contrast or no contrast?
- Is the answer choice grammatically correct?

First, what's the relationship between the two sentences? The speaker establishes a *contrast* between her sister's eating habits and her own. Now let's go through the answer choices.

By using the word *while*, **A** does a good job of expressing the relationship, but it has a parallelism error. It begins by saying *my sister eats*, so the second half of the sentence should say *I eat* (not *I'm eating*) in order for both halves of the sentence to match up. **B** also does a good job with the logical relationship, but it has a tense problem; the sister is eating in the present tense, but the speaker is eating sometime in the future. This changes the original meaning of the two sentences, in which both people are eating at the same time. Answer choice **C** doesn't express the logical relationship at all and is also a run-on sentence. Answer choice **D** expresses the relation-

the new SAT

ship but is awkward and wordy because of the phrase *and I am not the same*. That leaves answer choice **E**, which expresses the basic logical relationship between the two sentences, and does it grammatically.

9.10 ESSAY ANALYSIS—UP CLOSE

The SAT refers to the paragraphs on Improving Paragraphs questions as "essays" and "passages." We call them essays for the sake of simplicity, but the SAT refers to them both ways on the test. Essay Analysis questions often cover the essay as a whole. These questions require you to assess aspects of the entire essay, such as its "main idea." Other Essay Analysis questions pinpoint a sentence or two and ask you to evaluate aspects of the writer's "technique."

Sometimes you'll find that you don't even need to glance back to the essay to answer the question correctly. In this case, the question is usually referring back to the essay as a whole. On Essay Analysis questions that don't treat the passage as a whole, you probably *will* need to go back and reread a few sentences.

This question asks about the entire passage:

> Which sentence best summarizes the main idea of the passage?

In step 1 we suggest that you read the essay quickly and outline it in a flash. Now you can see how helpful that quick read and outline will be on questions like the one above. Instead of going back and fishing through the passage, you can use your own outline to refresh your memory of the essay's content and organization. You will also find that writing out these quick notes reinforces the main idea anyway, which will probably already be in your head.

The following is a different variety of Essay Analysis question that also requires you to analyze the entire essay:

> The writer uses all of the following techniques EXCEPT:
>
> (A) using concrete examples
> (B) using an anecdote to illustrate his thesis
> (C) discounting those who disagree with his opinion
> (D) stating and then disproving a theory
> (E) making reference to a work of fiction

This type of question does not allow you to prepare your own answer. You have to go right to the answer choices. Before you do that, however, make a big circle around the word EXCEPT. That's the key word in this question. The question asks you to *eliminate* all the techniques that the writer actually uses and to pick the one the writer does not use. To answer the question, you can refer back to the essay or you can use the outline you sketched in your first read of the essay. From there, you should try to eliminate answers as you verify that the writer does indeed use the technique in the answer choice. The correct answer will be the technique that the writer does *not* use, thanks to the EXCEPT in the question.

Now that you know how to approach tough questions like this one, keep in mind that it may make most sense to *skip* very demanding questions like this one. The SAT rewards students who correctly answer as many questions as possible. The SAT doesn't value a difficult question like the one above any more than it values the easiest question on the entire test. If you get stuck on a tough Essay Analysis question, feel free to move on to a question you can answer more quickly and confidently.

Analyzing a Single Sentence

Some analysis questions ask you to analyze one specific sentence. The best way to beat this type of Essay Analysis question is to go back to the essay and read the context sentences—the sentences before and after the sentence in the question. Here's an example for you:

> The primary purpose of sentence 4 is to
>
> (A) suggest a hypothetical situation
> (B) ask the reader to question the usefulness of theater
> (C) let the writer appear modest
> (D) contradict a widely held assumption about theater
> (E) reveal the writer's confusion about theatrical productions

To determine what sentence 4 does, head back to the paragraph that contains it and read sentences 3, 4, and 5. Then, before looking at the answer choices, decide what you think sentence 4's primary purpose is in the paragraph.

If you're having trouble making up your own answer to this kind of question, use the answer choices. Pay attention to the language each answer choice uses. Some of them may strike you as obviously wrong. Maybe the author is a braggart who doesn't sound *modest* at all; or perhaps she's revealing her mastery of theatrical productions, not her *confusion*. She could be clearly supporting a *widely held assumption*, not contradicting it. If you can make those determinations right away, cut those choices. That way you can eliminate the answers that you know are incorrect and raise your odds of selecting the correct answer from the two or three choices that remain.

Here's another kind of single-sentence Essay Analysis question:

> The writer could best improve sentence 8 by
>
> (A) admitting the flaws in his theory
> (B) giving concrete examples
> (C) explaining his own opinion
> (D) bringing up new problems
> (E) explaining modern theater

For this type of question, you *can* prepare your own answer first. Before you do, you need to follow step 3 and reread the context sentences. That means you should glance back at sentences 7, 8, and 9 to see if you can determine the problem with sentence 8 *before* you look at the answer choices. Next, come up with your own answer and take a look at the actual answer choices (step 4).

Once you've got an answer in mind, you can look at the actual answer choices and start eliminating choices that you determine must be incorrect (step 5). Often you can cut answers that seem too broad, farfetched, or ambitious. For example, do you think this writer could explain all of modern theater in sentence 8? No way. Cutting answer choices like that makes selecting the choice most like your own answer much easier, since fewer total choices remain.

9.11 A SAMPLE IMPROVING PARAGRAPHS ESSAY

Below is a sample essay followed by six typical SAT Improving Paragraphs questions. We also provide an explanation of how we applied our five-step strategy to answer each

the new SAT

question correctly. Take a shot at answering the questions yourself using the five steps before you look at our answers and explanations. Here's the sample essay:

(1) *In one scene in a short story I recently read, the main character goes back in time and happens to bring a few gold pieces back to the present with him.* (2) *The gold pieces turn out to be incredibly valuable.* (3) *This short story reminded me of the baseball card collecting craze, it being an interesting facet of American pop culture.* (4) *Buying and saving baseball cards means spending very little money on something that might turn out to be worth big bucks in the future.*

(5) *My dad collected baseball cards when he was a kid, and no one back then thought they'd be worth anything.* (6) *Someone like my dad used up his allowance every week just because he wanted to collect all of his favorite players—Roy Campanella, in my dad's case.* (7) *By dedicating the bulk of his weekly income to adding player after player to his collection, my father declared his dedication to the players.*

(8) *Baseball is a highly profitable sport, and so baseball card collecting has become one.* (9) *Everyone has heard of one baseball card in its original wrapping commanding an absurdly high price, and now everyone is positive that his or her shoebox filled with old baseball cards contains at least one card worth millions.* (10) *But if my dad had that one card, he won't know it.* (11) *Way before he realized it, his mother had gotten rid of them.*

1. Which sentence best summarizes the main idea of the passage?

(A)   sentence 1
(B)   sentence 2
(C)   sentence 3
(D)   sentence 4
(E)   sentence 7

2. In context, which revision does sentence 3 most need?

(A)   Add *In point of fact* at the beginning.
(B)   Delete the phrase *short story*.
(C)   Delete the words *it being*.
(D)   Replace the comma with a dash.
(E)   Replace *reminded* with *reminds*.

3. Which of the following sentences should be added before sentence 5, at the beginning of the second paragraph?

(A)   But there were people who didn't collect baseball cards with money in mind.
(B)   Clearly, early capitalism is a good idea.
(C)   In the collecting world, everyone has a different story.
(D)   Let me relate to you my own father's plan to make money.
(E)   Some pastimes have benefits you can't discern at first.

4. Which of the following best revises sentence 8, which is reproduced below?

    Baseball is a highly profitable sport, and so baseball card collecting has become one.

(A)   (as it is now)
(B)   Growing to be more and more like the sport that makes its existence possible has been baseball card collecting.
(C)   They say that baseball is now a highly profitable industry, as is this other pastime.
(D)   Like the sport itself, baseball card collecting has become a highly profitable industry.
(E)   At last, like the highly profitable industry of baseball, baseball card collecting is wholly changed.

5.   Of the following, which best revises the underlined part of sentence 10, which is reproduced below?

   But if my dad had that one card, he won't know it.

(A)   card, they would never realize it.
(B)   card; he would never realize it.
(C)   card, how could he realize it?
(D)   card, my dad won't ever realize it.
(E)   card—he never realized it.

6.   In the context of the paragraph, which is the best revision of sentence 11, which is reproduced below?

   Way before he realized it, his mother had gotten rid of them.

(A)   (as it is now)
(B)   Years before his cards became valuable, his mother had gotten rid of them.
(C)   Years before he has realized about the cards, his mother has gotten rid of them.
(D)   It was years before he realized about the cards that his mother got rid of them.
(E)   His mother gets rid of the cards years before he realizes about them.

Answers and Explanations

Before you answer any of these questions, remember to follow our five-step strategy for Improving Paragraphs questions. Here are the five steps once again:

Step 1. Read and outline the entire passage.
Step 2. Read the question.
Step 3. Reread the context sentences.
Step 4. Make up your own answer first.
Step 5. Read every answer and pick the one that comes closest to your answer.

You can often skip some of the five steps in our strategy plan, but having the five steps in mind will give you a plan of attack for each question. You can then pick and choose which steps to use to answer the question at hand. Below is a detailed discussion of each sample question and answer about the essay above.

1. The correct answer is D

This is an Essay Analysis question that asks you about the essay as a whole. The first step you should always take on Improving Paragraphs questions is to read the entire passage and outline it quickly. Here's an example of how we would outline the passage.

I.   bball card collecting / American culture / cheap cards now valuable
II.   Dad's cards = dedication / bball card collecting now profitable business, not just hobby
III.   Collections can be worth lots of $$$. Dad's collection junked by mom.

Notice that you don't have to write in complete sentences or spell out every word. Instead, do whatever it takes to make jotting down your outline as efficient and helpful as possible. Only *you* have to be able to understand what your outline says.

   After reading the essay once and jotting down an outline sketch like ours, you should read the first question (step 2). To answer this question as efficiently as possible, skip step 3. Since the question does not refer to one specific sentence, it doesn't make sense to reread context sentences. Step 4 *does* still apply to this passage, which means you should next come up with your own version of the main idea.

Use the quick outline you've jotted down to help determine the main idea of the passage. Is it just about baseball? Is it just about baseball card collecting? Try to narrow down the main idea to a more focused statement. For example, the most accurate description of this passage's main idea might be something like, "This passage is about how baseball card collecting evolved from being just a hobby to becoming a big business." You should then check your answer against the possible main idea sentences that the question directs you to assess specifically in the answer choices (step 5).

Your version of the main idea doesn't have to be as thorough as the one we suggested above—something like this will do just fine: *Collecting baseball cards can turn out to be very profitable.* That's just enough of a sketch to give you an idea of what you're looking for as you go back and check out the possible main idea sentences. Now let's take a closer look at those.

A: Sentence 1 reads, *In one scene in a short story I recently read, the main character goes back in time and happens to bring a few gold pieces back to the present with him.* That deals with the anecdote the writer uses to *introduce* his main idea—it's too specific to be the main idea sentence. Eliminate it.

B: Sentence 2 reads, *The gold pieces turn out to be incredibly valuable.* This is even more specific than the first sentence, so it also cannot be the correct expression of the essay's main idea. You can also eliminate **B**.

C: Sentence 3 reads, *This short story reminded me of the baseball card collecting craze, it being an interesting facet of American pop culture.* This sounds closer—it mentions baseball card collecting, which is part of the main idea of the essay. However, it sounds like a transition between the anecdote and the main thrust of the essay, rather than a summation of the overall main idea. Leave it for now, since it sounds better than the first two.

D: Sentence 4 reads, *Buying and saving baseball cards means spending very little money on something that might turn out to be worth big bucks in the future.* This sentence sounds very much like the main idea you generated on your own—it talks about card collecting, and it also mentions the idea that you can make money on card collecting. Sentence 4 is a better choice than sentence 3, which is a transition sentence and is not specific enough about the business side of baseball card collecting.

Look at **E**, just to be sure it's not a better answer choice than **D**. *By dedicating the bulk of his weekly income to adding player after player to his collection, my father declared his dedication to the players.* **E** is too specific. The passage's main point is not to explain the initial reason that kids take up card collecting; it's to explain what happens years after the collection is begun. **D** is the correct answer.

2. The correct answer is C.

Here we have a typical Sentence Revision question. Sentence 3 reads, *This short story reminded me of the baseball card collecting craze, it being an interesting facet of American pop culture.* You've read and outlined the essay (step 1), and you know what sentence the question covers (step 2), so now you're up to step 3. Rereading the context sentences is crucial on this question. Here's why: If you make the changes suggested by answer choice **A**, you get, *In point of fact, this short story reminded me of the baseball card collecting craze, it being an interesting facet of American pop culture.* Out of context, this change seems to fix the sentence just fine, except that it ends up a bit wordy. If you look at it in context, however, you can see that adding *in point of fact* is illogical: *The gold pieces turn out to be incredibly valuable. In point of fact, this short story reminded me of the baseball card collecting*

craze, it being an interesting facet of American pop culture. The phrase *in point of fact* signals that the writer is about to elaborate on a point that he or she started to make in the last sentence, but sentence 3 is actually a departure from sentence 2, not an elaboration on it. You can eliminate **A**. If you had skipped step 3 and just dove right in, you probably would have chosen **A** and moved on not knowing you had fallen into an SAT trap.

You always want to have your own fix in mind (step 4) as you review the answer choices in Sentence Revision questions. Ask yourself which part of the sentence sounds off or incorrect? The first half of the sentence looks and sounds perfect: This reminded me of the baseball card collecting craze. The tail end of the sentence also looks spotless: an interesting facet of American pop culture. The problem lies in the faulty phrase *it being*, which joins the two halves of the sentence. The correct answer must do something to remedy that awkward link. One suggestion you could keep in mind as your answer might be, "This reminded me of the baseball card collecting craze, an interesting facet of American pop culture," or "This reminded me of the baseball card collecting craze, which was an interesting facet of American pop culture."

Step 5 requires you to compare your answer with the answer choices given in the question. If you make the changes suggested by **B**, you get, *This reminded me of the baseball card collecting craze, it being an interesting facet of American pop culture.* Removing the phrase *short story* just makes the word *this* vague. It does not improve the sentence.

C gives you *This reminded me of the baseball card collecting craze, an interesting facet of American pop culture.* **C** is the correct answer choice because it removes the unnecessary *it being* phrase without making the sentence ungrammatical. The SAT loves concise solid sentences, so it's no surprise that **C** is the most compact and concise answer choice here. Notice also that **C** is a perfect match for the first of the two solutions that we suggested you plant in your head before reviewing the answer choices. Once you have a strong idea of the solution to a Sentence Revision question, finding the answer is often just a matter of plucking a match from the actual answer choices.

Let's check out **D** and **E** as well, just to be sure. **D** gives you *This reminded me of the baseball card collecting craze—an interesting facet of American pop culture.* A dash is usually used to signal an abrupt transition or a new thought. Here, the phrase that comes after the comma is an elaboration on the baseball card collecting phase, not a transition or a new thought, so a dash is inappropriate.

Finally, **E**'s changes: *This reminds me of the baseball card collecting craze, it being an interesting facet of American pop culture.* This revision doesn't really help or harm the sentence. So now you're at a crossroads. **C** is a better answer choice than **E** because it makes a needed revision to the sentence, whereas **E** just avoids making things worse. **C** it is.

3. The correct answer is A.

This is a Sentence Addition question that requires a firm grasp of the context sentences, so the best strategy to take on this question is to skip to step 3. Read sentences 4 and 5: (4) *Buying and saving baseball cards means spending very little money on something that might turn out to be worth big bucks in the future.* (5) *My dad collected baseball cards when he was a kid, and no one back then thought they'd be worth anything.*

Remember, the correct answer to Sentence Addition questions is almost always the one that smooths out a rough transition. If you can generate your own transi-

tional sentence and then see which answer choice matches it, great (steps 4 and 5). If not, try out the suggested sentences and see which one works.

A. *Buying and saving baseball cards means spending very little money on something that might turn out to be worth big bucks in the future. But there were people who didn't collect baseball cards with money in mind. My dad collected baseball cards when he was a kid, and no one back then thought they'd be worth anything.* **A** is the correct answer. It provides a smooth transition between the specific story of the writer's father and the idea that people can profit from their card collections.

Even if you were able to pick out **A** as the correct answer right away, it's helpful to understand why the other answer choices don't work. Often the difference between the right answer and each of the four other wrong answers is slight, and having an acute sense of the subtle differences the SAT likes to test can help you avoid SAT traps and boost your score.

B. *Buying and saving baseball cards means spending very little money on something that might turn out to be worth big bucks in the future. Clearly, early capitalism is a good idea. My dad collected baseball cards when he was a kid, and no one back then thought they'd be worth anything.* This solution is passable, with the exception of the phrase *early capitalism*, which is meaningless. Also, it doesn't tie together the two sentences, as **A** does.

C. *Buying and saving baseball cards means spending very little money on something that might turn out to be worth big bucks in the future. In the collecting world, everyone has a different story. My dad collected baseball cards when he was a kid, and no one back then thought they'd be worth anything.* This new sentence is okay, but it's more vague than the correct answer, and once again it doesn't do a good job of knitting together sentences 4 and 5. Also, the phrase *collecting world* is a little ambiguous. The passage is about baseball card collecting, not collecting in general.

D. *Buying and saving baseball cards means spending very little money on something that might turn out to be worth big bucks in the future. Let me relate to you my own father's plan to make money. My dad collected baseball cards when he was a kid, and no one back then thought they'd be worth anything.* **D**'s main problem is its tone. The writer takes a relaxed, chummy tone throughout this essay, and this new sentence has a serious tone that clashes with the rest of the prose. You can detect this inappropriate tone shift in phrases like *Let me relate to you* and in words like *father*, which contrasts sharply with the word choice in sentence 5, which uses the words *dad* and *kid*. **D** is inappropriately formal and should be eliminated.

E. *Buying and saving baseball cards means spending very little money on something that might turn out to be worth big bucks in the future. Some pastimes have benefits you can't discern at first. My dad collected baseball cards when he was a kid, and no one back then thought they'd be worth anything.* **E** relates almost entirely to sentence 5, without referring back to sentence 4 at all, whereas the correct answer refers to both 4 and 5 equally.

4. The correct answer is D.

This is another typical Sentence Revision question. Here the main problem is the vague phrase *has become one*, which disrupts the logical clarity of the sentence. Once you detect that problem, you can prepare your own answer (step 4) and then look for an answer choice that clears up the sentence in a way most similar to your own solution (step 5). Also, once you see that the sentence needs improvement, you can eliminate **A**, which keeps the sentence as it is.

B is grammatically incorrect. It contains a misplaced modifier, *baseball collecting*, and also suffers from awkward inconsistent use of tenses (*growing to be, has been*).

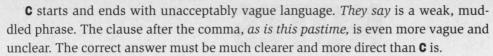
C starts and ends with unacceptably vague language. *They say* is a weak, muddled phrase. The clause after the comma, *as is this pastime,* is even more vague and unclear. The correct answer must be much clearer and more direct than **C** is.

D is the correct answer. It clears up that vague phrase *has become one*. The *one* is referred to specifically as *a highly profitable industry*.

E sounds strangely overblown. The original sentence does not claim that baseball card collecting is *wholly changed*, as if a vast transformation has taken place, so neither should the revised version.

5. The correct answer is D.

This Sentence Revision question asks you to revise a specific, underlined part of a sentence. Context sentences are irrelevant on these kinds of questions, so you can skip straight to step 4 and come up with your own solution to the problems in the underlined portion.

The main problem is tense. The first half of the sentence sets up a conditional sequence, but the verb is simple past tense: *if my dad had* and *won't know it* don't fit together correctly.

Of the answers, only **A** and **D** solve this tense problem. But **A** introduces a new problem by creating a mismatched pronoun. The plural *they* cannot act as a pronoun for the singular *my dad*. That means choice **D** must be the right answer.

6. The correct answer is B.

Another Sentence Revision question. The problem with the initial sentence is the overly vague phrase *way before he realized it*. Look at the sentence in context (step 3): (9) *Everyone has heard of one baseball card in its original wrapping commanding an absurdly high price, and now everyone is positive that his or her shoebox full of old baseball cards contains at least one card worth millions.* (10) *But if my dad had that one card, he won't know it.* (11) *Way before he realized it, his mother had gotten rid of them.*

Your revision must replace the vague phrase *way before he realized it* with a more specific phrase about realizing that his cards could be worth something. The point here is to bring out the emphasis on the cards' increased value, which is the point here, not the man's realization.

B is the correct answer. It replaces *way before he realized it* with the more specific phrase *years before his cards became valuable*, which replaces the vague word *way* with *years* and stresses the cards' increase in value rather than the man's realization.

If you didn't see that **B** was correct immediately, you could have eliminated wrong answers. Answer **A** can be eliminated, since you know the sentence is not perfect. **C** has a tense problem. Since everything in the sentence is happening in the past tense, *he has realized* should be *he realized*, and *has gotten rid of them* should be *got rid of them*. **D** is awkward and difficult to follow. **E** has a tense problem, like **C** (*his mother gets rid* should be *his mother got rid*). She got rid of the cards in the past, not in the present. Cutting **A, C, D,** and **E** leaves **B**, which is the best answer.

NOTES

NOTES

NOTES

NOTES

NOTES

NOTES

NOTES

NOTES

NOTES

NOTES

NOTES

THE
CRITICAL
READING
SECTION

MEET THE CRITICAL READING SECTION

SAT "VERBAL" IS DEAD. KAPUT. GONE THE WAY OF THE Dodo and the Sega Dreamcast. Or so the SAT wants you to believe. Actually, it's more accurate to say that most of the former SAT Verbal section is just wearing a fake mustache and traveling under an assumed name: "Critical Reading." The new Critical Reading section has all the familiar sentence completion and long reading questions as the section formerly known as "SAT Verbal," but now analogies have been cut, and new *short* reading questions have been added.

the new SAT

10.1 VERBAL VS. CRITICAL READING

In this corner, the Verbal section! In that corner, the Critical Reading section! Here's a table that compares the new Critical Reading section and the old Verbal section.

	Old Verbal	New Critical Reading
Analogies	YES	NO
Sentence Completion	YES	YES
Long Reading Passages	YES	YES
Short Reading Passages	NO	YES

Memorizing a list of tough vocabulary words and outwitting analogies went a long way toward getting you a good score on the old SAT Verbal section. That kind of preparation just won't cut it on the new Critical Reading section. Vocabulary still plays an important role on the test, but its role has changed. Questions no longer exclusively focus on vocabulary. Questions that do include tough vocab do so within the context of a sentence or a paragraph that provides clues to what the word means.

The emphasis on vocabulary *in context* on the new SAT makes excellent critical reading skills all the more important. Learning to read critically can help you answer questions correctly even when the meaning of certain words escapes you, and that could vastly improve your score on this section. So, while you should still study vocab (and we've got a list of the toughest words and techniques on how to remember them at the end of this section), you should also build up your reading muscles. And there's only one way to build up your muscles—exercise.

10.2 THE NEED TO READ

The best way to prepare for the Critical Reading section is to read. From the moment you read this sentence until the day you take the SAT, you should carve time out of your life to read. Read magazines. Read newspapers. Read books.

You already know how to read. But for the new SAT, you have to read *critically*, and that's a different skill. You need to develop an eye and an ear for the kinds of things the Critical Reading section tests:

- **Main idea**: What is the main subject of the passage?
- **Argument**: What position does the author take on the subject? What is the main *purpose* of the passage?
- **Tone**: What is the author's attitude or feelings toward the subject?
- **Technique**: What rhetorical devices (simile, metaphor, personification, etc.) does the author use to convey his or her tone, main ideas, and argument?

In our chapter "The Long of It," we offer tips on how to turn ordinary reading into productive Critical Reading preparation. We show you how to train your *critical* reading muscles so that when the SAT comes around, all you'll have to do is flex.

BASIC FACTS

The Critical Reading section is made up of three timed sections that test your critical reading skills for 70 minutes. Two of the timed sections are 25-minutes long, and one is 20 minutes long.

In all, the Critical Reading sections contain 67 questions.

- **19 Sentence Completions**: Single sentences with one or two blanks.
- **8 Short Reading questions**: Two single passages followed by 2 questions each; one dual passage followed by 4 questions
- **40 Long Reading questions** : A 400–500 word passage with 6 questions; a 500–600 word passage with 9 questions; a 700–800 word passagewith 12 questions; a dual passage with 13 questions.

The different types of questions break into the three timed sections in the following way:

- **25-minute Section with 24 Total Questions**: 8 Sentence Completions; 2 Short Reading Comp passages (each with 2 questions); Long Reading Comp passage with 12 questions.
- **25-minute Section with 24 Total Questions**: 5 Sentence Completions; the dual Short Reading Comp passage with 4 questions; Long Reading Comp with 6 questions; Long Reading Comp with 9 questions.
- **20-minute Section with 19 Total Questions**: 6 Sentence Completions; Long Reading Dual passage with 13 questions.

On some versions of the test the 800-word Long Reading Comp and the Dual Passage Long Reading Comp switch positions. When this happens, the 800-word LRC has 13 questions, while the Dual has 12.

HOW TO SCORE . . . CRITICAL READING

Just like Math and Writing, Critical Reading maxes out at a scaled score of 800. Also like Math and Writing, in order to get a scaled score, you first have to get a raw score.

The Critical Reading raw score follows the standard SAT rule of 1 point for each right answer, 0 points for each answer left blank, and a $-1/4$ point penalty for each wrong answer:

$$\text{Critical Reading raw score} = \text{\# of correct answers} - \frac{\text{\# of wrong answers}}{4}$$

Also, remember that because every single Critical Reading question follows the standard SAT scoring system, the basic guessing rules *always* apply. If you can eliminate just one answer on any question in the Critical Reading Section, always guess.

BEAT
SENTENCE
COMPLETIONS

SENTENCE COMPLETIONS ARE NOT ONLY ABOUT knowing vocabulary. Sentence Completions (which we call "SCs") are as much about understanding what's going on in the sentence as they are about knowing the vocab necessary to complete the blanks. In fact, if you know how to analyze the sentence surrounding the blank, you'll be able to figure out the answers without knowing the vocab at all. Showing you how to do that is what this chapter is all about.

SENTENCE COMPLETION INSTRUCTIONS

You know the drill. Read and learn the instructions for SCs before you show up to take the test.

Each sentence below has one or two blanks, each blank indicating that something has been omitted. Beneath the sentence are five words or sets of words labeled A through E. Choose the word or set of words that, when inserted in the sentence, <u>best</u> fits the meaning of the sentence as a whole.

    Example:

Medieval kingdoms did not become constitutional republics overnight; on the contrary, the change was ----.

(A)   unpopular
(B)   unexpected
(C)   advantageous
(D)   sufficient
(E)   gradual

Correct Answer: E

WHAT THE INSTRUCTIONS *DON'T* SAY

The directions for SCs are pretty clear. You need to read a sentence and select the answer choice that *best* completes the sentence. That means you need to find the answer choice that is the best of all the possible choices, not just an answer choice that *can* complete the sentence.

    The SC directions do include a mention of that subtle, yet crucial, fact, but they leave out three other key facts. Here are the three key facts and why you need to know them:

KEY FACT	WHAT IT IS	WHY IT'S IMPORTANT
1	Almost every SC contains all the information you need to define the word that fits in the blank.	You can use the context of the sentence to figure out what the missing words mean. You don't need to look at the answer choices first.
2	Every answer choice makes the sentence grammatically correct.	You won't be able to look at grammar to try to figure out the right answer. Only meaning matters.
3	SCs appear in order of difficulty within a timed section. The first third is easy, the second third moderately difficult, and the last third difficult.	If a question is easy or moderate, you can usually trust your first instincts. If you're on a difficult question, take a second to look out for SAT trickery before moving on.

HOW SCS WORK: A BUNCH OF PARTS

Every sentence is built out of a bunch of parts. The most important parts you need to know to beat SCs are **clauses** and **conjunctions**.

- **Clauses**: The parts of a sentence that contain a noun and a verb. Every complete sentence must contain at least one clause, and every clause should convey one idea. SCs always present you with *compound sentences*, which means they contain more than one clause. In compound sentences, clauses can either *support* or *contrast* each other. Clauses that support each other contain a consistent flow of ideas with no opposition within the sentence. For example, this sentence contains two clauses that support each other: "The test was easy, so I aced it." Clauses that contrast each other contain a flow of ideas that oppose each other. For example, this sentence contains clauses that contrast each other: "The test was easy, but I failed it."

- **Conjunctions**: Words that join clauses, like *so* and *but* in the previous examples, are called *conjunctions*. Conjunctions are important on SC questions because they often reveal how a sentence's clauses relate to each other. Knowing how clauses relate enables you to determine what kind of word(s) you need to fill in the blanks. In the sentence, "The test was easy, but I failed it," the conjunction *but* indicates that the two clauses *contrast*—although you would expect that the writer of this sentence would pass an easy test, the conjunction *but* signals a contrast, which sets up the unexpected idea that the writer of this sentence failed the test.

SC Electricity

One of the simplest ways to understand how sentences work is to imagine them as electrical circuits. Let's talk very basic electricity for a few minutes.

Here's how electricity works: An electric current flows along a path called a circuit, which carries the current from one point to another. Along the way, switches at certain key points of the circuit tell the current which way the flow should go.

Think of every sentence as a circuit. The clauses are the current and the conjunctions are the switches that direct the flow of the sentence.

- sentence = circuit
- clauses = current
- conjunctions = switches

Some sentences flow in one direction from start to finish. An example of a sentence in which the clauses flow one way is, "Sarah slept until noon and was wired all night." The two clauses, *Sarah slept until noon* and *was wired all night*, are joined by the conjunction *and*, a switch that tells you that the two clauses *support* each other. If someone sleeps until noon, you'd expect them to be wired all night; the *and* in this sentence signals that you're expectations will be met.

Other conjunctions signal a *contrast* between the clauses that make up a sentence. For example, in the sentence, "Sarah slept until noon but was still tired by nine p.m.," the conjunction *but* serves as a switch that signals a contrast, or opposition, between the two clauses in the sentence. You'd expect that Sarah would have trouble falling asleep, since she slept until noon; that *but* signals that you're expectations will *not* be met in this case.

SCS: A FIVE-STEP METHOD

We've developed a five-step method based on our electricity model to help you find the answer choice that best fills in the blank(s).

Here are the five steps, complete with an explanation of each:

Step 1. Spot the Switch
Step 2. Go with the Flow
Step 3 . Fill in the Blank
Step 4. Compare Your Answer to the Answer Choices
Step 5. Plug It In

Step 1: Spot the Switch

As we discussed, every electrical current flows along a path with one or more switches that direct which way the flow goes. Most SC sentences contain conjunction words that function like switches, pointing the meaning of the sentence in different directions. Some examples of these words include *so*, *however*, *thus*, and *although*. We call these words "switches."

The first thing you should do on every SC you come across is search for the switch. Not every sentence contains a switch, but many do. To make switch-spotting as easy as possible, here is a list of the switch words that most commonly appear on the SAT. There are two types of switches: one-way and two-way:

One-Way Switches

and	because	since	so	therefore	thus

Two-Way Switches

although	but	despite	however	instead	nevertheless
notwithstanding		rather	though	unless	while

Step 2: Go with the Flow

Every switch word can tell you which way the flow of the sentence goes. A one-way switch points out a one-way sentence. A two-way switch points out a two-way sentence.

- **One-way sentences** contain no contrast, which means they flow in one direction. All parts of the sentence support the main idea of the sentence.
- **Two-way sentences** contain a break in the flow of the sentence that makes one part of the sentence contrast with another part. Often the contrast comes after a comma or semicolon that divides the sentence.

Examples will make all of this much easier to see and understand.

One-Way Switches

Here's an example of an SC question that contains a one-way switch. Try to pick out the switch on your own before you read the explanation that follows.

Since the scientist's years of research finally confirmed his theories, everyone ---- him.

The switch in this sentence is *since*. It's a one-way switch, so it tells you that the sentence's flow goes one way. And knowing that the sentence is one-way allows you to figure out how the sentence works.

The part of the sentence before the comma says that a scientist did a ton of research that finally confirmed his original theories. The part after the comma, which contains the blank, describes the reaction to the scientist's research and theories. Because the sentence is one-way, the word in the blank must *support* the idea that the scientist's years of hard work have finally paid off.

Now that you've used the rest of the sentence to clue you into what the blank might mean, you can begin to come up with your own possible answers to fill in the blank. Ask yourself what people would do in that circumstance? They'd probably do something like *congratulate* or *cheer* the scientist *since* his research paid off, right? Exactly.

Two-Way Switches

A two-way switch indicates that the sentence contains a contrast and therefore flows two ways. Here's an almost identical version of the sentence you just saw. Only one word has been changed.

> Although the scientist's years of research finally confirmed his theories, everyone ---- him.

Once you've spotted the switch word *although*, you can use it to determine how the blank goes with the flow. The two-way switch word *although* indicates a *contrast*, so the blank must not support the idea of the scientist's research finally paying off. Once you've figured out which way the flow goes, you need to find the answer choice that goes with the flow of the sentence. Rather than *cheer* or *congratulate* the scientist, in this version of the sentence everyone must do something like *criticize* or *reject* the scientist.

No Switches

Not *every* sentence contains a switch. But whether there's a switch in a sentence or not, it's still vital that you figure out if the sentence flows one way or two ways.

And, luckily enough, there's a simple rule about sentences that don't have any switch words:

---

* A sentence without a switch will be one-way unless that sentence describes a change over time.

Sentences Describing a Change Over Time

There's one type of sentence that doesn't contain a switch word but can still flow two ways. These are sentences that compare two different periods of time. For example,

> Once a ---- movie director, Mickey Carson ended his life a pauper unable to finance the making of his own films.

Though this sentence does not contain a switch, it contains a two-way flow because it conveys an unexpected change over time. The main idea of the sentence focuses on a contrast: that Mickey Carson died a pauper even though he was once a ---- movie director. Words that you might come up with to go with the two-way flow of the sentence may include *successful*, *rich*, *celebrated*—all adjectives that contrast with the idea of a movie director who died in poverty.

If you can't find a switch word in a sentence, first check to see if the sentence describes a change over time. If it docs, you've got a two-way sentence. If it doesn't,

you've got a one-way sentence. Once you've determined that, come up with words that go with the flow as we just did in the previous example.

Following the Flow

On all SCs, if the sentence flows one way, ask yourself what main idea of the sentence the blank must *support*. If the sentence flows two ways, ask yourself which idea the blank must *contrast*. Here are some examples to test your ability to pick out the switch, follow the flow, and figure out which answer choices go with the flow.

> Despite the violently harsh weather conditions, the hikers ---- and made it back to their base camp.

What's the switch?	*despite*
Which way does the flow go?	two ways
What idea does the blank support or contrast?	contrasts with "the violently harsh weather conditions"

In this sentence, the switch word *despite* makes it clear that whatever fits into the blank has to contrast with the "violently harsh weather conditions." That means the sentence flows two ways. Now ask yourself what kind of word would go with the flow. The switch word *despite* tells you that there's a contrast in the sentence, which means the campers do make it back despite the harsh weather. Ask yourself what the campers would have to do to make it back despite threatening weather. They would have to *endure* or *survive*, right? That's the kind of word you would need to find among the answer choices.

Now try this example:

> Alex grew up near the beach, so he ---- how to surf at a very young age.

What's the switch?	*so*
Which way does the flow go?	one way
What idea does the blank support or contrast?	supports "grew up near the beach"

The switch word *so* in this example indicates that the sentence flows one way. That means all parts of the sentence must support the ideas that the sentence expresses. The word that fills in the blank must fit with the common conception of people who grow up by the beach. Ask yourself what their relationship to surfing would be at a young age. Would they learn to surf at a young age? Or know about surfing at a young age? Probably. That means you need to look for words like *learned* and *knew* in the answer choices. That would make the completed sentence read something like, *Alex grew up near the beach, so he learned how to surf at a very young age.*

Step 3: Fill in the Blank

You might have noticed that we haven't included the answer choices in our examples. We did that by design. Why?

Because you should try to come up with your own answer to fill in the blank or blanks in an SC *before* looking at the answer choices. That way you won't fall prey to SAT traps that the test may have planted among the answer choices. Coming up with your own answer first will also force you to stick with step 1 and step 2, which will prevent you from speeding along and making careless errors.

The answer that you generate to fill in the blank or blanks can be either a single word or a quick description of the type of word that you think should go in the blank.

Let's go back to a previous example, now with answer choices.

Despite the violently harsh weather conditions, the hikers ---- and made it back to their base camp.

(A)   surrendered
(B)   won
(C)   succeeded
(D)   collapsed
(E)   evacuated

What's the switch?	*despite*
Which way does the flow go?	two ways
What idea does the blank support or contrast?	contrasts with "the violently harsh weather conditions"

In step 2, we determined that the switch word *despite* indicates that the sentence flows two ways. That means the word in the blank must contrast with the idea of the violently harsh weather conditions. Ask yourself what the hikers would have to do despite the violently harsh weather conditions to make it back to camp. What word pops into your head? *Managed? Survived? Endured?* All of those choices are great. They go with the flow of the sentence and convey the idea of the hikers making it back despite the harsh weather. Now on to step 4.

Step 4: Compare Your Answer to the Answer Choices

Once you've used the information in the sentence to build your own answer, *then* you should go to the answer choices and look for a choice that matches yours.

In the example about the hikers, you can throw out *surrendered, collapsed*, and *evacuated*, because none of them even come close to your own answers.

That leaves you to choose between *succeeded* and *won*. Which is the better answer? Step 5 will help determine that.

Step 5: Plug It In

When you've got a new electrical device like a microwave or a TV, there's only one way to test whether it works: Plug it in. Same goes for testing out answer choices on *all* SCs. Always plug in the answer choice (or choices) you've selected to make sure your choice works in the sentence.

In the last example, we were trying to decide between *won* and *succeeded*. Plug both words in to determine which one fits *best* into the sentence.

Despite the violently harsh weather conditions, the hikers *won* and made it back to their base camp.

Despite the violently harsh weather conditions, the hikers *succeeded* and made it back to their base camp.

After plugging the two words in, *succeeded* seems like the better choice. The hikers weren't playing a game or involved in an contest, so the idea of having *won* something is inappropriate here.

You probably didn't have much trouble deciding between *won* and *succeeded* in this example. You may even be thinking that this plugging in step is a waste of time. It's not. Never skip step 5. Always plug in to check your answer choice.

IF VOCAB'S GOT YOU DOWN

Sentence Completions aren't all about vocab. But they are *somewhat* about vocab. And if you don't know the words huddling in those answer choices, things can get tough. But there *are* ways to attack SCs even if you don't know what all the words in the answer choices mean.

In fact, the first few steps for handling SCs with tough vocab are exactly the same as those for SCs with vocab you know:

1. Spot the Switch
2. Go with the Flow
3. Fill in the Blank

If you follow our five-step method, you shouldn't even look at the answer choices until after you've gone through the first three steps and figured out your own answer or phrase to fill in the blank. By ignoring the answer choices at first and instead focusing on the sentence, you eliminate the possibility that you'll be intimidated by hard vocabulary. This is important because it's *always* worthwhile to at least try to answer each SC. Why? Because once you've analyzed the sentence and have your own answer to fill the blank, it becomes much easier to eliminate answer choices, even if you don't completely know what they mean.

So, let's say you've gone through the first three steps. You've spotted the switches, if there are any. You've figured out the flow and how the blank fits into it. You've come up with your own answer. Then you go to the answer choices and realize you don't really know what they mean. What do you do? What tool can possibly save you from this mess? Word Charge.

Word Charge

Sentence Completion vocab words can often be broken down into one of two categories: positive or negative. That's "Word Charge." Nice happy words have a positive charge; dark unhappy words have a negative charge.

Word Charge is important on SCs for two reasons:

1. The Word Charge of the blank and the word that fills the blank must be the same. For example, a negative answer choice can never fill a blank that needs a positive word.
2. Even when you don't know the exact meaning of a word, you'll often have a sense of its "charge."

These two reasons add up to one great big fact: You can use Word Charge to sort through SC answer choices with tough vocab even if you don't know the exact meaning of the words. Below is a list of tough words to give you a chance to test out your sense of Word Charge. Cover up the column all the way on the right and try to guess each word's charge.

Word	Your Guess at Its Charge	Actual Charge
insidious		negative
diabolical		negative
effervescent		positive
truculent		negative
vivacious		Positive

Finding Word Charge: Word Roots

English has been developing as a language for a long time. It keeps getting bigger and bigger and adding new words. New words are made out of old words or out of parts of old words. These building blocks are called *word roots*. When you're looking for the Word Charge of a word you don't know, look within the word for roots of other words whose meanings you *do* know. The best place to look for word roots is in the *prefix*—the first 1 to 5 letters of a word.

Different roots have different basic meanings. For example, take the word *disconsolate*. You might not know this word. But you probably *do* have an idea of what the word *consolation* means. Ever heard of a "consolation prize"? That's the prize that game shows give to the losers. It's usually a board game of the show they're on or a gift certificate for a haircut. It's meant to *console* them for losing.

Even if you don't know the word *consolation*, you might know the word *console*, which lies at the root of the big scary word *disconsolate*. *Console* means to provide comfort in a time of sorrow or loss. The prefix *dis-* before *-consolate* means *not*. Put it all together and you can make a solid guess that *disconsolate* means "not consoled" or "grieving due to loss."

Learning even just a few key building blocks of words and what they mean can be extremely helpful in determining Word Charge. We provide a list of word roots that most commonly appear in SAT vocab in our chapter on new SAT Vocab (page 185).

Word Charge in Action

Okay, enough explanation. Time for an example:

> The East Coast Hamstaz was a terrible rap group in the early '90s; its music was dull and its lyrics ----.
>
> (A)   grandiloquent
> (B)   magnanimous
> (C)   truculent
> (D)   fatuous
> (E)   trenchant

Now answer this question step by step using our five-step SC method.

1. Spot the Switch

This sentence does not contain a switch. There's no word in the sentence that signals that the blank must support or contrast with the main ideas expressed in the sentence.

2. Go with the Flow

So, there's no switch, and a quick read-through of the sentence shows that it isn't about a change over time. This sentence must therefore flow one-way. The blank, which describes the Hamstaz lyrics, must therefore support the other ideas in the sentence:

What's the switch?	none
Which way does the flow go?	one way
What idea does the blank support or contrast?	supports "The East Coast Hamstaz was a terrible rap group"

3. Fill in the Blank

Now you know that the blank, which describes the lyrics of the rap group, supports the idea of the East Coast Hamstaz being a terrible rap group. Ask yourself: "Self, what must the lyrics of the Hamstaz have been like if the Hamstaz were a terrible rap group?" The lyrics must have been *bad*.

> The East Coast Hamstaz was a terrible rap and R&B group in the early '90s; its music was dull and its lyrics *bad*.

4. Compare Your Answer to the Answer Choices

So far, you've breezed through this one. Time to take a look at the answer choices and find the one that matches up with *bad*.

(A)	grandiloquent
(B)	magnanimous
(C)	truculent
(D)	fatuous
(E)	trenchant

What the . . . ? Which of these tough vocab words matches up with *bad*? Okay, keep cool. Don't give up just because the answer choices are filled with difficult vocabulary. Instead, use Word Charge.

In fact, you've already begun the Word Charge process. When you came up with your own answer for the blank in step 3, you also came up with the charge for the blank. The word that you thought should fill the blank was *bad*, which has a negative charge. That means you already know you need to find a negative word among the answer choices.

Take a run down the list and try to cut words that you think are positive based on their word roots or other clues you can decipher. Let's see: **A**, *grandiloquent*, sounds like a combination of *grand* and *eloquent*, both positive words. Cut it. **B**, *magnanimous*, sounds like "magnificent." Cut **B** too. Let's say that's as far as you can get with Word Charge. Stop there, and take a look at how far you've come.

By eliminating two answer choices, you've tipped the guessing odds strongly in your favor, without knowing the meaning of *any* of the answer choices. Sos the moral of the Word Charge story is, Word Charge may not always get you the correct answer, but it will help your score by making you a better guesser.

5. Plug It In

The last step is always to test-drive your answer choice by plugging it back in to the original sentence. In this example, you've used Word Charge to eliminate two answers, leaving you with three that seem to have the negative charge you need:

> The East Coast Hamstaz was a terrible rap and R&B group in the early '90s; its music was dull and its lyrics *bad*.
>
> | | |
> |---|---|
> | (A) | grandiloquent (CUT) |
> | (B) | magnanimous (CUT) |
> | (C) | truculent |
> | (D) | fatuous |
> | (E) | trenchant |

When you're faced with three words with charges you think you know, but with meanings you don't know at all, plugging in won't help. If that's the case, as in this example, the best thing you can do is pick any remaining answer immediately knowing that you've used Word Charge to tip the guessing odds in your favor. When you do have a sense of what the words mean, plug the answer you think is best back into the sentence to make sure it works. The correct answer to this question is **D**, fatuous, which means weak, silly, or foolish.

PRACTICE THE PROCESS

The best way to get the five-step SC process down cold is to practice. To that end, we give you examples of every type of SC under the sun: one-blankers, two-blankers, one-way, two-way, every single possible combination.

There are four different types of SCs.

1. One-Blank/One-Way
2. One-Blank/Two-Way
3. Two-Blank/One-Way
4. Two-Blank/Two-Way

Through the rest of this chapter we give you examples of each type, sometimes more than one. We then work out each example according to our five-step process.

SC Type 1: One-Blank/One-Way

About a third of the SAT SCs are one-blank/one-way. That's good news. They're the simplest type. Because the flow is one way, the blank will agree with the rest of the sentence. One-blank/one-way SCs almost never contain switch words.

There are two basic one-blank/one-way varieties:

- A **simple sentence** with no switch and with one missing word.
- A **compound sentence** with two halves split by a semicolon, colon, or comma. Usually, the first half of these SCs contains the blank, and the second half describes the word that goes in the blank.

Want some examples of what these actually look like? You got 'em.

Example: Simple Sentence

The ---- waves in Maui terrified the surfers.

1. Spot the Switch
This sentence contains no switch and isn't about a change over time, so it must be one-way.

2. Go with the Flow
Since the sentence is one-way, the blank must agree with the rest of the sentence. Well, what's the blank about? It refers to the size of the waves. Meanwhile, the rest of the sentence refers to the fact that the waves terrified the surfers.

What's the switch?	none
Which way does the flow go?	one way
What idea does the blank support or contrast?	Supports "waves that terrify the surfers"

3. Fill in the Blank
You know that the waves have to be the kind of waves that could terrify the surfers. What kind of waves could do that? How about *really big* waves.

The *really big* waves in Maui terrified the surfers.

4. Compare Your Answer to the Answer Choices

Now go to the answer choices and find the one that matches up with the answer you created just from looking at the sentence.

(A)	slight
(B)	gentle
(C)	tremendous
(D)	rolling
(E)	salty

The answer that seems to match *really big* best is **C**, *tremendous*.

5. Plug It In

The last step. Plug the choice you think is the answer back into the sentence.

The *tremendous* waves in Maui terrified the surfers.

Works perfectly. You're done.

Example: Compound Sentence with a Colon

Employees were constantly amazed by the CEO's ---- speeches: She seemed unable to put together a coherent sentence.

1. Spot the Switch

This sentence contains no switch and isn't about a change over time, so it must be one-way.

2. Go with the Flow

Since the sentence is one way, the blank must agree with the rest of the sentence. What's the blank about? It describes the CEO's speeches. The rest of the sentence also describes the speeches by saying that the CEO "seemed unable to put together a coherent sentence."

What's the switch?	none
Which way does the flow go?	one way
What idea does the blank support or contrast?	supports "the CEO can't put together a coherent sentence"

3. Fill in the Blank

Since the sentence is one way, you know that the blank describing the CEO's speeches must support the idea that she can't put together a coherent sentence. In other words, the CEO's speeches must be *bad*.

Employees were constantly amazed by the CEO's *bad* speeches: She seemed unable to put together a coherent sentence.

4. Compare Your Answer to the Answer Choices

Now go to the answer choices and find the one that matches up with the answer you created just from looking at the sentence.

(A)	excellent
(B)	voluminous
(C)	inarticulate
(D)	timid
(E)	efficient

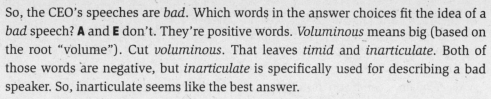
So, the CEO's speeches are *bad*. Which words in the answer choices fit the idea of a *bad* speech? **A** and **E** don't. They're positive words. *Voluminous* means big (based on the root "volume"). Cut *voluminous*. That leaves *timid* and *inarticulate*. Both of those words are negative, but *inarticulate* is specifically used for describing a bad speaker. So, inarticulate seems like the best answer.

Even if you didn't know the vocab, you still should have been able to use Word Charge to eliminate one, two, or even three of the answer choices.

5. Plug It In
The last step. Plug the choice you think is the answer back into the sentence.

> Employees were constantly amazed by the CEO's *inarticulate* speeches: She seemed unable to put together a coherent sentence.

Example: Compound Sentence with a Comma

> Many people consider the team ----, unmatched in skill or determination by any other team in the league.

1. Spot the Switch
This sentence contains no switch and isn't about a change over time, so it must be one-way.

2. Go with the Flow
Since the sentence is one-way, the blank must agree with the rest of the sentence. What's the blank about? How the team is perceived. The rest of the sentence also describes how the team is perceived—as "unmatched in skill or determination."

What's the switch?	none
Which way does the flow go?	one way
Which idea does the blank support or contrast?	supports "unmatched in skill or determination"

3. Fill in the Blank
Since the sentence is one-way, you know that the blank describing the team must fit with the fact that many people believe that the team is "unmatched in skill or determination." In other words, Hector must be *extremely good*.

> Many people consider the team *extremely good*, unmatched in skill or determination by any other team in the league.

4. Compare Your Answer to the Answer Choices
Now go to the answer choices and find the one that matches up with the answer you created just from looking at the sentence.

> (A)   middling
> (B)   destructive
> (C)   artistic
> (D)   quiescent
> (E)   invincible

You're looking for an answer choice that fits with the phrase *extremely good*, a very positive word. You should be able to eliminate *middling*, since it contains the root *middle*, which is the embodiment of average. You should also be able to eliminate *destructive*, since it's a negative term. That leaves *artistic*, *quiescent*, and *invincible*.

Artistic is a positive term but has little to do with team sports, the subject of the sentence. *Quiescent* means "quiet and calm," which also does not fit with the sports theme of the sentence. That leaves *invincible*, which means "cannot be defeated," a perfect fit for the idea of an *extremely good* team.

Once again, even if you didn't know all the vocab words, you could have cut several answers using Word Charge, putting you in a stronger position to guess.

5. Plug It In

Plug the choice you think is the answer back into the sentence.

> Many people consider the team *invincible*, unmatched in skill or determination by any other team in the league.

This five-step method is quickly making you invincible.

SC Type 2: One-Blank/Two-Way

On these SCs, the blank *contrasts* with the main idea of another clause in the sentence. Most one-blank/two-way sentences contain a switch that signals the contrast in the sentence. A few examples that convey a change over time will *not* contain a switch. We provide examples of both.

One-Blank/Two-Way with Switch

> Christina considered her pranks ----, but her former friends found her actions annoying and juvenile.

1. Spot the Switch

This sentence contains the two-way switch *but*. That means it must be two-way.

2. Go with the Flow

Since the sentence is two-way, the blank must contrast with the main ideas expressed in the rest of the sentence. The rest of the sentence describes how other people found Christina's pranks "annoying and juvenile." That means Christina's view of her pranks must contrast or oppose that perspective.

What's the switch?	*but*
Which way does the flow go?	two ways
What idea does the blank support or contrast?	contrasts "her pranks were annoying and juvenile"

3. Fill in the Blank

Since the sentence is two-way, you know that the blank describing Christina's view of her pranks must contrast with the common view of her actions, which is that they were "annoying and juvenile." So, to contrast "annoying and juvenile," maybe Christina thinks that her pranks are *funny and playful*.

> Christina thought her pranks were *funny and playful*, but her former friends found her actions annoying and juvenile.

4. Compare Your Answer to the Answer Choices

Now go to the answer choices and find which one of them matches up with the answer you created just from looking at the sentence.

(A)	hilarious
(B)	angry
(C)	colossal
(D)	trite
(E)	new

You're looking for an answer choice that fits with the phrase *funny and playful*, which is positive. You should be able to eliminate *angry* and *trite* ("corny"), since those are both negative. That leaves *hilarious, colossal,* and *new. Hilarious* is positive and means "extremely funny," so it's a very strong choice. *Colossal* has the same root as *colossus* and means "very big." It doesn't make much sense in a sentence that's about pranks or as a contrast to "annoying and juvenile." *New* is a positive word, but it also doesn't make sense as a contrast to "annoying and juvenile." *Hilarious* is the best choice.

Even if you didn't know all the vocab words, you should at least have been able to eliminate *angry* through Word Charge and *new* through the context of the sentence.

5. Plug It In

Plug the choice you think is the answer back into the sentence.

> Christina thought her pranks were *hilarious*, but her former friends found her actions annoying and juvenile.

One-Blank/Two-Way with No Switch

> Once a(n) ---- theory, the notion that the earth revolves around the sun is now accepted by virtually everyone.

1. Spot the Switch

This sentence contains no switch. However, the sentence does describe a change over time. Remember: Change-over-time sentences flow two ways even though they contain no switch.

2. Go with the Flow

Since the sentence is two-way, the blank must contrast with the ideas expressed in the rest of the sentence. The rest of the sentence describes how the idea of the earth revolving around the sun is accepted now "by virtually everyone." That means the blank must contrast with, or oppose, the idea that the earth revolving around the sun is widely accepted.

What's the switch?	none (change over time)
Which way does the flow go?	two ways
What idea does the blank support or contrast?	contrasts "accepted by virtually everyone"

3. Fill in the blank

Since the sentence is two-way, you know that the blank describing the old view of the theory must contrast with the current widespread acceptance of it. Previously, the theory must have been *not believed*.

> Once a(n) *not believed* theory, the notion that the earth revolves around the sun is now accepted by virtually everyone.

4. Compare Your Answer to the Answer Choices

Now go to the answer choices and find the one that matches up with the answer you created just from looking at the sentence.

> (A)   terrific
> (B)   pleasant
> (C)   esteemed
> (D)   beloved
> (E)   controversial

You're looking for an answer choice that fits with the phrase *not believed*, which is negative. Go down the list. *Terrific* is positive. So is *pleasant*, *esteemed*, and *beloved*. So *controversial* must be the answer. And it is.

You should note, though, that *not believed* and *controversial* really don't mean the same thing. Something that is controversial is believed by some people and not by others. That's the definition of a controversy: It's an argument between two passionate sides. Here's the lesson to learn from this example: When you make up your own answer, you should be flexible with it. If you find an answer choice that matches it exactly, awesome. If you don't, look for an answer choice that matches your answer's Word Charge and fits the context of the sentence.

5. Plug It In

Plug the choice you think is the answer back into the sentence.

> Once a(n) *controversial* theory, the notion that the earth revolves around the sun is now accepted by virtually everyone.

SC Type 3: Two-Blank/One-Way

Two-blank/one-way sentences sometimes contain switches like *and*, *because*, *since*, *so*, and *therefore*. Many two-blank/one-way sentences don't contain any switch at all.

Two-blank/one-way sentences come in two basic forms: blanks close together and blanks far apart. With blanks close together, you need to look at the half of the sentence that does not contain the blanks; with blanks far apart, you need to use clues from both halves of the sentence. That's the key difference between the two kinds of two-blank/one-way SCs.

Also note that with two-blank sentences, you have to take into account how *both* blanks function in the sentence when you're working on step 2.

Blanks Close Together

> The ---- conditions ---- even the intrepid explorer, who never again ventured out into the tundra.

1. Spot the Switch

This sentence contains no switch word and doesn't describe a change over time. That means it's one-way.

2. Go with the Flow

Since the sentence is one-way, both blanks must support the ideas expressed in the rest of the sentence. The rest of the sentence describes the explorer as intrepid and then says that even the explorer never again ventured into the tundra. That means the first blank must describe conditions that would convince even a bold explorer never to venture out again.

What's the switch?	none
Which way does the flow go?	one way
What idea does the blank support or contrast?	supports "even the intrepid explorer never went into the tundra again"

The second blank describes what the conditions did to the explorer to convince him never to venture out into the tundra again.

What's the switch?	none
Which way does the flow go?	one way
What idea does the blank support or contrast?	supports "even the intrepid explorer never went into the tundra again"

3. Fill in the Blank

Since the sentence is two-way, you know that the blanks describing the conditions and what happened to the intrepid explorer must agree with the fact that he never again went into the tundra. Would the explorer have refused to go back into the tundra if the conditions were nice? That wouldn't make sense. The conditions must have been *terrible*. And what would terrible conditions have done to the explorer? *Scared* him, or perhaps even *injured* him.

> The *terrible* conditions *scared* even the intrepid explorer, and he never again ventured out into the tundra.

4. Compare Your Answer to the Answer Choices

Now go to the answer choices and find the one that matches up with the answer you created just from looking at the sentence.

(A)	destructive..angered
(B)	gorgeous..moved
(C)	harsh..terrified
(D)	appalling..enveloped
(E)	serene..pleased

You're looking for two answer choices that fit with the words *terrible* and *scared*, both of which are negative. By Word Charge, you should be able to eliminate **B**, **D**, and **E**, since each of those pairs of words contains at least one word that's positive. Between **A**, *destructive..angered*, and **C**, *harsh..terrified*, answer **C** seems much stronger, since *terrified* is such a close fit with *scared*.

5. Plug It In

Plug the choice you think is the answer back into the sentence.

> The *harsh* conditions *terrified* even the intrepid explorer, and he never again ventured out into the tundra.

Blanks Far Apart

> Clarence Eichen was a ---- musician from a very young age, and he became the most ---- tuba performer in the world during the 1980s.

1. Spot the Switch
This sentence contains the one-way switch *and*. It must be one-way.

2. Go with the Flow
Since the sentence is one-way, both blanks must agree with the rest of the sentence. The rest of the sentence describes what sort of musician Eichen became. The first blank is about Eichen being a musician at a very young age.

What's the switch?	*and*
Which way does the flow go?	one way
What idea does the blank support or contrast?	supports "became the most ---- in the world"

The second blank describes what sort of performer Eichen became as an adult. The rest of the sentence describes what sort of musician he was as a child.

What's the switch?	*and*
Which way does the flow go?	one way
What idea does the blank support or contrast?	supports "was a ---- musician from a young age"

3. Fill in the Blank
The interesting thing about this sentence is that the two blanks refer to each other. That may make the sentence seem difficult to solve, since each blank stops you from guessing whether the other should be positive or negative. But since the sentence is one-way, you already do know something about the two blanks. Either they're both positive, or they're both negative. Either he was great as a boy and great as a man, or he was bad as a boy and bad as a man.

> Clarence Eichen was a *great* musician from a very young age, and he became the most *wonderful* tuba performer in the world during the 1980s.

or

> Clarence Eichen was a *bad* musician from a very young age, and he became the most *awful* tuba performer in the world during the 1980s.

4. Compare Your Answer to the Answer Choices
Now go to the answer choices and find the one that matches up with the answer you created just from looking at the sentence.

> (A) composed..tremulous
> (B) famous..accomplished
> (C) rigid..bellicose
> (D) calm..unstoppable
> (E) grave..humorous

None of the answer choices have two negatively charged pairs, so you don't have to worry about that. What you're looking for then, is a match for *great..wonderful*. You can eliminate **A**, **C**, and **E**, since *tremulous*, *rigid*, and *grave* all have negative charge.

Now, does it make logical sense to call someone a *calm* musician? In most situations, it doesn't. So the best match for *great..wonderful* is *famous..accomplished*.

5. Plug It In
Plug the choice you think is the answer back into the sentence.

> Clarence Eichen was a *famous* musician from a very young age, and he became the most *accomplished* tuba performer in the world during the 1980s.

SC Type 4: Two-Blank/Two-Way

In two-blank/two-way SCs, one-half of the sentence flows against the other half. This two-way contrast is usually, but not always, marked by the presence of a two-way switch. Below are examples of two-blank/two-way SCs, with and without switches.

Two-Blank/Two-Way with Switch

> Faulkner's use of adjective-filled language in his novels is now admired as an inimitable aspect of his unique style and a product of his literary ----; when his fiction was first published, however, many critics often ---- his style as needlessly ornate.

1. Spot the Switch
This sentence contains the two-way switch *however*. That means it's two-way.

2. Go with the Flow
The sentence is two-way, and the blanks each appear in different halves of the sentence. Since it's a two-way sentence, the two blanks (and the parts of the sentence before and after the semicolon) must contrast each other.

The first blank relates to the source of Faulkner's "unique style" that is "now admired." The second blank describes the reaction of early critics of Faulkner who considered his style "needlessly ornate."

What's the switch?	*however*
Which way does the flow go?	two ways
What idea does the blank support or contrast?	contrasts "when his fiction was first published, critics ---- his style as needlessly ornate."

The second blank describes how the critics reacted to Faulkner's style. This is in contrast to modern critics who "admire" it.

What's the switch?	*however*
Which way does the flow go?	two ways
What idea does the blank support or contrast?	contrasts "Faulkner's style is now admired."

3. Fill in the Blank
Since the sentence is two-way, you know that the two blanks must contrast, or oppose, each other. The first half of the sentence tells us that critics now admire Faulkner's style, which means the word you need to fill the blank will likely have a positive Word Charge. If the critics admired Faulkner's style, what might they have identified as its source? His literary *what*? How about *talent*?

The second half of the sentence tells us that critics at first considered his literary style "needlessly ornate." This indicates that the blank should be filled with a word that has negative Word Charge. How about *criticized*?

> Faulkner's use of intense, adjective-filled language in his novels is now admired as an inimitable aspect of his unique style and a product of his literary *talent*; but when his fiction was first published, many critics often *criticized* his style as needlessly ornate.

4. Compare Your Answer to the Answer Choices

Now go to the answer choices and find the one that matches up with the answer you created just from looking at the sentence.

> (A)   proclivities..extolled
> (B)   discrimination..praised
> (C)   abilities..examined
> (D)   genius..decried
> (E)   bombast..enlightened

You're looking for one answer choice that fits with the words *talent* and *criticized*. The first word is positive, the second negative. You should be able to eliminate **B**, **C**, and **E**, because *praised*, *examined*, and *enlightened* are all relatively common vocab words that are positive, and you want the second word to be negative.

That leaves **A** and **D**. Deciding between these two is hard, particularly because three of the four words are very difficult vocab words. At worst, you should plug both choices back into the sentence and then guess which one sounds best. At best, you'd sense either that *genius* is more positive than *proclivities* or that *extolled* has a positive charge, either of which would mark **D** as the correct answer.

5. Plug It In

Plug the choice you think is the answer back into the sentence.

> Faulkner's use of intense, adjective-filled language in his novels is now admired as an inimitable aspect of his unique style and a product of his literary *genius*; but when his fiction was first published, many critics often *decried* his style as needlessly ornate.

Two-Blank/Two-Way with No Switch

Two-way sentences that do *not* contain a switch word will compare a change over time.

> Once considered bad for your ----, bathing is now thought to be a crucial way of maintaining the ---- conditions that prevent plagues and epidemics.

1. Spot the Switch

This sentence contains no switch, but it does compare a change over time. That means it's two-way.

2. Go with the Flow

The sentence is two-way, and the blanks are each in different halves of the sentence. That means that the two blanks must contrast with each other.

What's the first blank about? It states that people once considered bathing harmful. This contrasts with the second half of the sentence, which says that bathing is now thought to "prevent plagues and epidemics."

What's the switch?	none
Which way does the flow go?	two ways
What idea does the blank support or contrast?	contrasts with "prevent plagues and epidemics"

The second blank describes the "conditions" that "prevent plagues and epidemics." It contrasts with the first half of the sentence, which says that people once thought that bathing was "bad for your ----."

What's the switch?	none
Which way does the flow go?	two ways
What idea does the blank support or contrast?	contrasts with "bad for your ----"

3. Fill in the Blank

Since the sentence is two-way, you know that the two blanks must contrast each other. The blank in the first half of the sentence explains in what way people thought bathing could harm them. This blank is contrasted with the modern thought that bathing "prevents plagues and epidemics." In other words, modern people think bathing "protects health," while in earlier times, people thought bathing was *bad* for your health.

As for the second blank, it describes the conditions that "prevent plagues and epidemics" and contrasts with the idea that bathing harms health. How about bathing creates *healthy* conditions?

> Once considered bad for your *health*, bathing is now thought to be a crucial way of maintaining the *healthy* conditions that prevent plagues and epidemics.

4. Compare Your Answer to the Answer Choices

Now go to the answer choices and find the one that matches up with the answer you created just from looking at the sentence.

> (A) behavior..superb
> (B) relations..helpful
> (C) development..ideal
> (D) ethics..unfortunate
> (E) well-being..sanitary

You're looking for two answer choices that fit with the words *health* and *healthy*. A quick look through the answer choices shows one answer that stands out from the rest: **E**. *Well-being* and *sanitary* both fit with the idea of health and the need for positive words.

5. Plug It In

Plug the choice you think is the answer back into the sentence.

> Once considered bad for your *well-being*, bathing is now thought to be a crucial way of maintaining the *sanitary* conditions that prevent plagues and epidemics.

And that's it! You're now ready for any Sentence Completion that the new SAT might send your way.

READING PASSAGES: THE LONG AND SHORT OF IT

TO MAKE A LONG STORY SHORT, THE SAT NOW CONTAINS two kinds of critical reading passages (which we call RPs):

- The familiar long RPs—multiparagraph passages followed by a series of questions.
- New short RPs—brief one-paragraph passages followed by two questions.

The test also contains dual passages for both long and short RPs that require you to read two passages and answer questions about how they relate. Long and short RP questions account for about two-thirds of the entire SAT Critical Reading section. Explaining what they're all about and how to beat them accounts for 100 percent of the next three chapters.

12.1 # BECOME A READING MACHINE

Whether you're dealing with long or short reading passages, you've got to have critical reading skills. But you can't just study for reading passages as easily as you can for math or grammar. If you don't know how to deal with triangles, you can study the precise rules that apply to *all* triangles. But if you're having trouble getting through reading passages, it's not quite as easy to figure out what to do.

So how *do* you study for reading passages? The answer is simple: Thou shalt read. Read! Read like mad. From this instant until the day you take the SAT, read, read, read. Reeeeeead. But don't read like you watch TV. You need to keep your mind *active* as you read, look between the lines and think about the mechanics, or the inner workings, of everything you read. For example,

1. **What's the author's main point or purpose?** Does the author, for instance, argue that lyrics to pop songs will corrupt America's youth?
2. **How does the author's attitude relate to the point being made?** Does the writer talk about pop stars in tones of disgust or of admiration?
3. **How does the author use language, sentence structure, and rhetorical devices, such as similes and metaphors?** Perhaps the writer is shocked by a pop star's new look and compares her to a siren, a character from Greek mythology who lured men to their dooms.

The point here is to train yourself to keep your brain on SAT alert while you read. Don't just coast. If you ask questions about what's going on as you read in your daily life, when the new SAT comes along, the RP questions will just feel like extensions of the reading mastery you've already established.

12.2 # SLAYING THE FIRE-BREATHING JARGON

The new SAT includes questions about rhetorical devices on both long and short RPs. Rhetorical devices are tools that authors use to convey meaning or add depth and richness to their writing. Terms such as *simile*, *metaphor*, and *personification* are rhetorical devices. Jargon's in, so now you've got to figure jargon out.

If you think this decision confirms that the new SAT overhaul is really more like The SAT Gone Wild, we don't necessarily disagree. But consider this: You'll have to recognize and analyze rhetorical devices in literature throughout high school and college. Learning these terms now will actually prove useful to your education beyond studying for the SAT. To help you get the most important rhetorical devices down cold, here's a list of the top 25 terms that will most likely appear on the new SAT:

-   **Alliteration**—The repetition of similar sounds, usually consonants, at the beginning of words. "Sweet scented stuff" is an example of alliteration in Robert Frost's poem "Out, Out—."
-   **Allusion**—A reference within a literary work to a historical, literary, or biblical character, place, or event. The following line from Shakespeare's *The Merchant of Venice* contains an allusion to the Roman mythological character Cupid: "Come, come, Nerissa; for I long to see quick Cupid's post that comes so mannerly."

- **Assonance**—The repetition of vowel sounds in a sequence of nearby words. "The monster spoke in a low mellow tone" has assonance in its repetition of the "o" sound.

- **Caricature**—A description or characterization that exaggerates or distorts a character's prominent features, usually for purposes of mockery. A cartoon of Abraham Lincoln with a giant top hat, a very thick beard, and extremely sunken eyes could be considered a caricature.

- **Cliché**—A familiar expression that has been used and reused so many times that it's lost its expressive power. "Happy as a clam" or "eyes like a hawk" are examples of clichés.

- **Epiphany**—A sudden, powerful, and often spiritual or life-changing realization that a character experiences in an otherwise ordinary moment.

- **Foreshadowing**—An author's deliberate use of hints or suggestions to give a preview of events or themes that do not develop until later in the narrative. Images such as a storm brewing or a crow landing on a fencepost often foreshadow ominous developments in a story.

- **Hyperbole**—An excessive overstatement or exaggeration of fact. "I've told you that a million times already" is a hyperbolic statement.

- **Idiom**—A common expression that has acquired a meaning that differs from its literal meaning, such as "It's raining cats and dogs" or "That cost me an arm and a leg."

- **Imagery**—Language that brings to mind sensory impressions. Homer's description of dawn as "rosy-fingered" in the *Odyssey* is an example of his use of imagery.

- **Irony**—**Irony** usually emphasizes the contrast between the way things are expected to be and the way they actually are. Here's an example of irony: Medieval people believed that bathing would harm them when in fact *not* bathing led to the unsanitary conditions that caused the bubonic plague.

- **Metaphor**—The comparison of one thing to another that does not use the terms *like* or *as*. Metaphors use a form of the verb "to be" to establish a comparison. A metaphor from Shakespeare's *Macbeth*: "Life is but a walking shadow."

- **Motif**—A recurring structure, contrast, idea, or other device that develops a literary work's major ideas. Urban decay is a motif in the novel *1984*, which is filled with scenes of a dilapidated, rundown city. Shadows and darkness is a motif in *A Tale of Two Cities*, a novel that contains many dreary, gloomy scenes and settings.

- **Onomatopoeia**—The use of words such as *pop* or *hiss* where the spoken sound resembles the actual sound. "The *whoosh* of the waves at the seashore," and "The *zoom* of the race cars speeding around the track" are two examples of **onomatopoeia**.

- **Oxymoron**—The association of two terms that seem to contradict each other, as in the expression "wise fool" or "jumbo shrimp."

- **Paradox**—A statement that seems contradictory on the surface but often expresses a deeper truth. The line from Oscar Wilde's *The Ballad of Reading Gaol*, "All men destroy the things they love" is a paradox.

- **Personification**—The use of human characteristics to describe animals, things, or ideas. Using the word "babbling" to describe a brook is an example of **personification**.

- **Pun**—A play on words that uses the similarity in sound between two words with distinctly different meanings. For example, the title of Oscar Wilde's play *The*

Importance of Being Earnest is a pun on the word *earnest*, which means "serious" or "sober," and the name "Ernest."

- **Rhetorical Question**—A question asked not to elicit an actual response but to make an impact or call attention to something. "Will the world ever see the end of war?" is an example of a rhetorical question.
- **Sarcasm**—A verbal tone in which it is obvious from context that the speaker means the opposite of what he or she says. "Mom, I'd love to see *Howard the Duck* with you" is probably a phrase you would say sarcastically.
- **Simile**—A comparison of two things that uses the words *like* or *as*. "Love is like a fire" is a simile.
- **Symbol**—An object, character, figure, place, or color used to represent an abstract idea or concept. The two roads in Robert Frost's poem "The Road Not Taken" **symbolize** the choice between two paths in life.
- **Theme**—A fundamental and universal idea explored in a literary work. The struggle to achieve the American Dream is a common theme in twentieth-century American literature.
- **Thesis**—The central argument that an author tries to make in a literary work. Some might consider J. D. Salinger's thesis in *The Catcher in the Rye* that society often forces people to be phoney.
- **Tone**—The author's or narrator's attitude toward the story or the subject. The tone of the *Declaration of Independence* is determined and confident.

12.3 RP SIZE AND RP SKILL

The difference between short RP questions and long RP questions is not in the questions. The questions are actually quite similar. The difference—prepare to be shocked—is in the *length* of the passages. Short RPs are about 100-words long and are followed by two questions. Long RPs are 500 to 800 words and include anywhere from eight to thirteen questions.

So, the questions on long and short RPs are similar, but the passages are of vastly different lengths. What should this mean to you? Two things:

1. **Long and short RPs test the same skills:** Your ability to understand what an author is trying to say and your ability to evaluate how an author uses language to make his or her points.
2. **Your strategy for dealing with long and short RPs has to be different.** The vast difference in the length of the passages affects how you should think about reading the passage and how you should deal with the questions after the passage.

In the following two chapters, we teach you the strategies you need to meet and beat both long and short RPs.

THE LONG OF IT

LONG READING PASSAGES POSE A DOUBLE CHALLENGE: Just like on every other section of the new SAT, you have to know how to deal with each individual question. But you also need a strategy for dealing with the passage. In this chapter, we show you how to deal with all the different types of questions the Critical Reading section might throw at you, *and* we explain the best strategy for how to read and remember the passage.

13.1 INSTRUCTIONS FOR READING PASSAGES

Here's your first RP exercise:

> Each passage below is followed by questions based on its content. Answer the questions following each passage on the basis of what is stated or implied in that passage and in any introductory material that may be provided.

13.2 WHAT THE INSTRUCTIONS DON'T TELL YOU

The instructions gloss over two important facts about reading passages and questions. Here they are:

- **Don't skip over the italicized contextual blurb**. Above each passage, you'll see an italicized introductory blurb that may offer some contextual information. The introduction looks a lot like instructions, and you know you're usually supposed to not waste time reading instructions that you can memorize long before taking the test. However, the context that the introduction provides will often help you understand the passage. So, read this introduction. Do not skip over it.
- **The order of the questions**. The questions following the passage are *not* ordered by difficulty. That means you should *not* adjust your pacing strategy on reading passages based on where a particular question appears relative to the other questions. The last few questions won't necessarily be tougher than the first few. Instead, RP questions are ordered by what part of the passage they refer to. Questions that test the beginning of the passage appear at the beginning of the group, questions that test the middle appear in the middle, and questions that cover the end appear at the end. General questions that cover the entire passage can appear either at the beginning or the end of the group of questions. General questions won't appear in the middle of the group.

13.3   A SAMPLE PASSAGE AND QUESTIONS

It's tough to talk about long RPs and questions without a sample passage and questions to look at. So, here's a sample passage about Galileo with the italicized introduction.

As you read the passage, note the little numbers to the left. Those numbers count off every five lines of the passage (the "5" means that you're reading the fifth line of the passage, the "10" means you're reading the tenth line, and so on). Questions that ask you to refer to a specific word or section of the passage will include the line numbers of that word or section.

Sample Passage

The following passage discusses the scientific life of Galileo Galilei in reference to the political, religious, artistic, and scientific movements of the age.

Line

Galileo Galilei was born in 1564 into a Europe wracked by cultural ferment and religious strife. The popes of the Roman Catholic Church, powerful in their roles as both religious and secular leaders, had proven vulnerable to the worldly and decadent spirit of the age, and their personal immorality brought the reputation of the papacy to historic lows. In 1517, Martin
5   Luther, a former monk, attacked Catholicism for having become too worldly and politically corrupt and for obscuring the fundamentals of Christianity with pagan elements. His reforming zeal, which appealed to a notion of an original, "purified" Christianity, set in motion the Protestant Reformation and split European Christianity in two.

In response, Roman Catholicism steeled itself for battle and launched the Counter-
10   Reformation, which emphasized orthodoxy and fidelity to the true Church. The Counter-Reformation reinvigorated the Church and, to some extent, eliminated its excesses. But the Counter-Reformation also contributed to the decline of the Italian Renaissance, a revival of arts and letters that sought to recover and rework the classical art and philosophy of ancient Greece and Rome. The popes had once been great patrons of Renaissance arts and sciences,
15   but the Counter-Reformation put an end to the Church's liberal leniency in these areas. Further, the Church's new emphasis on religious orthodoxy would soon clash with the emerging scientific revolution. Galileo, with his study of astronomy, found himself at the center of this clash.

Conservative astronomers of Galileo's time, working without telescopes, ascribed without
20   deviation to the ancient theory of geocentricity. This theory of astronomy held that the earth ("geo," as in "geography" or "geology") lay at the center of the solar system, orbited by both the sun and the other planets. Indeed, to the casual observer, it seemed common sense that since the sun "rose" in the morning and "set" at night, it must have circled around the earth. Ancient authorities like Aristotle and the Roman astronomer Ptolemy had championed this viewpoint,
25   and the notion also coincided with the Catholic Church's view of the universe, which placed mankind, God's principal creation, at the center of the cosmos. Buttressed by common sense, the ancient philosophers, and the Church, the geocentric model of the universe seemed secure in its authority. The Ptolemaic theory, however, was not impervious to attack. In the 16th century, astronomers strained to make modern observations fit Ptolemy's geocentric model of
30   the universe.

Increasingly complex mathematical systems were necessary to reconcile these new observations with Ptolemy's system of interlocking orbits. Nicholas Copernicus, a Polish astronomer, openly questioned the Ptolemaic system and proposed a heliocentric system in which the planets—including earth—orbited the sun ("helios"). This more mathematically
35   satisfying way of arranging the solar system did not attract many supporters at first, since the available data did not yet support a wholesale abandonment of Ptolemy's system. By the end of the 16th century, however, astronomers like Johannes Kepler (1571–1630) had also begun to embrace Copernicus's theory.

Ultimately, Galileo's telescope struck a fatal blow to the Ptolemaic system. But, in a sense,
40   the telescope was also nearly fatal to Galileo himself. The Catholic Church, desperately trying to hold the Protestant heresy at bay, could not accept a scientific assault on its own theories of the universe. The pressures of the age set in motion a historic confrontation between religion and science, one which would culminate in 1633 when the Church put Galileo on trial, forced him to recant his stated and published scientific beliefs, and put him under permanent house
45   arrest.

during the Renaissance the Catholic Church

The Seven Types of RP Questions

The SAT asks seven types of questions about RPs. These seven types of questions are the *same* for both long RPs and short RPs. So, if you're ready for these seven types, you're ready for every RP question that might appear on the new SAT.

Here's a list of the seven RP question types:

1. Main Idea
2. Attitude or Tone
3. Specific Information
4. Implied Information
5. Themes and Arguments
6. Technique
7. Words in Context

Below, we provide a more thorough explanation of each question type based on sample questions about the Galileo passage above. We provide an explanation of how to answer each question about the Galileo passage that will show you how to answer *all* questions of that type.

1. Main Idea

Main idea questions test your understanding of the entire passage. They don't include specific quotations from the passage. Instead, they ask broad questions that focus on the passage's primary purpose. Unlike themes and arguments questions (question type 5), main idea questions do not concern the author's opinions on the subject—they just focus on the subject or idea itself. Main idea questions cover things such as

- What's the primary purpose of the passage?
- What main idea is the author trying to convey?
- Why did the author write it?

A Sample Main Idea Question

Which of the following best states the main idea of the passage?

(A)   Science always conflicts with religion.
(B)   Science is vulnerable to outside social forces.
(C)   Ideally, scientific theories should reinforce religious doctrine.
(D)   Science operates in a vacuum.
(E)   Advanced technology is the only route to good scientific theories.

The best way to deal with main idea questions is to come up with a one-sentence summary of the passage. For this passage, you might come up with something like "Galileo's scientific discoveries in particular, and science in general, were affected by the religious and social forces of the time." Once you have the summary, go to the answer choices. In our example question, the answer that best fits the summary is **B**.

But since the passage takes a long time to discuss Galileo's run-ins with the Roman Catholic Church, you might have been tempted by **A**. If you're a bit unsure, a good way to back up your summary is to look at the opening and concluding sentences of the passage, and, if necessary, at the topic sentence of each paragraph (the topic sentence is the first sentence in each paragraph). In the Galileo passage, sentences like the first sentence of this passage—"Galileo Galilei was born in 1564 into a Europe wracked by cultural ferment and religious divisions"—make it clear that the passage is about a scientist in the midst of cultural and religious upheaval. The passage's descriptions of the struggle between the orthodoxy of the Church and the rising scientific revolution help establish the main idea of the passage: that science is vulnerable to outside social forces, **B**.

2. Attitude or Tone

These questions test whether you understand the author's view on the subject. To answer them correctly, you should write down whether the author is for or against his or her subject as you read the passage. It might also be helpful to jot down a few of the points or examples the writer uses to make his or her argument.

The differences in the answer choices for this type of question can be slight. For example, you might have to choose between "irritated" and "enraged." Both of these words suggest that the author has negative sentiments about the topic, but the difference lies in the *intensity* of those feelings. Detecting the words and phrases that convey the intensity of an author's feelings will help you distinguish between different extremes of a similar overall feeling. Determining that a certain topic upsets the author is only the first step. You then need to examine the author's word choice closely to pinpoint the degree of his or her feeling. Is the upset author mildly disturbed? Strongly disapproving? Or enraged? It might help to imagine how the author might sound if he or she read the passage aloud.

If you can't come to a firm decision about the intensity of a feeling, remember that even if all you know is whether the author's tone is positive, negative, or neutral, you'll almost definitely be able to eliminate at least some answer choices and turn the guessing odds in your favor.

A Sample Attitude or Tone Question

> The author's tone in this passage can best be described as
>
> (A) analytical
> (B) disturbed
> (C) skeptical
> (D) dramatic
> (E) reverent

It will help you to first decide whether the author's tone is positive, neutral, or negative, and *then* look at the answers in order to cross off those that don't fit. So, is the Galileo author positive, neutral, or negative? The passage describes an entire time period, covering the different sides, and while it discusses how the Counter-Reformation affected Galileo, it never condemns or praises either the reformation or Galileo. It seeks mainly to describe what happened. So, it's a pretty neutral passage, which means you can eliminate **B** and **C**, since those answer choices are negative, and **E**, since *reverent* ("expressing devotion") is extremely positive. That leaves *dramatic* and *analytical*.

The next step is to ask yourself how the passage would sound if its tone were *dramatic*: It would be full of highs and lows, exclamations and sudden shifts, and it may lurch all over the emotional spectrum. What about if it were *analytical*? It would be a little dry, very informational, with few highs and lows and lots of explanation meant to scrutinize all sides of the problem. Based on that description, analytical sounds like the most accurate way to sum up this writer's tone in the passage. **A** is the correct answer.

3. Specific Information

These questions ask about information that's explicitly stated in the passage. On long RPs, specific information questions usually pinpoint parts of the passage via line numbers or a direct quotation. Very often, specific information questions come in the form of NOT or EXCEPT formats in which you have to choose the one wrong answer out of the five answer choices.

A Sample Specific Information Question

> Which of the following was *not* a reason for Martin Luther's attack on the Catholic Church (lines 4–6)?
>
> (A)   pagan elements in its practices
> (B)   the amorality of its leadership
> (C)   its excessive attention to piety
> (D)   its corruption and worldliness
> (E)   the political involvement of the popes

There's no reason to ever try to answer this question type without going back to the passage. Take a brief look at the specific lines that the question addresses (in this example, lines 4–6). It's time well spent.

In this passage, lines 4–6 say that Luther attacked the Church for "having become too worldly and politically corrupt and for obscuring the fundamentals of Christianity with pagan elements." That takes out **A**, **B**, **D**, and **E**. so the answer is **C**.

4. Implied Information

Information is "implied" when certain facts, statements, or ideas convey the information but don't declare it outright. Think of these as "suggestion" questions. Implied information questions identify a particular part of the passage and ask you about less obvious information that's "between the lines." To find the correct answer, you may have to deduce what's being said or take a leap of logic. Remember that the leaps the SAT requires you to take are never very vast. Even though implied information questions ask you to reach a bit beyond what the passage states explicitly, they do not require you to think far outside the boundaries of the facts and opinions that the passage overtly contains. Often, you can spot implied information questions when you see words like *context*, *inferred*, *implied*, *indicated*, or *suggested*. Here is a sample of how the SAT phrases implied information questions.

A Sample Implied Information Question

> In the second paragraph, the passage implies that during the Renaissance, the Catholic Church
>
> (A)   saw little conflict between its own goals and those of the arts and sciences
> (B)   promoted the arts as a way to limit the social influence of scientists
> (C)   supported Martin Luther's views on religion and the Church
> (D)   had limited interaction with the religious affairs of commoners
> (E)   focused on spirituality as opposed to worldly matters

For this kind of question, it's important to come up with your own answer before looking at the answer choices. Outside of the context of the passage, any one of the answer choices might look acceptable to you. It can also be very helpful to think about the main idea of the passage to help you figure out the implied information. Since the author is trying to support a main idea, the information implied in that support will also be associated with the main idea.

This question asks about the Catholic Church during the Renaissance and identifies the second paragraph as the place to look. In that paragraph, it says that during the Renaissance, the Church "was a great patron of the arts and sciences." What does this suggest about the Church during that period? How about this: "The Church liked the arts and sciences during the Renaissance." Now go through the answer choices and look for a match: **A** is by far the best fit and the best answer.

5. Themes and Arguments

The main idea of a passage is its overall purpose. Themes are the recurring concepts that an author uses to establish the main idea. Arguments are the specific perspectives and opinions an author expresses on his or her main idea. Themes and arguments questions test your ability to look at particular parts of a passage and identify the underlying feelings they convey about the main idea. Themes and arguments questions often test your ability to put what the passage says, or how the author feels, into your own words.

The main idea of a passage might be that "the growing rat population is damaging Chicago." Three different themes that an author uses to establish the main idea could be disease, tourism, and city infrastructure. The author's arguments, or specific opinions, could be that the growing rat population has caused the spread of influenza in Chicago, has led to a steep drop in tourism to the city, and threatens to destroy some of the city's most important structures.

A Sample Themes and Arguments Question

> Which of the following best explains why the Catholic Church started the Counter-Reformation? (lines 8–10)
>
> (A)   to fight scientific heresy
> (B)   to clean out its own ranks
> (C)   to reinvigorate artists and intellectuals
> (D)   to elect a new pope
> (E)   to counter Protestant challenges

The first thing you should do on this type of question is go back to the passage and then come up with your own answer to the question. Once you have this answer in your head, *then* look at the answer choices. If you look at the answer choices before going back to the passage, you're much more likely to make a careless error.

This question tests whether you can follow the flow of argument within the text. More specifically, it tests your ability to differentiate between the causes and effects of the Counter-Reformation. Answers **A**, **B**, and **C** refer to *effects* of the Counter-Reformation, not the causes. But if you were to only look at the answers, any one of these choices might look familiar and therefore tempt you. Avoid temptation. Go back to the passage: "In 1517, Martin Luther, a former monk, attacked Catholicism for having become too worldly and politically corrupt and for obscuring the fundamentals of Christianity with pagan elements. His reforming zeal . . . set in motion the Protestant Reformation and split European Christianity in two. In response, Roman Catholicism steeled itself for battle and launched the Counter-Reformation, which emphasized orthodoxy and fidelity to the true Church." So, your answer to the question of why the Catholic Church started the Counter-Reformation would be something like, "In response to the Protestants and Martin Luther." Answer choice **E** is the best fit and the right answer.

6. Technique

Every author uses certain methods to convey his or her ideas. Technique questions require you to identify the specific literary tool or method the author of the passage uses in a specific part of the passage. This makes technique questions the most likely place for literary terms like *simile* and *metaphor* to appear.

Technique questions can focus on very small units in the passage, such as single words or simple parenthetical statements, or they can target larger units, such as a list, or even the relationship between entire paragraphs.

If you're having trouble figuring out why or how an author is using a particular technique, it can often be helpful to take a step back and look at the technique in light of the author's main point or idea. If you know the main idea, you can often use that information to figure out what an author is trying to accomplish in a particular area of a passage.

A Sample Technique Example

The author's description of Galileo's telescope as having "struck a fatal blow" is an example of a(n)

(A)   simile
(B)   metaphor
(C)   personification
(D)   allusion
(E)   irony

This question tests your knowledge of literary terms—a new subject on the new SAT. (If you're having trouble with literary terms, take some time to look over our literary terms list on page 158.) In this question, the telescope, an inanimate object, is described as having "struck a fatal blow." In other words, it's been given human qualities, which is the definition of *personification*.

7. Words in Context

These questions present a word or short phrase from the passage and then ask about the meaning of that word in the greater context of the passage. Such questions on long RPs include line numbers that direct you to where the words in the question appear in the passage.

The majority of words-in-context questions look like this:

The word "content" (line 34) is closest in meaning to which of the following words?

Words-in-context questions are a lot like sentence completions, only on these questions, the "blank" comes in the form of a word in quotes. You should try to ignore that word in quotes and imagine it as a blank. In other words, treat words-in-context questions as if they were Sentence Completions.

Why ignore those words in quotes? Because words-in-context questions often have answer choices with words that are indeed correct meanings of the tested word but not the correct meaning of the word *as it appears in the passage*. For example, the question above might contain answer choices such as *satisfied* and *subject*, both of which are correct meanings of the word *content*. But remember that these questions test the word *in context*. By approaching the sentence as if it were a sentence completion, you'll be forced to consider the context of the word in quotes.

A Sample Words in Context Example

1. The term "ferment" in line 1 most closely means

(A) alienation
(B) turmoil
(C) consolidation
(D) decomposition
(E) stagnation

So here's a words-in-context question. Treat it like it's a Sentence Completion: "Galileo Galilei was born in 1564 into a Europe wracked by cultural ---- and religious strife." The sentence is one-way (there are no switch words), so the blank needs to fit with the ideas of "wracked" and "strife," both of which bring up associations with fighting and chaos. See page 135 for Sentence Completion strategy.

13.4 LONG RP STRATEGY

By now you know that long and short RPs differ only in length—the questions the SAT asks about them test the same skills. Even so, length makes a big difference when it comes to strategy. Following are the steps you should follow to take on long RPs and their questions. Here's a quick list of all the steps:

Step 1. Force Yourself to Focus
Step 2. Read and Outline the Passage First
Step 3. Answer Specific Questions
Step 4. Answer General Questions

Step 1: Force Yourself to Focus

Almost everyone suffers from DLFD on SAT reading passages: Devastating Loss-of-Focus Disease. You know that hippy phrase, "Free your mind and the rest will follow?" That phrase is a lie. On the SAT, you have to lock up your mind, put it in solitary confinement, and then expect high scores to follow. You have to focus exclusively on the passage before you as if it were the only thing in your life. You must *trick* your mind into being very excited by this prospect. Say to yourself, "I am so excited to read this passage about the history of hot air balloons!"

This seems like a joke, but we're not joking. If you focus on the passage as you would something you really care about, you'll understand and remember much more of the passage. Do whatever you can to engage with the passage, even if it's about sea snails, and try to channel your manufactured passion into better focus and attention to detail. That's what will get you higher scores on reading passages. No joke.

Step 2: Read and Outline the Passage

Read the passage first, paying no attention to the answers. Looking at the answer first may seem like a good idea, but in practice it's just not possible to keep a load of questions in your head while also trying to read the passage.

You should never spend more than *five minutes* reading a long RP. Read the passage quickly, but don't just skim it. We think strategies like reading *only* the first and last sentence of each paragraph do more harm than good. Why? Because speed reading the first time around will force you to go back frequently to the passage when you get to the questions, which will cost you time. Instead, read the entire passage and focus intently on the most important parts of every long RP: The introduction, the conclusion, and the first and last sentences of each paragraph. This will ensure that you are not just reading but *actively* reading.

How to Read the Passage

Don't get bogged down trying to soak up every single fact and detail. Remember, questions that deal with specifics will give you line numbers, so going back to the passage won't be a big deal. You don't have to memorize the passage, you just have to get a solid gist of it.

Read the passage with an awareness of the big-picture questions that RP questions will ask you.

- What is the author's goal in writing the passage?
- What's the author's tone?
- What's the primary argument that the author makes?
- What literary techniques does the author use to convey his or her ideas?

It's also a good idea to take a few seconds after each paragraph to summarize for yourself what you just read and jot it down in your test booklet. This will help you retain the content of each passage and trace the overall structure and feel of the passage.

How to Outline a Reading Passage

When it comes time to answer questions about an RP, having a rough outline of the passage will be very helpful. When we say you should write an outline, we don't mean a thorough kind of outline with bullet points and roman numerals that you'd write for a teacher. We just mean you should keep a rough sketch in the margins of the RP in your test booklet.

Here's how: As you read each RP, keep a shorthand written record of your thoughts on the passage as you read through it. Write down the purpose of each paragraph as you go and jot down ideas about the tone, arguments, and techniques you spot along the way. That way, when you finish reading the passage, you'll already be armed with answers to some of the questions that you know will show up on the test, such as tone, main idea, themes and arguments, and technique. Underline topic sentences, draw in brackets to mark lists of examples that support the main argument, circle important names—mark anything relating to general themes and ideas, the main idea of each paragraph, and other aspects of the passage that strike you as important. This will reinforce what you read as you read it and give you a road map of the passage to use when you go back to answer specific questions.

Step 3: Answer Specific Questions

When you finish the passage, go straight to the questions. Specific questions refer to particular line numbers or paragraphs in the passage. We suggest you tackle these questions before the more general questions because those typically require more thought, time, and attention than specific questions.

Specific questions refer directly to words or lines in the passage. Before going back to the paragraph, articulate to yourself exactly what the question is asking. Don't look at the answers (this will help you avoid being caught by SAT traps). Next, go to the specified area in the passage and read just the few lines before and after it to get a sense of the context. Come up with your own answer to the question, then go back and find the answer that best matches yours.

Step 4: Answer General Questions

You should be able to answer general questions without looking back at the passage. General questions do not refer to specific locations in the passage. Instead, they ask about broad aspects of the passage such as its main idea, tone, and argument. Often the best way to answer general questions like these is to refer to the outline of the passage you made as you read through it. If you've already jotted down notes in your outline on the purpose of each paragraph, the tone, and the overall argument of the passage, you'll be all set to take on general questions with ease.

Your ability to answer general tone and main idea questions without looking back at the passage is also a good gauge of how well you're reading the passage. If you're having trouble with these sorts of questions and have to go back to the passage to answer them, you might be speeding through the passage too quickly or focusing too much on specific information.

13.5
CHALLENGED TO A DUAL (PASSAGE)

The new SAT contains one dual passage, which is SAT-speak for two separate passages that are somehow related. When you get to the dual passage, here's what you'll see:

- Italicized introduction
- Passage 1
- Passage 2
- Questions on passage 1
- Questions on passage 2
- Questions that ask you to relate the two passages

The secret to dual passages is: Do *not* follow this order. Instead, treat each passage separately, with the four-step method we just showed you. That results in the following five-step method for dual RPs:

Step 1. Read the introduction and the first passage.
Step 2. Answer the questions about *the first passage only*.
Step 3. Read the second passage.
Step 4. Answer the questions about *the second passage only*.
Step 5. Answer the questions that address both passages together.

Treating the passages separately makes sense for a number of reasons. First, it means that you'll be answering the questions on a particular passage when that passage is freshest in your mind. That will save you time, since you won't have to jump back and forth between questions and passages. Second, it means that you won't get so caught up looking for relationships between the two passages that you'll lose focus on the individual passages. By the time you've dealt with the two passages individually, you'll have naturally built up a strong enough understanding of each passage to be able to answer the questions that ask you to relate the two passages.

These "relating" passages questions usually ask you to compare a variety of aspects of the two passages, such as the main idea of the two passages, individual arguments in each passage, and the tones of each passage. Sometimes questions relating two passages get a bit more creative by asking you to predict how the author of one passage might think about information presented in the other passage.

THE SKINNY ON RP CONTENT

RPs on the new SAT split into two big categories:

- Nonfiction passages (on everything from science to art to history to literature)
- Fiction passages excerpted from literary works

Nonfiction Passages

These are the RPs that you expect to see on the SAT. You know, the ones with a bunch of paragraphs about a Native American tribe, the scientist who invented carbon dating, or a famous Civil War battle. These passages are always nonfiction with no distinct narrative voice. That means they're based on facts and read like newspaper or journal articles. The individual "voice" or identity of the author does not play much of a role in the discussion or the topic at hand in these passages.

None of these passages require you to have any background knowledge in the topics they cover. The passage or passages always contain every bit of information you need to answer the questions correctly. Below, we list a few details about the specific kinds of nonfiction, nonnarrative passages you can expect to encounter on the new SAT. But keep in mind that all of these subcategories test similar skills, namely, how well you can understand and evaluate what the passage contains.

Science Passages

Science passages range from discussions or debates about topics in science to descriptions of scientific events throughout history. For example, science subject matter may include a scientist arguing that genetics affect decisions about where people build their cities, a historian describing the disagreements between physicists in the early twentieth century, or an explanation of the earthworm's digestive system. All the science you need to know is presented in the passage—you should not expect to find anything like physics or chemistry formulas in science RPs.

History Passages

History RPs come in two forms: (1) passages taken from history, such as a historical address about an event or situation in society, and (2) passages in which historians write about and interpret history. Questions about history passages tend to focus heavily on your ability to understand the author's argument. History passages also frequently test your understanding of unfamiliar words in context. For example, a question about a passage on the Civil War may ask you to identify the definition of a word like *bayonet* based on the context of the passage.

Literary Criticism Passages

These passages usually discuss one of the following topics: a particular book or writer, a literary movement or trend, or some overarching literary concept. Questions following literary criticism RPs are almost always about the tone of the passage or the writer's point of view or overall opinion. Vocabulary is a dead giveaway of the writer's tone and argument in these passages.

Art Passages

Art passages discuss specific pieces of art, trends in art history, or particular artists. "Art" on the SAT usually means painting, architecture, or music. Art passages might involve the artist speaking about his or her own work, the artist speaking about his or her field in general, a critic discussing a specific work or artist, or a description of some controversy in the art world. Passages about specific artists usually try to locate that artist in the context of broader trends or movements.

Fiction Passages

Fiction is the wildcard that the new SAT has thrown into the long RP mix. *Every* Critical Reading section of the new SAT includes one fiction narrative passage. Fiction passages are very different from other RPs on the test, since they're the product of a writer's imagination. Instead of dealing with arguments or big concepts in science, literature, art, and history, fictional narratives require you to deal with characters, emotions, point of view, and literary style.

This means you have to think a little differently. As you read a fiction passage, think about why the author chose to write what he or she wrote. Why did the writer choose the images described in the passage? What rhetorical device like similes, metaphors, and personification did the author use? What is the tone? What is the writer's relationship to the characters, memories, or events being described? How do the characters feel about each other or about these memories or events?

Don't read too deeply into these passages. It won't ask you for a poetic interpretation or an innovative analysis of a passage. It will only ask you questions that you can answer based on what's right in front of you. That makes the best approach to fiction narrative interpreting only what you read directly in the passage. If you feel like you're stretching for an answer, you're probably not on the right track. Stick to the facts and ideas that the passage itself can support.

Hmmm . . . Have I Read This Before?

The reading passages on the old SAT were excerpts from obscure books that no high school student would ever have read. Using oddball sources helped bolster the test's fairness, since almost nobody would have read the books from which the passages were excerpted (unless you had perchance sat down one Saturday to read *Anook: Tales of an Eskimo Goat Herder*). So, their decision to use *Anook* and others like him made sense.

The new SAT aims to do a better job than the old SAT of mirroring what students actually learn in school. To encourage high schools to align what they teach, the SAT has now decided to use passages from popular works of literature that high school teachers often assign. The new SAT now includes excerpts from books commonly read in high school, like *Animal Farm* and *The Great Gatsby*. Does this mean your Critical Reading score can be dramatically affected by luck? Yes!

What can you do in response to this bizarre change? We've already encouraged you to read as much as you can in anticipation of the SAT, and the change to using popular works as sources only reinforces that advice. It's highly unlikely, however, that you'll have just read the book from which the passage you encounter is excerpted. Nobody knows exactly which books the SAT will use as sources for passages, so trying to read as many books as possible won't be an effective way to prepare for this change. The best thing to do is to continue reading and training yourself to read and think critically. Rather than reading only popular fiction, newspapers, or magazines, it's probably a good idea to start reading some of the classics commonly studied in high school. You can't read them all, of course, but you can read some of the most popular and important titles, which we've listed below. You can also read summaries and commentary on hundreds of literary classics for free online at *SparkNotes.com*. Here are the top twenty SparkNotes literature titles:

- *To Kill a Mockingbird*
- *The Great Gatsby*
- *The Scarlet Letter*
- *The Adventures of Huckleberry Finn*
- *Lord of the Flies*
- *The Catcher in the Rye*
- *The Odyssey*
- *Frankenstein*
- *Great Expectations*
- *The Crucible*
- *A Tale of Two Cities*
- *Heart of Darkness*
- *1984*
- *Of Mice and Men*
- *Brave New World*
- *The Canterbury Tales*
- *Things Fall Apart*
- *Pride and Prejudice*
- *Jane Eyre*
- *Fahrenheit 451*

THE SHORT OF IT

SHORT READING PASSAGE QUESTIONS ARE LIKE THE long-lost little brother of long RPs. They're a new addition to the SAT family, but they've got the same basic makeup as their older, longer siblings. Short RPs test the same skills and cover the same basic categories of science, literature, art, history, and narrative as long RPs. They even have the same instructions as long RPs. But there is one big difference: They're shorter. And that's enough to change your whole strategy, because it means you can read short RPs word for word.

14.1 WHAT SHORT READING PASSAGES LOOK LIKE

Short RPs are about 100 words long and are followed by just two questions. Short RP questions are just like long RP questions. Every question fits into one of the seven categories we covered for long RPs:

1. Main Idea
2. Attitude or Tone
3. Specific Information
4. Implied Information
5. Themes and Arguments
6. Technique
7. Words in Context

A Complete Short RP Example

Here's a sample short RP, complete with two questions. Read the passage and the questions straight through. Then we'll go over strategies for approaching short RPs like this one, including an explanation of how to answer the two questions about this passage using our four-step short RP strategy.

> Airplanes are such a common form of travel that it's easy to forget just how recently they were invented. Today, even a person in the middle of nowhere would not be surprised to see a plane in the sky. But before the Wright brothers flew their plane at Kitty Hawk, North Carolina, in 1910, most scientists thought flight by heavier-than-air machines would never be achieved. Never. In fact, the word "airplane" didn't come into common usage until after 1945.
>
> 1.   The reference to the "person in the middle of nowhere" primarily serves to
>
> (A)   introduce a new argument
> (B)   challenge common beliefs
> (C)   highlight the limitations of an accepted idea
> (D)   question modern morals
> (E)   indicate the scope of a change
>
> 2.   The author of the passage would most likely agree with each of the following statements EXCEPT
>
> (A)   airplanes are a relatively recent innovation
> (B)   the Wright brothers took the first airplane flight
> (C)   air travel remains the privilege of the elite
> (D)   the word "airplane" was rarely used in the early twentieth century
> (E)   airplanes can be seen almost anywhere

14.2 SHORT RP STRATEGY

For long RPs, we advised you to read the entire passage, make a sketchy outline, *then* check out the questions. We suggested that you follow those steps in that order because it'd be impossible to keep an 800-word passage and eight to thirteen questions in your head.

But short RPs are short and have just two questions. That means you *can* comfortably fit the entire passage and the two questions in your head. It also means you don't have to worry about keeping an outline, since you're dealing with only one paragraph. The change in the length of the passage therefore flips your whole strategy on its head: You should read the questions *before* you read the passage. That way, you'll have the *exact* questions you need to answer in mind as you read the passage.

Step 1. Read the two questions but *not* the answer choices.
Step 2. Read the passage, with special focus on answering the two questions.
Step 3. Come up with answers for the two questions in your own words.
Step 4. Match your answer to the correct answer.

Now let's see what happens when we apply this method to the two questions from our sample short RP.

Sample Short RP Answers and Explanations

Here's the first question again:

> 1.   The reference to the "person in the middle of nowhere" primarily serves to
>
> (A)   introduce a new argument
> (B)   challenge common beliefs
> (C)   highlight the limitations of an accepted idea
> (D)   question modern morals
> (E)   indicate the scope of a change

Let's say you ignore our four-step method and read through this passage, skipping step 1. You'd have no clue what the questions are, so you'd just breeze by the phrase about the "person in the middle of nowhere." Then you'd get to the first question and would have to go back to reread the entire sentence containing the "person in the middle of nowhere" phrase, wasting precious time.

Instead, if you had followed step 1 and read the questions first, you'd know what you were looking for. You'd then read the passage and keep an eye out for that particular phrase (step 2). You'd notice that the phrase "not even a person in the middle of nowhere would be surprised to see a plane in the sky" emphasizes how common airplanes are now, and it draws a contrast to a hundred years ago when scientists did not believe such flight was possible. That means the author uses that phrase to point out that today, no one, anywhere would be surprised to see a plane in the sky. That's your version of the answer to this technique question (step 3). Now take a look at the real answer choices and try to find one that matches yours closely (step 4). **E** matches almost perfectly. The author uses the reference to the "person in the middle of nowhere" to indicate the scope of the change from the days when airplanes were foreign to almost everyone.

Now, for the second question from the sample passage:

> 2.   The author of the passage would most likely agree with each of the following statements EXCEPT
>
> (A)   airplanes are a relatively recent innovation
> (B)   the Wright brothers took the first airplane flight
> (C)   air travel remains the privilege of the elite
> (D)   the word "airplane" was rarely used in the early twentieth century
> (E)   airplanes can be seen almost anywhere

Reading the questions first (step 1) can save you lots of time on EXCEPT questions. This themes and arguments question asks you to find the statement that the author would *not* agree with, so as you read the passage with the question in mind, you can check off the statements that the passage confirms as you read. Notice that on EXCEPT questions like this one, you have to read the answer choices first as well, since the question alone does not give you enough information to work with as you read the passage (step 2). Using this method will actually allow you to skip step 3 and 4, since the answer will be the only unchecked answer choice that remains after you've read the passage and checked off the statements with which the author would agree.

The author's main argument in this passage is that air travel has become entirely commonplace even though the invention of flight only happened 100 years ago. You can knock out **A**, since the author would certainly agree that air travel is a recent invention. Check off **B** since the author references the Wright brothers' famous first flight directly in the passage. **D** and **E** can get checks too, because they cover material that the author clearly supports in the passage: that airplanes can be seen even in the middle of nowhere and that the word *airplane* only came into common usage recently. Only **C** stands out as directly against the author's main theme and argument: rather than remaining exclusively for the wealthy, air travel can now be enjoyed by almost anyone. After having read the passage and checked off answer choices as you read, only **C** would remain, and that's the correct answer.

14.3 CHALLENGED TO A (SHORT) DUAL

Dual short RPs present you with *two* 100-word passages, and then *four* questions. The first question deals with the first passage, the second covers the second passage, and the last two questions cover the relationship between the passages.

As with the long dual passage, you should treat each short dual passage individually:

Step 1. Read the question about the first passage, and then read the first passage.

Step 2. Come up with your own answer and compare it to the actual answer choices in the question about the first passage.

Step 3. Read the question about the second passage, then read the second passage. Think about how the second passage relates to the first.

Step 4. Come up with your own answer and compare it to the actual answer choices in the question about the second passage.

Step 5. Answer the questions that address both passages together.

By the time you get to step 5, you'll be so familiar with the passages that you won't have to look back at them to answer the two questions that ask you to relate them.

Sample Short Dual RP

Here are two related brief passages followed by four questions: two that treat the passages together and two that treat them individually.

> Few things in life are as rewarding and fulfilling as owning a pet. Whether it's a dog, cat, bird, or fish, the appeal is the same—years of fun and unconditional love. Indeed, pets can actually satisfy many of the things people crave most: companionship, communication, loyalty, and plenty of amusement. Perhaps that's why pets are so popular among the elderly and people who live alone. As human relationships grow more complex with each new technological gadget, the simple bond between a pet and its owner offers a refreshing and comforting reprieve.
>
> In addition to protesting reprehensible practices like fur trapping and animal testing, animal rights groups have begun to attack owners of cats and dogs for keeping animals "imprisoned" in the home. Finally, these groups have started to make the justified comparison of owning a pet to keeping a domesticated animal like a sheep or a cow. Both pet ownership and domestication of animals stem from the same cruel source: human selfishness. No animal should be kept confined solely for the benefit of human beings, whether that benefit comes in the form of meat, leather, or the companionship of a pet.

Sample Dual Short RP Questions and Explanations

1. How might you sum up the author's main idea in the first passage?

(A) Owning a pet is cruel and unfair.
(B) Pets should always be leashed.
(C) Pet ownership has profound rewards.
(D) Pet ownership is technologically advanced.
(E) Pets need new forms of communication.

2. The word "reprehensible" in the second passage most nearly means

(A) demoralizing
(B) invigorating
(C) restorative
(D) disgraceful
(E) delightful

3. Based on information in these two passages, the authors disagree about whether

(A) animals should be kept as pets
(B) pets are beneficial for humans
(C) fur trapping should be illegal
(D) kennel conditions should be reformed
(E) human beings are inherently selfish

4. Which words among the pairs below best describe the tone of the first passage and of the second passage, respectively?

(A) alarmed and disengaged
(B) enthusiastic and critical
(C) despondent and exuberant
(D) elated and enervated
(E) wary and disapproving

Explanations

1. **C** Main Idea

Step 1 tells you to read this question before reading the first passage, since it's specifically about the first passage. You then know to think about coming up with your own quick description of the main idea of the first passage as you read. This author strongly supports pet ownership because it rewards pet owners with years of fun and love. So, that's your answer to describe main idea of the passage.

Now take a look at the actual answer choices and look for a description of the passage's main idea that comes closest to your description of the joys of pet ownerships (step 2). **A** is out because it describes having a pet as "cruel" and "unfair." **B**, **D**, and **E** are all SAT traps because each mentions something vaguely mentioned in the passage (leashes, technological innovations, and communication), but none captures the main idea. Only **C** matches the answer you generated to describe the main idea: Owning a pet brings profound, or deep, rewards to pet owners. **C** is the correct answer.

2.   **D**   Words-in-Context

Step 3 tells you to read the question(s) about the second passage *before* reading the second passage. You'd then know to pay close attention as you read the passage to the sentence with the word *reprehensible* so you don't have to go back and find it later.

And there it is, right in the first sentence. Since this is a words-in-context question, treat it like a Sentence Completion and use the rest of the paragraph to help you fill in the blank with your own answer. The sentence is: "In addition to protesting ---- practices like fur trapping and animal testing, animal rights groups have begun to attack owners of cats and dogs for keeping animals 'imprisoned' in the home." The switch words *in addition to* show that the sentence is one-way: The animal rights groups are acting consistently. And it's clear from the rest of the passage that the writer is really, really against pet ownership. So, it would seem that the blank must be filled with an extremely negative word like *awful*.

You can throw out answers **B**, **C**, and **E**, because each is a positive word. That leaves *demoralizing* and *disgraceful*. These two words are both negative, but *demoralizing* means "negatively affecting morale," which isn't quite strong enough to reflect this writer's anger about the mistreatment of animals. So the answer is **D**.

3.   **A**   Themes and Arguments

By the time you get to dual passage questions that ask about both passages together, you will have already read and answered specific questions about both passages. That means you don't need to read them again and can dive right in to generating your own answers and comparing them to the actual answer choices.

This question asks about what the authors of the two passage disagree about. The divergent views of the authors of these two passages are quite clear: One supports pet ownership enthusiastically and one objects to it strongly. Let's say that's the answer you generate on your own. Now let's see which answer choice matches it. Since you've established that the question of whether "animals should be kept as pets" is the core of their disagreement, **A** is the correct answer.

B is incorrect because while the first passage would agree with the statement, the second passage does not disagree; it just says that the question of whether having a pet is beneficial for the human is not the issue. **C** is an SAT trap. The SAT wants you to see "fur trapping," which the second passage mentions briefly, and pick that answer. But the first author does not mention fur trapping at all, so it is definitely not the main issue here. Cut **C**. Neither passage mentions kennels, so eliminate **D**. **E** is incorrect because only the author of the second passage would explicitly agree with the sentiment that human beings are selfish.

4.   **B**   Tone

This question asks about the tone of the two passages. Since you've read both passages thoroughly already, generate your own answer and compare it to the real answer choices.

What words might you already have in mind to describe the tone of these two passages? The first is positive, encouraging, and excited about the prospect of owning a pet. The second is negative, disapproving, and concerned about pet ownership in general. With that in mind, you should be able to select **B** as correct: The first passage is *enthusiastic* in tone, whereas the second is *critical*.

NEW SAT
VOCABULARY

WHILE VOCABULARY IS LESS IMPORTANT ON THE NEW SAT, that doesn't mean it's totally unimportant. Not at all. A great vocabulary will definitely still help you on the test, especially throughout the Critical Reading section. So, despite what the press might say, the era of the SAT word isn't really over. You'll never again have to figure out how *horrid* relates to *horticulture* (it doesn't), but a good vocabulary *will* help boost your score on the Critical Reading and Writing sections of the new SAT.

15.1   REMEMBERING SAT VOCAB

Anyone can study vocabulary by reading over a list of words and definitions. Simple. But not that helpful. It's another thing entirely to *remember* the words you study.

Mnemonics

Mnemonic[*] devices are tricks of the memorizing trade. A mnemonic could be an image, a rhyme, a formula—anything other than straight repetition of a word and its definition. So, let's say you want to memorize the word *mnemonic*. You could come up with an image of the word *mnemonic* branded into some guy's brain as he correctly answers a Sentence Completion. The image will stick in your head much more readily than any dry old definition. With mnemonics, you'll remember words permanently and with less effort.

When you use mnemonics, the more outlandish the image or rhyme you can make up, the better. The farther out the mnemonic, the more sticky it will be in your brain. If you're trying to memorize the word *sacrosanct*, which means "holy, or

---

[*] Pronounced *ni-'mä-nik*

something that should not be criticized," go all out. Imagine that scene in the *Raiders of the Lost Ark* when the holy "Ark of the Covenant" gets opened, and then everyone's face melts off because they dared to touch this holy, *sacrosanct* object. Boom. You know this word. You're not about to forget someone's face melting off. From now on, whenever you encounter an especially tough SAT vocab word, generate a detailed phrase or image that burns the meaning of the word into your memory.

Below are five mnemonic examples that we came up with to help you remember the definitions of some tough SAT vocab words:

SAT Word	Definition	Mnemonic	Word in a Sentence
buttress	a support	Having a big *butt* gives you extra support, like a *buttress*.	Without a strong *buttress*, the building's front structure would collapse.
conundrum	a problem or puzzle	Having only *one-drum* is a *conundrum* for a rock drummer.	The explorers figured out how to deal with the *conundrum* of having only two days to hike 100 miles.
cursory	brief and to the point	People tend to *curse* when they want to get straight to the point.	His boss took a *cursory* look at the memo and came to a decision.
malevolent	wanting harm to be done to others	*Violent males* tend to be *malevolent*.	The villain confirmed his *malevolent* wishes by cheering when the tree fell and crushed his neighbor's foot.
boon	a gift or blessing	Pirates consider booty a *boon*.	The teacher's decision to make the test open-book was a *boon* to her students.

Where the Wild Vocabs Are

SAT vocab lurks in lists and in life. You will be tempted to ignore life and focus only on the lists. That's up to you, but we think that's a mistake. You'll learn and retain more vocabulary if you focus on both.

Vocab in Lists

Studying vocab from a list of words seems easy, but it's actually quite tough. That list of words lulls you to sleep, so you think you're remembering what you study, but you're actually not. (This is another reason mnemonics are so helpful: You can't fool yourself into thinking you came up with a mnemonic. You've either got one or you don't.) You really need to focus to seal the meaning of the word into your mind. Breezing over a list won't make that happen.

There is another pitfall in studying vocab from lists. Your mind memorizes in context. One thing clues you into another. This can trick you into thinking that you know a word even when you don't—you may know it only when it's in the order from your list, not when it's sitting there alone in an answer choice. So, when you study from a list, don't always go through it in the same order. Switch things around, go backward, skip every other word. Keep your head on its toes. Or use flashcards and frequently reshuffle the deck.

Vocab in Life

Remember the other day when you were watching a movie like *The Matrix* and one of the characters said a word you didn't recognize, but you shrugged it off so you could just enjoy the show? Those days are over. From now until the day you take the new SAT, if you hear a word you don't know, try to guess its meaning from context, then look it up to see if you were right and make a mnemonic.

This takes some effort. And if you don't want to put out the effort to make the world your personal vocab oyster, well, we're not going to come track you down. But we will tell you that paying attention to words you encounter on lists *and* in life will go a long way toward building the vocabulary you need to beat the new SAT.

15.2 DEALING WITH WORDS YOU DON'T KNOW

No list will ever cover all the vocab words that might appear on the SAT. There are just too many words. In fact, we can pretty much guarantee that somewhere on the new SAT, you'll come across a word you haven't studied or just can't remember. No problem. We'll show you what to do.

Word Roots: The Building Blocks of Words

Lots of test-prep companies advise students to study Greek and Latin roots of English words to help figure out the meaning of an SAT vocabulary word. Some students even take Latin in high school with the sole aim of using it to learn vocabulary roots for the SAT. English words are often made up of bits and pieces derived from Latin or Greek, which we call *word roots*. For example, let's say you come across the word *antebellum* on the SAT and don't know what it means. The word root *ante* means "before," and *bellum* means "war," so you might think that antebellum means "before the war." You're correct! Here's a list of the 28 most common word roots that'll help you puzzle out the meanings of unfamiliar SAT words.

Word Root	What It Means	SAT Vocab Words
ante	before	antebellum, antediluvian
anti	against	antithesis, antipathy, antiseptic
auto	self	autocratic
bene	good, well	benefactor, benevolent, benediction
chron	time	anachronism, asynchronous
circum	around	circumnavigate, circumference, circumlocution, circumvent, circumscribe
con, com	with, together	convene, concatenate, conjoin, companionable
contra, counter	against	contradict, counteract, contravene
cred	to believe	credo, credible, credence, credulity, incredulous
dict	to speak	verdict, malediction, dictate, dictum, indict
dis	not	disperse, dissuade, distemper, disarray, disjointed
equi	equal	equidistant, equilateral, equilibrium, equinox, equitable, equanimity
ex, e	out, away	emit, enervate, excise, extirpate, expunge, exonerate, exacerbate

the new SAT

Word Root	What It Means	SAT Vocab Words
flu, flux	flow	effluence, effluvium, fluctuate, confluence
hyper	above, over	hyperbolic
in, im	not	inviolate, innocuous, intractable, impregnable, impermeable, impervious
inter	between	intermittent, introvert, interdict, interrogate
mal	bad	malformation, maladjusted, dismal, malady, malcontent, malfeasance
multi	many	multitude, multivalent
neo	new	neologism, neophyte
omni	all	omnipotent, omnivorous, omniscient
per	through	persuade, impervious, persistent, persecute
sanct	holy	sanctify, sanctuary, sanction, sanctimonious, sacrosanct
scrib, script	to write	inscription, prescribe, proscribe, ascribe, conscript, scribble, scribe
spect	to look	circumspect, retrospect, prospect, spectacle, aspect
tract	to drag, to draw	protract, detract, intractable
trans	across	transduce, intransigent
vert	to turn	extrovert, introvert

15.3 # THE TOP 250

Since vocab isn't as important on the new SAT as it was on the old SAT, it doesn't make sense to plow through 1,000-word-long lists. We're dedicated to getting you the most bang for your study time, so we searched through tons of old SAT tests and found 250 of the toughest and most frequently tested vocab words.

Of course, we know there'll be some of you out there who just can't get enough and who want the complete collection of 1,000 words. Well, we've got those for you also, free and online. Just go to **http://www.sparknotes.com** to download and memorize to your heart's content.

THE TOP 250 MOST DIFFICULT SAT WORDS

A

abjure *(v.)* to reject, renounce *(To prove his honesty, the president abjured the evil policies of his wicked predecessor.)*

abrogate *(v.)* to abolish, usually by authority *(The Bill of Rights assures that the government cannot abrogate our right to a free press.)*

acerbic *(adj.)* biting, bitter in tone or taste *(Jill became extremely acerbic and began to cruelly make fun of all her friends.)*

acrimony *(n.)* bitterness, discord *(Though they vowed that no girl would ever come between them, Biff and Trevor could not keep acrimony from overwhelming their friendship after they both fell in love with the lovely Teresa.)*

acumen *(n.)* keen insight *(Because of his mathematical acumen, Larry was able to figure out in minutes problems that took other students hours.)*

adumbrate *(v.)* to sketch out in a vague way *(The coach adumbrated a game plan, but none of the players knew precisely what to do.)*

alacrity *(n.)* eagerness, speed *(For some reason, Chuck loved to help his mother whenever he could, so when his mother asked him to set the table, he did so with alacrity.)*

anathema *(n.)* a cursed, detested person *(I never want to see that murderer. He is an anathema to me.)*

antipathy *(n.)* a strong dislike, repugnance *(I know you love me, but because you are a liar and a thief, I feel nothing but antipathy for you.)*

approbation *(n.)* praise *(The crowd welcomed the heroes with approbation.)*

arrogate *(v.)* to take without justification *(The king arrogated the right to order executions to himself exclusively.)*

ascetic *(adj.)* practicing restraint as a means of self-discipline, usually religious *(The priest lives an ascetic life devoid of television, savory foods, and other pleasures.)*

aspersion *(n.)* a curse, expression of ill-will *(The rival politicians repeatedly cast aspersions on each others' integrity.)*

assiduous *(adj.)* hard-working, diligent *(The construction workers erected the skyscraper during two years of assiduous labor.)*

B

blandish *(v.)* to coax by using flattery *(Rachel's assistant tried to blandish her into accepting the deal.)*

boon *(n.)* a gift or blessing *(The good weather has been a boon for many businesses located near the beach.)*

brusque *(adj.)* short, abrupt, dismissive *(The captain's brusque manner offended the passengers.)*

buffet 1. *(v.)* to strike with force *(The strong winds buffeted the ships, threatening to capsize them.)* 2. *(n.)* an arrangement of food set out on a table *(Rather than sitting around a table, the guests took food from our buffet and ate standing up.)*

burnish *(v.)* to polish, shine *(His mother asked him to burnish the silverware before setting the table.)*

buttress 1. *(v.)* to support, hold up *(The column buttresses the roof above the statue.)* 2. *(n.)* something that offers support *(The buttress supports the roof above the statues.)*

C

cacophony *(n.)* tremendous noise, disharmonious sound *(The elementary school orchestra created a cacophony at the recital.)*

cajole *(v.)* to urge, coax *(Fred's buddies cajoled him into attending the bachelor party.)*

calumny *(n.)* an attempt to spoil someone else's reputation by spreading lies *(The local official's calumny ended up ruining his opponent's prospect of winning the election.)*

capricious *(adj.)* subject to whim, fickle *(The young girl's capricious tendencies made it difficult for her to focus on achieving her goals.)*

clemency *(n.)* mercy *(After he forgot their anniversary, Martin could only beg Maria for clemency.)*

cogent *(adj.)* intellectually convincing *(Irene's arguments in favor of abstinence were so cogent that I could not resist them.)*

concomitant *(adj.)* accompanying in a subordinate fashion *(His dislike of hard work carried with it a concomitant lack of funds.)*

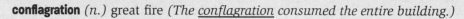

conflagration (n.) great fire (The <u>conflagration</u> consumed the entire building.)

contrite (adj.) penitent, eager to be forgiven (Blake's <u>contrite</u> behavior made it impossible to stay angry at him.)

conundrum (n.) puzzle, problem (Interpreting Jane's behavior was a constant <u>conundrum</u>.)

credulity (n.) readiness to believe (His <u>credulity</u> made him an easy target for con men.)

cupidity (n.) greed, strong desire (His <u>cupidity</u> made him enter the abandoned gold mine despite the obvious dangers.)

cursory (adj.) brief to the point of being superficial (Late for the meeting, she cast a <u>cursory</u> glance at the agenda.)

D

decry (v.) to criticize openly (The kind video rental clerk <u>decried</u> the policy of charging customers late fees.)

defile (v.) to make unclean, impure (She <u>defiled</u> the calm of the religious building by playing her banjo.)

deleterious (adj.) harmful (She experienced the <u>deleterious</u> effects of running a marathon without stretching her muscles enough beforehand.)

demure (adj.) quiet, modest, reserved (Though everyone else at the party was dancing and going crazy, she remained <u>demure</u>.)

deprecate (v.) to belittle, depreciate (Always over-modest, he <u>deprecated</u> his contribution to the local charity.)

deride (v.) to laugh at mockingly, scorn (The bullies <u>derided</u> the foreign student's accent.)

desecrate (v.) to violate the sacredness of a thing or place (They feared that the construction of a golf course would <u>desecrate</u> the preserved wilderness.)

desiccated (adj.) dried up, dehydrated (The skin of the <u>desiccated</u> mummy looked like old paper.)

diaphanous (adj.) light, airy, transparent (Sunlight poured in through the <u>diaphanous</u> curtains, brightening the room.)

diffident (adj.) shy, quiet, modest (While eating dinner with the adults, the <u>diffident</u> youth did not speak for fear of seeming presumptuous.)

discursive (adj.) rambling, lacking order (The professor's <u>discursive</u> lectures seemed to be about every subject except the one initially described.)

dissemble (v.) to conceal, fake (Not wanting to appear heartlessly greedy, she <u>dissembled</u> and hid her intention to sell her ailing father's stamp collection.)

dither (v.) to be indecisive (Not wanting to offend either friend, he <u>dithered</u> about which of the two birthday parties he should attend.)

the new SAT

E

ebullient *(adj.)* extremely lively, enthusiastic *(She became ebullient upon receiving an acceptance letter from her first-choice college.)*

effrontery *(n.)* impudence, nerve, insolence *(When I told my aunt that she was boring, my mother scolded me for my effrontery.)*

effulgent *(adj.)* radiant, splendorous *(The golden palace was effulgent.)*

egregious *(adj.)* extremely bad *(The student who threw sloppy joes across the cafeteria was punished for his egregious behavior.)*

enervate *(v.)* to weaken, exhaust *(Writing these sentences enervates me so much that I will have to take a nap after I finish.)*

ephemeral *(adj.)* short-lived, fleeting *(She promised she'd love me forever, but her "forever" was only ephemeral: she left me after one week.)*

eschew *(v.)* to shun, avoid *(George hates the color green so much that he eschews all green food.)*

evanescent *(adj.)* fleeting, momentary *(My joy at getting promoted was evanescent because I discovered that I would have to work much longer hours in a less friendly office.)*

evince *(v.)* to show, reveal *(Christopher's hand-wringing and nail-biting evince how nervous he is about the upcoming English test.)*

exculpate *(v.)* to free from guilt or blame, exonerate *(My discovery of the ring behind the dresser exculpated me from the charge of having stolen it.)*

execrable *(adj.)* loathsome, detestable *(Her pudding is so execrable that it makes me sick.)*

exigent *(adj.)* urgent, critical *(The patient has an exigent need for medication, or else he will lose his sight.)*

expiate *(v.)* to make amends for, atone *(To expiate my selfishness, I gave all my profits to charity.)*

expunge *(v.)* to obliterate, eradicate *(Fearful of an IRS investigation, Paul tried to expunge all incriminating evidence from his tax files.)*

extant *(adj.)* existing, not destroyed or lost *(My mother's extant love letters to my father are in the attic trunk.)*

extol *(v.)* to praise, revere *(Violet extolled the virtues of a vegetarian diet to her meat-loving brother.)*

F

fallacious *(adj.)* incorrect, misleading *(Emily offered me cigarettes on the fallacious assumption that I smoked.)*

fastidious *(adj.)* meticulous, demanding, having high and often unattainable standards *(Mark is so fastidious that he is never able to finish a project because it always seems imperfect to him.)*

fatuous *(adj.)* silly, foolish *(He considers himself a serious poet, but in truth, he only writes <u>fatuous</u> limericks.)*

fecund *(adj.)* fruitful, fertile *(The <u>fecund</u> tree bore enough apples to last us through the entire season.)*

feral *(adj.)* wild, savage *(That beast looks so <u>feral</u> that I would fear being alone with it.)*

fetid *(adj.)* having a foul odor *(I can tell from the <u>fetid</u> smell in your refrigerator that your milk has spoiled.)*

florid *(adj.)* flowery, ornate *(The writer's <u>florid</u> prose belongs on a sentimental Hallmark card.)*

fractious *(adj.)* troublesome or irritable *(Although the child insisted he wasn't tired, his <u>fractious</u> behavior—especially his decision to crush his cheese and crackers all over the floor—convinced everyone present that it was time to put him to bed.)*

G

garrulous *(adj.)* talkative, wordy *(Some talk-show hosts are so <u>garrulous</u> that their guests can't get a word in edgewise.)*

grandiloquence *(n.)* lofty, pompous language *(The student thought her <u>grandiloquence</u> would make her sound smart, but neither the class nor the teacher bought it.)*

gregarious *(adj.)* drawn to the company of others, sociable *(Well, if you're not <u>gregarious</u>, I don't know why you would want to go to a singles party!)*

H

hackneyed *(adj.)* unoriginal, trite *(A girl can only hear "I love you" so many times before it begins to sound <u>hackneyed</u> and meaningless.)*

hapless *(adj.)* unlucky *(My poor, <u>hapless</u> family never seems to pick a sunny week to go on vacation.)*

harangue 1. *(n.)* a ranting speech *(Everyone had heard the teacher's <u>harangue</u> about gum chewing in class before.)* 2. *(v.)* to give such a speech *(But this time the teacher <u>harangued</u> the class about the importance of brushing your teeth after chewing gum.)*

hegemony *(n.)* domination over others *(Britain's <u>hegemony</u> over its colonies was threatened once nationalist sentiment began to spread around the world.)*

I

iconoclast *(n.)* one who attacks common beliefs or institutions *(Jane goes to one protest after another, but she seems to be an <u>iconoclast</u> rather than an activist with a progressive agenda.)*

ignominious *(adj.)* humiliating, disgracing *(It was really <u>ignominious</u> to be kicked out of the dorm for having an illegal gas stove in my room.)*

impassive *(adj.)* stoic, not susceptible to suffering *(Stop being so <u>impassive</u>; it's healthy to cry every now and then.)*

imperious *(adj.)* commanding, domineering *(The imperious nature of your manner led me to dislike you at once.)*

impertinent *(adj.)* rude, insolent *(Most of your comments are so impertinent that I don't wish to dignify them with an answer.)*

impervious *(adj.)* impenetrable, incapable of being affected *(Because of their thick layer of fur, many seals are almost impervious to the cold.)*

impetuous *(adj.)* rash; hastily done *(Hilda's hasty slaying of the king was an impetuous, thoughtless action.)*

impinge 1. *(v.)* to impact, affect, make an impression *(The hail impinged the roof, leaving large dents.)* 2. *(v.)* to encroach, infringe *(I apologize for impinging upon you like this, but I really need to use your bathroom. Now.)*

implacable *(adj.)* incapable of being appeased or mitigated *(Watch out: Once you shun Grandma's cooking, she is totally implacable.)*

impudent *(adj.)* casually rude, insolent, impertinent *(The impudent young man looked the princess up and down and told her she was hot even though she hadn't asked him.)*

inchoate *(adj.)* unformed or formless, in a beginning stage *(The country's government is still inchoate and, because it has no great tradition, quite unstable.)*

incontrovertible *(adj.)* indisputable *(Only stubborn Tina would attempt to disprove the incontrovertible laws of physics.)*

indefatigable *(adj.)* incapable of defeat, failure, decay *(Even after traveling 62 miles, the indefatigable runner kept on moving.)*

ineffable *(adj.)* unspeakable, incapable of being expressed through words *(It is said that the experience of playing with a dolphin is ineffable and can only be understood through direct encounter.)*

inexorable *(adj.)* incapable of being persuaded or placated *(Although I begged for hours, Mom was inexorable and refused to let me stay out all night after the prom.)*

ingenuous *(adj.)* not devious; innocent and candid *(He must have writers, but his speeches seem so ingenuous it's hard to believe he's not speaking from his own heart.)*

inimical *(adj.)* hostile *(I don't see how I could ever work for a company that was so cold and inimical to me during my interviews.)*

iniquity *(n.)* wickedness or sin *("Your iniquity," said the priest to the practical jokester, "will be forgiven.")*

insidious *(adj.)* appealing but imperceptibly harmful, seductive *(Lisa's insidious chocolate cake tastes so good but makes you feel so sick later on!)*

intransigent *(adj.)* refusing to compromise, often on an extreme opinion *(The intransigent child said he would have 12 scoops of ice cream or he would bang his head against the wall until his mother fainted from fear.)*

inure (*v.*) to cause someone or something to become accustomed to a situation (*Twenty years in the salt mines inured the man to the discomforts of dirt and grime.*)

invective (*n.*) an angry verbal attack (*My mother's irrational invective against the way I dress only made me decide to dye my hair green.*)

inveterate (*adj.*) stubbornly established by habit (*I'm the first to admit that I'm an inveterate coffee drinker—I drink four cups a day.*)

J

jubilant (*adj.*) extremely joyful, happy (*The crowd was jubilant when the firefighter carried the woman from the flaming building.*)

juxtaposition (*n.*) the act of placing two things next to each other for implicit comparison (*The interior designer admired my juxtaposition of the yellow couch and green table.*)

L

laconic (*adj.*) terse in speech or writing (*The author's laconic style has won him many followers who dislike wordiness.*)

languid (*adj.*) sluggish from fatigue or weakness (*In the summer months, the great heat makes people languid and lazy.*)

largess (*n.*) the generous giving of lavish gifts (*My boss demonstrated great largess by giving me a new car.*)

latent (*adj.*) hidden, but capable of being exposed (*Sigmund's dream represented his latent paranoid obsession with other people's shoes.*)

legerdemain (*n.*) deception, slight-of-hand (*Smuggling the French plants through customs by claiming that they were fake was a remarkable bit of legerdemain.*)

licentious (*adj.*) displaying a lack of moral or legal restraints (*Marilee has always been fascinated by the licentious private lives of politicians.*)

limpid (*adj.*) clear, transparent (*Mr. Johnson's limpid writing style greatly pleased readers who disliked complicated novels.*)

M

maelstrom (*n.*) a destructive whirlpool which rapidly sucks in objects (*Little did the explorers know that as they turned the next bend of the calm river a vicious maelstrom would catch their boat.*)

magnanimous (*adj.*) noble, generous (*Although I had already broken most of her dishes, Jacqueline was magnanimous enough to continue letting me use them.*)

malediction (*n.*) a curse (*When I was arrested for speeding, I screamed maledictions against the policeman and the entire police department.*)

malevolent (*adj.*) wanting harm to befall others (*The malevolent old man sat in the park all day, tripping unsuspecting passersby with his cane.*)

manifold (*adj.*) diverse, varied (*The popularity of Dante's Inferno is partly due to the fact that the work allows for manifold interpretations.*)

maudlin *(adj.)* weakly sentimental *(Although many people enjoy romantic comedies, I usually find them maudlin and shallow.)*

mawkish *(adj.)* characterized by sick sentimentality *(Although some nineteenth-century critics viewed Dickens's writing as mawkish, contemporary readers have found great emotional depth in his works.)*

mendacious *(adj.)* having a lying, false character *(The mendacious content of the tabloid magazines is at least entertaining.)*

mercurial *(adj.)* characterized by rapid change or temperamentality *(Though he was widely respected for his mathematical proofs, the mercurial genius was impossible to live with.)*

modicum *(n.)* a small amount of something *(Refusing to display even a modicum of sensitivity, Henrietta announced her boss's affair in front of the entire office.)*

morass *(n.)* a wet swampy bog; figuratively, something that traps and confuses *(When Theresa lost her job, she could not get out of her financial morass.)*

multifarious *(adj.)* having great diversity or variety *(This Swiss Army knife has multifarious functions and capabilities. Among other things, it can act as a knife, a saw, a toothpick, and a slingshot.)*

munificence *(n.)* generosity in giving *(The royal family's munificence made everyone else in their country rich.)*

myriad *(adj.)* consisting of a very great number *(It was difficult to decide what to do Friday night because the city presented us with myriad possibilities for fun.)*

N

nadir *(n.)* the lowest point of something *(My day was boring, but the nadir came when I accidentally spilled a bowl of spaghetti on my head.)*

nascent *(adj.)* in the process of being born or coming into existence *(Unfortunately, my brilliant paper was only in its nascent form on the morning that it was due.)*

nefarious *(adj.)* heinously villainous *(Although Dr. Meanman's nefarious plot to melt the polar icecaps was terrifying, it was so impractical that nobody really worried about it.)*

neophyte *(n.)* someone who is young or inexperienced *(As a neophyte in the literary world, Malik had trouble finding a publisher for his first novel.)*

O

obdurate *(adj.)* unyielding to persuasion or moral influences *(The obdurate old man refused to take pity on the kittens.)*

obfuscate *(v.)* to render incomprehensible *(The detective did not want to answer the newspaperman's questions, so he obfuscated the truth.)*

oblique *(adj.)* diverging from a straight line or course, not straightforward *(Martin's oblique language confused those who listened to him.)*

obsequious *(adj.)* excessively compliant or submissive *(Mark acted like Janet's servant, obeying her every request in an obsequious manner.)*

obstreperous *(adj.)* noisy, unruly *(Billy's <u>obstreperous</u> behavior prompted the librarian to ask him to leave the reading room.)*

obtuse *(adj.)* lacking quickness of sensibility or intellect *(Political opponents warned that the prime minister's <u>obtuse</u> approach to foreign policy would embroil the nation in mindless war.)*

odious *(adj.)* instilling hatred or intense displeasure *(Mark was assigned the <u>odious</u> task of cleaning the cat's litter box.)*

officious *(adj.)* offering one's services when they are neither wanted nor needed *(Brenda resented Allan's <u>officious</u> behavior when he selected colors that might best improve her artwork.)*

opulent *(adj.)* characterized by rich abundance verging on ostentation *(The <u>opulent</u> furnishings of the dictator's private compound contrasted harshly with the meager accommodations of her subjects.)*

ostensible *(adj.)* appearing as such, seemingly *(Jack's <u>ostensible</u> reason for driving was that airfare was too expensive, but in reality, he was afraid of flying.)*

P

palliate *(v.)* to reduce the severity of *(The doctor trusted that the new medication would <u>palliate</u> her patient's discomfort.)*

pallid *(adj.)* lacking color *(Dr. Van Helsing feared that Lucy's <u>pallid</u> complexion was due to an unexplained loss of blood.)*

panacea *(n.)* a remedy for all ills or difficulties *(Doctors wish there was a single <u>panacea</u> for every disease, but sadly there is not.)*

paragon *(n.)* a model of excellence or perfection *(The mythical Helen of Troy was considered a <u>paragon</u> of female beauty.)*

pariah *(n.)* an outcast *(Following the discovery of his plagiarism, Professor Hurley was made a <u>pariah</u> in all academic circles.)*

parsimony *(n.)* frugality, stinginess *(Many relatives believed that my aunt's wealth resulted from her <u>parsimony</u>.)*

pathos *(n.)* an emotion of sympathy *(Martha filled with <u>pathos</u> upon discovering the scrawny, shivering kitten at her door.)*

paucity *(adj.)* small in quantity *(Gilbert lamented the <u>paucity</u> of twentieth-century literature courses available at the college.)*

pejorative *(adj.)* derogatory, uncomplimentary *(The evening's headline news covered an international scandal caused by a <u>pejorative</u> statement the famous senator had made in reference to a foreign leader.)*

pellucid *(adj.)* easily intelligible, clear *(Wishing his book to be <u>pellucid</u> to the common man, Albert Camus avoided using complicated grammar when composing The Stranger.)*

penurious *(adj.)* miserly, stingy *(Stella complained that her husband's <u>penurious</u> ways made it impossible to live the lifestyle she felt she deserved.)*

perfidious *(adj.)* disloyal, unfaithful *(After the official was caught selling government secrets to enemy agents, he was executed for his <u>perfidious</u> ways.)*

perfunctory *(adj.)* showing little interest or enthusiasm *(The radio broadcaster announced the news of the massacre in a surprisingly <u>perfunctory</u> manner.)*

pernicious *(adj.)* extremely destructive or harmful *(The new government feared that the Communist sympathizers would have a <u>pernicious</u> influence on the nation's stability.)*

perspicacity *(adj.)* shrewdness, perceptiveness *(The detective was too humble to acknowledge that his <u>perspicacity</u> was the reason for his professional success.)*

pertinacious *(adj.)* stubbornly persistent *(Harry's parents were frustrated with his <u>pertinacious</u> insistence that a monster lived in his closet. Then they opened the closet door and were eaten.)*

petulance *(n.)* rudeness, irritability *(The nanny resigned after she could no longer tolerate the child's <u>petulance</u>.)*

pithy *(adj.)* concisely meaningful *(My father's long-winded explanation was a stark contrast to his usually <u>pithy</u> statements.)*

platitude *(n.)* an uninspired remark, cliché *(After reading over her paper, Helene concluded that what she thought were profound insights were actually just <u>platitudes</u>.)*

plethora *(n.)* an abundance, excess *(The wedding banquet included a <u>plethora</u> of oysters piled almost three feet high.)*

polemic *(n.)* an aggressive argument against a specific opinion *(My brother launched into a <u>polemic</u> against my arguments that capitalism was an unjust economic system.)*

portent *(n.)* an omen *(When a black cat crossed my sister's path while she was walking to school, she took it as a <u>portent</u> that she would do badly on her spelling test.)*

precocious *(adj.)* advanced, developing ahead of time *(Derek was so academically <u>precocious</u> that by the time he was 10 years old, he was already in the ninth grade.)*

prescient *(adj.)* to have foreknowledge of events *(Questioning the fortune cookie's prediction, Ray went in search of the old hermit who was rumored to be <u>prescient</u>.)*

primeval *(adj.)* original, ancient *(The first primates to walk on two legs, called Australopithecus, were the <u>primeval</u> descendants of modern man.)*

probity *(n.)* virtue, integrity *(Because he was never viewed as a man of great <u>probity</u>, no one was surprised by Mr. Samson's immoral behavior.)*

proclivity *(n.)* a strong inclination toward something *(In a sick twist of fate, Harold's childhood <u>proclivity</u> for torturing small animals grew into a desire to become a surgeon.)*

promulgate *(v.)* to proclaim, make known *(The film professor <u>promulgated</u> that both in terms of sex appeal and political intrigue, Sean Connery's James Bond was superior to Roger Moore's.)*

propensity (*n.*) an inclination, preference (*Dermit has a propensity for dangerous activities such as bungee jumping.*)

propitious (*adj.*) favorable (*The dark storm clouds visible on the horizon suggested that the weather would not be propitious for sailing.*)

prosaic (*adj.*) plain, lacking liveliness (*Heather's prosaic recital of the poem bored the audience.*)

proscribe (*v.*) to condemn, outlaw (*The town council voted to proscribe the sale of alcohol on weekends.*)

protean (*adj.*) able to change shape; displaying great variety (*Among Nigel's protean talents was his ability to touch the tip of his nose with his tongue.*)

prurient (*adj.*) eliciting or possessing an extraordinary interest in sex (*David's mother was shocked by the discovery of prurient reading material hidden beneath her son's mattress.*)

puerile (*adj.*) juvenile, immature (*The judge demanded order after the lawyer's puerile attempt to object by stomping his feet on the courtroom floor.*)

pugnacious (*adj.*) quarrelsome, combative (*Aaron's pugnacious nature led him to start several barroom brawls each month.*)

pulchritude (*n.*) physical beauty (*Several of Shakespeare's sonnets explore the pulchritude of a lovely young man.*)

punctilious (*adj.*) eager to follow rules or conventions (*Punctilious Bobby, hall monitor extraordinaire, insisted that his peers follow the rules.*)

Q

quagmire (*n.*) a difficult situation (*We'd all like to avoid the kind of military quagmire characterized by the Vietnam War.*)

querulous (*adj.*) whiny, complaining (*If deprived of his pacifier, young Brendan becomes querulous.*)

quixotic (*adj.*) idealistic, impractical (*Edward entertained a quixotic desire to fall in love at first sight in a laundromat.*)

R

rancor (*n.*) deep, bitter resentment (*When Eileen challenged me to a fight, I could see the rancor in her eyes.*)

rebuke (*v.*) to scold, criticize (*When the cops showed up at Sarah's party, they rebuked her for disturbing the peace.*)

recalcitrant (*adj.*) defiant, unapologetic (*Even when scolded, the recalcitrant young girl simply stomped her foot and refused to finish her lima beans.*)

rectitude (*n.*) uprightness, extreme morality (*The priest's rectitude gave him the moral authority to counsel his parishioners.*)

replete (*adj.*) full, abundant (*The unedited version was replete with naughty words.*)

reprobate (*adj.*) evil, unprincipled (*The reprobate criminal sat sneering in the cell.*)

reprove *(v.)* to scold, rebuke *(Lara reproved her son for sticking each and every one of his fingers into the strawberry pie.)*

repudiate *(v.)* to reject, refuse to accept *(Kwame made a strong case for an extension of his curfew, but his mother repudiated it with a few biting words.)*

rescind *(v.)* to take back, repeal *(The company rescinded its offer of employment after discovering that Jane's resume was full of lies.)*

restive *(adj.)* resistant, stubborn, impatient *(The restive audience pelted the band with mud and yelled nasty comments.)*

ribald *(adj.)* coarsely, crudely humorous *(While some giggled at the ribald joke involving a parson's daughter, most sighed and rolled their eyes.)*

rife *(adj.)* abundant *(Surprisingly, the famous novelist's writing was rife with spelling errors.)*

ruse *(n.)* a trick *(Oliver concocted an elaborate ruse for sneaking out of the house to meet his girlfriend while simultaneously giving his mother the impression that he was asleep in bed.)*

S

sacrosanct *(adj.)* holy, something that should not be criticized *(In the United States, the Constitution is often thought of as a sacrosanct document.)*

sagacity *(n.)* shrewdness, soundness of perspective *(With remarkable sagacity, the wise old man predicted and thwarted his children's plan to ship him off to a nursing home.)*

salient *(adj.)* significant, conspicuous *(One of the salient differences between Alison and Nancy is that Alison is a foot taller.)*

sanctimonious *(adj.)* giving a hypocritical appearance of piety *(The sanctimonious Bertrand delivered stern lectures on the Ten Commandments to anyone who would listen, but thought nothing of stealing cars to make some cash on the side.)*

sanguine *(adj.)* optimistic, cheery *(Polly reacted to any bad news with a sanguine smile and the chirpy cry, "When life hands you lemons, make lemonade!")*

scurrilous *(adj.)* vulgar, coarse *(When Bruno heard the scurrilous accusation being made about him, he could not believe it because he always tried to be nice to everyone.)*

serendipity *(n.)* luck, finding good things without looking for them *(In an amazing bit of serendipity, penniless Paula found a $20 bill in the subway station.)*

servile *(adj.)* subservient *(The servile porter crept around the hotel lobby, bowing and quaking before the guests.)*

solicitous *(adj.)* concerned, attentive *(Jim, laid up in bed with a nasty virus, enjoyed the solicitous attentions of his mother, who brought him soup and extra blankets.)*

solipsistic *(adj.)* believing that oneself is all that exists *(Colette's solipsistic attitude completely ignored the plight of the homeless people on the street.)*

somnolent *(adj.)* sleepy, drowsy *(The somnolent student kept falling asleep and waking up with a jerk.)*

spurious *(adj.)* false but designed to seem plausible *(Using a spurious argument, John convinced the others that he had won the board game on a technicality.)*

staid *(adj.)* sedate, serious, self-restrained *(The staid butler never changed his expression no matter what happened.)*

stolid *(adj.)* expressing little sensibility, unemotional *(Charles's stolid reaction to his wife's funeral differed from the passion he showed at the time of her death.)*

stupefy *(v.)* to astonish, make insensible *(Veronica's audacity and ungratefulness stupefied her best friend, Heather.)*

surfeit *(n.)* an overabundant supply or indulgence *(After partaking of the surfeit of tacos and tamales at the All-You-Can-Eat Taco Tamale Lunch Special, Beth felt rather sick.)*

surmise *(v.)* to infer with little evidence *(After speaking to only one of the students, the teacher was able to surmise what had caused the fight.)*

surreptitious *(adj.)* stealthy *(The surreptitious CIA agents were able to get in and out of the house without anyone noticing.)*

sycophant *(n.)* one who flatters for self-gain *(Some see the people in the cabinet as the president's closest advisors, but others see them as sycophants.)*

T

tacit *(adj.)* expressed without words *(I interpreted my parents' refusal to talk as a tacit acceptance of my request.)*

taciturn *(adj.)* not inclined to talk *(Though Jane never seems to stop talking, her brother is quite taciturn.)*

tantamount *(adj.)* equivalent in value or significance *(When it comes to sports, fearing your opponent is tantamount to losing.)*

temerity *(n.)* audacity, recklessness *(Tom and Huck entered the scary cave armed with nothing but their own temerity.)*

tenuous *(adj.)* having little substance or strength *(Your argument is very tenuous, since it relies so much on speculation and hearsay.)*

timorous *(adj.)* timid, fearful *(When dealing with the unknown, timorous Tallulah almost always broke into tears.)*

torpid *(adj.)* lethargic, dormant, lacking motion *(The torpid whale floated, wallowing in the water for hours.)*

tractable *(adj.)* easily controlled *(The horse was so tractable, Myra didn't even need a bridle.)*

transient *(adj.)* passing through briefly; passing into and out of existence *(Because virtually everyone in Palm Beach is a tourist, the population of the town is quite transient.)*

transmute *(v.)* to change or alter in form *(Ancient alchemists believed that it was possible to transmute lead into gold.)*

trenchant *(adj.)* effective, articulate, clear-cut *(The directions that accompanied my new cell phone were trenchant and easy to follow.)*

truculent *(adj.)* ready to fight, cruel *(This club doesn't really attract the dangerous types, so why was that bouncer being so truculent?)*

turgid *(adj.)* swollen, excessively embellished in style or language *(The haughty writer did not realize how we all really felt about his turgid prose.)*

turpitude *(n.)* depravity, moral corruption *(Sir Marcus's chivalry often contrasted with the turpitude he exhibited with the ladies at the tavern.)*

U

ubiquitous *(adj.)* existing everywhere, widespread *(It seems that everyone in the United States has a television. The technology is ubiquitous here.)*

umbrage *(n.)* resentment, offense *(He called me a lily-livered coward, and I took umbrage at the insult.)*

unctuous *(adj.)* smooth or greasy in texture, appearance, manner *(The unctuous receptionist seemed untrustworthy, as if she was only being helpful because she thought we might give her a big tip.)*

undulate *(v.)* to move in waves *(As the storm began to brew, the placid ocean began to undulate to an increasing degree.)*

upbraid *(v.)* to criticize or scold severely *(The last thing Lindsay wanted was for Lisa to upbraid her again about missing the rent payment.)*

usurp *(v.)* to seize by force, take possession of without right *(The rogue army general tried to usurp control of the government, but he failed because most of the army backed the legally elected president.)*

V

vacillate *(v.)* to fluctuate, hesitate *(I prefer a definite answer, but my boss kept vacillating between the distinct options available to us.)*

vacuous *(adj.)* lack of content or ideas, stupid *(Beyoncé realized that the lyrics she had just penned were completely vacuous and tried to add more substance.)*

vapid *(adj.)* lacking liveliness, dull *(The professor's comments about the poem were surprisingly vapid and dull.)*

variegated *(adj.)* diversified, distinctly marked *(Each wire in the engineering exam was variegated by color so that the students could figure out which one was which.)*

venerate *(v.)* to regard with respect or to honor *(The tribute to John Lennon sought to venerate his music, his words, and his legend.)*

veracity *(n.)* truthfulness, accuracy *(With several agencies regulating the reports, it was difficult for Latifah to argue against its veracity.)*

verdant *(adj.)* green in tint or color *(The verdant leaves on the trees made the world look emerald.)*

vex *(v.)* to confuse or annoy *(My little brother vexes me by poking me in the ribs for hours on end.)*

vicarious *(adj.)* experiencing through another *(All of my lame friends learned to be social through <u>vicarious</u> involvement in my amazing experiences.)*

vicissitude *(n.)* event that occurs by chance *(The <u>vicissitudes</u> of daily life prevent me from predicting what might happen from one day to the next.)*

vilify *(v.)* to lower in importance, defame *(After the Watergate scandal, almost any story written about President Nixon sought to <u>vilify</u> him and criticize his behavior.)*

viscous *(adj.)* not free flowing, syrupy *(The <u>viscous</u> syrup took three minutes to pour out of the bottle.)*

vitriolic *(adj.)* having a caustic quality *(When angry, the woman would spew <u>vitriolic</u> insults.)*

vituperate *(v.)* to berate *(Jack ran away as soon as his father found out, knowing he would be <u>vituperated</u> for his unseemly behavior.)*

W

wanton *(adj.)* undisciplined, lewd, lustful *(Vicky's <u>wanton</u> demeanor often made the frat guys next door very excited.)*

winsome *(adj.)* charming, pleasing *(After such a long, frustrating day, I was grateful for Chris's <u>winsome</u> attitude and childish naivete.)*

wistful *(adj.)* full of yearning; musingly sad *(Since her pet rabbit died, Edda missed it terribly and was <u>wistful</u> all day long.)*

wizened *(adj.)* dry, shrunken, wrinkled *(Agatha's grandmother, Stephanie, had the most <u>wizened</u> countenance, full of leathery wrinkles.)*

Z

zenith *(n.)* the highest point, culminating point *(I was too nice to tell Nelly that she had reached the absolute <u>zenith</u> of her career with that one hit of hers.)*

zephyr *(n.)* a gentle breeze *(If not for the <u>zephyrs</u> that were blowing and cooling us, our room would've been unbearably hot.)*

NOTES

NOTES

NOTES

NOTES

NOTES

NOTES

NOTES

NOTES

NOTES

THE MATH SECTION

MEET THE MATH SECTION

SAT MATH SPANS TWO QUESTION TYPES, THREE TIMED sections, and four major math topics—that's a lot of stuff. This section covers all of it—the basic facts, the crucial score-building strategies, and, that's right, all the math tested on the new SAT. So, read this chapter, become an SAT Math guru, and then find yourself a mountain somewhere in Tibet. Up there you can give cryptic advice to awed high school students who've climb thousands of feet to see you, risking their own deaths at the hands of avalanches and abominable snowmen. Or forego this life of reverence and head off to the college of your choice.

16.1 THE NEW SAT MATH

There are four major changes that make the new SAT Math new. Three of those changes are good news: There are fewer math questions on the test, the entire math section is five minutes shorter, and those pesky Quantitative Comparisons have been eliminated. But the last change probably won't light a smile on your face: SAT Math now covers some topics in Algebra II. What does this all add up to (pardon the pathetic pun)? The math covered by the new SAT is more difficult. Yeah, it sucks.

But the truth is that the new Math isn't really all *that* much harder, and it'll still be stuff you've probably already seen in your high school math classes. Whether you've seen it before or not, we've got it covered in this book:

- **Numbers and Operations**
- **Algebra (I and II)**
- **Geometry**
- **Data Analysis, Statistics, and Probability**

On the test, questions covering these four major math topics are spread across three timed sections and 54 total questions.

- **25-minute section with 20 questions**: all questions are Multiple-Choice.
- **25-minute section with 18 questions**: 8 Multiple-Choice and 10 Grid-Ins.
- **20-minute section with 16 questions**: all questions are Multiple-Choice.

Them's the facts. There's nothing else to know about the SAT Math—unless you need directions to Tibet.

16.2 KNOWING STRATEGIES VS. KNOWING MATH

There are some test-prep books out there—we won't name names, cause we're nice—that claim the SAT only tests your ability to take the SAT and doesn't test any actual knowledge. Well, those test-prep books are written by at least one of the following types of people:

- Liars
- Fools

The fact is, someone who has all the math on the test down cold but doesn't know any of the strategies will almost always do better on the test than some other kid who's studied up on the strategies but doesn't know the Pythagorean theorem.

But who would ever go and study just the strategies, or just the math? The whole point is to study both. And we promise you: If you know the math and the strategies, you'll whip both of those hypothetical kids who focused only on one or the other.

16.3 THE MATH REFERENCE AREA

The math section on the SAT provides a reference area with the basic geometric formulas and information.

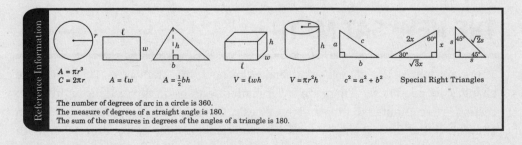

You might think that the SAT gives you this reference area because it asks lots of questions on these topics. Well, you're right. But the reference area is also a trap. Imagine a lazy student out there named Mike. Mike says to himself, "Why should I study all those formulas if they're just sitting there in the reference area?" Then he goes and takes a nap. On the day of the test, he's sitting there in his seat, sweating under the pressure, flipping maniacally back and forth between the reference area and the test questions, losing time and focus with every flip of the page.

Don't be like Mike. And don't just memorize the formulas. Figure out what they mean. The mathematical facts and rules in the reference area are the *foundation* for almost every geometry question on the test. Know all the formulas in the reference area as if they were tattooed on your body, as if they're part of you. You'll save time. You'll raise your score. You'll have funky mathematical tattoos.

16.4 ORDER OF DIFFICULTY

In each group of questions types, questions are ordered by difficulty. The first third of the questions are generally easy, the second third are a little harder, and the last third are difficult. So in the sections that are entirely Multiple-Choice the first third of the section will be easy, the scond third medium, and the last third hard. In the section that has both Multiple-Choice and Grid-ins, the pattern will start over for each group of questions. Knowing where you are in the order of difficulty can help you in a variety of ways:

- **On Individual Questions.** If you think you've got the answer to an easy question, don't second-guess yourself: You probably do. If you're looking at a difficult question, though, you might want to check your answer just to make sure you haven't fallen into a trap.
- **Overall Strategy.** Unless you're going for a 700 or above, you don't have to worry about answering every question on the test. You can use the order of difficulty to help you focus on answering the questions that you can. You should, for instance, answer every question in the first half of a timed math section. But if you're worried about time, you can probably get by without spending any real time at all on the final two questions.
- **Pacing.** You can also use the order of difficulty to manage your pacing. When you're given 25 minutes to answer 20 math questions in a timed section, you shouldn't just think to yourself that for every five minutes you should answer four questions. It takes more time to answer difficult problems than it does to answer easy problems. So in the early questions, you should be going *faster* than four questions answered per five minutes so you can save up time to figure out the harder problems.

16.5 BETTER, SMARTER, FASTER

Time management separates the students who kick major hindquarters on the Math section from those who merely do okay. If you take two students of equal skill in math, but give one a few extra minutes on an SAT Math section, who's gonna get a better score? The kid with more time.

You might be thinking, "Yeah, but no one's going to get more time." While no proctor is going to come along and give half the room 28 minutes on a section and hold the other half to 25, there is one person who can give you more time on a Math section: you!

Math Shortcuts

On the SAT Math, how much time you spend on a problem depends less on how much math you know and more on how you *approach* the problem. Take a look at the following example:

> Which has a greater area, a square with sides measuring 4 cm or a circle with a radius of the same length?

One student, we'll call him Bob, might solve this problem algebraically: Plug 4 into the formula for the area of a square and then the area of a circle. Area of a square $= s^2$, so the area of this square $= 4^2 = 16$. Area of a circle $= \pi r^2$, so the area of this circle must be $4\pi^2 = 16\pi$. 16π is obviously bigger than 16, so the circle must have a larger area than the square.

But another student, we'll call her Melanie, might choose a faster approach by quickly sketching the square and circle superimposed.

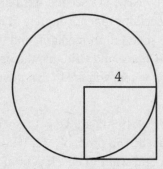

Bob and Melanie know the same amount of math, but because Melanie took the faster approach, she gave herself more time to work on other questions, a distinct advantage. A few more questions like this one, and Melanie will score considerably higher than Bob, even though the two of them know basically the same amount of math.

What Melanie did, essentially, was find a *shortcut*. Though she knew the same math that Bob did, Melanie found a way to answer the question more quickly. This doesn't make Melanie better at math, but it does make her a little bit better at taking the SAT.

The important question is, How can you learn to be more like Melanie? You need to do two things:

- **Be prepared.** You're not going to find a shortcut for a problem *unless* you know how to work it out the "long" way. An ability to find shortcuts is an expression of how *comfortable* you are with the math you know. Familiarity breeds shortcuts. The more you practice, and the more you look over the practice tests you take, the better you'll become at finding shortcuts.
- **Be on the lookout.** Be aware that there *are* shortcuts out there just waiting to be found. If you can invest a second to survey the question and think about a faster way, you'll be well served.

This is not to say that you should go into every question searching for a shortcut. A shortcut won't always exist. If you're on some blind quest for a shortcut, it might end up taking *longer* than the obvious long route to solving the problem.

Shortcuts are more common on SAT questions that cover particular SAT math. As we teach you the math you need to rock the SAT, we also point out the shortcuts you need to *really* rock the SAT Math.

SAT CALCULATOR SMARTS

By all means, use a calculator on the test. Bring the biggest, baddest calculator you've got, as long as it fits these specifications from the SAT:

- It isn't a hand-held minicomputer or laptop computer.
- It has no electronic writing pad or pen-input device.
- It isn't a pocket organizer (PDA).
- It doesn't have a QWERTY keyboard.
- It doesn't use paper tape.
- It doesn't make unusual noises (translation: *any* noises).
- It doesn't reqire an electrical outlet.

Any four-function, scientific, or graphing calculator is accepted as long as it doesn't break any of the above rules.

But just because you've got an awesome shiny hammer doesn't mean you should try to use it to pound in thumbtacks. Your calculator will help you on the SAT, but only if you use it intelligently.

Every question on the SAT can be solved *without* using a calculator, so you never *need* to start pushing buttons. In fact, on algebra questions involving variables, calculators are absolutely useless. So instead of reaching instinctively for your calculator every time, you should come up with a problem-solving plan for each question. Make sure you understand what the question requires and then decide whether to stick to your no. 2 pencil or to wield your formidable digital axe.

To see an example of what we mean, take a look at the following problem:

If $x = 3$, then what is the value of $f(x) = \dfrac{x^2 - 3x - 4}{11x - 44}$?

(A) −3
(B) −1.45
(C) 0
(D) .182
(E) .364

A trigger-happy calculator-user might immediately plug 3 in for x and start furiously working the keys. But the student who takes a moment to think about the problem will probably see that the calculation would be much simpler if the function were first simplified. To start, factor the 11 out of the denominator:

$$f(x) = \frac{x^2 - 3x - 4}{11(x - 4)}$$

Then, factor the numerator to its simplest form:

$$f(x) = \frac{(x - 4)(x + 1)}{11(x - 4)}$$

Cancel out, and you get

$$f(x) = \frac{(x + 1)}{11}$$

Now it's obvious that if you plug the 3 in for x, you get $\dfrac{4}{11}$, which equals .364.

Practical Calculator Rules

There are a few general rules of calculator use on the SAT that it pays to follow:

- Use a calculator for brute-force tasks, such as dealing with decimals.
- If you have to deal with a long string of numbers, do not jump to use your calculator. Instead, look for a way to cancel out some of the terms and simplify. A way will usually exist.
- Avoid using your calculator on fraction problems and on algebra questions with variables.
- Know your calculator before the test. Be comfortable and familiar with it so you don't waste time fiddling with buttons during the test. This is particularly true of graphing calculators, which have more buttons than 50 Cent has tattoos.
- Make sure your batteries are in good shape. Yes, we sound like your parents. But if your batteries run out during the test, you'll probably have to retake the test and tell your sad story to your entire extended family. That would be ugly.

Above all else, remember: Your calculator is a tool. You wouldn't wildly swing a hammer around, but some students seem to think they can just whip out their calculator and it will magically solve their problems. Those students seldom do all that well on the SAT Math section.

BEAT MULTIPLE-CHOICE AND GRID-INS

QUANTITATIVE COMPARISON QUESTIONS HAVE LEFT THE building. If you remember those nasty QCs from days of SAT yore, forget 'em. If you don't remember them, be glad you never met and move on to conquering the only math question types on the new SAT: multiple-choice and grid-ins.

17.1 MULTIPLE-CHOICE QUESTIONS

MC stands for all kinds of things. Rappers. Motorcycles. Master of ceremonies. Even Mariah Carey. On the new SAT, MC means good old multiple-choice questions: a question, maybe a graph or a geometric figure, and then five answer choices. About 70 percent of the entire SAT Math consists of these little babies. Know how to handle 'em, and you'll be crushing every MC on the block come test day.

For every math multiple-choice question on the test, you have two options:

- Solve the problem directly.
- Use the process of elimination.

In general, solving the problem is faster than going through the answer choices using process of elimination. Also, in general, if you're at all uncomfortable with the topic, it can be beneficial to try to eliminate answers instead of just solving the question.

Solving the Problem

Solving a problem directly is pretty straightforward as long as you feel comfortable with the math being tested. It's a two-step process.

1. **Read the question**, *but don't look at the answers*. Rephrase the question to make sure you understand it, and devise a plan to solve it.
2. **Solve the problem**. Once you have an answer —*and only then*— see if your answer is listed among the answer choices. By waiting to look at the answer choices until after you've solved the problem, you preempt those nasty SAT traps.

We can't stress enough that if you're trying to solve the problem directly, you should avoid looking at the answer choices until the end. Since trap answers are often the values you would get at the halfway point of the process of working out a problem, if you peek at the answers, you may get tricked into thinking you've solved the question before you actually have.

The Process of Elimination

On every multiple-choice question, the answer is right in front of you. It's just hidden among those five answer choices. This means you can sometimes short circuit the problem by plugging each answer into the question to see which one works. On certain occasions, working backward could actually be a faster method than just solving the problem directly.

Okay, example time:

A classroom contains 31 chairs, some which have arms and some of which do not. If the room contains 5 more armchairs than chairs without arms, how many armchairs does it contain?

(A) 10
(B) 13
(C) 16
(D) 18
(E) 21

If you want to solve the problem directly, you first have to assign variables:

Total number of chairs = 31

armchairs = x

chairs without arms = y

Next, take these variables and translate them into an equation based on the information in the question:

$$31 = x + y$$
$$y = x - 5$$

Then substitute one equation into the other:

$$31 = x + (x - 5)$$
$$31 = 2x - 5$$
$$36 = 2x$$
$$x = 18$$

There you are with the right answer, but it took a bit of time.

What if you plugged in the answers instead? And what if you plugged in intelligently, meaning: First plug in the value **C**.

Since answer choices on the SAT Math always either ascend or descend in value, starting with the middle value means that you'll never have to go through all five choices. For instance, in this question, if you plug in **C** (16) and discover that it's too small a number to satisfy the equation, you can eliminate **A** and **B** along with **C**. If 16 is too big, you can eliminate **D** and **E** along with **C**.

So let's plug in 16 and see what happens:

- The question says that there are 5 fewer armless chairs than armchairs, so if you have 16 armchairs, then you have 11 armless chairs, for a total of 27 chairs.
- Since you need the total numbers of chairs to equal 31, **C** is clearly not the right answer. But because the total number of chairs was too small, you can also eliminate **A** and **B**, the answer choices indicating fewer numbers of armchairs.
- If you then plug in **D** (18), you have 13 normal chairs and 31 total chairs. There's your answer. In this instance, plugging in the answers takes less time and seems easier.

As you take practice tests, you'll need to build up a sense of when working backwards can help you most. But here's a quick do and don't summary to help you along:

- **DO** work backward when the question describes an equation of some sort and the answer choices are all rather simple numbers.
- **DON'T** work backward when dealing with answer choices that contain variables or complicated fractions.

GRID-INS

Grid-ins cover the same topics and ask the same kind of questions as multiple-choice questions. They just don't have any answer choices. You have to work out the answer yourself and then "grid" it into a special answer-box thingy.

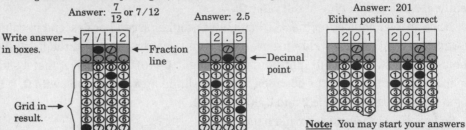

Directions for Student-Produced Response Questions

Each of the remaining 15 questions requires you to solve the problem and enter your answer by marking the ovals in the special grid, as shown in the examples below.

- Mark no more than one oval in any column.
- Because the answer sheet will be machine-scored, **you will receive credit only if the ovals are filled in completely.**
- Although not required, it is suggested that you write your answer in the boxes at the top of the columns to help you fill in the ovals accurately.
- Some problems may have more than one correct answer. In such cases, grid only one answer.
- No question has a negative answer.
- **Mixed numbers** such as $2\frac{1}{2}$ must be gridded as 2.5 or 5/2. If [2 1 / 2] is gridded, it will be interpreted as $\frac{21}{2}$, not $2\frac{1}{2}$.)

- **Decimal Accuracy:** If you obtain a decimal answer, **enter the most accurate value the grid will accommodate.** For example, if you obtain an answer such as 0.6666 . . . , you should record the result as .666 or .667. **Less accurate values such as .66 or .67 are not acceptable.** Acceptable ways to grid $\frac{2}{3}$ = .666 . . .

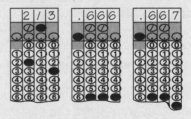

Note: You may start your answers in any column, space permitting. Columns not needed should be left blank.

The Grid

As you can see, grid-in instructions are a little intense. Here's a summary:

- **The computer that grades the test can't read anything but the ovals,** so you don't have to write anything in the spaces at the top. However, filling in the spaces at the top might help you to avoid making careless mistakes. So just write it out.
- **The grid cannot accommodate any number longer than four digits, any decimal or fraction that includes more than three numbers, or any negative signs.** Here's another way of looking at that: If the answer you come up with has more than four digits, is a fraction or decimal with more than three digits, or is a negative number, then your answer's wrong.
- **You must express a number as either a fraction or a decimal.** It doesn't matter which you choose.
- **You must transform all mixed numbers to fraction form.** For example, $4\frac{1}{2}$ must be written as $\frac{9}{2}$ or 4.5. If you were to try to write $4\frac{1}{2}$, the grading machine would read it as $\frac{41}{2}$, and you'd lose a point.
- **Sometimes the answer you come to will actually be a range of answers,** such as "any number between 4 and 5." When that happens, you could write in any number that fits the criteria—4.6, 4.2, $\frac{9}{2}$. But *no mixed numbers.*

Do Not Work Backward

Since there aren't any answer choices for grid-ins, you can't work backward. To answer these questions, you have to know the concepts and how to solve them directly. Luckily, that's exactly what the rest of this section covers.

NUMBERS

AND OPERATIONS

THE NEW SAT ESCHEWS THE SIMPLE AND TIME-HONORED term "Arithmetic" in favor of the clunky "Numbers and Operations." Not that it really matters, since both cover the exact same thing, and this gave us the chance to use the word *eschews*, which has nothing to do with teeth or chewing. *Eschew* means "to avoid," and as you know, the SAT tends to eschew simplicity a lot. Hence: Numbers and Operations.

the new SAT

The nifty table of contents above shows all the Numbers and Operations topics. For the new SAT, you should know this stuff so well you barely have to think about it, especially since a number of these will resurface in algebra questions.

18.1 KNOW YOUR NUMBERS

The SAT loves to throw around terminology about numbers. If you don't know the terminology, you won't know how to answer the question.

- **Whole Numbers.** The set of counting numbers, including zero $\{0, 1, 2, 3, \ldots\}$.
- **Natural Numbers.** The set of all whole positive numbers *except* zero $\{1, 2, 3, 4, 5, \ldots\}$.
- **Integers.** The set of all positive and negative whole numbers, including zero. Fractions and decimals are not included $\{\ldots, -3, -2, -1, 0, 1, 2, 3, \ldots\}$.
- **Rational Numbers.** The set of all numbers that can be expressed as integers in fractions. That is, any number that can be expressed in the form m/n, where m and n are integers.
- **Irrational Numbers.** The set of all numbers that cannot be expressed as integers in a fraction. Examples include π, $\sqrt{3}$, and $1.01001000100001000001\ldots$. A number must be either rational or irrational; no number can be both.
- **Real Numbers.** Every number on the number line. The set of real numbers includes all rational and irrational numbers.

18.2 ORDER OF OPERATIONS

PEMDAS is an acronym for the order in which mathematical operations should be performed as you move from left to right through an expression or equation:

- **P**arentheses
- **E**xponents
- **M**ultiplication
- **D**ivision
- **A**ddition
- **S**ubtraction

You may have had PEMDAS introduced to you as "Please Excuse My Dear Aunt Sally." Excuse us, but that's a supremely lame 1950s-style acronym. We prefer, Picking Eminem Made Dre A Star. Whatever. Just remember PEMDAS.

If an equation contains any or all of these PEDMAS elements, first carry out the math within the parentheses, then work out the exponents, then the multiplication, and the division. Addition and subtraction are actually a bit more complicated. When you have an equation to the point that it only contains addition and subtraction, perform each operation moving from left to right across the equation.

An example will make this easier to get:

$$\frac{(18-3) \times 2^2}{5} - 7 + (6 \times 3 - 1)$$

First work out the math in the parentheses (following PEMDAS even within the parentheses—always do multiplication before subtraction):

$$\frac{(18-3) \times 2^2}{5} - 7 + (18-1)$$

$$\frac{15 \times 2^2}{5} - 7 + 17$$

Now work out the exponents:

$$\frac{15 \times 4}{5} - 7 + 17$$

Then do the multiplication:

$$\frac{60}{5} - 7 + 17$$

Then the division:

$$12 - 7 + 17$$

Leaving you with just addition and subtraction. Now work from left to right:

$$5 + 17$$

And finally:

$$22$$

18.3 ODD AND EVEN NUMBERS

Even numbers are numbers that are divisible by 2 with no remainder. Remember that zero is included within this definition.

Even Numbers: . . . , –6, –4, –2, 0, 2, 4, 6, . . .

Odd numbers are numbers that, when divided by 2, leave a remainder of 1.

Odd Numbers: . . . , –5, –3, –1, 1, 3, 5, . . .

Operations and Odd and Even Numbers

For the SAT, you have to know how odd and even numbers act when they're added, subtracted, multiplied, and divided. The chart below shows addition, subtraction, and multiplication because multiplication and division are the same in terms of odd and even.

Addition	Subtraction	Multiplication
Even + Even = Even	Even – Even = Even	Even × Even = Even
Odd + Odd = Even	Odd – Odd = Even	Odd × Odd = Odd
Even + Odd = Odd	Even – Odd = Odd	Even × Odd = Even

If you know how odd and even numbers act when put through any of the four operations, you have a leg up in using the process of elimination. If the numbers in the answer choices are both odd and even, you should be able to use the rules of odd and even numbers to figure out if the answer you're looking for is odd or even. So even if you don't know the exact value of the answer you're looking for, you should be able to eliminate half of the answers based on whether they're odd or even.

THE POSITIVE, THE NEGATIVE, AND THE UGLY

Positive numbers are greater than zero. Negative numbers are less than zero. Zero itself is neither positive nor negative. On a number line, positive numbers appear to the right of zero and negative numbers appear to the left.

$$..., -5, -4, -3, -2, -1, 0, 1, 2, 3, 4, 5, ...$$

In equations and expressions, positive numbers look like normal numbers (for example, 7), while negative numbers have a negative sign in front of them (−7).

Negative numbers can be confusing. It's like you're suddenly told to read from right to left, but all of your instincts tell you to do the opposite. Why are we telling you this? To convince you to concentrate. The SAT Math preys on the careless, and negative numbers are one of the weapons it uses most often.

Negative Numbers and Operations

Negative numbers act differently from positive numbers when you add, subtract, multiply, or divide them.

Adding and Subtracting Signed Numbers

Adding a negative number is like *subtracting* a positive number...

$$3 + -2 = 1, \text{ just as } 3 - 2 = 1$$

...while subtracting a negative number is the same as *adding* a positive number.

$$3 - (-2) = 5, \text{ just as } 3 + 2 = 5$$

Multiplying and Dividing Negative Numbers

When negative numbers are involved in multiplication and division, they affect whether the outcome is positive or negative. You should know these rules cold.

Multiplying with Negative Numbers	Dividing with Negative Numbers
Positive × Positive = Positive	Positive ÷ Positive = Positive
Negative × Negative = Positive	Negative ÷ Negative = Positive
Positive × Negative = Negative	Positive ÷ Negative = Negative

Here's a helpful trick when dealing with a series of multiplied or divided positive and negative numbers: If there's an even number of negative numbers in the series, the outcome will be positive. If there's an odd number, the outcome will be negative.

The Ugly: Negative Numbers and Parentheses

When negative signs and parentheses collide, well, the heading says it all. The principle is simple: A negative sign outside parentheses is distributed across the parentheses. Take the question $3 + 4 - (3 + 1 - 8) = ?$. Solve this problem by following PEMDAS and first working out the parentheses:

$$3 + 4 - (4 - 8) = 3 + 4 - (-4) = 3 + 4 + 4 = 11$$

When you start dealing with algebra, however, you won't always have like terms and you won't be able to work out what's in the parentheses. You'll instead have to get rid of the parentheses by distributing the negative sign across it. Why can you do this? Because $3 + 4 - (3 + 1 - 8) = $ secretly has multiplication in it. It can also be written as $3 + 4 + (-1)(3 + 1 - 8) = $. So every number within the parentheses should be multiplied by -1. But remember that multiplication with a negative number changes the sign of the product. So the simplified expression is $3 + 4 - 3 - 1 + 8 = 11$. Whenever you see a negative sign before parentheses, take a deep breath and be careful of your signs.

Absolute Value

Negative numbers got you down? Absolute value can help. The absolute value of a number is the distance on a number line between that number and zero. Or, you could think of it as the positive "version" of every number. The absolute value of a positive number is that same number, and the absolute value of a negative number is the number without a negative sign.

The absolute value of x is written this way: $|x|$.

$$\text{If } x = 5, |x| = 5.$$
$$\text{If } x = -4.234, |x| = 4.234.$$
$$\text{If } x = 0, |x| = 0.$$

It is also possible to have expressions within absolute value brackets:

$$3 - 2 + |3 - 7|$$

You can't just make that -7 positive because it's sitting between absolute value brackets. You have to work out the math first:

$$3 - 2 + |-4|$$

Now you can get rid of the brackets and the negative sign from that 4.

$$3 - 2 + 4 = 5$$

18.5 DIVISIBILITY AND REMAINDERS

The SAT sometimes tests whether you can determine if one number is divisible by another. To check divisibility, you could take the immense amount of time necessary to do the division by hand and see if the result is a whole number. Or you can give yourself a shortcut and memorize this list of divisibility rules:

Divisibility Rules

1. All whole numbers are divisible by 1.
2. All numbers with a ones digit of 0, 2, 4, 6, or 8 are divisible by 2.

3. A number is divisible by 3 if its digits add up to a number divisible by 3. For example, 6,711 is divisible by 3 because 6 + 7 + 1 + 1 = 15, and 15 is divisible by 3.

4. A number is divisible by 4 if its last two digits are divisible by 4. For example, 80,744 is divisible by 4, but 7,850 is not.

5. A number is divisible by 5 if it ends in 0 or 5.

6. A number is divisible by 6 if it is even and also divisible by 3.

7. There are no rules for 7. It is a rebel.

8. A number is divisible by 8 if its last three digits are divisible by 8. For example, 905,256 is divisible by 8 because 256 is divisible by 8, and 74,513 is not divisible by 8 because 513 is not divisible by 8.

9. A number is divisible by 9 if its digits add up to a number divisible by 9. For example, 1,458 is divisible by 9 because 1 + 4 + 5 + 8 = 18 and 18 is divisible by 9.

10. A number is divisible by 10 if it ends in 0.

18.6 FACTORS

A factor is an integer that divides another integer evenly. If a/b is an integer, then b is a factor of a. The numbers 3, 4, and 6, for example, are factors of 12.

Factorization

Sometimes the SAT requires you to find all the factors of some integer or to just be able to run through the factors quickly. To make this happen, write down all the factors of a number in pairs, beginning with 1 and the number you're factoring. To factor 24:

- 1 and 24 (1 × 24 = 24)
- 2 and 12 (2 × 12 = 24)
- 3 and 8 (3 × 8 = 24)
- 4 and 6 (4 × 6 = 24)

If you find yourself beginning to repeat numbers, then the factorization's complete. After finding that 4 is a factor of 24, the next lowest factor is 6, but you've already written 6 down. You're done.

Prime Numbers

Everyone's always insisting on how unique they are. Punks wear leather. Goths wear black. But prime numbers actually are unique. They are the only numbers whose sole factors are 1 and themselves. All prime numbers are positive (because every negative number has −1 as a factor in addition to 1 and itself). Furthermore, all prime numbers besides 2 are odd.

The first few primes, in increasing order, are

$$2, 3, 5, 7, 11, 13, 17, 19, 23, 29, 31, 37, 41, 43, 47, 53, \ldots$$

You don't have to memorize this list, but getting familiar with it is a pretty good idea. Here's a trick to determine if a number is prime. First, estimate the square root of the number. Then, check all the prime numbers that fall below your estimate to see if they are factors of the number. For example, to see if 91 is prime, you should estimate the square root of the number: $\sqrt{91} \approx 10$. Now you should test 91 for divisibility by the prime numbers smaller than 10: 2, 3, 5, and 7.

- Is 91 divisible by 2? No, it does not end with an even number.
- Is 91 divisible by 3? No, 9 + 1 = 10, and 10 is not divisible by 3.
- Is 91 divisible by 5? No, 91 does not end with 0 or 5.
- Is 91 divisible by 7? Yes! 91 ÷ 7 = 13.

Therefore, 91 is not prime.

Prime Factorization

Come on, say it aloud with us: "Prime factorization." Now imagine Arnold Schwarzenegger saying it. Then imagine if he knew how to do it. Holy Moly. He would probably be governor of the entire United States.

To find the prime factorization of a number, divide it and all its factors until every remaining integer is prime. The resulting group of prime numbers is the prime factorization of the original integer. Want to find the prime factorization of 36? We thought so:

$$36 = 2 \times 18 = 2 \times 2 \times 9 = 2 \times 2 \times 3 \times 3$$

It can be helpful to think of prime factorization in the form of a tree:

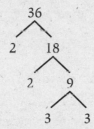

As you may already have noticed, there's more than one way to find the prime factorization of a number. Instead of cutting 36 into 2 and 18, you could have factored it to 6 × 6, and then continued from there. As long as you don't screw up the math, there's no wrong path—you'll always get the same result.

Greatest Common Factor

The greatest common factor (GCF) of two numbers is the largest factor that they have in common. Finding the GCF of two numbers is especially useful in certain applications, such as manipulating fractions (we explain why later in this chapter).

To find the GCF of two numbers, say, 18 and 24, first find their prime factorizations:

$$18 = 2 \times 9 = 2 \times 3 \times 3$$
$$24 = 2 \times 12 = 2 \times 2 \times 6 = 2 \times 2 \times 2 \times 3$$

The GCF is the "overlap," or intersection, of the two prime factorizations. In this case, both prime factorizations contain 2 × 3 = 6. This is their GCF.

Here's another, more complicated, example: What's the GCF of 96 and 144? First, find the prime factorizations:

$$96 = 2 \times 48 = 2 \times 2 \times 24 = 2 \times 2 \times 2 \times 12 = 2 \times 2 \times 2 \times 2 \times 6 = 2 \times 2 \times 2 \times 2 \times 2 \times 3 = 2^5 \times 3$$

$$144 = 2 \times 72 = 2 \times 2 \times 36 = 2 \times 2 \times 2 \times 18 = 2 \times 2 \times 2 \times 2 \times 9 = 2 \times 2 \times 2 \times 2 \times 3 \times 3 = 2^4 \times 3^2$$

The product of the "overlap" is $2^4 \times 3 = 48$. So that's their GCF.

MULTIPLES

A multiple is an integer that can divide evenly into another integer. If c/d is an integer, then c is a multiple of d. The numbers 45, 27, and 18, for example, are all multiples of 9. Here's a better example: What are some multiples of 4? The numbers 12, 20, and 96 are all multiples of 4. How do we know? Because

$$12 = 4 \times 3$$
$$20 = 4 \times 5$$
$$96 = 4 \times 24$$

Also, note that any integer, n, is a multiple of 1 and n, because $1 \times n = n$.

Least Common Multiple

The least common multiple (LCM) of two integers is the smallest multiple that the two numbers have in common. The LCM of two numbers is, like the GCF, useful when manipulating fractions. Also similar to the GCF, you can't find the LCM without using prime factorization. For example, what's the least common multiple of 4 and 6? Begin by prime factorizing:

$$4 = 2 \times 2, \text{ and } 6 = 2 \times 3$$

The LCM—get this, it's tricky—is equal to the multiplication of each factor by the maximum number of times it appears in either number. Since 2 appears twice in the prime factorization of 4, it will appear twice (2×2) in the LCM. Since 3 appears once, it will appear once. So the LCM of 4 and 6 is $2 \times 2 \times 3 = 12$.

One more example will help. What is the LCM of 14 and 38? Prime factorize:

$$14 = 2 \times 7$$
$$38 = 2 \times 19$$

Since 2 appears a maximum of once in either number, it will appear once in the LCM. Same goes for 7 and 19, making the LCM $2 \times 7 \times 19 = 266$.

KNOW YOUR FRACTIONS

The SAT loves fractions. Loves them. The number of questions on the test that cover fractions in some way is nothing short of stupefying. This means you must know fractions inside and out. Know how to compare them, reduce them, add them, and multiply them. Know how to divide them, subtract them, and convert them to mixed numbers. Know them. Love them like the SAT does. Make them your friend on the test, not your enemy.

To begin, here are the basics: A fraction is a part of a whole. It's composed of two expressions, a numerator and a denominator. The numerator of a fraction is the quantity above the fraction bar, and the denominator is the quantity below the fraction bar. For example, in the fraction $1/2$, 1 is the numerator and 2 is the denominator.

Equivalent Fractions

Fractions represent a part of a whole, so if you increase both the part and whole by the same multiple, you will not change the relationship between the part and the whole.

To determine if two fractions are equivalent, multiply the denominator and numerator of one fraction so that the denominators of the two fractions are equal (this is one place where knowing how to calculate LCM and GCF comes in handy). For example, $^1/_2 = {}^3/_6$ because if you multiply the numerator and denominator of $^1/_2$ by 3, you get:

$$\frac{1 \times 3}{2 \times 3} = \frac{3}{6}$$

As long as you multiply or divide *both* the numerator and denominator of a fraction by the *same* nonzero number, you will not change the overall value of the fraction.

Reducing Fractions

Reducing fractions makes life simpler. It takes unwieldy monsters like $^{450}/_{600}$ and makes them into smaller, friendlier critters. To reduce a fraction to its lowest terms, divide the numerator and denominator by their GCF. For example, for $^{450}/_{600}$, the GCF of 450 and 600 is 150. So the fraction reduces down to $^3/_4$, since $450 \div 150 = 3$ and $600 \div 150 = 4$.

A fraction is in its simplest, totally reduced form if its numerator and denominator share no further GCF (in other words, their GCF is 1). There is no number but 1, for instance, that can divide into both 3 and 4, so $^3/_4$ is a fraction in its lowest form.

Comparing Fractions

Large positive numbers with lots of digits, like 5,000,000, are greater than numbers with just a few digits, such as 5. But fractions don't work that way. While $^{200}/_{20,000}$ might seem like a nice, big, impressive fraction, $^2/_3$ is actually larger, because 2 is a much bigger part of 3 than 200 is of 20,000.

In certain cases, comparing two fractions can be very simple. If the denominators of two fractions are the same, then the fraction with the larger numerator is bigger. If the numerators of the two fractions are the same, the fraction with the smaller denominator is bigger.

However, you'll most likely have to deal with two fractions that have different numerators and denominators, such as $^{200}/_{20,000}$ and $^2/_3$. Don't worry. There is an easy comparison tool, which we now reveal: cross-multiplication. Just multiply the numerator of each fraction by the denominator of the other, then write the product of each multiplication next to the numerator you used to get it. Here's the cross-multiplication of $^{200}/_{20,000}$ and $^2/_3$:

$$600 = \frac{200}{20,000} \times \frac{2}{3} = 40,000$$

Since $40,000 > 600$, $^2/_3$ is the greater fraction.

Adding and Subtracting Fractions

Adding and subtracting fractions that have the same denominator is a snap. If the fractions have different denominators, though, you need an additional step.

Fractions with the Same Denominators

To add fractions with the same denominators, all you have to do is add up the numerators:

$$\frac{1}{20} + \frac{3}{20} + \frac{13}{20} = \frac{17}{20}$$

Subtraction works similarly. If the denominators of the fractions are equal, just subtract one numerator from the other:

$$\frac{13}{20} - \frac{2}{20} = \frac{11}{20}$$

Fractions with Different Denominators

If the fractions don't have equal denominators, then before you can actually get to the addition and subtraction, you first have to make the denominators the same. *Then* adding and subtracting will be a piece of cake, as in the example above. The best way to equalize denominators is to find the least common denominator (LCD), which is just the LCM of the two denominators. For example, the LCD of $^1/_2$ and $^2/_3$ is 6, since 6 is the LCM of 2 and 3.

But because fractions are parts of a whole, if you increase the whole, you also have to increase the part by the same amount. To put it more bluntly, multiply the numerator by the same number you multiplied the denominator. For the example $^1/_2$ + $^2/_3$, you know you have to get denominators of 6 in order to add them. For the $^1/_2$, this means you have to multiply the denominator by 3. And if you multiply the denominator by 3, you have to multiply the numerator by 3 too:

$$\text{numerator} = 1 \times 3 = 3$$
$$\text{denominator} = 2 \times 3 = 6$$

So, the new fraction is $^3/_6$. Repeat the same process for the second fraction, $^2/_3$, except this time you have to multiply both denominator and numerator by 2:

$$\text{numerator} = 2 \times 2 = 4$$
$$\text{denominator} = 3 \times 2 = 6$$

The new fraction is $^4/_6$. The final step is to perform the addition or subtraction. In this case, $^3/_6 + ^4/_6 = ^7/_6$.

Another approach is to skip finding the LCD and simply multiply the denominators together to get a common denominator. In some cases, such as our example, the product of the denominators will actually be the LCD ($2 \times 3 = 6 = $ LCD). But, other times, the product of the denominators will be greater than the LCD. For example, if the two denominators are 6 and 8, you could use $6 \times 8 = 48$ as a denominator instead of 24 (the LCD). There are two drawbacks to this second approach. The first is that you have to work with larger numbers. The second is that you have to take the extra step of reducing your answer. SAT answer choices almost always appear as reduced fractions. Trust us.

Multiplying Fractions

Multiplying fractions is a breeze, whether the denominators are equal or not. The product of two fractions is the product of their numerators over the product of their denominators:

$$\frac{a}{b} \times \frac{c}{d} = \frac{ac}{bd}$$

Want an example with numbers? You got one.

$$\frac{3}{7} \times \frac{2}{5} = \frac{3 \times 2}{7 \times 5} = \frac{6}{35}$$

Canceling Out

You can make multiplying fractions even easier by canceling out. If the numerator and denominator of any of the fractions you need to multiply share a common factor, you can divide by the common factor to reduce both numerator and denominator. For example, the fraction

$$\frac{4}{5} \times \frac{1}{8} \times \frac{10}{11}$$

To answer this fraction as it is, you have to multiply the numerators and denominators and then reduce. Sure, you could do it, but it would take some time. Canceling out provides a shortcut.

In this case, you can cancel out the numerator 4 with the denominator 8, and the numerator 10 with the denominator 5, which gives you

$$\frac{\cancel{4}^{1}}{\cancel{5}_{1}} \times \frac{1}{\cancel{8}_{2}} \times \frac{\cancel{10}^{2}}{11} = \frac{1}{1} \times \frac{1}{2} \times \frac{2}{11}$$

Then, canceling the 2's, you get

$$\frac{1}{1} \times \frac{1}{\cancel{2}_{1}} \times \frac{\cancel{2}^{1}}{11} = \frac{1}{1} \times \frac{1}{1} \times \frac{1}{11}$$

Canceling out can *dramatically* cut the amount of time you need to spend working with big numbers. When dealing with fractions, whether they're filled with numbers or variables, *always* be on the lookout for chances to cancel out.

Dividing Fractions

Multiplication and division are inverse operations. It makes sense, then, that to perform division with fractions, all you have to do is flip the second fraction and then multiply. Check it out:

$$\frac{a}{b} \div \frac{c}{d} = \frac{a}{b} \times \frac{d}{c} = \frac{ad}{bc}$$

Here's a numerical example:

$$\frac{1}{2} \div \frac{4}{5} = \frac{1}{2} \times \frac{5}{4} = \frac{5}{8}$$

Mixed Numbers

A mixed number is an integer followed by a fraction, like $1^1/_2$. But operations such as addition, subtraction, multiplication, and division can't be performed on mixed numbers, so you have to know how to convert them into fraction form.

Since we already mentioned $1^1/_2$, it seems only right to convert it. The method is easy: Multiply the integer (the big 1) of the mixed number by the denominator, and add that product to the numerator: $1 \times 2 + 1 = 3$ is the numerator of the improper fraction. Now, put that over the original denominator: $^3/_2$ is the converted fraction.

Here's another example:

$$3\,\frac{2}{13} = \frac{(3 \times 13) + 2}{13} = \frac{39 + 2}{13} = \frac{41}{13}$$

We said it once, we'll say it again: Converting mixed numbers is particularly important on grid-in questions, since you can't actually write a mixed number into the grid. If you tried to grid $1^1/_2$, the computer that scores your test will read it as $^{11}/_2$. Ouch!

Complex Fractions

Complex fractions are fractions of fractions.

$$\frac{\frac{a}{b}}{\frac{c}{d}}$$

Here's what you should be thinking: "Ugh." Complex fractions are annoying if you try to take them head on. But you don't have to. Instead, transform them into normal fractions according to this quick step: Multiply the top fraction by the reciprocal of the bottom fraction.

$$\frac{\frac{a}{b}}{\frac{c}{d}} = \frac{a}{b} \times \frac{d}{c} = \frac{ad}{bc}$$

And here's an example using actual numbers:

$$\frac{\frac{1}{3}}{\frac{4}{5}} = \frac{1}{3} \times \frac{5}{4} = \frac{5}{12}$$

18.9 DECIMALS

A decimal number is any number with a nonzero digit to the right of the decimal point. But for the SAT, it's more important to know that decimals are, like fractions, a way of writing parts of wholes. If you have to add, subtract, multiply, divide, or perform any other operation on a decimal for the SAT, we highly recommend that you use a calculator. It will save more time and you will make fewer mistakes.

Converting Decimals to Fractions

Even if you use a calculator, you should know how to convert decimals into fractions and vice versa. Both conversions are easy to do.

To convert a decimal number to a fraction,

1. Remove the decimal point and make the decimal number the numerator.
2. Let the denominator be the number 1 followed by as many zeros as there are decimal places in the decimal number.
3. Reduce this fraction.

To convert .3875 into a fraction, first eliminate the decimal point and place 3875 as the numerator:

$$.3875 = \frac{3875}{?}$$

Since .3875 has four digits after the decimal point, put four zeros in the denominator following the number 1:

$$.3875 = \frac{3875}{10000}$$

Then, by finding the GCF of 3875 and 10,000, which is 125, reduce the fraction:

$$\frac{3875}{10000} = \frac{31}{80}$$

To convert from fractions back to decimals is a cinch: divide the numerator by the denominator on your calculator:

$$31 \div 80 = 0.3875$$

18.10 PERCENTS

Percents are a specific type of fraction. *Percent* literally means "of 100" in Latin, so after you ace the SAT, go to college, drop out to become famous, and eventually amass 75% of all the money in the world, you'll then have $^{75}/_{100}$ of the world's money. Awesome.

Until then, you don't have that much money, and you still have to take the SAT (and pay for the privilege). So let's look at an example question:

> 4 is what percent of 20?

The first thing you have to know how to do is translate this sort of question into an equation. It's actually pretty straightforward as long as you see that "is" is the same as saying "equals," and "what" is the same as saying "x." So if 4 equals x percent of 20, then

$$4 = x\%(20)$$

Since a percent is actually a number out of 100, this means

$$4 = \frac{x}{100}(20)$$

Now just work out the math:

$$4 = \frac{20x}{100}$$

$$400 = 20x$$

$$x = 20$$

Therefore, 4 is 20% of 20.

Converting Percents into Fractions or Decimals

Converting percents into fractions or decimals is a crucial SAT skill. If you ever want to multiply or divide a number by a percent, you first have to convert it.

- To convert from a percent to a fraction, take the percentage number and place it as a numerator over the denominator 100. If you have 88 percent of something, then you can quickly convert it into the fraction $^{88}/_{100}$.
- To convert from a percent to a decimal, you must take a decimal point and insert it into the percent number two spaces from the right: 79% equals .79, while 350% equals 3.5.

What Percent of this Word Problem Don't You Understand, Bucko?

SAT word problems often seem to be phrased as if the person who wrote them doesn't know how to speak English. The SAT does this purposefully, because it thinks that verbal tricks are a good way to test your math skills. If that makes no sense to you, good. It makes no sense to us either. Here's an example of the kind of linguistic trickery we're talking about:

> What percent of 2 is 5?

Because the 2 is the smaller number and because it appears first in the question, you're first instinct may be to calculate what percent 2 is of 5.

But as long as you remember that "is"means "equals" and "what" means "x" you'll be able to correctly translate the word problem into math:

$$x\%(2) = 5$$

$$\frac{x}{100}(2) = 5$$

$$\frac{2x}{100} = 5$$

$$2x = 500$$

$$x = 250$$

So 5 is 250% of 2.

Percent Increase and Decrease

One of the most common ways the SAT tests percent is through the concept of percent increase and decrease.

- **Percent increase**—If the price of a $10 shirt *increases* 10%, the new price is the original $10 *plus* 10% of the $10 original.

- **Percent decrease**—If the price of a $10 shirt *decreases* 10%, the new price is the original $10 *minus* 10% of the $10 original.

One of the classic blunders students make on these questions is to figure out what the 10% increase or decrease is, but then, lost in a haze of joy and relief, to forget to carry out the necessary addition or subtraction. SAT traps take advantage of this. Be wary.

> A vintage bowling league shirt cost $20 in the 1990s. But during the 1970s, when the shirt was first made, it cost 15% less. What was the price of the shirt in the 1970s?
>
> (A) $3
> (B) $17
> (C) $23
> (D) $35
> (E) $280

First find the price decrease (remember that 15% = .15):

$$\$20 \times .15 = \$3$$

Now, since the price of the shirt was less back in the 1970s, subtract $3 from the $20 price from the early 1990s:

$$\$20 - \$3 = \$17$$

The answer is **B**. If you only finished the first part of this question and looked at the answers, you might see the $3 at answer **A** and forget to finish the calculation.

Double Percents

Some SAT questions ask you to determine a percent of a percent.

.25×2 = .5

> The original price of a banana in a store is $2. During a sale, the store reduces the price by 25% and Joe buys the banana. Joe then raises the price of the banana 10% from the price at which he bought it and sells it to Sam. How much does Sam pay for the banana?

.5×10 = $5.

This question asks you to determine the effect of two successive percent changes. The key to solving it is realizing that each percentage change is dependent on the last. You have to work out the effect of the first percentage change, come up with a value, and then use that value to determine the effect of the second percentage change.

When you're working on a percentage problem that involves a series of percentage changes, you should follow the same basic procedure that we explained for one percentage change, except here you should run through the procedure twice. For the first percentage change, figure out what's the whole, calculate the percentage of the whole, make sure to perform addition or subtraction if necessary, then take the new value and put it through these same steps for the second percentage change.

To answer the example problem, first find 25% of the original price:

$$\frac{25}{100} \times \$2 = \frac{50}{100} = \$.50$$

Now subtract that $.50 from the original price:

$$\$2 - \$.5 = \$1.50$$

Then increase $1.50 by 10%:

$$\frac{10}{100} \times \$1.50 = \frac{15}{100} = \$.15$$

Sam buys the banana for $1.50 + $.15 = $1.65. A total rip-off.

Some students, sensing a shortcut, are tempted to just combine the two percentage changes on double percent problems. This is not a real shortcut. It's more like a dark alley filled with cruel and nasty people who want you to do badly on the SAT.

If you reasoned on the last example problem that the first percentage change lowered the price 25% and the second raised the price 10%, meaning that the total change was a reduction of 15%, then

$$\frac{15}{100} \times \$2 = \frac{30}{100} = \$.30$$

Subtract that $.30 from the original price:

$$\$2 - \$.30 = \$1.70$$

We *promise* you that when the SAT gives you a double-percent problem, it will include this sort of wrong answer as a trap among the choices.

18.11 RATIOS

Ratios look like fractions and are related to fractions, but they don't quack like fractions. Whereas a fraction describes a part of a whole, a ratio compares one part to another part.

A ratio can be written in a variety of ways. Mathematically, it can appear as $^3/_1$ or as 3:1. In words, it would be written out as the ratio of 3 to 1. Each of these three forms of the ratio 3:1 mean the same thing, that there are three of one thing for every one of another. If you have three red alligators and one blue alligator, then you would have a ratio of 3:1 for red alligators to blue alligators. For the SAT, you must remember that ratios compare *parts to parts* rather than parts to a whole. Why do you have to remember that? Because of questions like this:

> For every 40 games a baseball team plays, it loses 12 games. What is the ratio of the team's losses to wins?
>
> (A)   3:10
> (B)   7:10
> (C)   3:7
> (D)   7:3
> (E)   10:3

The question says that the team loses 12 of every 40 games, but it asks you for the ratio of losses to *wins*, not losses to *games*. So the first thing you have to do is find out how many games the team wins in 40 games:

$$40 - 12 = 28$$

The team wins 28 games for every 40. So for every 12 losses, the team wins 28 games, for a ratio of 12:28. You can reduce this ratio by dividing both sides by 4 to get 3 losses for every 7 wins, or 3:7. Answer **C** is correct. If you didn't realize that the losses to games was a part to whole, you might have just reduced the ratio 12:40 to 3:10, and then chosen answer **A**. And there is no question that on ratio problems, the SAT will include an incorrect *part*: *whole* answer to try to trip you up.

Proportions

Just because you have a ratio of three red alligators to one blue alligator doesn't mean that you can *only* have three red alligators and one blue one. It could also mean that you have six red and two blue alligators or that you have 240 red and 80 blue alligators. Ratios compare only *relative magnitude*. In order to know how many of each color alligator you actually have, in addition to knowing the ratios, you also need to know how many total alligators there are.

The SAT often asks questions testing your ability to figure out an answer based on the ratio between items and the total number of all items:

Egbert has red, blue, and green marbles in the ratio of 5:4:3, and he has a total of 36 marbles. How many blue marbles does Egbert have?

For each group of 5 red marbles, you have a group of 4 blue marbles and a group of 3 green marbles. The ratio therefore tells you that out of every 12 marbles (since 5 + 4 + 3 = 12), 4 marbles will be blue.

The question also tells you that you have 36 total marbles, and since the ratio of blue marbles to total marbles will not change *no matter how many marbles you have*, you can solve this problem by setting up a proportion, which is an equation that states that two ratios are equal. In this case, you can set equal 4:12 and x:36, with x standing in for the number of blue marbles that you'd have out of a total of 36. To do math with proportions, it's most useful to set up proportions in fractional form:

$$\frac{4}{12} = \frac{x}{36}$$

Now isolate x by cross-multiplying, and then you can solve.

$$12x = 4 \times 36$$
$$12x = 144$$
$$x = 12$$

18.12 EXPONENTS

An exponent is a shorthand way of saying, "Multiply this number by itself this number of times." In a^b, a is multiplied by itself b times. Here's a numerical example: $2^5 = 2 \times 2 \times 2 \times 2 \times 2$. An exponent can also be referred to as a power: 2^5 is "two to the fifth power." Before jumping into the exponent nitty-gritty, learn these five terms:

- **Base.** The base refers to the 3 in 3^5. In other words, the base is the number multiplied by itself however many times specified by the exponent.
- **Exponent.** The exponent is the 5 in 3^5. The exponent tells how many times the base is to be multiplied by itself.
- **Squared.** Saying that a number is *squared* is a common code word to indicate that it has an exponent of 2. In the expression 6^2, 6 has been squared.
- **Cubed.** Saying that a number is *cubed* means it has an exponent of 3. In the expression 4^3, 4 has been cubed.
- **Power.** The term *power* is another way to talk about a number being raised to an exponent. A number raised to the third power has an exponent of 3. So 6 raised to the fourth power is 6^4.

One last word of exponent advice before we get started. We'll explain how to deal with exponents without using your calculator, but most good graphing calculators have a variety of exponent functions. Knowing how to use them could save you time, especially when exponent values get larger and involve fractions or negative numbers.

Common Exponents

It can be very helpful and a real time-saver on the SAT if you can easily translate back and forth between a number and its exponential form. For instance, if you can easily see that $36 = 6^2$, it can really come in handy if you're dealing with binomials, quadratic equations, or any number of other areas in algebra.

Here are some lists of common exponents. We'll start with the squares of the first ten integers:

$$1^2 = 1$$
$$2^2 = 4$$
$$3^2 = 9$$
$$4^2 = 16$$
$$5^2 = 25$$
$$6^2 = 36$$
$$7^2 = 49$$
$$8^2 = 64$$
$$9^2 = 81$$
$$10^2 = 100$$

Here are the first five cubes:

$$1^3 = 1$$
$$2^3 = 8$$
$$3^3 = 27$$
$$4^3 = 64$$
$$5^3 = 125$$

Finally, the first few powers of two are useful to know for various applications:

$$2^0 = 1$$
$$2^1 = 2$$
$$2^2 = 4$$
$$2^3 = 8$$
$$2^4 = 16$$
$$2^5 = 32$$
$$2^6 = 64$$
$$2^7 - 128$$
$$2^8 = 256$$
$$2^9 = 512$$
$$2^{10} = 1024$$

Adding and Subtracting Powers

Actually, you can't add or subtract *numbers* with exponents. Instead, work out each exponent to find its value, then add the two numbers. To add $3^3 + 4^2$, work out the exponents to get $(3 \times 3 \times 3) + (4 \times 4)$, and then, finally, $27 + 16 = 43$.

But if you're dealing with *algebraic expressions* that have the same bases and exponents, such as $3x^4$ and $5x^4$, then you *can* add or subtract them. For example, $3x^4 + 5x^4 = 8x^4$. Algebraic expressions that have different bases or exponents cannot be added or subtracted.

Multiply and Dividing Powers

Multiplying or dividing exponential numbers or terms that have the same base is so quick and easy it's like a little math oasis. When multiplying, just *add* the exponents together. This is known as the **Product Rule**:

$$3^6 \times 3^2 = 3^{(6+2)} = 3^8$$
$$x^4 \times x^3 = x^{(4+3)} = x^7$$

To divide two same-base exponential numbers or terms, *subtract* the exponents. This is known as the **Quotient Rule**:

$$\frac{3^6}{3^2} = 3^{(6-2)} = 3^4$$

$$\frac{x^4}{x^3} = x^{(4-3)} = x^1$$

Quick and easy. Right?

You want the bad news or the bad news? The same isn't true if you need to multiply or divide two exponential numbers that *don't* have the same base, such as, say, $3^3 \times 4^2$. When two exponents have different bases, you just have to do your work the old-fashioned way: Multiply the numbers out and multiply or divide the result accordingly: $3^3 \times 4^2 = 27 + 16 = 43$.

Raising a Power to a Power

To raise one exponent to another exponent, multiply the exponents. This is known as the **Power Rule**:

$$(3^2)^4 = 3^{(2 \times 4)} = 3^8$$

$$(x^4)^3 = x^{(4 \times 3)} = x^{12}$$

Again, easy. Just remember that you *multiply* exponents when raising one exponent to another, and you *add* exponents when multiplying two identical bases with exponents. The SAT expects lots of students to mix these operations up.

Fractions Raised to a Power

To raise a fraction to an exponent, raise both the numerator and denominator to that exponent:

$$\left(\frac{1}{3}\right)^3 = \frac{1}{27}$$

Negative Numbers Raised to a Power

Here's a fact you should already know: When you multiply a negative number by another negative number, you get a positive number, and when you multiply a negative number by a positive number, you get a negative number. Since exponents result in multiplication, a negative number raised to an exponent follows these rules:

- **A negative number raised to an even exponent will be positive.** For example $(-2)^4 = 16$. Why? Because $(-2)^4$ means $-2 \times -2 \times -2 \times -2$. When you multiply the first two −2s together, you get positive 4 because you're multiplying two negative numbers. When you multiply the +4 by the next −2, you get −8, since you're multiplying a positive number by a negative number. Finally, you multiply the −8 by the last −2 and get +16, since you're once again multiplying two negative numbers. The negatives cancel themselves out and vanish.

- **A negative number raised to an odd exponent will be negative.** To see why, just look at the example above, but stop the process at -2^3, which equals −8.

Special Exponents

You need to know a few special types of exponents for the SAT.

Zero

Any base raised to the power of zero is equal to 1. If you see any exponent of the form x^0, you should know that its value is 1. Strange, but true.

One

Any base raised to the power of one is equal to itself: $2^1 = 2$, $-67^1 = -67$ and $x^1 = x$. This fact is important to know when you have to multiply or divide exponential terms with the same base:

$$3x^6 \times x = 3x^6 \times x^1 = 3x^{(6+1)} = 3x^7$$

Negative Exponents

Any number or term raised to a negative power is equal to the reciprocal of that base raised to the opposite power. Uh. Got that? Didn't think so. An example will make it clearer:

$$x^{-5} = \frac{1}{x^5}$$

Here's a more complicated example:

$$\left(\frac{2}{3}\right)^{-3} = \left(\frac{1}{\frac{2}{3}}\right)^3 = \left(\frac{3}{2}\right)^3 = \frac{27}{8}$$

Here's a translation: If you see a base raised to a negative exponent, put the base as the denominator under a numerator of 1 and then drop the negative from the exponent. From there, just simplify.

Fractional Exponents

Exponents can be fractions too. When a number or term is raised to a fractional power, it is called taking the root of that number or term. This expression can be converted into a more convenient form:

$$x^{\left(\frac{a}{b}\right)} = \sqrt[b]{x^a}$$

The $\sqrt{}$ symbol is also known as the radical, and anything under the radical is called the radicand. We've got a whole section devoted to roots and radicals coming right up.

ROOTS AND RADICALS

Here's what you already know: (1) roots express fractional exponents; (2) it's often easier to work with roots by converting them into expressions that look like this:

$$x^{\left(\frac{a}{b}\right)} = \sqrt[b]{x^a}$$

Roots and powers are reciprocals. To square the number 3, multiply 3 by itself: $3^2 = 3 \times 3 = 9$. To get the root of 9, $\sqrt{9}$, you have to find the number that, multiplied by itself, will equal 9. That number is 3.

Square roots appear far more often than any other kind of root on the SAT, but cube roots, fourth roots, fifth roots, and so on could conceivably make an appearance. Each root is represented by a radical sign with the appropriate number next to it (a radical without any superscript denotes a square root). For example, cube roots are shown as $\sqrt[3]{\ }$, fourth roots as $\sqrt[4]{\ }$, and so on. Roots of higher degree operate the same way square roots do. Because $3^3 = 27$, it follows that the cube root of 27 is 3.

Here are a few examples:

$$\sqrt{16} = 4 \text{ because } 4^2 = 16$$
$$\sqrt[4]{81} = 3 \text{ because } 3^4 = 81$$
$$\sqrt{\frac{1}{4}} = \frac{1}{2} \text{ because } \left(\frac{1}{2}\right)^2 = \frac{1}{4}$$
$$\text{If } x^n = y, \text{ then } \sqrt[n]{y} = x$$

Adding and Subtracting Roots

You can't add or subtract roots. You have to work out each root separately and then add. To solve $\sqrt{9} + \sqrt{4} = ?$, *do not* add the 9 and 4 together to get $\sqrt{13}$. Instead, $\sqrt{9} + \sqrt{4} = 3 + 2 = 5$.

The SAT tests if you remember this rule by including trap answers that *do* add or subtract roots.

Multiplying and Dividing Roots

If you're multiplying or dividing two roots, you can multiply or divide the numbers under the root sign as long as the roots are of the same degree. You can multiply or divide two square roots for instance, but you can't multiply a square root and a cube root.

$$\sqrt[n]{x} \times \sqrt[n]{y} = \sqrt[n]{x \times y}$$
$$\sqrt{8} \times \sqrt{2} = \sqrt{8 \times 2} = \sqrt{16} = 4$$

A sequence is a series of numbers that proceed one after another according to some pattern. Here's one:

$$1, 2, 4, 8, 16,...$$

Each number in this sequence doubles the previous number. Once you know the pattern, you can come up with the number after 16, which is 32, the number after that, which is 64, and, if you felt like it, you could keep calculating numbers in the sequence for the rest of your life.

The SAT tests you on three specific types of sequences: arithmetic, geometric, and annoying.

Arithmetic Sequences

An arithmetic sequence is an ordered list of terms in which the difference between consecutive terms is constant. In other words, the same value or variable is added to each term in order to create the next term: If you subtract any two consecutive terms of the sequence, you will get the same difference.[*] An example is 1, 4, 7, 10, 13, ..., where 3 is the constant increment between values.

The notation of an arithmetic sequence is

$$a_n = a_1 + (n-1)d$$

For the SAT, you should be able to do three things with an arithmetic sequence:

1. Find the constant interval between terms.
2. Find any term in the sequence.
3. Calculate the sum of the first n terms.

Finding the Constant Interval (a.k.a., Finding *d*)

To find the constant interval, d, just subtract one term in an arithmetic sequence from the next. For the arithmetic sequence $a_n = 1, 4, 7, 10, 13, ...$, $d = 4 - 1 = 3$.

Okay, now here's a slightly more complicated form of this same d-finding question:

> In an arithmetic sequence, if $a_4 = 4$ and $a_7 = 10$, find d.

This question gives you the fourth and seventh terms of an arithmetic sequence:

$$a_n = a_1, a_2, a_3, 4, a_5, a_6, 10 ...$$

Since in arithmetic sequences d is constant between every term, you know that $a_4 + d = a_5$, $a_5 + d = a_6$, and $a_6 + d = 10$. In other words, the difference between the seventh term, 10, and the fourth term, 4, is $3d$. Stated as an equation,

$$10 = 4 + 3d$$

Now solve it.

$$3d = 6$$
$$d = 2$$

---

[*] This is the one time in the English language when the phrase "same difference" makes sense.

Finding Any Term in the Sequence (a.k.a., Finding the *n*th Term)

Finding the *n*th term is a piece of cake when you have a formula. And we have a formula:

$$a_n = a_1 + (n-1)d$$

where a_n is the *n*th term of the sequence and d is the difference between consecutive terms.

So, to find the 55th term in the arithmetic sequence $a_n = 1, 4, 7, 10, 13, ...,$ plug the values of $a_1 = 1$, $n = 55$, and $d = 3$ into the formula: $a_{55} = 1 + (55 - 1)3 = 1 + 162 = 163$.

Finding the Sum of the First *n* Terms

Finding the sum of the first n terms is also cake-like in its simplicity when you have a formula. And we do:

$$\text{Sum of the first } n \text{ terms} = n\frac{a_1 + a_n}{2}$$

Using the same example, the sum of the first 55 terms would be

$$Sum = 55\left(\frac{1+163}{2}\right) = 55\left(\frac{164}{2}\right) = 55(82) = 4510$$

Geometric Sequences and Exponential Growth

Whereas in an arithmetic sequence the *difference* between consecutive terms is always constant, in a geometric sequence the *quotient* of consecutive terms is always constant. The constant factor by which the terms of a geometric function differ is called the common ratio of the geometric sequence. The common ratio is usually represented by the variable r. Here is an example of a geometric sequence in which $r = 3$.

$$b_x = \frac{1}{3}, 1, 3, 9, 27, 81, \ldots$$

The general form of a geometric sequence is

$$b_x = b_1, b_1r, b_1r^2, b_1r^3, \ldots$$

As with arithmetic sequences, you should be able to perform three tasks on geometric sequences for the SAT:

1. Find r.
2. Find the *n*th term.
3. Calculate the sum of the first n terms.

Finding *r*

To find the common ratio of a geometric sequence, all you have to do is divide one term by the preceding term. For example, the value of r for the sequence 3, 6, 12, 24, ... is $6 \div 3 = 2$.

Finding the *n*th Term

Want to find the *n*th term of a geometric sequence? How about a formula to help you on your quest?

$$b_n = b_1 r^{n-1}$$

Here's the formula in action. The 11th term of the sequence 3, 6, 12, 24, ... is

$$b_{11} = 3(2^{10}) = 3072$$

Finding the Sum of the First *n* Terms

One final formula. To find the sum of the first *n* terms of a geometric sequence, use this one:

$$\text{Sum of the first } n \text{ terms} = b_1 \frac{1 - r^n}{1 - r}$$

So the sum of the first 10 terms of the same sequence is

$$3 \frac{1 - 2^{10}}{1 - 2} = 3069$$

Geometric Sequences and Negative Numbers

A geometric sequence is formed when each term is multiplied by some standard number to get the next phrase. So far we've only dealt with circumstances where that standard number was positive. But it can also be negative. Take a sequence that starts with the number 1 and multiplies each term by –2: 1, –2, 4, –8, 16, –32,... See the pattern? Whenever *r* is negative in a geometric sequence, the terms will alternate between positive and negative.

Annoying Sequences

Annoying sequences is a technical math term that we just made up. We made it up for one reason: These sequences annoy us, and we think they'll annoy you. Notice, though, that we didn't name them devastating sequences, or even difficult sequences. That's because they're neither difficult nor devastating. Just annoying.

In annoying sequences, the SAT makes up the rules. For instance, in the annoying sequence 1, 2, 3, 5, 8, 13, ..., there isn't any standard change between each term, but there is a pattern: after the first two terms, each term is equal to the sum of the previous two terms.

Annoying sequences most commonly show up in problems that ask you to find terms at absurdly high values of *n*. Here's an annoying sequence word problem:

> If the first two terms of a sequence are 1 and 2, and all the following terms in the sequence are produced by subtracting from the previous term the term before that, then what is the fiftieth term in the sequence?

The 50th term? How are you, with your busy life and no magic formula, supposed to write out the sequence until you get to the 50th term? Looks like you'll end up going to college in Siberia.

While Siberia *is* nice for one day each year in July, you don't have to worry. Whenever the SAT asks a question involving an insanely high term in a sequence, there's always a trick to finding it quickly. When the term is in an annoying sequence, the trick is usually a repeating pattern that will make the answer easy to find. So start writing out the sequence and look for the pattern. Once you see it, strike:

$$1, 2, 1, -1, -2, -1, 1, 2, 1, -1,...$$

Do you see the pattern? After six terms, this sequence starts to repeat itself: 1, 2, 1, -1, -2, -1 and then it starts over. So if the sequence repeats every six terms, then every sixth term will be a -1: the sixth term, the 12th term, all the way up to the 48th term. And if you know that the 48th term is a -1 and that the sequence starts over on the 49th, then you know that the 49th term will be a 1 and the 50th term will be a 2.

18.15 SETS

Set is a fancy math word for a group of items. Each item in a set is called an *element* or a *member*. The entire number of Hummers Jay-Z owns is a set, and each of the Hummers is an element of the set. A set contains only those things that can fit its definitions. Jay-Z's Ferraris and BMWs can't be in the set of his Hummers. If you have a set that is defined as $(1, 2, \sqrt{7})$, then the only things that can be in that set are $(1, 2, \sqrt{7})$.

Union and Intersection

The union of two sets is a set containing each element found in either set. If set A contains all the birds in the world, and set B contains all the fish in the world, then the union of those sets contains all the birds and all the fish in the world. If set A = (1, 6, 7, 8, 11, 13) and set B = (2, 4, 5, 8), then the union of set A and B is (1, 2, 4, 5, 6, 7, 8, 8, 11, 13).

The intersection of two sets are the elements common to each set. The intersection of the set that contains all the fish in the world with the set that contains all the birds in the world is an empty set ( ), because there are no animals that are both fish and birds. The intersection of set A = (1, 6, 7, 8, 11, 13) and set B = (2, 4, 5, 8) is (8), since both set A and set B contain an 8.

The Difficult Set Question

One particular type of set question almost always comes up on the SAT, and just as often throws students for a loop. In this type of question, the SAT describes two sets and a few people or things that fit into both sets. Then it asks how many total are in the two sets.

> Of the lions at the zoo, 13 eat zebra meat, 11 eat giraffe meat, and 7 eat both. How many lions are there in the zoo?

This question just *feels* hard. Lots of students who haven't read this book will skip it. But you have read this book, and you'll know the (surprisingly simple) formula for getting it right:

Total = number in set 1 + number in set 2 - number common to set 1 and 2

Once you know the formula, all you have to do is figure out which numbers in the word problem define set 1, which define set 2, and which define the overlap set. After that, just plug in the numbers and do some simple addition and subtraction. So how many lions are there in the zoo?

Total lions = 13 zebra eaters + 11 giraffe eaters − 7 eaters of both

Total Lions = 13 + 11 − 7 = 17

That's it for Numbers and Operations. Ready for SAT algebra? You bet you are.

ALGEBRA

THE BIGGEST CHANGE IN THE SAT MATH SECTION (besides the elimination of Quantitative Comparisons) is its increased focus on algebra. The new SAT covers more algebra, and in greater depth.

There is some silver lining to this dark cloud. First, the topics covered aren't that advanced: If you've taken three years of high school math, you should be familiar with them. Second, reading this chapter will prepare you for any algebra the new SAT throws at you.

19.1 TO ALGEBRA OR NOT TO ALGEBRA?

When faced with an algebra question on the SAT, you could, as you might expect, try to solve it by using standard algebra—setting up and working out the equation. But there are often alternative ways to attack. You might be able to plug the answer choices back into the question until one of them works out. You could pick numbers to substitute into the various expressions given as answer choices.

For problems you know how to solve, using algebra is probably the quickest method. In contrast, a problem that's giving you trouble may suddenly become much easier if you start plugging in numbers.

We're not telling you to pick just one method and always use it. Far from it. Flexibility is the key. Some methods work for some problems, and others work better with others. When you study your practice tests and look over the algebra questions you got wrong, think about more than just what the right answer was. Ask yourself if you approached the question correctly. Did you plug in answers when you should have used algebra? Did you use algebra when plugging in answers would have simplified the problem?

Here's an example of an algebra question. We solve it using each of the different problem-solving methods, explaining what you need to know about each one in the process.

A man flipped a coin 162 times. The coin landed with heads side up 62 more times than it landed with tails up. How many times did the coin land on heads?

(A)   100
(B)   104
(C)   108
(D)   112
(E)   116

Solving by Algebra

To answer this problem with algebra, you first have to translate it into algebra. You have to set up an equation. If you assign the variable x to stand for the number of times the coin landed on heads, then tails are represented by $x - 62$, since the coin landed on heads 62 times more times than it landed on tails. And since the coin was thrown 162 total times,

$$x + (x - 62) = 162$$
$$2x - 62 = 162$$
$$2x = 224$$
$$x = 112$$

As you can see, setting up the question takes a little bit of time and knowledge, but once you've set it up, the math is quick and easy.

Using algebra will only take you longer than plugging in if you have trouble coming up with the equation $x + (x - 62) = 162$. So here's a quick rule of thumb to help you decide whether to use algebra or to plug in: If you can quickly come up with the equation, then use algebra to solve algebra problems. If you have the sense that it will take you a while to figure out the equation, then plug in.

Solving by Plugging In

There are two ways to plug in: intelligently and maniacally. Don't be a maniac. How can you avoid this? Simple. The answer choices on the SAT that contain numbers (rather than variables) always appear in either ascending or descending order. The first answer choice will be the lowest and the last will be the largest, or vice versa.

Let's say the answer choices are in ascending order. If you start by plugging in the middle number, the answer choice for answer **C**, then even if that choice doesn't work, you can use the outcome to determine whether you need to plug in a smaller or larger number. If you need a smaller number, move to answer choice **B**. If you need a larger number, try **D**. If you follow this method, instead of having to check all five answer choices, you shouldn't ever have to check more than three. That'll save you time. $(5 - 3) / 5 \times 100 = 40\%$ of your time, to be exact.

To answer the coin-flip problem by plugging in, pick **C**, 108, as the first number to try. So, if the coin came up heads 108 times, then how many times did it land on tails? It landed on tails $162 - 108 = 54$. Are 108 heads 62 more than 54 tails? No: $108 - 54 = 54$. In order for the problem to work out you need more heads. You can eliminate **A** and **B** as possibilities. Choose **D**, 112, as your next plug-in number: $162 - 112 = 50$. Does $112 - 50 = 62$? Yes.

Picking Numbers

Picking numbers is a variation of plugging in. It should *only be used* when the answer choices contain variables. A modified version of our original sample question shows what kind of problem lends itself to picking numbers.

> A man flipped a coin z times. The coin landed on heads y more times than it landed on tails. If the number of times the coin landed heads is h, then, in terms of h and y, how many times was the coin flipped?
>
> (A) $z = h + y$
>
> (B) $z = h - y$
>
> (C) $z = \dfrac{h}{y}$
>
> (D) $z = 2h - y$
>
> (E) $z = \dfrac{2h}{y}$

Instead of testing your ability to set up and solve an equation, this question asks you only to set up an equation based on a word problem. While using algebra to set up the equation would be the faster tactic, for some people, thinking in terms of variables can be confusing. Picking numbers allows you to transform variables into concrete numbers.

To use the picking numbers method, select numbers and plug them into the answer choices. It doesn't matter what specific numbers you pick for each variable as long as you always plug the same number in for each variable and follow all guidelines given by the problem.

In the coin-flip problem, you are given three variables, z, y, and h. The question asks you to find z in terms of h and y. We'll pick some numbers. Let's say the coin landed on heads (h) 5 times, and that it landed on heads on 2 more flips (y) than it landed on tails. That would mean that the coin landed on tails 3 times, since $5 - 2 = 3$. Since the coin landed on heads on 5 flips, and on tails on 3 flips, the coin must have been flipped a total of $5 + 3 = 8$ times. Now plug 5 for h and 2 for y into all the equations and see which one comes out to 8: only **D**, which is the right answer.

In addition to giving you a method for solving tricky problems, picking numbers is also a good way to check your math for careless calculations.

Solving by Being an Amazing Genius

It's quite possible that you just looked at this problem and said to yourself, "Other than the 62 more heads, all the other flips were equally heads and tails. So: If I take the 62 out of the total of 162, then I know that the other 100 flips were 50 heads and 50 tails. Now I can just add 62 + 50 = 112. Man, I am an amazing genius!"

Yes, you are. No one knows how to teach other people how to be an amazing genius, though, and you can rest assured that almost no one taking the test will be an amazing genius on every question.

The moral of the story: Know that amazing-genius shortcuts exist, and keep a lookout for them, but don't stress over them. Only a fool would waste time looking for shortcuts. And you're no fool.

Algebra: The Bottom Line

There isn't any "right way" to answer an SAT algebra question. Some methods work best for some types of questions, and others for others. The best way to learn which methods work best for you is to take and study practice tests.

19.2 A VERY SHORT ALGEBRA GLOSSARY

There are six basic algebra terms you need to know for the SAT. You also need to know these terms to understand what we're talking about in this section of the book.

Constant. A quantity that does not change. A number.

Variable. An unknown quantity written as a letter. A variable can be represented by any letter in the English alphabet, most often x or y. Variables may be associated with specific things, like x number of apples or y dollars. Other times, variables have no specific association, but you'll need to manipulate them to show that you understand certain algebraic principles.

Coefficient. A coefficient is a number that appears next to a variable and tells how many of the variable there are. In the term $4x$, 4 is the coefficient.

Equation. Two expressions linked by an equal sign. Most of the algebra on the SAT consists of solving equations.

Term. The product of a constant and a variable. Or, a quantity separated from other quantities by addition or subtraction. For example, in the equation

$$3x^3 + 2x^2 - 7x + 4 = x - 1$$

the side to the left of the equal sign contains four terms $\{3x^3, 2x^2, -7x, 4\}$, while the right side contains two terms $\{x, -1\}$. (The constants, 4 and –1, are considered terms because they are coefficients of variables raised to the zero power: $4 = 4x^0$.) So every term, including constants, is the product of a constant and a variable raised to some power.

Expression. Any combination of terms. An expression can be as simple as a single constant term, like 5, or as complicated as the sum or difference of many terms, each of which is a combination of constants and variables, such as $\{(x^2 + 2)^3 - 6x\} / 7x^5$. Expressions don't include an equal sign—this is what differentiates expressions from equations. Expressions cannot be solved; they can only be simplified.

SUBSTITUTION QUESTIONS

We like substitution questions. Not because they have great personalities and a really good sense of humor. We love 'em because they're easy. They almost aren't algebra at all. Substitutions give you an algebraic equation and then tell you the value of the variable. Just plug in that variable and work out the answer.

> If $2y + 8x = 11$, what is the value of $3(2y + 8x)$?

You might see this equation bubbling over with variables and panic. Don't. It's simple. Since the question states that $2y + 8x = 11$, and you're looking for the value of $3(2y + 8x)$, all you have to do is substitute 11 for $2y + 8x$ in the expression, and you get $3(11) = 33$.

Not many substitution questions on the SAT are this simple, though. For more complicated substitution questions, you'll have to do some extra math either before or after the substitution.

Math Before Substitution

> If $3x - 7 = 8$, then $23 - 3x = ?$

In this problem, you have to find what $3x$ equals before you can substitute that value into the expression $23 - 3x$. To find $3x$, take that first equation,

$$3x - 7 = 8$$

and add 7 to both sides, giving

$$3x = 15$$

Now substitute that 15 into $23 - 3x$:

$$23 - 15 = 8$$

Math After Substitution

> If $a + b = 7$ and $b = 3$, then $4a = ?$

In this question, you have to plug the value for b into $a + b = 7$ in order to find a:

$$a + b = 7$$
$$a + 3 = 7$$
$$a = 4$$

Once you know that $a = 4$, just substitute into $4a$:

$$4 \times 4 = 16$$

For substitution questions in which you have to plug in values in more than one stage, make sure you work out that last substitution. When you're taking the SAT under real time pressure, you may be so consumed with getting to the next question that, for instance, you solve for $a = 4$ but then forget to substitute that value into $4a$. SAT traps are waiting for you to do just that. Recognize that 4 is an imposter answer and defeat them.

Multiple Substitutions

There's another type of substitution problem on the SAT that you'll probably have to deal with: multiple substitutions. On these questions, you have to do more than one substitution. For instance,

If $z = \dfrac{4y}{x^2}$, $y = 3x$, and $x = 2$, then what is the value of z?

To approach this problem, you just have to substitute 2 for x to find y, and then substitute those values into the equation for z. Substituting 2 for x into $y = 3x$ gives $y = 3(2) = 6$. Substituting for y and x in the equation for z, gives

$$z = \frac{4y}{x^2} = \frac{4(6)}{2^2} = \frac{24}{4} = 6$$

19.4 SOLVING EQUATIONS

To solve an equation, you have to isolate the variable you're solving for. You have to "manipulate" the equation until you get the variable alone on one side of the equal sign. By definition, the variable is then equal to everything on the other side of the equal sign. You've just solved for the variable. Congratulations.

The Fine Art of Manipulation

You can't manipulate an equation the way you manipulate your little brother or sister. When manipulating equations, there are rules. Here's the first and most fundamental (it's so important we're going to bold it): **Whatever you do to one side of an equation, you must do to the other side.** If you divide one side of an equation by 3, divide the other side by 3. If you take the square root of one side of an equation, take the square root of the other. If you fall in love with one side of the equation, fall in love with the other. Neither side will think you're a two-timer. They'll think you're a highly skilled mathematician.

By treating the two sides of the equation in the same way, you don't change what the equation means. You change the *form* of the equation—that's the point of manipulating it—but the equation remains true since both sides stay equal.

Take, for instance, the equation $3x + 2 = 5$. You can do anything you want to it, anything at all, and as long as you do that thing to both sides of the equation, x will always equal 1. For example, if you subtract 2 from both sides,

$$3x + 2 - 2 = 5 - 2$$

$$3x = 3$$

$$x = 1$$

And if you multiply both sides by 2,

$$2(3x + 2) = 2(5)$$

$$6x + 4 = 10$$

$$6x = 6$$

$$x = 1$$

In addition to the "do the same things to both sides of the equation" rule that you must follow, there are other rules of manipulation that you *should* follow. Nothing will go horribly wrong if you don't follow them, but it will take you longer to solve the question. Here are the rules:

1. Combine like terms to make the equation simpler.
2. Manipulate the equation in the reverse order of operations.

The second rule means that you should first subtract or add any extra terms on the same side as the variable. Then divide and multiply anything on the same side as the variable. Next, raise both sides of the equation to a power or take their roots according to any exponent attached to the variable. Finally, work out anything inside parentheses. Do the order of operations backward: SADMEP! The idea is to "undo" everything that has been done to the variable so that it will be isolated in the end. Example time:

$$2 + \frac{3(2\sqrt{x} + 3)}{2} = 17$$

In this equation, poor little x is being square rooted, multiplied by 2, added to 3, and encased in parentheses. You've got to get him out of there! Undo all of these operations in order to liberate x.

First, subtract 2 from both sides of the equation:

$$\frac{3(2\sqrt{x} + 3)}{2} = 15$$

Then multiply both sides by 2 to get rid of the fraction:

$$3(2\sqrt{x} + 3) = 30$$

Now divide both sides by 3 (later, parentheses):

$$2\sqrt{x} + 3 = 10$$

Subtract 3 from each side:

$$2\sqrt{x} = 7$$

Divide both sides by 2:

$$\sqrt{x} = \frac{7}{2}$$

And, finally, square each side to get rid of the square root:

$$x = \frac{49}{4}$$

Success! You've freed x from all of those bullying operations.

Location. Location. Location.

Isolating for x is all about where x is located. A variable in the numerator of a fraction is actually a pretty easy location to isolate. But if x is in the denominator of a fraction, things get more complicated.

$$\frac{1}{x+2} + 3 = 7$$

Following SADMEP, start by subtracting the 3:

$$\frac{1}{x+2} = 4$$

But now you have to get the x out of the denominator, and the only way to do that is to multiply both sides of the equation by that denominator, $x + 2$:

$$1 = 4(x+2)$$

Divide both sides by 4:

$$\frac{1}{4} = x + 2$$

Subtract 2 from each side:

$$-\frac{7}{4} = x$$

Simplification Tools

By now you know the rule: When solving an equation, never do something to one side of an equation that you don't do to the other. If you add 4 to one side, you have to add 4 to the other. But what if there were some simplification tools that didn't change the value of an expression? What if you could simplify one side of an equation without changing its value? That would rock. Why? Because it would allow you to make solving equations much simpler and save you time on the SAT.

Distributing

The first step to adding ferocious simplification tools to your arsenal is the rule of distribution, which states

$$a(b+c) = (a \times b) + (a \times c)$$

a can be any kind of term, meaning it could be a variable, a constant, or a combination of the two.

When you distribute a factor into an expression within parentheses, multiply each term inside the parentheses by the factor outside the parentheses. For example, in the previous problem, when you had $1 = 4(x + 2)$, you didn't actually have to divide both sides by 4. You could have distributed the 4 and pushed off all those messy fractions until the end: $1 = 4x + 8$; $4x = -7$; $x = {}^{-7}/_4$. So, if you have the expression $3y(y^2 - 6)$:

$$3y(y^2 - 6) = 3y^3 - 18y$$

Seems logical enough. But the true value of distributing becomes clear when you see a distributable expression in an equation: $3y(y^2 + 6) = 3y^3 + 36$ looks like it'd be hard to solve, since there aren't any equal terms to add or subtract away. But wait a sec . . . what if you distribute that $3y$?

$$3y^3 + 18y = 3y^3 + 36$$

Shocking revelation! It's suddenly clear that you can subtract $3y^3$ from both sides:

$$18y = 36$$
$$y = 2$$

Factoring

Factoring an expression is the opposite of distributing. $4x^3 - 8x^2$ is one mean-looking expression. Or so it seems, until you realize that all the terms share the greatest common factor $4x^2$, which you can factor out:

$$4x^3 - 8x^2 = 4x^2(x - 2)$$

With distributing and factoring, you can group or ungroup quantities in an equation to make your calculations simpler. Here are a few more examples:

$$
\begin{aligned}
3(x + y + 4) &= 3x + 3y + 12 & &3 \text{ is distributed.} \\
2x + 4x + 6x + 8x &= 2x(1 + 2 + 3 + 4) & &2x \text{ is factored out.} \\
x^2(x - 1) &= x^3 - x^2 & &x^2 \text{ is distributed.} \\
xy^2(xy^2 + x^2y) &= x^2y^4 + x^3y^3 & &xy^2 \text{ is distributed.} \\
14xy^2 - 4xy + 22y &= 2y(7xy - 2x + 11) & &2y \text{ is factored out.}
\end{aligned}
$$

Combining Like Terms

After factoring and distributing, you can take additional steps to simplify expressions or equations. Combining like terms is one of the simplest techniques you can use. It involves adding or subtracting the coefficients of variables that are raised to the same power. For example, by combining like terms, the expression

$$x^2 - x^3 + 4x^2 + 3x^3$$

can be simplified by adding the coefficients of the variable x^3 (-1 and 3) together and the coefficients of x^2 (1 and 4) together:

$$2x^3 + 5x^2$$

Variables that have *different* exponential values are *not* like terms and can't be combined. Two terms that do not share a variable are also not like terms and cannot be combined regardless of their exponential value.

$$You\ can't\ combine:\ x^4 + x^2 =$$
$$y^2 + x^2 =$$

19.5 ALGEBRA, ABSOLUTE VALUE, AND EXPONENTS

The new SAT puts more emphasis on subjects from Algebra II. In part, this means that the test asks more algebra questions that include absolute value, radicals, and exponents. All three mathematical concepts add certain complications to solving algebra equations.

Algebra and |Absolute Value|

To solve an equation in which the variable is within absolute value brackets, you have to follow a two-step process:

1. Isolate the expression within the absolute value brackets.
2. Divide the equation into two.

Divide the equation in two? What? Watch:

$$|x + 3| = 5.\ Solve\ for\ x.$$

Since $x + 3$ has absolute value brackets around it, for the expression to equal 5, the expresion $x + 3$ when outside of the absolute value brackets can equal either $+5$ or -5. So you're actually dealing with two equations:

$$x + 3 = 5$$
$$x + 3 = -5$$

To solve the problem, you need to solve both of them. First, solve for x in the equation $x + 3 = 5$. In this case, $x = 2$. Then, solve for x in the equation $x + 3 = -5$. In this case, $x = -8$. So the solutions to the equation $|x + 3| = 5$ are $x = \{-8, 2\}$.

Here's another example with a much more complicated equation:

Solve for x in terms of y in the equation $3\left|\dfrac{x+2}{3}\right| = y^2 - 1$.

First, isolate the expression within the absolute value brackets:

$$\left|\frac{x+2}{3}\right| = \frac{y^2 - 1}{3}$$

Remember that in terms of PEMDAS, absolute value brackets are like parentheses—do the math inside them first. So solve for the variable as if the expression within absolute value brackets were positive:

$$\frac{x+2}{3} = \frac{y^2-1}{3}$$

Multiply both sides of the equation by 3:

$$x + 2 = y^2 - 1$$

Subtract 2 from both sides:

$$x = y^2 - 3$$

Next, solve for the variable as if the expression within absolute value brackets were negative:

$$\frac{x+2}{3} = -\frac{y^2-1}{3}$$

Multiply both sides of the equation by 3:

$$x + 2 = -(y^2 - 1)$$

Distribute the negative sign (crucial step, make sure you do this or you'll fall into a trap!):

$$x + 2 = -y^2 + 1$$

Subtract 2 from both sides:

$$x = -y^2 - 1$$

The solution set for x is $\{y^2 - 3, -y^2 - 1\}$.

Algebra, Exponents, and Radicals

Exponents and radicals can have devilish effects on algebraic equations that are similar to those caused by absolute value.

Consider the equation $x^2 = 25$. Seems pretty simple, right? Just take the square root of both sides and you end up with $x = 5$. But remember the rule of multiplying negative numbers?

When two negative numbers are multiplied together the result is a positive. In other words, -5 squared also results in 25: $-5 \times -5 = 25$.

This means that whenever you have to take the square root to simplify a variable brought to the second power, the result will be *two* solutions, one positive and one negative: $\sqrt{x^2} = \pm x$. The only exception is if $x = 0$.

Want an example?

If $2x^2 = 72$, then what is the value of x?

To solve this problem, you first simplify the problem by dividing 2 out of both sides: $x^2 = 36$. Now you need to take the square root of both sides: $x = \pm 6$.

BEAT THE SYSTEM (OF EQUATIONS)

So you're kicking butt and taking names on those old one-variable equations, huh? Good. But some SAT questions contain two variables. Lucky for you, those questions also always contain two equations, and you can use the two equations in conjunction to solve the variables. These two equations together are called a system of equations. We said earlier that manipulating equations isn't like manipulating your younger brother or sister. But solving systems of equations *is* like manipulating your younger brother and sister. You use one equation against the other, and in the end you get whatever you want.

There are two types of systems of equations that you'll need to be able to solve for the SAT. The first, easier model involves substitution, and the second type involves manipulating equations simultaneously.

Substituting into the System

You know substitution: Find the value of one variable and then plug that into another equation to solve for a different variable.

If $x - 4 = y - 3$ and $2y = 6$, what is x?

You've got two equations and you have to find x. The first equation contains both x and y. The second equation contains only y. To solve for x, you first have to solve for y in the second equation and substitute that value for y in the first equation. If $2y = 6$, then $y = 3$. Now, substitute 3 in for y in $x - 4 = y - 3$:

$$x - 4 = 3 - 3$$

$$x - 4 = 0$$

$$x = 4$$

Here's one that's more likely to give you trouble on the SAT:

Suppose $3x = y + 5$ and $2y - 2 = 12k$. Solve for x in terms of k.

In order to solve for x in terms of k, you have to first get x and k into the same equation. To make this happen, you can solve for y in terms of k in the second equation, and then substitute that value into the first equation to solve for x. (You could also solve this problem by solving for y in the first equation and substituting that expression in for y in the second equation.)

$$2y - 2 = 12k$$
$$2y = 12k + 2$$
$$y = 6k + 1$$

Then substitute $y = 6k + 1$ into the equation $3x = y + 5$.

$$3x = y + 5$$
$$3x = (6k + 1) + 5$$
$$3x = 6k + 6$$
$$x = 2k + 2$$

Solving Simultaneous Equations

Simultaneous equations are equations that both contain the same variables. You can use the equations to solve for the variables by using one of the equations to solve for one variable in terms of the other, and then substituting that expression into the other equation.

Suppose $2x + 3y = 5$ and $x + y = 7$. What is x?

In this particular problem, you need to find x. But in order to find the value of x, you need to get that pesky y variable out of one of the equations, right? Here's how to do it. First solve one of the equations for y in terms of x:

$$x + y = 7$$

$$y = 7 - x$$

Now substitute $7 - x$ for y in the equation $2x + 3y = 5$:

$$2x + 3(7 - x) = 5$$

$$2x + 21 - 3x = 5$$

$$-x = -16$$

$$x = 16$$

Here's what just happened. You manipulated one equation to separate the two variables on either side of the equal sign. Then you substituted one side of that equal sign into the other equation so that only the variable whose value you had to find was left. Bold move!

Another Way to Solve Simultaneous Equations

So that's how you can solve every simultaneous equation question on the SAT. But wait! There's another, even faster way to solve simultaneous equations.

Some students find this method tricky, but it is definitely faster, and it works. The choice of which method to use is up to you. Take a look at the following question:

$2x + 3y = 5$ and $-1x - 3y = -7$. What is x?

The amazing thing about simultaneous equations is that you can actually add or subtract the entire equations from each other. Observe:

$$\begin{array}{r} 2x + 3y = 5 \\ +(-1x) - 3y = -7 \\ \hline x = -2 \end{array}$$

Here's another example:

$6x + 2y = 11$ and $5x + y = 10$. What is $x + y$?

By subtracting the second equation from the first,

$$6x + 2y = 11$$
$$\underline{-(5x + y = 10)}$$
$$x + y = 1$$

In order to add or subtract simultaneous equations, you need to know what variable you want to solve for, and then add or subtract accordingly. But we've got to admit something: So far, we've purposely chosen very easy examples to show how this method works. You won't always have two equations that you can immediately add or subtract from each other to isolate one variable:

$2x + 3y = -6$ and $-4x + 16y = 13$. What is the value of y?

You're asked to solve for y, which means you've got to get rid of x. But how can you get rid of x if one equation has $2x$ and the other has $-4x$? Well, you can't. But remember, you can change the form of the equation without changing the actual equation, as long as you do the same thing to both sides of the equation. For instance, you could multiply both sides of $2x + 3y = -6$ by 2, which would give you

$$2(2x + 3y) = 2(-6)$$

$$4x + 6y = -12$$

You can add this equation to $-4x + 16y = 13$ to isolate y.

$$4x + 6y = -12$$
$$\underline{+(-4x) + 16y = 13}$$
$$22y = 1$$
$$y = \frac{1}{22}$$

On the SAT, you will almost always be able to manipulate one of the two equations in a pair of simultaneous equations so that they can be added and subtracted to isolate the variable you want. The question is whether you can see how to do it. Our recommendation? Since it's faster, it always pays to take a second to try to see how to isolate the variable by adding or subtracting the equations. If you can't, then go ahead and solve the simultaneous equations using the first method we described.

19.7 INEQUALITIES

Life isn't always fair. That's why there are inequalities. An inequality is like an equation, but instead of relating equal quantities, it specifies exactly how two quantities are *not* equal. There are four types of inequalities:

1. $x > y$ — x is greater than y
2. $x < y$ — x is less than y
3. $x \geq y$ — x is greater than or equal to y
4. $x \leq y$ — x is less than or equal to y

Solving inequalities is exactly like solving equations except for one very important difference: **When both sides of an inequality are multiplied or divided by a negative number, the direction of the inequality switches.**

Here are a few examples:

$$\frac{x}{2} - 3 < 2y$$
$$\frac{x}{2} < 2y + 3$$
$$x < 2(2y + 3)$$
$$x < 4y + 6$$

$$\frac{4}{x} \geq -2$$
$$4 \geq -2x$$
$$-2 \leq x$$

Notice that in the last example the inequality had to be flipped, since both sides had to be divided by –2 between the second and third steps.

To help remember that multiplication or division by a negative number reverses the direction of the inequality, remember that if $x > y$, then $-x < -y$, just as $5 > 4$ and $-5 < -4$. The larger the number, the harder it falls (or the smaller it becomes when you make it negative).

Ranges

Inequalities are also used to express the range of values that a variable can take. $a < x < b$ means that the value of x is greater than a and less than b. Consider the following word problem:

A company manufactures car parts. As is the case with any system of mass production, small errors in production of every part occur. To make viable car parts, the company must make sure the unavoidable errors occur only within a specific range. The company knows that a particular part they manufacture will not work if it weighs less than 98% of its target weight or more than 102% of its target weight. If the target weight of this piece is 20.5 grams, what is the range of weights the part must fall within for it to function?

The car part must weigh between $.98 \times 21.5 = 21.07$ grams and $1.02 \times 21.5 = 21.93$ grams. The problem states that the part cannot weigh *less* than the minimum weight or *more* than the maximum weight in order for it to work. This means that the part will function at boundary weights themselves, and the lower and upper bounds are included. The answer to the problem is $21.07 \leq x \leq 21.93$, where x is the weight of the part in grams.

Finding the range of a particular variable is essentially an exercise in close reading. Every time you come across a question involving ranges, you should carefully peruse the problem to pick out whether or not a particular variable's range includes its bounds. This inclusion is the difference between "less than or equal to" ($\leq$) and simply "less than" ($<$).

Operations on Ranges

Ranges can be added, subtracted, or multiplied.

If $4 < x < 7$, what is the range of $2x + 3$?

To solve this problem, simply manipulate the range like an inequality until you have a solution. Begin with the original range:

$$4 < x < 7$$

Multiply the inequality by 2:

$$8 < 2x < 14$$

Add 3 to the inequality, and you have the answer:

$$11 < 2x + 3 < 17$$

And always remember the crucial rule about multiplying inequalities: If you multiply a range by a negative number, you *must* flip the greater-than or less-than signs. If you multiply the range $2 < x < 8$ by –1, the new range will be $-2 > -x > -8$.

Absolute Value and Inequalities

Absolute values do the same thing to inequalities that they do to equations. You have to split the inequality into two equations and solve for each. This can result in solutions to inequalities in which the variable falls between two values (as in a range) or a combination of two "disjointed ranges."

Single Range

If the absolute value is less than a given quantity, then the solution is a single range with a lower and an upper bound. An example of a single range would be the numbers between –5 and 5, as seen in the number line below:

On the SAT, you'll most likely be asked to deal with single ranges in the following way:

Solve for x in the inequality $|2x - 4| \le 6$.

First, split the inequality into two. Remember to flip around the inequality sign when you write out the inequality for the negative number.

$$2x - 4 \le 6$$

$$2x - 4 \ge -6$$

Solve the first:

$$2x - 4 \leq 6$$
$$2x \leq 10$$
$$x \leq 5$$

Then solve the second:

$$2x - 4 \geq -6$$
$$2x \geq -2$$
$$x \geq -1$$

So x is greater than or equal to –1 and less than or equal to 5. In other words, x lies between those two values. So you can write out the value of x in a single range, $-1 \leq x \leq 5$.

Disjointed Ranges

You won't always find that the value of the variable lies between two numbers. Instead, you may find that the solution is actually two separate ranges: one whose lower bound is negative infinity and whose upper bound is a real number, and one whose lower bound is a real number and whose upper bound is infinity. Yeah, words make it sound confusing. A number line will make it clearer.

An example of a disjointed range would be all the numbers smaller than –5 and larger than 5, as shown below:

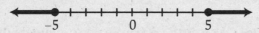

On the SAT, disjointed ranges come up on problems like the following:

Solve for x in the inequality $|3x + 4| > 16$.

You know the drill. Split 'er up, then solve each part:

$$3x + 4 > 16$$

$$3x + 4 < -16$$

Solving the first part:

$$3x + 4 > 16$$
$$3x > 12$$
$$x > 4$$

And the second:

$$3x + 4 < -16$$
$$3x < -20$$
$$x < -\frac{20}{3}$$

Notice, though, that x is greater than the positive number and smaller than the negative number. In other words, the possible values of x don't lie *between* the two numbers, they lie *outside* the two numbers. So you need two separate ranges to show the possible values of x: $-\infty < x < -20/3$ and $4 < x < \infty$.

19.8 BINOMIALS AND QUADRATIC EQUATIONS

With its new emphasis on Algebra II, the new SAT asks quite a few more questions on binomials. What is a binomial? Quite simply, it is an expression that has two terms: $x + 5$ and $x^2 - 6$ are both binomials.

Multiplying Binomials

The multiplication of binomials is its own SAT topic and a fundamental skill for dealing with the dreaded quadratic equations. Luckily, the best acronym ever made (other than SCUBA) will help you remember how to multiply binomials. This acronym is **FOIL**, and it stands for **F**irst, **O**uter + **I**nner, **L**ast. The acronym tells you the order in which you multiply the terms of two binomials to get the correct product.

For example, let's say you were kidnapped by wretched fork-tongued lizard-men whose only weakness was binomials. Now what if the lizard-king asked to you to multiply the binomials:

$$(x + 1)(x + 3)$$

What would you do? Follow FOIL, of course. First, multiply the first terms of each binomial:

$$x \times x = x^2$$

Next, multiply the outer terms of the binomials:

$$x \times 3 = 3x$$

Then, multiply the inner terms:

$$1 \times x = x$$

And multiply the last terms:

$$1 \times 3 = 3$$

Add all these terms together:

$$x^2 + 3x + x + 3$$

Finally, combine like terms, and you get

$$x^2 + 4x + 3$$

Here are a few more examples of multiplied binomials to use to test yourself.

$$(y + 3)(y - 7) = y^2 - 7y + 3y - 21 = y^2 - 4y - 21$$
$$(-x + 2)(4x + 6) = -4x^2 - 6x + 8x + 12 = -4x^2 + 2x + 12$$
$$(3a + 2b)(6c - d) = 18ac - 3ad + 12bc - 2bd$$

Quadratic Equations

Quadratics are the robots who return from the future to destroy humankind at the end of *Terminator 3*. Well, the future is now: The new SAT forces you to take on quadratic equations. But the future also isn't that tough. Here's the first thing: A quadratic expression takes the form $ax^2 + bx + c$, where $a \neq 0$. And here's the second: Note how closely $ax^2 + bx + c$ resembles the products formed when binomials are multiplied. Coincidence? Fat chance.

A quadratic equation sets a quadratic equal to zero: $ax^2 + bx + c = 0$. The values of x for which the equation holds are called the roots, or solutions, of the quadratic equation. Some of the SAT questions on quadratic equations ask you to find their roots.

There are two basic ways to find roots: by factoring and by using the quadratic formula. Factoring is faster, but doesn't always work. The quadratic formula takes longer to work out, but works on every quadratic equation.

On the SAT, you'll be able to factor almost every quadratic expression or equation that appears, but every once in a while the test may throw in a quadratic that you need to know the quadratic formula to solve. In other words, you probably don't need to know the quadratic formula, and if you're pressed for time you could survive if you didn't spend time studying it. But if you want to slam dunk the new SAT, memorize it.

Factoring Quadratics

Here's why quadratic expressions resemble the product of two binomials: Quadratic expressions *are* the product of two binomials. Factoring a quadratic means breaking the quadratic back into its binomial parts. Factoring might as well be called LIOF; it's FOIL in reverse. Check out this quadratic expression:

$$x^2 + 10x + 21$$

For starters, you know that the binomials have the form $(x + m)(x + n)$, where m and n are constants. How do you know this? Because of that x^2. When you FOIL to get the first term, you multiply the two first terms of the binomials. To get x^2, you have to multiply x by x. As for figuring out what m and n are, you have two clues to work with.

1. The sum of m and n is 10, since the $10x$ is derived from multiplying the OUTER and INNER terms of the binomials and then adding the resulting terms together ($10x = mx + nx$, so $m + n$ must equal 10).

2. The product of m and n equals 21, since 21 is the product of the two last terms of the binomials. The only pair of numbers that fit the bill for m and n are 3 and 7 ($3 + 7 = 10$ and $3 \times 7 = 21$), so $x^2 + 10x + 21 = (x + 3)(x + 7)$.

But what if this had been a quadratic *equation* rather than a plain old quadratic expression? Well, first of all, it would have looked like this: $x^2 + 10x + 21 = 0$. Second, once you'd factored it to get $(x + 3)(x + 7) = 0$, you could solve for its roots. Because the product of two terms is zero, one of the terms must be equal to zero. Since $x + 3 = 0$ or $x + 7 = 0$, the solutions (also known as the roots) of the quadratic must be $x = -3$ and $x = -7$.

Quadratics with Negative Terms

Once you get the hang of it, factoring a quadratic with negative terms is no harder than dealing with one with only positive terms.

Consider the quadratic equation $x^2 - 4x - 21 = 0$. Here's what we know about this equation: The first term of each binomial is x, since the first term of the quadratic is x^2; the product of m and n is -21; and the sum of a and b equals -4. The equation also tells you that either m or n must be negative, but that *both* cannot be negative, because only the multiplication of one positive and one negative number can result in a negative number. Now you need to look for the numbers that fit these requirements for m and n. The numbers that multiply together to give you -21 are -21 and 1, -7 and 3, -3 and 7, and 21 and -1. Of these, the pair that sums to -4 is -7 and 3. The factoring of the equation is $(x - 7)(x + 3) = 0$. So the roots of the equation are $x = 7$ and $x = -3$.

Two Special Quadratics

There are two special quadratics that pop up all the time on the SAT. If you know what they look like and can identify them quickly, you'll save time. These two quadratics are called the "perfect square" and the "difference of two squares."

Perfect square quadratics are the product of a term squared (multiplied by itself). There are therefore two kinds of perfect square quadratics: those formed by the squaring of a binomial of the form $(a + b)^2$ and those formed by the squaring of binomials that look like $(a - b)^2$.

---

1. $a^2 + 2ab + b^2 = (a + b)(a + b) = (a + b)^2$

Example: $a^2 + 6ab + 9 = (a + 3)^2$

---

2. $a^2 - 2ab + b^2 = (a - b)(a - b) = (a - b)^2$

Example: $a^2 - 6ab + 9 = (a - 3)^2$

Note that when you solve for the roots of a perfect square quadratic equation, the solution for the equation $(a + b)^2 = 0$ will be $-b$, while the solution for $(a + b)^2 = 0$ will be b.

The difference of two-squares quadratic equations follow the form below:

$$(a + b)(a - b) = a^2 - b^2$$
$$\text{Example: } (a + 3)(a - 3) = a^2 - 9$$

See how the middle term drops out? The disappearance of the middle term causes lots of students to fail to recognize when they're dealing with a difference of two-squares quadratic.

Practice Quadratics

Since the ability to factor quadratics relies in large part on your ability to "read" the information in the quadratic, the best way to sharpen your eye is to practice, practice, practice. Take a look at the following examples and try to factor them on your own before you peek at the answers.

$$x^2 + x - 2 = 0 \qquad \text{Roots}: \{-2, 1\}$$
$(x + 2)(x - 1)$

$$x^2 + 13x + 42 = 0 \qquad \text{Roots}: \{-7, -6\}$$
$(x + 7)(x + 6)$

$$x^2 - 8x + 15 = 0 \qquad \text{Roots}: \{3, 5\}$$
$(x - 3)(x - 5)$

$$x^2 - 5x - 36 = 0 \qquad \text{Roots}: \{-4, 9\}$$
$(x - 9)(x + 4)$

$$x^2 - 10x + 25 = 0 \qquad \text{Roots}: \{5\}$$
$(x - 5)(x - 5)$

$$x^2 - 25 = 0 \qquad \text{Roots}: \{5, -5\}$$
$(x - 5)(x + 5)$

19.9 VARIATION

One way that the new SAT tests whether you understand an equation is to ask questions about the relationship between certain variables. For example,

If z triples while x doubles, what happens to y?

$$y = \frac{x}{z}$$

The easiest way to solve such problems is to just plug in:

$$y = \frac{2x}{3z}$$

So the value of y will be $^2/_3$ of what it was.

Essentially, these sorts of problems are testing to see if you understand how an equation works and how different variables interact. While in a simple equation like the first example, this is easy to see, it becomes a little more complicated as the equations get more complex:

If z triples while x doubles, what happens to y?

$$y = \frac{x^3}{2z}$$

Once again, you can still find the answer by plugging in $2x$ for x and $3z$ for z. You just have to do some additional math:

$$y = \frac{(2x)^3}{2(3z)} = \frac{8x^3}{6z} = \frac{4x^3}{3z}$$

The value of y will be $^8/_3$ of what it was. Since the original expression was $y = x^3/2z$, we must figure out what fraction times $^1/_2$ is equal to $^4/_3$:

$$\left(\frac{1}{2}\right)f = \frac{4}{3}$$

$$f = \frac{\frac{4}{3}}{\frac{1}{2}} = \left(\frac{4}{3}\right)\left(\frac{2}{1}\right) = \frac{8}{3}$$

It's also possible that you'll have to know some variation jargon for the new SAT. There are two terms you need to know: *direct* and *inverse*. A direct relationship between two variables exists when, if one variable increases, the other variable increases. In the equation

$$y = \frac{x}{z}$$

y and x share a direct relationship, since if x increases, so does y.

An inverse relationship is just the opposite. In the same example, y and z have an inverse relationship, because if z were to increase, y would decrease.

19.10 HOW DO FUNCTIONS FUNCTION?

Functions are one of the most important additions to the Math section of the new SAT. So, what's a function? A function describes a relationship between one or more inputs and one output. The inputs to a function are variables such as x; the output of the function for a particular value of x is usually represented as $f(x)$ or $g(x)$. In the function $f(x) = 2x$, the output of the function is always equal to two times the value of x. So, if $x = 1$, then $f(x) = 2$, and if $x = 12$, then $f(x) = 24$.

So far, it may seem as if a *function* is just another word for *equation*. Based on the way the SAT generally tests functions, it's fine to think of functions that way. However, all functions follow a special rule that you've got to know:

For every input x, a function can have only one value for $f(x)$.

You might be asking yourself what this math babble means. Here's an example that should help translate. Take the equation $|y| = x$. Because y sits between absolute value brackets, if $x = 2$, then y could be equal to *either* 2 or –2. This equation can't be a function, because for each value of x, there are two possible values of y.

19.11 EVALUATING FUNCTIONS

Evaluating a function simply means finding $f(x)$ at some specific value x. To put it more bluntly, these are glorified substitution questions. We glorify them above all because they're easy. Here's an example:

If $f(x) = x^2 - 3$, what is $f(5)$?

See how that $f(5)$ substituted a 5 for the x in $f(x)$? Well, every time you see an x in the equation, replace it with a 5:

$$f(5) = 5^2 - 3 = 22$$

You almost don't even have to think at all when answering these questions. If the entire Math section was just a bunch of evaluating functions questions, amoebas could get 800s and Ivy League schools would welcome every well-rounded single-celled organism who applied.

Ah, but life and the new SAT ain't that easy. Here's one wrinkle the new test may throw at you. You may have to evaluate a function at a variable rather than a constant. For example,

If $f(x) = \dfrac{3x}{4-x}$, what is $f(x + 1)$?

Okay, slightly harder than substituting in a number, but still not difficult. Search out all the occurrences of x in the function and replace it with $(x + 1)$:

$$f(x+1) = \frac{3(x+1)}{4-(x+1)}$$
$$= \frac{3x+3}{4-x-1}$$
$$= \frac{3x+3}{3-x}$$

As long as you remembered to distribute that negative sign across the $(x + 1)$ to make $-x - 1$ in that second step, you're all set.

Performing Operations on Functions

Functions can be added, subtracted, multiplied, and divided like any other quantities. A few key rules will make these operations easier. For any two functions $f(x)$ and $g(x)$,

Rule		Example
Addition	$(f+g)(x) = f(x) + g(x)$	If $f(x) = x^2$ and $g(x) = 2x$: $(f+g)(x) = x^2 + 2x$
Subtraction	$(f-g)(x) = f(x) - g(x)$	If $f(x) = x^2 + 5$ and $g(x) = x^2 + 2x + 1$: $(f-g)(x) = x^2 + 5 - x^2 - 2x - 1 = -2x + 4$
Multiplication	$(f \times g)(x) = f(x) \times g(x)$	If $f(x) = x$ and $g(x) = x^3 + 8$: $(f \times g)(x) = x \times (x^3 + 8) = x^4 + 8x$
Division	$\dfrac{f}{g}(x) = \dfrac{f(x)}{g(x)}, g(x) \neq 0$	If $f(x) = 2x$ and $g(x) = x^2$: $\dfrac{f}{g}(x) = \dfrac{2x}{x^2} = \dfrac{2}{x}, g(x) \neq 0$

Here's a quick rule to follow for all of these operations on functions: Work out the value for both functions separately, and then perform the operation on those two values. Remember that any time you divide functions,

$$\frac{f(x)}{g(x)}$$

the resulting function is undefined whenever the $g(x)$ in the denominator equals zero. Division by zero is always a no-no.

Wacko Symbols Questions (Algebra in Disguise)

The SAT seems to give itself a cooky thrill by creating odd symbols and then defining those symbols as mathematical functions. For example, a typical symbol SAT question might say,

Let $a @ b$ be defined as $\dfrac{a^2}{b}$, where $b \neq 0$. What is the value of $4 @ 2$?

These symbols questions are just snazzy, dressed-to-kill, evaluating functions questions. Answer them by plugging in:

$$4 @ 2 = \frac{4^2}{2} = \frac{16}{2} = 8$$

Some students get frazzled when they see odd symbols in their test booklet, which is exactly what the SAT wants. Don't get tripped up on these otherwise easy questions.

19.12 COMPOUND FUNCTIONS

You know those Russian nesting dolls? Each doll has a smaller and smaller doll inside it? Compound functions are like that. A compound function is a function that operates on another function. It's written out like this: $f(g(x))$. To evaluate a compound function, first evaluate the internal function, $g(x)$. Next, evaluate the outer function at the result of $g(x)$. It's just double substitution: a classic SAT question that looks much meaner than it really is.

Try this example on for size:

Suppose $h(x) = x^2 + 2x$ and $j(x) = |\frac{x}{4} + 2|$. What is $j(h(4))$?

First evaluate $h(4)$:

$$h(4) = 4^2 + 2(4)$$
$$= 16 + 8$$
$$= 24$$

Now plug 24 into the definition of j:

$$j(24) = |\frac{24}{4} + 2|$$
$$= |6 + 2|$$
$$= 8$$

Just make sure you pay attention to the order in which you evaluate the compound function. Always evaluate the inner function first. If the question had asked you to evaluate $h(j(4))$, you'd get a completely different answer:

$$h(j(4)) = h(|\frac{4}{4} + 2|)$$
$$= h(|1 + 2|)$$
$$= h(3)$$
$$= 3^2 + 2(3)$$
$$= 9 + 6$$
$$= 15$$

As with ordinary evaluating functions questions, the SAT doesn't always give you a constant with which to evaluate compound functions.

Suppose $f(x) = 3x + 1$ and $g(x) = \sqrt{5x}$. What is $g(f(x))$?

When you aren't given a constant, just substitute the definition of $f(x)$ as the input to $g(x)$. It's as if you're being asked to evaluate a signle function at a variable rather than a constant.

$$g(f(x)) = g(3x + 1)$$
$$= \sqrt{5(3x + 1)}$$
$$= \sqrt{15x + 5}$$

Compound Wacko Symbols Questions

The SAT also sometimes asks compound symbols questions. These are exactly the same as compound function questions.

Let $a\#b\#c\#d$ be defined for all numbers by $a\#b\#c\#d = ab - cd$. If $x = 6\#3\#5\#4$, then what is the value of $7\#x\#3\#11$?

Strange symbols are flying all over the place, and the question is asking you to calculate the value of a strange symbol with a variable in it?! No problem. The answer to this question is only two steps away:

1. Calculate the value of x.
2. Calculate the value of $7\#x\#3\#11$ (which won't be very hard, since by step 2, you'll know exactly what x equals).

Since

$$a\#b\#c\#d = ab - cd$$
$$x = 6\#3\#5\#4 = (6)(3) - (5)(4) = 18 - 20 = -2$$
$$x = -2$$

Now plug $x = -2$ into $7\#x\#3\#11$:

$$7\#x\#3\#11 = 7\# - 2\#3\#11 = (7)(-2) - (3)(11) = -14 - 33 = -47$$

19.13 DOMAIN AND RANGE

Difficult SAT questions on functions test to see if you are the master of your domain and range. Here are the keys to the kingdom.

Domain of a Function

The domain of a function is the set of inputs (x values) for which the function is defined. Consider the functions $f(x) = x^2$ and $g(x) = 1/x$. In $f(x)$, any value of x can produce a valid result, since any number can be squared. In $g(x)$, though, not every value of x can generate an output: When $x = 0$, $g(x)$ is undefined. While the domain of $f(x)$ is all values of x, the domain of $g(x)$ is $x < 0$ and $x > 0$. The domain of the function $h(x) = \sqrt{x}$ is even more restricted. Since a negative number has no square root, $h(x)$ has a domain of $x > 0$.

Finding the Domain of a Function

To find the domain of a given function, first look for any restrictions on the domain. There are two main restrictions for function domain questions to look out for on the SAT:

1. **Division by zero.** Division by zero is mathematically impossible. A function is therefore undefined for all the values of x for which division by zero occurs. For example, $f(x) = {}^1/x\text{-}2$ is undefined at $x = 2$, since when $x = 2$, the function is equal to $f(x) = {}^1/0$.

2. **Negative numbers under square roots.** The square root of a negative number does not exist, so if a function contains a square root, such as $f(x) = \sqrt{x}$, the domain must be $x > 0$.

There are easy-to-spot warning signs that indicate you should look out for either division by zero or negative numbers under square roots. The division by zero warning sign is a variable in the denominator of a fraction. The negative number under square roots warning sign is a variable under a square root (or a variable raised to the 1/2 power). Once you've located the likely problem spots, you can usually find the values to eliminate from the domain pretty easily.

You must be itching for an example. Allow us to scratch that itch:

> What is the domain of $f(x) = \dfrac{x}{x^2 + 5x + 6}$?

$f(x)$ has variables in its denominator: red flag for the possibility of division by zero. You may need to restrict the function's domain to ensure that division by zero doesn't occur. To find the values of x that cause the denominator to equal zero, set up an equation equal to zero: $x^2 + 5x + 6 = 0$. A quadratic equation. Ahoy! Factor it: $(x + 2)(x + 3) = 0$. So, for $x = \{-2, -3\}$, the denominator is zero and $f(x)$ is undefined. The domain of $f(x)$ is the set of all real numbers x such that $x \neq -2, -3$. This can also be written in the form $\{x: x \neq -2, -3\}$.

Here's another example:

> What is the domain of $f(x) = \dfrac{2\sqrt{x-4}}{x-7}$?

This function has both warning signs: a variable under a square root and a variable in the denominator. It's best to examine each situation separately:

1. The denominator would equal zero if $x = 7$.
2. The quantity under the square root, $x - 4$, must be greater than or equal to zero in order for the function to be defined. Therefore, $x \geq 4$.

The domain of the function is therefore the set of real numbers x such that $x \geq 4$, $x \neq 7$.

The Range of a Function

A function's range is the set of all values of $f(x)$ that can be generated by the function. The easiest way to think about range is to visualize it on a graph. The domain, which is all the valid values of x in the function, is the x-axis, while the range, all the values of $f(x)$, is the y-axis. Take a look at the following two graphs:

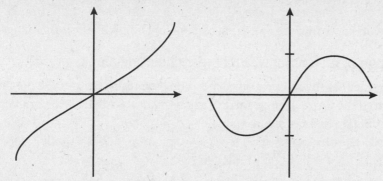

What values of the y-axis are reached on each graph? In the graph on the left, you can see that every possible value of y, from negative infinity to positive infinity, is included in the range. The range could be written as $-\infty \leq f(x) \leq \infty$. Contrast this with the graph on the right, where the range is quite limited: Only the values between -1 and 1 are part of the range. So the range is $-1 \leq f(x) \leq 1$.

There are two main warning signs of functions with limited ranges: absolute value and even exponents.

- **Absolute value.** The absolute value of a quantity is always positive. So, in a simple case, $f(x) = |x|$, you know that $f(x)$ must always be positive, and so the range includes only zero and positive numbers: $f(x) \geq 0$. Never assume that any function with an absolute value symbol has the same range, though. The range of $g(x) = -|x|$ is zero and all of the negative numbers: $f(x) \leq 0$.
- **Even Exponents.** Any time you square a number (or raise it to any multiple of 2) the resulting quantity will be positive.

Finding the Range

Calculating the range of a complex function is similar to finding the domain. First, look for absolute values, even exponents, or other reasons that the range would be restricted. Then adjust that range step by step as you run down the same checklist you use to find the domain.

What is the range of $f(x) = \dfrac{|x-3|}{2}$?

In this case, the absolute value around $|x - 3|$ screams out that the range of $f(x)$ excludes all negative numbers: $f(x) \geq 0$. $|x - 3|$ is then divided by 2, so you have to divide the range by 2. But this division doesn't actually change the range, since both zero and infinity remain unchanged when halved.

Now for a more complicated example:

What is the range of $\dfrac{\sqrt{|x-6|+4}}{2}$?

Tackle this example step by step.

1. The absolute value restricts the range to $0 \leq f(x) \leq \infty$.
2. Add 4 to each bound of the range. This action only affects the lower bound: $4 \leq f(x) \leq \infty$.
3. Taking the square root once again affects only the lower bound: $2 \leq f(x) \leq \infty$.
4. Finally, divide the bounds of the range in half to determine the range of the entire function: $1 \leq f(x) \leq \infty$.

Note that addition, subtraction, multiplication, division, and other mathematical operations don't affect infinity. That's why it's particularly important to look for absolute values and even roots. Once you can find a bound on a range that isn't infinity, you know that the operations on the function will affect that range.

The Range of a Function with a Prescribed Domain

Another way that the range of a function could be restricted is if the domain is itself restricted. If the SAT is feeling particularly nasty, it'll nail you with this kind of complicated domain and range question:

$f(x) = 2x^2 + 4$ for $-3 < x < 5$. What is the range of $f(x)$?

The first thing you have to realize is that there's no reason to assume that the range of the function will be at its high and low points at exactly the bounds of the restricted domain. If you assume that the range of $f(x) = 2x^2 + 4$ has its high point at 5 and its low point at -3, well, that's exactly what the SAT wants you to assume.

Here's where having a graphing calculator is immensely helpful on the new SAT. If you graph $f(x) = 2x^2 + 4$, you'll see

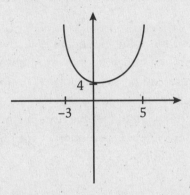

You can see from this graph that the low point of the range comes when $x = 0$ and the high point comes when $x = 5$. Plug 0 and 5 into the function to get the low and high bounds of the function for the range $-3 < x < 5$. $f(0) = 4$. $f(5) = 54$. So the range is $0 < f(x) < 54$.

19.14 FUNCTIONS AS MODELS

The old SAT constantly got hammered for being a test that didn't have much to do with the real world. The test-writers decided that they didn't want to hear it anymore with the new SAT, and so they created Functions as Models questions, which have nothing to do with Giselle or Tyson Beckford but present information about a real-life scenario and then ask you to pick a function in equation or graph form that best describes the scenario.

A Function as Models question with graphs looks something like this:

> If temperature is $f(x)$ and time is x, which of the following best describes a bucket of cold water left outside on a hot day?
>
>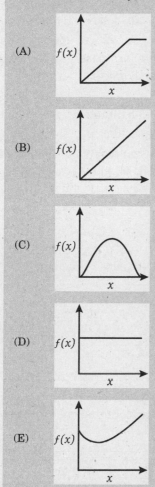

So, what'll happen to a bucket of cold water left outside on a hot day? It'll heat up, of course, so the answer's **B** ... except that this is the real world and the question contains a trick. **B** shows that bucket heating up *forever*, when in fact, the water in the bucket can't actually get any hotter than the day itself. So at some point, that rise in temperature has to hit a plateau: **A** is the answer.

A Functions as Models problem that deals with written-out functions looks like this:

> A bookstore is selling a particular book for $15 per copy. At this price it has been selling 20 copies of the book each day. The store owner estimates that for every dollar reduction in the selling price of the book, daily sales will increase by 20 copies. What is the daily sales, S, as a function of price, p?
>
> (A) $S = -20p + 320$
>
> (B) $S = 15p + 20$
>
> (C) $S = \frac{3}{5}p$
>
> (D) $S = -20p - 15$
>
> (E) $S = p + 5$

The key to solving this sort of problem is to first define what kind of mathematical function this "real-world" scenario is describing. Take another look at the question: At $15, the book sells 20 copies, and for each dollar the price goes down, the book sells another 20 copies. In other words, for each dollar decrease in price, sales increase by a fixed amount. Sound like anything to you? How about a linear function, like $S = mp + b$, where m is the slope and b is the y-intercept. The "fixed increase" for every change of p is the slope. Since the slope *in*creases 20 units for each dollar *de*crease in price, that slope must be negative: –20. You could now eliminate all the answers but **A** and **D**. To find the definitive right answer, though, you have to find b. You can do that by plugging in numbers from the question. You know that when the book costs \$15 dollars (p), it sells 20 copies (S). So, $20 = –20(15) + b$; $20 = –300 + b$; $b = 320$. There you go. **A** is the answer.

If you're a little algebra-phobic, all this might seem very hard to you. But there's another way to go about it. Use the information in the question to build a graph. From the information in the question, you know that at the price of \$15, the store sells 20 copies, and that for each dollar less, the store sells 20 more copies. So, in other words, you know the points on this graph: (15,20), (14,40), (13,60)...

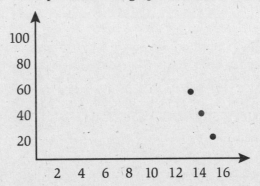

This graph doesn't give you the answer, but it does make it clear that you're dealing with a linear graph of slope –20, and that if you just keep on counting back to where $p = 0$, you'll get the y-intercept, or 320.

19.15 DEFEATING WORD PROBLEMS

Before you can solve an equation, you first need an equation to solve. Word problems give you all the information you need to answer the question—but in English. On the SAT, you must be able to translate that information into math.

> In a sack of 50 marbles, there are 20 more red marbles than blue marbles. All of the marbles in the sack are either red or blue. How many blue marbles are in the sack?

When you're turning a word problem into an equation (or equations) there are four things you have to do:

1. Know what the question is asking.
2. Assign variables.
3. Define mathematical relationships between the variables.
4. Show the problem who's boss.

1. Know what the question is asking.

Well, isn't it obvious what the question is asking? It wants to know how many blue marbles are in the sack. It doesn't get any more obvious than that. You're right, but there are reasons we stress this point so seriously. "How many blue marbles are in the sack?" is not what the question is asking you. What it's really asking is, "How many blue marbles are in a sack that contains 50 total marbles, out of which 20 more are red than blue?" This is the true question, because it identifies all the relationships and contains all the information that the question describes. SAT word problems can make even simple equations sound complicated and messy. Restating the question is a good way to clean things up.

2. Assign variables.

The question tells you the total number of marbles, and it says that there are red and blue marbles. You don't need a variable for total marbles, since you know the total is 50, but you do need variables for the red and blue marbles, since those are unknown quantities. Pick whatever ones you like. How about r and b?

3. Define mathematical relationships between variables.

Okay. You know from the question that the 50 total marbles are made up of red and blue marbles. So $50 = r + b$. The question also tells you that the sack contains 20 more red marbles than blue marbles. So the number of red marbles is 20 more than the number of blue marbles: $r = b + 20$. Just like that, you've taken all the information and put it into mathematical form.

4. Show the problem who's boss.

Once you've got the word problem translated, solving is a cinch. You're looking for how many blue marbles are in a sack that contains 50 total marbles, out of which 20 more are red than blue. So, in the equation with total marbles, red marbles, and blue marbles, you're looking for blue marbles. A little manipulating does the trick: $b = 50 - r$. And since you know that $r = b + 20$, you can substitute $b + 20$ for r to get $b = 50 - (b + 20)$. Solve: $r = 50 - r - 20$; $2r = 30$; $r = 15$.

An Example

Here's a longer, more complicated problem. Conquer it with the same four-step technique:

> Gus needs to paint his house, which has a surface area of x square feet. The brand of paint he buys (at a price of p dollars a can) comes in cans that cover y square feet each. How much will it cost him to paint his house?

1. Know what the question is asking.

What is the cost of the paint Gus needs to buy if he needs to cover a total of x square feet, when each can costs p dollars and covers y square feet?

2. Assign variables.

The question assigns almost all of the variables for you: x is total square feet that need painting in the house, p is the price of a can of paint, and y is the square feet that each can of paint can cover. Nice! You just need a variable for that total cost. How about t?

3. Define mathematical relationships between variables.

Since p is the price of a can of paint, and you need to find the total cost of buying paint, you must find the number of cans of paint that Gus has to buy . . . look at that! You need another variable for numbers of cans of paint. How about n? (This happens sometimes: You'll find out that there is a variable you need that is implied by the problem but not explicitly mentioned.) So $t = np$.

Now to find n. Use the information the problem gives you. It tells you the total square feet (x) and the square feet covered per can (y), which means that if you were to divide x by y, you'd get the number of cans:

$$n = \frac{x}{y}$$

4. Show the problem who's boss.

You've got the relationships between the variables mapped out. Plug the equation for n into the $t = np$ and you've got the total cost:

$$t = \frac{xp}{y}$$

Unlike the rule of doing the same thing to both sides of the equation, there's no universal rule stating that you must follow the three steps we've just explained. But we think following these steps will help you get a handle on every SAT world problem, no matter how long and gnarly it is.

19.16 THE MOST COMMON WORD PROBLEMS

Word problems come in all shapes and sizes. But each and every year, the SAT includes certain particular varieties. We've got the skinny on 'em.

Rates

A rate is a ratio of related qualities that have different units. For example, speed is a rate that relates the two quantities of distance and time. Here is the general rate formula:

$$\text{quantity } A \times \text{rate } r = \text{quantity } B$$

No matter the specifics, the key to a rate word problem is in correctly placing the given information in the three categories: A, r, and B. Then, you can substitute the values into the rate formula. We look at the three most common types of rate: speed, work, and price.

Speed

In the case of speed, time is quantity A and distance is quantity B. For example, if you traveled for 4 hours at 25 miles per hour, then

$$4 \text{ hours} \times 25 \ \frac{\text{miles}}{\text{hour}} = 100 \text{ miles}$$

Usually, the new SAT won't simply give you one of the quantities and the rate and ask you to plug it into the rate formula. Since rate questions are always in the form of word problems, the information that you'll need to solve the problem is often given in the befuddling complicated manner you've grown to know and hate.

Here's an example:

Jim rollerskates 6 miles per hour. One morning, Jim starts rollerskating and doesn't stop until he has gone 60 miles. How many hours did he spend rollerskating?

This question provides more information than simply the speed and one of the quantities. You get unnecessary facts such as how Jim is traveling (by rollerskates) and when he started (in the morning). Ignore them and focus on the facts you need to solve the problem.

- **Quantity A:** x hours rollerskating
- **Rate:** 6 miles per hour
- **Quantity B:** 60 miles

$$x \text{ hours of rollerskating } = 60 \text{ miles} \div 6 \text{ miles per hour } = 10 \text{ hours}$$

Here's a more difficult rate problem:

At a cycling race, the cyclist from California can cycle 528,000 feet per hour. If the race is 480 miles long, how long will it take her to finish the race? (1 mile = 5280 feet)

You should immediately pick out the given rate of 528,000 feet per hour and notice that the total distance traveled is 480 miles. You should also notice that the question presents a units problem: The given rate is in *feet* per hour, while the total distance traveled is given in *miles*.

Sometimes a question gives you inconsistent units, as in this example. *Always* read over the problem carefully and don't forget to adjust the units—the SAT makes sure that the answer you would come to if you had forgotten to correct for units appears among the answer choices.

For the cycling question, since the question tells you that there are 5,280 feet in a mile, you can find the rate for miles per hour:

$$528,000 \text{ feet per hour} \div 5,280 \text{ feet per mile} = 100 \text{ miles per hour}$$

Now you can plug the information into the rate formula:

- **Time:** x hours cycling
- **Rate:** 100 miles per hour
- **Distance:** 480 miles

$$480 \text{ miles} \div 100 \text{ miles per hour} = 4.8 \text{ hours}$$

Work

Work sucks. You're there from 9 to 5 and, at best, you get two weeks off per year, and you've got a boss constantly checking up on you. Work word problems on the SAT are a breeze in comparison. On work word problems, you'll usually find the first quantity measured in time (t), the second quantity measured in work done (w), and the rate measured in work done per time (r). For example, if you knitted for 8 hours and produced 2 sweaters per hour, then

$$8 \text{ hours} \times 2 \ \frac{\text{sweaters}}{\text{hour}} = 16 \text{ sweaters}$$

Here's a sample work problem. It's one of the harder rate word problems you might come across on the SAT:

Four workers can dig a 40-foot well in 4 days. How long would it take for 8 workers to dig a 60-foot well? Assume that these 8 workers work at the same pace as the 4 workers.

First, examine what that problem says: 4 workers can dig a 40-foot well in 4 days. You know how much total work was done and how many people did it, you just don't know the rate at which the workers worked. You need that rate, since the 8 workers digging the 60-foot wells are working at the same rate. Since $r = w \div t$, you can get the rate by dividing 40 by 4, which equals 10. The workers together dig at a pace of 10 feet per day.

Now for that group of 8 workers digging a 60-foot well. The total work (w) done by the 8 workers is 60 feet, and they work at a rate (r) of 10 feet per day per 4 workers. Can you use this information to answer the question? Oh yeah. The rate of 10 feet per day per 4 workers converts to 20 feet per day per 8 workers, which is the size of the new crew. Now you can use the rate formula:

- **Time:** x days of work
- **Rate:** 20 feet per day per 8 workers
- **Work Done (in this case, distance dug):** 60 feet

60 feet ÷ 20 feet per day per 8 workers = 3 days of work for 8 workers

This last problem required a little bit of creativity—but nothing you can't handle. Just remember the classic rate formula and use it wisely.

Price

In rate questions dealing with price, you'll usually find the first quantity measured in numbers of items, the second measured in price, and the rate in price per item. If you have 8 basketballs, and you know that each basketball costs $25,

$$8 \text{ basketballs} \times \$25 \, \frac{\text{price}}{\text{basketball}} = \$200$$

Exponential Growth and Decay

Exponential growth and decay problems are like percent change problems on steroids: You must perform a percent change over and over again. You can use exponents on these repeated percent change questions. Here's an example:

If a population of 100 grows by 5% per year, how large will the population be in 50 years?

You could do two things to solve this problem. You could multiply each successive generation by 5% fifty times to get the final answer, or you could use this formula:

$$\text{Final Amount} = \text{Original Amount} \times (1 + \text{Growth Rate})^{(\text{number of changes})}$$

The formula is probably the better bet. So, to solve this problem,

$$\text{final amount} = 100 \times 1.05^{50} = 1146.74 \approx 1147$$

Exponential decay only slightly modifies the formula:

$$\text{Final Amount} = \text{Original Amount} \times (1 - \text{Growth Rate})^{(\text{number of changes})}$$

Exponential decay is often used to model population decreases as well as the decay of physical mass.

We'll work through a few example problems to get a feel for both exponential growth and decay problems.

A Simple Exponential Growth Problem

A population of bacteria grows by 35% every hour. If the population begins with 100 specimens, how many are there after 6 hours?

You've got an original population of 100, a growth rate of .35 every hour, and 6 hours. To solve the problem, you just need to plug the appropriate values into the formula for exponential growth.

$$\text{final amount} = 100 \times 1.35^6 \approx 605 \text{ specimens}$$

A Simple Exponential Decay Problem

A fully inflated beach ball loses 6% of its air every day. If the beach ball originally contains 4000 cubic centimeters of air, how many cubic centimeters does it hold after 10 days?

Since the beach ball loses air, you know this is an exponential decay problem. The decay rate is .06, the original amount is 4000 cubic centimeters of air, and the time is 10 days. Plugging the information into the formula,

$$\text{final amount} = 4000 \times (0.94)^{10} \approx 2154 \text{ cubic centimeters}$$

A More Annoying Exponential Growth Problem

A bank offers a 4.7% interest rate on all savings accounts, per month. If 1000 dollars is initially put into a savings account, how much money will the account hold two years later?

This problem is a bit tricky because the interest rate is per month, while the time period is given in years. You need to make the units match up. In the two-year time period given by the question, there will be $2 \times 12 = 24$ months

$$\text{final amount} = 1000 \times 1.047^{24} \approx 3011.07 \text{ dollars}$$

Here's another compounding problem:

Ben puts $2000 into a savings account that pays 5% interest compounded annually. Justin puts $2500 into a different savings account that pays 4% annually. After 15 years, whose account will have more money in it if no more money is added or subtracted from the principal?

Ben's account will have $2000 $\times$ $1.05^{15} \approx$ $4157.85 in it after 15 years. Justin's account will have $2500 $\times$ $1.04^{15} \approx$ $4502.36 in it. Justin's account will still have more money in it than Ben's after 15 years. Notice, however, that Ben's account *is* gaining on Justin's account.

And with that, you've covered everything you need to know to rock SAT algebra. Geometry's next.

GEOMETRY

OF THE FOUR MAJOR SAT MATH TOPICS, GEOMETRY IS the least affected by the new SAT. Sure, it throws in some new tidbits here and there, like tangent lines, transformations, and a new emphasis on proper geometric notation. But, essentially, if you could handle the geometry for the old SAT, you're set for the new SAT as well.

20.1   A BASIC REVIEW OF THE BASICS

Here's a quick review of the fundamental concepts and ideas of geometry. SAT questions assume you know these topics and will throw around basic geometry jargon, so you need to have the fundamentals down pat.

Points

A point is a way to describe a specific location in space. Below, the point *B* is pictured. Isn't it lovely?

B

A point has no length or width. Though in the picture, point *B* is a black dot, in real life points take up no space. Points are useful for identifying specific locations but are not objects in themselves. They only appear as objects when drawn on a page.

Lines

A line is an infinite set of points assembled in a straight formation. A line has no thickness but is infinitely long in both directions. To form a line, take any two points, *A* and *B*, and draw a straight line through them. The resulting line is a called line *AB*.

A line can be drawn through any two points.

Line Segments

A line segment is the portion of a line that lies between two points on that line—in this example, the portion between points *A* and *B* make up a line segment. Whereas a line has infinite length, a line segment has a finite length. A line segment is named by the two points it lies between

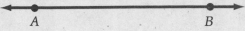

A line segment can be drawn between any two points.

Rays

Imagine a line and a line segment mating. The result is a ray, a cross between a line and a line segment. It extends infinitely in one direction but not the other.

A ray is named by its endpoint and another point that it passes through.

Okay. Painless basic geometric knowledge: acquired. That was quick. Now on to the real meat and potatoes of the geometry that the new SAT tests.

20.2 A NOTE ON NOTATION

The new SAT now uses standard geometric notation to indicate lines, line segments, rays, length, and congruence. Why is this a big deal? Because it makes interpreting questions and drawing figures more difficult. It's possible that if you don't know the notation, you won't know what the question is asking you to do. So here's a list of the correct notation. Memorize it.

What	Notation
Line *AB*	$\overleftrightarrow{AB}$
Line segment *AB*	$\overline{AB}$
Ray *AB*	$\overrightarrow{AB}$
Length of $\overline{AB}$	AB

Finally, you need to know the term *congruent*, which means "exactly the same" or "equal." The new SAT may also test to see if you know the symbol that indicates congruence. To say that angle *A* is congruent to angle *B*, you'd write: $A \cong B$.

ANGLES AND LINES

An angle is a geometric figure consisting of two lines, rays, or line segments that share a common endpoint called a *vertex*:

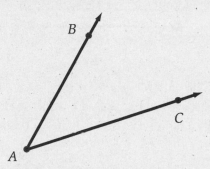

In the angle above, the vertex is point A. The angle can be called either angle *CAB* or angle *BAC*. The only rule for naming an angle is that the vertex must be the middle "initial" of the angle. The SAT may also refer to angles using symbols: ∠A.

Degrees

Angles are measured in degrees, which have nothing to do with Nelly or temperature. Geometric degrees are sometimes denoted by this little guy: °. There are 360° in a complete rotation around a point (that's why a circle has 360°).

Two Lines Meet in a Bar...

When two lines meet, they produce angles. And when two lines meet, they form four angles! That must be exhausting.

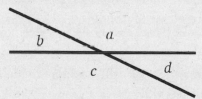

These aren't just any old four angles, either. Together, the angles encompass one full revolution around the point of intersection of the two lines. So, the four angles produced by two intersection lines total 360°: angle $a + b + c + d = 360°$.

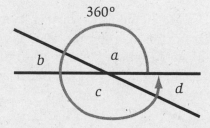

If you know the value of three of the four angles formed by intersecting lines, you can always find the value of the fourth.

Types of Angles

The different types of angles are named and categorized according to their number of degrees.

Zero Angles

A zero angle has, you guessed it, 0°. To visualize a zero angle, first picture two lines that form some angle greater than 0°. Then imagine one of the lines rotating toward the other until they both fall on the same line. The angle they create has shrunk from its original measure to 0°, forming a zero angle:

Right Angles

For some reason, an angle with a measure of 90° is called a right angle. For some other reason, right angles are symbolized with a square drawn in the corner of the angle. Whenever you see that reliable little square, you know you're dealing with a right angle.

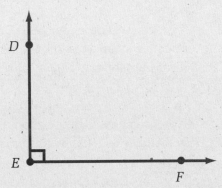

Right angles are extremely important on the SAT. They appear in math questions all the time. Knowing their special properties will help you solve right angle questions. We give you a detailed look at those properties a little later in this chapter. For now, just remember: *Always* be on the lookout for right angles on the SAT.

Straight Angles

An angle with a measure of 180° is called a straight angle. It looks just like a line. Don't confuse straight angles with zero angles, which look like a single ray.

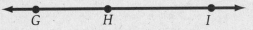

Acute and Obtuse Angles

An angle can also be classified according to whether its measure is greater or less than 90°. If an angle measures less than 90°, it's called an acute angle. If it measures more than 90°, it's called an obtuse angle. Right angles are neither acute nor obtuse. They're just right. In the picture below, $\angle ABC$ is acute, while $\angle DEF$ is obtuse.

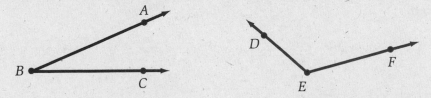

Complementary and Supplementary Angles

Special names are given to pairs of angles whose sums equal either 90° or 180°. Angles whose sum is 90° are called complementary angles, while angles whose sum is 180° are called supplementary angles.

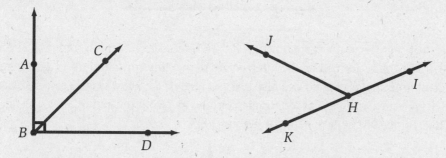

In the picture above, $\angle ABC$ and $\angle CBD$ are complementary, since together they make up a right angle. Angles $\angle JHK$ and $\angle JHI$ are supplementary, since they make up a straight line.

On the SAT, you'll have to use the rules of complementary and supplementary angles to figure out the degree measure of an angle.

In the diagram below, AC is a line. What is x in degrees?

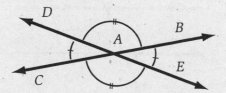

The picture tells you that $\angle ABD$ is 113°, but how many degrees is $\angle DBC$? Well, since you know that AC is a line, $\angle ABC$ must be a straight angle (meaning it equals 180°). So $\angle ABD$ and $\angle DBC$ are supplementary angles that add up to 180°. To find out the value of $\angle DBC$, you can simply take 180° and subtract 113°. $\angle DBC = 67°$.

Vertical Angles

When two lines (or line segments) intersect, the angles that lie opposite each other, called vertical angles, are *always* equal.

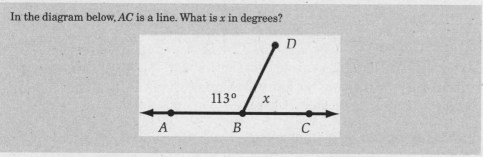

Angles $\angle DAC$ and $\angle BAE$ are vertical angles and are therefore equal. Angles $\angle DAB$ and $\angle CAE$ are also vertical (and equal) angles. We promise that the SAT will ask you at least one question involving vertical angles. Promise.

Parallel and Perpendicular Lines

Pairs of lines that never intersect are parallel. Parallel lines appear to line up right next to each other because they never meet in space. However, on the SAT, you can't assume two lines are parallel just because they look parallel. The SAT will tell you if two lines are parallel.

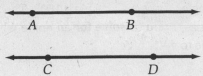

Lines (or segments) are perpendicular if their intersection forms a right angle. And if one of the angles formed by the intersection of two lines or segments is a right angle, then all four angles created will also be right angles. By the way, this also shows that the degree measurement of four angles formed by two intersecting lines will add up to 360°, since 90° + 90° + 90° + 90° = 360°.

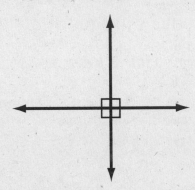

As with parallel lines, don't assume that lines on the SAT are perpendicular unless the SAT tells you they are. The SAT will tell you either in words ("lines a and b are parallel") or by using the little reliable box to show that the angles are 90°.

Parallel Lines Cut by a Transversal

A transversal is a line that cuts through two parallel lines. The SAT loves to cut parallel lines with transversals. Who knows why? Not us. But we know how to get those questions right, and you will too.

A transversal creates eight angles when it intersects with two parallel lines. The eight angles created by these two intersections have special relationships to each other.

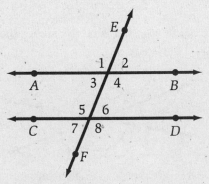

You now have a choice to make: (1) spend all day figuring out these relationships, or (2) use our list.

Good choice:

- Angles 1, 4, 5, and 8 are equal to each other because they're vertical angles.
- Angles 2, 3, 6, and 7 are equal to each other because they're vertical angles.
- The sum of any two adjacent angles, such as 1 and 2 or 7 and 8, equals 180°, because these are supplementary angles.

By using these three rules, you can figure out the degrees of angles that may seem unrelated. For example, since angles 1 and 2 sum to 180°, and since angles 2 and 7 are equal, the sum of angles 1 and 7 also equals 180°. The SAT will almost definitely include a question that asks you to solve for an angle whose measurement at first glance seems impossible to determine.

TRIANGLES

Triangles pop up all over the Math section. There are questions specifically about triangles, questions that ask about triangles inscribed in polygons and circles, and questions about triangles in coordinate geometry.

Three Sides, Four Fundamental Properties

Every triangle, no matter how special, follows four main rules.

1. Sum of the Interior Angles

If you were trapped on a deserted island with tons of SAT questions about triangles, this is the one rule you'd need to know:

The sum of the interior angles of a triangle is 180°.

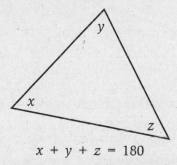

$$x + y + z = 180$$

If you know the measures of two of a triangle's angles, you'll always be able to find the third by subtracting the sum of the first two from 180.

2. Measure of an Exterior Angle

The exterior angle of a triangle is always supplementary to the interior angle with which it shares a vertex and equal to the sum of the measures of the remote interior angles. An exterior angle of a triangle is the angle formed by extending one of the sides of the triangle past a vertex. In the image below, d is the exterior angle.

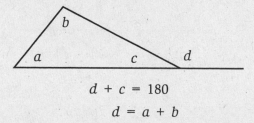

$$d + c = 180$$
$$d = a + b$$

Since d and c together form a straight angle, they are supplementary: $d + c = 180°$. According to the first rule of triangles, the three angles of a triangle always add up to 180°, so $a + b + c = 180°$. Since $d + c = 180°$ and $a + b + c = 180°$, d must equal $a + b$.

3. Triangle Inequality Rule

If triangles got together to write a declaration of independence, they'd have a tough time, since one of their defining rules would be this:

The length of any side of a triangle will always be less than the sum of the lengths of the other two sides and greater than the difference of the lengths of the other two sides.

There you have it: Triangles are unequal by definition.

Take a look at the figure below:

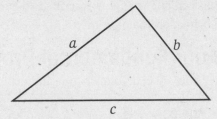

The triangle inequality rule says that $c - b < a < c + b$. The exact length of side a depends on the measure of the angle created by sides b and c. Witness this triangle:

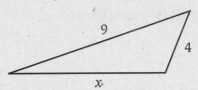

Using the triangle inequality rule, you can tell that $9 - 4 < x < 9 + 4$, or $5 < x < 13$. The exact value of x depends on the measure of the angle opposite side x. If this angle is large (close to $180°$) then x will be large (close to 13). If this angle is small (close to $0°$), then x will be small (close to 5).

The triangle inequality rule means that if you know the length of two sides of any triangle, you will always know the range of possible side lengths for the third side. On some SAT triangle questions, that's all you'll need.

4. Proportionality of Triangles

Here's the final fundamental triangle property. This one explains the relationships between the angles of a triangle and the lengths of the triangle's sides.

In every triangle, the longest side is opposite the largest angle and the shortest side is opposite the smallest angle.

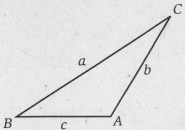

In this figure, side a is clearly the longest side and $\angle A$ is the largest angle. Meanwhile, side c is the shortest side and $\angle C$ is the smallest angle. So $c < b < a$ and $C < B < A$. This proportionality of side lengths and angle measures holds true for all triangles.

See if you can use this rule to solve the question below:

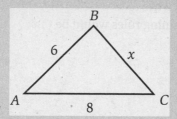

What is one possible value of *x* if angle $C < A < B$?

(A)   1
(B)   6
(C)   7
(D)   10
(E)   15

According to the proportionality of triangles rule, the longest side of a triangle is opposite the largest angle. Likewise, the shortest side of a triangle is opposite the smallest angle. The largest angle in triangle *ABC* is $\angle B$, which is opposite the side of length 8. The smallest angle in triangle *ABC* is $\angle C$, which is opposite the side of length 6. This means that the third side, of length *x*, measures between 6 and 8 units in length. The only choice that fits the criteria is 7. **C** is the correct answer.

Special Triangles

Special triangles are "special" not because they get to follow fewer rules than other triangles but because they get to follow more. Each type of special triangle has its own special name: *isosceles*, *equilateral*, and *right*. Knowing the properties of each will help you tremendously, humongously, a lot, on the SAT.

But first we have to take a second to explain the markings we use to describe the properties of special triangles. The little arcs and ticks drawn in the figure below show that this triangle has two sides of equal length and three equal angle pairs. The sides that each have one tick through them are equal, as are the sides that each have two ticks through them. The angles with one little arc are equal to each other, the angles with two little arcs are equal to each other, and the angles with three little arcs are all equal to each other.

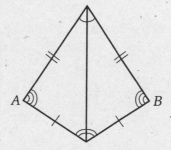

Isosceles Triangles

In ancient Greece, Isosceles was the god of triangles. His legs were of perfectly equal length and formed two opposing congruent angles when he stood up straight. Isosceles triangles share many of the same properties, naturally. An isosceles triangle has two sides of equal length, and those two sides are opposite congruent angles.

These equal angles are usually called as base angles. In the isosceles triangle below, side $a = b$ and $\angle A = \angle B$:

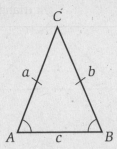

If you know the value of one of the base angles in an isosceles triangle, you can figure out all the angles. Let's say you've got an isosceles triangle with a base angle of 35°. Since you know isosceles triangles have two congruent base angles by definition, you know that the other base angle is also 35°. All three angles in a triangle must always add up to 180°, right? Correct. That means you can also figure out the value of the third angle: 180° – 35° – 35° = 110°.

Equilateral Triangles

An equilateral triangle has three equal sides and three congruent 60° angles.

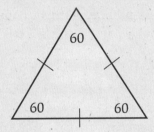

Based on the proportionality rule, if a triangle has three equal sides, that triangle must also have three equal angles. Similarly, if you know that a triangle has three equal angles, then you know it also has three equal sides.

Right Triangles

A triangle that contains a right angle is called a right triangle. The side opposite the right angle is called the hypotenuse. The other two sides are called legs. The angles opposite the legs of a right triangle are complementary (they add up to 90°).

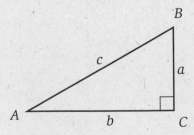

In the figure above, $\angle C$ is the right angle (as indicated by the box drawn in the angle), side c is the hypotenuse, and sides a and b are the legs.

If triangles are an SAT favorite, then right triangles are SAT darlings. In other words, know these rules. And know the Pythagorean theorem.

The Pythagorean Theorem

The Greeks spent a lot of time reading, eating grapes, and riding around on donkeys. They also enjoyed the occasional mathematical epiphany. One day, Pythagoras discovered that the sum of the squares of the two legs of a right triangle is equal to the square of the hypotenuse. "Eureka!" he said, and the SAT had a new topic to test.

Here's the Pythagorean theorem: In a right triangle, $a^2 + b^2 = c^2$:

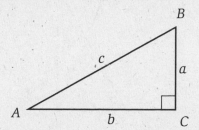

where c is the length of the hypotenuse and a and b are the lengths of the two legs.

The Pythagorean theorem means that if you know the measures of two sides of a right triangle, you can *always* find the third. "Eureka!" you say.

Pythagorean Triples

Because right triangles obey the Pythagorean theorem, only a specific few have side lengths that are all integers. For example, a right triangle with legs of length 3 and 5 has a hypotenuse of length $\sqrt{3^2 + 5^2} = \sqrt{9 + 25} = \sqrt{34} = 5.83$.

The few sets of three integers that do obey the Pythagorean theorem and can therefore be the lengths of the sides of a right triangle are called Pythagorean triples. Here are some common ones:

$$\{3, 4, 5\}$$

$$\{5, 12, 13\}$$

$$\{7, 24, 25\}$$

$$\{8, 15, 17\}$$

In addition to these Pythagorean triples, you should also watch out for their multiples. For example, $\{6, 8, 10\}$ is a Pythagorean triple, since it is a multiple of $\{3, 4, 5\}$.

The SAT is full of right triangles whose side lengths are Pythagorean triples. Study the ones above and their multiples. Identifying Pythagorean triples will help you cut the amount of time you spend doing calculations. In fact, you may not have to do any calculations if you get these down cold.

Extra-Special Right Triangles

Right triangles are pretty special in their own right. But there are two *extra*-special right triangles. They are 30-60-90 triangles and 45-45-90 triangles, and they appear all the time on the SAT.

In fact, knowing the rules of these two special triangles will open up all sorts of time-saving possibilities for you on the test. Very, very often, instead of having to work out the Pythagorean theorem, you'll be able to apply the standard side ratios of either of these two types of triangles, cutting out all the time you need to spend calculating.

30-60-90 Triangles

The guy who named 30-60-90 triangles didn't have much of an imagination. These triangles have angles of 30°, 60°, and 90°. What's so special about that? This: The side lengths of 30-60-90 triangles always follow a specific pattern. Suppose the short leg, opposite the 30° angle, has length x. Then the hypotenuse has length $2x$, and the long leg, opposite the 60° angle, has length $x\sqrt{3}$. The sides of every 30-60-90 triangle will follow this ratio of 1: $\sqrt{3}$: 2 .

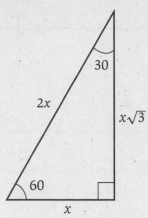

This constant ratio means that if you know the length of *just one* side in the triangle, you'll immediately be able to calculate the lengths of all the sides. If, for example, you know that the side opposite the 30° angle is 2 meters long, then by using the 1: $\sqrt{3}$: 2 ratio, you can work out that the hypotenuse is 4 meters long, and the leg opposite the 60° angle is $2\sqrt{3}$ meters.

And there's another amazing thing about 30-60-90 triangles. Two of these triangles joined at the side opposite the 60° angle will form an equilateral triangle.

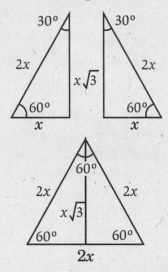

Here's why you need to pay attention to this extra-special feature of 30-60-90 triangles. If you know the side length of an equilateral triangle, you can figure out the triangle's height: Divide the side length by two and multiply it by $\sqrt{3}$. Similarly, if you drop a "perpendicular bisector" (this is the term the SAT uses) from any vertex of an equilateral triangle to the base on the far side, you'll have cut that triangle into two 30-60-90 triangles.

Knowing how equilateral and 30-60-90 triangles relate is incredibly helpful on triangle, polygon, and even solids questions on the SAT. Quite often, you'll be able to break down these large shapes into a number of special triangles, and then you can use the side ratios to figure out whatever you need to know.

45-45-90 Triangles

A 45-45-90 triangle is a triangle with two angles of 45° and one right angle. It's sometimes called an isosceles right triangle, since it's both isosceles and right. Like the 30-60-90 triangle, the lengths of the sides of a 45-45-90 triangle also follow a specific pattern. If the legs are of length x (the legs will always be equal), then the hypotenuse has length $x\sqrt{2}$:

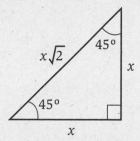

Know this $1:1:\sqrt{2}$ ratio for 45-45-90 triangles. It will save you time and may even save your butt.

Also, just as two 30-60-90 triangles form an equilateral triangles, two 45-45-90 triangles form a square. We explain the colossal importance of this fact when we cover polygons a little later in this chapter.

Similar Triangles

Similar triangles have the same shape but not necessarily the same size. Or, if you prefer more math-geek jargon, two triangles are "similar" if the ratio of the lengths of their corresponding sides is constant (which you now know means that their corresponding angles must be congruent). Take a look at a few similar triangles:

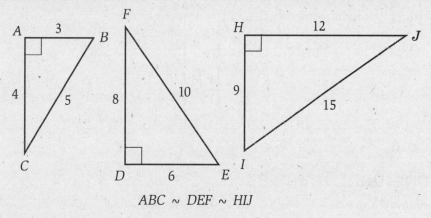

$$ABC \sim DEF \sim HIJ$$

As you may have assumed from the figure above, the symbol for "is similar to" is $\sim$. So, if triangle ABC is similar to triangle DEF, we write $ABC \sim DEF$.

There are two crucial facts about similar triangles.

- Corresponding angles of similar triangles are identical.
- Corresponding sides of similar triangles are proportional.

For $ABC \sim DEF$, the corresponding angles are $\angle A = \angle D$, $\angle B = \angle E$, and $\angle C = \angle F$. The corresponding sides are $^{AB}/_{DE} = {}^{BC}/_{EF} = {}^{CA}/_{FD}$.

The SAT usually tests similarity by presenting you with a single triangle that contains a line segment parallel to one base. This line segment creates a second, smaller, similar triangle. In the figure below, for example, line segment DE is parallel to CB, and triangle ABC is similar to triangle AE.

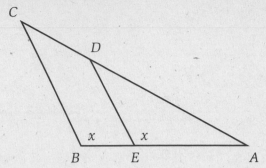

After presenting you with a diagram like the one above, the SAT will ask a question like this:

If $CB = 6$ and $AD = \frac{2}{3}AC$, what is DE?

Notice that this question doesn't tell you outright that DE and CB are parallel. But it does tell you that both lines form the same angle, $x°$, when they intersect with BA, so you should be able to figure out that they're parallel. And once you see that they're parallel, you should immediately recognize that $ABC \sim AED$ and that the corresponding sides of the two triangles are in constant proportion. The question tells you what this proportion is when it tells you that $AD = {}^2/_3AC$. To solve for DE, plug it into the proportion along with CB:

$$\frac{2}{3} = \frac{DE}{CB}$$
$$\frac{2}{3} = \frac{DE}{6}$$
$$3 \times DE = 12$$
$$DE = 4$$

Congruent Triangles

Congruent triangles are identical. Some SAT questions may state directly that two triangles are congruent. Others may include congruent triangles without explicit mention, however.

Two triangles are congruent if they meet any of the following criteria:

1. All the corresponding sides of the two triangles are equal. This is known as the Side-Side-Side (SSS) method of determining congruency.

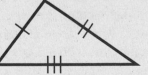 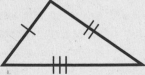

2. The corresponding sides of each triangle are equal, and the mutual angles between those corresponding sides are also equal. This is known as the Side-Angle-Side (SAS) method of determining congruency.

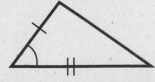 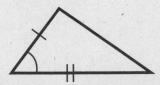

3. The two triangles share two equal corresponding angles and also share any pair of corresponding sides. This is known as the Angle-Side-Angle (ASA) method of determining congruency

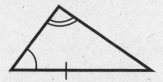 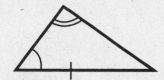

Perimeter of a Triangle

The perimeter of a triangle is equal to the sum of the lengths of the triangle's three sides. If a triangle has sides of lengths 4, 6, and 9, then its perimeter is $4 + 6 + 9 = 19$. Easy. Done and done.

Area of a Triangle

The formula for the area of a triangle is

$$A = \frac{1}{2}bh$$

where b is the length of a base of the triangle, and h is height (also called the altitude). The heights of a few triangles are pictured below with their altitudes drawn in as dotted lines.

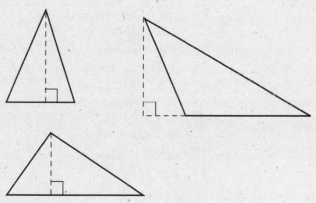

We said "a base" above instead of "the base" because you can actually use any of the three sides of the triangle as the base; a triangle has no particular side that has to be the base. You get to choose.

The SAT may test the area of a triangle in a few ways. It might just tell you the altitude and the length of the base, in which case you could just plug the numbers into the formula. But you probably won't get such an easy question. It's more likely that you'll have to find the altitude, using other tools and techniques from plane geometry. For example, try to find the area of the triangle below:

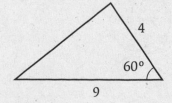

To find the area of this triangle, draw in the altitude from the base (of length 9) to the opposite vertex. Notice that now you have two triangles, and one of them (the smaller one on the right) is a 30-60-90 triangle.

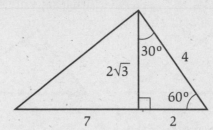

The hypotenuse of this 30-60-90 triangle is 4, so according to the ratio $1 : \sqrt{3} : 2$, the short side must be 2 and the medium side, which is also the altitude of the original triangle, is $2\sqrt{3}$. *Now* you can plug the base and altitude into the formula to find the area of the original triangle: $^1/_2bh = {}^1/_2(9)(2\sqrt{3}) = 9\sqrt{3}$.

20.5 POLYGONS

A polygon is a two-dimensional figure with three or more straight sides. (So triangles are actually a type of polygon.) Polygons are named according to the number of sides they have.

Number of Sides	Name
3	triangle
4	quadrilateral
5	pentagon
6	hexagon
7	heptagon
8	octagon
9	nonagon
10	decagon
12	dodecagon
n	n-gon

All polygons, no matter how many sides they possess, share certain characteristics:

- The sum of the interior angles of a polygon with n sides is $(n-2)180°$. For instance, the sum of the interior angles of an octagon is $(8-2)180° = 6(180°) = 1080°$.
- The sum of the exterior angles of any polygon is $360°$.
- The perimeter of a polygon is the sum of the lengths of its sides. The perimeter of the hexagon below is $5 + 4 + 3 + 8 + 6 + 9 = 35$.

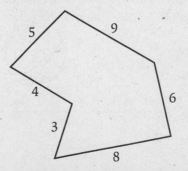

Regular Polygons

The polygon whose perimeter you just calculated was an irregular polygon. But most of the polygons on the SAT are regular: Their sides are of equal length and their angles congruent. Neither of these conditions can exist without the other. If the sides are all equal, the angles will all be congruent, and vice versa. In the diagram below, you'll see, from left to right, a regular pentagon, a regular octagon, and a square (also known as a regular quadrilateral):

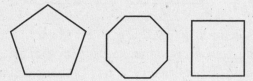

Quadrilaterals

Good news: Most polygons on the SAT have just four sides. You won't have to tangle with any dodecahedrons on the SAT you take. But this silver cloud actually has a dark lining: There are *five* different types of quadrilaterals that pop up on the test. These five quadrilaterals are trapezoids, parallelograms, rectangles, rhombuses, and squares.

Trapezoids

A trapezoid may sound like a new *Star Wars* character. Certainly, it would be less annoying than Jar Jar Binks. But it's actually the name of a quadrilateral with one pair of parallel sides and one pair of nonparallel sides.

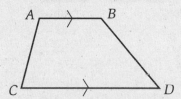

In this trapezoid, *AB* is parallel to *CD* (shown by the arrow marks), whereas *AC* and *BD* are not parallel.

The formula for the area of a trapezoid is

$$A = \frac{s_1 + s_2}{2} h$$

where s_1 and s_2 are the lengths of the parallel sides (also called the bases of the trapezoid), and h is the height. In a trapezoid, the height is the perpendicular distance from one base to the other.

To find the area of a trapezoid on the SAT, you'll often have to use your knowledge of triangles. Try to find the area of the trapezoid pictured below:

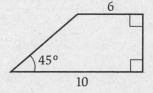

The question tells you the length of the bases of this trapezoid, 6 and 10. But to find the area, you first need to find the height. To do that, split the trapezoid into a rectangle and a 45-45-90 triangle by drawing in the height.

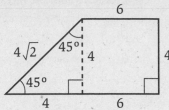

Once, you've drawn in the height, you can split the base that's equal to 10 into two parts: The base of the rectangle is 6, and the leg of the triangle is 4. Since the triangle is 45-45-90, the two legs must be equal. This leg, though, is also the height of the trapezoid. So the height of the trapezoid is 4. Now you can plug the numbers into the formula:

$$A = \frac{6 + 10}{2}(4) = 8(4) = 32$$

Parallelogram

A parallelogram is a quadrilateral whose opposite sides are parallel.

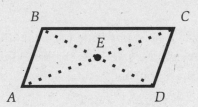

In a parallelogram,

- Opposite sides are equal in length: $BC = AD$ and $AB = DC$
- Opposite angles are equal: $\angle ABC = \angle ADC$ and $\angle BAD = \angle BCD$
- Adjacent angles are supplementary: $\angle ABC + \angle BCD = 180°$
- The diagonals bisect (split) each other: $BE = ED$ and $AE = EC$
- One diagonal splits a parallelogram into two congruent triangles: $\triangle ABD = \triangle BCD$
- Two diagonals split a parallelogram into two pairs of congruent triangles: $\triangle AEB = \triangle DEC$ and $\triangle BEC = \triangle AED$

The area of a parallelogram is given by the formula

$$\text{Area} = bh$$

where b is the length of the base, and h is the height.

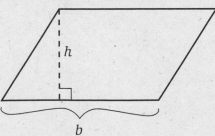

Rectangles

A rectangle is a quadrilateral in which the opposite sides are parallel and the interior angles are all right angles. Another way to look at rectangles is as parallelograms in which the angles are all right angles. As with parallelograms, the opposite sides of a rectangle are equal.

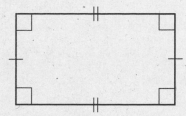

The formula for the area of a rectangle is

$$A = bh$$

where b is the length of the base, and h is the height.

The diagonals of a rectangle are always equal to each other. And one diagonal through the rectangle cuts the rectangle into two equal right triangles. In the figure below, the diagonal BD cuts rectangle $ABCD$ into congruent right triangles ABD and BCD.

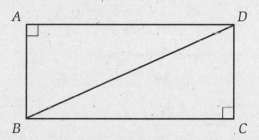

Since the diagonal of the rectangle forms right triangles that include the diagonal and two sides of the rectangle, if you know two of these values, you can always calculate the third with the Pythagorean theorem. If you know the side lengths of the rectangle, you can calculate the diagonal. If you know the diagonal and one side length, you can calculate the other side. Also, keep in mind that the diagonal might cut the rectangle into a 30-60-90 triangle. That would make your calculating job even easier.

Rhombus

A rhombus is a specialized parallelogram in which all four sides are of equal length.

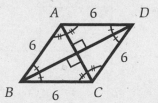

In a rhombus,

- All four sides are equal: $AD = DC = CB = BA$
- The diagonals bisect each other and form perpendicular lines (but note that the diagonals are not equal in length)

- The diagonals bisect the vertex angles ($\angle ADB = \angle CDB$, $\angle DCA = \angle BCA$)

The formula for the area of a rhombus is

$$A = bh$$

where b is the length of the base and h is the height.

To find the area of a rhombus on the SAT (you guessed it), you'll probably have to split it into triangles:

If *ABCD* is a rhombus, *AC* = 4, and *ABD* is an equilateral triangle, what is the area of the rhombus?

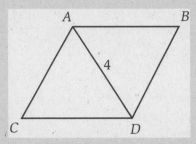

Since *ABD* is an equilateral triangle, the length of each side of the rhombus must be 4, and angles *ADB* and *ABD* are 60°. All you have to do is find the height of the rhombus. Draw an altitude from *A* to *DC* to create a 30-60-90 triangle.

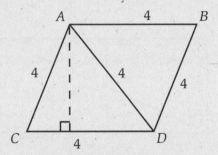

Figure Not Drawn to Scale

Since the hypotenuse of the 30-60-90 triangle is 4, you can use the ratio $1 : \sqrt{3} : 2$ to calculate that the length of this altitude is $2\sqrt{3}$. The area formula for a rhombus is *bh*, so the area of this rhombus is $4 \times 2\sqrt{3} = 8\sqrt{3}$.

Square

A square combines the special features of the rectangle and rhombus: All its angles are 90°, and all four of its sides are equal in length.

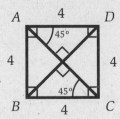

The square has two more crucial special qualities. In a square,

- Diagonals bisect each other at right angles and are equal in length.
- Diagonals bisect the vertex angles to create 45° angles. (This means that one diagonal will cut the square into two 45-45-90 triangles, while *two* diagonals break the square into *four* 45-45-90 triangles.)

The formula for the area of a square is

$$A = s^2$$

where s is the length of a side of the square.

Because a diagonal drawn into the square forms two congruent 45-45-90 triangles, if you know the length of one side of the square, you can always calculate the length of the diagonal:

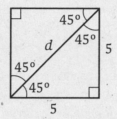

Since d is the hypotenuse of the 45-45-90 triangle that has legs of length 5, according to the ratio $1:1:\sqrt{2}$, you know that $d = s\sqrt{2}$.

Similarly, if you know the length of the diagonal, you can calculate the length of the sides of the square.

20.6 CIRCLES

A circle is the collection of points equidistant from a given point, called the *center*. A circle is named after its center point. The distance from the center to any point on the circle is called the radius, (r), the most important measurement in a circle. If you know a circle's radius, you can figure out all its other characteristics. The diameter (d) of a circle is twice as long as the radius ($d = 2r$) and stretches between endpoints on the circle, passing through the center. A chord also extends from endpoint to endpoint on the circle, but it does not necessarily pass through the center. In the figure below, point C is the center of the circle, r is the radius, and AB is a chord.

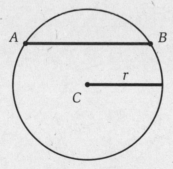

Tangent Lines

Tangents are lines that intersect a circle at only one point. Tangents are a new addition to the SAT. You can bet that the new SAT will make sure to cram at least one tangent question into every test.

Just like everything else in geometry, tangent lines are defined by certain fixed rules. Know these rules and you'll be able to handle anything the SAT throws at you.

Here's the first: A radius whose endpoint is the intersection point of the tangent line and the circle is always perpendicular to the tangent line. See?

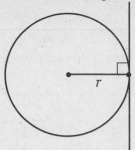

And the second rule: Every point in space outside the circle can extend exactly two tangent lines to the circle. The distance from the origin of the two tangents to the points of tangency are always equal. In the figure below, $XY = XZ$.

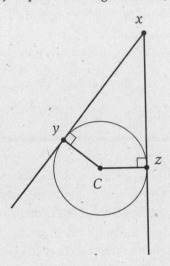

Tangents and Triangles

Tangent lines are most likely to appear in conjunction with triangles.

What is the area of triangle QRS if RS is tangent to circle Q?

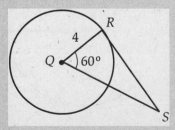

You can answer this question only if you know the rules of circles and tangent lines. The question doesn't tell you that QR is the radius of the circle; you just have to know it: Because the circle is named circle Q, point Q must be the center of the circle, and any line drawn from the center to the edge of the circle is the radius. The question also doesn't tell you that QR is perpendicular to RS. You have to know that they're perpendicular because QR is a radius and RS is a tangent that meet at the same point.

If you know how to deduce those key facts about this circle, then the actual math in the question is simple. Since QR and RS are perpendicular, and angle RQS is 60°, triangle QRS is a 30-60-90 triangle. The image tells you that side QR, the side opposite the 30° angle equals 4. Side QR is the height of the triangle. To calculate the area, you just have to figure out which of the other two sides is the base. Since the height and base of the triangle must be perpendicular to each other, side *RS* must be the base. To find *RS*, use the $1:\sqrt{3}:2$ ratio. *RS* is the side opposite 60°, so it's the $\sqrt{3}$ side: $RS = 4\sqrt{3}$. The area of triangle QRS is $\frac{1}{2}(4)(4\sqrt{3}) = 8\sqrt{3}$.

Central Angles and Inscribed Angles

An angle whose vertex is the center of the circle is called a *central angle*.

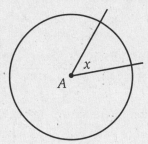

The degree of the circle (the slice of pie) cut by a central angle is equal to the measure of the angle. If a central angle is 25°, then it cuts a 25° arc in the circle.

An inscribed angle is an angle formed by two chords originating from a single point.

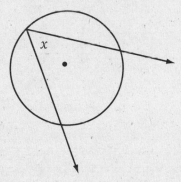

An inscribed angle will always cut out an arc in the circle that is *twice* the size of the degree of the inscribed angle. If an inscribed angle has a degree of 40, it will cut an arc of 80° in the circle.

If an inscribed angle and a central angle cut out the same arc in a circle, the central angle will be twice as large as the inscribed angle.

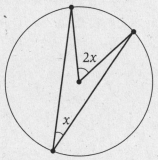

Circumference of a Circle

The circumference is the perimeter of the circle. The formula for circumference of a circle is

$$C = 2\pi r$$

where *r* is the radius. The formula can also be written $C = \pi d$, where *d* is the diameter. Try to find the circumference of the circle below:

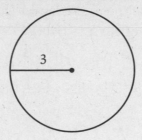

Plugging the radius into the formula, $C = 2\pi r = 2\pi\,(3) = 6\pi$.

Arc Length

An arc is a *part* of a circle's circumference. An arc contains two endpoints and all the points on the circle between the endpoints. By picking any two points on a circle, two arcs are created: a major arc, which is by definition the longer arc, and a minor arc, the shorter one.

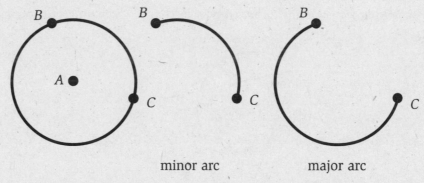

minor arc   major arc

Since the degree of an arc is defined by the central or inscribed angle that intercepts the arc's endpoints, you can calculate the arc length as long as you know the circle's radius and the measure of either the central or inscribed angle.

The arc length formula is

$$\text{arc length} = \frac{n}{360} \times 2\pi r$$

where *n* is the measure of the degree of the arc, and *r* is the radius.

Here's the sort of question the SAT might ask:

Circle *D* has radius 9. What is the length of arc *AB*?

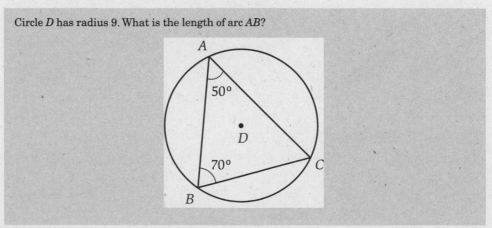

In order to figure out the length of arc *AB*, you need to know the radius of the circle and the measure of ∠*C*, the inscribed angle that intercepts the endpoints of *AB*. The question tells you the radius of the circle, but it throws you a little curveball by not providing you with the measure of $\angle C$. Instead, the question puts $\angle C$ in a triangle and tells you the measures of the other two angles in the triangle. Like we said, only a little curveball: You can easily figure out the measure of $\angle C$ because, as you (better) know, the three angles of a triangle add up to 180°.

$$\angle c = 180° - (50° + 70°)$$
$$\angle c = 180° - 120°$$
$$\angle c = 60°$$

Since angle c is an inscribed angle, arc AB must be 120°. Now you can plug these values into the formula for arc length:

$$AB = \frac{120}{360} \times 2\pi 9$$
$$AB = \frac{1}{3} \times 18\pi$$
$$AB = 6\pi$$

Area of a Circle

If you know the radius of a circle, you can figure out its area. The formula for area is:

$$\text{Area} = \pi r^2$$

where r is the radius. So when you need to find the area of a circle, your real goal is to figure out the radius.

Area of a Sector

A sector of a circle is the area enclosed by a central angle and the circle itself. It's shaped like a slice of pizza. The shaded region in the figure below is a sector:

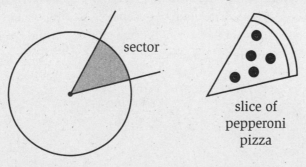

sector

slice of
pepperoni
pizza

There are no analogies on the SAT anymore, but here's one anyway: The area of a sector is related to the area of a circle just as the length of an arc is related to the circumference. To find the area of a sector, find what fraction of 360° the sector makes up and multiply this fraction by the area of the circle.

$$\text{Area of Sector} = \frac{n}{360} \times \pi r^2$$

where n is the measure of the central angle that forms the boundary of the sector, and r is the radius.

Try to find the area of the sector in the figure below:

The sector is bounded by a 70° central angle in a circle whose radius is 6. Using the formula, the area of the sector is

$$A = \frac{70}{360} \times \pi(6)^2 = \frac{7}{36} \times 36\pi = 7\pi$$

Polygons and Circles

We've talked already about triangles in circle problems. But all kinds of polygons have also been known to make cameos on SAT circle questions. Here's an example:

What is the length of minor arc *BE* if the area of rectangle *ABCD* is 18?

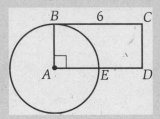

To find the length of minor arc *BE*, you have to know two things: the radius of the circle and the measure of the central angle that intersects the circle at points *B* and *E*. Because *ABCD* is a rectangle, and rectangles only have right angles, figuring out the measure of the central angle is simple. ∠*BAD* is 90°, so the measure of the central angle is 90°.

Finding the radius of the circle is a little tougher. From the diagram, you can see that the radius is equal to the height of the rectangle. To find the height of the rectangle, you can use the fact that the area of the rectangle is 18, and the length is 6. Since A = *bh*, and you know the values of both *a* and *b*,

$$h = A \div b$$
$$= 18 \div 6$$
$$= 3$$

Now that you've got the radius and measure of the angle, plug them into the arc length formula to find the length of minor arc *BE*.

$$BE = \frac{90}{360} \times 2\pi(3)$$

$$BE = \frac{1}{4} \times 6\pi$$

$$BE = \frac{6\pi}{4}$$

$$BE = \frac{3\pi}{2}$$

20.7 SOLID AS A ROCK

Solids are three-dimensional shapes, with the dimension of depth added to length and height. With solids, there's good news and bad news. The bad news is that solids can be difficult to visualize. But the good news more than makes up for it: The only solids on the new SAT are cubes, rectangular solids, and right cylinders. Learn to visualize these three shapes now, before the test, and you'll be fine.

Rectangular Solids

A rectangular solid is a prism with a rectangular base and edges that are perpendicular to its base. It looks a lot like a cardboard box.

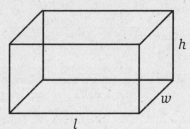

A rectangular solid has three important dimensions: length (l), width (w), and height (h). If you know these three measurements, you can find the solid's surface area, volume, and diagonal length.

Volume of a Rectangular Solid

The formula for the volume of a rectangular solid takes the formula for area of a rectangle and adds another dimension. The area of a rectangle is $A = lh$ (area equals length times height). The formula for the volume of a rectangular solid adds on width:

$$\text{Volume} = lwh$$

Here's a good old-fashioned example:

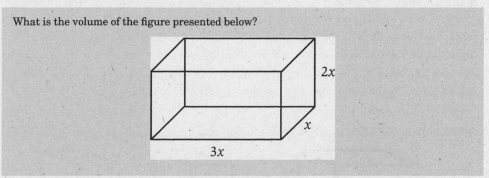

What is the volume of the figure presented below?

Just plug the values into the volume formula and you're good to go: $V = (3x)(2x)(x) = 6x^3$.

Surface Area of a Rectangular Solid

The surface area of a solid is the area of its outermost skin. In the case of rectangular solids, imagine a cardboard box all closed up. The surface of that closed box is made of six rectangles: the sum of the areas of the six rectangles is the surface area of the box. To make things even easier, the six rectangles come in three congruent pairs. We've marked the congruent pairs by shades of gray in the image below: One pair is clear, one pair is light gray, and one pair is dark gray.

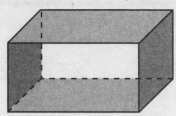

Two faces have areas of $l \times w$, two faces have areas of $l \times h$, and two faces have areas of $w \times h$. The surface area of the entire solid is the sum of the areas of the congruent pairs:

$$\text{Surface Area} = 2lw + 2lh + 2wh$$

Wanna practice? Alright. What's the surface area of this guy?

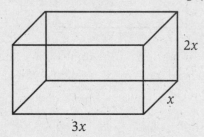

Plug in. Plug in. Plug in.

$$\begin{aligned}
\text{Surface Area} &= 2lw + 2lh + 2wh \\
&= 2(3x)(x) + 2(3x)(2x) + 2(x)(2x) \\
&= 6x^2 + 12x^2 + 4x^2 \\
&= 22x^2
\end{aligned}$$

Meat Cleaver Problems

The SAT won't just hand you surface area questions on a silver platter. It'll make you work for them. One of the ways the SAT likes to make you work goes like this. A question will describe a solid, give you all of its measurements, and then tell you that the box has been cut in half. You'll then have to find the combined surface area of the two new boxes. For example, pictured below is a rectangular solid that has a length of 8, a depth of 4, and a height of 4. Then, out of the blue, a giant cleaver comes down and cuts the solid into two cubes.

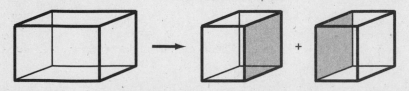

As you can see from the diagram, when the rectangle was cut in two, two new surfaces suddenly appeared (these are the darkened surfaces). But notice that the total volume of the two cubes has remained the same. So here's a rule: *Whenever a solid is cut into smaller pieces, its surface area increases, but its volume is unchanged.* The SAT loves to test this little factoid.

Diagonal Length of a Rectangular Solid

The diagonal of a rectangular solid, *d*, is the line segment whose endpoints are opposite corners of the solid. Every rectangular solid has four diagonals, each with the same length, that connect each pair of opposite vertices. Here's one diagonal drawn in:

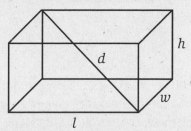

It's possible that an SAT question will test to see if you can find the length of a diagonal. Now you can:

$$d = \sqrt{l^2 + w^2 + h^2}$$

where *l* is the length, *w* is the width, and *h* is the height. The formula is like a pumped up Vin Diesel version of the Pythagorean theorem. Check it out in action:

What is the length of diagonal *AH* in the rectangular solid below if *AC* = 5, *GH* = 6, and *CG* = 3?

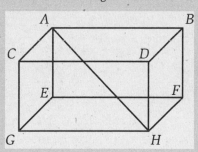

The question gives the length, width, and height of the rectangular solid, so you can just plug those numbers into the formula:

$$AH = \sqrt{5^2 + 6^2 + 3^2} = \sqrt{25 + 36 + 9} = \sqrt{70}$$

Cubes

A cube is a square brought into 3-D. The length, width, and height of a cube are equal, and each of its six faces is a square.

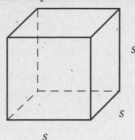

Volume of a Cube

The formula for finding the volume of a cube is essentially the same as the formula for the volume of a rectangular volume. However, since a cube's length, width, and height are all equal, the formula for the volume of a cube is

$$\text{Volume of a Cube} = s^3$$

where s is the length of one edge of the cube.

Surface Area of a Cube

Since a cube is just a rectangular solid whose sides are all equal, the formula for finding the surface area of a cube is the same as the formula for finding the surface area of a rectangular solid, except with s substituted in for l, w, and h:

$$\text{Surface Area of a Cube} = 6s^2$$

Diagonal Length of a Cube

The formula for the diagonal of a cube is also adapted from the formula for the diagonal length of a rectangular solid, with s substituted for l, w, and h.

$$\sqrt{3s^2} = s\sqrt{3}$$

Right Circular Cylinders

A right circular cylinder looks like one of those cardboard things that toilet paper comes on, except it isn't hollow. In fact, one way to think of a right circular cylinder is as a rectangle curved around so that its ends meet.

A right circular cylinder has two connected congruent circular bases and looks like this:

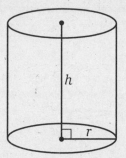

The height of a cylinder, h, is the length of the line segment whose endpoints are the centers of the bases. The radius of a cylinder, r, is the radius of its base. For the new SAT, all you need to know about a right circular cylinder is how to calculate its volume.

Volume of a Cylinder

The volume of a cylinder is the product of the area of its base and its height. Because a cylinder has a circular base, the volume of a cylinder is equal to the area of the circle that is the base times the height:

$$\text{Volume of a Cylinder} = \pi r^2 h$$

Try to find the volume of the cylinder below:

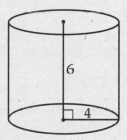

This cylinder has a radius of 4 and a height of 6. Using the volume formula,

$$\text{Volume} = \pi(4)^2(6) = 96\pi$$

Sketchy Word Problems

The SAT has been known to ask word problems about solids. Because solids are so difficult to visualize, these problems can seem brutally difficult. So here's the rule: *Always sketch out what the question is describing.* Once you see what the question's talking about, you seldom have to do much more than plug the right numbers into the right equation.

20.8 GEOMETRIC VISUALIZATIONS

Geometric-visualization questions give you an image on paper and ask you to twist or flip it in your mind.

If a square piece of paper were folded into a rectangle, as seen in Fig. I, and then cut, as seen in Fig. II, what would the paper look like when it was unfolded again?

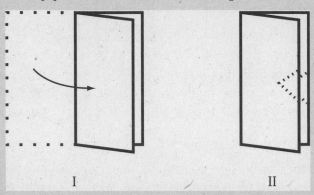

I   II

There are no formulas on these types of questions, no surefire method of attack. All we're really doing is warning you that they're lurking out there, and telling you to draw a sketch *before* looking at the answer choices. The answer, incidentally, is

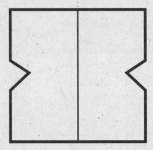

20.9 COORDINATE GEOMETRY

The new SAT has stepped up the emphasis on coordinate geometry, which is the study of geometric shapes on the coordinate plane. If you think the coordinate plane is a ferocious type of new jet fighter, don't worry. We're about to clear this all up for you.

The Coordinate Plane

The coordinate plane is where all the magic happens. It's the space in which coordinate geometry exists. Pretty snazzy.

Every point on a coordinate plane can be mapped by using two perpendicular number lines. The x-axis defines the space from left to right. The y-axis defines the space up and down. And the two meet at a point called the origin.

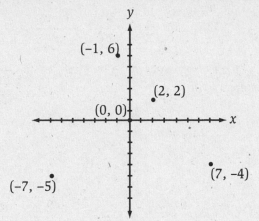

Every point on the plane has two coordinates. Because it's the center of the plane, the origin gets the coordinates (0,0). The coordinates of all other points indicate how far they are from the origin. These coordinates are written in the form (x, y). The x-coordinate is the point's location along the x-axis (its distance either to the left or right of the origin). If the point is to the right of the origin, the x-coordinate is positive. If the point is to the left of the y-axis, the x-coordinate is negative.

The y-coordinate of a point is its location along the y-axis (either up or down from the origin). If the point is above the x-axis, its y-coordinate is positive, and if the point is below the x-axis, its y-coordinate is negative. So the point labeled (2,2) is 2 to the right and 2 above the origin. The point labeled (-7,-5) is 7 to the left and 5 below the origin.

Are We There Yet? Distance on the Coordinate Plane

The SAT tests to see if you can find the distance between any two points on the coordinate plane. It also tests to see if you can find the midpoint between two points on the test. This news should make you happy. Why? Because these are easy questions that you can answer easily as long as you know the two necessary formulas. Now we're going to make sure you know those two formulas. Memorize them.

The Distance Between Two Points

If you know the coordinates of any two points—we'll call them (x_1, y_1) and (x_2, y_2)—you can find their distance from each other with the aptly named distance formula:

$$\text{Distance} = \sqrt{(x_2 - x_1)^2 + (y_2 - y_1)^2}$$

Let's say you were suddenly overcome by the desire to calculate the distance between the points (4,-3) and (-3,8). Just plug the coordinates into the formula:

$$\text{Distance} = \sqrt{(-3 - 4)^2 + (8 - (-3))^2}$$
$$= \sqrt{49 + 121}$$
$$= \sqrt{170}$$

Finding Midpoints

As for the midpoint between the two points (x_1, y_1) and (x_2, y_2), the formula to use is

$$\text{Midpoint} = \left(\frac{x_1 + x_2}{2}, \frac{y_1 + y_2}{2}\right)$$

In other words, the x- and y-coordinates of the midpoint are the averages of the x- and y-coordinates of the endpoints. To find the midpoint of the points $(6,0)$ and $(3,7)$,

$$\begin{aligned}
\text{Midpoint} &= \left(\frac{6 + 3}{2}, \frac{0 + 7}{2}\right) \\
&= \left(\frac{9}{2}, \frac{7}{2}\right) \\
&= (4.5, 3.5)
\end{aligned}$$

Lines in the Coordinate Plane

You already know that a line is just an infinite set of points arrayed in a straight formation. But once you stick one of those "infinite set of points" into a coordinate plane, it has all sorts of properties you can analyze. And the SAT will make sure you know how to analyze 'em.

The Slope of a Line

A line's slope is a measurement of how steeply that line climbs or falls as it moves from left to right. If you want the technical jargon, slope is a line's vertical change divided by its horizontal change. Or, if you prefer the poetic version,

Slope is "the rise over run."

If you've got two points on a line, once again (x_1, y_1) and (x_2, y_2), the slope of that line can be calculated using the following formula:

$$\text{Slope} = \frac{y_2 - y_1}{x_2 - x_1}$$

The variable most often used to represent slope is m.

So, for example, the slope of a line that contains the points $(-2, -4)$ and $(6, 1)$ is

$$m = \frac{1 - (-4)}{6 - (-2)} = \frac{1 + 4}{6 + 2} = \frac{5}{8}$$

Positive and Negative Slopes

The slopes of some lines are positive, the slopes of others are negative. Whether a line has a positive or negative slope is easy to tell just by looking at a graph of the line. If the line slopes uphill as you trace it from left to right, the slope is positive. If a line slopes downhill as you trace it from left to right, the slope is negative. Uphill = positive. Downhill = negative.

You can get a sense of the magnitude of the slope of a line by looking at the line's steepness. The steeper the line, the greater the slope; the flatter the line, the smaller the slope. Note that an extremely positive slope is *larger* then a moderately positive slope, while an extremely negative slope is *smaller* then a moderately negative slope.

Check out the lines below and try to determine whether the slope of each line is negative or positive and which has the greatest slope:

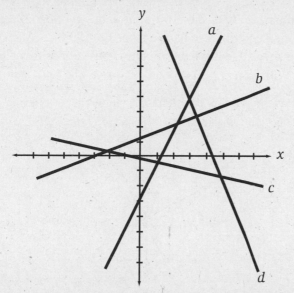

Lines *a* and *b* have positive slopes, and lines *c* and *d* have negative slopes. In terms of slope magnitude, line *a* > *b* > *c* > *d*.

Slopes You Should Know by Sight

There are certain easy-to-recognize slopes that it pays to recognize by sight. Knowing how to pick them out instantly will save you precious time.

- A horizontal line has a slope of zero. Since there is no "rise," $y_2 - y_1 = 0$, $m = (y_2 - y_1)/(x_2 - x_1) = 0/(x_2 - x_1) = 0$.
- A vertical line has an undefined slope. In this case, there is no "run," and $x_2 - x_1 = 0$. So, $m = (y_2 - y_1)/(x_2 - x_1) = (y_2 - y_1)/0$, and any fraction with zero in its denominator is, by definition, undefined.
- A line that makes a 45° angle with a horizontal line has a slope of either 1 or –1, depending on whether it's going up or down from left to right. In this case, the rise equals the run: $y_2 - y_1 = x_2 - x_1$, or $y_2 - y_1 = -(x_2 - x_1)$.

Of the four lines pictured below, which has a slope of 0, which has a slope of 1, which has a slope of –1, which has an undefined slope?

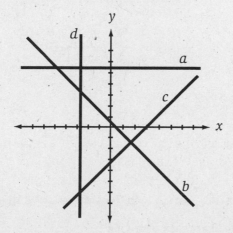

Line *a* has slope 0 because it's horizontal. Line *b* has slope –1 because it slopes downward at 45° as you move from left to right. Line *c* has slope 1 because it slopes upward at 45° as you move from left to right. Line *d* has undefined slope because it is vertical.

The Slopes of Parallel and Perpendicular Lines

The slopes of parallel and perpendicular lines always have the same relationships.

- The slopes of parallel lines are always the same. If one line has a slope of m, any line parallel to it will also have a slope of m.

- The slopes of perpendicular lines are always the opposite reciprocals of each other. A line with slope m is perpendicular to a line with a slope of $-1/m$.

In the figure below, lines q and r both have a slope of 2, so they are parallel. Line s is perpendicular to both lines q and r, so it has a slope of $-1/2$.

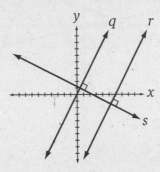

Equation of a Line

Coordinate geometry is actually where algebra and geometry meet. Coordinate geometry allows you to "graph" algebraic equations. For the new SAT, you need to know the equation of a line and how to graph that equation. The equation of a line is

$$y = mx + b$$

where m is the slope of the line, and b is the y-intercept of the line (the y-coordinate of the point where the line intersects the y-axis). As long as you know the slope of the line and the y-intercept, you can write the equation of the line.

To sketch a line whose equation you know, first plot the y-intercept, and then use the slope of the line to plot another point. Connect the two points to form your line. The figure below graphs the line $y = -2x + 3$.

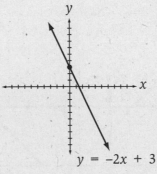

$$y = -2x + 3$$

Since the y-intercept is at 3, the line crosses the y-axis at $(0, 3)$. And since the slope is equal to -2, the line descends two units for every one unit it moves in the positive x direction. In other words, from $(0,3)$, the line moves one unit to the right and two units down, to point $(1,1)$. You could graph the line using those two points.

Finding the x- and y-Intercepts of a Line

The y-intercept of a line is the y-coordinate of the point where the line intersects the y-axis. The x-intercept of a line is the x-coordinate of the point where the line intersects the x-axis. You can find either the x- or y-intercept of a line by using the slope-intercept form of the line equation.

Finding the intercepts is very straightforward. To find the y-intercept, set $x = 0$ and solve for y. To solve for the x-intercept, set $y = 0$ and solve for x. For example, if you've got the line equation $y = -3x + 2$, the y-intercept equals 2, since $y = -3(0) + 2 = 2$. To find the x-intercept, set $y = 0$ and solve:

$$0 = -3x + 2$$

$$3x = 2$$

$$x = \frac{2}{3}$$

Parabolas Attack! Quadratic Equations Invade the Coordinate Plane

When a quadratic equation is graphed on the coordinate plane, the result is a parabola, which is a giant man-eating insect. Actually, it's a harmless, U-shaped curve that can open either upward or downward.

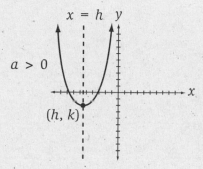

If the SAT covers parabolas at all, it'll most likely do one of these things:

1. Give you an equation and ask you to choose which graph matches the equation.
2. Give you a graph and ask you to choose which equation matches the graph.

You can answer either of these questions as long as you can read the quadratic equation to identify the location of a parabola's vertex and determine whether the parabola opens upward or downward. Here's how to do it.

The equation for a parabola looks like this:

$$y = ax^2 + bx + c$$

where a, b, and c are constants. By plugging a, b, or c into the correct formulas, you can figure out where the vertex is and whether the parabola opens upward or downward:

1. The vertex of the parabola is located at point $(-b/2a, c - b^2/4a)$.
2. The parabola opens upward if $a > 0$, and downward if $a < 0$.

So, if you're given the quadratic equation $y = 2x^2 - 3x + 4$, you know that the parabola opens upward, since $a > 0$. And you could figure out the vertex by plugging in. The x-coordinate would be

$$-\frac{b}{2a} = -\left(\frac{-3}{4}\right) = \frac{3}{4}$$

And the y-coordinate would be

$$c - \frac{b^2}{4a} = 4 - \frac{(-3)^2}{4(2)} = 4 - \frac{9}{8} = 2\frac{7}{8}$$

Put it all together, and you've got a parabola that looks something like this:

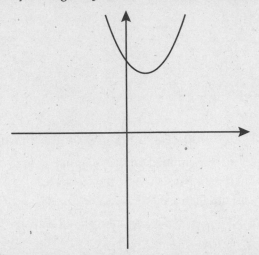

Of course, if you had a graphing calculator, you wouldn't have to go through any of this calculation at all. This is one of the many reasons we steadfastly demand that you have a graphing calculator and know how to use it for the new SAT.

Transformations

There's just one more bit of coordinate geometry you have to know for the new SAT: how slight changes to a function change the way that the graph of that function looks in the coordinate plane. There are two different kinds of transformations you have to know how to deal with: shifts and stretches.

Shifts

Imagine a graph. No, better yet, look at this graph:

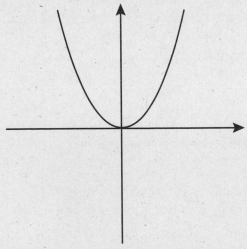

It's a pretty simple graph: a parabola that has a vertex at the origin. To put it into math, $f(x) = x^2$. A shift of this graph would occur when the parabola remains exactly the same shape but is shifted over either vertically or horizontally so that the vertex no longer rests on the origin.

Vertical Shift   Horizontal Shift

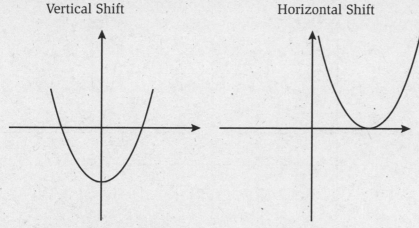

To get a vertical or horizontal shift, you have to do slightly different things, but each type of shift has one thing in common: addition or subtraction.

Horizontal Shifts

To get a horizontal shift, in which the graph moves either to the left or right, you use addition. But this time, you need to add within the parentheses. So, if you want to move the graph of the function $f(x)$ two spaces to the right, you make the function $f(x + 2)$. If you want to move it four spaces to the left, you make the function $f(x - 4)$.

Vertical Shifts

Vertical shifts are extremely easy. If you want the image to shift up two spots, just add the number 2 to it. If you want it to shift down four spots, subtract the number 4. So, an equation of a parabola that is two spaces above the origin would look like this: $f(x) + 2 = x^2 + 2$. And an equation that's four spaces below would look like this $f(x) - 4 = x^2 - 4$.

Stretches

Imagine a graph. No better yet, look at that same example we showed you before.

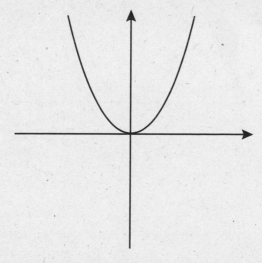

Stretching a graph makes it either fat or thin.

Fat

Thin

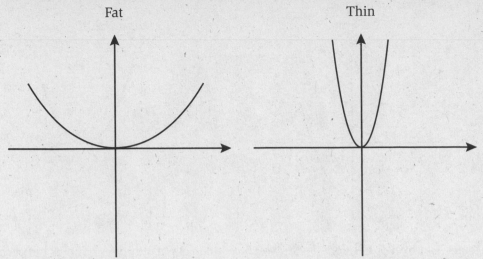

A graph stretches when a function is multiplied, whether that multiplication is $3f(x)$ or $f(3x)$. If a function is multiplied by a number greater than 1, it gets taller and thinner, while if it is multiplied by a number less than 1, it gets stubbier and wider.

That's all the SAT covers on geometry. Just one more SAT Math chapter to go. It's got the longest name—Data, Statistics, and Probability—but it's the shortest of the bunch. Almost there. . . .

DATA, STATISTICS, AND PROBABILITY

THESE ARE THE SAT MATH TOPICS THAT SLIPPED through the cracks. Not quite Numbers and Operations, not nearly Geometry, but still something the new SAT wants you to know.

21.1 STATISTICAL ANALYSIS

Statistical analysis sounds like dental surgery. Scientific and sticky and gross. But SAT statistical analysis is actually not so bad. On these questions, the SAT gives you a data set—a collection of measurements or quantities. An example of a data set is the set of math test scores for the 20 students in Ms. Mathew's fourth-grade class:

71, 83, 57, 66, 95, 96, 68, 71, 84, 85, 87, 90, 88, 90, 84, 90, 90, 93, 97, 99

You are then asked to find one or more of the following values:

1. Arithmetic Mean
2. Median
3. Mode
4. Range

Arithmetic Mean (a.k.a. Average)

Arithmetic mean means the same thing as average. It's also the most commonly tested concept of statistical analysis on the SAT. The basic rule of finding an average isn't complicated: It's the value of the sum of the elements contained in a data set divided by the number of elements in the set.

$$\text{Arithmetic Mean} = \frac{\text{the sum of the elements of a set}}{\text{the number of elements in the set}}$$

Take another look at the test scores of the 20 students in Ms. Mathew's class. We've sorted the scores in her class from lowest to highest:

57, 66, 68, 71, 71, 83, 84, 84, 85, 87, 88, 90, 90, 90, 90, 93, 95, 96, 97, 99

To find the arithmetic mean of this data set, sum the scores and then divide by 20, since there are 20 students in her class:

$$\text{mean} = \frac{57 + 66 + 68 + \cdots + 96 + 97 + 99}{20}$$
$$\text{mean} = \frac{1600}{20}$$
$$\text{mean} = 80$$

But the SAT is Sneaky When It's Mean

But that's not the way that the SAT usually tests mean. It likes to be more complicated and conniving. For example,

> If the average of four numbers is 22, and three of the numbers are 7, 11, and 18, then what is the fourth number?

Here's the key: If you know the average of a group and also know how many numbers are in the group, you can calculate the sum of the numbers in the group. The question above tells you that the average of the numbers is 22 and that there are four numbers in the group. If the average of four numbers is 22, then the four numbers, when added together, must equal $4 \times 22 = 88$. Since you know three of the four numbers in the set, and since you now know the total value of the set, you can write

$$7 + 11 + 18 + \text{unknown number} = 88$$

Solving for the unknown number is easy. All you have to do is subtract the sum of 7, 11, and 18 from 88: $x = 88 - (7 + 11 + 18) = 88 - 36 = 52$.

As long as you realize that you can use an average to find the sum of all the values in a set, you can solve pretty much every question about arithmetic mean on the SAT:

> The average of a set of seven numbers is 54. The average of three of those seven numbers is 38. What is the average of the other four numbers?

This question seems really tough, since it keeps splitting apart its set of seven mysterious numbers. Students often freak out when SAT questions ask them for numbers that seem impossible to determine. Chill out. You don't have to know the exact numbers in the set to answer this problem. All you have to know is how averages work.

There are seven numbers in the entire set, and the average of those numbers is 54. The sum of the seven numbers in the set is $7 \times 54 = 378$. And, as the problem states, three particular numbers from the set have an average of 38. Since the sum of three items is equal to the average of those three numbers multiplied by three, the sum of the three numbers in the problem is $3 \times 38 = 114$. Once you've got that, you can calculate the sum of the four remaining numbers, since that value must be the total sum of the seven numbers minus the sum of the mini-set of three: $378 - 114 = 264$. Now, since you know the total sum of the four numbers, you can get the average by dividing by 4: $264 \div 4 = 66$.

And here's yet another type of question the SAT likes to ask about mean: the dreaded "changing mean" question.

> The mean age of the 14 members of a scuba diving club is 34. When a new member joins, the mean age increased to 37. How old is the new member?

Actually, you shouldn't dread "changing mean" questions at all. They're as simple as other mean questions. Watch. Here's what you know from the question: the original number of members, 14, and the original average age, 34. And you can use this information to calculate the sum of the ages of the members of the original group by multiplying $14 \times 34 = 476$. From the question, you also know the total members of the group after the new member joined, $14 + 1 = 15$, and you know the new average age of the group, 37. So, you can find the sum of the ages of the new group as well: $15 \times 37 = 525$. The age of the new member is just the sum of the age of the new group minus the sum of the age of the old group: $555 - 476 = 79$. That is one ancient scuba diver.

Median

The median is the number whose value is exactly in the middle of all the numbers in a particular set. Take the set $\{6, 19, 3, 11, 7\}$. If the numbers are arranged in order of value, you get

$$\{3, 6, 7, 11, 19\}$$

It's clear that the middle number in this group is 7, so 7 is the median.

If a set has an even number of items, it's impossible to isolate a single number as the median. Here's the last set, but with one more number added:

$$\{3, 6, 7, 11, 19, 20\}$$

In this case, the median equals the average of the two middle numbers. The two middle numbers in this set are 7 and 11, so the median of the set is $(7+11)/2 = 9$.

Mode

The mode is the number within a set that appears most frequently. In the set $\{10, 11, 13, 11, 20\}$, the mode is 11, since it appears twice and all the others appear once. In a set where more than one number appears at the same highest frequency, there can be more than one mode: The set $\{2, 2, 3, 4, 4\}$ has modes of 2 and 4. In the set $\{1, 2, 3, 4, 5\}$, where all of the numbers appear an equal number of times, there is no mode.

Range

The range measures the spread of a data set, or the difference between the smallest element and the largest. For the set of test scores in Ms. Mathew's class, $\{57, 66,$

68, 71, 71, 83, 84, 84, 85, 87, 88, 90, 90, 90, 90, 93, 95, 96, 97, 99}, the range is 99 − 57 = 42.

21.2 GRAPHS, CHARTS, AND TABLES

There are countless ways to organize and present data. Luckily, the SAT uses only three of them: graphs, charts, and tables. On easy graphs, charts, and tables questions, the SAT just tests to see if you can understand the data being presented. More complicated questions ask you to perform some type of operation on data found in a chart or graph, such as calculating a mean or a percent.

Simple Charts, Graphs, and Tables Questions

Reading charts and graphs questions is pretty straightforward. The SAT shows you a chart. You answer a question about the data in the chart.

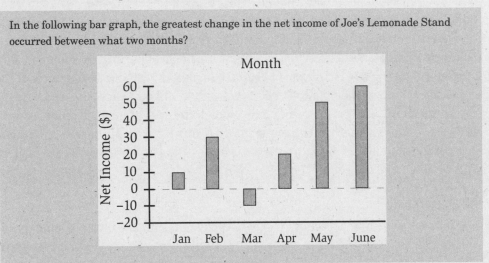

In the following bar graph, the greatest change in the net income of Joe's Lemonade Stand occurred between what two months?

Maybe you looked at this question and realized that you didn't know what the term "net income" means. Well, whether you did or didn't know the term, *it doesn't matter*. The graph tells you that the bars represent net income; you don't have to know what net income is to see between which months the net income differed most.

For this graph, a quick look makes it clear that the two biggest differences in terms of net income per month are between April and May, and between February and March. The net income in April was $20 and the net income in May was $50, making the April–May difference $30. The net income in February was $30 and the net income in March was −$10, so the February–March difference was $40. The answer, therefore, is February to March. This question throws a tiny trick at you by including negative numbers as net income. If you don't realize that March is negative, then you might choose the April–May difference.

When dealing with graphs and charts, be sure to pay attention to negative and positive values. And ignore distracting information—like the meaning of net income—that makes easy questions seem complex.

Performing Operations on Data

The second type of charts and graphs question asks you to take a further step. You have to use the data in the chart or graph to perform some operation on it. For instance, you could be asked to figure out the mean of the data shown in a graph. Or, you could be asked something like this:

What was the percent increase in the net income from April to May?

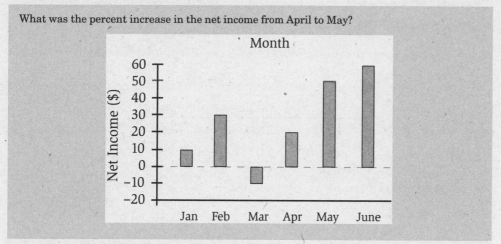

To find the percent increase in net income from April to May, you have to find out how much the net income increased between April and May and then compare that increase to the original net income in April. The difference in net income between April and May is

$$\text{May net income (\$50)} - \text{April net income (\$20)} = \$30$$

Now, to calculate the percent increase, you have to divide the change in net income by the original income in April:

$$\frac{30}{20} = 1.5$$

But there's a final trick in the question. The answer is *not* 1.5%. Remember, to get percents, you have to multiply by 100. The answer is $\$1.5 \times 100 = 150\%$. The SAT will certainly include 1.5% as one of its answer choices to try to fool you.

Double Table Questions

The new SAT puts special emphasis on questions that ask you to relate the data contained in two different tables.

Costs of Ice Cream

	Vanilla	Chocolate
1 scoop	$1.00	$1.25
2 scoops	$1.50	$1.75
3 scoops	$1.75	$2.00

Ice Cream Cones Eaten in a Year

	1 scoop	2 scoops	3 scoops
Tiny Tim	5	12	8
King Kong	16	10	6

If Tiny Tim only eats vanilla ice cream and King Kong only eats chocolate, how much do the two of them spend on ice cream in a year?

You need to be able to see the relationship between the data in the two tables and the question to figure out the answer. Here's what the two tables tell you:

1. How much one-scoop, two-scoop, and three-scoop cones cost for both vanilla and chocolate.
2. How many one-, two-, and three-scoop cones Tiny Tim and King Kong ate in a year.

Since the question tells you that Tiny Tim only eats vanilla and King Kong only eats chocolate, you know that Tiny Tim eats 5 one-scoop vanilla cones ($1.00), 12 two-scoop vanilla cones ($1.50), and 8 three-scoop vanilla cones ($1.75). So, in one year, Tiny Tim spent

$$(5 \times 1) + (12 \times 1.5) + (8 \times 1.75) = 5 + 18 + 14 = 37$$

dollars on ice cream. King Kong, meanwhile, spent

$$(16 \times 1.25) + (10 \times 1.75) + (6 \times 2) = 20 + 17.5 + 12 = 49.5$$

dollars. So, together, these two pigged out on $86.50 of ice cream.

Scatterplots

The new SAT may also give you a special kind of graph called a scatterplot. A scatterplot lives up to its name. It's a graph with a whole lot of points scattered around:

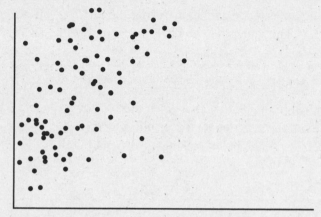

But the thing about a scatterplot is that the plots aren't scattered randomly. They have some sort of trend. And if you see the trend, you can draw a line that makes an average of the all the plots scattered around. Here's a line for the previous example:

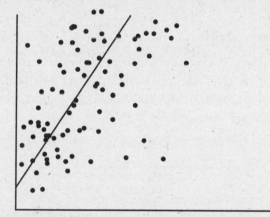

On the SAT, you won't have to do more than identify which line is the right one for a particular scatterplot and perhaps tell whether the slope of that line is negative or positive. You already know how to tell positive and negative slope, so these should be a breeze.

21.3 PROBABILITY

The probability is high that at least one question on the SAT will cover probability. The probability is even higher that the probability formula will help you on SAT probability questions. Here's the formula:

$$\text{Probability} = \frac{\text{number of times a certain event might occur}}{\text{total number of events that might occur}}$$

Let's say you go on a game show and are put in a room that contains 52 doors. Behind 13 of the doors are awesome prizes, including new cars, diamond watches, and infinity millions of dollars. Behind the rest of the doors are goats. What's the probability that you'll draw an awesome prize?

$$P = \frac{\text{awesomeness}}{\text{doors}} = \frac{13}{52} = \frac{1}{4}$$

And what's the probability that you'll end up with the goat?

$$P = \frac{\text{goats}}{\text{doors}} = \frac{(52 - 13)}{52} = \frac{39}{52} = \frac{3}{4}$$

Here's a more complicated example, involving the SAT's favorite probability prop: marbles! That SAT sure knows how to have a good time with marbles.

> Joe has 3 green marbles, 2 red marbles, and 5 blue marbles, and if all the marbles are dropped into a dark bag, what is the probability that Joe will pick out a green marble?

There are three ways for Joe to pick a green marble (since there are three different green marbles), but there are ten total possible outcomes (one for each marble in the bag). Therefore, the probability of picking a green marble is

$$P = \frac{3}{10}$$

When you calculate probability, always be careful to divide by the total number of chances. In the last example, you may have been tempted to leave out the three chances of picking a green marble from the total possibilities, yielding $P = {}^3/_7$. Brutal wrongness.

Backwards Probability

The SAT might also ask you a "backwards" probability question. For example, if you have a bag holding twenty marbles, and you have a $^1/_5$ chance of picking a blue marble, how many blue marbles are in the bag? All you have to do is set up the proper equation, following the model of $P = {}^m/_n$:

$$\frac{1}{5} = \frac{x}{20}$$

in which x is the variable denoting the number of blue marbles. Cross-multiplying through the equation, you get $5x = 20$, which reduces to $x = 4$.

The Range of Probability

The probability, P, that any event will occur is always $0 \le P \le 1$. A probability of 0 for an event means that the event will *never* happen. A probability of 1 means the event will *always* occur. Drawing a bouquet of flowers from a standard deck of cards has a probability of 0. Becoming Lord (or Lady) of the Universe after scoring 2400 on the new SAT has a probability of 1.

The Probability That an Event Will *Not* Occur

Some SAT questions ask you to determine the probability that an event will *not* occur. In that case, just figure out the probability of the event occurring, and subtract that number from 1.

Probability an event will not occur = 1 − probability of the event occurring

Probability and Multiple Unrelated Events

More difficult SAT probability questions deal with multiple unrelated events. For these questions, the probability of both events occurring is the product of the outcomes of each event: $P_A \times P_B$, where P_A is the probability of the first event, and P_B is the probability of the second event.

A perfect example of two unrelated events is this: Drawing a spade from a full deck of cards *and* rolling a one with a six-sided die is the product of the probability of each event. Neither outcome will affect the outcome of the other. The probability of both events occuring is

$$P = \frac{13}{52} \times \frac{1}{6}$$
$$= \frac{1}{4} \times \frac{1}{6}$$
$$= \frac{1}{24}$$

The same principle can be applied to finding the probability of a series of events. Take a look at the following problem:

A teacher keeps a jar full of different flavored jelly beans on her desk and hands them out randomly to her class. But one greedy student likes only the licorice-flavored ones. One day after school, the student sneaks into the dark classroom and steals three jelly beans. If the jar has 50 beans in all—15 licorice, 10 cherry, 20 watermelon, and 5 blueberry—what is the probability that the student got at least one licorice-flavored bean?

In order to find the probability of three consecutive events, first find the probability of each event separately. The first jelly bean has a $^{15}/_{50}$ chance of being licorice-flavored. The second jellybean, however, is a different story. There are now only 49 jelly beans left in the jar, so the probability of getting another licorice-flavored one is $^{14}/_{49}$. The probability of getting a third licorice-flavored jelly bean is $^{13}/_{48}$. The odds of all three happening are:

$$P = \frac{15}{50} \times \frac{14}{49} \times \frac{13}{48}$$
$$= \frac{3}{10} \times \frac{2}{7} \times \frac{13}{48}$$
$$= \frac{1}{10} \times \frac{1}{7} \times \frac{13}{8}$$
$$= \frac{13}{560}$$

The moral of this sad tale of larceny and candy is that crime pays only $^{13}/_{560}$ of the time.

Geometric Probability

The new SAT occasionally asks questions to which it has given the exciting name "geometric probability." The SAT could have saved itself some time by just saying that it's going to ask you questions about playing darts.

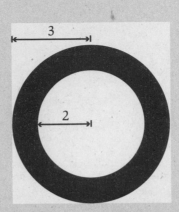

What is the probability of throwing a dart into the shaded area of the dartboard pictured above?

Here you have to find the area of some shaded (or unshaded) region, and divide that by the total area of the figure. In this question, the dartboard is a circle of radius 3. The shaded region is the area of the circle minus a circle of radius 2.

$$P = \frac{(\pi 3^2) - (\pi 2^2)}{\pi 3^2} = \frac{9\pi - 4\pi}{9\pi} = \frac{5\pi}{9\pi} \approx \frac{5(3.14)}{9(3.14)} \approx 0.56$$

and 0.56 equals 56%.

21.4 PERMUTATIONS AND COMBINATIONS

If the new SAT is a haunted forest, permutation and combination problems are the deepest, darkest, rarest trees. No, they are the mysterious fluorescent fungus growing on those trees. Permutation and combination problems are almost always hard, and most students skip them because they take so long. But if you're going for a Math score above 700, you should know how to deal with them. And to deal with permutations and combinations, you first have to know about factorials. If you're rushed for study time, though, and you're not trying to score a 700 on the Math section, this would be a good section to skip.

Factorials!

The factorial of a number, represented by $n!$, is the product of the natural numbers up to and including n:

$$n! = n \times (n-1) \times (n-2) \times \cdots \times 3 \times 2 \times 1$$

The factorial of n is the number of ways that the n elements of a group can be ordered. So, if you become a wedding planner and you're asked how many different ways six people can sit at a table with six chairs, the answer is $6! = 6 \times 5 \times 4 \times 3 \times 2 \times 1 = 720$.

Permutations

Mutations are genetic defects that result in three-headed fish. A permutation, however, is an ordering of elements. For example, say you're running for office in California, and there are six different offices to be filled—governor, lieutenant governor, secretary, treasurer, spirit coordinator, and head cheerleader. If there are six candidates running, and the candidates are celebrities who don't care which office they're elected to, how many different ways can the California government be composed? Except that California politics are funny, this question is no different from the question about the ordering of six people in six chairs around the table. The answer is 6! = 720 because there are six candidates running for office and there are six job openings.

But, what if a terrible statewide budget crisis caused three California government jobs to be cut? Now only the three offices of governor, lieutenant governor, and spirit coordinator can be filled. The same six candidates are still running. How many different combinations of the six candidates could fill the three positions? Time for permutations.

In general, the permutation, nP_r, is the number of subgroups of size r that can be taken from a set with n elements:

$$_nP_r = \frac{n!}{(n-r)!}$$

For the California election example, you need to find $_6P_3$:

$$_6P_3 = \frac{6!}{6-3!} = \frac{6!}{3!} = \frac{6 \times 5 \times 4 \times 3 \times 2 \times 1}{3 \times 2 \times 1} = \frac{720}{6} = 120$$

Notice that on permutations questions, calculations become much faster if you cancel out. Instead of multiplying everything out, you could have canceled out the $3 \times 2 \times 1$ in both numerator and denominator, and just multiplied $6 \times 5 \times 4 = 120$.

Permutations and Calculators

Graphing calculators and most scientific calculators have a permutation function, labeled nP_r. Though calculators do differ, in most cases, you must enter n, then press the button for permutation, and then enter r. This will calculate a permutation for you, but if n is a large number, the calculator often cannot calculate $n!$. If this happens to you, don't give up! Remember, the SAT never deals with huge numbers: Look for ways to cancel out.

Combinations

A combination is an unordered grouping of a set. An example of a combination scenario in which order doesn't matter is a hand of cards: a king, an ace, and a five is the same as an ace, a five, and a king.

Combinations are represented as nC_r, where unordered subgroups of size r are selected from a set of size n. Because the order of the elements in a given subgroup doesn't matter, this means that $\binom{n}{r}$ will be less than $_nP_r$. Any one combination can be turned into more than one permutation. $\binom{n}{r}$ is calculated as follows:

$$\binom{n}{r} = \frac{_nP_r}{r!} = \frac{n!}{(n-r)!r!}$$

Here's an example:

> Suppose six people are running for three leadership positions, each of which has the same duties and title. How many ways can this be done?

In this example, the order in which the leaders are assigned to positions doesn't matter—the leaders aren't distinguished from one another in any way, unlike in the California government example. This distinction means that the question can be answered with a combination rather than a permutation. So, to figure out how many different groups of three can be taken from a group of six, do this:

$$_6C_3 = \frac{6!}{(6-3)!3!} = \frac{6 \times 5 \times 4 \times 3 \times 2 \times 1}{(3 \times 2 \times 1)(3 \times 2 \times 1)} = \frac{120}{6} = 20$$

There are only 20 different ways to elect three leaders, as opposed to 120 ways when the leadership jobs were differentiated.

Combinations and Calculators

As with permutations, there should be a combination function on your graphing or scientific calculator labeled nC_r. Use it the same way you use the permutation key.

That's it, everything, the whole SAT mathematical banana—from Numbers and Operations to Data, Statistics, and Probability. You've now covered every little bit of math that might appear on the SAT. To make your job even easier, at the start of this section is a chart that summarizes the most important SAT math facts, rules, and formulas for quick reference and easy studying.

SAT PRACTICE TEST 1 ANSWER SHEET

SECTION 6

1. Ⓐ Ⓑ Ⓒ Ⓓ Ⓔ	10. Ⓐ Ⓑ Ⓒ Ⓓ Ⓔ	19. Ⓐ Ⓑ Ⓒ Ⓓ Ⓔ	28. Ⓐ Ⓑ Ⓒ Ⓓ Ⓔ
2. Ⓐ Ⓑ Ⓒ Ⓓ Ⓔ	11. Ⓐ Ⓑ Ⓒ Ⓓ Ⓔ	20. Ⓐ Ⓑ Ⓒ Ⓓ Ⓔ	29. Ⓐ Ⓑ Ⓒ Ⓓ Ⓔ
3. Ⓐ Ⓑ Ⓒ Ⓓ Ⓔ	12. Ⓐ Ⓑ Ⓒ Ⓓ Ⓔ	21. Ⓐ Ⓑ Ⓒ Ⓓ Ⓔ	30. Ⓐ Ⓑ Ⓒ Ⓓ Ⓔ
4. Ⓐ Ⓑ Ⓒ Ⓓ Ⓔ	13. Ⓐ Ⓑ Ⓒ Ⓓ Ⓔ	22. Ⓐ Ⓑ Ⓒ Ⓓ Ⓔ	31. Ⓐ Ⓑ Ⓒ Ⓓ Ⓔ
5. Ⓐ Ⓑ Ⓒ Ⓓ Ⓔ	14. Ⓐ Ⓑ Ⓒ Ⓓ Ⓔ	23. Ⓐ Ⓑ Ⓒ Ⓓ Ⓔ	32. Ⓐ Ⓑ Ⓒ Ⓓ Ⓔ
6. Ⓐ Ⓑ Ⓒ Ⓓ Ⓔ	15. Ⓐ Ⓑ Ⓒ Ⓓ Ⓔ	24. Ⓐ Ⓑ Ⓒ Ⓓ Ⓔ	33. Ⓐ Ⓑ Ⓒ Ⓓ Ⓔ
7. Ⓐ Ⓑ Ⓒ Ⓓ Ⓔ	16. Ⓐ Ⓑ Ⓒ Ⓓ Ⓔ	25. Ⓐ Ⓑ Ⓒ Ⓓ Ⓔ	34. Ⓐ Ⓑ Ⓒ Ⓓ Ⓔ
8. Ⓐ Ⓑ Ⓒ Ⓓ Ⓔ	17. Ⓐ Ⓑ Ⓒ Ⓓ Ⓔ	26. Ⓐ Ⓑ Ⓒ Ⓓ Ⓔ	35. Ⓐ Ⓑ Ⓒ Ⓓ Ⓔ
9. Ⓐ Ⓑ Ⓒ Ⓓ Ⓔ	18. Ⓐ Ⓑ Ⓒ Ⓓ Ⓔ	27. Ⓐ Ⓑ Ⓒ Ⓓ Ⓔ	

SECTION 7

1. Ⓐ Ⓑ Ⓒ Ⓓ Ⓔ	6. Ⓐ Ⓑ Ⓒ Ⓓ Ⓔ	11. Ⓐ Ⓑ Ⓒ Ⓓ Ⓔ	16. Ⓐ Ⓑ Ⓒ Ⓓ Ⓔ
2. Ⓐ Ⓑ Ⓒ Ⓓ Ⓔ	7. Ⓐ Ⓑ Ⓒ Ⓓ Ⓔ	12. Ⓐ Ⓑ Ⓒ Ⓓ Ⓔ	17. Ⓐ Ⓑ Ⓒ Ⓓ Ⓔ
3. Ⓐ Ⓑ Ⓒ Ⓓ Ⓔ	8. Ⓐ Ⓑ Ⓒ Ⓓ Ⓔ	13. Ⓐ Ⓑ Ⓒ Ⓓ Ⓔ	18. Ⓐ Ⓑ Ⓒ Ⓓ Ⓔ
4. Ⓐ Ⓑ Ⓒ Ⓓ Ⓔ	9. Ⓐ Ⓑ Ⓒ Ⓓ Ⓔ	14. Ⓐ Ⓑ Ⓒ Ⓓ Ⓔ	19. Ⓐ Ⓑ Ⓒ Ⓓ Ⓔ
5. Ⓐ Ⓑ Ⓒ Ⓓ Ⓔ	10. Ⓐ Ⓑ Ⓒ Ⓓ Ⓔ	15. Ⓐ Ⓑ Ⓒ Ⓓ Ⓔ	

SECTION 8

1. Ⓐ Ⓑ Ⓒ Ⓓ Ⓔ	5. Ⓐ Ⓑ Ⓒ Ⓓ Ⓔ	9. Ⓐ Ⓑ Ⓒ Ⓓ Ⓔ	13. Ⓐ Ⓑ Ⓒ Ⓓ Ⓔ
2. Ⓐ Ⓑ Ⓒ Ⓓ Ⓔ	6. Ⓐ Ⓑ Ⓒ Ⓓ Ⓔ	10. Ⓐ Ⓑ Ⓒ Ⓓ Ⓔ	14. Ⓐ Ⓑ Ⓒ Ⓓ Ⓔ
3. Ⓐ Ⓑ Ⓒ Ⓓ Ⓔ	7. Ⓐ Ⓑ Ⓒ Ⓓ Ⓔ	11. Ⓐ Ⓑ Ⓒ Ⓓ Ⓔ	15. Ⓐ Ⓑ Ⓒ Ⓓ Ⓔ
4. Ⓐ Ⓑ Ⓒ Ⓓ Ⓕ	8. Ⓐ Ⓑ Ⓒ Ⓓ Ⓔ	12. Ⓐ Ⓑ Ⓒ Ⓓ Ⓔ	16. Ⓐ Ⓑ Ⓒ Ⓓ Ⓔ

SECTION 9

1. Ⓐ Ⓑ Ⓒ Ⓓ Ⓔ	5. Ⓐ Ⓑ Ⓒ Ⓓ Ⓔ	9. Ⓐ Ⓑ Ⓒ Ⓓ Ⓔ	13. Ⓐ Ⓑ Ⓒ Ⓓ Ⓔ
2. Ⓐ Ⓑ Ⓒ Ⓓ Ⓔ	6. Ⓐ Ⓑ Ⓒ Ⓓ Ⓔ	10. Ⓐ Ⓑ Ⓒ Ⓓ Ⓔ	14. Ⓐ Ⓑ Ⓒ Ⓓ Ⓔ
3. Ⓐ Ⓑ Ⓒ Ⓓ Ⓔ	7. Ⓐ Ⓑ Ⓒ Ⓓ Ⓔ	11. Ⓐ Ⓑ Ⓒ Ⓓ Ⓔ	
4. Ⓐ Ⓑ Ⓒ Ⓓ Ⓔ	8. Ⓐ Ⓑ Ⓒ Ⓓ Ⓔ	12. Ⓐ Ⓑ Ⓒ Ⓓ Ⓔ	

SECTION 1

ESSAY

Time — 25 minutes

You have twenty-five minutes to plan and write an essay on the topic assigned below. DO NOT WRITE ON ANOTHER TOPIC. AN ESSAY ON ANOTHER TOPIC IS NOT ACCEPTABLE.

The essay is assigned to give you an opportunity to show how well you can write. You should, therefore, take care to express your thoughts on the topic clearly and effectively. How well you write is much more important than how much you write, but to cover the topic adequately you will probably need to write more than one paragraph. Be specific.

Your essay must be written on the following two pages. You will find that you have enough space if you write on every line, avoid wide margins, and keep your handwriting to a reasonable size. It is important to remember that what you write will be read by someone who is not familiar with your handwriting. Try to write or print so that what you are writing is legible to the reader.

Directions: Think carefully about the issue presented in the following excerpt and the assignment below.

> Politicians and government leaders often use the expression that "the ends always justify the means" to justify actions they deem essential to achieving certain results, such as going to war in order to preserve peace.

Assignment: Do the ends always justify the means? Plan and write an essay in which you develop your point of view on this issue. Support your position with reasoning and examples taken from your reading, studies, experience, or observations.

DO NOT WRITE YOUR ESSAY IN YOUR TEST BOOK. You will receive credit only for what you write on your answer sheet.

WHEN YOUR SUPERVISOR ANNOUNCES THAT TWENTY-FIVE MINUTES HAVE PASSED, YOU MUST STOP WRITING THE ESSAY AND GO ON TO SECTION 2 IF YOU HAVE NOT ALREADY DONE SO. IF YOU FINISH YOUR ESSAY BEFORE THIS ANNOUNCEMENT, GO ON TO SECTION 2 AT ONCE.

BEGIN WRITING YOUR ESSAY ON THE ANSWER SHEET.

SECTION 1—ESSAY

Time — 25 minutes

SECTION 1—ESSAY

Time — 25 minutes

Section 2

Turn to Section 2 of your answer sheet to answer the questions in this section.

Time—25 Minutes 24 Questions	For each question in this section, select the best answer from among the choices given and fill in the corresponding oval on the answer sheet.

Each sentence below has one or two blanks, each blank indicating that something has been omitted. Beneath the sentence are five words or sets of words labeled A through E. Choose the word or set of words that, when inserted in the sentence, <u>best</u> fits the meaning of the sentence as a whole.

Example:

Medieval kingdoms did not become constitutional republics overnight; on the contrary, the change was ----.

(A) unpopular
(B) unexpected
(C) advantageous
(D) sufficient
(E) gradual

Ⓐ Ⓑ Ⓒ Ⓓ ●

1. Unable to grasp the question in front of her, Karen was ----.

(A) furious
(B) abstinent
(C) perplexed
(D) prepared
(E) earnest

2. Despite years of intermittent ----, politicians in the war-torn region continue to strive for ----.

(A) disagreement .. hatred
(B) war .. religion
(C) prosperity .. starvation
(D) bloodshed .. peace
(E) turmoil .. negotiation

3. While he may have once hoped to ---- Europe from the system of monarchy, Napoleon quickly became a ----, consolidating his power at the expense of his subjects' freedom.

(A) free .. hero
(B) salvage .. warrior
(C) dominate .. tyrant
(D) administrate .. thug
(E) liberate .. despot

4. In prehistoric North and South America, some ground sloths were ----, much larger than modern-day tree sloths.

(A) feral
(B) gargantuan
(C) amorphous
(D) anthropocentric
(E) docile

5. The doctor suspected that her patient had leukemia, but until she could make her diagnoisis ----, she kept it to herself.

(A) medically
(B) unequivocally - without question
(C) reputably
(D) precariously
(E) ambiguously

6. Unlike the signing of the *Magna Carta* in 1215, which guaranteed the rights of only a limited group of elite English nobles, the signing of the United States *Constitution* was intended to guarantee the rights of the ---- as well.

(A) aristocracy
(B) commoners
(C) gentry
(D) clergy
(E) oligarchy

7. Colleagues showered Bernice with ---- after she solved the conundrum that had ---- theorists for more than a decade.

(A) commendations .. benefited
(B) accolades .. confounded
(C) disparagement .. calibrated
(D) contempt .. flabbergasted
(E) tribute .. denigrated

8. Cindy admitted she was the cause of the ----; she encouraged the two boys to fight for the right to take her to the junior prom.

(A) altercation - fight
(B) selection
(C) dalliance
(D) artifice
(E) reconciliation

GO ON TO THE NEXT PAGE

Section 2

Each short passage below is followed by questions based on its content. Answer the questions based on what is <u>stated</u> or <u>implied</u> in each passage.

Questions 9–10 are based on the following passage.

Iron is an essential mineral and an important component of proteins in your body. But while iron is necessary for the metabolic processes of life, too much iron in the body can cause liver and heart damage. To complicate matters, iron has a
5 moderate to high potential for toxicity because very little iron is excreted from the body. In fact, most adults can only lose iron through significant blood loss. Thus, iron can accumulate to excessive and dangerous levels in body tissues and organs over time when its normal storage sites are already filled to capacity.

9. This passage would most likely appear in which of the following type of publication?

   (A) a research journal for scientists
   (B) a health textbook
   (C) a brochure about a deadly insect
   (D) a techno... magazine
   (E) a newsletter for surgeons

10. What does the phrase "potential for toxicity" most likely mean as it is used in the passage?

   (A) Iron can easily corrode.
   (B) Iron can cause cardiac arrest.
   (C) Iron can cure various diseases.
   (D) Iron is always poisonous in the body.
   (E) Iron can build up to dangerous levels in the body.

Questions 11–12 are based on the following passage.

Before November 18, 1883, there were no time zones in America, but that didn't mean people across the country followed one single time back then. Quite the contrary. Before 1883, people all over the country set their clocks by the rising and setting of the sun.
5 The impetus for the establishment of specific and regulated time zones was the rise of the transcontinental railroad. New cross-country trains promised to revolutionize travel and commerce in the United States, but in order to run smoothly they needed to follow clear schedules everyone could count on. The time zones
10 regularized the time in each region of the country, which allowed for set dependable transportation schedules.

11. Based on information in the passage, what development led to the decision to institute time zones in the United States?

   (A) a boom in commerce
   (B) the advent of a new technology
   (C) a population explosion
   (D) the physical size of the country
   (E) regional rivalries

12. The phrase "quite the contrary" is used primarily to

   (A) sum up a national debate
   (B) highlight a controversy
   (C) argue for a new historical perspective
   (D) challenge a radical belief
   (E) emphasize a historical fact

GO ON TO THE NEXT PAGE

Section 2

Questions 13–24 are based on the following passage.

The passage below is excerpted from an essay written by Theodore Roosevelt after he attended an art exhibit in New York. The essay was published in 1913.

The recent "International Exhibition of Modern Art" in New York was really noteworthy. Davies, Kuhn, Gregg, and their fellow members of the Association of American Painters and Sculptors did a work of very real value in securing such an exhibition of the

5 works of both foreign and native painters and sculptors. Primarily their purpose was to give the public a chance to see what has recently been going on abroad. No similar collection of the works of European "moderns" has ever been exhibited in this country. The exhibitors were quite right as to the need of showing our

10 people in this manner the art forces which of late have been at work in Europe, forces which cannot be ignored.

This does not mean that I in the least accept the view that these men take of the European extremists whose pictures were here exhibited. It is true, as the champions of these extremists

15 say, that there can be no life without change, no development without change, and that to be afraid of what is different or unfamiliar is to be afraid of life. It is no less true, however, that change may mean death and not life, and retrogression instead of development.

20 Probably we err in treating most of these pictures seriously. It is likely that many of them represent in the painters the astute appreciation of the power to make folly lucrative which the late P. T. Barnum [P. T. Barnum was the owner of Barnum and Bailey Circus] showed with his fake mermaid. There are thousands of

25 people who will pay small sums to look at a fake mermaid; and now and then one of this kind with enough money will buy a Cubist picture, or a picture of a misshapen nude woman, repellent from every standpoint.

In some ways it is the work of the American painters and

30 sculptors which is of most interest in this collection, and a glance at this work must convince anyone of the good that is coming out of the new movements, fantastic though many of the developments of these new movements are. There was one note entirely absent from the exhibition, and that was the note of the

35 commonplace. There was not a touch of simpering, self-satisfied conventionality anywhere in the exhibition. Any sculptor or painter who had in him something to express and the power of expressing it found the field open to him. He did not have to be afraid because his work was not along ordinary lines. There was

40 no stunting or dwarfing, no requirement that a man whose gift lay in new directions should measure up or down to stereotyped and fossilized standards.

For all of this there can be only hearty praise. But this does not in the least mean that the extremists whose paintings and

45 pictures were represented are entitled to any praise, save, perhaps, that they have helped to break fetters. Probably, in any reform movement, any progressive movement, in any field of life, the penalty for avoiding the commonplace is a liability to extravagance. It is vitally necessary to move forward and to shake

50 off the dead hand, often the fossilized dead hand, of the reactionaries; and yet we have to face the fact that there is apt to be a lunatic fringe among the devotees of any forward movement. In this recent art exhibition the lunatic fringe was fully in evidence, especially in the rooms devoted to the Cubists and the

55 Futurists, or Near-Impressionists. I am not entirely certain which of the two latter terms should be used in connection with some of the various pictures and representations of plastic art, and, frankly, it is not of the least consequence.

The Cubists are entitled to the serious attention of all who find

60 enjoyment in the colored puzzle-pictures of the Sunday newspapers. Of course there is no reason for choosing the cube as a symbol, except that it is probably less fitted than any other mathematical statement for any but the most formal decorative art. There is no reason why people should not call themselves

65 Cubists, or Octagonists, or Parallelopipedonists, or Knights of the Isosceles Triangle, or Brothers of the Cosine, if they so desire; as expressing anything serious and permanent, one term is as fatuous as another. Take the picture which for some reason is called "A Naked Man Going Down Stairs." There is in my

70 bathroom a really good Navajo rug which, on any proper interpretation of the Cubist theory, is a far more satisfactory and decorative picture. Now, if, for some inscrutable reason, it suited somebody to call this rug a picture of, say, "A Well-Dressed Man Going Up a Ladder," the name would fit the facts just about as

75 well as in the case of the Cubist picture of the "Naked Man Going Down Stairs." From the standpoint of terminology, each name would have whatever merit gleaned in a rather cheap straining for effect; and from the standpoint of decorative value, of sincerity, and of artistic merit, the Navajo rug is infinitely ahead of the

80 picture.

GO ON TO THE NEXT PAGE

13. Which of the following statements best describes Roosevelt's attitude toward change as stated in the second paragraph of the passage?

    (A) Change is necessary but should be undertaken carefully.
    (B) Change is always positive.
    (C) Change is only good if it is reactionary.
    (D) Change is a European phenomenon.
    (E) Change is usually a bad thing.

14. By saying that "probably we err in treating most of these pictures seriously" in line 20, Roosevelt means that

    (A) these paintings belong in museums and not private homes
    (B) the painters wanted to convey generally lighthearted messages through their paintings despite popular interpretation
    (C) people shouldn't pay too much for these paintings
    (D) these paintings are more important as examples of current artistic trends than as serious and timeless pieces of art
    (E) the people who put together the exhibition have bad taste

15. Roosevelt references the legendary circus owner P. T. Barnum in the third paragraph to suggest that

    (A) art has no commercial value
    (B) both art and circuses exploit women
    (C) low-quality entertainment often sells quite well, so sales shouldn't be a factor in identifying great art
    (D) it is better to go to the circus than to buy these paintings
    (E) these paintings depict circus scenes

16. Which of the following best expresses the meaning of the word "fantastic" in line 32?

    (A) outrageous and excessive
    (B) wonderful and exciting
    (C) likely to appeal to new fans
    (D) based on fantasy
    (E) welcome and well-thought-out

17. Roosevelt's reaction to "conventionality" in line 36 is best described by which of the following?

    (A) dismissive
    (B) supportive
    (C) terrified
    (D) awestruck
    (E) carefree

18. Roosevelt uses the term "fossilized" in line 42 to do which of the following?

    (A) Emphasize how much time has passed since the stone age.
    (B) Suggest that artists break from outdated ideas from past art movements.
    (C) Establish a connection to a recent controversial scientific theory.
    (D) Question the importance of learning from mistakes made by other artists.
    (E) Challenge a new style of American art.

19. The author's tone in lines 43–53 can best be described as

    (A) contemplative
    (B) suggestive
    (C) disappointed
    (D) bored
    (E) sarcastic

20. The word "fatuous," as used in line 68, is closest in meaning to which of the following?

    (A) obese
    (B) excessive
    (C) foolish
    (D) elementary
    (E) inspiring

21. The author uses the comparison in lines 68–80 between the Cubist painting and the Navajo rug primarily to

    (A) illustrate the aesthetic qualities he values in art
    (B) belittle the Navajo rug
    (C) suggest all art should be utilitarian
    (D) claim that the painting should be walked on
    (E) argue about the definition of American art

22. In the final paragraph, Roosevelt's discussion of the painting's title implies primarily that

    (A) the picture is wrongly titled
    (B) paintings shouldn't have titles
    (C) the Navajo rug looks more like the subject of the picture's title than the painting does
    (D) he believes that art should be realistic
    (E) the titles of pictures should be made up by viewers

GO ON TO THE NEXT PAGE

Section 2

23. Roosevelt finds the art exhibition noteworthy mainly for

    (A) the artistic talent on view
    (B) its inclusion of both American and European artists
    (C) its emphasis on Cubist art
    (D) its rejection of the commonplace
    (E) its convenient location in New York City

24. In the essay, Roosevelt is primarily concerned with

    (A) artists
    (B) progress
    (C) the relationship between Europe and America
    (D) nomenclature
    (E) anthropology

S T O P

IF YOU FINISH BEFORE TIME IS CALLED, YOU MAY CHECK YOUR WORK ON THIS TEST ONLY.
DO NOT TURN TO ANY OTHER SECTION IN THIS TEST.

Section 3

Time—25 Minutes
20 Questions

In this section solve each problem, using any available space on the page for scratchwork. Then decide which is the best of the choices given and fill in the corresponding oval on the answer sheet.

Notes:

1. The use of a calculator is permitted. All numbers used are real numbers.

2. Figures that accompany problems in this test are intended to provide information useful in solving the problems. They are drawn as accurately as possible EXCEPT when it is stated in a specific problem that the figure is not drawn to scale. All figures lie in a plane unless otherwise indicated.

3. Unless otherwise specified, the domain of any function f is assumed to be the set of all real numbers x for which $f(x)$ is a real number.

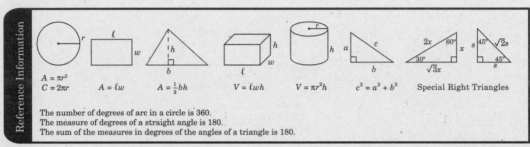

Reference Information

$A = \pi r^2$
$C = 2\pi r$

$A = \ell w$

$A = \frac{1}{2}bh$

$V = \ell wh$

$V = \pi r^2 h$

$c^2 = a^2 + b^2$

Special Right Triangles

The number of degrees of arc in a circle is 360.
The measure of degrees of a straight angle is 180.
The sum of the measures in degrees of the angles of a triangle is 180.

1. If it takes Allison six minutes to complete a lap around a park, how much of a lap will she cover in four minutes, assuming she runs at a constant pace?

6 minutes to complete a lap.

(A) $\frac{1}{24}$

(B) $\frac{1}{6}$

(C) $\frac{1}{4}$

(D) $\frac{1}{2}$

(E) $\frac{2}{3}$

2. Which of the following numbers is greater than $\frac{5}{8}$ and less than $\frac{3}{4}$?

(A) 0.25

(B) 0.5

(C) 0.7

(D) 0.8

(E) 0.9

7.625
< .75

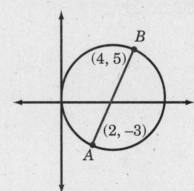

3. If $\overline{AB}$ is a diameter of the circle, what are the coordinates of the center of the circle?

(A) (0,0)

(B) (2,2)

(C) (3,1)

(D) (6,2)

(E) (6,8)

$\dfrac{2x_1 + x_2}{2} \qquad \dfrac{y_1 + y_2}{2}$

$\dfrac{4+2}{2} = 3 \quad \dfrac{5+3}{2} \quad \dfrac{2}{2} = 1$

$(4,5) \quad (2,-3)$
$\;\; x,y \qquad x,y$

GO ON TO THE NEXT PAGE

Section 3

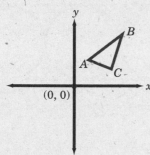

(0, 0)

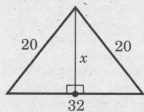

4. Which of the sides of the triangle pictured above has a negative slope?

   (A) AB
   (B) AC
   (C) BC
   (D) AB and BC
   (E) AC and AB

5. If Mark is older than Judy, and Judy is older than Brian but younger than Lisa, then which of the following statements must be true?

   (A) Mark is older than Lisa.
   (B) Lisa is older than Mark.
   (C) Brian is older than Lisa.
   (D) Brian is younger than Mark.
   (E) Lisa is younger than Brian.

6. There is a large cookie jar filled with 45 cookies. If the cookies are distributed in a 2:3:4 ratio among three children, what is the greatest number of cookies that any one child receives?

   (A) 2
   (B) 4
   (C) 15
   (D) 20
   (E) 36

7. If $xy = x$ and $x \neq 0$, then what is the value of yz?

   (A) 0
   (B) 1
   (C) x
   (D) y
   (E) z

8. How many integer values of x satisfy the inequality $|x - 4| \leq 2.5$?

   (A) 4
   (B) 5
   (C) 6
   (D) 7
   (E) infinitely many

9. What is the value of x?

   (A) $\sqrt{624}$
   (B) 20
   (C) 16
   (D) 12
   (E) 10

10. If $3x + 4y = 7$ and $2y = 6x + 6$, then what is xy?

    (A) $-\dfrac{1}{3}$
    (B) $-\dfrac{2}{3}$
    (C) 2
    (D) 6
    (E) 7

11. If the mean of a and b is 10 and the mean of c and d is 12, what is the mean of $\{a, b, c, d, 26\}$?

    (A) 13
    (B) 14
    (C) 15
    (D) 16
    (E) 17

12. A rectangle with an area of 108 is divided into three equal squares. What is the perimeter of the rectangle?

    (A) 18
    (B) $12\sqrt{3}$
    (C) 36
    (D) 48
    (E) 72

GO ON TO THE NEXT PAGE

Section 3

13. Starting with the second term, the even terms of a sequence are consecutive powers of two, such that the second term is 2^1, the fourth term is 2^2, and so on. The odd terms, starting with the third term, are the averages of the terms immediately preceding them and the terms immediately following them. For example, the third term is the average of the second and fourth term. The first term is 1.5. What is the sum of the third, fifth, and seventh terms of this sequence?

   (A) 11
   (B) 12
   (C) 15
   (D) 16
   (E) 21

14. The square of a prime number must always be what?

   I. Odd
   II. Prime
   III. Positive

   (A) I only
   (B) II only
   (C) III only
   (D) II and III only
   (E) I, II, and III

15. For which of the following graphs does $f(-x) = -f(x)$?

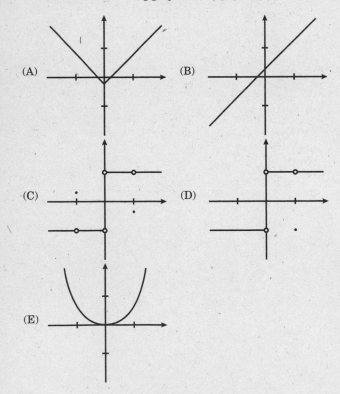

16. The circumference of each of the three identical circles is 10π. What is the perimeter of the rectangle?

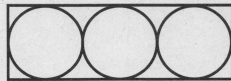

   (A) 20
   (B) 30
   (C) 40
   (D) 60
   (E) 80

17. If the mean of 3, 4, and r is the same as the mean of 4, 6, and s, what is the difference between r and s?

   (A) 1
   (B) 2
   (C) 3
   (D) 4
   (E) 5

18. What is the range of f if $-2 \le x \le 4$ and $f(x) = 2x^2 - 3$?

   (A) $y \le -3$
   (B) $y \ge -3$
   (C) $-3 \le y \le 1$
   (D) $1 \le y \le 29$
   (E) $-3 \le y \le 29$

GO ON TO THE NEXT PAGE

Section 3

19. Which of the following scatterplots has a line with a slope smaller than −1?

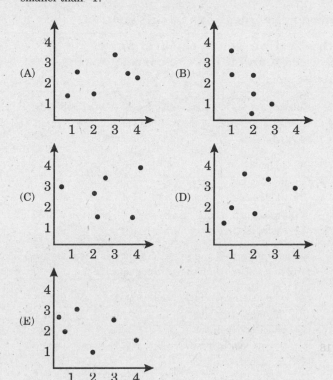

20. p is a prime number. How many factors does p^n have?

   (A) p
   (B) n
   (C) pn
   (D) $n + p$
   (E) $n + 1$

S T O P

IF YOU FINISH BEFORE TIME IS CALLED, YOU MAY CHECK YOUR WORK ON THIS TEST ONLY.
DO NOT TURN TO ANY OTHER SECTION IN THIS TEST.

Section 4

Turn to Section 4 of your answer sheetto answer the questions in this section.

Time—25 Minutes
24 Questions

For each question in this section, select the best answer from among the choices given and fill in the corresponding oval on the answer sheet.

Each sentence below has one or two blanks, each blank indicating that something has been omitted. Beneath the sentence are five words or sets of words labeled A through E. Choose the word or set of words that, when inserted in the sentence, best fits the meaning of the sentence as a whole.

Example:

Medieval kingdoms did not become constitutional republics overnight; on the contrary, the change was ----.

(A) unpopular
(B) unexpected
(C) advantageous
(D) sufficient
(E) gradual

1. Although the *New Yorker* is often regarded as an ---- publication, it is actually very ----, with one of the largest circulations of any magazine in the country.

    (A) outdated . . superficial
    (B) elitist . . popular
    (C) ambivalent . . well-written
    (D) enjoyable . . demeaning
    (E) excellent . . slipshod

2. Understanding the United States tax code is a ---- undertaking; nevertheless, many people continue to rush through their taxes as though it were a(n) ---- task.

    (A) formidable . . undemanding
    (B) noble . . exceptional
    (C) rewarding . . enriching
    (D) civic . . irresponsible
    (E) miniscule . . straightforward

3. Though he was ----, the young entrepreneur tried ---- to come out ahead at the negotiating table.

    (A) terrified . . valiantly
    (B) unnerved . . timidly
    (C) egomaniacal . . doggedly
    (D) amoral . . shrewdly
    (E) wealthy . . desperately

4. Knowing that her controversial findings were likely to be heavily scrutinized, Yolanda ---- documented every aspect of her research.

    (A) callously
    (B) dexterously
    (C) meticulously
    (D) passively
    (E) undeniably

5. Known for their ---- and ---- waters, Florida's beaches are a favored vacation destination throughout the year.

    (A) opaque . . unsanitary
    (B) calming . . incendiary
    (C) unsoiled . . pellucid
    (D) picturesque . . inaccessible
    (E) residual . . posterior

GO ON TO THE NEXT PAGE

Section 4

The two short passages below are followed by questions based on their content. Answer the questions based on what is <u>stated</u> or <u>implied</u> in each passage.

Passage 1

Many people assume that the stock market has been around for ages, but it's only existed for about a century. During that time no greater wealth creation mechanism has surfaced on the face of the earth. The stock market is the paragon of capitalism. Where
5 else can any lowly citizen invest his or her funds in the world's most powerful companies? Only on the stock exchange can every member of society have a voice and even a vote about future business decisions that can impact economies on a grand scale, both in the United States and abroad.

Passage 2

The stock market is like a breeding ground for greedy thieves. For almost a century it's been luring unwitting individual investors into the trap of owning shares in public companies. The notion that everyone can have a say in the future of a multibillion dollar
5 corporation sounds great on paper, but in practice it's an illusory sham. Individual investors end up getting bilked more often than they end up getting rich—only the stock market analysts and big-time traders benefit. Just look at the Great Depression! Would you have wanted to own stock in publicly traded companies then?

6. The description of the stock market as a "breeding ground for greedy thieves" in the second passage is an example of (a)

(A) onomotopeia
(B) paradox
(C) semaphore
(D) soliloquy
(E) metaphor

7. How would you describe the attitudes of the authors of these two passages toward the stock market?

(A) The author of passage 1 is laudatory, while the author of passage 2 is disapproving.
(B) The author of passage 1 is reverent, while the author of passage 2 is fawning.
(C) The author of passage 1 is resigned, while the author of passage 2 is frustrated.
(D) The author of passage 1 is alarmed, while the author of passage 2 is uneasy.
(E) The author of passage 1 is awestruck, while the author of passage 2 is grateful.

8. All of the following words are ways to describe the stock market as it is depicted in the two passages EXCEPT

(A) democratic
(B) misleading
(C) capitalist
(D) perilous
(E) deliberate

9. The author of the second passage would most likely use all of the following evidence to disprove the statement in the first passage that the stock market is a great "wealth creation mechanism" EXCEPT

(A) stock market analysts dupe investors
(B) the stock market is manipulated by the wealthy
(C) the Great Depression ravaged individual investors
(D) the stock market embodies the fundamental tenets of capitalism
(E) individual investors do not have a strong impact on the decisions major corporations make

GO ON TO THE NEXT PAGE

Section 4

The passage below is followed by questions based on its content. Answer the questions on the basis of what is <u>stated</u> or <u>implied</u> in the passage and in any introductory material that may be provided.

Questions 10–15 are based on the following passage. The passage is adapted from a description of the present appearance and geological history of a particular volcano. The passage is written by the American naturalist John Muir.

Shasta is a fire-mountain, an old volcano gradually accumulated and built up into the blue deep of the sky by successive eruptions of ashes and molten lava which, shot high in the air and falling in darkening showers, and flowing from chasms and craters, grew
5   outward and upward like the trunk of a knotty, bulging tree. Not in one grand convulsion was Shasta given birth, nor in any one special period of volcanic storm and stress, though some mountains more than a thousand feet in height have been cast up like molehills in a night.
10   Sections cut by the glaciers, displaying some of the internal framework of Shasta, show that comparatively long periods of quiescence intervened between many eruptions. During these periods of calm the cooling lavas ceased to flow, and took their places as permanent additions to the bulk of the growing
15   mountain. Thus eruption succeeded eruption with alternating haste and deliberation, until Mount Shasta surpassed even its present sublime height.

Then followed a strange contrast. The glacial winter came on. The sky that so often had been darkened with storms of cinders
20   and ashes and lighted by the glare of volcanic fires was filled with snow, which, descending upon the cooling mountain, gave birth to glaciers that eventually formed one grand conical glacier—a creeping mantle of ice upon a fountain of smoldering fire, crushing, grinding, and remodeling the entire mountain from
25   summit to base.

How much effect the glaciers wielded we have no means of determining. The porous, crumbling rocks of Shasta are poorly adapted to provide a record of the mountain's glacial past. This much, however, is plain: the summit of the mountain was
30   considerably lowered and the sides deeply grooved during the time when Shasta served as a center of dispersal for the glaciers of the entire region.

When at length the glacial period began to draw near its close, the ice mantle gradually melted off around the base of the
35   mountain. In receding and breaking up into its present fragmentary condition, the once great glacier left behind it a ring of irregular heaps of moraine matter on which forests now grow. The receding glacier left behind porous gravel and sand that yields freely to the power of running water. In fact, several
40   centuries ago when an eruption melted massive quantities of ice and snow, a flood of extraordinary magnitude washed the sand and gravel from the higher slopes to the mountain's base, creating conspicuous delta-like beds around the base. Upon these

flood-beds of soil flowery chaparral now grows.
45   Thus, by forces seemingly antagonistic and destructive, Nature accomplishes her designs—now a flood of fire, now a flood of ice, now a flood of water. Then in the fullness of time an outburst of organic life—Shasta the fire-mountain becomes forest and garden, with all its wealth of fruit and flowers, and the air
50   stirred into one universal hum by rejoicing insects.

10. Which of the following statements can be inferred from lines 5–11?

(A) All mountains form in the same way.
(B) Volcanoes are all under one thousand feet in height.
(C) Most mountains take a long time to form.
(D) Different mountains are created in unique ways.
(E) Volcanoes all have glaciers.

11. The term "deliberation" in line 16 most nearly means

(A) a slow, steady pace
(B) contemplation
(C) disagreement
(D) indecisiveness
(E) short intervals of time

12. Which of the following is NOT a function of the phrase "glacial winter" in line 18?

(A) to serve as a metaphor comparing geological processes to seasons
(B) to dramatize the process of glaciation
(C) to refer to an Ice Age
(D) to suggest a marked contrast from periods of volcanic activity
(E) to describe a particularly cold winter of long ago

13. From the passage, it's possible to surmise that Muir bases his version of Mount Shasta's geological history primarily on

(A) the mountain's flora and fauna
(B) the position and types of rock formations on the mountain
(C) local legends
(D) settler's histories
(E) his knowledge of other mountains

GO ON TO THE NEXT PAGE

Section 4

14. In which of the following would Muir be most interested?

    (A) New data on earthquakes around Mount Shasta

    (B) A history of attempts to climb Mount Shasta

    (C) Local legends regarding the mountain

    (D) An anthropological study of Native American tribes living near Shasta

    (E) An exhibition of paintings of Mount Shasta

15. Which of the following best expresses the thematic concerns of this passage?

    (A) "Time Passes"

    (B) "One Mountain Long Ago"

    (C) "Shasta's Majestic Height"

    (D) "Shasta: A Study in Contradictory Forces"

    (E) "The Plants and Animals of Mount Shasta"

GO ON TO THE NEXT PAGE

Section 4

The passage below is followed by questions based on its content. Answer the questions on the basis of what is <u>stated</u> or <u>implied</u> in the passage and in any introductory material that may be provided.

Questions 16–24 are based on the following passage. The passage below is excerpted from the novel O! Pioneers *by Willa Cather, which is set in rural Nebraska near the end of the nineteenth century.*

On Wednesday morning Carl got up before it was light, and stole downstairs and out of the kitchen door just as old Ivar was making his morning ablutions at the pump. Carl nodded to him and hurried up the draw, past the garden, and into the pasture
5 where the milking cows used to be kept.

    The dawn in the east looked like the light from some great fire that was burning under the edge of the world. The color was reflected in the globules of dew that sheathed the short gray pasture grass. Carl walked rapidly until he came to the crest of
10 the second hill, where the Bergson pasture joined the one that had belonged to his father.

    There he sat down and waited for the sun to rise. It was just there that he and Alexandra used to do their milking together, he on his side of the fence, she on hers. He could remember exactly
15 how she looked when she came over the close-cropped grass, her skirts pinned up, her head bare, a bright tin pail in either hand, and the milky light of the early morning all about her. Even as a boy he used to feel, when he saw her coming with her free step, her upright head and calm shoulders, that she looked as if she
20 had walked straight out of the morning itself. Since then, when he had happened to see the sun come up in the country or on the water, he had often remembered the young Swedish girl and her milking pails.

    Carl sat musing until the sun leaped above the prairie, and in
25 the grass about him all the small creatures of day began to tune their tiny instruments. Birds and insects without number began to chirp, to twitter, to snap and whistle, to make all manner of fresh shrill noises. The pasture was flooded with light; every clump of ironweed and snow-on-the-mountain threw a long
30 shadow, and the golden light seemed to be rippling through the curly grass like the ocean tide sweeping in.

    He crossed the fence into the pasture that was now the Shabatas' and continued his walk toward the pond. He had not gone far, however, when he discovered that he was not the only
35 person abroad. In the draw below, his gun in his hands, was Emil, advancing cautiously, with a young woman beside him. They were moving softly, keeping close together, and Carl knew that they expected to find ducks on the pond.

    At the moment when they came in sight of the bright spot of
40 water, he heard a whirr of wings and the ducks shot up into the air. There was a sharp crack from the gun, and five of the birds fell to the ground. Emil and his companion laughed delightedly, and Emil ran to pick them up. When he came back, dangling the ducks by their feet, Marie held her apron and he dropped them into it.

45 As she stood looking down at them, her face changed. She took up one of the birds, a rumpled ball of feathers with the blood dripping slowly from its mouth, and looked at the live color that still burned on its plumage.

16. The word "stole" in line 1 most nearly means

    (A) took illegally
    (B) clambered noisily
    (C) did illicitly
    (D) stumbled clumsily
    (E) moved stealthily

17. From the passage, it is possible to infer that Carl is which of the following?

    (A) a small child
    (B) a young man returning to his childhood home
    (C) trying to write a novel
    (D) an old man about to go on a journey
    (E) naive about the farming life

18. What is Alexandra's relationship to Carl?

    (A) sister
    (B) neighbor
    (C) daughter
    (D) cousin
    (E) supervisor

19. In the third paragraph, the author uses Carl's memories to

    (A) explain how Carl first came to rural Nebraska
    (B) provide a sense of Carl's feelings for Alexandra
    (C) highlight the beauty of the fields
    (D) indicate that Carl feels lonely and isolated
    (E) show that Carl is poor and owns no land

20. In lines 28–31, the metaphor comparing the morning light to the tides of the ocean does all of the following EXCEPT

    (A) suggest that Carl has seen a lot of the world beyond the farm
    (B) suggest that the scene can be meaningful even to those who have not seen morning light on the prairie
    (C) suggest that Carl wishes he were at the ocean
    (D) imply the calmness of the scene
    (E) add to the beauty of the description

GO ON TO THE NEXT PAGE

Section 4

21. The reference to "the pasture that was now the Shabatas'" in lines 32–33 suggests that

    (A) the old neighbors were bad farmers
    (B) Carl is mistaken in his memories
    (C) significant time has passed since Carl's last visit
    (D) the farms are dwindling away and won't exist much longer
    (E) Carl is vandalizing the property

22. Emil's shooting of the ducks contrasts sharply with which of the following in this passage?

    (A) Carl's feeling of hunger
    (B) the pastoral depiction of farm life
    (C) the description of the sunset
    (D) the environmental dangers of farm life
    (E) Carl's response to Nebraska's harsh climate

23. The description of the bird as "a rumpled ball of feathers" in line 46 is an example of a

    (A) metaphor
    (B) paradox
    (C) simile
    (D) theme
    (E) conflict

24. The tone of this passage is best described as

    (A) reflective, then wistful
    (B) cheerful, then troubled
    (C) distracted, then confused
    (D) nostalgic, then uneasy
    (E) worried, then serene

S T O P

IF YOU FINISH BEFORE TIME IS CALLED, YOU MAY CHECK YOUR WORK ON THIS TEST ONLY.
DO NOT TURN TO ANY OTHER SECTION IN THIS TEST.

Section 5

Turn to Section 5 of your answer sheet to answer the questions in this section.

Time—25 Minutes
18 Questions

In this section solve each problem, using any available space on the page for scratchwork. Then decide which is the best of the choices given and fill in the corresponding oval on the answer sheet.

Notes:
1. The use of a calculator is permitted. All numbers used are real numbers.

2. Figures that accompany problems in this test are intended to provide information useful in solving the problems. They are drawn as accurately as possible EXCEPT when it is stated in a specific problem that the figure is not drawn to scale. All figures lie in a plane unless otherwise indicated.

3. Unless otherwise specified, the domain of any function f is assumed to be the set of all real numbers x for which $f(x)$ is a real number.

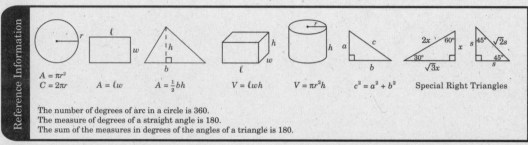

Reference Information

$A = \pi r^2$
$C = 2\pi r$

$A = \ell w$

$A = \frac{1}{2}bh$

$V = \ell wh$

$V = \pi r^2 h$

$c^2 = a^2 + b^2$

Special Right Triangles

The number of degrees of arc in a circle is 360.
The measure of degrees of a straight angle is 180.
The sum of the measures in degrees of the angles of a triangle is 180.

1. A public health study found that in a certain town, 30% of the citizens are malnourished. If that town has a population of 1320, how many of its citizens are malnourished?

    (A) 19
    (B) 44
    (C) 396
    (D) 528
    (E) 924

    $1320 \times .30$

2. If $w = 2y^2 - 2$, $y = \sqrt{\frac{x}{2} + 3}$, and $x = 4$, then what is the value of w?

    (A) $\sqrt{5}$
    (B) $\sqrt{8}$
    (C) 5
    (D) 8
    (E) 10

    $2\frac{\cancel{4}}{2} + 3$

    $\sqrt{5}$

    $2(\sqrt{5})^2 - 2$

    $10 - 2$

    8

3. A truck contains exactly 7 barrels. Each barrel contains at least 120 apples but no more than 180 apples. Which of the following could be the number of apples on the truck?

    (A) 600
    (B) 800
    (C) 1000
    (D) 1300
    (E) 1600

4. If $xy = 42$ and $x^2 - y^2 = 13$, then what is the value of $(x - y)^2$?

    (A) 1
    (B) 13
    (C) 55
    (D) 85
    (E) 169

    $x = 7$
    $y = 6$

GO ON TO THE NEXT PAGE

Section 5

Cost of Items		
	Small	Large
Hats	$12	$12
Shirts	$18	$20
Pants	$30	$35

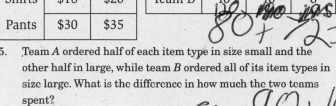

Item Type Orders			
	Hats	Shirts	Pants
Team A	12	8	6
Team B	10	18	6

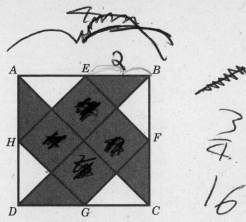

5. Team A ordered half of each item type in size small and the other half in large, while team B ordered all of its item types in size large. What is the difference in how much the two teams spent?

(A) 0
(B) 7
(C) 37
(D) 39
(E) 62

6. 20 percent of 70 percent of an integer is equal to x percent of 40 percent of that same integer. What is the value of x?

(A) 20
(B) 35
(C) 50
(D) 60
(E) 75

7. In square $ABCD$, points E, F, G, and H are the midpoints of their respective sides. What is the area of the shaded portion if $\overline{AB} = 4$?

(A) 2
(B) 4
(C) 8
(D) 12
(E) 16

8. If $5 \le x + 3y \le 8$, and $z \le 5$, what is the greatest possible value of $2x + 6y + z$?

(A) 3
(B) 13
(C) 18
(D) 21
(E) 40

GO ON TO THE NEXT PAGE

Section 5

Directions: for Student-Produced Response Questions 9-18, use the grids at the bottom of the answer sheet page on which you have answered questions 1-8.

Each of the remaining 10 questions requires you to solve the problem and enter your answer by marking the ovals in the special grid, as shown in the examples below.

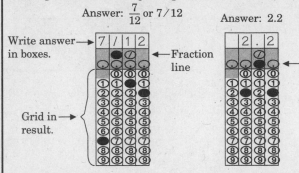

Answer: $\frac{7}{12}$ or 7/12

Answer: 2.2

Answer: 201
Either postion is correct

Write answer in boxes. ← Fraction line

← Decimal point

Grid in result.

Note: You may start your answers in any column, space permitting. Columns not needed should be left blank.

- Mark no more than one oval in any column.

- Because the answer sheet will be machine-scored, **you will receive credit only if the ovals are filled in completely.**

- Although not required, it is suggested that you write your answer in the boxes at the top of the columns to help you fill in the ovals accurately.

- Some problems may have more than one correct answer. In such cases, grid only one answer

- No question has a negative answer.

- **Mixed numbers** such as $2\frac{1}{2}$ must be gridded as 2.5 or 5/2. If $\boxed{2\,1\,/\,2}$ is gridded, it will be interpreted as $\frac{21}{2}$, not $2\frac{1}{2}$.)

- **Decimal Accuracy:** If you obtain a decimal answer, **enter the most accurate value the grid will accommodate.** For example, if you obtain an answer such as 0.6666 . . . , you should record the result as .666 or .667. **Less accurate values such as .66 or .67 are not acceptable.** Acceptable ways to grid $\frac{2}{3}$ = .666 . . .

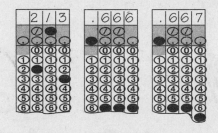

9. If $x = 2$, what is the area of the shaded region?

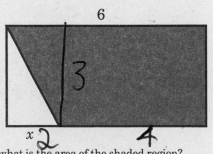

10. Arnold buys a new suit, on sale at 15% off. After a year he sells the suit for $200, which is 20% less than the price he paid to buy it. How much did the suit cost before it was put on sale? (round your answer to the nearest dollar)

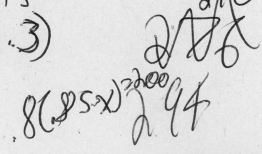

GO ON TO THE NEXT PAGE

Section 5

11. A bowl of soup at temperature x is left out in a cold room. For every minute that the soup is in the room, its temperature drops by $10t$ degrees, where t is the number of minutes that the soup has been in the room. If $x = 150$, how many minutes will it take for the soup's temperature to reach 40 degrees?

 $11 \, min$

12. Set A contains the elements $\{5, 4, 8, 9, 14, 10, 1\}$. Set B contains the elements $\{10, 7, 6, 13, 1, 4, 9, 12\}$. What is the mean of the intersection of A and B?

13. If $h(x) = \sqrt{x^2 - 5}$, then what is the value of $h(3) + h(-3)$?

14. If line l is the perpendicular bisector of a line segment with endpoints $(-2,1)$ and $(1,-1)$, then what is the slope of line l?

15. If $2^x = 4^y = 16^z$, what is $\frac{x}{y} + \frac{x}{z}$?

16. A line passes through the point $(2,3)$ and is parallel to the line $y = -\frac{1}{2}x + 3$? What is the x-intercept of the line?

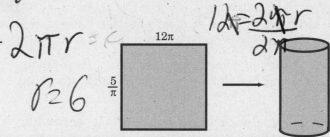

$2\pi r = c$

26

$\frac{12 = 2\pi r}{2\pi}$

17. If the rectangle in the figure is rolled into a cylinder according to the figure above (so that the edges of length $5/\pi$ touch), what is the volume of the cylinder?

$\pi r^2 h = 180$

$\pi 6^2 \frac{5}{\pi}$

18. A jar holds 3 black marbles and 2 white marbles. Two marbles are taken out one after the other. What is the probability that the first marble removed will be black and the second removed will be white?

S T O P

IF YOU FINISH BEFORE TIME IS CALLED, YOU MAY CHECK YOUR WORK ON THIS TEST ONLY.
DO NOT TURN TO ANY OTHER SECTION IN THIS TEST.

Section 6

Time—25 Minutes
35 Questions

For each question in this section, select the best answer from among the choices given and fill in the corresponding oval on the answer sheet.

Directions: The following sentences test correctness and effectiveness of expression. In choosing answers, follow the requirements of standard written English; that is, pay attention to grammar, choice of words, sentence construction, and punctuation.

In each of the following sentences, part of the sentence or the entire sentence is underlined. Beneath each sentence you will find five ways of phrasing the underlined part. Choice A repeats the original; the other four are different.

Choose the answer that best expresses the meaning of the original sentence. If you think the original is better than any of the alternatives, choose it; otherwise choose one of the others. Your choice should produce the most effective sentence—clear and precise, without awkwardness or ambiguity.

EXAMPLE:

Laura Ingalls Wilder published her first book and she was sixty-five years old then.

(A) and she was sixty-five years old then
(B) when she was sixty-five
(C) at age sixty-five years old
(D) upon the reaching of sixty-five years
(E) at the time when she was sixty-five

SAMPLE ANSWER:

Ⓐ ● Ⓒ Ⓓ Ⓔ

1. International travel has become cheaper, but hotel prices and car rental fees has caused the total price of vacations abroad to increase significantly.

   (A) has caused the total price of vacations abroad to increase significantly
   (B) have caused an increase in the total price of vacations abroad
   (C) significantly rise the total cost of vacations abroad
   (D) will significantly raise the total price of vacations abroad
   (E) caused the total price of vacations abroad to be increasing significantly

2. Women who were competing in the Olympic games for the first time in 1928.

   (A) Women who were competing in the Olympic games
   (B) The Olympic games who were where women were competing
   (C) Women competing in the Olympic games
   (D) Women, competing in the Olympic games who were,
   (E) Women competed in the Olympic games

3. My brother Abraham lived in a cabin in Alaska, and it was not winterized, and he refused to move or to install a heating system.

   (A) My brother Abraham lived in a cabin in Alaska, and it was not winterized, and he refused to move or to install a heating system.
   (B) Although his cabin in Alaska was not winterized, my brother Abraham refused to move or to install a heating system.
   (C) My brother Abraham refused to move or to install a heating system, in addition to his cabin in Alaska not being winterized.
   (D) Although my brother Abraham refused to move or to install a heating system, but he lived in a cabin in Alaska which was not winterized.
   (E) Although he had lived in a cabin in Alaska, my brother Abraham refused to move or to install a heating system even though it was not winterized.

GO ON TO THE NEXT PAGE

Section 6

4. Coach Rogers had the endorsement of the school's athletic department, <u>this support</u> allowed him the time and budget necessary to lead the football team to an undefeated season.

   (A) this
   (B) consequently
   (C) and this
   (D) their
   (E) however

5. All of the provinces are ruled by democratically elected tribunals, <u>each with its own set of rules and regulations</u>.

   (A) each with its own set of rules and regulations
   (B) each with their own set of rules and regulations
   (C) each being subject to their own set of rules and regulations
   (D) which has its own set of rules and regulations
   (E) they each have their set of rules and regulations

6. A good translator must understand the subtleties of language <u>as well as remaining faithful to the tone</u> of the author's original text.

   (A) as well as remaining faithful to the tone
   (B) as well as remaining as faithful to the tone
   (C) and remain faithful to the tone
   (D) and to remain faithful to the tone
   (E) and to remain faithful in the tone

7. Columbus discovered most of the islands in the West Indies <u>but failed to find the gold their backers demanded</u>.

   (A) but failed to find the gold their backers demanded
   (B) and failed to find the gold his backers demanded
   (C) and failed to find the gold their backers demanded
   (D) but failed to find the gold his backers demanded
   (E) but was a failure at finding the gold his backers demanded

8. Arguably one of the finest examples of modern architecture, <u>the public's reaction to the new Getty Center in Los Angeles was enthusiastic</u>.

   (A) the public's reaction to the new Getty Center in Los Angeles was enthusiastic
   (B) the public's reaction to the new Getty Center in Los Angeles was enjoyably enthusiastic
   (C) the new Getty Center's reaction was enjoyable and enthusiastic
   (D) the new Getty Center garnered an enthusiastic reaction from the public
   (E) the new Getty Center was reacted by enjoyment and enthusiasm

9. When my grandmother designed her garden, <u>she had evoked Monet's famous garden at Giverny but was not directly copying it</u>.

   (A) she had evoked Monet's famous garden at Giverny but was not directly copying it
   (B) Monet's famous garden at Giverny was being evoked without being directly copied by her
   (C) she was evoking, without a direct copy, Monet's famous garden at Giverny
   (D) she evoked, but had not directly copied, Monet's famous garden at Giverny
   (E) she evoked, but did not directly copy, Monet's famous garden at Giverny

10. A favorite of teenagers and adults for decades, Madonna is popular <u>not so much for her music but for her ability to remain one step ahead of the trend</u>.

    (A) not so much for her music but for her ability to remain one step ahead of the trend
    (B) not so much for her music but for being able to remain one step ahead of the trend
    (C) not so much because of her music but because of her ability to be remaining one step ahead of the trend
    (D) not for her music but for her being able to remain one step ahead of the trend
    (E) not so much for her music as for her ability to remain one step ahead of the trend

11. While in Trieste, <u>James Joyce's writing career did not start promisingly, failing so terribly</u> as a writer that he was forced to tutor students in foreign languages for a number of years.

    (A) James Joyce's writing career did not start promisingly, failing so terribly
    (B) James Joyce's writing career did not start promisingly, having failed so terribly
    (C) James Joyce's writing career did not start promisingly but failed so terribly
    (D) James Joyce did not have a promising start to his career, failing so terribly
    (E) James Joyce did not start his career promisingly but failed it so terribly

GO ON TO THE NEXT PAGE

Section 6

12. Although cutting taxes may sound like an attractive
       A   B
proposition, they may impair the county's ability to maintain
         C
services that everyone depends on. No error
         D   E

13. Devoid of many fixed lines, Frank Gehry's buildings features
    A   B   C
extreme curves and sloping surfaces. No error
              D   E

14. The group of students, teachers, and librarians have endorsed
        A   B   C
the fantastic new series of study guides. No error
     D   E

15. Clara was soon to learn that she could make herself understood
           A   B
more easily by speaking Spanish and not by writing it. No error
      C   D   E

16. Weighing in at over 300 pounds, the boxer was the heavier of all
    A   B   C
the fighters in the tournament. No error
             D   E

17. Although many foster children are fortunate to have family and
                                  A
friends which are eager to help them, an equal number
       B
complain of inadequate support systems and feelings of
  A C   D
isolation. No error
        E

18. The malodorous sight of the deer carcass, which lay by the side
     A   B   C
of the road after the accident, caused Gretchen to gasp. No error
                              D   E

19. Proponents of the new hormone therapy advocate early
    A   B
intervention, frequent checkups, and to comply with
                           C
recommended dosages. No error
         D   E

20. Many people continue to scoff at the notion that pet ownership
                 A   B
can significantly reduce the onset of stress-related illness.
     C   D
No error
 E

21. Ruth Stout, widely regarded as one of the first proponents of
          A   B
organic gardening, espoused theories that were as
                           C
unconventional as they were effective. No error
            D   E

22. Disputes in the private sector forced top executives to propose a
    A   B
series of alternative solutions toward rampant insider trading.
                  C   D
No error
 E

23. Victims of the police officers' use of force, later ruled excessive by
                           A   B
the court, spoke passionately about the suffrage
                      C
they had endured after the incident. No error
     D   E

24. The entire delegation, except for the ambassador himself,
                                  A
were on board the plane that arrived late yesterday in Los
   B   C   D
Angeles. No error
       E

25. The vacationers who arrived at the beach were
                     A
invariably struck by the tranquil atmosphere that prevailed
   B   C
despite the threat of the approaching tropical storm. No error
                       D   E

GO ON TO THE NEXT PAGE

26. The early novels of Richard Thompson are <u>filled</u> with <u>such</u>
    _A   _B
    exceptional sequences <u>of</u> coincidence that <u>scarcely no</u> modern
    _C   _D
    reader finds them believable. <u>No error</u>
    _E

27. The <u>economic</u> dollar cost <u>of purchasing</u> a country home <u>proved</u>
    _A   _B   _C
    too great for the struggling family, which had only recently seen
    <u>its</u> financial fortunes improve. <u>No error</u>
    _D   _E

28. The popularity <u>of</u> a <u>recognizable</u> brand <u>will</u> always dominate
    _A   _B   _C
    <u>its generic equivalent</u>. <u>No error</u>
    _D   _E

29. <u>Fully</u> one hundred percent <u>of</u> the sales respresentatives present
    _A   _B
    at the conference resolved to respond <u>for</u> the challenge with
    _C
    <u>alacrity</u>. <u>No error</u>
    _D   _E

GO ON TO THE NEXT PAGE

Section 6

Questions 30–35 are based on the following passage.

(1) *When I was younger, I thought that knowing about history was pointless; it seemed like one of those things that parents and teachers want you to learn in order to give you discipline and to make sure you do homework.* (2) *But now I know if you want to understand yourself in context of the world, it doesn't hurt to study history.* (3) *A lot of people think of Abraham Lincoln as the tall guy who fought slavery and got shot but there was a lot more to him.* (4) *He was a pioneer in the true sense of the word.* (5) *(Then again, there are definitely people who disagree and maybe it doesn't matter if you are ignorant of your past, depending on your job and how far you want to go in the world.)*

(6) *For instance, did you know that we weren't even discovered on purpose but inadvertently?* (7) *The reason I thought this was helpful to know was that a lot of other things happen by accident—scientific breakthroughs and medical advancements—and it is good to know that success can sometimes come in the midst of what feels like failure.* (8) *Newton and Gregor Mendel exemplified this principle with their persistence.* (9) *Although they weren't necessarily Americans, per se.* (10) *Consequently, knowing how hard your ancestors fought to ensure your liberty and free rights is very poignant and makes you appreciate things you could otherwise take for granted.* (11) *Once you know that the Boston Tea Party wasn't some riotous celebration but a serious battle, one looks at life differently.*

(12) *Even with the noble leaders of our past and all of the rights we have fought to maintain, our country is still very young.* (13) *Reading newspapers and taking responsibility for understanding your past will create a better future.* (14) *And that, my friend, is our only way forward.*

30. What is the best revision of sentence 2 (reproduced below)?

> But now I know if you want to understand yourself in context of the world, it doesn't hurt to study history.

(A) But now I know if you would like to understand yourself in context of the world, it won't hurt to study history.

(B) Now I know that studying history can help you understand yourself in the context of the world.

(C) However, now I know studying history can put you in the context of the world.

(D) However, now I know if one wants to understand oneself in the context of the world, you should study history.

(E) Now I know that studying history doesn't hurt you when you put yourself in the context of the world.

31. Which of the following sentences is LEAST essential to the second paragraph?

(A) sentence 7
(B) sentence 8
(C) sentence 9
(D) sentence 10
(E) sentence 11

32. Which of the following would be the best replacement for *Consequently* at the beginning of sentence 10?

(A) Furthermore
(B) Although
(C) Because
(D) Despite
(E) Finally

33. Which version of the underlined portion of sentence 11 (reproduced below) is the best?

> Once you know that the Boston Tea Party wasn't some riotous celebration <u>but a serious battle, one looks at life differently.</u>

(A) (as it is now)
(B) but a serious battle to make one look at life differently
(C) but a serious battle that will make one look differently at life
(D) but a serious battle, you looked at life differently
(E) but a serious battle, you will look at life differently

GO ON TO THE NEXT PAGE

Section 6

34. All of the following strategies are used by the writer EXCEPT

    (A) the first person
    (B) citing specific historical incidents
    (C) parenthetical clauses
    (D) point-by-point refutation of an opposing point of view
    (E) colloquial language

35. What is the best way to combine sentences 13 and 14 (reproduced below)?

    Reading newspapers and taking responsibility for understanding your past will create a better future. And that, my friend, is our only way forward.

    (A) To understand our past, we must move forward toward reading newspapers and taking responsibility.
    (B) A better future depends on moving forward to taking responsibility and reading newspapers.
    (C) Reading newspapers and taking responsibility for moving forward is the best way to understand our past.
    (D) Reading newspapers and taking responsibility for understanding our past is the best way to move toward a better future.
    (E) My friend, take responsibility and read newspapers to understand our past and move forward toward a better future.

S T O P

IF YOU FINISH BEFORE TIME IS CALLED, YOU MAY CHECK YOUR WORK ON THIS TEST ONLY.
DO NOT TURN TO ANY OTHER SECTION IN THIS TEST.

Section 7

Time—20 Minutes
19 Questions

For each question in this section, select the best answer from among the choices given and fill in the corresponding oval on the answer sheet.

Each sentence below has one or two blanks, each blank indicating that something has been omitted. Beneath the sentence are five words or sets of words labeled A through E. Choose the word or set of words that, when inserted in the sentence, best fits the meaning of the sentence as a whole.

Example:

Medieval kingdoms did not become constitutional republics overnight; on the contrary, the change was ----.

(A) unpopular
(B) unexpected
(C) advantageous
(D) sufficient
(E) gradual

---

1. Ice ages, in which the average temperature of the planet ---- significantly, tend to develop gradually; ice and cold do not ---- appear out of nowhere.

(A) grows . . swiftly
(B) decreases . . suddenly
(C) changes . . indirectly
(D) lessens . . slowly
(E) extends . . merely

2. He is often hailed as a ---- writer, but Mark Twain's later work probes unsettling and ---- truths.

(A) troubling . . funny
(B) distressing . . bothersome
(C) hilarious . . disorganized
(D) patriotic . . regional
(E) comic . . disturbing

3. In Upton Sinclair's book *The Jungle*, the author ---- the world of meatpacking companies, scrutinizing its often unsavory practices.

(A) romanticizes
(B) evades
(C) revamps
(D) exposes
(E) prohibits

4. In retrospect many historians consider the Vietnam War's Tet Offensive downright ----, since it culminated in so many casualties and so few gains.

(A) punctual
(B) foolhardy
(C) fickle
(D) bold
(E) admirable

5. Louisa's ---- of historical matters was ---- by the erroneous comments she made regarding the events leading up to the American Revolution.

(A) mastery . . highlighted
(B) ignorance . . illustrated
(C) love . . evidenced
(D) negligence . . eviscerated
(E) obstruction . . articulated

6. Born ----, baby howler monkeys will explore every inch of their surroundings without any sense of fear, since they are not ---- of the possibility of danger at such a young age.

(A) inquisitive . . cognizant
(B) malleable . . perspicacious
(C) pugnacious . . wary
(D) adventurous . . impudent
(E) timorous . . apprehensive

GO ON TO THE NEXT PAGE

Section 7

The passages below are followed by questions based on their content. Answer the questions on the basis of what is <u>stated</u> or <u>implied</u> in the passages and in any introductory material that may be provided.

<u>Questions 7–19</u> are based on the following passages.

The following passages were adapted from articles published in two New York newspapers, the Herald *and the* Times, *around 1870. Both articles discuss the sport of baseball, which was just becoming popular at the time..*

Passage 1

Some few years ago there was no manly outdoor sport in which the youth of the country could indulge and which could be claimed as national. The game baseball in a crude form was practiced among others, and by a few gentlemen was being systematized

5 and perfected. The *Herald*, observing that in the game were all the elements which could commend it as a favorite pastime, styled it the National Game, and from that time to the present the young men—and many of the old men—of the country have adopted it as a means of recreation, amusement, and physical development.

10 That the game possesses the requisites for affording recreation and relaxation from daily labor is plainly shown by the thousands who flock to witness contests between any of the leading organizations. That it promotes the physical development is attested beyond a doubt by the improved physiques of those

15 who practice with the bat and ball. Every portion of the physical system is brought into action, while the mind is subjected, at the same time, to a recreative course of treatment. The eye is trained to take in at once the entire situation; the hearing is quickened, to enable the players to note the slightest click of "tip" and to

20 understand the call of the umpire or the order of the captains when the other faculties are intent on some other point; the judgment is exercised so as to enable the player to decide instantly on the best course of action to benefit his party, and the muscular strength is developed by the running, throwing,

25 pitching, and batting in which all take part during the contest.

The game has now been reduced to a science, and the objection which was formerly made to it, on the ground that, compared to cricket, it was child's play, can no longer be raised. It was considered by some as being too dangerous; fingers were broken

30 and the players were otherwise wounded, while in cricket the men could pad themselves so that they would not be hurt. Is it an objection to swimming that people are drowned sometimes? Or to skating that people are hurt by collisions or falls? Besides, the fact that the players at baseball unflinchingly face the dangers shows

35 the inherent bravery of the American people and their determination to obtain even amusement at the risk of danger.

Aside from these considerations, the formation of clubs and state and national associations presents an advantage to the youth of this country. In these associations the members are

40 almost unconsciously trained in the system of legislation. Business is conducted on the same plan as the legislative and corporate bodies throughout the country, and the members of the club become fitted for the proper performance of their duties as sovereigns. There is still another advantage to be derived from

45 the associations which may be formed in the leading amateur organizations, such as the Empire, Knickerbocker and Eagle clubs of New York, Excelsior and Star of Brooklyn, Eureka of Newark, and National of Albany; for in them gentlemen of the highest standing in business and social circles may be found,

50 aiding by their presence and their influence the progress and permanency of the national game.

Passage 2

The game of baseball is, in many respects, worthy of encouragement. In a community by far too much given to sedentary occupations and dyspepsia, it furnishes an incentive to

55 active open-air exercise, and we should be glad to see it even more resorted to than it is, among the class who would profit most by its benefits. Our merchants and lawyers and over-worked clerks, after their day of harassing mental labor, would derive more advantage from a brisk game of baseball than from the favorite

60 drive on the road with its accompaniments of dust and dissipation.

To be sure we do not share the opinion of some of its more enthusiastic advocates, that skill in our national pastime implies an exercise of the moral virtues, and we have taken occasion to

65 express our dissent from the views of the president of a Western club, who appears to rank the science of ball playing with the learned professions. Moderately used, however, in its legitimate sphere as an amusement, baseball is certainly a wholesome and invigorating sport.

70 It is one of the defects of our national characters, however, that no sooner do we get hold of a good thing of this sort, than we proceed to make it hurtful by excess. Baseball as a recreation was well enough, but baseball established as a business calls upon us to revise our notions of its usefulness. Nor is professional

75 baseball, as at present practiced, entitled to the only praise that might be urged in its favor; it is not even a healthy physical exercise. On the contrary, it is so dangerous to life and limb, that in insurance language it would be labeled extra hazardous. Fatal accidents on the ballfield have been so common of late as hardly to

GO ON TO THE NEXT PAGE

80 excite remark, and maiming is the rule and not the exception
among members of the first-class clubs. One of the best players of
the Red Stockings was so injured in a recent match that he is
unable to walk without crutches. In fact, a veteran baseball
player, whose teeth have not been knocked out, or whose bones
85 have not been repeatedly broken, is a lucky rarity. The moral
aspect of our national game is even less reassuring. At its best, it
is an excuse for gambling; at its worst, a device for viler
"jockeying" and swindling than ever disgraced the turf.

7. In passage 1, line 6, "styled" most nearly means

    (A) deemed
    (B) coiffed
    (C) arranged
    (D) decorated
    (E) annulled

8. In lines 10–25, the author notes that baseball serves as a venue
    for all of the following EXCEPT

    (A) relaxation
    (B) reflex training
    (C) physical exercise
    (D) entertainment
    (E) financial gain

9. In lines 31–33, the author mentions the dangers involved in
    swimming and skating so as to

    (A) discourage readers from swimming and skating
    (B) highlight the dangers of baseball
    (C) encourage readers to skate or swim rather than play
        baseball
    (D) downplay the dangers of baseball
    (E) encourage readers to play baseball in addition to
        swimming and skating

10. The author's tone in lines 41–44 could most accurately be
    characterized as

    (A) patriotic
    (B) xenophobic
    (C) anticlerical
    (D) wrathful
    (E) soothing

11. In lines 44–51, the author of passage 1 suggests that the
    participation of important businessmen

    (A) corrupts the moral foundations of baseball
    (B) causes instability in the game
    (C) reflects baseball's ability to promote products through
        advertising
    (D) solidifies baseball as a national institution
    (E) demonstrates how baseball players are simply looking to
        make a quick buck

12. In line 58, "harassing" most closely means

    (A) haranguing
    (B) tiring
    (C) molesting
    (D) pesky
    (E) facile

13. The author of passage 2 argues that baseball

    (A) is a useful expression of social precepts
    (B) should serve exclusively as a means of gaining exercise and
        relaxation
    (C) functions as a unifying force for the American nation
    (D) encourages the development of interstate trade
    (E) induces religious piety in its spectators

14. In lines 77–78, the author of passage 2 characterizes baseball as

    (A) innocuous
    (B) scientific
    (C) perilous
    (D) bellicose
    (E) reassuring

15. The "Red Stockings" (line 82) most likely refers to a

    (A) political party
    (B) corporation
    (C) baseball team
    (D) business venture
    (E) umpires' union

16. In lines 86–88, the author of passage 2 asserts that "[a]t its best,
    [baseball] is an excuse for gambling" in order to

    (A) encourage the development of sports-related gambling
    (B) justify his personal gambling habit
    (C) argue for the expansion of baseball in the West
    (D) illustrate that baseball encourages immoral practices
    (E) reassure his readers that baseball is not dangerous

17. In paragraph 4, the author of passage 1 argues that playing
    baseball helps the youth by

    (A) training them to succeed in business and politics
    (B) building their bodies for factory work
    (C) exposing them to new ideas and people
    (D) augmenting hand-eye coordination
    (E) teaching them that that in life there are winners and losers

GO ON TO THE NEXT PAGE

18. Reading the phrase "it is so dangerous to life and limb, that in insurance language it would be labeled extra hazardous" (passage 2, lines 77–78), the author of passage 1 would most likely

(A) strongly agree
(B) strongly disagree
(C) claim that baseball is safer than swimming
(D) contend that more study must be done to before baseball can be called either safe or dangerous
(E) argue that it is good that baseball is dangerous

19. Which of the following issues is NOT explicitly discussed in either passage?

(A) sports injuries
(B) patriotism
(C) the moral implications of baseball
(D) the details of how baseball teams are funded
(E) spectatorship

S T O P

IF YOU FINISH BEFORE TIME IS CALLED, YOU MAY CHECK YOUR WORK ON THIS TEST ONLY.
DO NOT TURN TO ANY OTHER SECTION IN THIS TEST.

Section 8

Time—20 Minutes
16 Questions

In this section solve each problem, using any available space on the page for scratchwork. Then decide which is the best of the choices given and fill in the corresponding oval on the answer sheet.

Notes:

1. The use of a calculator is permitted. All numbers used are real numbers.

2. Figures that accompany problems in this test are intended to provide information useful in solving the problems. They are drawn as accurately as possible EXCEPT when it is stated in a specific problem that the figure is not drawn to scale. All figures lie in a plane unless otherwise indicated.

3. Unless otherwise specified, the domain of any function f is assumed to be the set of all real numbers x for which $f(x)$ is a real number.

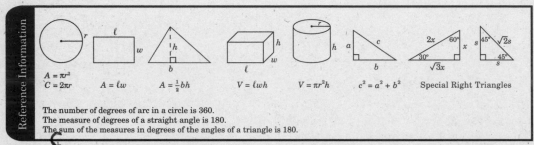

$A = \pi r^2$
$C = 2\pi r$

$A = \ell w$

$A = \frac{1}{2}bh$

$V = \ell wh$

$V = \pi r^2 h$

$c^2 = a^2 + b^2$

Special Right Triangles

The number of degrees of arc in a circle is 360.
The measure of degrees of a straight angle is 180.
The sum of the measures in degrees of the angles of a triangle is 180.

1. If a one-way bus ride costs $0.90, and John rides to and from school on the bus every school day, which is the best estimate of how much John will spend on bus rides in the month of February? Assume that there are 21 school days in the month of February.

   (A) $.50 × 20
   (B) 2 × $50 × 25
   (C) $1.00 × 20
   (D) 2 × $.50 × 20
   (E) 2 × $1.00 × 20

2. If $x = ab$, and a doubles while b triples, by what factor will the value of x change?

   (A) 1
   (B) 2
   (C) 3
   (D) 4
   (E) 6

3. If 28 is divided by 5 and 30 is divided by 7, what is the product of the remainders?

   (A) 2
   (B) 3
   (C) 5
   (D) 6
   (E) 35

4. If $z = x^2 - x$ and $x = 2\sqrt{j}$, what is the value of z when $j = 3$?

   (A) $12 - 2\sqrt{3}$
   (B) $36 - 2\sqrt{3}$
   (C) $4\sqrt{3}$
   (D) $2\sqrt{3}$
   (E) 2

5. Thirty of a building's windows have shades. If 2 of every 5 windows are shaded, then how many windows does the building have?

   (A) 12
   (B) 15
   (C) 30
   (D) 75
   (E) 150

GO ON TO THE NEXT PAGE

Section 8

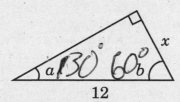

12

6. If $a = \dfrac{b}{2}$, then what is the value of x?

(A) 6
(B) $6\sqrt{2}$
(C) $6\sqrt{3}$
(D) $12\sqrt{2}$
(E) $12\sqrt{3}$

7. If $f(x) = x^2 - 2$ and $g(x) = \dfrac{x}{2} - 1$, then $f(g(8)) =$

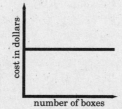

(A) 3
(B) 7
(C) 8
(D) 30
(E) 62

8. A company produces boxes. It incurs a one-time cost to build its factory and then a constant unit cost for each box it produces. Which of the following graphs could represent the company's costs?

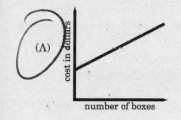

(A)

(B)

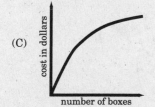

(C)

(D)

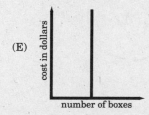

(E)

9. Points $A, B, C, D, E,$ and F lie on the same plane. Points $A, B,$ and C lie on one line. A line connecting points B and D is perpendicular to a line connecting points A and C. A line connecting points $C, E,$ and F is parallel to a line connecting points B and D. Given this information, which of the following pairs of line segments must be perpendicular to each other?

(A) $\overline{AB}$ and $\overline{CF}$
(B) $\overline{BD}$ and $\overline{CF}$
(C) $\overline{AD}$ and $\overline{EC}$
(D) $\overline{AB}$ and $\overline{BC}$
(E) $\overline{BD}$ and $\overline{EC}$

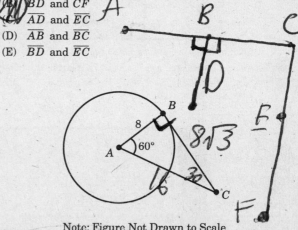

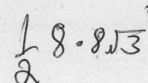

Note: Figure Not Drawn to Scale

10. What is the area of triangle ABC, if AB is the radius of circle A and line segment BC is tangent to the circle?

(A) $8\sqrt{3}$
(B) 16
(C) 32
(D) $32\sqrt{3}$
(E) $64\sqrt{3}$

GO ON TO THE NEXT PAGE

Section 8

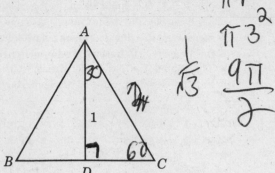

11. ABC is an equilateral triangle. $\overline{AD} = 1$. What is the length of $\overline{AC}$?

(A) $\dfrac{1}{2}$

(B) $\dfrac{\sqrt{3}}{2}$

(C) $\dfrac{2}{\sqrt{3}}$

(D) $\sqrt{2}$

(E) 1.5

12. Donna is the head of the school recycling drive. It takes her 15 minutes to crush 1 trash bag full of aluminum cans. If the school collected 180 trash bags full of cans, and there are 3 hours to crush cans, how many people does Donna need to recruit to help her? Assume that everyone crushes cans at the same rate and that Donna is working too.

(A) 4

(B) 11

(C) 12

(D) 14

(E) 15

13. For all $x \neq \pm 2$, the expression $\dfrac{2x^2 - 5x + 2}{x^2 - 4} =$

(A) $\dfrac{1 - 2x}{x}$

(B) $\dfrac{2x + 1}{x - 2}$

(C) $\dfrac{2x - 1}{x - 2}$

(D) $\dfrac{2x + 1}{x + 2}$

(E) $\dfrac{2x - 1}{x + 2}$

14. Given the equations $\dfrac{(y + 2)}{2} = \dfrac{x^2 + x}{x + 1}$ and $y = 4x$, what is the value of x?

(A) -2

(B) -1

(C) 1

(D) 2

(E) 4

15. Points A, B, and C are the centers of three adjacent circles. ABC is an equilateral triangle. What is the area of the shaded region if the diameter of one circle is 6?

(A) $9\sqrt{3} - \dfrac{9\pi}{2}$

(B) $9\sqrt{3} - 9\pi$

(C) $18 - \dfrac{9\pi}{2}$

(D) $9(\sqrt{3} - 2\pi)$

(E) $18(2 - \pi)$

16. Set Z contains the z flute players in Ms. Meyers' class and Set W contains the w trumpet players. Set Y consists of all those students who play flute or trumpet, excluding those n students who play both flute and trumpet ($n > 0$). Which of the following shows the number of students in Set Y?

(A) $z + w + k$

(B) $z + w - k$

(C) $z - (w + k)$

(D) $z + w - 2k$

(E) $(z - w) + k$

S T O P

IF YOU FINISH BEFORE TIME IS CALLED, YOU MAY CHECK YOUR WORK ON THIS TEST ONLY.
DO NOT TURN TO ANY OTHER SECTION IN THIS TEST.

Section 9

Turn to Section 9 of your answer sheet to answer the questions in this section.

Time—10 Minutes
14 Questions

For each question in this section, select the best answer from among the choices given and fill in the corresponding oval on the answer sheet.

Directions: The following sentences test correctness and effectiveness of expression. In choosing answers, follow the requirements of standard written English; that is, pay attention to grammar, choice of words, sentence construction, and punctuation.

In each of the following sentences, part of the sentence or the entire sentence is underlined. Beneath each sentence you will find five ways of phrasing the underlined part. Choice A repeats the original; the other four are different.

Choose the answer that best expresses the meaning of the original sentence. If you think the original is better than any of the alternatives, choose it; otherwise choose one of the others. Your choice should produce the most effective sentence—clear and precise, without awkwardness or ambiguity.

EXAMPLE:

Laura Ingalls Wilder published her first book and she was sixty-five years old then.

SAMPLE ANSWER:

(A) and she was sixty-five years old then
(B) when she was sixty-five
(C) at age sixty-five years old
(D) upon the reaching of sixty-five years
(E) at the time when she was sixty-five

---

1. Alice will pursue a career in education, athletics, <u>or to become a lawyer</u>.

    (A) or to become a lawyer
    (B) or becoming a lawyer
    (C) or law
    (D) or a lawyer
    (E) or to be legal

2. Alexa had just arrived at home <u>when she learns</u> that she had won the contest.

    (A) when she learns
    (B) when she learned
    (C) and then she finds out
    (D) when she had come to learn
    (E) when she was then informing

3. <u>For more than at least three decades,</u> Jackie Palmer trained to become the world's best golfer.

    (A) for more than perhaps three decades
    (B) for at least three decades
    (C) for nothing less than at least three decades
    (D) for three decades, perhaps
    (E) for three decades and over

4. Rick, Sue, and Andrea were jogging <u>when, losing her balance,</u> <u>she fell and scraped her knee</u>.

    (A) when, losing her balance, she fell and scraped her knee
    (B) when Sue scraped her knee, fell, and lost her balance
    (C) when she lost her balance, fell, and scraped her knee
    (D) when Sue, losing her balance, fell, and scraped her knee.
    (E) when Sue lost her balance, fell, and scraped her knee

5. By rebuilding their industrial facilities after the flood, the townspeople kept their community prosperous, <u>a successful turn of events nobody expects</u>.

    (A) a successful turn of events nobody expected
    (B) and nobody expected this to succeed
    (C) a successful turn of events that nobody had expected
    (D) a turn of events that was expected by nobody to be successful
    (E) a successful turn of events nobody expected

GO ON TO THE NEXT PAGE

Section 9

6. Overall wellness takes into account both physical fitness and mentally healthy as well.

   (A) and mentally healthy as well
   (B) and also the mind
   (C) and mental health
   (D) or mental health as well
   (E) and mental healthy as well

7. Since the burglar is a minor, this will not receive the harshest legal penalties.

   (A) this will not receive
   (B) he will not receive
   (C) he receives
   (D) he receives not only
   (E) this does not receive

8. Though it's great to watch celebrities on the big screen, it's just not the same seeing them in person is always more memorable.

   (A) it's just not the same seeing them in person is always more memorable
   (B) seeing them in person is always the same and more memorable
   (C) it's just not the same as seeing them in person, which is always more memorable
   (D) seeing them in person is always more memorable but just not the same
   (E) it's just not the same as to see them in person, which is always more memorable

9. Without proper parental guidance, many errors in judgment were made by her.

   (A) many errors in judgment were made by her
   (B) her errors were many in judgment
   (C) she made many errors in judgment
   (D) her errors made in judgment were many
   (E) her many errors in judgment were made

10. It is not fair to say that all librarians only like to read and therefore are not doing anything else.

   (A) and therefore are not doing anything else
   (B) and therefore don't do anything else
   (C) and are doing nothing else, therefore
   (D) and are not therefore do anything else
   (E) and therefore are not to do anything else

11. After visiting another country, a change in your entire outlook on life can happen.

   (A) a change in your entire outlook on life can happen
   (B) you can be changing your entire outlook on life
   (C) a change can happen to your entire outlook on life
   (D) changes can happen to your entire outlook on life
   (E) you can change your entire outlook on life

12. Many people believe that robots are capable of replacing not only outdated machines, and also human beings.

   (A) and also human beings
   (B) but also of human beings
   (C) but also human beings
   (D) or human beings
   (E) but human beings

13. Many people in the United States tend to speak English at work but speak other languages at home.

   (A) but speak other languages at home
   (B) if other languages are spoken at home
   (C) but are speaking other languages at home
   (D) but are tending to speak other languages at home
   (E) but at home tend to speak other languages

14. With its furry coat and ducklike bill, zoologists failed to classify the platypus accurately for decades.

   (A) With its furry coat and ducklike bill, many zoologists failed to classify the platypus accurately for decades
   (B) With its furry coat and ducklike bill, zoologists failed accurately to classify the platypus for decades
   (C) Due to its furry coat and ducklike bill, zoologists failed for decades to accurately classify the platypus
   (D) With its furry coat and ducklike bill, the platypus failed accurate classification by zoologists for decades
   (E) Due to the platypus's furry coat and ducklike bill, zoologists failed to classify the platypus accurately for decades

S T O P

IF YOU FINISH BEFORE TIME IS CALLED, YOU MAY CHECK YOUR WORK ON THIS TEST ONLY.
DO NOT TURN TO ANY OTHER SECTION IN THIS TEST.

PRACTICE TEST 1
EXPLANATIONS

TEST 1 ANSWERS

Question Number	Answer	Right	Wrong	Question Number	Answer	Right	Wrong
Section 2				**Section 4, continued**			
1	C	___	___	8	E	___	___
2	D	___	___	9	D	___	___
3	E	___	___	10	D	___	___
4	B	___	___	11	A	___	___
5	B	___	___	12	E	___	___
6	B	___	___	13	B	___	___
7	B	___	___	14	A	___	___
8	A	___	___	15	D	___	___
9	B	___	___	16	E	___	___
10	E	___	___	17	B	___	___
11	B	___	___	18	B	___	___
12	E	___	___	19	B	___	___
13	A	___	___	20	C	___	___
14	D	___	___	21	C	___	___
15	C	___	___	22	B	___	___
16	A	___	___	23	A	___	___
17	A	___	___	24	D	___	___
18	B	___	___	**Section 5**			
19	E	___	___	1	C	___	___
20	C	___	___	2	D	___	___
21	A	___	___	3	C	___	___
22	D	___	___	4	A	___	___
23	D	___	___	5	D	___	___
24	B	___	___	6	B	___	___
Section 3				7	D	___	___
1	E	___	___	8	D	___	___
2	C	___	___	9	15	___	___
3	C	___	___	10	294	___	___
4	B	___	___	11	11	___	___
5	D	___	___	12	6	___	___
6	D	___	___	13	4	___	___
7	E	___	___	14	3/2	___	___
8	B	___	___	15	6	___	___
9	D	___	___	16	8	___	___
10	B	___	___	17	180	___	___
11	B	___	___	18	3/10	___	___
12	D	___	___	**Section 6**			
13	E	___	___	1	B	___	___
14	C	___	___	2	E	___	___
15	C	___	___	3	B	___	___
16	E	___	___	4	C	___	___
17	C	___	___	5	A	___	___
18	E	___	___	6	C	___	___
19	B	___	___	7	D	___	___
20	E	___	___	8	D	___	___
Section 4				9	E	___	___
1	B	___	___	10	E	___	___
2	A	___	___	11	D	___	___
3	A	___	___	12	C	___	___
4	C	___	___	13	C	___	___
5	C	___	___	14	B	___	___
6	E	___	___	15	D	___	___
7	A	___	___	16	C	___	___

Question Number	Answer	Right	Wrong	Question Number	Answer	Right	Wrong
Section 6, continued				**Section 7, continued**			
17	B	___	___	17	A	___	___
18	A	___	___	18	E	___	___
19	C	___	___	19	D	___	___
20	E	___	___	**Section 8**			
21	E	___	___	1	E	___	___
22	C	___	___	2	E	___	___
23	C	___	___	3	D	___	___
24	B	___	___	4	A	___	___
25	E	___	___	5	D	___	___
26	D	___	___	6	A	___	___
27	A	___	___	7	B	___	___
28	D	___	___	8	A	___	___
29	C	___	___	9	A	___	___
30	B	___	___	10	D	___	___
31	C	___	___	11	C	___	___
32	A	___	___	12	D	___	___
33	E	___	___	13	E	___	___
34	D	___	___	14	B	___	___
35	D	___	___	15	A	___	___
Section 7				16	D	___	___
1	B	___	___	**Section 9**			
2	E	___	___	1	C	___	___
3	D	___	___	2	B	___	___
4	B	___	___	3	B	___	___
5	B	___	___	4	E	___	___
6	A	___	___	5	C	___	___
7	A	___	___	6	C	___	___
8	E	___	___	7	B	___	___
9	D	___	___	8	C	___	___
10	A	___	___	9	C	___	___
11	D	___	___	10	B	___	___
12	B	___	___	11	E	___	___
13	B	___	___	12	C	___	___
14	C	___	___	13	A	___	___
15	C	___	___	14	E	___	___
16	D	___	___				

CALCULATING YOUR SCORE

Writing Section Raw Score

A. Essay score (from 1–6)

_____
A

B. Section 6 Multiple-Choice: _____ – (_____ ÷ 4) =
no. correct   no. incorrect

_____
B

C. Section 9 Multiple-Choice: _____ – (_____ ÷ 4) =
no. correct   no. incorrect

_____
C

D. Unrounded Multiple-Choice Score (B + C)

_____
D

E. Total Rounded Multiple- Choice Raw Score
(Rounded to the nearest whole number)

_____
E

F. Total Scaled Score
(See the Writing conversion table on the following pages)

_____
SAT Writing
Score

G. Writing Multiple-Choice Subscore
(See the Writing Multiple-Choice conversion table on the following pages)

_____
Writing MC
Score

Math Section Raw Score

A. Section 3 Raw Score: _____ – (_____ ÷ 4) =
no. correct   no. incorrect

_____
Subtotal A

B. Section 5 Raw Score: _____
no. correct

_____
Subtotal B

C. Section 8 Raw Score: _____ – (_____ ÷ 4) =
no. correct   no. incorrect

_____
Subtotal C

D. Total Unrounded Raw Score
(Total A + B + C)

_____
D

E. Total Rounded Raw Score (Rounded to the nearest whole number)

_____
E

F. Scaled Score
(See the conversion table on the following pages)

_____
SAT Math
Score

the new SAT

Critical Reading Section Raw Score

A. Section 2 Raw Score:

$\underline{\hspace{4cm}}$ − ($\underline{\hspace{4cm}}$ ÷ 4) = $\underline{\hspace{3cm}}$

no. correct   no. incorrect   A

B. Section 4 Raw Score:

$\underline{\hspace{4cm}}$ − ($\underline{\hspace{4cm}}$ ÷ 4) = $\underline{\hspace{3cm}}$

no. correct   no. incorrect   B

C. Section 7 Raw Score:

$\underline{\hspace{4cm}}$ − ($\underline{\hspace{4cm}}$ ÷ 4) = $\underline{\hspace{3cm}}$

no. correct   no. incorrect   C

D. Total Unrounded Raw Score
(Total A + B + C)

$\underline{\hspace{4cm}}$

D

E. Total Rounded Raw Score
(Rounded to the nearest whole number)

$\underline{\hspace{4cm}}$

E

F. Scaled Score
(See the conversion table on the next page)

$\underline{\hspace{4cm}}$

SAT Critical
Reading
Score

the
new
SAT

CONVERTING YOUR RAW SCORES

Raw Score	Critical Reading Scaled Score	Math Scaled Score
67	800	
66	790	
65	770	
64	760	
63	750	
62	740	
61	720	
60	710	
59	700	
58	690	
57	680	
56	670	
55	670	
54	660	800
53	650	780
52	640	760
51	640	740
50	630	730
49	620	710
48	610	700
47	610	690
46	600	670
45	590	660
44	590	650
43	580	650
42	580	640
41	570	630
40	560	620
39	560	610
38	550	600
37	540	590
36	540	590
35	530	580
34	530	570
33	520	560
32	510	560
31	510	550
30	500	540
29	500	530
28	490	520
27	480	520
26	480	510
25	470	500
24	470	490
23	460	490
22	450	480
21	450	470
20	440	460
19	430	460

the new SAT

Raw Score	Critical Reading Scaled Score	Math Scaled Score
18	430	450
17	420	440
16	410	430
15	410	430
14	400	420
13	390	410
12	380	400
11	380	390
10	370	380
9	360	380
8	350	370
7	340	360
6	330	340
5	320	330
4	310	320
3	300	310
2	280	290
1	270	280
0	250	260
-1	250	250
-2	240	240
-3	230	230
-4	220	220
-5	210	210
-6	200	200

Writing Subscores

- **Essay Subscore**: Subtotal A from Writing Score (page 382)
- **Multiple-Choice Subscore**: Calculate by plugging in Subtotal E from your writing score (page 382) into the score conversion table below

Raw Score	Multiple-Choice Subscore	Raw Score	Multiple-Choice Subscore
49	80	30	59
48	79	29	58
47	77	28	57
46	76	27	56
45	75	26	55
44	74	25	54
43	72	24	53
42	71	23	52
41	70	22	51
40	69	21	51
39	68	20	50
38	67	19	49
37	66	18	48
36	65	17	47
35	64	16	46
34	63	15	45
33	62	14	44
32	61	13	43
31	60	12	42

Raw Score	Multiple-Choice Subscore	Raw Score	Multiple-Choice Subscore
11	41	2	32
10	40	1	30
9	39	0	29
8	38	-1	27
7	37	-2	25
6	36	-3	24
5	35	-4	23
4	34	-5	22
3	33	-6	21

Writing Scaled Score

Writing Scaled Score

MC raw score	Essay Score					
	6	5	4	3	2	1
49	800	790	780	470	720	700
48	790	780	760	730	700	680
47	780	770	750	720	690	670
46	770	760	740	710	680	660
45	770	750	740	700	670	650
44	760	750	730	690	660	640
43	750	740	710	680	650	630
42	750	730	700	670	640	620
41	740	730	690	660	630	610
40	740	720	690	650	620	600
39	740	710	680	640	610	590
38	730	700	670	630	610	590
37	720	690	660	630	600	580
36	710	680	650	620	590	570
35	710	680	640	610	580	560
34	700	670	640	600	570	550
33	690	660	630	590	560	540
32	680	650	620	580	560	540
31	670	640	610	580	550	530
30	660	630	600	570	540	520
29	650	630	590	560	530	510
28	640	620	590	550	520	510
27	640	610	580	540	510	490
26	630	600	570	530	500	490
25	620	590	560	520	500	480
24	610	580	550	510	490	470
23	600	570	540	510	480	460
22	590	570	530	500	470	450
21	590	570	530	500	470	450
20	580	560	520	490	460	440
19	570	550	520	480	450	430
18	570	540	520	470	440	420
17	560	530	510	460	430	420
16	550	520	500	450	430	410
15	540	510	490	450	420	400
14	530	500	480	440	410	390
13	520	500	470	430	400	380
12	510	490	460	420	390	370

Writing Scaled Score

MC raw score	Essay Score					
	6	5	4	3	2	1
11	510	480	450	410	380	360
10	500	470	450	400	370	350
9	490	460	440	390	360	350
8	480	450	430	390	360	340
7	470	440	420	380	350	330
6	460	430	410	370	340	320
5	450	430	400	360	330	310
4	450	420	390	350	320	300
3	440	410	390	340	310	290
2	430	400	380	330	300	280
1	420	380	370	320	290	270
0	400	370	350	310	280	260
-1	380	360	340	290	270	260
-2	370	340	320	270	260	250
-3	360	330	310	260	250	240
-4	350	320	290	250	240	230
-5	340	310	280	240	230	220
-6	340	310	280	240	220	210

ESSAY

A 6 Essay

Often, even the most noble end does not justify the means required to achieve it. The decision to drop an atomic bomb on Hiroshima at the end of World War II provides one example of the ends not justifying the means. The current debate over human cloning also shows how the ends don't always justify the means. Finally, the example of famed wildlife photographer Jacques Perrott, who died while photographing polar bears, proves that the ends don't always work to justify the means.

In wartime, leaders often justify their decisions to use force by claiming it was necessary to achieve a peaceful outcome—but the passage of time often proves that these supposedly necessary means weren't morally justifiable. For example, Hiroshima. The Allied leaders said that in order to end World War II, they needed to strike with deadly, overwhelming force. When Hiroshima was bombed, the city and it's population were decimated. It's almost impossible to justify the slaughter of thousands of civilians, even when ending a war is the stated aim.

Most scientists agree that human cloning is unethical, but a few claim that legalizing cloning would make research possible that could lead to life-saving discoveries. Some scientists, notably Dr. Artis Antinori, suggest that cloning should be allowed because some people desperately want children. In a news conference, Antinori said that the end (saved lives) justified any means necessary, including cloning. Most lawmakers and scientists agree, however, that even if human cloning made parents happy and saved lives, the moral, psychological, and ethical implications make cloning objectionable.

Wildlife photographer Jacques Perott believed the ends always justified the means, and that belief cost him his life. Perott became famous by traveling to some of the most remote locations on earth to photograph exotic animals up close. The outspoken Perrott frequently boasted of his fearless conviction that taking these risks justified the rewards—photographs of species few had dared to capture on film. Perrott died while on an expedition to photograph polar bears in Antarctica, proving that rare photographs (the ends) are not worth the dangerous risks (the means) required to obtain them.

As the examples of Hiroshima, human cloning, and the tragedy of Jacques Perott demonstrate, the ends don't always justify the means. Sometimes, as in the case of cloning, we don't have the luxury of hindsight to teach us why the ends don't always merit the means. Then we must learn from our past history that no matter how noble the ends, the perils and ramifications of the means must always be considered.

Discussion

This essay follows our Universal SAT Essay Template almost perfectly. Below is a quick checklist of the criteria for our template.

UNIVERSAL SAT ESSAY TEMPLATE CRITERIA	YES OR NO?
Thesis statement in first sentence of paragraph 1	YES
Three examples listed in paragraph 1 in order from best to worst	YES
Topic sentence for example in paragraph 2	YES
3–4 development sentences to support paragraph 2's example	YES
Topic sentence for example in paragraph 3	YES
3–4 development sentences to support paragraph 3's example	YES
Topic sentence for example in paragraph 4	YES
3–4 development sentences to support paragraph 4's example	YES
Conclusion paragraph contains rephrased thesis statement	YES
About 15 sentences total	YES

Let's take a closer look at the essay based on our four key SAT essay ingredients: positioning, organization, examples, and command of language.

POSITIONING

The writer takes a strong and clear stance on the essay topic right from the start. The first sentence contains a thesis statement, and the first paragraph spells out the three examples the writer will use to support his or her position.

ORGANIZATION

The writer organizes this essay into precisely the organization we suggest in our Universal SAT Essay Template. It contains five paragraphs of at least three sentences each. The paragraphs are organized into an introduction, three example paragraphs starting with the strongest example, and a conclusion that broadens the argument.

EXAMPLES

The writer spells out the three examples he or she will use to prove his or her position on the topic. In this case, the writer takes the position that the ends don't always justify the means. To prove it, the writer uses three diverse examples: one from history (Hiroshima), one from current events (human cloning), and one from the arts (the photographer). The writer uses each example to prove his or her thesis statement. The development of each example works to advance the argument rather than provide needless details or off-topic discussion.

COMMAND OF LANGUAGE

Even 6 essays don't have to be perfect. SAT essay graders should expect at least a few errors in every SAT essay. This essay contains a few minor slips regarding the writer's command of language. *For example, Hiroshima* is a sentence fragment. The phrase *the land and it's people* contains the common mistake of using the contraction "it's" (which is short for "it is") instead of the possessive "its." However, a few small errors like these, which likely result from time constraints, will not keep a great essay from getting the 6 it deserves.

Notice that this essay also contains just the right amount of Special Sauce. The words the writer chooses are effective and appropriate. A few flashes of impressive vocabulary, such as *decimated* and *ramifications,* are sure to impress any SAT essay grader if used properly. The writer also varies the sentence structure frequently, making the essay interesting and easy to read.

A 3 Essay

I disagree with the above statement. The end doesn't always justify the means. Sometimes it does, but not always. It all depends on the case in question.

For example, in a Dorothy L. Sayers novel there is a character who wants to get a fortune. Who doesn't? This is a justifiable end. But in order to do it, he has to kill his cousin, whose the one with the fortune. To do this, he eats a little arsenic every day, slowly building up an imunity to it. Finally he can eat doses of arsenic that would be leethal to most, but he can eat them without blinking an eye. Then he serves an ommelette to his cousin that's completely filled with arsenic. He eats the same ommelet, so the police don't think he could be blamed for poisoning his cousin. This was a good end, but an evil means.

Then, there is the recent mayoral election in New York City. Both men wanted to win the race. They both thought they would be the best mayor for New York City. So to them, winning the race is a great end. But in order to get there, in the last days of the campain they ran a series of mudslinging ads, accusing the other person of sexual harrassment, buying the office, etc. etc. When two politicians lower the tone of a race like that, there is no excuse.

And what about football players who take steroids? They want to make their performance on the field good.

Discussion

This essay fails to follow our Universal SAT Template in several ways. Check out the NOs below to see precisely where it misses the mark.

UNIVERSAL SAT ESSAY TEMPLATE CRITERIA	YES OR NO?
Thesis statement in first sentence of paragraph 1	NO
Three examples listed in paragraph 1 in order from best to worst	NO
Topic sentence for example in paragraph 2	NO
3–4 development sentences to support paragraph 2's example	YES
Topic sentence for example in paragraph 3	YES
3–4 development sentences to support paragraph 3's example	YES
Topic sentence for example in paragraph 4	NO

3–4 development sentences to support paragraph 4's example	NO
Conclusion paragraph contains rephrased thesis statement	NO
About 15 sentences total	YES

As you can tell, this "3" essay doesn't fail to fulfill *every* requirement of our Universal SAT Essay Template. Let's take a closer look at this essay based on our four key SAT essay ingredients: positioning, organization, examples, and command of language.

POSITIONING

According to our template, the thesis statement must come in the first sentence of the essay and should take a firm, clear stance on the topic. The writer does take a strong and clear stance on the essay topic with the statement *The end doesn't always justify the means*. The writer should have used that sentence to begin the essay instead of the somewhat weak opening line he or she chose: *I disagree with the above statement*. The writer then undercuts his or her position by saying that the end sometimes justifies the means. That kind of wishy-washy, indecisive language has no place in any SAT essay. This writer also fails to create an essay summary by laying out all three examples in the first paragraph. Instead, the grader has a sense of the writer's position, but no clue where the essay is headed.

ORGANIZATION

The writer organizes this essay into four paragraphs, which is a good start. The *best* SAT essays should contain five paragraphs, however: three middle paragraphs for supporting examples surrounded by a strong introduction and conclusion. This essay has a weak introduction that establishes the writer's position but does not spell out his or her examples. We then get two paragraphs of examples, neither of which presents a very clear topic sentence or well-organized development. The sentences in this essay often don't work together to advance the argument—and that's the *only* purpose of every sentence in the SAT essay.

EXAMPLES

The writer does include three examples to support his or her position that the ends don't always justify the means. However, the writer really only covers two of these examples, as the third example gets cut off after a brief mention of atheletes and steroids. The most serious problem with the examples in this essay is their lack of development. The writer does not include clear topic sentences linking the essay to the thesis statement, and many of the development sentences are off topic (Both men wanted to win the race) or inappropriate (*who doesn't?*). The example about atheletes and steroids could have supported the thesis statement effectively, but the writer ran out of time and failed to develop it at all.

COMMAND OF LANGUAGE

The main problem with this essay is its lack of sophisticated prose. The essay reads like a transcript of the writer's spoken ramblings on the topic, complete with numerous spelling and grammar errors. Some examples include *campain*, *ommelet*, *whose*, and *leethal*. Another consistent flaw is the author's tendency to rely on vague words like *this* and *it*: *in order to do it, to do this*. Using *this* and *there* and *it* too much keeps the reader in the dark. Instead of writing *in order to do it*, for example, the writer should say *in order to gain the fortune*. This gives the grader a more solid sense that the writer is in control.

This essay doesn't really contain any Special Sauce. The writer's word choice is often too casual. The sentence structure often repeats (*But in order to do it, . . . To do this,*)—lending the entire essay a dull, plodding feel that makes it difficult to read.

SECTION 2

Sentence Completions

1. **C**   One-Blank/One-Way   *Easy*

The sentence contains no switch and isn't about a change over time, so it must flow one way. That means that the blank, which describes the way "Karen was," must agree with the fact that she was "unable to grasp the question in front of her." A word to describe a person "unable to grasp a question" will have negative Word Charge and mean something like *confused*. The answer choice that best agrees with the idea of confused is **C**, *perplexed*. None of the other answer choices gets across the idea of being confused at all.

2. **D**   Two-Blank/Two-Way   *Easy*

The sentence contains a switch word: *despite*. This is a two-way switch, so the sentence must be two-way: the first half of the sentence and the second half must contrast, or disagree. The blank in the first half of the sentence states what has been going on for years, while the blank in the second states what "hope" still remains. The fact that the two halves of the sentence contrast indicates that the word charge needed to fill the blanks will be opposite (that knocks out **A** and **E**). Also, since there's a "hope" in the second half of the sentence, the word charge of that blank must be positive. You're not going to have a "hope" of a negative thing. That knocks out **C**. The next step is to plug the remaining answer choices for **B** and **D** into the sentence. Here's **B**: "Despite years of intermittent *war*, politicians in the war-torn region continue to strive for *religion*." And here's **D**: "Despite years of intermittent *bloodshed*, politicians in the region continue to strive for *peace*." Answer **D** is the better choice, because it makes more sense for politicians to offer the hope of peace than to offer the hope of religion.

3. **E**   Two-Blank/Two-Way   *Medium*

The switch *while* tells you that the sentence is two-way. The two halves of the sentence must contrast. Napoleon was once one way, but now he's a different way that involves limiting the freedom of his subjects. So, the word charge of the first word is positive, while the second is negative. The need for a positive first word allows you to cut **C** and **D**, while the need for a negative second word ges rid of **A** and **B**. That leaves answer **E**, which fits into the question perfectly. Napoleon once wanted to *liberate* Europe, but then he became a *despot* ("tyrant").

4. **B**   One-Blank/One-Way   *Medium*

The sentence contains no switch or comparison over time, so the sentence is one way. The blank word describes "some prehistoric ground sloths," and the blank must fit with the idea that these ancient ground sloths are "much larger than modern-day tree sloths." The word that fills the blank must be something like "really big." That fits the definition of *gargantuan* precisely.

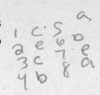

the new SAT

5. **B**   One-Blank/One-Way   *Medium*

The sentence contains the switch word *but*, which means it's two-way. The blank in the second half of the sentence describes the type of knowledge the doctor has to have in order to act, and this blank has to contrast with the word *suspect*. *Suspect* means to "think without proof." A word that contrasts would mean something like "know absolutely" and have a positive word charge. That throws out *medically*, *precariously*, and *ambiguously* as answer choices. *Reputably* means "having a good reputation," so while it has a positive Word Charge, it doesn't have the right meaning. That leaves *unequivocally*, which means "without question" and is the right answer.

    This question contained some difficult vocabulary. Even if you didn't know the meaning of all the words, you could have tried to eliminate incorrect answer choices by using word charge.

6. **B**   One-Blank/Two-Way   *Difficult*

The switch word in this sentence is *unlike*, which means that the sentence is two-way and contrasts. So, the blank describing the Constitution will contrast with the fact that the Magna Carta "guaranteed the rights of only a limited group of elite English nobles." What contrasts with giving rights to only a few elite people? Giving rights to the common people. So, look through the answer choices for a word that fits with *normal*, and there it is: answer **B**, *commoners*.

7. **B**   Two-Blank/One-Way   *Difficult*

This sentence contains no switch or comparison over time, so it's one-way. That means you know that the way Bernice was treated after solving the conundrum will result directly from how the conundrum affected the theorists for more than a decade. If the conundrum (a problem or a question that's tough to solve) had troubled the theorists in any way, it seems likely they would treat Bernice well. Alternatively, if the status of the conundrum as unsolved somehow helps the theorists, then it seems likely they would be less pleased with Bernice. To put it another way, the word charge of the blanks is opposite. With that knowledge you can throw out **A**, which has two positive word charges, **D**, which has two negative word charges, and **C**, since calibrated doesn't have a word charge either way (calibrated means "measured"). That leaves **B** and **D**, and to decide between these two, you have to know the meaning of *confounded* and *denigrated*. *Confound* means to "confuse"; *denigrate* means to "speak ill of." Conundrums don't "speak ill of" people, but they do confuse people. So **B** is the answer.

8. **A**   One-Blank/Two-Way   *Difficult*

The sentence contains no switch word and does not make a comparison over time, so it's one-way. That means that the event described by the blank must fit with the fact that the "two boys fought over Cindy." The word that fits the blank must therefore have negative word charge and be something like "argument." The only answer choice that fits these requirements is *altercation*, which means "fight."

Short Reading Passages

9. **B**   Attitude or Tone   *Easy*

Questions that ask you to classify the type of audience that would be appropriate for a given passage are really asking you to evaluate the tone of the passage. Is it cynical, critical, advisory, informative? Is it complicated or basic? This passage about the impact of iron on the body is intended for an audience not too familiar with the subject, since its content is so basic. It would not be appropriate in any publication for doctors or scientists, so cut **A** and **E**. The passage does not mention insects or technology, so **C** and **D** can go. That leaves **B**, a health textbook. The passage is written in an introductory, informative tone that would certainly be appropriate in a book about the body and basic health.

10.   **E**   Implied Information   *Medium*

Implied information is information you must deduce based on other information that is stated explicitly. In this passage, the phrase "potential for toxicity" clearly means something bad, right? Cut **C** immediately because it suggests that the phrase means something positive: curing a disease. The remaining choices are all pretty bad: corrosion, danger, and so on. You can cut **A** because it discusses a property of iron as a metal, not in the context of the human body. There's no basis for **B** in the body, so you can cut that too. **D** should go because it violates the law of absolutely wrong: Iron is definitely not *always* poisonous in the body. But iron, when it builds up to excessive levels in the body, can become toxic, or dangerous to the body. That makes **E** your answer.

11.   **B**   Specific Information   *Easy*

This question wants to know why people needed to introduce time zones in the United States. The passage tells you very bluntly that time zones happened because of the transcontinental railroad. All you need to do is find the answer choice that sounds closest to "because of the transcontinental railroad." The only answer here that might trip you up is **A**, a boom in commerce. But that commercial boom did not yet exist: It was a desired effect of the time-zone change, not a cause. The need for time zones came about because of the emergence of the railroads, a new technology: **B** it is.

12.   **E**   Technique   *Medium*

Technique questions often ask you to assess why an author uses a certain phrase or literary device. In this case, the author uses "quite the contrary" to focus the reader's attention on the historical fact that the country had *no* time zones or common times before 1883. The author is saying, essentially, "From the information I gave you, you might think this; but really it's this way." He pulls off this rhetorical flourish to emphasize that time in the United States before 1883 was completely unregulated. So **E** is the answer.

Long Reading Passage (Roosevelt)

13.   **A**   Themes and Arguments   *Medium*

In the second paragraph, Roosevelt says it is true that there can be no life without change. But he goes on to say, "It is no less true, however, that change may mean death and not life." In these two lines, Roosevelt notes the necessity of change but also indicates a certain wariness about it. Answer **A** reflects Roosevelt's belief in the importance of change while also marking his caution.

14. **D**   Themes and Arguments   *Medium*

While the paragraph in which this statement appears seems to focus on the exhibition and potential sale of these paintings, the statement in question actually concerns the more generalized importance of the works. In the first paragraph, Roosevelt praises the exhibit for exposing Americans to contemporary European art, but he goes on to criticize the quality of the works as pieces of art. Only **D** captures the idea that it is important to be open to change, but just as important to be skeptical about what those changes mean.

15. **C**   Technique   *Difficult*

Answers **B**, **D**, and **E** can be eliminated because none of the three have anything to do with the passage. Roosevelt isn't comparing an art show to a circus. He's comparing a person who buys a piece of Cubist art to a person who pays to look at fake exhibits. As for the remaining two choices, since Roosevelt claims that people are foolish enough both to go to sideshows and to buy paintings of this sort, the paintings must have some commercial value to someone, so **A** can't be right (it also fails the Law of Absolutely Wrong). **C** is the correct answer because Roosevelt mentions Barnum to illustrate another time when people paid for something of little apparent value.

16. **A**   Words in Context   *Medium*

If you approach this question as if it were a Sentence Completion question, you can immediately cut answers **C** and **E**, since they don't make much sense when substituted for the word "fantastic" in line 32. Once you consider the context, you should also be able to eliminate **B** and **D**. "Based on fantasy" suggests that the paintings Roosevelt describes contain fantastical figures like elves and wizards—they don't. "Wonderful and exciting" does not fit with the construction of the sentence, which contrasts the "fantastic" work against the "good" that is coming from the exhibition. With the next sentence, which claims the exhibit is lacking in the commonplace, you should be able to see that **A** is the right answer.

17. **A**   Attitude or Tone   *Medium*

Roosevelt writes about "simpering, self-satisfied conventionality." In other words, Roosevelt dismisses convention as closed-minded, simpering, weak, and inexpressive.

18. **B**   Technique   *Medium*

Roosevelt uses the term *fossilized* in reference to the "dead hand" of reactionaries, or those who wish to bring back the ways of the past. Roosevelt instead favors breaking out of the constraints of old trends and styles. These old ways threaten to hold back forward-thinking artists, to keep them frozen in past art movements just as a fossil keeps bones stuck in stone. That makes **B** the correct answer, since Roosevelt advocates breaking from the deeply rooted and outdated ideas of past art movements in order to move the art world forward.

19. **E**   Attitude or Tone   *Easy*

Roosevelt is mocking Cubism by thinking of names for art movements that he feels would be equally ridiculous. Only answer choice **E** captures the idea of making fun.

20. **C** Words in Context *Medium*

Words-in-context questions are like Sentence Completions with the added help of the context around the sentence as well. In this case, Roosevelt is mocking the name chosen by the leaders of the Cubist art movement. Since he's clearly mocking their *fatuous* choice of the term Cubist, fatuous most likely has a negative Word Charge. You can throw out **D** and **E**, since **D** is a neutral term and **E** is totally positive. If you then plug in the other words, *obese* makes little sense, though it is a bit of a trap, since it has some relation to the "fat" part of "fatuous." That leaves *excessive*, which means "over the top," and *inane*, which means "idiotic." Since Roosevelt is mocking the names of the movements as pointless and silly, *foolish* is the right choice.

21. **A** Technique *Medium*

The comparison between the Cubist painting and the Navajo rug lets Roosevelt illustrate what he values in art: accurate representations of reality and "sincerity." None of the other answers work. Roosevelt clearly likes his Navajo rug, so he's not belittling it. Nowhere does he say that art should be utilitarian, while the idea that the painting should be used as something to walk on is just plain weird. Finally, Roosevelt is making an argument about Cubist art in general; he isn't specifically commenting on American art.

22. **D** Implied Information *Difficult*

Although many of the statements given as possible answers are suggestions that Roosevelt makes in this paragraph, his main point is to convey what he values in art: realism. He dislikes the painting's title because it does not look like what its title suggests.

23. **D** Main Idea *Easy*

Roosevelt praises the art in the exhibit for its thorough break with commonplace convention, but for little else. While he does mention that it is an important collection because it shows Americans what is happening in Europe, he does not mention the idea of New York City explicitly.

24. **B** Main Idea *Difficult*

While the essay nominally discusses art, Roosevelt is not really interested in the artists themselves. He is much more concerned with exploring how progress occurs in society. Roosevelt argues that change is necessary, but that change for its own sake is not enough. All you have to realize to get the question right, though, is that Roosevelt cares about progress and how to achieve it.

SECTION 3

1. **E** Numbers and Operations: Ratios *Easy*

The question tells you that Allison can run one full lap in six minutes. To figure out how much of a lap she can run in four minutes, just set up a ratio of laps over minutes: $\frac{4}{6} = \frac{x}{1}$. You could cross-multiply and then work out the problem, but there's a faster way. Simplify: $\frac{4}{6} = x$ and then reduce $\frac{2}{3} = x$.

2.   **C**   Numbers and Operations: Decimals   *Easy*

Change the fractions in the questions into decimals, and you're home free. Get out your calculator, and divide numerator 5 by denominator 8, and you get $\frac{5}{8}$ = 0.625. Divide 3 by 4, and you get $\frac{3}{4}$ = 0.75. Only answer **C** has a number that falls between the range 0.625 and 0.75.

3.   **C**   Geometry: Circles   *Easy*

Since line segment $\overline{AB}$ is a diameter of the circle, to find the center of the circle, you have to find the midpoint of $\overline{AB}$. Use the midpoint formula: $Midpoint = \left(\frac{x_1 + x_2}{2}, \frac{y_1 + y_2}{2}\right)$. The x-coordinate of the midpoint is $\frac{4 + 2}{2}$ = 3 , and the y-coordinate of the midpoint is equal to $\frac{5 + (-3)}{2}$ = 1 . So, the midpoint and the center of the circle is (3, 1).

4.   **B**   Geometry: Coordinate Geometry   *Easy*

To differentiate between positive and negative slope that appear on a graph, you have to know two things: A line with positive slope goes up as you trace it from left to right, whereas a line with negative slope goes down as you trace it from left to right. The only side of the triangle with a negative slope is $\overline{AC}$.

5.   **D**   Data Analysis, Statistics, Probability: Logic   *Easy*

The SAT loves this kind of logic question. It's not so difficult, but it contains lots of information. What you need to do is organize all that information. Here's a helpful way to do just that: Write the names vertically in your test booklet as you learn about each person. So, when you see that Mark is older than Judy, write his name above hers:

      Mark

      Judy

The next sentence tells you that Judy is older than Brian but younger than Lisa, so you can put Brian's name under Judy's. While you know Lisa is older than Judy (and therefore also older than Brian), the question gives you no clue about how her age compares with Mark's. Just list her name with a question mark next to Mark's to show that you know she and Mark are the oldest, but that you don't know which one is older:

      Mark | Lisa (?)

      Judy

      Brian

Since there's no more information in the question, go straight to the answers. Choices **A** and **B** are tricky because they *could* be true, but neither *must* be true. You don't know whether Lisa or Mark is older. Choices **C** and **E** are definitely not true based on the relationship list you wrote out on your answer sheet. **D** is correct because Mark is clearly listed above Brian.

6.   **D**   Numbers and Operations: Ratios   *Easy*

Given a 2:3:4 ratio, you can set up the equation $2x + 3x + 4x = 45$, to find exactly how the 45 cookies are divided among the three kids. Solve the equation: $9x = 45$, so $x = 5$. One child receives $2x$ cookies, one receives $3x$, and the last receives $4x$, or 10, 15, and 20 cookies respectively. The greatest number of cookies that any one child receives is 20 cookies.

7.   **E**   Algebra: Solving Equations   *Medium*

To figure out the value of yz, you first have to find the value of y. And to find y, you can use the equation $xy = y$.

$$xy = x$$
$$y = \frac{x}{x}$$
$$y = 1$$

Now just substitute $y = 1$ into the second equation: $1 \times z = z$.

8.   **B**   Algebra: Inequalities   *Medium*

Since absolute value always results in positive numbers, the problem $|x - 4| \leq 2.5$ is really asking you to find the values of x that make $x - 4$ either smaller than 2.5 or greater than -2.5. Written out mathematically, you get: $-2.5 \leq x - 4 \leq 2.5$. Now you can solve these two inequalities by adding 4 to both sides: $1.5 \leq x \leq 6.5$. The question asks how many integers satsify the inequality. The answer is that 5 integers satisfy the inequality: 2, 3, 4, 5, and 6.

9.   **D**   Geometry: Triangles   *Medium*

The figure shows an isosceles triangle divided by a perpendicular bisector. In order to solve the question, you have to know that a perpendicular bisector cuts the base of the triangle into two equal lengths. In this case, $32 \div 2 = 16$. Now you've got two right triangles, each with a hypotenuse of 20, and with one leg of length 16. And you can use the Pythagorean theorem to find x:

$$x^2 + 16^2 = 20^2$$
$$x^2 + 256 = 400$$
$$x^2 = 144$$
$$x = 12$$

10.   **B**   Algebra: Systems of Equations   *Medium*

Here's a classic systems of equations problem. To figure out x and y, you need to use one equation to solve the other. Since y is already isolated on the left side of the equation in $2y = 6x + 6$, use this one to solve for y: $y = 3x + 3$. Now plug this value for y into the other equation:

$$3x + 4(3x + 3) = 7$$
$$3x + 12x + 12 = 7$$
$$15x = -5$$

the new SAT

$$x = -\frac{1}{3}$$

Plug that value into $3x + 4y = 7$ and you get $-1 + 4y = 7$, so $4y = 8$ and $y = 2$. The question asks you to solve for $xy = \left(-\frac{1}{3}\right)(2) = -\frac{2}{3}$.

11.   **B**   Data Analysis, Statistics, Probability: Statistical Analysis   *Medium*

To find the mean of $\{a, b, c, d, 26\}$, you have to know the values of a, b, c, and d. Since the average is equal to the sum divided by the number of elements in the set, the sum = average × number. So, the sum of a and $b = 10 \times 2 = 20$, and the sum of c and $d = 12 \times 2 = 24$. Therefore, the sum of a, b, c, d, and $26 = 20 + 24 + 26 = 70$. Since there are five numbers in this group, its average is $70 \div 5 = 14$.

12.   **D**   Geometry: Polygons   *Medium*

First things first. Sketch this sucker: a rectangle with area of 108 divided into three equal squares:

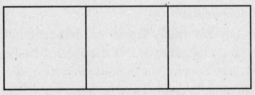

Answering this question correctly requires you to know that the three squares together take up the same area as the rectangle. So, each square individually must have an area of $108 \div 3 = 36$. A square of area 36 has a side of length $\sqrt{36} = 6$. Plug in those side lengths to your sketch:

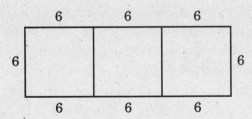

The perimeter is 48.

13.   **E**   Numbers and Operations: Sequences   *Difficult*

The question asks you to find the sum of the third, fifth, and seventh terms of the sequence. Since those terms are found by getting the average of the even terms around them, you need to find the second, fourth, sixth, and eighth terms. Following the instructions in the question, these four terms are $\{2^1, 2^2, 2^3, 2^4\}$, which works out to: $\{2, 4, 8, 16\}$. The third, fifth, and seventh terms are therefore 3, 6, and 12. Their sum is 21.

14.   **C**   Numbers and Operations: Factors and Multiples   *Medium*

To solve questions like this one that contain three different possibilities, use the process of elimination. Statement III is true: primes are greater than zero, and the square of a positive number is positive. Eliminate answers **A** and **B**, since they don't contain III. The other two criteria are both false. By definition, any perfect square has its square root as a factor and is therefore non-prime. And, since 2 is a prime number, and its square, 4, is also even, the square of a prime can be even. That leaves only **C**.

15. **C** Geometry: Coordinate Geometry   *Medium*

Whenever there's a function in which $f(-x) = -f(x)$, that function is said to be "symmetric with respect to the origin." Put simply, this sort of function will be a mirror image of itself on either side of the origin. Only graph **C** fits that description (graphs **A** and **E** are mirror images across the *y*-axis, but not across the origin). Even if you didn't know the mirror image rule, you could have solved the problem by plugging in. For instance, in which graph does $f(-5) = -f(5)$? If you trace equal distances into the positive and the negative along the *x*-axis, it should quickly be clear that only on graph **C** does $f(-x) = -f(x)$.

16. **E** Geometry: Circles   *Difficult*

To find the perimeter of the rectangle, you have to know its length and height. The image shows that the height is equal to the diameter of one of the circles, while the length is equal to the diameter of all three circles. If you can find the diameter of the circles, you can find the perimeter of the rectangle. Since the question tells you that the circumference of each circle is 10π, you can use the circumference formula ($C = \pi d$) to find the diameter: $d = 10$. This means the height of the rectangle is 10 and its length is 30. Therefore, the perimeter of the rectangle is $10 + 10 + 30 + 30 = 80$.

17. **C** Data Analysis, Statistics, Probability: Statistical Analysis   *Medium*

In order for the means of two sets of numbers with the same numbers of elements to be the same, the sum of the elements in each set must be the same. You can therefore write an equation in which the sums of the elements in each set are equal: $3 + 4 + r = 4 + 6 + s$. Simplifying this equation brings you $7 + r = 10 + s$. Now isolate one variable to see it in terms of the other. Subtract 7 from both sides: $r = 3 + s$. The difference between *r* and *s* is 3.

18. **E** Algebra: Domain and Range   *Difficult*

This is a "difficult" Math question because lots of students taking the SAT will be frightened and confused just by the concept of range. But you shouldn't be because range questions are usually fairly simple. As you know from reading this book, the range is the highest and lowest value of *y* within a given domain of *x*. In this problem, the domain of *x* stretches between –2 and 4. Just plug the equation $f(x) = 2x^2 - 3$ into your graphing calculator (remember, a graphing calculator is crucial for the test). When you look at the resulting graph, you should see that its highest point occurs at $x = 4$ and its lowest at $x = 0$. The fastest thing to do next is to plug both 0 and 4 into the equation, and see that the range of the function between $-2 \le x \le 4$ is $-3 \le y \le 29$.

If you don't have a graphing calculator, you could have solved this problem by plugging every integer between –2 and 4 into the function and then finding the highest and lowest values.

19. **B** Data Analysis, Statistics, Probability: Graphs, Charts, and Tables   *Difficult*

Before even worrying about the scatterplots in the answer choices, make sure you know what to look for. The phrase "a slope smaller than –1" means that you're looking for a slope even more negative than –1. In other words, you're looking a slope that will slant downward from left to right at a steepness *greater* than a slope of –1.

the new SAT

Now you can sketch in your scatterplot's lines: Only **B** and **E** have negative slopes at all, and **B** is by far the steeper of the two, so that's the right answer.

20. **E** Numbers and Operations: Factors and Multiples *Difficult*

A prime number is a number whose only factors are itself and 1, so the factors of p are one and p—in other words, it has two factors. The factors of p^2 are 1, p, and p^2—it has three factors. The factors of p^3 are 1, p, p^2, and p^3—it has four factors. At this point, the pattern should become clear: The number of factors is one more than the exponent of p. p^n has $n + 1$ factors.

SECTION 4

Sentence Completions

1. **B** Two-Blank/Two-Way *Easy*

The switch word *although* indicates that the sentence is two-way. The *New Yorker* is regarded in one way, but it's actually different from this perception. The third clause in this sentence ("with one of the largest circulations . . .") provides a key clue to how the *New Yorker* really is: the second blank must match the idea of the *New Yorker* having lots of readers. The only answer that fits both the need for a contrast and the fact that the magazine has a large readership is *elitist . . popular*. Though the *New Yorker* is often seen as elitist or snobby, it's actually very popular and has a huge circulation. This choice provides contrast and matches the other information provided by the sentence.

2. **A** Two-Blank/Two-Way *Medium*

The switch word in this sentence is *nevertheless*, which signals that the sentence is two-way. The two halves of the sentence, divided by a semicolon, must therefore contrast. The blank in the first half of the sentence describes what sort of "undertaking" it is to try to understand the tax code, while the blank in the second half of the sentence describes how people treat filling out their taxes. In addition, the second half of the sentence describes people as "rushing through" their taxes, so you know that people treat their taxes as if they *aren't hard to do*. The first blank therefore has to contrast with the idea of "not hard," while the second blank agrees with it. The only answer choice that fits the bill is **A**, *formidable . . undemanding*.

3. **A** Two-Blank/Two-Way *Medium*

The sentence contains the switch word *though*, which tells you that this is a two-way sentence: Something about the entrepreneur will conflict with his effort to come out ahead at the negotiating table. *Unnerved . . timidly*, *egomaniacal . . doggedly*, and *amoral . . shrewdly* could describe a young entrepreneur, but they don't create a clear contrast between the two halves of the sentence. *Wealthy . . desperately* is also incorrect, since the young entrepreneur would not be *desperate* to win the negotiation if he already had plenty of money. *Terrified . . valiantly* makes sense when plugged into the sentence, and it creates the contrast that this two-way sentence requires: The young entrepreneur was *terrified*, but he tried *valiantly* (a fancy word for "bravely") to do well anyway.

4. **C**   One-Blank/One-Way   *Medium*

This sentence contains no switch and does not make a comparison over time. That means the sentence is one-way from start to finish. The blank describes the way that Yolanda documented her research, and this is directly related to her knowledge that her "controversial findings were likely to be scrutinized." Since she's expecting her work to be closely looked over, it would make logical sense that Yolanda would be "careful." Do any words in the answer choices match up with the meaning of the word careful? Yes. *Meticulously* means exactly that.

5. **C**   Two-Blank/One-Way   *Difficult*

This sentence contains no switch and does not make a comparison over time, so it's one-way. The two blanks describing Florida's water must therefore fit with the fact that Florida's beaches are "favored vacation destinations." In other words, the words that fill the blank must be positive. You can therefore eliminate any answer that has one negative word in it. **A** is out, because *unsanitary* is negative. **B** is gone, because *incendiary* is negative. **D** is wrong, because *inaccessible* is negative. And **E** is gone, because while neither *residual* nor *posterior* is exactly negative, neither is positive either. That leaves **C**. *Unsoiled* means clean, and *pellucid* means clear. Clean and clear water = appealing beaches.

Dual Short Reading Passage

6. **E**   Technique   *Medium*

Author's Technique questions on the new SAT sometimes ask you to identify specific literary terms like *paradox* and *simile* in Critical Reading passages. The description of the stock market as a "breeding ground" is a comparison. Which words on the list of answer choices means a comparison? Only metaphor does, so **E** is the answer. These questions can be tough because unlike words-in-context questions, for example, the surrounding context of the sentence and the passage won't help you if you can't tell a metaphor from a semaphore. (That's why we have a list of the top twenty-five literary terms you must know to beat the Critical Reading section of the new SAT. Learn those terms.)

7. **A**   Relating Two Passages   *Difficult*

This question is all about attitude. The authors of these two passages definitely disagree about the stock market. Passage 1 loves the stock market; passage 2 hates it. You need to find the answer choice that sums up that split as closely as possible. Start by looking at the words you know well and find those that don't match the love/hate split. **C** and **D** describe passage 1's author as "resigned" and "alarmed." That ain't love. Cut 'em. It's down to **A**, **B**, and **E**. Now try to find an inaccurate description of passage 2's tone among the remaining choices. **E** calls passage 2 *grateful*. Passage 2's author would only be grateful if the stock market got shut down. Cut **E**.

The two choices left, **A** and **B**, contain three tough words: *fawning*, *laudatory*, and *reverent*. The fourth word, *disapproving*, keeps **A** alive because passage 2 definitely has a disapproving tone. The word to focus on next is *fawning*. Assuming you don't know its definition, use word charge to guess the general meaning of the word. Does a word that sounds like the word for a baby deer match passage 2's tone? No, and indeed, fawning means "showering with praise and admiration." That means the correct answer is **A**, which describes passage 1 as *laudatory* (praising, approving) and passage 2 as *disapproving*.

8. **E** Relating Two Passages *Difficult*

The setup of this passage makes it feel tougher than it really is. It's an EXCEPT question, which means you need to find the one answer choice that's not like the others. It also asks you to combine information from both passages. The question is actually asking something like this: "Which of the following descriptions do the authors of these two passages not use in their opinions about the stock market?" That phrasing makes it clearer that the authors did not necessarily use these exact words. The question really just wants to know which of the words is the oddball. The authors say nothing about the stock market being *deliberate*, **E**. You might even be able to pick out **E** without reading the passages, since describing a stock market as "deliberate" (intentional, willful) just doesn't make sense.

9. **D** Relating Two Passages *Difficult*

Take it slow. This question is not as brutal as it seems at first glance. Like the EXCEPT example in question 4 above, figuring out precisely what this question wants will make finding its correct answer much more simple. Here, we have a twist above and beyond just EXCEPT—the word *dis*prove. That means the question wants you to pick the answer choice that the author of passage 2 would not use to prove that the author of passage 1 has got it all wrong about the stock market being a great way to get rich. Once you've broken the question down to its bare bones, you need to find the information that would not help passage 2's case against the market. All of the answers *except* **D** come straight from passage 2's argument. **D** comes from passage 1, so passage 2 certainly wouldn't use that bit of info to refute passage 1's ideas about the market.

Long Reading Passage (Shasta)

10. **D** Implied Information *Medium*

The cited lines contrast the way that Mount Shasta was formed to other "volcanoes over one thousand feet" tall that form very quickly. In other words, the sentence is saying that not all mountains form in the same way (bye **A**), that there are many volcanoes over one thousand feet tall (see ya **B**), that many mountains shoot up quickly (sayonara **C**). The cited lines don't mention glaciers at all (adios **E**). That leaves **D**, the correct answer choice.

11. **A** Words in Context *Medium*

In normal usage, "deliberation" means "contemplation," which is answer **B**. However, as always with word-in-context questions, you must go back and look at how the word is being used in the passage. In this case, Muir uses the technique of personification to describe Shasta. Sometimes eruptions in of mountains occur in haste, other times in deliberation. Because the passage is comparing "deliberation" with "haste," it implies that "deliberation" in this context must mean something that is the opposite of haste. Only **A** fits this need.

12. E   Technique   *Difficult*

The phrase "glacial winter" shows Muir's elaborate and often poetic style of writing. In this case, he uses "Glacial winter" as a metaphor that relates the geologic process of glaciation to the season of winter, to give the glaciation of Shasta a kind of drama, to refer specifcally to an Ice Age that gripped the Earth (and Shasta), and to contrast the Ice Age to Shasta's earlier volcanic activity. What it doesn't do is describe a particular winter. One winter is much too short of a time to allow for the growth of a glacier.

13. B   Specific Information   *Easy*

Throughout the passage, Muir focuses on the rock formations and the evidence of how they have changed and shifted through time to explain the geological history of Shasta. For instance, in the first sentence of the second paragraph, he writes: "Sections cut by the glaciers, displaying some of the internal framework of Shasta, show that comparatively long periods of quiescence intervened between many eruptions."

14. A   Implied Information   *Easy*

Muir is interested in geology, the rock formations on the mountain and the history of how those formations arrived at their current state. He is not concerned with human or behavior, or with legends, myths, or art about the mountain.

15. D   Main idea   *Difficult*

Throughout the passage Muir emphasizes contradiction: glaciers and volcanoes, fire and ice, rock and lush plant life. While Muir is interested in how the passage of time affects a mountain, the title "Time Passes" is too general for a passage that focuses so closely on Shasta. "One Mountain Long Ago" also does not meet the criteria of the passage, since Shasta still exists. While Muir does mention Shasta's height and does discuss the animals and plants on the mountain, he focuses on neither. Instead, Muir returns over and over to the contradictory forces that merged to create Shasta.

Long Reading Passage (Cather)

16. E   Words in Context   *Medium*

In common, everyday usage, *stole* means "took illegally." But if you plug it into the passage, you get "he took illegally downstairs." Utter nonsense. That one's an SAT trap. Throw it out. The passage around the sentence tells you that Carl got up before dawn, so you know that Carl went quietly down the stairs. The only answer choice that comes close to fitting the meaning of the context is **E**, *moved stealthily*.

17. B   Implied Information   *Medium*

From Carl's constant recollections, you can conclude that Carl has likely returned to his childhood home after an absence of some time: He thinks about memories of the girl next door and also stares at his father's pasture and the neighbor's pasture, both of which now have new owners. Carl's memories indicate he has some knowledge of farming, and there is no mention at all of his trying to write a novel. Carl is definitely not a small child, since he is remembering his life when he was a child. There's also no reason to think Carl is going on a journey.

18. **B** Implied Information   *Easy*

The passage never comes right out and says that Alexandra and Carl were neighbors, but it does imply it in two ways. The first is through the mention of the fence. If Carl and Alexandra were related, or if she worked on his farm as a farmhand, why would they work in pastures on opposite sides of a fence? The second is through tone: Carl has powerful, romantic feelings about Alexandra, which eliminates the possibility of her being a family member, so you can cut **A**, **C**, and **D**. **E** does not make sense in light of the relationship described in the passage. **B** does.

19. **B** Technique   *Easy*

The third paragraph focuses on Carl's memories of Alexandra, and describes how Carl felt about Alexandra even when they were little children: "she looked as if she had walked straight out of the morning itself." This memory shows the high regard and deep feelings that Carl has for Alexandra.

20. **C** Technique   *Medium*

The metaphor used in this passage does several things. First, it suggests that Carl has been far enough away from the farm to have seen the tides coming in on the ocean. More subtly, by comparing the farm to the ocean, the metaphor creates a link to those who have never seen a farm. Finally, the comparison of the rippling wind through the fields to the "sweeping" tide creates the sense of calmness that surrounds Carl as he sits on the hill. But in no way does the metaphor imply that Carl doesn't *want* to be at the farm.

21. **C** Implied Information   *Medium*

The writer of this passage uses this quick reference to help show how much time has passed and how much has changed since Carl's last time at the farm: The order of things he took for granted as a child is no longer the same. That makes **C** the correct answer.

22. **B** Technique   *Difficult*

The word *pastoral* most often refers to idyllic portrayals of rural life. The shooting of the ducks breaks up the serene, idealized, *pastoral* description of farm life that makes up most of the passage. Therefore, **B** is the correct answer.

23. **A** Technique   *Difficult*

This question requires you to know a few common literary terms. We include a list of the top terms you need to know for the new SAT in our Critical Reading chapter. Comparisons that do not include *like* or *as* are called *metaphors*. The comparison of the bird to a ball of feathers is a metaphor, so **A** is the correct answer.

24. **D** Attitude or Tone   *Difficult*

In the first part of the passage, Carl is quietly looking back on his youth. The two best words in the answer choice that match this feeling of quiet contemplation are *reflective* and *nostalgic*. The question then becomes: Is the end of the passage *wistful* or *uneasy*? Well, ending as it does, focused on a dead duck, its color and warmth draining from its increasingly lifeless body, *uneasy* seems the better choice.

SECTION 5

Math Multiple Choice

1. **C**   Numbers and Operations: Percents   *Easy*

The word problem tells you that 30% of 1320 people in a town are malnourished. That means the town has $0.30 \times 1320 = 396$ malnourished citizens.

2. **D**   Algebra: Substitution   *Easy*

This is a substitution question: Just plug in the numbers and work out the math.

First, plug 4 in for x in $y = \sqrt{\frac{4}{2}} + 3 = \sqrt{5}$. So $w = 2(\sqrt{5})^2 - 2 = 2(5) - 2 = 8$.

3. **C**   Algebra: Inequalities   *Easy*

This is a word inequality problem. If you translate the word problem into math you get: if $120 \le x \le 180$, then what are the possible values for $7x$? To answer the problem, all you have to do is multiply the entire inequality by 7: $840 \le 7x \le 1260$. The only number that falls into this range is 1000.

4. **A**   Numbers and Operations: Exponents   *Medium*

The fastest way to solve this problem is to use the equation $xy = 42$ to find the possible values of x and y, and then check to see which are right in the equation $x^2 - y^2 = 13$. The factors of 42 are: 1 and 42, 2 and 21, 3 and 14, and 6 and 7. A little plugging in makes it clear that $x = 7$ and $y = 6$, since $7^2 - 6^2 = 49 - 36 = 13$. Now plug 7 and 6 into $(x-y)^2$ and you get $(7-6)^2 = 1^2 = 1$.

5. **D**   Data Analysis, Statistics, Probability: Graphs, Charts, Tables   *Medium*

You must interpret the question and two charts to be able to set up equations to solve this problem. The first chart tells you how many of each item (regardless of size) each team ordered, the second chart tells the cost of each item in size small and large, and the question gives information that will let you figure out how many large or small items each team ordered. Given all that information, you know that team A ordered 12 hats, 8 shirts, and 6 pants, and that it bought half of each item type in large and half in small. So, team A spent: $6(12) + 6(12) = \$144$ on hats; $4(18) + 4(20) = \$152$ on shirts; and $3(30) + 3(35) = \$195$ on pants. In total, team A spent $144 + 152 + 195 = \$491$. Team B, meanwhile, only bought uniform items in size large. Team B therefore spent $10(12) + 10(20) + 6(35) = \$530$. Finally, to find the difference between what the two teams spent, just subtract: $530 - 491 = 39$.

6. **B**   Numbers and Operations: Percents   *Medium*

This question tests double percents, and the key to the question is knowing how to translate the word problem into actual math. The most important thing to realize is that the phrase "20 percent of 70 percent" of x is telling you to take the 70 percent of x first. Many students will think that just because the "20 percent" is mentioned first it should be taken first. Once you realize that, the math is fairly simple. For this question, you can pick a number as long as it's an integer. The best number to pick is 100, since all percents work off of 100. So, first you need to take 70 percent of 100: 70. Then 20 percent of 70: 14. Now you have to set that 14 equal to "x percent of 40 percent of 100." 40 percent of 100 is 40, now you just have to find the percentage of 40 that's equal to 14. $x = \frac{14}{40} \times 100 = 35$.

7.　**D**　Geometry: Polygons　　　　　　　　　　　　　　　　*Difficult*

There's a long way and a quick way to figure out the answer to this problem. The long way is to figure out the area of each shaded area and add them all together. The quick way is to count up the number of shaded areas and the number of unshaded areas, and figure out the percentage of the big square that's shaded. Remember that each triangle counts as half of a square. There are four shaded squares and four shaded triangles, which adds up to six shaded squares. There are four unshaded triangles, which adds up to two unshaded squares. Since $\frac{6}{8} = \frac{3}{4}$, three-fourths of the entire square is shaded. Now since you know from the question that $\overline{AB} = 4$, you can calculate the area of the entire square: $4^2 = 16$. Since the shaded region is three-fourths of the entire square: $\frac{3}{4} \times 16 = 12$.

8.　**D**　Algebra: Inequalities　　　　　　　　　　　　　　　*Difficult*

To get the highest possible value of $2x + 6y + z$, you have to find the highest possible value of the quantity $2x + 6y$ and the variable z. From the information given, you know that the highest z can be is 5. If you multiply the first inequality by 2, you get $10 \le 2x + 6y \le 16$, so the highest possible value of $2x + 6y$ is 16. This means that the highest possible value of the expression is $16 + 5 = 21$.

Grid-Ins

9.　**15**　Geometry: Polygons　　　　　　　　　　　　　　　　*Easy*

The area of the shaded region is the difference between the areas of the rectangle and the triangle. The area of the rectangle is $6 \times 3 = 18$. The area of the triangle is $\frac{1}{2}(2)(3) = 3$. The difference of the areas is $18 - 3 = 15$.

10.　**294**　Numbers and Operations: Percents　　　　　　　　　*Easy*

This is a double-percent word problem. Your first task is to translate the words into math. So, what does the question want you to find? The value of the suit before it was put on sale. Give that unknown value the variable x. When Arnold bought the suit it was at 15% off. Since a price of 15% off is just another way of saying that he bought the suit for 85% of the total price (x), you can define the amount for which Arnold bought the suit as $.85x$. The question then tells you that Arnold sold the suit at 20% off of $.85x$, which is the same as saying he sold it for 80% of $.85x$, and which can be written as $(.8)(.85)x$. Since the question tells you that he sold the suit for $200, you can set up an equation that allows you to solve for x: $(.8)(.85)x = 200$; $.68x = 200$; $x = 294.12$. The question asks you to round to the nearest dollar, so the answer is 294.

11. **11** Algebra: Functions as Models   *Medium*

The question describes the function that defines the temperature of the soup at any moment: $x - 10t$. You're asked to figure out how long the soup has been in the room if it originally was 150 degrees and is now 40 degrees. Like all function questions, it's just a matter of plugging the right numbers into the right place: $40 = 150 - 10t$. Now, work out the math: $-110 = -10t$, which simplifies to $t = 11$.

12. **6** Numbers and Operations: Sets   *Medium*

The intersection of sets A and B contains the elements common to both sets. Those elements are 4, 9, 10, and 1. To find the mean, you have to find the sum of the elements and then divide by the number of elements. The sum of the elements is $4 + 9 + 10 + 1 = 24$. The number of elements is 4. So the mean is $24/4 = 6$.

13. **4** Algebra: Functions   *Medium*

This is one of those sneaky function problems that's really just a glorified algebraic substitution question. In this question, you have to substitute 3 into the function, then substitute −3 into the function, and add the two results.

   If you take a second to look at the function, you could save some time. Since x appears only once in the function and is squared, you should be able to see that 3 and −3 will result in the same value, since both 3 and −3 give the value 9 when squared. So you only have to work out the function once, then double the answer: $h(x) = \sqrt{3^2 - 5} = \sqrt{4} = 2$. Now, just double 2 to get 4.

14. **3/2** Geometry: Coordinate Geometry   *Medium*

To answer this question, you have to know that the slopes of perpendicular lines are negative reciprocals. To figure out the slope of line l, you have to figure out the slope of the line segment connecting $(-2,1)$ and $(1,-1)$ first. The fastest way to find this slope is to use the two points to figure out the "rise over run" of the line: $\frac{1-(-1)}{(-2)-1} = \frac{2}{-3}$. The negative reciprocal, which is the slope of the line perpendicular to l of $-\frac{2}{3}$, is $\frac{3}{2}$.

15. **6** Numbers and Operations: Exponents   *Difficult*

The first step of this problem is to recognize that each base is a power of 2 and can therefore be rewritten as $2n$. The rewritten equation looks like this:

$$2^x = 2^{2y} = 2^{4z}$$

With all bases equal, you can equate the exponents to solve for the three variables: $x = 2y = 4z$. Then just substitute into $\frac{x}{y} + \frac{x}{z} : \frac{2y}{y} + \frac{4z}{z} = 2 + 4 = 6$.

16. **8** Geometry: Coordinate Geometry   *Difficult*

You need to find the x-intercept of the line that passes through point $(2,3)$ and is parallel to $y = \frac{1}{2}x + 3$. First, you have to find the equation of the line. Since you're given a point, $(2,3)$, and the slope $-\frac{1}{2}$, you can use the point-slope equation $y - y_1 = m(x - x_1)$

to figure out the equation of the line: $y - 3 = -\frac{1}{2}(x - 2)$. If you work this equation out, you wind up with $y = -\frac{1}{2}x + 4$, which is the equation of the line. Now you need to find the x-intercept, which is the point where the line intercepts with the x-axis. Don't be tricked here! Under pressure, you might assume that a line will intersect with the x-axis when $x = 0$. Instead, picture a graph in your head. A line will actually intersect with the x-axis when $y = 0$. Plug 0 in for y in the equation, and solve: $0 = -\frac{1}{2}x + 4$, which means that $\frac{1}{2}x = 4$, and finally $x = 8$.

17. **180** Geometry: Geometric Visualizations   *Difficult*
The volume of a right circular cylinder with radius r and height h is $\pi r^2 h$—the area of the circular base multiplied by the height of the cylinder. The diagram shows that the cylinder will have the same height as the rectangle. You should also be able to see that the side of the rectangle that has length 12π becomes the circumference of the base of the cylinder when the rectangle is rolled as shown. Once you see that, you can use the formula for circumference $2\pi r$ to find the radius of the cylinder: $12\pi = 2\pi r$, which simplifies to $r = 6$. Now you can solve for the volume of the cylinder:

$$\begin{aligned} \text{Volume} &= \pi r^2 h \\ &= 36\pi \frac{5}{\pi} \\ &= 36 \times 5 = 180 \end{aligned}$$

18. **3/10** Data Analysis, Statistics, Probability: Probability   *Difficult*
When you draw two marbles from a jar, the crucial fact you must remember is that after you draw the first marble, the jar contains one less marble. For this question, you have to determine the probability of drawing one black marble and one white marble.

The probability of drawing the black marble first is $\frac{3}{5}$; the probability of drawing the white marble second after drawing a black marble is $\frac{2}{4}$. The probability of both happening is the product of their individual probabilities: $\frac{3}{5} \times \frac{2}{4} = \frac{6}{20} = \frac{3}{10}$.

SECTION 6

Improving Sentences

1. **B** Subject-Verb Agreement   *Easy*
The original sentence has an error of subject-verb agreement—*hotel prices* and *car rental fees* are plural and require a plural verb, but *has increased* is singular. **B** accommodates the compound subject *hotel prices and car rental fees*, with the plural, *have increased*. **B** also improves clarity and flow by using fewer words than the original to express the same idea.

2.   **E**   Fragments   *Medium*

The original sentence is a fragment, and **A**, **B**, **C**, and **D** all fail to solve the problem. **B** has the additional problem of applying *who* to the Olympics. *Who* applies to people, not to events. **E** provides the sentence with the two essential elements of a complete sentence: a subject and a properly conjugated verb (*Women competed*).

3.   **B**   Coordination and Subordination   *Medium*

The error in the original sentence is faulty coordination. The sentence gives equal weight to three clauses of varying significance and needs to be revised so that it demonstrates how the clauses relate to each other. **B** is the best answer choice because it shows that in spite of the cabin's lack of heat, the brother refuses to move or to install a heating system. The fact that **B** drops the explicit statement that Abraham lives in the cabin is actually a good thing; that clause is unnecessary because the sentence implies that he lives there.

4.   **C**   Run-Ons   *Medium*

The original sentence is a run-on. Two independent clauses, such as the ones in this question, should be linked by a semicolon or a coordinating conjunction (such as *and*) preceded by a comma. **D** commits the same problem as the original sentence: It divides two independent clauses using only a comma. The transitional adverbs in **B** and **E** lack proper punctuation; transitional adverbs (*consequently*, *however*) should come after a semicolon and before a comma. Even if punctuated correctly, words like these should be considered carefully to determine how they might change a sentence's meaning. In this case, *however* suggests a contrast that isn't indicated by the sentence. That leaves **C**, which provides the coordinating conjunction *and*.

5.   **A**   No Error   *Medium*

No error. If you chose **B**, remember that *each* is a singular noun. *Its* refers to each singular province. *Their* would be correct only if it referred to a plural noun.

6.   **C**   Parallelism   *Medium*

The phrase *as well as* is often a clue to a parallelism error. Lo and behold, this sentence has one. Parallelism requires the verb *understand* to be matched by a second verb in the same form—*remain*. **D** is almost correct, except for its use of the infinitive form *to remain*. **C** is the best answer: It eliminates the parallelism problem by cutting the phrase "as well as" and keeping the verbs *understand* and *remain* consistent.

7.   **D**   Conjunctions   *Medium*

Columbus is just one guy, so the reference should be to *his* backers, not *their* backers. That knocks out **A** and **C** as possible answers. Now you have to decide between the conjunctions *and* and *but* to keep whittling the list down to the answer. The sentence contrasts Columbus's success at finding the islands with his failure to find the gold. So, the necessary conjunction is *but*, which makes this contrast explicit. That leaves **D** and **E**. Between those two, **D** is the better choice because it gets across the same message in fewer words.

8.   **D**   Misplaced Modifiers   *Difficult*

Misplaced modifiers abound in Improving Sentence questions, so you should always make sure that a modifying phrase is next to its subject. In this sentence, once you recognize that the Getty Center itself, and not the reaction to the museum, is *one of the finest examples of modern architecture*, you can eliminate choices **A**, **B**, and **C**. Of the remaining choices, **D** makes sense, but **E** does not.

9.   **E**   Tenses   *Difficult*

E is the best answer because it stays in the past tense—*she evoked, but did not directly copy*. **A** and **D** switch tenses (*had evoked but was not directly copying*, for example). **C** changes the meaning of the sentence. **B** is grammatically correct, but its use of the passive voice slightly obscures the meaning of this sentence. Therefore **E** is a better answer than **B**.

10.   **E**   Idioms   *Difficult*

Idioms are tricky because you must know by heart how to use them correctly. This sentence uses an idiom that's worth committing to memory: *not so much FOR this AS for that*.

11.   **D**   Misplaced Modifiers   *Difficult*

James Joyce, not his writing career, was in Trieste. Once you realize that James Joyce should be the subject of the sentence, you can eliminate **A**, **B**, and **C**. Of the two remaining choices, **D** is a better answer than **E**. Answer **E** implies that Joyce failed his career rather than failed *at* his career.

Identifying Sentence Errors

12.   **C**   Pronouns   *Easy*

When there are pronouns in a sentence, check them for errors of agreement (singular/plural) or case (subject/object). In this sentence, *they* refers to the act of *cutting taxes*, which is singular. The question tries to confuse you by using the plural word *taxes*. But the sentence says that it is the act of *cutting taxes* that might harm the country, so you need to change the plural pronoun *they* to the singular *it*.

13.   **C**   Subject-Verb Agreement   *Easy*

Buildings is a plural noun; *features* is a singular verb. Remember, adding an "s" to the end of a verb makes the verb singular, not plural. It's easy to overlook this sort of error since you're so trained to think of "s" as making a word plural. The moral? Check subject and verb agreement.

14.   **B**   Subject-Verb Agreement   *Easy*

Any time you see a phrase like *group of students, teachers, and librarians*, in which a singular subject is followed by plural nouns in a prepositional phrase, go on alert. In this case, *of students, teachers, and librarians* draws your attention away from the true subject of the sentence—*group*, a singular noun. If you can ignore the distracting filler between *group* and *have endorsed*, you'll see that the correct verb is singular: *has endorsed*.

15.   **D**   Faulty Comparison   *Medium*

The sentence, as you can see from the phrase *more easily*, compares Clara's ability to speak and write Spanish. Clara understands Spanish more easily by speaking it *than* she does by writing it. To use *and* instead of *than* is to link the two ideas, not to compare them.

16. **C** Abverbs and Adjectives *Medium*

When comparing two nouns, you should use a word ending in *-er*, also known as a comparative modifier. When you compare three or more, as happens in this sentence, you need to use a word ending in *-est*, a superlative modifier. As one of many fighters, the boxer is the heaviest of all, not the *heavier*.

17. **B** Pronouns *Medium*

Family and friends are people; therefore, *who* should replace *which*. *Who* is a pronoun used as a replacement for people, while *which* is a stand-in for things.

18. **A** Wrong Word *Medium*

Malodorous means "foul-smelling." Here *malodorous* is incorrectly used to refer to the *sight* of the dead deer. This is an example of an instance in which a Writing section question tests vocabulary.

19. **C** Parallelism *Medium*

Whenever you see a list in an Identifying Sentence Errors question, check for parallel structure errors. In this case, you've got two nouns modified by adjectives—*early intervention*, *frequent checkups*—and then you've got an infinitive verb—*to comply with recommended dosages*.

20. **E** No Error *Medium*

21. **E** No Error *Medium*

22. **C** Idioms *Medium*

The executives want to find a solution *to* something, not *toward* something. Idiom questions are usually somewhat tough: You simply need to know that the noun *solution* must be followed by *to*, not *from*, *for*, *of*, or *toward*.

23. **C** Wrong Word *Medium*

If they were victims of violence, they experienced *suffering*. *Suffrage* is a term that refers to the right to vote. This is a case of a vocabulary question disguised as an Identifying Sentence Errors question.

24. **B** Subject-Verb Agreement *Medium*

Delegation is a singular noun, so it has to take a singular verb. But in the sentence, the plural verb *were* refers to the delegation. So, *were* is wrong. Remember to check subject-verb agreement, especially if the noun and the verb are separated by some other phrase, as they are in this sentence.

25. **E** No Error   *Medium*

26. **D** Double Negative   *Difficult*

Your ears should prick up like a fox's whenever you see words like *scarcely* and *hardly*. Used on their own they're fine, but when they're placed next to other negative words like *no*, they become double negatives. The sentence should read *scarcely any*.

27. **A** Redundancy   *Difficult*

Economic is redundant because the sentence already contains the phrase *dollar cost*, which makes it clear even without the word *economic* that the sentence is about money. If you thought *its* sounded funny, just link it to the noun it modifies, *family*, which is one of those pesky collective singulars (like *audience*, *group*, *community*) that sound plural but aren't.

28. **D** Parallelism   *Difficult*

As written, the sentence compares different things. It should say, The *popularity of a recognizable brand* will always dominate the *popularity* of its generic equivalent. Or, alternatively, *A recognizable brand will always dominate its generic equivalent.* Think of it this way—you can't say you like your Labrador's hair better than your entire poodle. To make a grammatically correct comparison, you can only compare your Labrador's *hair* to the *hair* of your poodle.

29. **C** Idioms   *Difficult*

In correct idiomatic English, you can't say *respond for*. The word *to* has to follow *respond* in order for it to be grammatically correct.

Improving Paragraphs

30. **B** Sentence Revision   *Medium*

The original sentence has two main problems: It begins with the conjunction *but*, and it uses the ambiguous pronoun *it*. Choice **B** gets rid of the conjunction and eliminates the problem of the ambiguous pronoun by turning the two clauses (*if you want to understand yourself...* and *it doesn't hurt to study history*) into a single, grammatically correct clause, without changing the meaning of the sentence. Choice **A** begins with *but*, so you can rule it out immediately. Choice **C** changes the meaning of the sentence by claiming that studying history will put you physically in the "context of the world." Choice **D** mixes pronouns, shifting from *one* to *you*. Although choice **E** begins correctly, it alters the meaning of the sentence.

31. **C** Essay Analysis   *Medium*

This essay discusses the importance of knowing something about history. Although the second paragraph contains several disconnected and irrelevant thoughts, sentence 9, which states that Newton and Mendel weren't American, is especially off topic. The importance of studying history has nothing to do with whether these two guys were American. Parenthetical asides can be informative, but this particular parenthetical clause is a useless digression from the author's main argument.

32. A Essay Analysis *Medium*

In sentence 10, the writer provides an additional piece of information to support his or her argument. *Furthermore* indicates that the sentence is an added supportive thought. *Although* and *Despite* aren't good replacements because they suggest a contrast or opposition that is not in the sentence. *Because* suggests a causal link that doesn't exist with the preceding sentence. *Finally* implies that this sentence is the last in a series of points, but the paragraph fails to build points in any logical manner.

33. E Sentence Revision *Medium*

The original sentence incorrectly switches pronoun case from *you* in the first clause to *one* in the second. **E** offers pronoun agreement (*you* and *you*) and uses sensible verb tenses. The first clause says *once you know*, suggesting that you don't know yet, so the use of the future tense in the second clause (*you will look*) is logical. Choice **D**, which also has correct pronoun agreement, illogically uses the past tense in the second half of the sentence: *you looked*.

34. D Essay Analysis *Easy*

Any time you see a question that requires you to look for an exception, tread carefully. The test-makers highlighted the word EXCEPT because they know that speedy testtakers tend to seize on the first answer that says what the author *did* do. In this case, **D** is correct because the author did not argue against anyone else's position.

Colloquial language means informal, conversational language. The tone of this essay is extremely colloquial: The writer addresses *you* and talks about himself.

35. D Sentence Combination *Difficult*

Questions that ask you to combine sentences usually demand that you simplify and clarify the meaning of the two sentences in your revision. In this example, the author's sudden addition of the colloquial phrase *my friend* is awkward and inappropriate, so you can eliminate choice **E**. The sentences combined should emphasize the following objective: By staying informed and knowing history, people can move forward to make a better future. In sentence **A**, the goal is understanding the past, which distorts the original meaning of the two sentences. Cut it. **B** preserves a better future as the main goal, but it also distorts the order of the original sentences and creates grammatical imperfections. **C** is incorrect because it makes moving forward our responsibility, whereas the original sentences say that understanding our past is our responsibility. **D** preserves and clarifies the meaning of the original two sentences and cuts out the casual language. It's the best answer.

SECTION 7

Sentence Completions

1. B Two-Blank/One-Way *Easy*

This sentence contains no switch or comparison over time, which means it is one-way. The first blank describes what happens to the temperature during an ice age. So, what happens to temperatures during an ice age? They must "drop," or else it wouldn't make sense to call it an ice age. That means the only possible answer choices are **B** and **D**, since only those two match the meaning of "drop." The second blank describes how ice and cold do *not* act, and this must agree with the idea that ice ages "tend to develop gradually." In other words, you're looking for a word to fill the blank so that "not ----" means "slowly." This means that **D** is a trap. The word *slowly* matches the total meaning you want, but combine it with the "not" before the blank and you've got "not slowly," which basically means fast. In **B**, you've got *suddenly*, which combined with the "not" gives just the meaning you're looking for. "Not suddenly" means "slowly," so **B** is the right answer.

2.   **E**   Two-Blank/Two-Way   *Easy*

The switch word *but* tells you that the sentence is two-way. The way that Twain is "hailed as a writer" does not match with his later work, so the two halves of the sentence have to contrast. Further, since the second half of the sentence contains the word *unsettling* in association with the blank, the blank has to have negative word charge and must mean something like "troubling." Those two facts knock out **A**, **B**, and **D**, so the choice is between **C** and **E**. Only **E** has an answer choice that matches the meaning of "troubling," so **E** is the correct answer.

3.   **D**   One-Blank/One-Way   *Medium*

The sentence contains no switch and no comparison over time: it's one-way. The blank, which describes what Upton Sinclair did to the "world of meatpacking companies," must fit with the idea that he "scrutinized its often unsavory practices." Since scrutinized means study intently, Upton Sinclair must have written a book about what he learned about the meatpacking industry. It wouldn't make sense for Upton to do all that heavy studying and then *romanticize*, *evade*, or *revamp* (improve) what he found. It's also beyond his power to *prohibit* (forbid) the "world of meatpacking companies" from doing anything. But as an author who studies the "unsavory practices" of the meatpacking companies, he does have the power to *expose*.

4.   **B**   One-Blank/One-Way   *Medium*

In this question, the one-way switch *since* signals that the sentence is one-way. The blank should agree with the facts presented in the rest of the sentence. The blank describes "the Tet Offensive," and the rest of the sentence describes the offensive as culminating "in so many casualties and so few gains." To put it another way, the blank describing the Tet Offensive should have negative word charge. That knocks out *punctual* ("on time"), *bold*, and *admirable*, so you have to decide between *foolhardy* and *fickle*. It may be hard to choose if you don't know the vocabulary, though the root of *foolhardy* may give you a clue. Foolhardy doesn't quite mean "foolish," but it does mean "reckless." Fickle basically means "erratic." *Foolhardy* is the best choice.

5.   **B**   Two-Blank/One-Way   *Medium*

The sentence contains no switch and does not make a comparison over time, so it's one-way. The two blanks must fit with the facts presented in the sentence. The first blank describes Louisa's relationship with "historical matters." Since the sentence is one-way, and since the sentence states that Louisa made "erroneous comments" about American history, you can deduce that her knowledge of history must be *weak*. That knocks out all the answer choices but *ignorance..illustrated* and *negligence..eviscerated*. The second blank describes the relationship between Louisa's erroneous comments and her weak grasp of history: The erroneous comments "demonstrated" her weak grasp of history. *Illustrated* and "demonstrated" are a perfect match, so **B** is the answer.

6. **A**   Two-Blank/One-Way   *Difficult*

This sentence contains a one-way switch: *since*. This means that the sentence is one-way and that the two blanks fit into a single flow without any contrast. In the sentence, the first blank describes how baby howler monkeys are when they're born. The first blank is then described further: baby howler monkeys will explore every inch of their surroundings." So, a good word to describe baby howlers would be "curious." The second blank comes after the *since*, which means that it explains something in the sentence: in this case, it explains why baby howlers are without fear. More specifically, the blank explains how the baby howlers are in relation to "the possibility of danger." Since the baby howlers are basically fearless, it makes sense that they either "don't care" about the possibility of danger or they are "unaware" of the possibility of danger. But note that "not" before the blank: It means that you're looking for a word that means either "care" or "aware."

To sum up, you're looking for a first blank that means something like "curious" and a second blank that means either "don't care" or "unaware." The only answer choices that come close to fitting "curious" in meaning are *inquisitive* and *adventurous*. Onto the second blank: *cognizant* (which means "aware") and *impudent* (which means "bold and contemptuous"). *Cognizant* fits the need perfectly, so the answer is **A**.

Long Reading Comprehension

7. **A**   Words in Context   *Easy*

All of the answer choices but *annulled* are legitimate synonyms for *styled*. Plug them back into the sentence to see which one fits best. Answers **B**, **C**, and **D**, which all interpret the word literally, don't look so hot. Only **A** fits with the context and identifies correctly that *styled* is used metaphorically to mean "deemed," or *described as*.

8. **E**   Specific Information   *Easy*

In the lines specified, the author explains that baseball provides relaxation, reflex training, exercise, and entertainment. Nowhere does it mention financial gain for the players.

9. **D**   Technique   *Medium*

In the indicated part of the passage, the author is responding to the objection that baseball is a dangerous sport by pointing out potential dangers in other sports that are generally considered safe. His goal is not to encourage or discourage people from participating in other sports, but to show that any sport can be defined as dangerous if examined closely enough. This allows him to make the claim that baseball is dangerous seem like an irrational overreaction

10. **A**   Attitude or Tone   *Difficult*

The vocabulary in this one is a little tough, which might make the question seem hard. (*Xenophobic* means "frightened of foreigners," while *anticlerical* means "against clerics or priests.") But you could have gotten the answer even if you didn't know those difficult words. In the specified lines, the author comments on the

the new SAT

"inherent bravery" and "determination" of Americans. In other words, he's pretty proud of his country. In still other words, the writer is *patriotic*.

11. D   Attitude or Tone   *Difficult*

In these lines, the author explicitly says that he sees the participation of high-level businessmen as adding stature to the game and "aiding" it to become the national pastime. So, the businessmen, in the writer's opinion, are helping to build baseball into an institution.

12. B   Words in Context   *Medium*

The author identifies baseball as a game that helps "over-worked" clerks find relaxation. The "harassing" mental labor is part of this over-work, and so the best word to take the place of harassing is *tiring*, answer **B**. Choosing the right answer might be difficult, since both *haranguing* and *molesting* are generally better synonyms for "harassing," but in the context of this passage, they just don't make much sense.

13. B   Main Idea   *Difficult*

The author of passage 2 is not a huge baseball fan. He thinks the competitive aspect of the game makes it dangerous and, in terms of gambling, immoral. But he does say that the game could be somewhat valuable as exercise. Or, to put it in his words, "In a community by far too much given to sedentary occupations and dyspepsia, it furnishes an incentive to active open-air exercise."

14. C   Themes and Arguments   *Medium*

The author describes baseball as both "dangerous" and "hazardous." The only word among the answer choices that fits this idea of danger is **C**, *perilous*.

   Even if you didn't know what all the words in the answer choices meant, you still should have been able to eliminate some answers. For instance, *scientific* and *reassuring* are words you probably know, and neither has anything to do with danger.

15. C   Specific Information   *Easy*

The "Red Stockings" are mentioned in relation to "one of the best players on the Red Stockings" getting hurt. Of the five answer choices, only a *baseball team* has players.

16. D   Themes and Arguments   *Medium*

In this phrase, the author is saying that even at its very best, baseball *still* encourages gambling and other heinous and immoral things. The word "best" is used ironically. At its best, in the author's opinion, it's still bad and *encourages immoral practices*.

17. A   Relating Two Passages   *Medium*

The author of passage 1 claims in these lines that by playing on a baseball team, youths are "almost unconsciously trained" in the American system of legislation and business. The author believes that youths who play baseball will be better trained for success in the American world.

18. E   Relating Two Passages   *Medium*

In order to answer this question, you have to have a sense of how the author of passage 1 feels about the danger inherent in playing baseball. The author of passage 1, in fact, does mention what he thinks about the danger in baseball: "the fact that the players at baseball unflinchingly face the dangers shows the inherent bravery of the American people and their determination to obtain even amusement at the risk of danger." The author of passage 1 thinks the dangers in baseball help to show the greatness of Americans.

19. D   Relating Two Passages   *Medium*

To answer this question, you basically have to go back through the passages and cross out each answer choice when it's mentioned. As it turns out, neither author talks about the details of how baseball teams are funded.

Yes, the author of passage 1 does mention "business interests" involved in the games. But the answer choice says "the details of how baseball teams are funded," and neither passage gives those details at all.

SECTION 8

1. E   Algebra: Solving Equations   *Easy*

You don't actually have to solve this word problem, but you do have to set it up as if you're going to solve it. Here's all the information that the question gives you: It costs $0.90 to take the bus one way, John takes the bus two ways each day (to and from school), and in February he takes the bus on 21 days. To find the total cost, you have to multiply these numbers: $2 \times 0.90 \times 21$. You now have to pick the answer that's the best estimate. That would be **E**, which correctly rounds $0.90 up to $1.00 and rounds 21 down to 20.

2. E   Algebra: Variation   *Easy*

Since x is equal to the product of a and b, if a doubles (is multiplied by 2) and b triples (is multiplied by 3), x will increase by a factor of 6: $6x = (2a)(3b)$.

3. D   Numbers and Operations: Divisibility and Remainders   *Medium*

When you divide one number by another, the remainder is the numerator in the resulting mixed number: $28 \div 5 = 5\frac{3}{5}$, which has a remainder of 3. Likewise, $30 \div 7 = 4\frac{2}{7}$, which has a remainder of 2. When the remainders are multiplied, the product is $3 \times 2 = 6$.

4. A   Algebra: Substitution   *Easy*

Double substitution: Plug in j to find x, then plug in x to find z. Plugging 3 into the equation for j gives $x = 2\sqrt{3}$. Plugging that value for x into the equation for z gives $z = (2\sqrt{3})^2 - 2\sqrt{3}$. Now, just work it out: $z = (4 \times 3) - 2\sqrt{3} = 12 - 2\sqrt{3}$.

5. D   Numbers and Operations: Ratios   *Easy*

Here's a ratio problem, but it's a little tricky. To get it right, you have to notice that the building has 30 *shaded* windows, not 30 *total* window; 30 is a *part* of the ratio, not the *whole*. So, when you set up the ratio, that 30 has to be on top: $\frac{30}{x} = \frac{2}{5}$. Cross-multiply to get $2x = 150$, and then simplify to $x = 75$.

By the way, did you notice the SAT trap lurking in the answer choices? If you got mixed up and put that 30 on the bottom of the ratio, after cross-multiplying, you'd have $5x = 60$. That simplifies to $x = 12$, which is incorrect.

6.   **A**   Geometry: Triangles   *Easy*

The first step is figuring out what a and b equal. Since the third angle in the triangle is a right angle (meaning it's 90 degrees), $a + b = 90$. You know from the question that $a = \frac{b}{2}$, and you can rearrange this equation to see that $b = 2a$. Plugging in, you get $a + 2a = 90$, so $a = 30$. You've got a 30-60-90 triangle on your hands! Awesome. The figure shows that the hypotenuse of the triangle is 12. The side opposite the 30-degree angle in a 30-60-90 triangle is equal to half of the hypotenuse: $\frac{1}{2} \times 12 = 6$.

7.   **B**   Algebra: Functions   *Medium*

This is a compound function question. Solve for $g(x)$, and then plug that answer into $f(x)$. First, plug 8 into $g(x)$: $g(8) = \frac{8}{2} - 1 = 4 - 1 = 3$. Now, plug that answer, 3, into $f(x)$: $f(3) = 3^2 - 2 = 9 - 2 = 7$.

8.   **A**   Algebra: Functions as Models   *Medium*

In this question, the company faces the one-time cost of building its factory before producing any boxes and then a constant cost for each box it makes. So, to produce 0 boxes, there is a cost, which means that the line that indicates the cost of producing boxes must start farther up the y-axis than the origin. This eliminates all the answer choices but **A** and **D**. The cost of making each box is constant, so each additional box made adds a new cost. In other words, the line can't be flat. The correct answer is a graph with a positive y-intercept and a constant positive slope: **A**.

9.   **A**   Geometry: Angles and Lines   *Medium*

A geometry word problem: Sketch away. From the question, you know that A, B, and C are all on one line and that B and D are on a line perpendicular to the line $\overline{ABC}$. Finally, you know that C, E, and F are on a line parallel to line $\overline{BD}$.

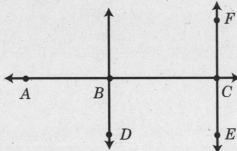

   As this diagram shows, the only lines perpendicular to each other are $\overline{AB}$ and $\overline{CF}$.

10.   **D**   Geometry: Circles   *Difficult*

The key to this question is knowing that a line tangent to a circle is perpendicular to a radius of the circle drawn to the point of tangency. If you didn't know that rule when you came upon this question, learn it. It's essential. If you did know it, you're golden: You've got a simple 30-60-90 triangle to deal with. To find the height of this triangle, you need to know the length of the base and the height. Since this is a right triangle, the base is equal to BC and the height is equal to AB. The question tells you that $AB = 8$, and from the $1 : \sqrt{3} : 2$ ratio of the sides of a 30-60-90 triangle, you should automatically know that the length of BC must equal $8\sqrt{3}$. Now, just work out the triangle area equation: $A = \frac{1}{2}bh = \frac{1}{2}(8 \times 8\sqrt{3}) = 32\sqrt{3}$.

11. **C** Geometry: Triangles   *Difficult*

Because segment $\overline{AD}$ starts at the apex of the equilateral triangle and is perpendicular to the base, you should know that it is a perpendicular bisector that cuts the triangle into two congruent 30-60-90 triangles. Once you see you're dealing with a 30-60-90 triangle, you can use the side length ratio: $1:\sqrt{3}:2$, which tells you that the ratio of the longer leg, $\overline{AD}$, to the hypotenuse, $\overline{AC}$, is $\sqrt{3}:2$. In this triangle, since $\overline{AD} = 1$, you can set up a proportion: $\dfrac{1}{x} = \dfrac{\sqrt{3}}{2}$. Cross-multiply and simplify, and you end up with $x = \dfrac{2}{\sqrt{3}}$.

12. **D** Algebra: Solving Equations   *Difficult*

Here's a rate problem that deals with work (crushing cans). This one is a little complicated, since it asks you to figure out how many people Donna needs to complete the work in a given amount of time (3 hours). Here's the rate formula for work: time × rate = work done. The question tells you the amount of work that has to get done (180 bags of cans crushed), and it tells you that it takes a person 15 minutes ($\frac{1}{4}$ of an hour) to crush one full bag. This means that one person crushes 4 bags in one hour.

So, now you know that in 3 hours, some number of people, x, working at a rate of 4 bags an hour, must crush a total of 180 bags of cans. In equation form, $3 \times x(4) = 180$. Therefore, $12x = 180$, which simplifies to $x = 15$. But that is *not* the right answer. It's an SAT trap. Since Donna will be working too, all she needs is 14 people to help her. The answer is **D**.

13. **E** Algebra: Binomials and Quadratics   *Medium*

To solve this question, you have to factor both the numerator and denominator of the expression in order to simplify it. Once you realize that you have to factor (and you should be wary that you might need to factor *whenever* you see a binomial on the new SAT), you actually have to do the factoring. The denominator is a difference of two squares: $x^2 - 4 = (x+2)(x-2)$. The numerator is a lot more complicated to factor, but since you know what the factors of the denominator are and that you will have to simplify, you can feel pretty comfortable assuming that one of the factors of the numerator will match up with one of the factors of the denominator for canceling out: $2x^2 - 5x + 2 = (2x-1)(x-2)$. Now that you've got them factored, you can go ahead and simplify: $\dfrac{(2x-1)(x-2)}{(x+2)(x-2)} = \dfrac{2x-1}{x+2}$.

14. B   Algebra: Binomials and Quadratics   *Difficult*

The algebra needed for this problem looks intense, but before you get intimidated, remember that the SAT won't ever give you a question with really crazy algebra. It's going to give you a question in which almost everything cancels out. Keep that in mind as you solve for x. To get x, plug in $4x$ for y: $\frac{4x+2}{2} = \frac{x^2+x}{x+1}$. The first thing to do is simplify the left side of the equation: $2x+1 = \frac{x^2+x}{x+1}$. Now that you've simplified the left, it's time to simplify the right. Eliminate the fraction by multiplying both sides of the equation by $x+1$. This means you'll have to use FOIL on the left side of the equation when you multiply $2x+1$ by $x+1$. The result of all this FOILing is this equation: $2x^2+3x+1 = x^2+x$.

The key to solving the problem is recognizing that you're dealing with quadratics at this point. If you realize that, then you'll know that you need to get one side of the equation to equal 0. The easiest way to accomplish this is to subtract x^2+x from both sides, giving $x^2+2x+1 = 0$. All that's left is to factor the quadratic, resulting in $(x+1)(x+1) = 0$—which means that x must equal -1.

15. A   Geometry: Circles   *Difficult*

The area of the shaded region is equal to the area of triangle ABC minus the area of the segments of the circles that are created by angles A, B, and C, so you must find the area of the triangle and the area of the three wedges. The area of the triangle is equal to $\frac{1}{2}bh$. Since the base, which connects points B and C is equal to the radius of circle B plus the radius of circle C, the base is equal to the diameter of one of the circles, which the question tells you is 6. The height of the triangle is a perpendicular bisector that divides the triangle into two 30-60-90 triangles. This means you can calculate the length of the height by using the Pythagorean theorem.

$$h^2 + 3^2 = 6^2$$
$$h^2 = 27$$
$$h = \sqrt{27}$$
$$h = 3\sqrt{3}$$

So, the area of triangle ABC is $\frac{1}{2} \times 6 \times 3\sqrt{3} = 9\sqrt{3}$. At this point, you can eliminate choices **D** and **E** as answers, since they don't have $9\sqrt{3}$ as the area of the triangle.

Next, you have to calculate the area of the circle segments created by the angles A, B, and C. Since ABC is an equilateral triangle, you know that each angle is $60°$, and since $\frac{60}{360} = \frac{1}{6}$, each wedge is equal to $\frac{1}{6}$ of an entire circle. The area of the three wedges together is $3 \times \frac{1}{6} = \frac{1}{2}$ the area of the circle. Since the radius of each circle is equal to $6 \div 2 = 3$, the area of each circle is $\pi 3^2 = 9\pi$, and the area of the three combined wedges is equal to $\frac{9\pi}{2}$. The area of the shaded region, therefore, is equal to $9\sqrt{3} - \frac{9\pi}{2}$.

16. **D**   Numbers and Operations: Sets   *Difficult*

Set Y consists of those students who are in either Set Z or Set W, but leaves out those who are in both. If you were to draw a Venn diagram of the Set Y, it would look like this (Set Y is the lined area):

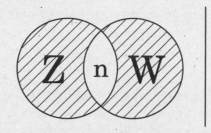

The key to solving this question is realizing that in order to find the shaded part of Set Y you have to subtract k from y, and in order to find the shaded part of Set W you also have to subtract k from w. So the entire shaded region, which is Set Z $= (y - k) + (w - k)$, which can be simplified to Set Z $= y + w - 2k$.

SECTION 9

Improving Sentences

1.   **C**   Parallelism   *Easy*

Remember the rules of parallelism. Here you've got two nouns that refer to professions (*education* and *athletics*), but the final item in the list (*or to become a lawyer*) isn't parallel. To accord to the first two items, and therefore to preserve the sentence's parallel structure, you've got to replace *or to become a lawyer* with a noun that refers to the profession of being a lawyer—that's law, which makes **C** the correct answer. **A**, **B**, and **E** introduce unnecessary verbs that break up the parallel structure, and **D** contains a noun that refers to a specific position within law (lawyer), rather than to the entire profession (as *education* and *athletics* do).

2.   **B**   Tenses   *Easy*

The tenses in this sentence are out of whack. The tense used in the first and final clauses (*had just arrived*, *had won*) makes the present tense *she learns* incorrect. To rectify the tense situation, *learns* must be changed to the past tense *learned*. So you can cut **A** right off the bat. The next choice to eliminate is **C** since it also uses present tense (*finds*). **D** uses the wrong tense (*had*) as well, so that's also out. **E** uses an –ing verb (*informing*) improperly. That leaves **B**, the only choice that uses the simple past tense verb that this sentence needs.

3.   **B**   Wordiness   *Easy*

The phrase *more than at least* is redundant since *more than* implies that something took place for "at least" the specified period of time. So cut **A**. **C** makes things even more redundant and complicated. **D** introduces unnecessary uncertainty with *perhaps*. **B** and **E** convey the same idea as the underlined portion of the sentence, but only **B** is grammatically correct.

4.　**E**　Other　　　　　　　　　　　　　　　　　　*Medium*

Here the pronoun *she* is ambiguous because the subject of the sentence contains two females: does *she* refer to Sue or Andrea? Since you've identified an error in the sentence, cut **A**. **C** contains the same ambiguous pronoun as A. **B** clears up the pronoun confusion, but presents the events out of order. **D** and **E** both solve the pronoun issue, but only E does so with correct grammar.

5.　**C**　Tenses　　　　　　　　　　　　　　　　　　*Medium*

This sentence describes events in the past, but the underlined portion contains a noun written incorrectly in the present-tense. To convey what people were expecting before an event that occurred in the past (*the flood*), you need to use the past perfect tense (the tense with had). Only answer choice **C** contains the tense you need (*had expected*), which makes **C** the correct answer.

6.　**C**　Parallelism　　　　　　　　　　　　　　　　*Medium*

Here's a case of faulty parallel structure. The phrase *physical fitness* must match up with its equivalent in order for the two nouns to be parallel. What's the mental equivalent of physical fitness? *Mental health*, so **C** either or **D** is most likely correct. The conjunction *or* in **D** is incorrect, so cut **D**. **C** gets the job done correct and simply, which makes it the correct answer.

7.　**B**　Other　　　　　　　　　　　　　　　　　　*Easy*

The pronoun that refers to *the burglar* must be *he* or *she*, not *this*. That makes it easy to cut **A** and **E**. **C** uses the correct pronoun *he*, but when plugged back into the sentence, **C** doesn't make sense: the burglar does not receive the harshest penalties because he's a minor. The phrase *not only* in **D** turns the sentence into nonsense. Only **B** works. B uses the correct pronoun he and conveys the intended meaning of the sentence: the burglar won't receive the harshest penalties because he is a minor.

8.　**C**　Run-On　　　　　　　　　　　　　　　　　*Medium*

The underlined portion makes this sentence a run-on: it smooshes together what should be two separate clauses: *it's just not the same* and *seeing them in person is always more memorable*. Since the sentence contains an error, cut **A**. Of the remaining choices, which one best solves the run-on dilemma? **B** uses the conjunction *and*, but the result doesn't make sense. **D** tries a similar fix with the conjunction *but*, but with similarly nonsensical results. Now you're down to **E** and **C**. **E**, though, has a grammar problem with the incorrect verb form *to see*. **C** solves that problem by using *seeing*.

9.　**C**　Misplaced Modifiers　　　　　　　　　　　*Medium*

The underlined portion of this sentence makes it sound like the *many errors in judgment* lacked *proper parental guidance*. Instead the sentence intends to say that the female person (referred to in the *by her* clause) made the errors as a result of improper parental guidance. The problem results from a combination of a misplaced modifier and the passive voice phrase *were made by her*. That means **A** is definitely out. **B**, **D**, and **E** solve the misplaced modifier problem by placing *her* directly after the comma instead of *many errors in judgment*, but **E** still contains the passive voice. So cut **E**. **D** is excessively wordy and somewhat nonsensical, cut that too. That leaves B and **C**. **B** looks right at first glance, but read more carefully and you'll see that it doesn't make sense (it should say *her errors in judgment were many*). Even then it wouldn't be as correct and effective as choice **C**, which drops *her* and eliminates the passive voice by using the active phrase *she made many errors in judgment*.

10. **B**   Parallelism   *Medium*

The verbs in the first few clauses of this sentence are all written in the simple present tense (*it is*, *to read*). The verb in the final clause is written in what's called the continuous present tense (*are not doing*). That should set off your parallelism alarm—**A** must be incorrect, and the correct answer must make these verb forms align. **C**, **D**, and **E** all use the continuous present (*are doing*, *are not doing*), so they can't possibly solve the parallelism problem. Only **B** uses the simple present form of the verb (*don't do*).

11. **E**   Misplaced Modifier   *Medium*

When was the last time a "change" visited another country? Never. But the way this sentence is written makes it sound like the change in your outlook, rather than you, just visited another country. That's what we call a misplaced modifier. To solve it, find the answer choice that replaces the *change* with *you*. That makes it easy to eliminate **A**, **C**, and **D**. Of the remaining choices, **B** uses a clunky bunch of incorrect verbs (*can be changing*), a problem not present in **E**, the correct answer.

12. **C**   Idioms   *Medium*

Idioms are often tough because they require you to hear that something is amiss in the sentence. The English idiom *not only* is followed by the phrase *but also*, not *and also*. That makes **A** and **D** incorrect since they use *and* and *or*. The remaining choices all use *but*, but only **C** does so with correct idiomatic grammar.

13. **A**   No Error   *Difficult*

14. **E**   Misplaced Modifier   *Difficult*

This sentence looks great, but looks can be deceiving. Take another look and you'll see that as it's written, this sentence says zoologists have furry coats and ducklike bills. Maybe some zoologists do, but here those qualities should clearly be attributed to the platypus, the subject of the sentence. Fixing misplaced modifiers often requires reshuffling the order of the clauses in a sentence. Here you need to make it clear that the furry coat and ducklike bill belong to the platypus, not the zoologists. Next the sentence needs to make it clear that the platypus's bizarre physical attributes made the animal difficult to classify. Since **A** contains the misplaced modifier, cut that choice right away. **B** and **C** make the same mistake, so those should also go. **D** solves the misplaced modifier problem but introduces other mistakes—the platypus didn't fail, the zoologists did. That makes **E** the only choice that solves the misplaced modifier problem and conveys the meaning of the sentence with correct grammar.

SAT PRACTICE TEST 2 ANSWER SHEET

SECTION 6

1. Ⓐ Ⓑ Ⓒ Ⓓ Ⓔ	10. Ⓐ Ⓑ Ⓒ Ⓓ Ⓔ	19. Ⓐ Ⓑ Ⓒ Ⓓ Ⓔ	28. Ⓐ Ⓑ Ⓒ Ⓓ Ⓔ
2. Ⓐ Ⓑ Ⓒ Ⓓ Ⓔ	11. Ⓐ Ⓑ Ⓒ Ⓓ Ⓔ	20. Ⓐ Ⓑ Ⓒ Ⓓ Ⓔ	29. Ⓐ Ⓑ Ⓒ Ⓓ Ⓔ
3. Ⓐ Ⓑ Ⓒ Ⓓ Ⓔ	12. Ⓐ Ⓑ Ⓒ Ⓓ Ⓔ	21. Ⓐ Ⓑ Ⓒ Ⓓ Ⓔ	30. Ⓐ Ⓑ Ⓒ Ⓓ Ⓔ
4. Ⓐ Ⓑ Ⓒ Ⓓ Ⓔ	13. Ⓐ Ⓑ Ⓒ Ⓓ Ⓔ	22. Ⓐ Ⓑ Ⓒ Ⓓ Ⓔ	31. Ⓐ Ⓑ Ⓒ Ⓓ Ⓔ
5. Ⓐ Ⓑ Ⓒ Ⓓ Ⓔ	14. Ⓐ Ⓑ Ⓒ Ⓓ Ⓔ	23. Ⓐ Ⓑ Ⓒ Ⓓ Ⓔ	32. Ⓐ Ⓑ Ⓒ Ⓓ Ⓔ
6. Ⓐ Ⓑ Ⓒ Ⓓ Ⓔ	15. Ⓐ Ⓑ Ⓒ Ⓓ Ⓔ	24. Ⓐ Ⓑ Ⓒ Ⓓ Ⓔ	33. Ⓐ Ⓑ Ⓒ Ⓓ Ⓔ
7. Ⓐ Ⓑ Ⓒ Ⓓ Ⓔ	16. Ⓐ Ⓑ Ⓒ Ⓓ Ⓔ	25. Ⓐ Ⓑ Ⓒ Ⓓ Ⓔ	34. Ⓐ Ⓑ Ⓒ Ⓓ Ⓔ
8. Ⓐ Ⓑ Ⓒ Ⓓ Ⓔ	17. Ⓐ Ⓑ Ⓒ Ⓓ Ⓔ	26. Ⓐ Ⓑ Ⓒ Ⓓ Ⓔ	35. Ⓐ Ⓑ Ⓒ Ⓓ Ⓔ
9. Ⓐ Ⓑ Ⓒ Ⓓ Ⓔ	18. Ⓐ Ⓑ Ⓒ Ⓓ Ⓔ	27. Ⓐ Ⓑ Ⓒ Ⓓ Ⓔ	

SECTION 7

1. Ⓐ Ⓑ Ⓒ Ⓓ Ⓔ	6. Ⓐ Ⓑ Ⓒ Ⓓ Ⓔ	11. Ⓐ Ⓑ Ⓒ Ⓓ Ⓔ	16. Ⓐ Ⓑ Ⓒ Ⓓ Ⓔ
2. Ⓐ Ⓑ Ⓒ Ⓓ Ⓔ	7. Ⓐ Ⓑ Ⓒ Ⓓ Ⓔ	12. Ⓐ Ⓑ Ⓒ Ⓓ Ⓔ	17. Ⓐ Ⓑ Ⓒ Ⓓ Ⓔ
3. Ⓐ Ⓑ Ⓒ Ⓓ Ⓔ	8. Ⓐ Ⓑ Ⓒ Ⓓ Ⓔ	13. Ⓐ Ⓑ Ⓒ Ⓓ Ⓔ	18. Ⓐ Ⓑ Ⓒ Ⓓ Ⓔ
4. Ⓐ Ⓑ Ⓒ Ⓓ Ⓔ	9. Ⓐ Ⓑ Ⓒ Ⓓ Ⓔ	14. Ⓐ Ⓑ Ⓒ Ⓓ Ⓔ	19. Ⓐ Ⓑ Ⓒ Ⓓ Ⓔ
5. Ⓐ Ⓑ Ⓒ Ⓓ Ⓔ	10. Ⓐ Ⓑ Ⓒ Ⓓ Ⓔ	15. Ⓐ Ⓑ Ⓒ Ⓓ Ⓔ	

SECTION 8

1. Ⓐ Ⓑ Ⓒ Ⓓ Ⓔ	5. Ⓐ Ⓑ Ⓒ Ⓓ Ⓔ	9. Ⓐ Ⓑ Ⓒ Ⓓ Ⓔ	13. Ⓐ Ⓑ Ⓒ Ⓓ Ⓔ
2. Ⓐ Ⓑ Ⓒ Ⓓ Ⓔ	6. Ⓐ Ⓑ Ⓒ Ⓓ Ⓔ	10. Ⓐ Ⓑ Ⓒ Ⓓ Ⓔ	14. Ⓐ Ⓑ Ⓒ Ⓓ Ⓔ
3. Ⓐ Ⓑ Ⓒ Ⓓ Ⓔ	7. Ⓐ Ⓑ Ⓒ Ⓓ Ⓔ	11. Ⓐ Ⓑ Ⓒ Ⓓ Ⓔ	15. Ⓐ Ⓑ Ⓒ Ⓓ Ⓔ
4. Ⓐ Ⓑ Ⓒ Ⓓ Ⓔ	8. Ⓐ Ⓑ Ⓒ Ⓓ Ⓔ	12. Ⓐ Ⓑ Ⓒ Ⓓ Ⓔ	16. Ⓐ Ⓑ Ⓒ Ⓓ Ⓔ

SECTION 9

1. Ⓐ Ⓑ Ⓒ Ⓓ Ⓔ	5. Ⓐ Ⓑ Ⓒ Ⓓ Ⓔ	9. Ⓐ Ⓑ Ⓒ Ⓓ Ⓔ	13. Ⓐ Ⓑ Ⓒ Ⓓ Ⓔ
2. Ⓐ Ⓑ Ⓒ Ⓓ Ⓔ	6. Ⓐ Ⓑ Ⓒ Ⓓ Ⓔ	10. Ⓐ Ⓑ Ⓒ Ⓓ Ⓔ	14. Ⓐ Ⓑ Ⓒ Ⓓ Ⓔ
3. Ⓐ Ⓑ Ⓒ Ⓓ Ⓔ	7. Ⓐ Ⓑ Ⓒ Ⓓ Ⓔ	11. Ⓐ Ⓑ Ⓒ Ⓓ Ⓔ	
4. Ⓐ Ⓑ Ⓒ Ⓓ Ⓔ	8. Ⓐ Ⓑ Ⓒ Ⓓ Ⓔ	12. Ⓐ Ⓑ Ⓒ Ⓓ Ⓔ	

SECTION 1

ESSAY

Time — 25 minutes

You have twenty-five minutes to plan and write an essay on the topic assigned below. DO NOT WRITE ON ANOTHER TOPIC. AN ESSAY ON ANOTHER TOPIC IS NOT ACCEPTABLE.

The essay is assigned to give you an opportunity to show how well you can write. You should, therefore, take care to express your thoughts on the topic clearly and effectively. How well you write is much more important than how much you write, but to cover the topic adequately you will probably need to write more than one paragraph. Be specific.

Your essay must be written on the following two pages. You will find that you have enough space if you write on every line, avoid wide margins, and keep your handwriting to a reasonable size. It is important to remember that what you write will be read by someone who is not familiar with your handwriting. Try to write or print so that what you are writing is legible to the reader.

Directions: Think carefully about the issue presented in the following excerpt and the assignment below.

An old proverb states that "Knowledge in youth is wisdom in age." Some take this saying to mean that the education one acquires throughout youth only becomes wisdom over time, as one ages and broadens his or her experience. Others view the proverb as a dismissal of the notion that only the aged and experienced can ever be truly wise.

Assignment: Do the ends always justify the means? Plan and write an essay in which you develop your point of view on this issue. Support your position with reasoning and examples taken from your reading, studies, experience, or observations.

DO NOT WRITE YOUR ESSAY IN YOUR TEST BOOK. You will receive credit only for what you write on your answer sheet.

WHEN YOUR SUPERVISOR ANNOUNCES THAT TWENTY-FIVE MINUTES HAVE PASSED, YOU MUST STOP WRITING THE ESSAY AND GO ON TO SECTION 2 IF YOU HAVE NOT ALREADY DONE SO. IF YOU FINISH YOUR ESSAY BEFORE THIS ANNOUNCEMENT, GO ON TO SECTION 2 AT ONCE.

BEGIN WRITING YOUR ESSAY ON THE ANSWER SHEET.

SECTION 1—ESSAY

Time — 25 minutes

SECTION 1—ESSAY

Time — 25 minutes

Section 2

Turn to Section 2 of your answer sheet to answer the questions in this section.

Time—25 Minutes
24 Questions

For each question in this section, select the best answer from among the choices given and fill in the corresponding oval on the answer sheet.

Each sentence below has one or two blanks, each blank indicating that something has been omitted. Beneath the sentence are five words or sets of words labeled A through E. Choose the word or set of words that, when inserted in the sentence, best fits the meaning of the sentence as a whole.

Example:

Medieval kingdoms did not become constitutional republics overnight; on the contrary, the change was ----.

(A) unpopular
(B) unexpected
(C) advantageous
(D) sufficient
(E) gradual   Ⓐ Ⓑ Ⓒ Ⓓ ●

1. In *Moby-Dick*, the symbolic meaning of the color white is ----; some readers take it to represent death, some take it to represent divinity. b=correct

(A) beautiful
(B) ambiguous
(C) benign
(D) infinite
(E) persuasive

2. Thanks to his many ---- and friendly ----, Henri easily got the job at the new software company.

(A) connections..evidence
(B) achievements..demeanor
(C) flaws..humor
(D) talents..desperation
(E) demotions..appetite

3. It caused a ---- at its premiere, but Stravinsky's "Rite of Spring" no longer seems so audaciously modern; in fact, it is actually quite ---- by the standards of avant-garde music today.

(A) sensation..shocking
(B) scandal..tame
(C) stir..imposing
(D) backlash..infuriating
(E) riot..advanced

4. In contrast to his ghost story *A Christmas Carol*, which is brief and tightly organized, Charles Dickens's *David Copperfield*, is ----.

(A) jovial
(B) reminiscent
(C) dubious
(D) implausible
(E) sprawling

5. The influence of the popular vote on the outcome of a presidential election is ----; it informs the Electoral College, which is the body that actually chooses the new president.

(A) absolute
(B) obscure
(C) arbitrary
(D) negligible
(E) indirect

6. Instead of ---- for his pranks, the character Puck in Shakespeare's *A Midsummer Night's Dream* actually brags about them.

(A) living
(B) singing
(C) striving
(D) apologizing
(E) fighting

GO ON TO THE NEXT PAGE

Section 2

7. Though often ---- by literary critics, Rod McKuen was ---- by his readers, who made him the most popular poet of the 1960s.

   (A) emasculated..tarnished
   (B) redeemed..celebrated
   (C) denounced..ignored
   (D) derided..venerated
   (E) extolled..loathed

8. The sales representative was expected to ---- the whole district, seeking orders from each new business.

   (A) discern
   (B) canvass—go door to door.
   (C) validate
   (D) incorporate
   (E) castigate

GO ON TO THE NEXT PAGE

Section 2

Each short passage below is followed by questions based on its content. Answer the questions based on what is <u>stated</u> or <u>implied</u> in each passage.

Questions 9–10 are based on the following passage.

Don't move. You're surrounded. Right now tens of thousands of arthropods are crawling all over your skin like a tiny army on the march. These microscopic organisms, commonly known as dust mites, make their homes in soft furniture and clumps of dust, and
5 are particularly prevalent in humid environments. Sweeping or vacuuming can cause mites in dust balls to become airborne. They then end up on the skin, or worse, ingested through the nose and mouth. In 1921, scientists began to suspect that dust contained some allergen that caused allergic reactions and even respiratory
10 afflictions like asthma. It was not until 1964 that a group of investigators identified dust mites as the culprit.

9. The description of dust mites as a "tiny army" is an example of (a)

    (A) onomotopeia
    (B) alliteration
    (C) clarification
    (D) paradox
    (E) simile

10. Based on information contained in the passage, dust mites do all of the following EXCEPT

    (A) cause disease
    (B) live in dust clumps
    (C) spread via air
    (D) cause allergies
    (E) destroy furniture

Questions 11–12 are based on the following passage.

The Oregon Trail was a two-thousand-mile passageway across the plains of the Midwest and through the Rocky Mountains. Early settlers followed the Trail en route to the territories we now know as Idaho, Washington, Nevada, California, and Utah. The first
5 two people to traverse the trail were Marcus and Narcissa Whitman in 1836. A rush of people followed starting a few years later in 1843. The journey was arduous. Settlers had to face the perils of disease, food shortages, and conflicts with Native Americans. To top it all off, they had no supplies and no support.
10 None. It's amazing that the American West was settled at all.

11. The author's tone in this passage is

    (A) shocked and stupefied
    (B) dispassionate and technical
    (C) respectful and admiring
    (D) joyful and celebratory
    (E) nostalgic and sentimental

12. The statement "None" near the end of the passage primarily serves to emphasize

    (A) the isolation and loneliness of the settlers
    (B) the settlers' understanding of their newfound surroundings
    (C) the factors stacked up against people on the Oregon Trail
    (D) the author's surprise that the settler's were successful
    (E) the negative effects of settlement on Native Americans

GO ON TO THE NEXT PAGE ➤

The passage below is followed by questions based on its content. Answer the questions on the basis of what is <u>stated</u> or <u>implied</u> in the passage and in any introductory material that may be provided.

Questions 13–24 are based on the following passage, in which the narrator, Huckleberry Finn, discusses his time as a young boy spent at the house of the Widow Douglas, a woman who has taken him in.

The Widow rung a bell for supper, and you had to come to time. When you got to the table you couldn't go right to eating, but you had to wait for the Widow to tuck down her head and grumble a little over the victuals, though there warn't really anything the
5 matter with them,—that is, nothing only everything was cooked by itself. In a barrel of odds and ends it is different; things get mixed up, and the juice kind of swaps around, and the things go better.

After supper she got out her book and learned me about Moses
10 and the Bulrushers, and I was in a sweat to find out all about him; but by and by she let it out that Moses had been dead a considerable long time; so then I didn't care no more about him, because I don't take no stock in dead people.

Pretty soon I wanted to smoke, and asked the Widow to let me.
15 But she wouldn't. She said it was a mean practice and wasn't clean, and I must try to not do it any more. That is just the way with some people. They get down on a thing when they don't know nothing about it. Here she was a-bothering about Moses, which was no kin to her, and no use to her, being gone, you see, yet
20 finding a power of fault with me for doing a thing that had some good in it. And she took snuff, too; of course that was all right, because she done it herself.

Her sister, Miss Watson, a tolerable slim old maid, with goggles on, had just come to live with her, and took a set at me
25 now with a spelling-book. She worked me middling hard for about an hour, and then the Widow made her ease up. I couldn't stood it much longer. Then for an hour it was deadly dull, and I was fidgety. Miss Watson would say, "Don't put your feet up there, Huckleberry;" and "Don't scrunch up like that, Huckleberry—set
30 up straight;" and pretty soon she would say, "Don't gap and stretch like that, Huckleberry—why don't you try to?" Then she told me all about the bad place, and I said I wished I was there. She got mad then, but I didn't mean no harm. All I wanted was to go somewheres; all I wanted was a change, I warn't particular.
35 She said it was wicked to say what I said; said she wouldn't say it for the whole world; she was going to live so as to go to the good place. Well, I couldn't see no advantage in going where she was going, so I made up my mind I wouldn't try for it. But I never said so, because it would only make trouble, and wouldn't do no good.
40 By and by everybody was off to bed. I went up to my room with a piece of candle, and put it on the table. Then I set down in a chair by the window and tried to think of something cheerful, but it warn't no use. I felt so lonesome I most wished I was dead. The stars were shining, and the leaves rustled in the woods ever so
45 mournful; and I heard an owl, away off, who-whooing about somebody that was dead, and a whippowill and a dog about somebody that was going to die; and the wind was trying to whisper something to me, and I couldn't make out what it was, and so it made the cold shivers run over me. Then away out in the
50 woods I heard that kind of a sound that a ghost makes when it wants to tell about something that's on its mind and can't make itself understood, and so can't rest easy in its grave, and has to go about that way every night grieving. I got so down-hearted and scared I did wish I had some company. Pretty soon a spider went
55 crawling up my shoulder, and I flipped it off and it lit in the candle; and before I could budge it was all shriveled up. I didn't need anybody to tell me that that was an awful bad sign and would fetch me some bad luck, so I was scared and most shook the clothes off of me. I got up and turned around in my tracks three
60 times and crossed my breast every time; and then I tied up a little lock of my hair with a thread to keep witches away. But I hadn't no confidence. You do that when you've lost a horseshoe that you've found, instead of nailing it up over the door, but I hadn't ever heard anybody say it was any way to keep off bad luck when you'd killed a spider.

13. The word "victuals" most nearly means

(A) prayer
(B) food
(C) silverware
(D) books
(E) barrels

14. The disagreement between the Widow and Huckleberry about smoking and snuff in the third paragraph demonstrates that

(A) the Widow does not care about the narrator
(B) Huckleberry can see through the hypocrisy of others
(C) Huckleberry is bound to end up in "the bad place"
(D) Huckleberry is extremely religious
(E) Huckleberry is trying to make the Widow angry

15. The word "mean" in line 15 most nearly means

(A) cruel
(B) vicious
(C) small
(D) dangerous
(E) unpleasant

GO ON TO THE NEXT PAGE

16. The quotes of Miss Watson in lines 28–31 serve primarily to

    (A) establish her as bossy and domineering
    (B) show that the narrator is a troublemaker
    (C) highlight how much she loves Huckleberry
    (D) demonstrate that the narrator needs lessons in manners
    (E) cause the reader to dislike Huckleberry

17. The effect of the sentence that begins "All I wanted..." (line 33) is to

    (A) show that the Huckleberry is restless and feels confined
    (B) illuminate the relationship between Miss Watson and the Widow
    (C) contrast Huckleberry to the Widow
    (D) destroy Huckleberry's credibility as a narrator
    (E) corroborate previous comments from Miss Watson

18. The description of the leaves in line 44 is an example of

    (A) metaphor
    (B) hyperbole
    (C) paradox
    (D) personification
    (E) alliteration

19. From the narrator's reaction to accidentally burning the spider, he could best be described as

    (A) cold-hearted
    (B) gentle
    (C) superstitious
    (D) pragmatic
    (E) dreamy

20. How does the fourth paragraph function in relation to the third paragraph?

    (A) It reiterates and builds upon feelings and themes from the third paragraph.
    (B) It clarifies ambiguities left unexamined in the third paragraph.
    (C) It describes events foreshadowed in the third paragraph.
    (D) It offers analysis of a scene presented in the third paragraph.
    (E) It extends a metaphor created in the third paragraph.

21. The entire passage suggests that Huck regards the civilized world of the Widow Douglas and Miss Watson with

    (A) disdain
    (B) skepticism
    (C) sadness
    (D) animosity
    (E) ambivalence

22. Through his narration of the passage, Huckleberry is portrayed as

    (A) cruel, haughty, and vindictive
    (B) independent, free-thinking, and lonely
    (C) selfish, argumentative, and greedy
    (D) sad, desperate, and terrified
    (E) stupid, uneducated, and ignorant

23. The tone of the passage could best be described as

    (A) casual and informal
    (B) witty and urbane
    (C) despairing and bereft
    (D) ominous and portentous
    (E) angry and defiant

24. In the passage, Huckleberry responds to the attempts of the Widow and Miss Watson to educate him by

    (A) running away from the Widow Douglas's house
    (B) taking his anger out on the spider in his bedroom
    (C) goading them into intense and interminable arguments
    (D) making nasty asides to the reader about their appearance and stupidity
    (E) pointing out to the reader the inconsistencies in Miss Watson's and the Widow's own logic and beliefs

S T O P

IF YOU FINISH BEFORE TIME IS CALLED, YOU MAY CHECK YOUR WORK ON THIS TEST ONLY.
DO NOT TURN TO ANY OTHER SECTION IN THIS TEST.

Section 3

Turn to Section 3 of your answer sheet to answer the questions in this section.

Time—25 Minutes
20 Questions

In this section solve each problem, using any available space on the page for scratchwork. Then decide which is the best of the choices given and fill in the corresponding oval on the answer sheet.

Notes:

1. The use of a calculator is permitted. All numbers used are real numbers.

2. Figures that accompany problems in this test are intended to provide information useful in solving the problems. They are drawn as accurately as possible EXCEPT when it is stated in a specific problem that the figure is not drawn to scale. All figures lie in a plane unless otherwise indicated.

3. Unless otherwise specified, the domain of any function f is assumed to be the set of all real numbers x for which $f(x)$ is a real number.

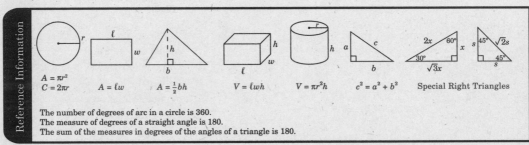

The number of degrees of arc in a circle is 360.
The measure of degrees of a straight angle is 180.
The sum of the measures in degrees of the angles of a triangle is 180.

1. If $x = 3$ and $y = x$, what is the value of xy^2?

(A) 27
(B) 9
(C) 6
(D) 3
(E) 1

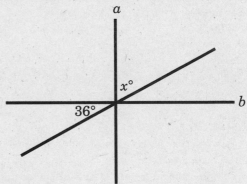

2. In the figure above, if lines a and b are perpendicular, what is the value of x?

(A) 36
(B) 54
(C) 64
(D) 144
(E) 180

GO ON TO THE NEXT PAGE

Section 3

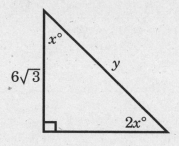

3. For which of the following sets of numbers is the mode equal to the mean?

   (A) {1,2,2,7}
   (B) {1,1,3,7}
   (C) {3,4,4,5}
   (D) {0,1,1,6}
   (E) {−1,−1,3,7}

For questions 4–6, let $\bar{n}$ be the sum of the individual digits of n. For example, $\overline{134} = 1 + 3 + 4 = 8$.

4. What is $\dfrac{\overline{4371} - \overline{3441}}{\overline{231}}$?

   (A) 0.25
   (B) 0.5
   (C) 3
   (D) 7
   (E) 12

5. If $\leftarrow n$ means to reverse the order of the digits in n, then what is $\overline{1,234,533,234} - \overline{\leftarrow 1,234,533,234}$?

   (A) −2
   (B) −1
   (C) 0
   (D) 1
   (E) 2

6. If n is an integer and $10 < n < 90$, what is $\overline{(n + 1090)}$?

   (A) n
   (B) $\bar{n}$
   (C) $\overline{n-1}$
   (D) 100
   (E) $\bar{n} + 1$

7. If $x + 2y = 7$ and $x + y = 6$, what is x?

   (A) 1
   (B) 2
   (C) 5
   (D) 6
   (E) 7

8. What is the value of y?

   (A) $3\sqrt{3}$
   (B) 6
   (C) $6\sqrt{3}$
   (D) 12
   (E) $12\sqrt{3}$

9. $a - b = 2b$ and $b = 2$. What is the value of $2a$?

   (A) 2
   (B) 3
   (C) 6
   (D) 12
   (E) 36

10. A piece of string is x yards long. If it is cut into 5 equal pieces, each 1.5 feet in length, what is x? Assume that no string is left over. (Note: 3 feet = 1 yard.)

    (A) $\dfrac{1}{2}$
    (B) $\dfrac{7}{4}$
    (C) 2
    (D) $\dfrac{5}{2}$
    (E) $\dfrac{15}{2}$

11. The sum of x and y is 10 more than 3 times z. Which of the following equations describes x and y in terms of z?

    (A) $\dfrac{x + y - 10}{3} = z$
    (B) $3(x + y) = z$
    (C) $x + y - 30 = z$
    (D) $x + y + 30 = z$
    (E) $\dfrac{x + y + 10}{3} = z$

GO ON TO THE NEXT PAGE

Section 3

12. A line with slope $\frac{3}{5}$ passes through $(h,0)$ and $(11h,6)$. What is h?

    (A) $\frac{3}{5}$

    (B) 1

    (C) $\frac{11}{15}$

    (D) $\frac{5}{3}$

    (E) $\frac{33}{5}$

13. Two congruent triangles are joined to form a square. If the longest side of each triangle measures $5\sqrt{2}$, what is the area of the square?

    (A) 4

    (B) 5

    (C) 10

    (D) 25

    (E) 50

14. If $\frac{x}{2}$ is an integer, and $x \neq 0$, what must be true of $x^2 - \frac{x}{3}$?

    I.   It is an integer
    II. It is even
    III. It is positive

    (A) I only

    (B) II only

    (C) III only

    (D) I, II, and III only

    (E) None of these is necessarily true

15. If $p < 0$ and $-1 < s < 1$, then what number value for ps^2 is <u>not</u> possible?

    (A) −5

    (B) −1

    (C) −.5

    (D) 0

    (E) .5

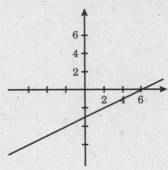

16. The figure above shows the graph of $f(x) = \frac{x}{2} - 3$. Which of the following most closely resembles the graph of $f(x + 3)$?

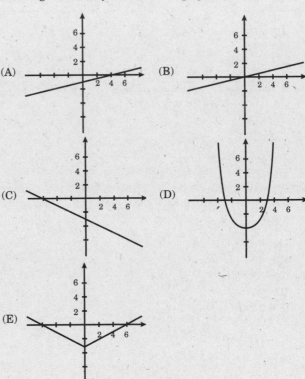

17. A gas pump pumps x gallons of gas every y minutes. If gas costs z dollars per gallon, and the pump automatically stops after dispensing gas for m minutes, how much does the dispensed gas cost?

    (A) $\$ \frac{mxz}{y}$

    (B) $\$ \frac{mx}{z}$

    (C) $\$ \frac{myz}{x}$

    (D) $\$ \frac{m}{xyz}$

    (E) $\$ \frac{xz}{my}$

GO ON TO THE NEXT PAGE

Section 3

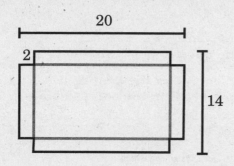

18. The figure above is produced by taking squares of length 2 out of the corners of a rectangle. The resulting figure is then folded along the gray lines in order to form an open box. What is the volume of the box?

(A) 160
(B) 280
(C) 320
(D) 480
(E) 560

19. Scientists leave a population of six rabbits on a deserted island and then chart the size of the population each year. After four years, the population doubles. After another four years, the population doubles again. If the geometric growth of the population continues at this rate, how many more rabbits will be on the island after 20 years than are on the island after 12 years?

(A) 24
(B) 48
(C) 72
(D) 96
(E) 144

20. A go-kart is pushed off a 50-meter-long hill. After rolling down the hill, it continues to roll for another 150 meters until it stops. Which of the following graphs could show the speed of the go-kart as a function of distance?

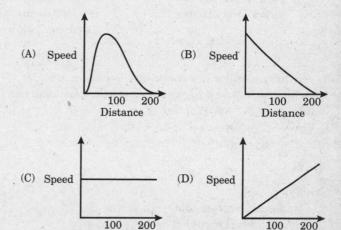

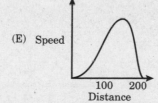

GO ON TO THE NEXT PAGE

Section 4

Turn to Section 4 of your answer sheetto answer the questions in this section.

Time—25 Minutes
24 Questions

For each question in this section, select the best answer from among the choices given and fill in the corresponding oval on the answer sheet.

Each sentence below has one or two blanks, each blank indicating that something has been omitted. Beneath the sentence are five words or sets of words labeled A through E. Choose the word or set of words that, when inserted in the sentence, best fits the meaning of the sentence as a whole.

Example:

Medieval kingdoms did not become constitutional republics overnight; on the contrary, the change was ----.

(A) unpopular
(B) unexpected
(C) advantageous
(D) sufficient
(E) gradual

1. Although Henrietta was quite ----, she was undisciplined and therefore often encountered academic ----.

(A) intelligent..catastrophe
(B) lazy..success
(C) thoughtful..superiority
(D) uninspired..prowess
(E) irresponsible..failure

2. The ---- Supreme Court decision in the case *Roe v. Wade* continues to divide the United States.

(A) novel
(B) oblique
(C) untenable
(D) controversial
(E) figurative

3. In all her endeavors, Tamara was an ---- employee: responsible, efficient, and, above all, courteous.

(A) ineffective
(B) unhelpful
(C) irrelevant
(D) exemplary
(E) absorbing

4. After espousing views inconsistent with official Christian religious doctrine, Joan of Arc was deemed a ---- and subsequently burned at the stake.

(A) perpetrator
(B) populist
(C) murderer
(D) heretic
(E) zealot

5. Ignorant of the most basic social ----, Paul offended even the most forgiving host with his ---- table manners.

(A) conventions..refined
(B) graces..resplendent
(C) vicissitudes..deleterious
(D) precepts..atrocious
(E) expropriations..portentous

GO ON TO THE NEXT PAGE

Section 4

Each short passage below is followed by questions based on its content. Answer the questions based on what is <u>stated</u> or <u>implied</u> in each passage.

Passage 1

Without a doubt the Internet has improved the way we all communicate. Just a decade ago getting in touch with old friends and relatives required a lengthy search through interstate phone books at the local library. Today it's as simple as searching the
5 Web. Everything from online yearbooks to comprehensive ancestry and genealogy databases make finding that missing special someone easy. I can't even imagine going back to the days of standing on line at the library when today I can go online to get just what I need in a flash.

Passage 2

The Internet has led to a total breakdown in the boundaries of privacy. Over the past few years everyone's private business has become a public affair. Many people revel in the instant access to all kinds of information on the Web, but they may not be aware
5 that details from their own private lives can be uploaded to a Web site and published for all the world to see. Unlike newspapers and books, Internet pages don't age. Once your name, address, and credit history make it to the Web, you'll have a tough time getting them off. It's a problem snowballing out of anyone's control.

6. The use of the phrase "Just a decade ago" in the first passage serves primarily to

   (A) express shock at how quickly time passes
   (B) highlight the extent of a change
   (C) use historical precedent as a point of argument
   (D) make light of the fears of others
   (E) argue for the elimination of restrictions

7. The tone of the first and second passages above could best be described as which of the following, respectively?

   (A) cautious and confident
   (B) enthusiastic and perturbed
   (C) anxious and uneasy
   (D) afraid and conniving
   (E) malevolent and mawkish

8. The opinions of the authors of these two passages differ regarding

   (A) public access to private information on the Internet
   (B) new laws that impact the content that can appear on Web pages
   (C) whether reading books is a better way to learn than reading on the Internet
   (D) the danger created by the anonymity of the Internet
   (E) the Internet's growing popularity in developing nations

9. The authors of the two passages would most likely disagree about all of the following EXCEPT

   (A) the free flow of all types of information benefits everyone
   (B) the Internet's ability to track an individual's online activities allows for better customer service
   (C) the Internet causes more fundamental problems than it solves
   (D) there needs to be more oversight and regulation of information on the Web
   (E) the Internet has drastically affected society

GO ON TO THE NEXT PAGE

Section 4

The two short passages below are followed by questions based on their content. Answer the questions based on what is <u>stated</u> or <u>implied</u> in each passage.

Questions 10–15 are based on the following passage.

In the following passage, the author discusses the different ways in which art was perceived during medieval times as opposed to during the modern era.

Art did not mean the same thing in medieval Europe that it means today. An object that a modern person might classify as art would not have been recognized as such in medieval times. The way in which people today think about art was essentially formed
5 during the Renaissance, the flowering of culture that ended the medieval age and transformed the cultural world.

In medieval Europe, artists were thought of as craftsmen, as people who worked with their hands rather than with their minds. The ruling class, the clergy and the nobles, saw artists as
10 tools. A clergyman or nobleman might commission an artist to produce a piece, but it was the commissioner who took credit for bringing that art into the world. The medieval artist was seen as merely an extension of the patron who commissioned the work of art to be made. The artist was the hand; the patron was the mind.
15 This medieval conception of the roles of patron and artist explains why so many medieval artists are anonymous today. In the early 1100s, when a priest named Abbot Suger wrote his record of the rebuilding of the choir and façade of the church of Saint Denis—a project that art historians today mark as the beginning of the
20 Gothic style that would soon come to dominate European architecture—he never mentioned the name of the architect. The name of the artist was considered unimportant.

Just as medieval and modern conceptions of the artist are at odds, so too are medieval and modern understandings of what
25 makes great art. Today, many people judge a piece of art by its originality, and the words "new" and "unique" are often understood as synonyms for "good." But to link originality to quality would have seemed quite foreign to people in medieval times. Back then, it was believed that unoriginality was actually
30 the pinnacle of art: people in medieval times wanted their artists to make near-perfect copies of earlier works rather than try to make some kind of personal expression through "unique" art.

The art historian Ernst Gombrich likens this medieval attitude toward art to our present-day attitude toward classical
35 music. He explains that when we go to a concert, we are not displeased if the orchestra adheres closely to the score. What we want to hear, for example, is a worthy rendition of the great music of Bach—we do not want improvisation. The excellence or mediocrity of the orchestra is measured by its ability to play Bach,
40 not to surpass Bach.

Similarly, a medieval artist who was asked to paint the Virgin Mary holding the Christ Child did not depart from the forms he had learned regarding how the Virgin Mary and the Christ Child ought to be portrayed. The artist could display himself as a
45 master or a bungler by his skill at recreating those forms, but it was the forms that were important. An artist who placed his own ideas and skill above the traditional religious forms might have been condemned as a blasphemer.

10. The author argues that art

(A) has remained constant throughout the centuries
(B) was appreciated more during the Middle Ages and the Renaissance than it is today
(C) too often incorporated or mimicked other works
(D) was, in medieval times, unsophisticated
(E) was seen differently at different periods of history

11. The sentence that describes the artist as a "hand" and the patron as a "mind" (line 14) is an example of:

(A) metaphor
(B) irony
(C) paradox
(D) alliteration
(E) personification

12. In the phrase "when a priest named Abbot Suger ... name of the architect" in lines 17–21 the author is doing which of the following?

(A) providing a concrete example
(B) offering a textual analysis
(C) seeking support from other authorities
(D) considering opposing viewpoints
(E) defining an important term

13. In the fourth paragraph, the author discusses classical music today

(A) to help describe medieval conceptions of art
(B) as an illustration of the discrepancy in funding between concerts and art exhibits
(C) as evidence in the argument calling for increased artistic representations of religious images
(D) to justify adapting art according to one's own improvisation
(E) as a warning against comparing works from different time periods

GO ON TO THE NEXT PAGE

14. In lines 48-50 the sentence "An artist who placed his own ideas and skill...blasphemy" explains why

    (A) medieval artists who produced poor work were punished
    (B) medieval artwork was often improperly credited to the wrong artist
    (C) medieval artists concentrated on following old forms rather than trying to break new ground
    (D) the medieval public was unable to discern between what is art and what is not
    (E) the Renaissance changed the nature of art

15. According to the author, the modern critical judgment of art generally considers

    (A) the time period of a piece of art's creation
    (B) the country of origin and the source of commission for a piece of art
    (C) how readily a piece of art can be compared to classical music
    (D) the dominant style from which the piece of art arises
    (E) the innovative ideas and original features contained within a piece of art

GO ON TO THE NEXT PAGE

Section 4

The passage below is followed by questions based on its content. Answer the questions on the basis of what is <u>stated</u> or <u>implied</u> in the passage and in any introductory material that may be provided.

Questions 16–24 are based on the following passage.

In the following passage, the author discusses the difference between pure science and applied science, and the moral considerations that must be applied to each.

Pure science is a science of discovery, a science of figuring out the physical, chemical, and biological laws governing the universe. A scientist engaged in pure science gains knowledge of a limited sort. He or she may gain an understanding of the actions of
5 particles under certain circumstances, or of the processes which make up the nitrogen cycle, but a researcher who discovers the why's and how's of scientific laws does not attempt to change those laws. Pure scientific research does not directly change the world and therefore does not impinge on the rights or privacy of
10 particular individuals or communities.

Applied science, in contrast, by its definition involves an effort to harness the knowledge gained by pure science for the purpose of achieving specific ends. Applied science aims to change or affect the world. As a result of this aim, applied science holds the
15 potential to greatly benefit humanity and ease humanity's existence in the world. Yet for precisely the same reason that applied science can be such a boon to mankind, because it attempts to affect or change the world in some way, it also holds the potential to cause great harm, whether that harm is explicit,
20 such as the atomic bomb built specifically to destroy, or more subtle, such as the dangers inherent in nuclear reactors that were once trumpeted as the solution to the energy needs of the future. It is only when science becomes manifest in society through application that it can impinge on human rights.

25 Such an assertion seems to free pure scientists and pure science from any responsibility to individuals or society: since pure science seeks to map the laws of the universe rather than bend those laws to human will, there is no danger that the attempt might backfire. Of course, the assertion of such a strict
30 separation between pure and applied science is itself open to criticism. But that distinction seems to hold up rather well for the sciences of matter: physics, chemistry, astronomy.

For example, even in the case of atomic physics, the discovery of which led to the development of the atomic bomb, there exists a
35 marked contrast between the initial discovery of fission and the subsequent effort to develop the bomb during World War II. The scientists involved in building the atomic bomb for the United States justified their efforts in a variety of manners, many claiming a moral imperative to finish developing the bomb before
40 fascist Germany. Whether those justifications ring hollow or true is not the issue (at least not here). Rather, the importance lies in the fact that the scientists saw their justifications as necessary at

all; such a need for justification indicates the existence of a moral ethical space around the bomb building process. J. Robert
45 Oppenheimer, who coordinated the project to build the atomic bomb, powerfully referenced that moral dimension by resorting to biblical language, noting that "the physicists have known sin."

In contrast, no moral dimension surrounded the chemist Otto Hahn as he experimented with the idea of nuclear fission in 1938.
50 Hahn, in fact, had created his experiments expressly to disprove the possibility of fission as a natural phenomenon. Hahn could have made no moral judgment about his work because he had no idea what he might find. Hahn was searching for the truth, whereas the scientists working on the bomb were after specific
55 results whose ethical and moral implications could and should have been weighed.

16. The author's tone in this passage is best described as

(A) angry
(B) concerned
(C) uninterested
(D) pleased
(E) disappointed

17. The phrase "becomes manifest" in line 23 means

(A) becomes obvious in
(B) is introduced to
(C) is fated to
(D) becomes burdensome to
(E) becomes revolutionary for

18. Lines 29–31 discuss challenges to the author's distinction between pure and applied science in order to

(A) weaken the overall argument
(B) suggest other avenues of exploration
(C) admit the author's ignorance
(D) confuse the reader
(E) preempt disagreement

GO ON TO THE NEXT PAGE

Section 4

19. In line 31 the author claims that all of the following fit the rigid distinction between pure and applied sciences EXCEPT

   (A) Physics
   (B) Chemistry
   (C) Astronomy
   (D) Sciences of Matter
   (E) Biology

20. The author uses the parenthetical interjection "at least not here" in line 41 to suggest that

   (A) these particular justifications for building the atomic bomb should be questioned, though the author will not do so in this passage
   (B) any justifications are morally irrelevant
   (C) other essays on this subject concentrate on frivolous matters
   (D) scientists cannot evaluate their own moral reasoning
   (E) applied science needs no justification

21. Which of the following would this author consider an example of pure science?

   (A) researching ways to combat air pollution
   (B) cleaning up hazardous waste
   (C) discovering which rock formations are likely to bear gold
   (D) developing a technique to extract oil from small deposits
   (E) measuring the mass of the earth

22. How would this author feel about an experiment designed to measure the fission rates of various materials?

   (A) This experiment would be pure science and therefore always acceptable.
   (B) The author's feelings would depend on whether the experimenter is aware of potential human uses of fission.
   (C) It depends on the moral worth of the scientist involved.
   (D) This experiment is morally unacceptable.
   (E) The experiment probably would not work.

23. The term "truth" in line 53 means

   (A) the best way to use scientific discoveries
   (B) the ethical context of scientific knowledge
   (C) the physical laws governing the universe
   (D) an understanding of the scientific method
   (E) the intentions of the scientist performing the experiment

24. Which of the following statements best reflects the author's feelings about applied science?

   (A) It is only objectionable if it involves producing weapons.
   (B) It is always objectionable.
   (C) It has no moral component.
   (D) It is potentially beneficial but its consequences need to be considered.
   (E) All scientific research is useful and desirable.

S T O P

IF YOU FINISH BEFORE TIME IS CALLED, YOU MAY CHECK YOUR WORK ON THIS TEST ONLY.
DO NOT TURN TO ANY OTHER SECTION IN THIS TEST.

Section 5

Turn to Section 5 of your answer sheet to answer the questions in this section.

Time—25 Minutes
18 Questions

In this section solve each problem, using any available space on the page for scratchwork. Then decide which is the best of the choices given and fill in the corresponding oval on the answer sheet.

Notes:
1.   The use of a calculator is permitted. All numbers used are real numbers.

2.   Figures that accompany problems in this test are intended to provide information useful in solving the problems. They are drawn as accurately as possible EXCEPT when it is stated in a specific problem that the figure is not drawn to scale. All figures lie in a plane unless otherwise indicated.

3.   Unless otherwise specified, the domain of any function f is assumed to be the set of all real numbers x for which $f(x)$ is a real number.

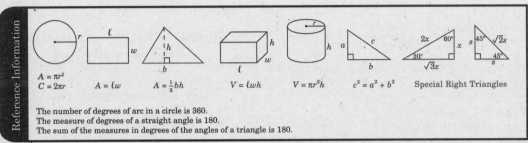

Reference Information

$A = \pi r^2$
$C = 2\pi r$

$A = \ell w$

$A = \frac{1}{2}bh$

$V = \ell wh$

$V = \pi r^2 h$

$c^2 = a^2 + b^2$

Special Right Triangles

The number of degrees of arc in a circle is 360.
The measure of degrees of a straight angle is 180.
The sum of the measures in degrees of the angles of a triangle is 180.

1.   In the equation $y = \dfrac{x^2}{w^2 z}$, if x doubles, w halves, and z quadruples, by what factor will y change?

(A) $\dfrac{1}{4}$

(B) 1

(C) 2

(D) 4

(E) 8

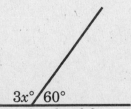

2.   In the figure above, what is the value of x?

(A) 10
(B) 30
(C) 40
(D) 120
(E) 300

3.   The greatest prime factor of 74 is x. The greatest prime factor of 96 is y. What is the value of $x - y$?

(A) −27
(B) 0
(C) 5
(D) 7
(E) 34

4. $f(x) = 2x + 7$ for all real x. What is the slope of the equation $y = f(x + 4)$?

(A) 2
(B) 4
(C) 6
(D) 7
(E) 15

GO ON TO THE NEXT PAGE

Section 5

5. When x is divided by 4, the remainder is 3. When x^2 is divided by 4, what must the remainder be?

(A) 1
(B) 3
(C) 7
(D) 12
(E) 49

6. A particular zebra is the 10th fastest animal in its herd and also the 10th slowest animal in its hard. If every zebra in the herd is of a different speed, then how many zebra are there in the herd?

(A) 18
(B) 19
(C) 20
(D) 21
(E) 22

7. A class holds a bake sale to raise money for a trip. The number of dollars, S, that the students will earn by selling n cupcakes is given by the function $S(n) = 3n - 15$. What is the least number of cupcakes the students must sell in order to make a profit?

(A) 3
(B) 4
(C) 5
(D) 6
(E) 7

8. If $\frac{1}{2}xy = \frac{2}{3}yz$, what is $\frac{x}{z}$? Assume that $y \neq 0$ and $z \neq 0$.

(A) $\frac{3}{4}$
(B) $\frac{4}{3}$
(C) $\frac{7}{4}$
(D) 3
(E) 4

GO ON TO THE NEXT PAGE

Section 5

Directions: for Student-Produced Response Questions 9-18, use the grids at the bottom of the answer sheet page on which you have answered questions 1-8.

Each of the remaining 10 questions requires you to solve the problem and enter your answer by marking the ovals in the special grid, as shown in the examples below.

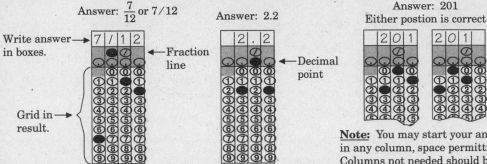

Answer: $\frac{7}{12}$ or 7/12

Write answer in boxes. ← Fraction line

Grid in result.

Answer: 2.2 ← Decimal point

Answer: 201
Either postion is correct

Note: You may start your answers in any column, space permitting. Columns not needed should be left blank.

- Mark no more than one oval in any column.

- Because the answer sheet will be machine-scored, **you will receive credit only if the ovals are filled in completely.**

- Although not required, it is suggested that you write your answer in the boxes at the top of the columns to help you fill in the ovals accurately.

- Some problems may have more than one correct answer. In such cases, grid only one answer

- No question has a negative answer.

- **Mixed numbers** such as $2\frac{1}{2}$ must be gridded as 2.5 or 5/2. If $\boxed{2\ 1\ /\ 2}$ is gridded, it will be interpreted as $\frac{21}{2}$, not $2\frac{1}{2}$.)

- **Decimal Accuracy:** If you obtain a decimal answer, **enter the most accurate value the grid will accommodate.** For example, if you obtain an answer such as 0.6666 . . . , you should record the result as .666 or .667. **Less accurate values such as .66 or .67 are not acceptable.** Acceptable ways to grid $\frac{2}{3}$ = .666 . . .

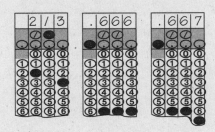

9. What is the area of a square with vertices at $(-1, 3)$, $(2, 3)$, $(2, 0)$, and $(-1, 0)$?

10. The buffet at a business lunch contains 35 sandwiches, 35 sodas, and 50 cookies. If the people at the lunch eat 22 sandwiches, drink 28 sodas, and eat 38 cookies, then what fraction of the total number of food items remain after the lunch is finished?

11. The mean of a, b, c, and d is 24. The mean of a, b, and c is 20. What is d?

GO ON TO THE NEXT PAGE

Section 5

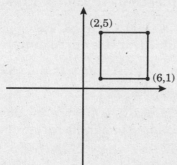
(2,5)
(6,1)

12. What would be the area of a square inscribed in the square pictured in the figure above?

13. $(x^a)^b \times (x^2)^3 = x^9$ for any x. What is the value of ab?

14. What is the y value at the point where the lines $y = \frac{-x}{2} + 6\frac{3}{4}$ and $y = 3x - \frac{1}{4}$ intersect?

Number of Fences	Fence Length
3	3
7	6
8	8
11	5

15. If Joe can paint fences at the rate of 5 feet per hour while Jack can paint at the rate of 10 feet per hour, then how many total hours will it take Joe and Jack to paint all the fences if Joe paints all the 3-foot and 6-foot fences, and Jack paints all the 8-foot and 5-foot fences? (round your answer to the nearest hour)

16. 64 cubes are stacked together to form a single larger cube. Each face of this larger cube is then painted red. If the large cube is then disassembled, and each of the small cubes is dropped into a bag, what is the probability of drawing from the bag a cube that has exactly two of its faces painted red?

17. The expression $\frac{2x^2 - 5x - 12}{x - 4}$ is how much more than $2x$?

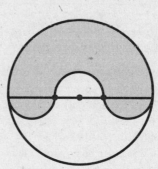

18. Each of the small semicircles has an area of 8π. What is the area of the shaded region divided by π?

S T O P

IF YOU FINISH BEFORE TIME IS CALLED, YOU MAY CHECK YOUR WORK ON THIS TEST ONLY.
DO NOT TURN TO ANY OTHER SECTION IN THIS TEST.

Section 6

Directions: The following sentences test correctness and effectiveness of expression. In choosing answers, follow the requirements of standard written English; that is, pay attention to grammar, choice of words, sentence construction, and punctuation.

   In each of the following sentences, part of the sentence or the entire sentence is underlined. Beneath each sentence you will find five ways of phrasing the underlined part. Choice A repeats the original; the other four are different.

   Choose the answer that best expresses the meaning of the original sentence. If you think the original is better than any of the alternatives, choose it; otherwise choose one of the others. Your choice should produce the most effective sentence—clear and precise, without awkwardness or ambiguity.

EXAMPLE:

Laura Ingalls Wilder published her first book
and she was sixty-five years old then.

(A) and she was sixty-five years old then
(B) when she was sixty-five
(C) at age sixty-five years old
(D) upon the reaching of sixty-five years
(E) at the time when she was sixty-five

SAMPLE ANSWER:

1. Jorge reluctantly agreed to dress up as Santa Claus for the office party, since it involved wearing a heavy, itchy fake belly.

   (A) since it involved wearing a heavy, itchy fake belly
   (B) because it involved wearing a heavy, itchy, fake belly
   (C) but it involved the necessity to wear of a heavy, itchy fake belly
   (D) even though it involved wearing a heavy, itchy fake belly
   (E) it involved wearing a heavy, itchy fake belly

2. The would-be novelist in the café with the world-weary smile says he models himself after Hemingway.

   (A) in the café with the world-weary smile says he models himself
   (B) in the café says he models himself, with a world-weary smile
   (C) says he modeled himself, in the café with the world-weary smile,
   (D) says he models himself, with a world-weary smile, in the café,
   (E) with the world-weary smile in the café says he models himself

3. Even though the rain delay lasted for more than three hours, although only a handful of fans left the stadium.

   (A) although only a handful of fans
   (B) only a handful of fans
   (C) yet even so, only a handful of fans
   (D) and yet only a handful of fans
   (E) and it caused only a handful of fans

GO ON TO THE NEXT PAGE

4. Goya, who began his career painting portraits of royalty, turned to more violent subjects after an illness left him deaf.

   (A) Goya, who began his career painting portraits of royalty, turned
   (B) Goya began his career painting portraits of royalty, he turned
   (C) Goya who once having begun his career painting portraits of royalty, turned
   (D) Goya, because he began his career painting portraits of royalty, turned
   (E) Goya began his career painting portraits of royalty since he turned

5. In advance of the troops, the general who came to scout out the terrain and weigh the tactical benefit of a night attack.

   (A) the general who came to scout out the terrain
   (B) the general, who comes to scout out the terrain
   (C) the general coming to scout out the terrain
   (D) the general came to scout out the terrain
   (E) the general that came to scout out the terrain

6. With her dark eyes and having a cunning look, the older woman was perfect for the part of a murder suspect.

   (A) With her dark eyes and having a cunning look
   (B) Dark eyes and a cunning look
   (C) With her dark eyes and cunning look
   (D) Dark eyes and with her cunning look
   (E) With having a cunning look and dark eyes

7. The open call for a new reality show attracted thousands of applicants, each with a desire to become famous.

   (A) each with a desire to become famous
   (B) they each wanted to become famous
   (C) which all had a desire to become famous
   (D) each having a desire to become famous
   (E) when they each had a desire to become famous

8. Paying off your credit card bill in full every month, while sometimes difficult, is better than to pay outrageous interest rates.

   (A) better than to pay outrageous interest rates
   (B) better, still, than it is paying outrageous interest rates
   (C) not as bad as to pay outrageous interest rates
   (D) compared to paying outrageous interest rates, is better
   (E) better than paying outrageous interest rates

9. Isabella Stuart Gardner, Boston socialite, decided in mid-life to become a serious art collector, and as a result an impressive number of European Renaissance paintings began to be purchased.

   (A) an impressive number of European Renaissance paintings began to be purchased
   (B) an impressive number of European Renaissance paintings were purchased by her
   (C) she began to purchase an impressive number of European Renaissance paintings
   (D) beginning to be purchased were an impressive number of European Renaissance paintings
   (E) the purchasing of an impressive number of European Renaissance paintings

10. In 1974 the ballet dancer Mikhail Baryshnikov defected to the United States, leaving behind the Kirov Ballet to join the New York City Ballet.

   (A) leaving behind the Kirov Ballet to join the New York City Ballet
   (B) and joining the New York City Ballet and leaving the Kirov Ballet
   (C) he joined the New York City Ballet after leaving the Kirov Ballet
   (D) for the leaving of the Kirov Ballet in favor of the New York City Ballet
   (E) and as a result was leaving behind the Kirov Ballet, joining the New York City Ballet

11. One of the most inventive and respected dancers in the world, tap dancing was elevated by Fred Astaire from an entertainment to an art.

   (A) tap dancing was elevated by Fred Astaire
   (B) tap dancing, elevated by Fred Astaire
   (C) tap dancing received elevation from Fred Astaire
   (D) Fred Astaire got elevation from tap dancing
   (E) Fred Astaire elevated tap dancing

GO ON TO THE NEXT PAGE

Section 6

12. Each of the manuscripts in the enormous body of work
                                        A
left unpublished at the author's death poses their own
 B   C   D
problems—and pleasures. No error
                   E

13. Radha has decide to go on the camping trip despite the
           A   B   C
strenuous objections of her friends. No error
              D   E

14. The Eiffel Tower, more than any of Paris's dozens of other tourist
               A   B   C
attractions, have become the symbol of the city. No error
         D   E

15. The amateur-collector kit came complete with instructions
                        A
that explained how to prevent the butterfly to escape the net.
 B   C   D
No error
 E

16. The characters in Kafka's fiction are so isolated and feel so
                     A   B
guilty, that from the beginning the reader feels pessimistic
      C
about their chances for happiness. No error
     D   E

17. Of the dozens of beverages the company makes, its customers
  A   B   C
like seltzer water better. No error
          D   E

18. Today's museums perform several functions: they present new
       A   B
works of art, education for visitors, and exhibit collections.
        C   D
No error
 E

19. Before one attempts to take a political stand on the issue,
you should investigate in depth the pros and cons of both sides of
   A   B   C   D
the argument. No error
           E

20. The first years of Hank Aaron's pro-baseball career were more
                                       A
difficult than other players; he had to endure threats and racist
        B   C
comments from fans and even from his own teammates. No error
                  D   E

21. The restaurant owner requires waiters to take both a course on
                  A   B
wine and a seminar on people skills before he will allow them to
          C   D
serve in his restaurant. No error
               E

22. The tour guide cleared his throat and clapped his hands
                 A   B
together, his usual sign that the start of the tour was eminent.
                C   D
No error
 E

23. I never expected it could be so difficult to take an exam, but this
            A   B
term each have all been very exhausting. No error
      C   D   E

24. The tenor sang so loud that he completely lost his voice,
            A   B
and could not speak for weeks afterwards, much less sing.
   C   D
No error
 E

GO ON TO THE NEXT PAGE

Section 6

25. <u>Wanting to</u> take an active role <u>in public life</u>, Clint Eastwood
    A   B

    <u>ran for and won</u> the position <u>of mayor of</u> Carmel, California.
    C   D

    <u>No error</u>
    E

26. Edith Wharton's character Lily Bart <u>cannot scarcely</u> stand
                                          A

    <u>to marry</u> a poor man, <u>yet at the same time</u> she does not wish
    B   C

    <u>to marry</u> a rich man she dislikes. <u>No error</u>
    D   E

27. A crucial part <u>of developing</u> <u>an appreciation</u> for the work of the
                    A   B

    novelist Muriel Spark <u>is gaining</u> <u>an understanding</u> of her dry,
                           C   D

    subtle humor. <u>No error</u>
                   E

28. The teachers' strike <u>continued</u> until someone <u>came up with</u> a
                          A   B

    plan <u>where</u> the union could work out <u>its</u> differences with the
         C   D

    school board. <u>No error</u>
                   E

29. Neither the liberal <u>nor</u> the conservative candidate
                         A

    <u>were prepared</u> at this time <u>to suggest</u> a <u>date for</u> the next debate.
    B   C   D

    <u>No error</u>
    E

GO ON TO THE NEXT PAGE

Section 6

Questions 30–35 are based on the following passage.

(1) *Obesity is a big problem in the United States.* (2) *Sixty-one percent of adults suffer from it, but around 300,000 people die every year from diseases directly related to obesity.* (3) *Obesity is related to diabetes, high blood pressure, and getting heart disease.*

(4) *Only a healthy diet combined with a regular exercise program can help people lose weight.* (5) *This sounds simple enough, but it proves nearly impossible for most people.* (6) *Many overweight people go on diets to lose weight, trying everything from pills to shakes and formulas advertised on late-night infomercials.* (7) *You can lose weight by almost any method out there.* (8) *One study showed that ninety-five percent of people who lost weight on diets that didn't include exercise gained back all of the weight after they stopped dieting.* (9) *This makes sense, it's unrealistic to expect people to continue drinking only shakes for the rest of their lives.* (10) *Ideally, therefore, reliance on trendy diets would be replaced by a lifelong change in eating and exercise habits.*

(11) *It is not just physical habits that must be changed in order to control obesity.* (12) *Psychology must be considered, too.* (13) *Our intensely weight-conscious society has turned eating from a simple necessity into a loaded psychological endeavor.*

30. Which of the following is the best way to revise the underlined portion of sentence 2, which is reprinted below?

> *Sixty-one percent of adults suffer from it, but around 300,000 people die every year from diseases directly related to obesity.*

(A) suffer from it, but around
(B) suffer, from it but around
(C) suffer from it, and
(D) suffer from it, although
(E) suffer because of it, but around

31. Which of the following is the best way to revise sentence 3, which is reprinted below?

> *Obesity is related to diabetes, high blood pressure, and getting heart disease.*

(A) Obesity is related to diabetes, high blood pressure, and getting heart disease.
(B) Obesity, related to diabetes, high blood pressure, and getting heart disease.
(C) Obesity is related, to diabetes and high blood pressure and to getting heart disease.
(D) Obesity has been related to diabetes high blood pressure, and heart disease.
(E) Obesity is related to diabetes, high blood pressure, and heart disease.

32. Which of the following should be inserted at the beginning of the second paragraph, directly before sentence 4?

(A) Something must be done to stop this dangerous problem.
(B) Faithfully following diets like the Atkins diet can help some people.
(C) Losing weight and keeping it off turns out to be a fairly manageable proposition.
(D) It's important to remember that obesity is not simply a physical problem—it's a psychological one, too.
(E) Obesity poses a serious health risk.

33. Which of the following revisions is most needed in sentence 6?

(A) replace "from" with a comma
(B) change "trying" to "they try"
(C) change "and" to "to"
(D) omit the word "advertised"
(E) insert "most of which do not work" after the word "infomercials"

GO ON TO THE NEXT PAGE

Section 6

34. Which of the following revisions is the best way to combine sentences 7 and 8, reprinted below?

> *You can lose weight by almost any method out there. One study showed that ninety-five percent of people who lost weight on diets that didn't include exercise gained back all of the weight after they stopped dieting.*

(A) You can lose weight by almost any method out there; studies show that ninety-five percent of people who lost weight on diets that didn't include exercise gained back all of the weight after they stopped dieting.

(B) Studies show that ninety-five percent of people who lost weight on diets that didn't include exercise gained back all of the weight after they stopped dieting, but you can lose weight by almost any method out there.

(C) You can lose weight via almost any method out there; studies show that ninety-five percent of people who lost weight on diets that didn't include exercise gained back all of the weight after they stopped dieting.

(D) Studies show that even though ninety-five percent of people who lost weight on diets that didn't include exercise gained back all of the weight after they stopped dieting, you can lose weight by almost any method out there.

(E) Although you can lose weight by almost any method out there, studies show that ninety-five percent of people who lost weight on diets that didn't include exercise gained back all of the weight after they stopped dieting.

35. Which of the following is the best way to revise the underlined portion of sentence 9, which is reprinted below?

> *This makes <u>sense, it's unrealistic</u> to expect people to continue drinking only shakes for the rest of their lives.*

(A) sense it's unrealistic
(B) sense; it's unrealistic
(C) sense, its unrealistic
(D) sense, yes it's
(E) sense it is unrealistic

S T O P

Section 7

Each sentence below has one or two blanks, each blank indicating that something has been omitted. Beneath the sentence are five words or sets of words labeled A through E. Choose the word or set of words that, when inserted in the sentence, best fits the meaning of the sentence as a whole.

Example:

Medieval kingdoms did not become constitutional republics overnight; on the contrary, the change was ----.

(A) unpopular
(B) unexpected
(C) advantageous
(D) sufficient
(E) gradual

1. Elroy had lost money in the stock market before, but he was convinced that his new investments would bring him ----.

(A) deficit
(B) profit
(C) shares
(D) health
(E) power

2. Terrified of the prospect of war, the ambassador did everything he could to bring about ---- between the two nations.

(A) demoralization
(B) aggression
(C) misconception
(D) prejudice
(E) reconciliation

3. The numerous firings and layoffs that the company has suffered ---- the financial difficulties that have characterized its last few years.

(A) refute
(B) devastate
(C) confirm
(D) endanger
(E) nurture

4. In choosing a president, many Americans are most interested in ----, basing their votes on issues of character and morality.

(A) temerity
(B) exuberance
(C) irreverence
(D) gravity
(E) integrity

5. The jurors viewed the defendant's refusal to testify at her trial as a ---- acknowledgment of her guilt.

(A) libelous
(B) tacit
(C) saccharine
(D) magnanimous
(E) tranquil

6. The author quickly lost sight of his original plan to write a ---- comedy, and instead penned a weighty ---- on a highly tragic theme.

(A) flippant..meditation
(B) maudlin..satire
(C) scintillating..farce
(D) banal..narrative
(E) wretched..proposition

GO ON TO THE NEXT PAGE

Section 7

The passages below are followed by questions based on their content. Answer the questions on the basis of what is <u>stated</u> or <u>implied</u> in the passages and in any introductory material that may be provided.

Questions 7–19 are based on the following passages. Hamlet, published in 1603, was written by William Shakespeare. The play tells the story of Hamlet, a prince of Denmark, whose father dies and whose mother remarries her former husband's brother, Claudius. Soon after the marriage, Hamlet encounters his father's ghost, who claims to have been murdered by Claudius and demands that Hamlet take revenge. Yet Hamlet hesitates to take action. The passages below are adaptations of two essays that discuss Hamlet's psychology.

Passage 1

The death of Hamlet's father was a natural evil, and as such he endures it. That he is excluded by his mother's marriage from succeeding immediately to the royalty that belongs to him seems to affect him slightly; he seems above vehemence and vain
5 ambition. He is moved by finer principles, by an exquisite sense of virtue and moral beauty. The impropriety of Gertrude's behavior, her ingratitude to the memory of her former husband, and the depravity she displays in the choice of a successor afflict Hamlet's soul and cast him into utter agony. Here then is the principle and
10 spring of all his actions.

The man whose sense of moral excellence is uncommonly exquisite will find it a source of pleasure and of pain in his commerce with mankind. Susceptible to every moral impression, he delights at the display of virtuous actions, and the contrary
15 excite uneasiness.

The triumph and inward joy of a son, on account of the fame and high desert of a parent, is by nature very sublime and tender. His sorrow is no less acute and overwhelming if those connected to him by such intimate relations have acted unbecomingly and
20 incurred disgrace. Such is the condition of Hamlet. Exquisitely sensible of moral beauty and deformity, he discerns depravity in Gertrude, his mother. Led by the same moral principle to admire and glory in the high desert of his father, even this admiration contributes to his uneasiness. Aversion to his uncle, arising from
25 the same origin, augments his anguish.

Agitated and overwhelmed with afflicting images, no soothing, no exhilarating affection can have admission into his heart. His imagination is visited by no vision of happiness; and he wishes for deliverance from his afflictions, by being delivered from a painful
30 existence.

Passage 2

Of all the characters of Shakespeare, that of Hamlet has been generally thought the most difficult to be reduced to any fixed or settled principle. With the strongest purposes of revenge, he is irresolute and inactive; amidst the gloom of deepest melancholy,
35 he is gay and jocular; and while he is described as a passionate lover, he seems indifferent about the object of his affections. It may be worthwhile to inquire whether any leading idea can be found, upon which these apparent contradictions may be reconciled. I will venture to lay before my readers some
40 observations on this subject.

The basis of Hamlet's character seems to be an extreme sensibility of mind, apt to be strongly impressed by its situation, and overpowered by the feelings which that situation excites. Naturally a virtuous man, Hamlet finds himself in circumstances
45 which unhinge his noble principles of action, which, in another situation, would have delighted mankind, and made himself happy. That kind of distress which he suffered was, beyond all others, calculated to produce this effect. His misfortunes were not the misfortunes of accident, which, though they may overwhelm
50 at first, the mind will soon call up reflection to alleviate, and hopes to cheer: they were such as reflection only serves to irritate, such as rankle in the soul's tenderest part; they arose from an uncle's villainy, a mother's guilt, a father's murder! Yet, amidst the gloom of melancholy, and the agitation of passion, in which his
55 calamities involve him, there are occasional breakings-out of a mind richly endowed by nature. We perceive gentleness in his demeanor, wit in his conversation, taste in his amusements, and wisdom in his reflections.

That Hamlet's character, thus formed by nature, and thus
60 modeled by situation, is often variable and uncertain, I am not disposed to deny. I will content myself with the supposition that this is the very character which Shakespeare meant to give Hamlet. Finding such a character in real life, of a person endowed with feelings so delicate as to border on weakness, with sensibility
65 too exquisite to allow for determined action, he has placed it where it could be best exhibited, in scenes of wonder, of terror, and of indignation, where its varying emotions might be most strongly marked amidst the workings of imagination, and the war of passions.

70 This management of the character creates in us the most interest in his behalf. Had Shakespeare made Hamlet pursue his vengeance with a steady determined purpose, had he led him through difficulties arising from accidental causes, and not from the doubts and hesitations of his own mind, the anxiety of the
75 spectator might have been highly raised; but it would have been anxiety for the event, not for the person. As it is, we feel not only the virtues, but the weakness of Hamlet, as our own.

GO ON TO THE NEXT PAGE

7. According to passage 1, what is the general cause of Hamlet's unhappiness?

   (A) his psychological instability, which prevents him from being able to act
   (B) his intense jealousy that his uncle inherited the throne after his father died
   (C) his essential cowardice, combined with a powerful desire not to seem cowardly to those around him
   (D) his grief over his father's death
   (E) his acute moral sensitivity, aggravated by his reactions to the behavior of his parents and his uncle

8. According to the author of passage 1, what exactly does Gertrude do to disturb Hamlet so greatly (lines 6–9)?

   (A) She knowingly marries the man who murdered his father.
   (B) She fails to honor his father's memory, and exhibits very poor judgment in choosing a new husband.
   (C) She demonstrates that it was only the example of his father that kept her behavior in check.
   (D) She begins to abuse her power over the common people.
   (E) She supports Claudius's attempt to take over the throne of Denmark.

9. What is the meaning of the word "commerce" in passage 1, line 13?

   (A) economic activity
   (B) salesmanship
   (C) moral judgment
   (D) interaction
   (E) emotional response

10. What is the logical implication of the author's observation about a child's reactions to his parents' behavior in passage 1, lines 16–17?

    (A) A sensitive child will feel intense pride or shame based on the moral worth of his or her parents.
    (B) An intelligent child will realize that the behavior of parents does not always reflect on their child.
    (C) A child will be quick to seek revenge on anyone who insults or injures a beloved parent.
    (D) Children always have strong feelings about their parents.
    (E) Parents do not always think of their children's feelings before they act.

11. How would you describe the author's tone in the final paragraph of passage 1 (lines 26–30)?

    (A) defiant
    (B) dramatic and descriptive
    (C) measured and scholarly
    (D) resigned
    (E) confrontational

12. In line 35, what is "jocular" used to mean?

    (A) morbid, melancholy
    (B) violent, confrontational
    (C) giddy, happy
    (D) vengeful
    (E) confused, inactive

13. In the second paragraph of passage 2, what two kinds of misfortune does the author compare?

    (A) misfortunes that one can remedy and misfortunes that one can do nothing about
    (B) misfortunes arising from accidental circumstance and misfortunes arising from the intentionally wicked behavior of others
    (C) misfortunes that detrimentally effect all concerned and misfortunes that harm some and benefit others
    (D) misfortunes that cause frustration and misfortunes that cause despair
    (E) misfortunes caused by others and misfortunes that one brings upon oneself

14. According to lines 63–69, why might Shakespeare have chosen to make Hamlet's character so inconsistent and variable?

    (A) Shakespeare was attempting to portray his idea of psychological complexity, which involved self-contradiction.
    (B) The demands of the plot required the main character to act one way at one time and another way at another time.
    (C) It was necessary to provide comic relief in the intensely disturbing story.
    (D) He wanted to make Hamlet puzzling and mysterious to his audience.
    (E) Shakespeare observed similar traits in real individuals and chose to examine them on the stage.

GO ON TO THE NEXT PAGE

Section 7

15. According to the final paragraph of passage 2 (lines 70–77), what does Shakespeare do to make us feel Hamlet's strengths and weaknesses "as our own"?

   (A) He makes Hamlet struggle against his own thoughts and feelings rather than against outer events.

   (B) He makes all the characters around Hamlet seem suspect so that Hamlet is the only person with whom the reader can identify.

   (C) He imbues Hamlet's personal struggles with deep truths common to all human experience.

   (D) He makes Hamlet the victim of fate rather than the victim of circumstance.

   (E) He portrays the moral universe of the play in very stark terms of good and evil so that all viewers will be drawn to one side or the other.

16. According to passage 2, what is the main cause of Hamlet's inability to act on his desire for revenge?

   (A) His moral awareness causes him to deliberate endlessly on the moral questions involved in killing Claudius.

   (B) Despite the pain she has caused him, he still loves his mother too much to kill her husband.

   (C) He worries that, in killing Claudius, he would lower himself to Claudius's level and be no better than a common murderer.

   (D) He is acutely hurt by his family's traumatic situation, causing his natural inconsistency to rise to the fore.

   (E) He is naturally fearful and worries about the repercussions of killing the King of Denmark.

17. What aspect of Hamlet's character, very important to the author of passage 2, does the author of passage 1 fail to address?

   (A) Hamlet's violent temper
   (B) Hamlet's sensitivity to his family's behavior
   (C) Hamlet's variable, inconstant behavior
   (D) Hamlet's melancholy mood
   (E) Hamlet's temptation to sin

18. Both passages indicate that Hamlet's mother

   (A) has been a moral example for Hamlet
   (B) is a beloved figure in Denmark
   (C) is innocent of Hamlet's father's death
   (D) deeply loves Claudius, her new husband
   (E) behaves immorally and inappropriately

19. What is the main difference between the two passages' descriptions of Hamlet's sensitivity?

   (A) Passage 1 emphasizes Hamlet's sensitivity to the behavior of his mother, father, and uncle, while passage 2 focuses on his sensitivity to his own feelings.

   (B) Passage 1 argues that Hamlet's sensitivity is to morality, while passage 2 is concerned with his sensitivity to insults and injuries.

   (C) Passage 1 is concerned with Hamlet's sensitivity to beauty, while passage 2 is concerned with his sensitivity to insults and injuries.

   (D) Passage 1 discusses Hamlet's sensitivity to moral behavior, while passage 2 discusses Hamlet's sensitivity to events in general.

   (E) Passage 1 explores the effects of Hamlet's sensitivity, while passage 2 explores its causes.

S T O P

IF YOU FINISH BEFORE TIME IS CALLED, YOU MAY CHECK YOUR WORK ON THIS TEST ONLY.
DO NOT TURN TO ANY OTHER SECTION IN THIS TEST.

Section 8

Time—20 Minutes
15 Questions

In this section solve each problem, using any available space on the page for scratchwork. Then decide which is the best of the choices given and fill in the corresponding oval on the answer sheet.

Notes:

1. The use of a calculator is permitted. All numbers used are real numbers.

2. Figures that accompany problems in this test are intended to provide information useful in solving the problems. They are drawn as accurately as possible EXCEPT when it is stated in a specific problem that the figure is not drawn to scale. All figures lie in a plane unless otherwise indicated.

3. Unless otherwise specified, the domain of any function f is assumed to be the set of all real numbers x for which $f(x)$ is a real number.

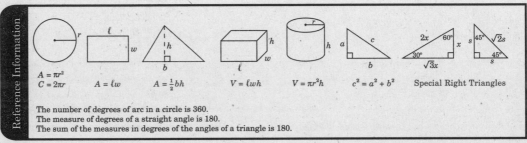

$A = \pi r^2$
$C = 2\pi r$

$A = \ell w$

$A = \frac{1}{2} bh$

$V = \ell wh$

$V = \pi r^2 h$

$c^2 = a^2 + b^2$

Special Right Triangles

The number of degrees of arc in a circle is 360.
The measure of degrees of a straight angle is 180.
The sum of the measures in degrees of the angles of a triangle is 180.

---

1. If $x + 9$ is an even integer, then which of the following integers could be x?

   (A) −4
   (B) −2
   (C) 0
   (D) 3
   (E) 6

3. If $x + y + z = 10$, $x + y = 3$, and $y + z = 8$, what is y?

   (A) −5
   (B) −1
   (C) 1
   (D) 2
   (E) 5

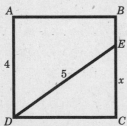

2. If *ABCD* is a square, what is the value of x?

   (A) 3
   (B) 4
   (C) 5
   (D) 6
   (E) 7

GO ON TO THE NEXT PAGE

Section 8

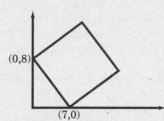

(0,8)

(7,0)

4. What is the area of the square pictured above?

(A) 49
(B) 56
(C) 64
(D) 112
(E) 113

5. $\sqrt{xyz} = (xyz)^{2m}$. What is the value of m? Assume that x, y, and z are all positive integers.

(A) $\dfrac{1}{16}$
(B) $\dfrac{1}{4}$
(C) $\dfrac{1}{2}$
(D) 1
(E) 4

6. The graph in the figure above could be a reasonable result of which of the following functions?

(A) The weight of a steel rod of standard width as a function of length
(B) The age of a rock as a function of time
(C) The height of a man as a function of time
(D) The temperature of a bowl of soup as a function of time
(E) The volume of a sphere as a function of radius

7. If $\dfrac{1}{x-y} < \dfrac{1}{y-x}$, then which of the following must be true?

I. $x > y$
II. $x > -y$
III. $xy > 0$

(A) I only
(B) II only
(C) III only
(D) I and III only
(E) I, II, and III

8. How do the graphs of the equations $y = x + 2$ and $y = \dfrac{x^2 - 4}{x - 2}$ compare?

(A) They are completely different
(B) They are identical
(C) They are completely different, except at point $x = 2$, where they intersect
(D) They are identical, except at point $x = 2$
(E) They are identical, except at point $x = 4$

9. Set A contains the 11 students in Mrs. Applethwaite's advanced music class who know how to play the flute. Set B contains the 7 students who know how to play the piano. If every student in Mrs. Applethwaite's class knows how to play either the flute, the piano, or both, and the entire class contains 13 students, then how many students occupy Set C, which is the intersection of Set A and Set B?

(A) 4
(B) 5
(C) 6
(D) 13
(E) 18

10. A square is inscribed within a circle that is itself inscribed within another square. If the length of one side of the smaller square is 4, then what is the area of the larger square?

(A) $\sqrt{32}$
(B) 32
(C) 64
(D) 72
(E) $96\sqrt{3}$

GO ON TO THE NEXT PAGE

Section 8

11. If $2y^{-2} = \frac{1}{2}x^{\frac{1}{2}}$, and $y = 4$, then what is the value of x?

    (A) $\frac{1}{16}$

    (B) $\frac{1}{4}$

    (C) $\frac{1}{2}$

    (D) 2

    (E) 4

12. For what value of x is $xyz + 2$ equal to $4 - xyz$?

    (A) yz

    (B) $2yz$

    (C) $\frac{yz}{2}$

    (D) $\frac{1}{yz}$

    (E) $6 + 2yz$

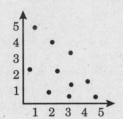

13. Which of the following is the best description of the slope, m, of the line for the scatterplot pictured above?

    (A) $m = 2$

    (B) $m = 1$

    (C) $m = 0$

    (D) $m = -\frac{1}{2}$

    (E) $m = -1$

14. If $f(x) = \sqrt{3x - 3}$ and $g(x) = \frac{1}{x-1}$, what is the domain of $g(f(x))$?

    (A) $x > \frac{4}{3}$

    (B) $x \neq \frac{4}{3}$ and $x \neq 4$

    (C) $x > 1$

    (D) $1 < x < \frac{4}{3}$ and $x > \frac{4}{3}$

    (E) $x < 1$ and $x > \frac{4}{3}$

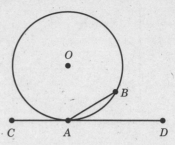

Figure Not Drawn to Scale

15. In the figure above, chord AB and the radius of circle O are both equal to 6, and line segment CD is tangent to point A. If a triangle AOD is drawn, such that line segment OD passes through point B, then what would be the area of triangle AOD?

    (A) $6\pi - 9\sqrt{3}$

    (B) $9\sqrt{3}$

    (C) 36

    (D) $18\sqrt{3}$

    (E) $36(\pi - 1)$

16. A company has 40 more men than women as employees. If the company has y female employees, then what percent of the employees are women in terms of y?

    (A) $\frac{y}{y - 40}$

    (B) $\frac{y}{y + 40}$

    (C) $\frac{y}{2y + 40}$

    (D) $\frac{100y}{y + 40}$

    (E) $\frac{100y}{2y + 40}$

S T O P

IF YOU FINISH BEFORE TIME IS CALLED, YOU MAY CHECK YOUR WORK ON THIS TEST ONLY.
DO NOT TURN TO ANY OTHER SECTION IN THIS TEST.

Section 9

Turn to Section 9 of your answer sheet to answer the questions in this section.

Time—10 Minutes
14 Questions

For each question in this section, select the best answer from among the choices given and fill in the corresponding oval on the answer sheet.

Directions: The following sentences test correctness and effectiveness of expression. In choosing answers, follow the requirements of standard written English; that is, pay attention to grammar, choice of words, sentence construction, and punctuation.

In each of the following sentences, part of the sentence or the entire sentence is underlined. Beneath each sentence you will find five ways of phrasing the underlined part. Choice A repeats the original; the other four are different.

Choose the answer that best expresses the meaning of the original sentence. If you think the original is better than any of the alternatives, choose it; otherwise choose one of the others. Your choice should produce the most effective sentence—clear and precise, without awkwardness or ambiguity.

EXAMPLE:

Laura Ingalls Wilder published her first book and she was sixty-five years old then.

(A) and she was sixty-five years old then
(B) when she was sixty-five
(C) at age sixty-five years old
(D) upon the reaching of sixty-five years
(E) at the time when she was sixty-five

SAMPLE ANSWER:

1. Elvis Presley recorded his first album and he was only seventeen.

   (A) and he was only seventeen
   (B) when only he was seventeen
   (C) but he was only seventeen
   (D) when he was only seventeen
   (E) when seventeen only

2. Almost all the known planets have moons, but only Saturn is having rings.

   (A) and only Saturn is having rings
   (B) but only Saturn has rings
   (C) and Saturn had been ringed
   (D) and only Saturn had rings
   (E) but Saturn only has rings

3. Driving above the speed limit is never justified, even in an emergency, it is against the law.

   (A) an emergency, it is against the law
   (B) an emergency is against the law
   (C) an emergency, because it is against the law
   (D) an emergency, because to speed is against the law
   (E) an emergency, driving above the speed limit is against the law

4. More sheep lives in New Zealand than people.

   (A) More sheep lives in New Zealand than people
   (B) More sheep are living in New Zealand than people are living in New Zealand
   (C) Living in New Zealand are more sheep than people
   (D) In New Zealand lives more sheep than people
   (E) More sheep live in New Zealand than people

GO ON TO THE NEXT PAGE

5. Oceanographers hope someday to explore the deepest regions of the sea <u>by using submarines piloted by robots</u>.

    (A) by using submarines piloted by robots
    (B) by robotically piloted submarines
    (C) by the use of robots piloting submarines
    (D) and to use robots
    (E) and robots will pilot the submarines that explore there

6. Maya Angelou <u>to advance the women's rights movement</u>.

    (A) also to help advance the women's rights movement
    (B) has advanced helping the women's rights movement
    (C) has helped to advance the women's rights movement
    (D) has helped the advanced women's rights movement
    (E) is helping in the advancing of women's rights

7. Though justice should be blind, it's just not accurate <u>claiming that any system of law can be truly impartial</u>.

    (A) claiming that any system of law can be truly impartial
    (B) for a system of law to be truly impartial is also impossible
    (C) to claim that any system of law can be truly impartial
    (D) for claiming that no system of law is truly impartial
    (E) than truly impartial law systems are impossible

8. Cartographers must always create maps <u>that are accurate and have also been easy to use</u>.

    (A) that are accurate and have also been easy to use
    (B) that are easy to use and be accurate
    (C) that are easy to use with accuracy
    (D) of accuracy and ease of use
    (E) that are accurate and easy to use

9. To give the public a forum to evaluate politicians, such as presidential candidates, <u>the government holds political debates</u>.

    (A) the government holds political debates
    (B) political debates are held by the government
    (C) political debates, by the government, are held
    (D) the government is held to political debates
    (E) political debates are to be held by the government

10. The real estate developer was unflagging in his refusal to answer the board's questions <u>and he eventually reversed his position</u> and told them what they wanted to hear.

    (A) and he eventually reversed his position
    (B) since he eventually reversed his position
    (C) but he eventually reversed his position
    (D) therefore he eventually reversed his position
    (E) because he eventually reversed his position

11. In addition to being a phenomenal nonfiction writer, the author Alfred Biegel <u>was exploring Antarctica courageously</u>.

    (A) was exploring Antarctica courageously
    (B) also was exploring Antarctica courageously
    (C) explored Antarctica courageously
    (D) was an explorer of Antarctica, and courageous
    (E) was also a courageously exploring Antarctica visitor

GO ON TO THE NEXT PAGE

Section 9

12. <u>Even though they work in extremely cramped conditions, such as aboard small spacecrafts, astronauts who have returned from successful space missions tend not to complain at all about the lack of space aboard their crafts</u>.

(A) Even though they work in extremely cramped conditions, such as aboard small spacecrafts, astronauts who have returned from successful space missions tend not to complain at all about the lack of space aboard their crafts.

(B) Even though, after returning from successful missions, they tend not to be complaining about the lack of space aboard their crafts, astronauts work in extremely cramped conditions, such as aboard small spacecrafts.

(C) Even though they return from successful missions having tended not to complain about the lack of space aboard their crafts, astronauts work in extremely cramped conditions, such as aboard small spacecrafts.

(D) Even though they tend not to complain about working in extremely cramped conditions, such as aboard small spacecrafts, astronauts return from successful space missions tending not to complain at all about the lack of space aboard their crafts.

(E) Astronauts who have returned from successful space missions, tending not to complain at all about the lack of space aboard their crafts, work in extremely cramped conditions, such as aboard small spacecrafts.

13. Since California has hundreds of miles of coastline and tends to experience earthquakes, <u>this leads many experts to speculate they will someday fall into the ocean</u>.

(A) this leads many experts to speculate they will someday fall into the ocean

(B) many experts speculate that the state will someday fall into the ocean

(C) many experts speculate that it will someday fall into the ocean

(D) someday it will fall into the ocean, many experts speculate

(E) it may fall into the ocean someday, as speculated by experts

14. Most people know that rock climbing is very dangerous, <u>but few know that it's also one of the most effective means of exercise</u>.

(A) but few know that it's also one of the most effective means of exercise

(B) and few know that it's also one of the most effective means of exercise

(C) but few know that as a means of exercise it's the most effective

(D) but few know that it's more effective as a means of exercise

(E) so few know that it's also most effective as a means of exercise

S T O P

IF YOU FINISH BEFORE TIME IS CALLED, YOU MAY CHECK YOUR WORK ON THIS TEST ONLY.
DO NOT TURN TO ANY OTHER SECTION IN THIS TEST.

PRACTICE TEST 2
EXPLANATIONS

TEST 2 ANSWERS

Question Number	Answer	Right	Wrong	Question Number	Answer	Right	Wrong
Section 2				**Section 4, continued**			
1	B	___	___	8	A	___	___
2	B	___	___	9	E	___	___
3	B	___	___	10	E	___	___
4	E	___	___	11	A	___	___
5	E	___	___	12	A	___	___
6	D	___	___	13	A	___	___
7	D	___	___	14	C	___	___
8	B	___	___	15	E	___	___
9	E	___	___	16	B	___	___
10	E	___	___	17	B	___	___
11	C	___	___	18	E	___	___
12	C	___	___	19	E	___	___
13	B	___	___	20	A	___	___
14	B	___	___	21	E	___	___
15	E	___	___	22	B	___	___
16	A	___	___	23	C	___	___
17	A	___	___	24	D	___	___
18	D	___	___	**Section 5**			
19	C	___	___	1	D	___	___
20	A	___	___	2	C	___	___
21	B	___	___	3	E	___	___
22	B	___	___	4	E	___	___
23	A	___	___	5	A	___	___
24	E	___	___	6	B	___	___
Section 3				7	D	___	___
1	A	___	___	8	B	___	___
2	B	___	___	9	9	___	___
3	C	___	___	10	4/15	___	___
4	B	___	___	11	36	___	___
5	C	___	___	12	8	___	___
6	E	___	___	13	3	___	___
7	C	___	___	14	23/4	___	___
8	D	___	___	15	22	___	___
9	D	___	___	16	3/8	___	___
10	D	___	___	17	3	___	___
11	A	___	___	18	80	___	___
12	B	___	___	**Section 6**			
13	D	___	___	1	D	___	___
14	C	___	___	2	E	___	___
15	E	___	___	3	B	___	___
16	A	___	___	4	A	___	___
17	A	___	___	5	D	___	___
18	C	___	___	6	C	___	___
19	E	___	___	7	A	___	___
20	A	___	___	8	E	___	___
Section 4				9	C	___	___
1	A	___	___	10	A	___	___
2	D	___	___	11	E	___	___
3	D	___	___	12	D	___	___
4	D	___	___	13	A	___	___
5	D	___	___	14	D	___	___
6	B	___	___	15	D	___	___
7	B	___	___	16	E	___	___

Question Number	Answer	Right	Wrong	Question Number	Answer	Right	Wrong
Section 6, continued				Section 7, continued			
17	D	___	___	17	C	___	___
18	C	___	___	18	E	___	___
19	A	___	___	19	D	___	___
20	C	___	___	Section 8			
21	E	___	___	1	D	___	___
22	D	___	___	2	A	___	___
23	C	___	___	3	C	___	___
24	A	___	___	4	E	___	___
25	E	___	___	5	B	___	___
26	A	___	___	6	C	___	___
27	E	___	___	7	A	___	___
28	C	___	___	8	D	___	___
29	B	___	___	9	B	___	___
30	C	___	___	10	B	___	___
31	E	___	___	11	A	___	___
32	A	___	___	12	D	___	___
33	C	___	___	13	E	___	___
34	E	___	___	14	D	___	___
35	B	___	___	15	D	___	___
Section 7				16	E	___	___
1	B	___	___	Section 9			
2	E	___	___	1	A	___	___
3	C	___	___	2	B	___	___
4	E	___	___	3	C	___	___
5	B	___	___	4	E	___	___
6	A	___	___	5	A	___	___
7	E	___	___	6	C	___	___
8	B	___	___	7	C	___	___
9	D	___	___	8	E	___	___
10	A	___	___	9	A	___	___
11	B	___	___	10	C	___	___
12	C	___	___	11	B	___	___
13	B	___	___	12	A	___	___
14	E	___	___	13	B	___	___
15	A	___	___	14	A	___	___
16	D	___	___				

CALCULATING YOUR SCORE

Writing Section Raw Score

A. Essay Score (from 1–6)

_____
A

B. Section 6 Multiple-Choice: _____ – (_____ ÷ 4) = _____
                        no. correct   no. incorrect   B

C. Section 9 Multiple-Choice: _____ – (_____ ÷ 4) = _____
                        no. correct   no. incorrect   C

D. Unrounded Multiple-Choice Score (B + C)

_____
D

E. Total Rounded Multiple- Choice Raw Score
(Rounded to the nearest whole number)

_____
E

F. Total Scaled Score
(See the Writing conversion table on the following pages)

_____
SAT Writing
Score

G. Writing Multiple-Choice Subscore
(See the Writing Multiple-Choice conversion table on the following pages)

_____
Writing MC
Score

Math Section Raw Score

A. Section 3 Raw Score: _____ – (_____ ÷ 4) = _____
                 no. correct   no. incorrect   Subtotal A

B. Section 5 Raw Score: _____
                 no. correct   Subtotal B

C. Section 8 Raw Score: _____ – (_____ ÷ 4) = _____
                 no. correct   no. incorrect   Subtotal C

D. Total Unrounded Raw Score
(Total A + B + C)

_____
D

E. Total Rounded Raw Score (Rounded to the nearest whole number)

_____
E

F. Scaled Score
(See the conversion table on the following pages)

_____
SAT Math
Score

Critical Reading Section Raw Score

A. Section 2 Raw Score:

_____ − (_____ ÷ 4) = _____

no. correct ⟶ no. incorrect ⟶ A

B. Section 4 Raw Score:

_____ − (_____ ÷ 4) = _____

no. correct ⟶ no. incorrect ⟶ B

C. Section 7 Raw Score:

_____ − (_____ ÷ 4) = _____

no. correct ⟶ no. incorrect ⟶ C

D. Total Unrounded Raw Score
(Total A + B + C)

_____

D

E. Total Rounded Raw Score
(Rounded to the nearest whole number)

_____

E

F. Scaled Score
(See the conversion table on the next page)

_____

SAT Critical
Reading
Score

the
new
SAT

CONVERTING YOUR RAW SCORES

Raw Score	Critical Reading Scaled Score	Math Scaled Score
67	800	
66	790	
65	770	
64	760	
63	750	
62	740	
61	720	
60	710	
59	700	
58	690	
57	680	
56	670	
55	670	
54	660	800
53	650	780
52	640	760
51	640	740
50	630	730
49	620	710
48	610	700
47	610	690
46	600	670
45	590	660
44	590	650
43	580	650
42	580	640
41	570	630
40	560	620
39	560	610
38	550	600
37	540	590
36	540	590
35	530	580
34	530	570
33	520	560
32	510	560
31	510	550
30	500	540
29	500	530
28	490	520
27	480	520
26	480	510
25	470	500
24	470	490
23	460	490
22	450	480
21	450	470
20	440	460
19	430	460

Raw Score	Critical Reading Scaled Score	Math Scaled Score
18	430	450
17	420	440
16	410	430
15	410	430
14	400	420
13	390	410
12	380	400
11	380	390
10	370	380
9	360	380
8	350	370
7	340	360
6	330	340
5	320	330
4	310	320
3	300	310
2	280	290
1	270	280
0	250	260
-1	250	250
-2	240	240
-3	230	230
-4	220	220
-5	210	210
-6	200	200

Writing Subscores

- **Essay Subscore**: Subtotal A from Writing Score (page 470)
- **Multiple-Choice Subscore**: Calculate by plugging in Subtotal E from your writing score (page 470) into the score conversion table below

Raw Score	Multiple-Choice Subscore	Raw Score	Multiple-Choice Subscore
49	80	30	59
48	79	29	58
47	77	28	57
46	76	27	56
45	75	26	55
44	74	25	54
43	72	24	53
42	71	23	52
41	70	22	51
40	69	21	51
39	68	20	50
38	67	19	49
37	66	18	48
36	65	17	47
35	64	16	46
34	63	15	45
33	62	14	44
32	61	13	43
31	60	12	42

the new SAT

Raw Score	Multiple-Choice Subscore
11	41
10	40
9	39
8	38
7	37
6	36
5	35
4	34
3	33

Raw Score	Multiple-Choice Subscore
2	32
1	30
0	29
-1	27
-2	25
-3	24
-4	23
-5	22
-6	21

Writing Scaled Score

MC raw score	Writing Scaled Score — Essay Score					
	6	5	4	3	2	1
49	800	790	780	470	720	700
48	790	780	760	730	700	680
47	780	770	750	720	690	670
46	770	760	740	710	680	660
45	770	750	740	700	670	650
44	760	750	730	690	660	640
43	750	740	710	680	650	630
42	750	730	700	670	640	620
41	740	730	690	660	630	610
40	740	720	690	650	620	600
39	740	710	680	640	610	590
38	730	700	670	630	610	590
37	720	690	660	630	600	580
36	710	680	650	620	590	570
35	710	680	640	610	580	560
34	700	670	640	600	570	550
33	690	660	630	590	560	540
32	680	650	620	580	560	540
31	670	640	610	580	550	530
30	660	630	600	570	540	520
29	650	630	590	560	530	510
28	640	620	590	550	520	510
27	640	610	580	540	510	490
26	630	600	570	530	500	490
25	620	590	560	520	500	480
24	610	580	550	510	490	470
23	600	570	540	510	480	460
22	590	570	530	500	470	450
21	590	570	530	500	470	450
20	580	560	520	490	460	440
19	570	550	520	480	450	430
18	570	540	520	470	440	420
17	560	530	510	460	430	420
16	550	520	500	450	430	410
15	540	510	490	450	420	400
14	530	500	480	440	410	390
13	520	500	470	430	400	380
12	510	490	460	420	390	370

Writing Scaled Score

MC raw score	Essay Score					
	6	5	4	3	2	1
11	510	480	450	410	380	360
10	500	470	450	400	370	350
9	490	460	440	390	360	350
8	480	450	430	390	360	340
7	470	440	420	380	350	330
6	460	430	410	370	340	320
5	450	430	400	360	330	310
4	450	420	390	350	320	300
3	440	410	390	340	310	290
2	430	400	380	330	300	280
1	420	380	370	320	290	270
0	400	370	350	310	280	260
-1	380	360	340	290	270	260
-2	370	340	320	270	260	250
-3	360	330	310	260	250	240
-4	350	320	290	250	240	230
-5	340	310	280	240	230	220
-6	340	310	280	240	220	210

ESSAY

A 6 Essay

It is not always true that wisdom only comes with age because children and young people often demonstrate wisdom. You can see this in Henry James's novel What Maisie Knew; *you can also find it in Martin Amis's novel* The Rachel Papers. *Finally, there is the example of Bobby Fischer, a chess prodigy who astounded players worldwide by beating even the most experienced adult chess players. In all of these examples, young people demonstrate wisdom beyond their years.*

What Maisie Knew *is about a very young girl whose parents are in the process of a messy, acrimonious divorce. Throughout the novel, Maisie perceives human relationships with a much keener and kinder eye than the adults around her. James points out that it is not the ability to grasp the concepts of divorce and alimony and adultery that makes someone wise: Its the ability to understand people's behavior. Maisie senses every twitch and change in mood in everyone around her, and its this ability that makes her wise beyond her years.*

The Rachel Papers *stars a teenage character named Charles who demonstrates more wisdom than any of the adults around him. He examines his human relationships in a way that eludes his own father. Charles is extremely concerned with treating people with kindness, whereas his father cheats on Charles's mother and finds nothing wrong with his infidelity. Charles makes close notes of every important conversation he has with his family, and studies his papers for clues to their significance—just another sign of his maturity and wisdom.*

Bobby Fischer became a grandmaster of chess at age fifteen. The young Fischer astounded even the most seasoned chess players starting at age 12 when he first joined the Manhattan Chess Club, where the best players in the world square off. Fischer's success was bolstered by his strong IQ and amazing memory, both of which helped him routinely defeat adults five times his age.

The young characters in the novels of Henry James and Martin Amis show their readers a different kind of wisdom—a thoughtfulness and insight into human relations that young people possess, and older people can lack. The example of Bobby Fischer proves that children can possess intellectual capabilities that rival or even exceed those of adults. If everyone swore off the notion that "With age comes wisdom," young people would be empowered to have much more of an impact on the world.

Discussion

Below is a quick checklist that shows how this essay stacks up against our criteria for our Universal SAT Essay Template.

OUR UNIVERSAL SAT ESSAY TEMPLATE CRITERIA	YES OR NO?
Thesis statement in first sentence of paragraph 1	YES
Three examples listed in paragraph 1 in order from best to worst	YES
Topic sentence for example in paragraph 2	YES
3–4 development sentences to support paragraph 2's example	YES
Topic sentence for example in paragraph 3	YES
3–4 development sentences to support paragraph 3's example	YES
Topic sentence for example in paragraph 4	YES
3–4 development sentences to support paragraph 4's example	YES
Conclusion paragraph contains rephrased thesis statement	YES
About 15 sentences total	YES

Let's take a closer look at the essay based on our four key SAT essay ingredients: positioning, organization, examples, and command of language.

POSITIONING

The writer takes a strong and clear stance on the essay topic right from the start. The first sentence contains a thesis statement, and the first paragraph spells out the three examples the writer will use to support his or her position: two from literature (Henry James and Martin Amis) and one from recent history (Bobby Fischer).

ORGANIZATION

The writer organizes this essay based precisely on the structure we suggest in our Universal SAT Essay Template. It contains five paragraphs of at least three sentences each. The paragraphs are organized into an introduction, three example paragraphs starting with the strongest example, and a conclusion that sums up and broadens the argument.

EXAMPLES

The writer spells out the three examples he or she will use to prove the position on the topic. In this case, the writer takes the position that the phrase, "With age comes wisdom" is disproven by the existence of many examples of exceptionally "wise" young people. To prove it, the writer uses three diverse examples: one from a Henry James novel (*What Maisie Knew*), one from a Martin Amis novel (*The Rachel Papers*) and one from recent history (Bobby Fischer). The writer could have chosen a more diverse mix of examples to impress the grader with a greater breadth of knowledge. Even so, since the writer uses these examples so effectively to prove the thesis statement, any grader would likely not deduct points due to the examples' lack of breadth.

COMMAND OF LANGUAGE

As this essay proves, "6" essays can have errors. In fact, SAT essay graders should expect at least a few errors in *every* SAT essay. This essay contains a few minor slips regarding the writer's command of language, such as the misspelling *its* instead of *it's*. This sentence includes a faulty comparison: *Maisie sees human relationships with a much keener and kinder eye than the adults around her.* This comparison suggests that Maisie sees relationships more clearly than she sees adults; what the writer means to suggest, however, is that Maisie sees relationships more clearly than adults see relationships. Overall, the errors in this essay are minor and few, nothing substantial enough to cause a grader to lower this writer's score.

A few flashes of impressive vocabulary combined with appropriate word choice give this essay just enough Special Sauce to convey the writer's strong command of language. The writer also varies the sentence structure frequently, making the essay interesting and easy to read. One exception is the writer's repeated use of the word *wisdom*. It's obviously tough to limit use of this word since it appears in the prompt. Still, the writer's command of language would have been even more impressive if the writer used a synonym.

A 1 Essay

I'm not sure what can be said about such a wise old saying in such a short space of time and room to right!!! I think, to me, this statement is saying that you can only be smart, wise, knowladgeble, etc., if you are older/getting on in years. And if that person is older, than he/she will really know what kind of advice to give somone like me a high school student, like what to do to have a good life or how to get the most out of life. I think this statement is usually true. For example, I have a grandmother, Grandma Ruth, who helps me so much. You look at her and your not sure if she's really "with it" because she's really old, but she's sharp as a tack! She remembers all our birthdays and how old we are. She always gives me good advise whenever I have a problem.

Then sometimes its not true, though. Because my little brother is the smartest, and he's defenately not old!! Sometimes I'll bring a friend home and he'll say something that seems wierd at the time, like Oh I don't like that person, but in the end it always turns out that he was right, I shouldn't have trusted that person.

So on both sides of this argument there are things to say.

Discussion

This essay fails to follow our Universal SAT Template from start to finish. Below is a quick checklist of the criteria for our Universal SAT Essay Template. Note the NOs to see exactly where this essay's key deficiencies lie.

OUR UNIVERSAL SAT ESSAY TEMPLATE CRITERIA	YES OR NO?
Thesis statement in first sentence of paragraph 1	NO
Three examples listed in paragraph 1 in order from best to worst	NO
Topic sentence for example in paragraph 2	NO
3–4 development sentences to support paragraph 2's example	YES
Topic sentence for example in paragraph 3	NO
3–4 development sentences to support paragraph 3's example	NO

OUR UNIVERSAL SAT ESSAY TEMPLATE CRITERIA	YES OR NO?
Topic sentence for example in paragraph 4	NO
3–4 development sentences to support paragraph 4's example	NO
Conclusion paragraph contains rephrased thesis statement	NO
About 15 sentences total	NO

Let's take a closer look at the essay based on our four key SAT essay ingredients: positioning, organization, examples, and command of language.

POSITIONING

The writer takes only a flimsy stance on the topic. He or she tries to define the topic, agrees with it, then disagrees with it. A wishy-washy stance like this one is a bad idea on the SAT essay. So is wasting time defining what you think the SAT topic means. SAT essay topics are always very straightforward, and the graders don't care about what you think the topic means. Graders care about whether you agree or disagree with the topic's claims and can back up your stance with solid supporting examples. This writer wastes time trying to explain what the topic means and complicates this meandering approach even further by *never* taking a firm stance on the topic.

ORGANIZATION

According to our Universal SAT Essay Template, an ideal SAT essay should contain five paragraphs, each with at least three sentences. This essay contains one paragraph of eight sentences, one paragraph of two sentences, and one paragraph of one sentence. The lack of structure and balance makes the essay feel disorganized and rootless. The writer does not pay attention to internal paragraph structure either. As a result, the essay lacks topic sentences, clear paragraph development, and any sense of transition. Each paragraph contains a jumble of ideas rather than one idea clearly articulated and developed.

EXAMPLES

The writer's examples in this essay are as fuzzy and weak as the essay's stance on the topic. We get the sense at first that the writer agrees with the topic's claim, but the example of Grandma Ruth that the writer provides does not support that position effectively. The writer then backs off and uses the example of his or her younger brother to show how the topic's claim can be proven false. Both examples show that this writer is thinking within a very narrow range of personal experience. He or she fails to introduce and develop examples from any outside discipline like history or literature to support a position on the topic sentence.

COMMAND OF LANGUAGE

"1" essays have severe language problems, and this essay is no exception. Some of the most glaring mistakes here are spelling errors: *room to right* should be *room to write*, *knowladgeble* should be *knowledgeable*, *somone* should be *someone*, *your not sure* should be *you're not sure*, and *wierd* should be *weird*. You get the picture: This writer has serious problems with command of language. The writer also fails to write in a tone that's appropriate for a formal essay. He or she includes exclamations and informal diction (*You look at her and your not sure*) that make this essay feel more like a diary entry than an SAT essay. Word choice is similarly conversational (*my little brother is the smartest*), and sentence structure is varied only because the essay is written so haphazardly. In short, this writer skipped the Special Sauce.

SECTION 2

Sentence Completions

2

SECTION 2 | PRACTICE TEST 2 EXPLANATIONS

the new SAT

1. B   One-Blank/One-Way   *Easy*

This question contains no switch and is not about a comparison over time, so it's one way. That means the word in the blank must agree with the facts and ideas presented in the sentence. The blank in this sentence refers to the "meaning of the color white" in *Moby-Dick*. The rest of the sentence explains that different people think it means different things. So a good word to describe the meaning of the color white in *Moby-Dick* might be *variable* or *unclear*. There is one word among the answer choices that means just that: *ambiguous*. *Infinite* is a strong runner-up, but here's why it's incorrect: The sentence indicates that there are a lot of ways to interpret white in *Moby-Dick*; it doesn't say that there are unlimited ways. Infinite is overkill.

2. B   Two-Blank/One-Way   *Easy*

The phrase *thanks to* works as a one-way switch: It tells you that Henri got the job because of the facts stated in the first part of the sentence. Of course, those facts are blank, so you're looking for words to fill those blanks that are both positive (since they got Henri the job) and somehow related to getting work and dealing with people. Since you're looking for two positive words, that means you can throw out any answer choices with a negative word. That knocks out **C** because of the word *flaws*, **D** because of the word *desperation*, and **E** because of the word *demotions*. The second blank has to go with the word "friendly ----" so you can plug in the remaining choices to see which works: "friendly *evidence*" or "friendly *demeanor*." Evidence doesn't make much sense next to friendly. But demeanor is a synonym of "behavior" or "way of being" and matches up well.

3. B   Two-Blank/Two-Way   *Medium*

The two-way switch word *but* indicates that the sentence is two way. The way that the "Rite of Spring" is perceived has changed. It used to be perceived in one way that is associated with "audaciously modern," but today it is actually perceived in a different way. So, the two blanks have to contrast. The phrase <u>audaciously modern</u>, which describes how the "Rite of Spring" used to be perceived, <u>means that in the past the music was seen as new and bold and shocking</u>: That's what *audacious* means. In the past, the "Rite of Spring" was seen as "shocking," while today it's seen as "old and un-shocking." The only answer choice that provides the needed *new and shocking..old and unshocking* mix is **B** *scandal..tame*. "Rite of Spring" was once scandalous (audaciously modern), but today it seems tame.

4. E   One-Blank/Two-Way   *Medium*

The switch *in contrast* makes it clear that this is a two-way sentence: There is a contrast between the two books. The blank describes how *David Copperfield* is, and it must contrast with the fact that *A Christmas Carol* is "tightly organized." A good phrase to fit the blank would be "loose and disorganized." *Sprawling*, which means loose and unwieldy, matches what you need exactly.

5. **E** One-Blank/One-Way *Medium*

The sentence contains no switch and does not make a comparison over time: It's one-way. The blank must fit with the other facts and information presented in the sentence. The blank describes the "influence of the popular vote," and the second half of the sentence explains that the vote doesn't actually decide the election. Instead, it "informs" the Electoral College, which is the body that actually chooses the president. In other words, in the political system in the sentence, the election of the president is one step removed from the popular vote. So, what word means "at a distance," "removed," or "not entirely direct"? *Indirect* does.

6. **D** One-Blank/Two-Way *Medium*

The switch word *instead* tells you that the sentence is two-way: The two halves of the sentence must disagree. The blank, which describes how you might expect Puck to act after pulling one of his pranks, must contrast with Puck's actual attitude about his pranks. Since in actuality Puck brags about his pranks, you know he's proud of them. What you need, therefore ,is a word that contrasts with the idea of pride. What words come to mind? *Shame*, *guilt*, and so on. The one word among the answer choices that describes the actions of a person who feels guilt is *apologizing*. People apologize for actions they feel bad about.

7. **D** Two-Blank/Two-Way *Difficult*

The two-way switch *though* signals that the second half of the sentence will contrast with the first: Rod McKuen's readers and his critics disagree about his status and skill. That means you know you need words that contrast. You can throw out *emasculated..tarnished*, since both words are negative, and *redeemed..celebrated*, since both are positive. To get the answer, you need to use the information provided at the end of the sentence: McKuen was the most popular poet of the 1960s. That means that the public had to think of him positively (the second blank), while the literary critics thought he stunk (second blank). You're looking for a *negative..positive* pair. *Derided . . venerated* fits the bill: The critics derided McKuen (mocked and disparaged him), but his readers venerated (glorified) him by making him the most widely read poet of his time.

8. **B** One-Blank/One-Way *Difficult*

The sentence contains no switch and does not make a comparison over time. The blank, which explains what the sales representative was expected to do, must fit with the description "seeking orders from each new business." In other words, the sales representative was supposed to go door to door. This question is tricky, though, because the vocabulary is difficult. There is an answer choice that exactly fits the meaning of "go door to door": *canvass*. You've probably heard of the word *canvas*, which is a type of fabric. Artists paint on canvas. Some shoes are made of canvas. But here you're dealing with *canvass*. That extra "s" makes a big difference. Canvass means "to solicit action from the residents of an area." That meaning makes canvass fit the sentence very well.

Let's say you weren't sure what canvass meant. You could still have worked to eliminate some of the other answers. *To discern* means to detect with the eyes, or to notice. The blank in this sentence needs a stronger action than just going around the neighborhood looking around. Cut that one. A salesperson might *validate*, or establish as valid, a region for future sales, but this salesperson is actually seeking orders, not just scouting around. *Incorporate* and *castigate* (bring together; criticize) make no sense in the context of the sentence. Only canvass makes the sentence make sense. Even if you didn't know the meaning of canvass, cutting choices like *incorporate* and *castigate* could put you in a strong position to guess.

Short Reading Passages

9. **E**   Technique   *Medium*

This question requires you to know a bunch of literary terms. If you had already used our list of the top twenty-five literary terms you need to know for the new SAT, this question would be a breeze. A simile is a comparison involving the words *like* or *as*. The passage says dust mites travel on the skin "like a tiny army on the march."

10. **E**   Specific Information   *Difficult*

Specific Information questions with the nasty EXCEPT twist can be conquered most effectively by rephrasing them in your head. What does this question really want you to identify among the answer choices? It wants you to pick out the one trait that the passage does *not* associate with dust mites. What don't dust mite do? The passage says that they live in dust clumps, spread through the air, and can cause allergies and diseases like asthma. That takes care of four answers, leaving only **E**, destroy furniture. The passage does indeed mention furniture, but it says dust mites live in furniture; it does not specify whether they destroy it.

11. **C**   Attitude or Tone   *Difficult*

Tone questions like this one require you to look closely at words that clue you in on the author's attitude toward the subject. It's clear that the conditions the author describes on the Oregon Trail were awful. What's his or her take on the people who actually survived the journey? The author's final comment about it being "amazing" that the West ever got settled at all reveals that he or she admires the startling determination and resourcefulness of those who made it all the way along the Trail. A bunch of the answer choices here might cause some confusion. **B** is easiest to eliminate, since *dispassionate and technical* suggests that the author takes a scientific, emotionless view of the Oregon Trail settlers. **A** and **D** have trace elements of the author's actual tone: The author finds the settlers' success amazing, which isn't too far from *shocked*; and he or she certainly feels their amazing success was cause to celebrate. But even so, both **A** and **D** are too extreme and absolute. **E** is tricky because the author definitely takes a sentimental, looking-backward type of tone when describing the settlers along the Trail. But the author is too far removed to be nostalgic about the Oregon Trail settlers. One gets nostalgic about stuff like summer camp. Overall, the tone is *respectful and admiring.* He or she looks back in amazement at the struggles the settlers endured and appreciates their efforts. That makes **C** the best answer.

12. **C**   Technique   *Difficult*

This question wants to know why the author includes the short sentence "None." One-word sentences tend to jolt the reader into paying particular attention to an author's point, kind of like an exclamation point. Once you've established that the reason to include a sentence is to emphasize a particular point, you have to determine what that point is. That's truly why the author includes this short sentence, and that's the correct answer here. The "None" refers to the lack of supplies and support that the settlers suffered from on the trail. It does not refer to their isolation or loneliness explicitly, so cut **A**. It has nothing to do with their understanding of their environment, so cut **B**. It does relate directly to underscoring the odds that the settlers had to overcome to make it on the Trail, so keep **C**. **D** is tough because the last sentence of the passage makes it clear that the settlers' success surprised the author, but that's not why he or she includes the "None" sentence, which is all this question asks you to evaluate. **E** refers to Native Americans, a subject the passage mentions, but not in the context of how the Native Americans were affected by the settlement of the American West. So, only **C** survives.

Long Reading Passage (Huck Finn)

13. **B**   Words in Context   *Easy*

Here's a Words-in-Context question. What's the context? Huck's describing what happens when the Widow calls him down to dinner. Then, the Widow tucks "down her head and grumbles a little over the ----, though there warn't really anything wrong with them . . . only everything was cooked by itself." Huck is describing the "victuals" as getting cooked, which means the word must mean *food*.

14. **B**   Themes and Arguments   *Difficult*

When Huck argues with the Widow, she tells him that smoking is a "mean" activity, yet, Huck observes, she chews tobacco herself. Huck then says that the Widow thinks that chewing tobacco is alright, because she does it herself. In other words, the Widow will make allowances for her own habit precisely because it's hers, but she won't make allowances for another person's habits. She's a hypocrite.

If you had trouble coming to this answer directly, you could have worked backward through the answers. Huck is definitely not religious—so **D** is out. But there's no sense of doom that Huck will have to go to the "bad place." In fact, the bad place hasn't even been mentioned at that point in the passage. Goodbye **C**. The Widow's concern about Huck shows that **A** is wrong: She does care—she's just bossy. She shows her care by being bossy. Finally, as for **E**, Huck asks the Widow if he can smoke and she says no. He then tells the reader about it, but he doesn't say anything else to the Widow, so how could he be trying to make her angry?

15. **E**   Words in Context   *Medium*

Treat this question like a Sentence Completion: "She said it was a ---- practice and wasn't clean." The only answer that fits the idea of dirtiness is **E**, *unpleasant*.

16. **A**   Implied Information   *Medium*

The quotes of Miss Watson all show her telling Huck what to do, how to be, how to act. And it's all about little ticky-tack stuff: where Huck should put his feet, how he should stand, and so on. Either Huck's a troublemaker or Miss Watson is bossy. Since the narrative is from Huck's point of view, it doesn't make much sense for Huck to try to show that he's the one at fault—so it must be that Miss Watson's domineering.

17. **A**   Implied Information   *Medium*

The brief argument Huck has with Miss Watson about going "to the bad place" leads into Huck's comment that he didn't mean to make her angry, that he just wanted a change, something new. He's basically saying that in the Widow's house, he feels stuck, confined. He wants to go somewhere, anywhere, so much, that he'd just as soon go to Hell. This may make Huck unreligious, but even more, it makes it clear that he feels restless.

18. **D**   Technique   *Medium*

Here's the description of the leaves: "The leaves rustled in the woods ever so mournful." Leaves don't actually have feelings. They can't be mournful unless they are being *personified*.

19. **C**   Specific Information   *Easy*

After he accidentally kills the spider, Huck says that he knew that it meant he was bound to run into some bad luck. He believes in omens and luck and stuff like that. In a word, he's *superstitious*.

20. **A**   Themes and Arguments   *Difficult*

In the third paragraph, Huck describes his disagreement with the Widow and shows how she will not let him smoke. In the fourth, he describes the conflict with Miss Watson, showing how bullied he feels and how much he wants to get away. Through both paragraphs, there's a sense of restlessness and loneliness. So, the fourth paragraph is a strengthening and building on the previous paragraph: **A**.

21. **B**   Attitude or Tone   *Medium*

Throughout the passage, Huck keeps questioning conventional wisdom. He explains how food cooked all in one heap is actually better than food cooked in separate dishes; he picks out the Widow's hypocrisy about tobacco; he questions the importance of Moses, since Moses is long dead; he decides the "good place" can't be all that good if Miss Watson's going to be there ordering everyone around. Huck constantly uses his common sense and personal knowledge to question the civilized world that the Widow and Miss Watson take for granted. And while Huck is *skeptical* about the so-called civilized world, he never gets outright angry or disdainful. **B** is the best answer.

22. **B**   Main Idea   *Medium*

There are two main themes in the passage: The first is that Huck keeps poking holes in the standard, civilized notions that the Widow and Miss Watson hold so dear. This makes Huck independent and free-thinking. The second theme is that Huck feels trapped, restless, and lonely: He'd risk the "bad place" just to get out of the house, and he describes himself at one point as "lonesome."

23. **A**   Attitude or Tone   *Easy*

The tone of the passage is largely created by the style in which it is written. Huck talks to the reader in his own dialect, as if he's speaking rather than writing. This makes the passage as a whole feel immensely *casual and informal*. While there are moments in which Huck describes himself as being sad, and other moments when he talks about omens and other superstitions, the tone of the passage is overwhelmingly light and friendly because of Huck's way to speaking. **A** is the best answer.

24.   **E**   Specific Information   *Difficult*

The Widow and Miss Watson try to educate Huck about manners, the Bible, spelling, and other "civilized" matters. Each time Huck responds with a kind of friendly skepticism. His common sense keeps pointing out holes in what the Widow or Miss Watson is saying or doing: the Widow's hypocrisy about tobacco; Miss Watson telling him he's going to go to hell for putting his feet up. Huck does *not* use his observations to try to start fights or make fun of the Widow or Miss Watson, so **C** and **D** are out. Answer **A** is a bit of an SAT trap. In the book where this excerpt came from, Huck does eventually run away, but in this passage, he does not. He kills the spider accidentally, so answer **B** is also wrong, which leaves **E**, the best description of what Huck keeps doing in the passage.

SECTION 3

1.   **A**   Algebra: Substitution   *Easy*

Since $x = 3$, substitute 3 for x in $y = x$, and you see that $y = 3$. Now you can substitute 3 in for both x and y in xy^2: $3(3)^2 = 3^3 = 27$.

2.   **B**   Geometry: Angles and Lines   *Easy*

Because a and b are perpendicular, the four angles formed by their intersection are right angles, or 90°. The angle you have to find, x, makes up just a part of one of those 90° angles. So x is smaller than 90°. That means you can eliminate answers **D** and **E**. The diagonal line that forms x is a transversal, so it creates opposite angles. This means that you know the angle adjacent to x is 36°, since that angle's opposite angle is 36°. Now you can do the simple math: $x + 36 = 90$, which comes to $x = 54$.

3.   **C**   Data Analysis, Statistics, Probability: Statistical Analysis   *Easy*

The mean of a set of numbers is the sum of the numbers divided by the number of elements in the set. The mode of a set of numbers is the element within the set that occurs most frequently. With that in mind, you should eliminate **B** and **E**, since the mean of a set will always be a number between the highest and lowest numbers in the set, and the mode of those sets is very low. Once you do the math on the other three, it becomes clear that only in **C** are the mean and mode equal (both equal 4).

4.   **B**   Algebra: Functions   *Easy*

Remember, weird symbol questions are just function questions in disguise. And function questions are usually nothing more than glorified substitution questions. So, here you've just got a glorified substitution question in disguise.

The instructions for this weird symbol indicate that you are to add all the digits under the line. So, follow the instructions:

$$\frac{\overline{4371} - \overline{3441}}{\overline{231}} = \frac{(4+3+7+1) - (3+4+4+1)}{(2+3+1)} = \frac{15-12}{6} = \frac{3}{6} = \frac{1}{2}$$

The answer choices are in decimal, but it shouldn't be hard to see that you're looking for **B**, 0.5.

5.   **C**   Algebra: Functions   *Medium*

This is a classic SAT problem—it's more about saving time than being good at math. All you've got to do to solve this question is turn the digits around and add them up. But the question is actually testing your understanding of the properties of addition rather than your ability to add. If you know that the order the numbers are in doesn't matter when adding numbers, you can see that $\overline{1,234,533,234} - \overline{\leftarrow 1,234,533,234}$ will sum to 0 without having to do any calculation at all.

6.   **E**   Algebra: Functions   *Easy*

Don't worry about tough algebra on this question. Instead, just pick numbers. Choose a value for n that fits the criteria of $10 < n < 90$. Next, calculate $\overline{n + 1090}$, and see which one of the answer choices is correct. For example, let $n = 23$ and add it to 1090 to get 1113. $\overline{1113} = 1 + 1 + 1 + 3 = 6$. Because $\overline{23} = 2 + 3 = 5$, you can see that the only answer that works is **E**, $\overline{n} + 1$.

7.   **C**   Algebra: Systems of Equations   *Easy*

Systems of equations! So, do the system of equations thing. Subtract one equation from the other:

$$
\begin{array}{r}
x + 2y = 7 \\
-(x + \ y = 6) \\
\hline
y = 1
\end{array}
$$

Now substitute 1 for y into $x + y = 6$, and you get $x = 5$.

8.   **D**   Geometry: Triangles   *Medium*

To find y, you first need to find the measures of the angles in the triangle. Since the sum of the angles in any triangle is equal to 180°, and since all of the angles have the same variable, x, you can find each angle by setting the sum of the angles equal to 180°:

$$
\begin{aligned}
x + 2x + 90 &= 180 \\
3x + 90 &= 180 \\
3x &= 90 \\
x &= 30
\end{aligned}
$$

You're dealing with a 30-60-90 triangle. Whip out that trusty 30-60-90 side length ratio of $1 : \sqrt{3} : 2$, and you'll see that the longer leg (which you know) has a ratio with the hypotenuse, y, of $\sqrt{3} : 2$. Set up a proportion, and work it out:

$$
\frac{6\sqrt{3}}{y} = \frac{\sqrt{3}}{2}
$$

$$
12\sqrt{3} = y\sqrt{3}
$$

$$
y = 12
$$

9.   **D**   Algebra: Substitution   *Medium*

This is a substitution problem with a little trick. Before you can substitute $b = 2$ into the equation $a - b = 2b$, you have to isolate the a on one side of the equation by adding b to both sides: $a = 2b + b$. Now, substitute the 2 in for b, and you get $a = 2(2) + 2 = 4 + 2 = 6$. But wait! **C**, 6, is actually an SAT trap! Remember that the question asks you to find the value of $2a$, which is 12.

10. **D**   Numbers and Operations: Fractions   *Medium*

To figure out the length of the string, just multiply the length of each piece by the number of equal pieces: 5 × 1.5 = 7.5 feet. But remember, the question is looking for the length in yards, not feet, so the answer $\frac{15}{2}$ is an SAT trap. You can convert feet to yards by dividing by 3: 7.5 ÷ 3 = 2.5, or $\frac{5}{2}$.

11. **A**   Algebra: Solving Equations   *Easy*

This problem requires you to transform a mathematical description into an equation. The "is" stands for the " = " sign. The left side of the equation is "the sum of x and y," which can be written as $x + y$. The right side of the equation is "10 more than 3 times z," which can be written as $3z + 10$. The correct equation is $x + y = 3z + 10$. You have to write an equation that "describes x and y in terms of z," which means you have to isolate z on one side of the equation. To isolate z, subtract 10 from both sides: $x + y - 10 = 3z$. Divide both sides by 3, and there's answer **A** staring back at you: $\frac{x + y - 10}{3} = z$

12. **B**   Geometry: Coordinate Geometry   *Difficult*

Since you know the slope of this line, you can solve for h by using the point slope formula for a line. Since the point slope equation is $y - y_1 = m(x - x_1)$, you can use the information given in the equation to set up a proportion and then solve for h:

$$\frac{6 - 0}{11h - h} = \frac{3}{5}$$
$$\frac{6}{10h} = \frac{3}{5}$$
$$\frac{3}{5h} = \frac{3}{5}$$

At this point, you should be able to see that $h = 1$. (If not, you can cross-multiply as usual when you have two equal fractions to see that $15h = 15$.)

13. **D**   Geometry: Triangles   *Medium*

The only kind of triangles that can fit together to form a square are right isosceles triangles. They are joined at the hypotenuse, their longest side, so the legs of the triangles form the sides of the square. The best way to see all this is to draw it out yourself:

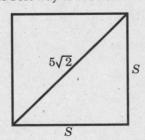

You want to find the area of the square. This means that you first need to find the length of its sides. These sides are also the legs of the isosceles triangles, which means you can find their measure by using the good old Pythagorean theorem: $s^2 + s^2 = (5\sqrt{2})^2$. So, $2s^2 = 50$, and s^2, which is the area of the square, equals 25.

14. C   Numbers and Operations: Basic Operations   *Difficult*

First, determine as much as possible about x. Since x divided by 2 is an integer, you know that x must be even. You know that x doesn't equal 0 because the question tells you so. Now, onto those three pesky criteria. Try to prove each wrong, and then eliminate any answer choices that hold them.

1. Is $x^2 - {}^x/_3$ an integer? x^2 is certainly an integer, but ${}^x/_3$ is not necessarily an integer, since not all even numbers are divisible by 3. So, the answer is no.
2. Is $x^2 - {}^x/_3$ even? Since all even numbers are integers, and we know that $x^2 - {}^x/_3$ is *not* always an integer, it certainly can't always be even.
3. Is $x^2 - {}^x/_3$ positive? x^2 must be positive, and x^2 will be larger than ${}^x/_3$ for all values of x, so, yes, $x^2 - {}^x/_3$ is always positive.

15. E   Numbers and Operations: Exponents   *Difficult*

According to the question, p is always negative, and by definition, s^2 is either 0 or positive (all squares are positive or 0). Therefore, ps^2 must always be negative or 0, since a negative number times a number that is either positive or 0 will always be negative or 0. So **E**, .5, is not a possible answer because it's a positive number.

16. A   Geometry: Coordinate Geometry   *Medium*

This is a transformation question. Your mission is to determine what a slight change to a function will do to the graph of that function. When you're given graphs in the answer choices, the most effective way to solve transformation questions is to plug numbers into both functions and see which answer-choice graphs fit the values you get. If you plug 0 for x in $f(x)$, you get $f(x) = \dfrac{0}{2} - 3 = -3$, and you'll see $f(x) = -3$ as the value for $x = 0$ on the graph. If you now plug 0 into $f(x + 3)$, you'll see where that point should be plotted on the graph. $f(x + 3) = \dfrac{0 + 3}{2} - 3 = 1\dfrac{1}{2} - 3 = -1\dfrac{1}{2}$. Scan the answer choices to see which graphs show the point $f(x + 3) = -1\dfrac{1}{2}$ when $x = 0$. Only the graph in choice **A** does, so that's your answer.

17. A   Algebra: Solving Equations   *Difficult*

To find the total cost, you have to figure out how many gallons of gas were pumped and then multiply that amount by z. Since you only know how many gallons of gas have been pumped in intervals of y minutes, you have to figure out how many of those intervals passed by dividing m, the total time, by y, the interval: $\dfrac{m}{y}$. To figure out how many gallons were pumped in this time, multiply by x, the amount of gas pumped every y minutes: $\dfrac{mx}{y}$. At z dollars per gallon, the total cost of the dispensed gas is $\dfrac{mxz}{y}$.

18.　**C**　Geometry: Geometric Visualizations　　　　*Difficult*

If the figure is folded as shown, you're left with a box with a rectangular base of width 16 and length 10. The height of the box is 2. Therefore, the volume of the box is 16 × 10 × 2 = 320.

19.　**E**　Numbers and Operations: Sequences　　　　*Difficult*

This word problem is a geometric sequence problem in disguise. It tells you the first two terms in the sequence and asks you to find other terms in order to subtract one from another.

　First, figure out which terms you need to know. The population doubles every four years, and the question asks you to know the number of rabbits on the island after 12 and 20 years. So, after 0 years, there were 6 rabbits on the island; after 4 years, there were 12; after 8, there were 24; after <u>12, there were 48</u>; after 16, there were 96; and after <u>20, there were 192</u>. Now just do the subtraction: 192 – 48 = 144.

20.　**A**　Algebra: Functions as Models　　　　*Difficult*

Imagine a go-kart pushed off a hill. What will happen to the go-kart's speed? Well, first it will speed up, and then after it gets off the hill, it will slow down. If it hits a wall or something, it will slow down immediately. The go-kart in this problem doesn't hit a wall though. All it does is speed up, then slow down. The only graphs that show the go-kart's speed as first speeding up and then slowing down are **A** and **E**. To decide between them, you have to look at the details of the question. The go-kart is on the hill for 50 meters, and then it rolls for another 150 meters before stopping. So, the go-kart will speed up for 50 meters, and then spend the next 150 meters slowing down. **A** is the answer that best graphs this pattern.

SECTION 4

Sentence Completions

1.　**A**　Two-Blank/Two-Way　　　　*Medium*

The switch word *although* tells you that this is a two-way sentence. You know you're dealing with contrast, so you can cut choices in which both words create either a negative or positive connotation: *irresponsible . . failure* and *thoughtful . . superiority* should both go. Next, think about the second half of the sentence. The blank describes what happens because Henrietta lacks discipline, so you need a negative word to complete this half of the sentence. Therefore, you can throw out *lazy . . success* and *uninspired . . prowess*, since the second words of both those pairs are positive. The only remaining choice, *intelligent . . catastrophe*, is the correct answer.

2.　**D**　One-Blank/One-Way　　　　*Medium*

The sentence contains no switch and does not make a comparison over time: It's one-way. The facts presented in the sentence must agree. The blank describes the Supreme Court decision, and the rest of the sentence states that the decision "divides the United States." So, you're looking for a word like *divisive* or a word that means "makes people angry." *Controversial*, which means "giving rise to disagreement," is a good word to use to describe a deeply divisive issue. That's the best answer.

3.   **D**   One-Blank/One-Way   *Medium*

The sentence contains no switch or comparison over time: It's one-way. The blank describes what sort of employee Tamara is, and the rest of the sentence describes her as "responsible, efficient, and courteous." In other words, Tamara is a "really good" employee, so you're looking for a positive word that means "very good." Among the answer choices, only *exemplary* and *absorbing* have positive connotations. When you plug these into the sentence, you get, "Tamara was an *absorbing* employee" or "Tamara was an *exemplary* employee." An *absorbing* employee would be an employee that everyone else likes to watch. An *exemplary* employee would be someone who is a near-perfect employee. *Exemplary* fits the sentence best. That's your answer.

4.   **D**   One-Blank/One-Way   *Difficult*

The sentence contains no switch or comparison over time: It's one-way. The blank describes what Joan of Arc was "deemed" after she "espoused views inconsistent with official Christian religious doctrine." So, you're looking for a word that describes someone who goes against religious doctrine. *Heretic* means exactly that, but it's a tough vocab word.

   If you didn't know the word *heretic*, you could still try to eliminate answers. *Perpetrator* means someone who is guilty of some crime, but not necessarily related to religion. *Populist* describes a political person whose most pressing concern is the common people. Joan of Arc might have been a populist, but the answer you need must relate to her religious rebelliousness. *Murderer* is an SAT trap that might tempt you just because Joan was executed. She was certainly not a murderer, though. A *zealot* believes fanatically in something, such as religion, but not necessarily religion. Only *heretic* conveys the two ideas you need: religion and dissent.

5.   **D**   Two-Blank/One-Way   *Difficult*

The sentence contains no switch or comparison over time: It's one way. The way Paul acts is consistent throughout the sentence. The first blank describes what social matter Paul is ignorant of, and the second blank describes Paul's table manners. The sentence also explains that Paul could "offend even the most forgiving host." Paul must not be too good at social situations. He probably is ignorant of basic social "rules," and his table manners probably are "bad." So, you're looking for a first blank that means something like rules and a second blank that is negative. You can eliminate **A** and **B**, since *refined* or *resplendent* are positive: Such table manners would impress, not offend. Of the remaining choices, only **D**, *precepts*, has a meaning similar to "rules." That's the answer.

Dual Short Reading Passage

6.   **B**   Technique   *Easy*

The phrase "just a decade ago" attempts to give some perspective to the vast changes that the Internet has brought about in only a short time. The "shock" that the author marvels at here is not the speed with which time passes, but the extent of the change that's occurred in a relatively short period of time. That makes **B** the correct answer.

7. B Attitude or Tone *Difficult*

The first author presents the Net as a boon for research. The second portrays it as a dangerous tool for snoops. You know you need an answer choice with a positive word and then a negative word to describe the tones taken by these two authors. That makes the first step cutting choices with two positive or two negative words. **C** is easy to cut, since *anxious* and *uneasy* are synonyms and both are negative. If you find the vocab in **D** and **E** too tough, note that you can cut them both based just on their first words. You know *afraid* is negative (and you need a positive word to describe the chipper first author), and you should be able to deduce that *malevolent* is negative based on the word root -*mal*, which pretty much always means something bad, as in *malpractice*, *malcontent*, and *malnourished*. That leaves only **A** and **B**. Using the same first-word-elimination technique, you can cut **A** because the first author is not at all cautious about the Internet. On the contrary, that author gushes about how great it is with seemingly no reservations. Only **B** remains, and its two descriptive words, *enthusiastic* and *perturbed* (troubled, bothered) sum up these two tones perfectly.

8. A Relating Two Passages *Easy*

These two authors definitely disagree about the merits of the Internet. But this question asks you to delve a bitter deeper into why they disagree. The author of the first passage loves that he or she can waltz into a library and look up personal information about his or her ancestors. The second author hates the idea that the Web compromises privacy. Nobody mentions anonymity—quite the opposite, actually. So **D** is wrong. The topics of law, **B**, reading books, **C**, and developing nations, **E** also never factor into these passages. The only choice that does figure centrally is **A**, the debate over public access to private information on the Web.

9. E Relating Two Passages *Easy*

In this EXCEPT question, the authors should disagree about every answer choice except one. Put simply, which of the choices would both authors agree on? The best way to answer this is to go down the list of answers, eliminating each one you can.

A is out because their disagreement focuses on the problem of freely available information on the Net. Neither mentions customer service, so **B** is out. **C** requires the first author to view the Net as problematic, but that's not the case. The first author would disagree that there should be more regulation of the Web, so **D** is no good. Both authors would agree, though, that the Internet has had a huge impact on society. So, **E** works best.

Long Reading Passage (Art)

10. E Main Idea *Easy*

This questions covers the main point of the entire passage. You can answer this question by looking at the first sentence of the passage, which acts as a topic sentence. That sentence states that "Art did not mean the same thing" in medieval times as it does today. To paraphrase: the meaning of art changed over time. Now you can look through the answer choices and find the one that best matches this paraphrase. Answer **A** is incorrect because it explicitly states that art has not changed over the centuries. Answer **B** is also incorrect, because while the author focuses on how the two time periods in question appreciate art, he never compares how much. Answer

C is wrong because while the author does discuss how medieval art often incorporates or mimics other works, he doesn't make a value judgement about this fact. Answer **D** is incorrect because the author never makes a claim of this sort at all. This leaves answer choice **E** as the best choice.

11. **A**   Technique   *Medium*

In order to help illustrate its discussion of the relationship between artist and patron in medieval times, the line indicated by the question describes the artist as a "hand" and the patron as a "mind." A comparison of one thing to another without use of the words "like" or "as" is a metaphor. None of the other literary terms in the answer choices indicate the comparison that is part of a metaphor. (If you didn't know the literary terms in the answer choices, check out the list on page 158 of this book).

12. **A**   Technique   *Easy*

The best way to approach this question is to go back to the passage and look at the context around the indicated lines. In this case, the author tells the story about Abbot Suger after explaining that few medieval artists are known today because patrons were considered more important. The story about Abbot Suger, then, is an example supporting an earlier statement.

13. **A**   Themes an Arguments   *Medium*

This questions asks you to figure out how the paragraph about music in the passage functions as a part of the entire passage. When you're trying to figure out the purpose of a paragraph it's often helpful to look at the paragraphs topic sentence (i.e. first sentence): "The art historian Ernst Gombrich likens this medieval attitude toward art to our present-day attitude toward classical music." In other words, the art historian Ernst Gombrich is using the example of classical music to help explain how people in medieval times thought about all art. This matches with answer **A** perfectly. If you were having trouble picking out the right answer, though, you could have tried to eliminate answers. Choices **B** and **C** can be eliminated because the author neither mentions funding discrepancies nor calls for increased representations of the Virgin and Child. Answer **D** can be eliminated since the paragraph about classical music states that classical musicians are expected not to improvise. Answer **E** is wrong because the passage's author actually does compare art from two periods, quite the opposite of warning people not to compare art from different times.

14. **C**   Implied Information   *Difficult*

Answering this question begins with understanding the words "condemned of blasphemy." Even if you don't know the word *blasphemy*, the word *condemned* suggests that an artist in medieval times who placed his "own ideas and skill" above religious forms would be punished. The fear of punishment therefore explains why artists would avoid making new and unique art and instead focus on following old forms.

15. **E**   Themes and Arguments   *Medium*

The first part of answering this question is figuring out what the question wants. The most important phrase in the question is "modern critical judgments," which lets you know that you need to remember or find the parts of the passage that discuss art in modern times, specifically the section that discusses critical interpretation and judgment. While paragraphs 1 and 3 discuss art in modern times, only paragraph 3

the new SAT

includes details about critical judgments of art. It is in this paragraph that the author states plainly that people judge art by its originality, which corresponds to answer **E**.

Long Reading Passage (Science)

16. **B**   Attitude or Tone   *Easy*

One good way to answer questions about tone is to ask yourself what the author is trying to do in this essay. Well, he or she is discussing the differences between pure and applied science and highlighting some of the moral and ethical dangers inherent in applied science. Is this the goal of an *angry* person? No, an angry person would use much stronger language and be much less open-minded about the benefits of applied science. A *concerned* person? Yes. An *uninterested* person wouldn't take a stand one way or the other. A *pleased* person wouldn't discuss the pitfalls of applied science. A *disappointed* person would be more upset, less analytical. Concerned is it.

17. **B**   Themes and Arguments   *Difficult*

The contextual sentences around "becomes manifest" describe how science can only interfere with people's rights or well-being when a particular scientific effort has some sort of effect on society. If you plug in the different answer choices for "becomes manifest," only **B** provides the meaning that science is introduced to and has an effect in society.

18. **E**   Technique   *Difficult*

This question asks you to think about some of the strategies this author may be using to persuade his or her reader. One good way to approach a question like this is by thinking about the effect the passage has on you as you read it. Do you remember the challenge discussed by the author in these lines when you finish reading the whole piece? Probably not, so you can eliminate answer **A**, since this section seems to have little effect on the overall argument. You can also eliminate answers **C** and **D**, since the author is trying to make a point about applied science, and it would be silly to admit ignorance or confuse the reader while trying to make a point. That leaves **B** and **E**. While the author's comment about possible challenges to the definitions of pure and applied science does indicate an area for further study, that is not the goal of the passage. The author wants to convince you, the reader, of his point. The author acknowledges the reader's potential doubts so that the reader will set them aside for the time being. In other words, the author anticipates possible criticisms and preemptively defuses them.

19. **E**   Specific Information   *Easy*

In the indicated lines, the author argues that the rigid distinction between pure and applied science stands firm for the sciences of matter (physics, chemistry, and astronomy). Because the author does not mention biology, you can assume that it is not a science of matter and does not conform to the rigid distinction between pure and applied science.

20. **A**   Technique   *Difficult*

The author's parenthetical insertion is a technique called an "aside": something that is suggestive but outside the scope of the main argument. The author uses this parenthetical interjection to suggest that the history of justifications surrounding the atomic bomb is, indeed, worthy of examination, but outside the scope of the topic of the passage.

21. E   Implied Information   *Medium*

This question tests your understanding of the author's distinction between pure and applied science. To this author, pure science is research that has no relation to human industry or other activities. The only answer that could be correct is **E**.

22. B   Implied Information   *Medium*

This author assigns moral considerations only to experiments designed to affect human life. If a scientist were experimenting with fissionable materials but the potentially destructive uses of such knowledge were unknown at the time, this experiment would fall under the category of pure science. However, if the scientist were aware that fission could be used to make weapons, then the experiment would have a moral component. Also, notice that both answers **A** and **D** can be eliminated by the Law of Absolutely Wrong.

23. C   Words in Context   *Difficult*

In the context of this passage *truth* has a very specific meaning, which is tied in to the author's conception of "pure science." According to this passage, Otto Hahn was not looking to affect the world by building a bomb or a nuclear generator. He was investigating the objective physical laws of the universe.

24. D   Main Idea   *Easy*

The main point of this essay is that applied science can have profound effects on mankind. Although the author spends most of the essay discussing potential negative consequences, he takes care to mention that applied science is often beneficial to mankind.

   C should be fairly easy to eliminate, since the whole passage is about the moral implications of applied science. **A** is a little more difficult to eliminate, but if you remember that the passage discusses the moral issues of nuclear reactors in addition to nuclear bombs, you can see that for the author, questions of morality are not just limited to weapons.

SECTION 5

Multiple Choice Questions

1. D   Algebra: Variation   *Easy*

You can solve variation questions like this simply and quickly by setting all the variables equal to 1 and then following the changes described in the question. Whatever value you get for y is your answer. $y = \dfrac{(2 \times 1)^2}{\left(\frac{1}{2}\right)^2 (4)} = \dfrac{4}{\left(\frac{1}{4}\right)4} = \dfrac{4}{1} = 4$.

2. C   Geometry: Angles and Lines   *Easy*

Since the two angles in the image together form a straight line, you know that their sum is 180°. Solve the equation $3x + 60 = 180$ to find that $x = 40$. The one tricky part of this question is making sure that you solve for x, not $3x$.

the new SAT

3. **E** Factors and Multiples *Easy*

The factors of 74 are 2 and 37, so 37 is the greatest prime factor. If you set up a factor tree for 96 you get:

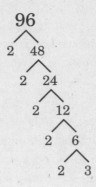

So the greatest prime factor for 96 is 3. To solve the problem you need to find $x - y$, which is $37 - 3 = 34$.

4. **E** Algebra: Functions *Medium*

When you work out $y = f(x + 4)$, you end up with $y = 2x + 15$. Since the equation for a line is $y = mx + b$, where m is equal to the slope, the slope of the line in $y = f(x + 4)$ is 2.

5. **A** Numbers and Operations: Divisibility and Remainders *Medium*

The easiest way to answer this question is to pick a number for which the first statement applies, square it, and divide by 4. You only have to try this with one number because the question implies that the property must hold for all numbers. So, choose a number that, when divided by 4, will give a remainder of 3 (choosing small numbers, such as 7 or 11, will make your calculations easier). Squaring 7 gives 49, which, when divided by 4, is 12 with a remainder of 1.

6. **B** Statistical Analysis *Medium*

This seems like an easy question: if the zebra is the 10th fastest and the 10th slowest then there must be 20 animals in the herd right. So just go mark C… and you'll be wrong. This question is a trick, pure and simple. It's also a good example of why you should always show work. A Zebra that is the tenth fastest and slowest will be slower than 9 zebras and faster than 9 zebras. Take a look at this number line:

Fastest

5 6 7 8 9 10 9 8 7 6 5 4 3 2 1

So that means there are actually 19 zebras in the herd.

7. **D** Functions as Models *Medium*

This question gives you a function that defines how much money the class will make based on the number (n) cupcakes it sells. Well, that's easy enough: all you have to do to find how much money the class will make is plug in for n. For instance, if the class sold 10 cupcakes, it will make $3(10) - 15 = 30 - 15 = \$15$. But what the question asks you to figure out is how many cupcakes the class has to sell *in order to make a profit*. We italicized that little phrase because its crucial that you pay attention to it. A lot of students will read this phrase and think the question is asking how many cupcakes the class will have to sell in order to get back to $0. But $0 is not a profit. So what the question is really asking is what is the least number of cupcakes does the class have to sell to make more than $0 dollars. This means that the number of cupcakes you're looking for will be 1 more than the number of cupcakes it will take to break even (reach $0). The number of cupcakes it will take to reach $0 is given by the equation $0 = 3n - 15; 3n = 15; n = 5$. And this means that in order to make a profit, the students will have to sell $5 + 1 = 6$ cupcakes.

8. **B** Algebra: Solving Equations *Difficult*

You're given an equation relating x and z, and you must manipulate it until you have an expression for $\frac{x}{z}$. Since you're given two equal fractions, you can cross-multiply to get two equal expressions:

$$\frac{xy}{2} = \frac{2yz}{3}$$

$$3xy = 4yz$$

Now, simply rearrange the terms of this equation to isolate the desired term.

$$3xy = 4yz$$
$$3x = 4z$$
$$\frac{3x}{z} = 4$$
$$\frac{x}{z} = \frac{4}{3}$$

Grid-Ins

9. **9** Geometry: Coordinate Geometry *Medium*

A geometry problem without an image? Sketch it! Plotting the vertices, you get

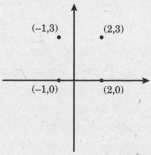

This sketch should show you that the sides of the square are equal to 3, which means the area is 9.

10. **4/15** Numbers and Operations: Fractions *Easy*

To find the fraction of "food items" left over, you need to find the total number of left-over items and the total number of original items. The number of original items is easy: Just add up what the question says was in the buffet at the beginning of the lunch: $35 + 35 + 50 = 120$. To find what was left over, subtract the number of items eaten from the original total. The question tells you that $22 + 28 + 38 = 88$ items were eaten. $120 - 88 = 32$. Now, you just need to reduce the fraction: $\frac{32}{120} = \frac{4}{15}$.

11. **36**   Data Analysis, Statistics, Probability: Statistical Analysis   *Medium*
A key fact you need to know to answer this question is that the sum of a group of numbers is equal to the mean of the group multiplied by the number of elements in the group. So, in order for the mean of the four numbers a, b, c, and d to be 24, their sum must be $4(24) = 96$. Likewise, since the mean of a, b, and c is 20, the sum of those three variables must be $3(20) = 60$. The two groups are identical except that the first group contains d, while the second doesn't, and the first group has a sum that is 36 more than the second group. So, $d = 36$.

12. **8**   Geometry: Coordinate Geometry   *Medium*
The corners of one square inscribed in another will touch the midpoints of the sides of the larger sqaure. This is more than a bit of good geometry trivia. It means that you can figure out the side lengths of the square inscribed in the square shown by the question:

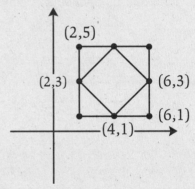

Pick any two of these midpoints and run them through the distance formula. Just for the heck of it, we'll pick the points $(4,1)$ and $(6,3)$: $D = \sqrt{(6-4)^2 + (3-1)^2} = \sqrt{4+4} = \sqrt{8}$. Now that you know the side length, square it to get the area: $A = (\sqrt{8})^2 = 8$.

13. **3**   Numbers and Operations: Exponents   *Medium*
When an exponent gets raised to another exponent, you just multiply the two exponents together. When common bases with exponents are multiplied, you can just add the exponents. As long as you know those two rules of exponents, this problem's algebra is simple. The first step is to convert $(x^a)^b$ and $(x^2)^3$ to x^{ab} and x^6 respectively. You can then combine these two terms to get $(x^{ab}) \times (x^6) = x^{ab+6}$. The question tells you that $x^{ab+6} = x^9$, so $ab + 6 = 9$ and $ab = 3$.

14. **23/4** Geometry: Coordinate Geometry   *Difficult*
There are two ways to solve this question. You could graph the equations, or you could work out the math. It may seem easier to graph the equations and try to see the answer on the graph, but using a calculator to solve this question can take quite a bit of time. If you know the secret of intersecting lines, then the math is really very easy. Here's the secret: Intersecting lines are equal at the point of intersection.

Mathematically, $3x - \frac{1}{4} = -\frac{1}{2}x + 6\frac{3}{4}$. Working out the math is simple algebra: $3\frac{1}{2}x = 7$, so $x = 2$. Plug that in to $y = 3x - \frac{1}{4}$, and you get $y = 5\frac{3}{4} = \frac{23}{4}$.

15. **22**   Data Analysis, Statistics, Probability: Graphs, Charts, Tables   *Medium*

This question isn't very difficult, but it does have several steps. Since you know the rates at which Joe and Jack paint fences, the first thing you have to do is use the chart to calculate how many feet of fence each of them has to paint. Since Joe paints the 3-foot and 6-foot fences, he has to paint $(3 \times 3) + (7 \times 6) = 51$ feet. Jack is painting the 8-foot and 5-foot fences, so he has $(8 \times 8) + (11 \times 5) = 119$ feet of fence to paint. Now, just divide the amount of fence by Joe and Jack's work rates. To paint 51 feet of fence working at 5 feet an hour, it will take Joe $\frac{51}{5} = 10\frac{1}{5}$ hours. To paint 119 feet of fence at a rate of 10 feet per hour, it will take Jack $\frac{119}{10} = 11\frac{9}{10}$. When you add the hours together, you get $22\frac{1}{10}$, which rounds down to 22.

16. **3/8**   Geometry: Geometric Visualizations   *Difficult*

The first thing you should do is sketch the cube that the question describes. A cube containing 64 smaller cubes will be $4 \times 4 \times 4$, and look like this:

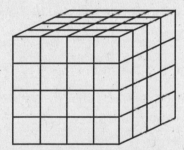

You have to figure out how many of the 64 cubes that make up the large cube have exactly two faces showing. A little investigation should allow you to see that the cubes showing two faces are those on the edges that aren't corners:

(This drawing doesn't show the faces on the back side of the cube.) If you count up all the cubes, including the invisible ones on the back side, you'll get 24. So, the probability of pulling a cube with two red faces from the bag is $\frac{24}{64} = \frac{3}{8}$.

17. **3**   Algebra: Binomials and Quadratics   *Difficult*

This question is difficult because it contains a quadratic that you have to factor. Spotting a few clues in the expression will make factoring much easier. Since the question is looking for some value larger than $2x$, you can bet that the big quadratic once factored and simplified will look something like $2x + b$. Also, so that the expresson simplifies down, it's likely that the $x - 4$ in the denominator will probably get cancelled out by an $x - 4$ in the numerator. Now you have a good idea about each of the factors: $(2x + b)(x - 4)$. A little trial and error should get you the value for b: $2x^2 - 5x - 12 = (2x + 3)(x - 4)$. Cancel out the $x - 4$ in the numerator and denominator, and you're left with $2x + 3$. So, your answer is 3.

18. **80** Geometry: Circles *Difficult*

The shaded region is basically a half-circle with two smaller half-circles added and one small half-circle subtracted. The area of the small semicircles is given in the problem. Finding the area of the larger circle is a little more complicated, since you aren't given any information about the radius of the larger circle directly. However, you can figure out the radius of the larger circle if you notice that the diameters of the three smaller circles, lined up end-to-end, span the entire diameter of the larger circle. All you have to do is figure out the diameters of the smaller circles:

The area of the small semicircle is 8π, so the area of a full small circle is 16π. Working backwards with the formula for the area of a circle, you can calculate that the radius of one of the small circles is

$$\pi r^2 = (\pi)(16)$$
$$r^2 = 16$$
$$r = 4$$

Since the radius of each small semicircle is 4, the diameter of each is 8. There are three small diameters in the diameter of the large circle, so the large diameter is $8 \times 3 = 24$. Now, you can find the area of the large half-circle using the formula $A = \pi r^2$. Remember to divide the whole thing by 2, since you're looking for the area of a *half*-circle: $A = \dfrac{\pi r^2}{2} = \dfrac{\pi(12)^2}{2} = \dfrac{144\pi}{2} = 72\pi$. The area of the shaded region is equal to the large semi-circle minus two small semicircles plus one semicircle: $72\pi + 16\pi - 8\pi = 80\pi$. Remember to divide by π to get 80, the correct answer.

SECTION 6

Improving Sentences

1. **D** Conjunctions *Easy*

With the word *reluctantly*, the sentence makes it clear that Jorge wasn't keen on the idea of playing Santa, so why would he do it *since* it involved wearing an uncomfortable costume? That does not compute. You need a conjunction between the two clauses that makes it clearer that he wore the costume despite that he didn't really want to: a conjunction like *even though*. There it is in **D**.

B can't be right because it has the same problem as the original sentence. **C** includes the phrase *necessity to wear*, and *necessity* is one of those words that must be followed by a gerund like *of wearing*. **E**, when added to the original sentence, makes a run-on.

2. **E**   Misplaced Modifiers   *Easy*

This sentence is incorrect because of a misplaced modifier. Look at the problem: *the café with the world-weary smile*. When it stands on its own like that, you can probably see the problem: The sentence makes it sound like the café has the world-weary smile, when it means to say the would-be novelist has the world-weary smile. **E** corrects the problem.

   B is a bit strange. It makes it sound as if the novelist's technique for modeling himself after Hemingway is to employ a world-weary smile. This is not what the original sentence suggests. **C** repeats the original problem. The phrases in **D** are arranged so that they completely obscure logical meaning.

3. **B**   Coordination and Subordination   *Easy*

This sentence suffers from bad coordination. The coordinating word, *although*, muddles the meaning of the sentence and makes it sound as if the rain delay continued despite that only a few fans departed. The correct answer, **B**, simply removes the incorrect *although*, thereby making the meaning of the sentence clear: Most fans stuck it out and stayed on through the long rain delay.

   Answers **C** and **D** use phrases synonymous with the original, problematic *although*. **E**, even though it changes *although* to *and*, does not solve the problem. It makes the relationship between the two clauses just as strange as it is in the original sentence.

4. **A**   No Error   *Medium*

5. **D**   Fragments   *Medium*

Fragment. Remember, if you feel like the sentence grinds to a halt before it's made its point, it might be a fragment. Here, you're left thinking, "The general did what?" The sentence never finishes what it begins. The correct answer, **D**, tells you what the general did: He came to scout out the terrain.

6. **C**   Tenses   *Medium*

Parallelism is the issue here. The sentence talks about the two characteristics that make the old woman good for the part of a murder suspect: *dark eyes* and *having a cunning look*. Because that first quality is described as a noun, the second quality must be described as a noun, too. In **C**, it is: *cunning look*.

7. **A**   No Error   *Medium*

8. **E**   Tenses   *Medium*

The infinitive *to pay* is incorrect. The sentence begins with the gerund *paying*, and for the sake of parallelism, the second half of the sentence should also use a gerund. Therefore, **E** is the correct answer.

   C can be eliminated because it does not fix the infinitive problem. **B** is not the right answer because of its wordiness. There's no reason for that *still* or the phrase *it is*. **D** is wordy and awkward: The phrase *is better* shouldn't be tacked onto the end of the sentence like that.

9. **C**   Passive Voice   *Medium*

The second half of the sentence uses the passive voice. Although you can figure it out from context, you're never told the identity of the performer of the action: Who is buying the paintings? The right answer, **C**, makes explicit the fact that *she* (Gardner) was the one buying the paintings.

10. **A**   No Error   *Medium*

11. **E**   Misplaced Modifiers   *Medium*
The problem here is a misplaced modifier. Look at the problem in isolation: *One of the most inventive and respected dancers in the world, tap dancing.* Tap dancing is not a respected dancer; Fred Astaire is. The answer choice that best expresses this is **E**.

   B makes the sentence into a run-on and doesn't fix the misplaced modifier. **C** does not fix the misplaced modifier. **D** changes the meaning of the sentence; it suggests that Fred Astaire benefited from tap dancing, whereas the original sentence suggests that tap dancing benefited from Fred Astaire.

Identifying Sentence Errors

12. **D**   Pronouns   *Easy*
When the writer of this sentence refers back to *each of the manuscript*s, he talks about *their own problems*. This is incorrect, because the phrase *each of the manuscripts* actually refers to each manuscript individually—it's a singular phrase. So, this singular phrase should be matched with the singular phrase *its own problems*.

13. **A**   Tense   *Easy*
This sentence contains a tense error. The verb *has decide* is not a valid verb tense. It has to be *has decided*.

14. **D**   Subject-Verb Agreement   *Easy*
The key to spotting the error in this sentence is to notice how far apart the subject (*The Eiffel Tower*) is from its verb (*have become*). If you eliminate the intervening clause *more than any of Paris's dozens of other tourist attractions*, you get *The Eiffel Tower have become*. Sound wrong? It is. *The Eiffel Tower* is a single subject. The verb form *have become* is plural. **D** is the right answer.

15. **D**   Gerunds   *Easy*
The infinitive *to prevent* must be followed by a gerund. If those grammar terms freak you out, think of it like this: You can't say *to prevent to escape*. No matter how passionately you utter a phrase like this—"Nothing can prevent you to escape the clutches of my love"—it's still wrong. Sounds like a bad translation from an Austrian romance novel. The rules of English dictate instead that a gerund (ending in *-ing*) follows an infinitive (*to _____*): *to prevent the butterfly from escaping*.

16. **E**   No Error   *Medium*

17. **D**   Abverbs and Adjectives   *Medium*
If you're comparing three or more items, you need a superlative, a word that usually ends in *-est*, such as *juiciest*, *lamest*, or *jolliest*. Comparative words, which often end in *-er*, such as *better*, can only compare two items. Since *dozens* of items are being

considered in this sentence, you need a superlative, not a comparative. Since *better* is a comparative, it is wrong, and **D** is the answer.

18. **C**   Parallelism   *Medium*

When you encounter a list, check it carefully for parallelism errors. This list begins and ends with verb phrases (*present new works* and *exhibit collections*), but the middle item is a noun (*education*). Remember, items in a list must take parallel form. Therefore, *education for visitors* should be changed to something like *provide education for visitors* or *offer education to visitors*, and **C** is the correct answer.

19. **A**   Pronouns   *Medium*

Pronouns referring to the same thing cannot change halfway through a sentence. If a sentence begins with "one" as its subject, it can't switch to a "you" subject halfway through—and vice versa. This sentence begins with the phrase *before one attempts*, but midway through, it switches pronouns: *you should investigate*.

20. **C**   Faulty Comparison   *Medium*

This sentence has a faulty comparison. Technically, this sentence says that other players weren't as difficult for Hank Aaron as were the first years of his career. What the writer means to say is that the first years of Aaron's career were more difficult than the first years of other players' careers.

21. **E**   No Error   *Medium*

22. **D**   Wrong Word   *Medium*

Eminent means "prominent, well-known." *Imminent* means "impending, about to begin." This writer wanted the latter word and used the former. Unfortunately, barring a lucky guess, the only way to get this question right is to study our list of pesky, commonly confused words.

23. **C**   Pronouns   *Medium*

This sentence might sound fine on first reading, but you should always look carefully at pronoun usage. People use pronouns incorrectly in speech so frequently that it can be difficult to notice pronoun errors on the test. In this sentence, the problematic pronoun is *they*. Because the sentence starts out by talking about *an exam* (singular) it cannot refer to that one exam as *they*. Instead of *they have all been exhausting*, the sentence should read something like *each one has been exhausting*. Alternatively, the sentence could use plurals throughout: *I never expected it could be so difficult to take exams, but this semester they have all been very exhausting*.

24. **A**   Abverbs and Adjectives   *Medium*

Look at the first clause, *the tenor sang so loud that he completely lost his voice*. *Sang* is a verb, and it is described by the adjective *loud*. This is a problem, because adjectives can't describe verbs. A corrected version of the sentence would read *the tenor sang so loudly*. *Loudly* is grammatically correct; it is an adverb, and adverbs exist specifically to describe verbs. **A** is your answer.

25. **E**   No Error   *Medium*

26. **A**   Double Negative   *Difficult*

Cannot is a negative word. *Scarcely* is also a negative word, but a less obvious one. Be careful whenever you encounter words like *scarcely*, and its cousins *hardly* and *barely*. They're all negative words that don't sound negative, and it's easier to miss a double negative when one of those tricky negative-but-doesn't-sound-negative words is in the mix. So the right answer is **A**—*cannot scarcely* should be either *cannot* or *scarcely*.

27. **E**   No Error   *Difficult*

28. **C**   Wrong Word   *Difficult*

The problem here is with the word *where*, which refers to a physical place. *A plan* is not a physical place. The sentence should read *someone came up with a plan by which the union could work out its differences.*

29. **B**   Subject-Verb Agreement   *Difficult*

Neither/nor constructions always result in singular nouns. Neither this individual guy nor that individual guy *was . . . .* So, in this sentence, *were prepared* is incorrect.

Improving Paragraphs

30. **C**   Sentence Revision   *Easy*

The word *but* is not correct in the original sentence. *But* makes the fact that 300,000 people die from obesity sound like it *contradicts* the fact that sixty-one percent of people suffer from obesity. Actually, these two facts make perfect sense when considered together. Therefore, the connecting word should be *and*, as it is in **C**.

31. **E**   Sentence Revision   *Medium*

The sentence contains a list. The first thing you should do is search for faulty parallelism: The items in the list must be all noun phrases or all gerunds. In the original sentence, the first two items are noun phrases, but the third is a gerund. **E** turns the gerund *getting heart disease* into the noun phrase *heart disease*, fixing the problem.

32. **A**   Sentence Addition   *Difficult*

Before you go about choosing an answer, examine the essay and see what's missing from the beginning of that second paragraph. The second paragraph begins abruptly, jumping right from talking about the problems that obesity causes to talking about how people should diet. A transition would be useful—and you should remember, too, that transitions are favorite additions on this section of the test. **A** is the correct answer, since it provides a transition from a discussion of facts about the problem of obesity (in the first paragraph) to a discussion of solutions aimed at preventing obesity on a physical level (in the second paragraph).

33. **C**   Sentence Revision   *Difficult*

The best way to deal with this type of sentence is to treat it as an Identifying Sentence Errors question. Where is the worst error in the sentence? In this question, the problem is in the list of things people try. If you're saying a range of items, as this sentence does in the phrase *from pills to shakes and formulas*, you have to use the word *to*, not *and*, in between each item. That makes **C** the correct answer.

34.   **E**   Sentence Combination   *Difficult*

The best way to deal with this question is to figure out the answer before you look at the answer choices. Ask yourself how the two sentences relate to one another. Basically, they're saying that even though you can lose weight, you'll gain it back once you stop dieting. Once you have that relation clear, go to the answer choices. **E** most effectively gets across that relationship.

35.   **B**   Sentence Revision   *Medium*

This sentence is a run-on. The clauses on each side of the comma are complete ideas, and the comma isn't strong enough to hold them together. To fix it, **B** throws a semicolon between the two clauses.

SECTION 7

Sentence Completions

1.   **B**   One-Blank/Two-Way   *Easy*

The two-way switch *but* tells you that the sentence presents a contrast. What happened to Elroy in the past with the stock market will not, according to Elroy, happen again. The blank describes what Elroy thinks is going to happen this time. In the past, Elroy "lost money in the stock market," so the blank must make it clear that this time he expects to make money. The only answer that fits the idea of making money is *profit*.

Several of the other answer choices feature words associated with investment and finance (*deficit*, *shares*, and *power*), but those are all traps.

2.   **E**   One-Blank/One-Way   *Medium*

The sentence contains no switch and does not make a comparison over time: It's one-way. So the blank, which describes the aims of the ambassador, must fit with the fact that the ambassador is "terrified of war." Therefore, the ambassador must be hoping to bring about "peace." You're looking for a positive word that fits with the idea of creating peace. The words *demoralization*, *aggression*, *misconception*, and *prejudice* are all negative and all likely to cause war, not prevent it. The best answer is *reconciliation*, a word that implies forgiveness and settling differences, a prerequisite to peace.

3.   **C**   One-Blank/One-Way   *Medium*

This sentence is a little tricky. The word you'd normally look at to determine whether the sentence is one way or two way is actually the blank! So, instead of looking at that word, you have to look at the context on either side of the blank. To the left of the blank the sentence says that the company has suffered many firings while to the right it talks about the financial difficulties the company's had. The two sides of the sentence go together (they're both bad news for the company). So the word you choose for the blank has to link the two sides of the sentence, as opposed to contrasting them. Only *confirm* and *nurture* preserve a noncontrasting relation-

the new SAT

ship between the two sides of the sentence. And since nurture implies that the firings would have caused the financial difficulties, which doesn't make any sense, confirm is the right answer.

4. **E** One-Blank/One-Way   *Medium*

The sentence contains no switch and no comparison over time: It's one-way. The blank must fit with the rest of the information presented in the sentence. The blank describes what "many Americans" look for in a president, and the rest of the sentence explains that these Americans vote based on issues of character and morality. The blank must be something like "good values." So, which answer choices match "good values"? *Temerity* (boldness)? Nope. *Exuberance* (excitement)? Nope. *Irreverence* (disrespect)? Nope. *Gravity* might seem like a more tempting choice since, seriousness and thoughtfulness are often found in a person of good, moral character. But a thoughtful, serious person could be completely immoral, so cut gravity too. The best answer is *integrity*. Someone with integrity demonstrates a strict adherence to a moral code.

5. **B** One-Blank/One-Way   *Medium*

The sentence contains no switch and does not make a comparison over time: It's one-way. The defendant's actions must be directly related to the way that the jury views her guilt, which is what the blank describes. In this sentence, the defendant refuses to testify, and the blank describes what kind of "acknlowledgment of guilt" the jurors see this refusal to speak as being. To put it another way, the jury sees the defendant's refusal to testify as an "unspoken" admission of guilt, so you're looking for a word like *unspoken*. *Tacit* means exactly that: something implied or not stated directly.

But perhaps you didn't know the definition of *tacit*. The best thing to do in that case is to eliminate whatever you can. *Libelous* seems like a fitting word for a sentence about a trial, but that's why it's such a good SAT trap. When put into the context of the sentence, it doesn't make sense to describe a defendant's silent admission of guilt as "libelous," or defamatory. The sentence gives you no reason to think the jury would see the defendant's admission as *solemn* (somber) or *magnanimous* (noble). Cut those. Finally, the idea of a *tranquil* acknowledgment doesn't make sense (*tranquil* means peaceful), so you can eliminate that choice as well.

6. **A** Two-Blank/Two-Way   *Difficult*

The sentence contains the two-way switch *although*, which signals that the two halves of the sentence contrast. The author meant to write some kind of comedy, and ended up writing some sort of tragedy. The first blank describes the type of comedy the author meant to write, and the second describes the book on "a highly tragic theme" the author ended up writing. The first blank should be filled with a word like *funny* or *silly* and the second blank should have a serious and weighty word like *tome* or possibly even something having to do with deep thought, like *reflection* or *philosophy*. You can cut *hackneyed . . satire*, *banal . . narrative*, and *wretched . . proposition* since the first word in each of these choices has a strongly negative connotation that doesn't fit with a comedy. You can also cut *scintillating . . farce*, since there's no such thing as a weighty farce (a farce is a kind of light comedy). The only choice that fits the sentence well is *flippant . . meditation*. The author meant to write a flippant (light and witty) comedy, but instead penned a weighty meditation on a tragic theme. You've got your comedy, your tragedy, your contrast, and you're all set.

Long Reading Passage (Hamlet)

7.   E   Main Idea   *Medium*

Each of these answer choices might, on its own terms, be valid explanations for Hamlet's melancholy. It's necessary to read through the passage for both specific clues and a general sense of the author's argument. **B** and **D** can be discarded, since the author specifically states that Hamlet did not feel jealousy over his uncle's ascension to the throne or an unnatural grief over his father's death. The passage makes no reference to Hamlet's cowardice, **C**, or to his psychological instability, **A**, but it does refer several times to his "exquisite sense" of morality, **E**, and to the centrality of his mother and uncle's behavior in his own moral consciousness—as he loved and admired his father for his virtue, he comes to despise his mother for her vice.

8.   B   Specific Information   *Medium*

The major difficulty of this question, as with the passage generally, is figuring out just what the heck this overly complex critic is trying to say. Here's what: Hamlet is troubled by Gertrude's "ingratitude to the memory of her former husband, and the depravity she displays in the choice of a successor." This makes **B** the only feasible answer choice: Gertrude dishonors the memory of her former husband, Hamlet's father, and displays "depravity" in choosing a new husband, Claudius.

9.   D   Words in Context   *Easy*

The word *commerce* usually has an economic overtone (it is the root of the word *commercial*). But remember, this is a Words-in-Context sentence. Go back to the context: "The man whose sense of moral excellence is uncommonly exquisite will find it a source of pleasure and of pain in his ---- with mankind." The sentence discusses the idea that a person who cares so deeply about "moral excellence" will have trouble in his relationship or dealings with the rest of mankind. The only word among the answer choices that captures this idea of relationship is **D**, *interaction*.

10.   A   Implied Information   *Difficult*

Choice **C** is tempting because it involves a theme of revenge that is also central to Hamlet, and choices **D** and **E** are tempting because they are generally true to the spirit of passage. But the critic of passage 1 never outright says **C**, and **D** and **E** both fail the Law of Absolutely Wrong. The writer says that a child will feel "joy" and "triumph" for morally worthy parents, and "acute" sorrow for unworthy parents. In other words, **A** is the right answer: *intense pride or shame based on the moral worth of his or her parents*.

11.   B   Words in Context   *Easy*

The author never seems angry or hostile, so *defiant* and *confrontational* should be eliminated. By the same token, for the author to be *resigned* would imply that he is prepared to meet an unpleasant or unsatisfactory outcome, and no such outcome is suggested by this paragraph. So, the most compelling of the possible answer choices are **B** and **C**—the author is either *dramatic and descriptive* or *measured and careful*. Because the author is clearly a literary critic of some kind, you may be tempted to answer *measured and careful*, since that's the stereotype of scholars in general. But take a look at the language the guy uses, ranging from colorful description ("Agitated and overwhelmed . . .") to repetition ("no soothing, no exhilarating . . ."), to present Hamlet's situation in suitably grand terms. **B** is the correct answer choice.

the new SAT

12. **C**   Words in Context   *Medium*

Each answer choice accurately describes one facet of Hamlet's behavior during the course of the play. They do not, however, all fit the definition of the word *jocular*, and they do not all fit the context of the sentence in which the word is found. In the passage in question, the author lists several ways in which Hamlet's inner contradictions make him a difficult character to understand: He is committed to revenge, but fails to act; he is a passionate lover, yet seems uninterested in the woman he loves; and he is deeply melancholy, yet often acts in a "jocular" manner. In each case, Hamlet's behaviors seem to be directly self-contradictory; from that observation, you can assume that *jocular* means the opposite of melancholy or depressed. This is underscored by the fact that in the sentence, *jocular* is used along with the word *gay*, which means *happy*.

13. **B**   Themes and Arguments   *Difficult*

Each choice represents a complex, plausible, possible answer to this relatively difficult question. In order to arrive at the correct answer, you have to look at the section of the passage indicated in the question. In general, the passage compares misfortunes that one can forget easily ("the mind will soon call up reflections to alleviate, and hopes to cheer") and misfortunes that linger in the mind (those that "reflection only serves to irritate"). The first, forgettable kind of misfortunes are categorized as "misfortunes of accident"; the second, memorable kind of misfortunes are not categorized, but are exemplified: "they arose from an uncle's villainy, a mother's guilt, a father's murder!"

Each of these seems to be an example of preconceived, intentional wrongdoing, which contrasts with the accidental circumstance at work in the first kind of misfortune. Thus, the answer must be **B**, which compares accidental misfortune to misfortune caused by the bad behavior of others.

14. **E**   Specific Information   *Medium*

The author of passage 2 writes that Shakespeare might have encountered "such a character" in real life and chosen to translate his attributes to the stage, where they could be observed through the workings of imagination and the conflict of the passions.

15. **A**   Main Idea   *Medium*

The passage says that Shakespeare makes the reader feel "anxiety for the person"— that is, for Hamlet—rather than "anxiety for the event," or suspense based on an uncertain outcome. He says that Shakespeare accomplishes this by making Hamlet's difficulties arise from the thoughts and feelings of his own mind rather than from accidental circumstance or a deliberate, focused attempt to achieve his goals. Because Hamlet's thoughts and feelings are the main focus of the play, the reader is able to feel Hamlet's struggles very personally and even consider Hamlet's state of mind more important than the outward plot of the play. **A** is the best answer choice— Hamlet becomes important to readers not because of his moral position or his outward situation, but because his inner situation is the main focus of the story and provides the play's major conflict.

16. **D**   Main Idea   *Difficult*

One entire paragraph of passage 2 discusses Hamlet's sensitivity to his surroundings and the pain his family has caused him. Another paragraph describes Hamlet's natural inconsistency and variability. The author implies that Hamlet's sensitive and reflective nature is exacerbated by his situation, causing his erratic streak to emerge as he oscillates between commitment to revenge and helpless uncertainty.

17. **C** Themes and Arguments *Difficult*

This question requires you to catalog the various aspects of Hamlet's character that each author discusses and to compare those catalogs to see what the passage 1 author leaves out that the Passage 2 author puts in. The easiest way to go about this task is to run down the list of possible answers and try to find each of them in each passage.

Neither passage mentions Hamlet's temper or his temptation to sin, so **A** and **E** can be eliminated. **B** and **D** can be eliminated for just the opposite reason: Both passages discuss Hamlet's sensitivity to his family's behavior and his melancholy mood. The only answer choice that remains is **C**, which, when you check the passages, is confirmed as the correct answer: the passage 2 author explores the question of Hamlet's inconsistency at some length, while the passage 1 author is more focused on the causes of his melancholy disposition.

18. **E** Relating Two Passages *Easy*

Passage 1 describes the "impropriety" of Gertrude's behavior in marrying Claudius so soon after her first husband's death and says that Hamlet detects moral "depravity" in her actions. The second passage identifies "a mother's guilt" as one of Hamlet's most terrible burdens, implying that Gertrude is guilty of some crime. Neither passage mentions her love for Claudius, her innocence in the matter of the murder, her popularity in Denmark, or her former role as a moral example for Hamlet.

19. **D** Relating Two Passages *Medium*

Because of the long answer choices and wide variety of ideas they discuss, this question appears far more complicated than it really is. Both passages discuss Hamlet's sensitivity fairly early on. The passage 1 author emphasizes Hamlet's acute moral feelings, saying that he responds to virtue and vice with extremely powerful reactions. The author of passage 2 comments on Hamlet's general sensitivity, saying that he is "apt to be strongly impressed by his situation" and even "overpowered by the feelings which that situation excites." So, passage 1 emphasizes Hamlet's moral sensitivity, while passage 2 emphasizes his more general sensitivity to events, making **D** the best answer choice. Though they reference a wide variety of ideas, many of which are important to the play, none of the other answer choices seems particularly relevant to the specific texts in question.

SECTION 8

1. **D** Numbers and Operations: Basic Operations *Easy*

To answer this question, you have to know the rules of odd and even numbers like the back of the neck of the person who sits in front of you in math class. Sure, on this question, you could just try out each answer choice and it wouldn't really take sooooo long, but remember: Saving time is crucial on the SAT Math section. Easy questions like this one can help you save time for the test's tougher questions. Okay. Now to solve it: Since 9 is an odd number, and $x + 9$ equals an even number, by the rules of addition of odd and even numbers, x must also be odd. The only odd answer choice is 3, so that's it.

2.   **A**   Geometry: Polygons   *Easy*

Because *ABCD* is a square, you know that the length of side *CD* is equal to 4. *ECD* is a right triangle because all of the angles in a square are right angles. You also know that *ED*, which equals 5, is the hypotenuse because it is the side opposite the right angle. With this information, you can use the Pythagorean theorem: $c^2 = a^2 + x^2$, where *c* is 5 and *a* is 4. Once you work out the theorem, you get $x = 3$. You could have skipped working out the Pythagorean theorem if you had recognized right away that the triangle has to be a 3-4-5 triangle.

3.   **C**   Algebra: Systems of Equations   *Easy*

In this systems of equations, the only difference between the first two equations is the presence of the term *z*. That makes it easy to solve for *z* by subtracting the second equation from the first:

$$(x + y + z) - (x + y) = 10 - 3$$
$$x + y + z - x - y = 7$$
$$z = 7$$

Once you have the value of *z*, you can plug it into the third equation to get $y = 1$.

4.   **E**   Geometry: Coordinate Geometry   *Medium*

The area of the square is the length of the side squared, so the first thing you have to do is find the length of a side of the square. Lo and behold! A right triangle is formed by the two axes and the square, with the hypotenuse as one side of the square. Now you can use the Pythagorean theorem to find the side length of the square.

$$s^2 = 7^2 + 8^2$$
$$s^2 = 49 + 64$$
$$s^2 = 113$$

At this point, you *could* solve for *s* and then square it to get the area of the square, but why bother? The area of the square is equal to s^2, and you just showed that $s^2 = 113$. In other words, you're already done.

5.   **B**   Numbers and Operations: Roots and Radicals   *Medium*

To answer this question correctly, you have to know that a radical sign can also be written as a fractional exponent. So, $\sqrt{x} = x^{\frac{1}{2}}$. Once you know that, you can see that in this question, $2m = \frac{1}{2}$, which means $m = \frac{1}{4}$.

6.   **C**   Algebra: Functions as Models   *Medium*

To answer this question, think about what the graph is doing, then see which described situation best fits the graph. In the figure, the graph *y* increases as *x* increases until, at some point, *y* hits a plateau and stays flat as *x* continues to increase. Now, look at the answer choices. While the weight of a steel rod, the volume of a sphere, and the age of a rock will all increase as length, time, and radius increase respectively, they will never flatten out. In contrast, a man does stop growing at some point in his life. His height will flatten out.

7.　**A**　Algebra: Inequalities　　　　　　　　　　　　　*Medium*

Dealing with fractions and inequalities can make your head spin. Treat them like you would an unwanted guest: Get rid of them. Since $\frac{1}{x-y} < \frac{1}{y-x}$, the denominator of the fraction on the left has to be larger than the denominator on the right (the larger the denominator, the smaller the fraction). So, $x - y > y - x$.

Now this question is a whole lot easier to handle. Take a look at I, II, and III, and notice that the question asks which of these *must* be true. Look for ways to prove each scenario wrong. When testing each possibility, make sure you take negative numbers into account. For choice I, since $x - y > y - x$, x must always be larger than y. Does x have to be larger than $-y$, though? No. If $x = -1$ and $y = -2$, then $-y$ is larger than x, but the inequality still works out, since $-1 - (-2) = 3$, and 3 is greater than $-2 - (-1) = -3$. So, II is untrue. And III? For $xy > 0$, x and y must both be positive or both be negative. Will the inequality work out if one is positive and the other negative? (Remember that we know that $x > y$, so x has to be the positive one in this experiment.) If $x = 2$ and $y = -1$, the inequality still holds true, since $2 - (-1) = 3$ and 3 is greater than $-1 - 2 = -3$. So, **A** is the answer.

8.　**D**　Algebra: Binomials and Quadratics　　　　　　*Medium*

This type of question preys on people who depend too much on their calculator. If you just plug both equations into your calculator and graph them, you might conclude that the two equations are identical and get the question wrong. The SAT trap answer, **B**, would snare you. Instead of jumping immediately to the calculator, take a brief second to look at the question, asking yourself where it might be trying to trick you. You might then notice that the second equation can't have a value at $x = 2$, since the denominator is $x - 2$, and a fraction with a denominator of 0 is undefined. *Now*, either graph the two equations on your calculator or work out the math.

On your calculator, the two graphs will probably look exactly the same, because the calculator's standard setting is too broad to show the undefined spot at $x = 2$ for the second equation. But since you know that the undefined spot at $x = 2$ exists, you know the answer is **D**. If you work out the math, you'll see that the equation $y = \frac{x^2 - 4}{x - 2}$ can be factored to give $y = \frac{(x+2)(x-2)}{x-2}$. In all situations but $x = 2$, the $x - 2$ in the numerator and denominator cancel out to give $y = x + 2$, the same as the first equation. But, of course, at $x = 2$, the equation is undefined.

9.　**B**　Numbers and Operations: Sets　　　　　　　*Difficult*

Whenever you're faced with a sets problem in which you're told about two separate sets and a few items or people who fit into both sets, remember a simple formula: Total = number in the first set + number in the second set – the number common to both sets. For this question, $13 = 11 + 7 - x$, where x is the number of students who know how to play both flute and piano. Do the math: $x = 5$.

10. **B**   Geometry: Solids   *Difficult*

First things first: sketch what the question describes—a square inscribed in a circle inscribed in a square, and the side of the inmost square is 4.

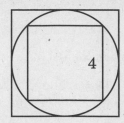

This is a simple question mathematically, but lots of students get it wrong because they miss the one key point: The diagonal of the inscribed square is equal to the diameter of the circle, just as the length of the outside square is equal to the diameter of the circle. A slight modification of the image will make this clearer.

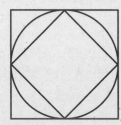

Now to find the diagonal of the square: A diagonal in a square cuts a triangle into two 45-45-90 triangles, so the diagonal is equal to the length of the side, 4, times $\sqrt{2}$. The diagonal length, which is also the length of a side of the larger square, is $4\sqrt{2}$. Square that to get the area of the large square: $\left(4\sqrt{2}\right)^2 = 16 \times 2 = 32$.

11.   **A**   Algebra: Absolute Value and Exponents   *Medium*

This question is a pretty straightforward test of what you know about negative and fractional exponents. Since the question tells you that $y = 4$, you can plug that number right into $2y^{-2}$ and get $2(4^{-2}) = 2\left(\dfrac{1}{4^2}\right) = 2\left(\dfrac{1}{16}\right) = \dfrac{1}{8}$. Now you can solve for $\dfrac{1}{2}x^{\frac{1}{2}} = \dfrac{1}{8}$. First, simplify the equation by multiplying both sides by 8: $4x^{\frac{1}{2}} = 1$. Remember that a fractional exponent is the same as a radical sign, so $\sqrt{x} = \dfrac{1}{4}$, which means that $x = \dfrac{1}{16}$.

12.   **D**   Algebra: Solving Equations   *Difficult*

To find the value of x at which the two equations are equal, just set the equations equal to each other, and then solve for x:

$$xyz + 2 = 4 - xyz$$
$$2xyz = 4 - 2$$
$$2xyz = 2$$
$$xyz = 1$$
$$x = \frac{1}{yz}$$

13.   **E**   Data Analysis, Statistics, Probability:Graphs, Charts, and Tables*Medium*
The line that best "averages out" all of the plots scattered about in this particular scatterplot is:

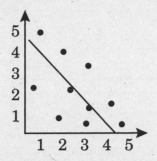

The slope is clearly negative, leaving only **D** and **E** as possible right answers. If you then take a closer look, you can see that the line travels about one unit on the *y*-axis for each unit on the *x*-axis, meaning its slope is closest to –1.

14.   **D**   Algebra: Domain and Range   *Difficult*
To solve this domain and range question, you first have to figure out what function you're dealing with. Since you have $g(f(x))$, you need to plug $\sqrt{3x-3}$ into function g wherever x appears: $g(f(x)) = \dfrac{1}{\sqrt{3x-3}-1}$. The question asks you for the range of the function, which means it's asking you for the values of x at which the function is valid. Since you're dealing with a function that is a fraction and also contains a radical, there are two ways that the function might not be valid at a particular value of x: First, there might be a negative value under the radical sign. Second, the denominator of the fraction could be equal to 0. To solve the problem, you need to find the numbers that will create such issues for this function and define the range accordingly. First, deal with the radical. The expression under the radical must be positive. In other words, you need $3x-3 > 0$; $3x > 3$; $x > 1$. That's one component of your range: x must be greater than 1 (once you know this, you can eliminate answers **B** and **E**). You also need the numerator of the fraction not to equal 0: $\sqrt{3x-3}-1 \neq 0$, which means that $\sqrt{3x-3} \neq 1$. If you square both sides, you see that $3x-3 \neq 1$, so $3x \neq 4$ and $x \neq \dfrac{4}{3}$. The answer choice that shows the proper range is **D**.

15.   **D**   Geometry: Circles   *Difficult*
There are the two key facts you need to know to solve this problem:

1. A tangent line is perpendicular to a radius drawn to the point of tangency.
2. If a chord on a circle is equal to the radius of a circle, the angle formed by drawing radii to the endpoints of the chord equals 60 degrees.

Using this information, it's time to update the given diagram:

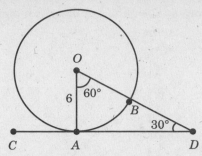

Suddenly, all you've got to contend with is a 30-60-90 triangle. The side opposite the 30° angle equals 6, so the side opposite the 60° angle must equal $6\sqrt{3}$, and the area of the triangle will equal $A = \frac{1}{2}(6)(6\sqrt{3}) = 18\sqrt{3}$. Boom. Done.

16.　**E**　Numbers and Operations: Percents　　　　　　　　　　*Difficult*

Percents are parts of wholes. In this question, you know that the part is y, but you don't know the whole. In fact, you need to figure out the expression that signifies the whole. From the question, you know that y is the number of women in the company, and that the number of men is equal to $y + 40$ (since there are 40 more male employees than female employees). The key is to realize that in order to find the total number of employees at the company, you have to add the number of male and female employees. So the whole is equal to $y + (y + 40) = 2y + 40$. So the part over the whole would be $\frac{y}{2y+40}$. But wait! There's one more trick in this problem (this is the trick that makes it difficult). If you divide y by $2y + 40$ the result will be a decimal, not a percentage. In order to get a percentage, you have to multiply the value by 100. So the right answer is $\frac{100y}{2y+40}$.

SECTION 9

Improving Sentences

1.　**A**　Conjunctions　　　　　　　　　　　　　　　　　　　　*Easy*

This sentence uses the conjunction *and* incorrectly. Conjunctions such as *and* are used to link nouns or clauses containing nouns ("I like the rock concerts *and* the symphony"). But the sentence in this question doesn't need a conjunction because the final clause describes the original subject (Elvis). **D** solves the problem by replacing *and* with *when*.

2.　**B**　Tenses　　　　　　　　　　　　　　　　　　　　　　　*Easy*

The clause following the conjunction *but* should be in the same tense as the clause that preceded it. Here instead we have two different tenses: the simple present (*have moons*) and the continuous present (*is having rings*). The correct answer choice has to have both verbs in the simple present. You know therefore that **A**, **C**, and **D** are out, leaving you with **B** and **E**. Both look correct at first glance since they've got the simple present verb form (*has rings*), but **E** implies that Saturn does not have moons, which makes the sentence as a whole contradictory, because it states that all the planets have moons.

3. **C** Run-On   *Easy*

Run-on sentences like this one join two or more independent clauses without a conjunction (*and*, *or*, *but*, *because*, *since*, and so on). To make the sentence make sense, the correct answer must introduce a conjunction that separates the clauses of the sentence appropriately. Cut **A**, **B**, and **E** since none of those choices contains a conjunction. **C** and **D** contain the conjunction *because* (technically called a "subordinating conjunction"). **C** is the better choice because **D** contains the redundant verb "to speed."

4. **E** Subject-Verb Agreement   *Medium*

The subject of this sentence, *sheep*, is plural and therefore requires a plural verb. Instead this sentence has got the singular verb *lives*. Both **A** and **D** contain the singular verb form, so cut both. **B** contains a long redundant clause (*are living in New Zealand*), so cut **B**. **C** and **E** both contain plural verbs, but **C** uses the clunky continuous present (*are living*) and employs an awkward sentence structure. **E** cleans things up nicely by using the correct verb form and a simple correct subject-verb grammatical structure.

5. **A** No Error   *Medium*

6. **C** Fragment   *Easy*

This sentence reads like a newspaper headline—it needs another verb in order for it to make sense and to convey its intended meaning. **B** and **D** put the verb *advanced* in the wrong place. **E** should use the infinitive *to advance* rather than *in the advancing*. The only choice that does work is **C**, which makes the sentence read: Maya Angelou has helped to advance the women's rights movement.

7. **C** Idioms   *Medium*

The phrase *it's just not accurate* must be followed by the preposition *to* if another verb such as *claim* follows it. The correct answer choice must therefore contain a construction like it's *just not accurate to claim*.

8. **E** Parallelism   *Medium*

Parallelism requires the verb forms within a clause to align properly. Here we've got a simple present verb (*are*) mixed in with a present perfect verb (*have been*). The best solution to this problem is to cut the second verb and use the verb *are* to refer to both *accurate* and *easy to use*. That means you can cut **A**, **B**, and **D**, none of which use just are. **C** and **E** both do, but **C** changes *accurate* to *accuracy*, which changes the meaning of the sentence. **E** is the best answer.

9. **A** No Error   *Medium*

10. **C** Coordination and Subordination   *Medium*

The word *and* that links the developer's refusal with his eventual reversal won't cut it here. Instead you need a word that conveys the contrast between the developer's original stance, and the one he later takes in deciding to answer the board's questions. The best word that does do that among the options in the answer choices is *but*. *Therefore*, *because*, *since*, and *and* all fail to convey a contrast between the developer's initial attitude and his changed position.

11.   **B**   Tenses   *Medium*

This one's somewhat tricky. Many of the answer choices seem so wrong that you might be tempted to choose **A**. Choices **B**, **D**, and **E** are all filled with problems. The original sentence has one fatal tense flaw: the continuous past verb form *was exploring* should actually be the simple past form, *explored*. The adverb *courageously* works just fine with explored, so **C** is the best answer choice.

12.   **A**   No Error   *Difficult*

13.   **B**   Other   *Difficult*

The subject of this sentence is California, but the pronoun that refers to California is *they*. Here's the tricky part: even the pronoun *it* would not suffice here, however, because *it* could refer to either California or its coastline. That leaves **B** as the only possible answer.

14.   **A**   No Error   *Difficult*

SAT PRACTICE TEST 3 ANSWER SHEET

SECTION 6

1. Ⓐ Ⓑ Ⓒ Ⓓ Ⓔ	10. Ⓐ Ⓑ Ⓒ Ⓓ Ⓔ	19. Ⓐ Ⓑ Ⓒ Ⓓ Ⓔ	28. Ⓐ Ⓑ Ⓒ Ⓓ Ⓔ
2. Ⓐ Ⓑ Ⓒ Ⓓ Ⓔ	11. Ⓐ Ⓑ Ⓒ Ⓓ Ⓔ	20. Ⓐ Ⓑ Ⓒ Ⓓ Ⓔ	29. Ⓐ Ⓑ Ⓒ Ⓓ Ⓔ
3. Ⓐ Ⓑ Ⓒ Ⓓ Ⓔ	12. Ⓐ Ⓑ Ⓒ Ⓓ Ⓔ	21. Ⓐ Ⓑ Ⓒ Ⓓ Ⓔ	30. Ⓐ Ⓑ Ⓒ Ⓓ Ⓔ
4. Ⓐ Ⓑ Ⓒ Ⓓ Ⓔ	13. Ⓐ Ⓑ Ⓒ Ⓓ Ⓔ	22. Ⓐ Ⓑ Ⓒ Ⓓ Ⓔ	31. Ⓐ Ⓑ Ⓒ Ⓓ Ⓔ
5. Ⓐ Ⓑ Ⓒ Ⓓ Ⓔ	14. Ⓐ Ⓑ Ⓒ Ⓓ Ⓔ	23. Ⓐ Ⓑ Ⓒ Ⓓ Ⓔ	32. Ⓐ Ⓑ Ⓒ Ⓓ Ⓔ
6. Ⓐ Ⓑ Ⓒ Ⓓ Ⓔ	15. Ⓐ Ⓑ Ⓒ Ⓓ Ⓔ	24. Ⓐ Ⓑ Ⓒ Ⓓ Ⓔ	33. Ⓐ Ⓑ Ⓒ Ⓓ Ⓔ
7. Ⓐ Ⓑ Ⓒ Ⓓ Ⓔ	16. Ⓐ Ⓑ Ⓒ Ⓓ Ⓔ	25. Ⓐ Ⓑ Ⓒ Ⓓ Ⓔ	34. Ⓐ Ⓑ Ⓒ Ⓓ Ⓔ
8. Ⓐ Ⓑ Ⓒ Ⓓ Ⓔ	17. Ⓐ Ⓑ Ⓒ Ⓓ Ⓔ	26. Ⓐ Ⓑ Ⓒ Ⓓ Ⓔ	35. Ⓐ Ⓑ Ⓒ Ⓓ Ⓔ
9. Ⓐ Ⓑ Ⓒ Ⓓ Ⓔ	18. Ⓐ Ⓑ Ⓒ Ⓓ Ⓔ	27. Ⓐ Ⓑ Ⓒ Ⓓ Ⓔ	

SECTION 7

1. Ⓐ Ⓑ Ⓒ Ⓓ Ⓔ	6. Ⓐ Ⓑ Ⓒ Ⓓ Ⓔ	11. Ⓐ Ⓑ Ⓒ Ⓓ Ⓔ	16. Ⓐ Ⓑ Ⓒ Ⓓ Ⓔ
2. Ⓐ Ⓑ Ⓒ Ⓓ Ⓔ	7. Ⓐ Ⓑ Ⓒ Ⓓ Ⓔ	12. Ⓐ Ⓑ Ⓒ Ⓓ Ⓔ	17. Ⓐ Ⓑ Ⓒ Ⓓ Ⓔ
3. Ⓐ Ⓑ Ⓒ Ⓓ Ⓔ	8. Ⓐ Ⓑ Ⓒ Ⓓ Ⓔ	13. Ⓐ Ⓑ Ⓒ Ⓓ Ⓔ	18. Ⓐ Ⓑ Ⓒ Ⓓ Ⓔ
4. Ⓐ Ⓑ Ⓒ Ⓓ Ⓔ	9. Ⓐ Ⓑ Ⓒ Ⓓ Ⓔ	14. Ⓐ Ⓑ Ⓒ Ⓓ Ⓔ	19. Ⓐ Ⓑ Ⓒ Ⓓ Ⓔ
5. Ⓐ Ⓑ Ⓒ Ⓓ Ⓔ	10. Ⓐ Ⓑ Ⓒ Ⓓ Ⓔ	15. Ⓐ Ⓑ Ⓒ Ⓓ Ⓔ	

SECTION 8

1. Ⓐ Ⓑ Ⓒ Ⓓ Ⓔ	5. Ⓐ Ⓑ Ⓒ Ⓓ Ⓔ	9. Ⓐ Ⓑ Ⓒ Ⓓ Ⓔ	13. Ⓐ Ⓑ Ⓒ Ⓓ Ⓔ
2. Ⓐ Ⓑ Ⓒ Ⓓ Ⓔ	6. Ⓐ Ⓑ Ⓒ Ⓓ Ⓔ	10. Ⓐ Ⓑ Ⓒ Ⓓ Ⓔ	14. Ⓐ Ⓑ Ⓒ Ⓓ Ⓔ
3. Ⓐ Ⓑ Ⓒ Ⓓ Ⓔ	7. Ⓐ Ⓑ Ⓒ Ⓓ Ⓔ	11. Ⓐ Ⓑ Ⓒ Ⓓ Ⓔ	15. Ⓐ Ⓑ Ⓒ Ⓓ Ⓔ
4. Ⓐ Ⓑ Ⓒ Ⓓ Ⓔ	8 Ⓐ Ⓑ Ⓒ Ⓓ Ⓔ	12. Ⓐ Ⓑ Ⓒ Ⓓ Ⓔ	16. Ⓐ Ⓑ Ⓒ Ⓓ Ⓔ

SECTION 9

1. Ⓐ Ⓑ Ⓒ Ⓓ Ⓔ	5. Ⓐ Ⓑ Ⓒ Ⓓ Ⓔ	9. Ⓐ Ⓑ Ⓒ Ⓓ Ⓔ	13. Ⓐ Ⓑ Ⓒ Ⓓ Ⓔ
2. Ⓐ Ⓑ Ⓒ Ⓓ Ⓔ	6. Ⓐ Ⓑ Ⓒ Ⓓ Ⓔ	10. Ⓐ Ⓑ Ⓒ Ⓓ Ⓔ	14. Ⓐ Ⓑ Ⓒ Ⓓ Ⓔ
3. Ⓐ Ⓑ Ⓒ Ⓓ Ⓔ	7. Ⓐ Ⓑ Ⓒ Ⓓ Ⓔ	11. Ⓐ Ⓑ Ⓒ Ⓓ Ⓔ	
4. Ⓐ Ⓑ Ⓒ Ⓓ Ⓔ	8. Ⓐ Ⓑ Ⓒ Ⓓ Ⓔ	12. Ⓐ Ⓑ Ⓒ Ⓓ Ⓔ	

SECTION 1
ESSAY

Time — 25 minutes

You have twenty-five minutes to plan and write an essay on the topic assigned below. DO NOT WRITE ON ANOTHER TOPIC. AN ESSAY ON ANOTHER TOPIC IS NOT ACCEPTABLE.

The essay is assigned to give you an opportunity to show how well you can write. You should, therefore, take care to express your thoughts on the topic clearly and effectively. How well you write is much more important than how much you write, but to cover the topic adequately you will probably need to write more than one paragraph. Be specific.

Your essay must be written on the following two pages. You will find that you have enough space if you write on every line, avoid wide margins, and keep your handwriting to a reasonable size. It is important to remember that what you write will be read by someone who is not familiar with your handwriting. Try to write or print so that what you are writing is legible to the reader.

<u>Directions</u>: Think carefully about the issue presented in the following excerpt and the assignment below.

> Imagination is more important than knowledge. For knowledge is limited to all we now know and understand, while imagination embraces the entire world, and all there ever will be to know and understand. —Albert Einstein (1879–1955)

<u>Assignment:</u>   Do the ends always justify the means? Plan and write an essay in which you develop your point of view on this issue. Support your position with reasoning and examples taken from your reading, studies, experience, or observations.

DO NOT WRITE YOUR ESSAY IN YOUR TEST BOOK. You will receive credit only for what you write on your answer sheet.

WHEN YOUR SUPERVISOR ANNOUNCES THAT TWENTY-FIVE MINUTES HAVE PASSED, YOU MUST STOP WRITING THE ESSAY AND GO ON TO SECTION 2 IF YOU HAVE NOT ALREADY DONE SO. IF YOU FINISH YOUR ESSAY BEFORE THIS ANNOUNCEMENT, GO ON TO SECTION 2 AT ONCE.

BEGIN WRITING YOUR ESSAY ON THE ANSWER SHEET.

SECTION 1—ESSAY

Time — 25 minutes

SECTION 1—ESSAY

Time — 25 minutes

Section 2

Turn to Section 2 of your answer sheet to answer the questions in this section.

Time—25 Minutes
24 Questions

For each question in this section, select the best answer from among the choices given and fill in the corresponding oval on the answer sheet.

Each sentence below has one or two blanks, each blank indicating that something has been omitted. Beneath the sentence are five words or sets of words labeled A through E. Choose the word or set of words that, when inserted in the sentence, best fits the meaning of the sentence as a whole.

Example:

Medieval kingdoms did not become constitutional republics overnight; on the contrary, the change was ----.

(A) unpopular
(B) unexpected
(C) advantageous
(D) sufficient
(E) gradual   Ⓐ Ⓑ Ⓒ Ⓓ ●

 positive word

1. Many physicists considered string theory a ---- field because it presented so many unproven theories and research opportunities.   *C=correct*

   (A) safe
   (B) disappointing — *upsetting*
   (C) promising
   (D) turbuluent — *violently agitated or disturbed.*
   (E) dubious — *fraught w/ uncertainty ; undecided*

2. Though his first experiment ended in disappointment, the chemist hoped his second try would bring ----.

   (A) collapse
   (B) hypothesis
   (C) success
   (D) renewal   *C*
   (E) flaws

3. Although Spartacus wished to ---- his army after vanquishing the Roman forces, his men insisted on remaining ---- and continuing to fight.   *C*

   (A) reward..affluent
   (B) execute..macabre
   (C) outfit..neutral
   (D) disband..together
   (E) encourage..immoral

4. Because he wasn't British, many members of the English Parliament saw Prince Albert as a meddler in English affairs and treated him with ---- after he married Queen Victoria in 1840.   *C=correct*

   (A) impatience
   (B) ecstasy
   (C) contempt
   (D) interest
   (E) sadness

5. The Battle of Hastings in 1066 was a ---- event in English history, since the Norman victory over the Saxons changed the future course of the nation.   *B=correct*

   (A) petty
   (B) seminal
   (C) disastrous
   (D) disputable
   (E) glorious

6. Ms. Gutierrez told her students that a good paper must be factually ---- and conform to all rules of proper ----.   *C*

   (A) obvious..explanations
   (B) negative..behavior
   (C) inconsistent..punctuation
   (D) correct..grammar
   (E) continuous..spelling

GO ON TO THE NEXT PAGE

Section 2

7. Reindeer are often portrayed in American culture as merely ---- creatures, though in fact they are ---- to the survival of the people known as the Sami.

   (A) dim-witted..unnecessary
   (B) critical..instrumental
   (C) fanciful..crucial
   (D) Arctic..unhelpful
   (E) festive..detrimental

8. Despite having suffered through years of ---- rule, the people of Zambonia refused to forget the ---- traditions of their ancestors and continued to struggle for freedom.

   (A) benevolent..idiosyncratic
   (B) autocratic..egalitarian
   (C) destructive..despicable
   (D) idyllic..democratic
   (E) legislative..acrimonious

Section 2

Each short passage below is followed by questions based on its content. Answer the questions based on what is <u>stated</u> or <u>implied</u> in each passage.

Questions 9–10 are based on the following passage.

As I turned the corner, I heard a great rattle and jar from inside the house I was passing. No doubt a fight in that house! Or so I thought. Before I could turn, there came a terrific shock; the ground rolled under me in waves, interrupted by a violent joggling
5 up and down, and there was a heavy grinding noise as of brick houses rubbing together. I fell against the frame house and hurt my elbow. A third and more severe shock came, and as I reeled on the pavement trying to keep my footing, I saw a sight! The entire front of a four-story brick building on Third Street sprung
10 outward like a door and fell sprawling across the street!

9. The word "reeled" as used in the passage is closest in meaning to which of the following?

   (A) ensnared
   (B) decoyed
   (C) quavered
   (D) swivel
   (E) staggered

10. In the first instants of the earthquake, the author mistakes the earth's movement for a

   (A) jet flying overhead
   (B) family argument
   (C) construction project on a nearby building
   (D) rattle from a nearby window
   (E) a passing locomotive

Questions 11–12 are based on the following passage.

Dry ice is formed from frozen carbon dioxide, a gas which is a normal part of the atmosphere—that's right, the gas that you exhale while breathing and that plants take in for photosynthesis. Dry ice is particularly useful for your freezing needs because of its
5 extremely cold temperature (80 degrees Celsius lower than normal ice), and because it is easy to handle using nothing more than insulated gloves. Not enough for you? Dry ice also has the added benefit of skipping the wet liquid stage entirely. Instead, it changes directly from a solid state to a gas in normal atmospheric
10 conditions, a process called sublimation. All the freezing, none of the runny mess.

11. The author's main goal in this passage is to

   (A) pass along some interesting facts about dry ice
   (B) warn of the potential dangers of exposure to carbon dioxide
   (C) ridicule normal ice as a cooling agent
   (D) teach about the mysterious process of sublimation
   (E) convince people to use dry ice

12. One possible reason for the author of the passage to say that carbon dioxide is "a normal part of the atmosphere" is to

   (A) dispute recent scientific findings
   (B) allay fears that dry ice might be dangerous
   (C) illustrate how easy dry ice is to make
   (D) compare dry ice to ice made from water
   (E) dismiss dry ice as a cooling agent

GO ON TO THE NEXT PAGE

Section 2

The passage below is followed by questions based on its content. Answer the questions on the basis of what is <u>stated</u> or <u>implied</u> in the passage and in any introductory material that may be provided.

Questions 13-24 are based on the following passage.

In the following passage, the author discusses Herman Melville's novel Billy Budd. *The passage focuses on the importance and meaning of names, specifically in relation to the different subtitles that Melville considered for the novel.*

Because it went unpublished during Melville's lifetime, there has never been a clear consensus on the proper title for the work most commonly and concisely known as *Billy Budd*. Melville had a passion for subtitling his work, and *Billy Budd* stands as no
5 exception. Though it is generally referred to simply as *Billy Budd*, in scanning the literature regarding the work, one is equally likely to come upon the titles *Billy Budd, Sailor* or *Billy Budd, Foretopman*, and always bound to notice a further subtitle, "An Inside Narrative." All of these additional titles go further than the
10 abbreviated version to illustrate one of Melville's major themes in the work: the constant dilemma of an individual forced to function in a society.

In the opening lines of *Moby-Dick*, Melville introduces his narrator in a rather curious and roundabout way. He does not say,
15 "I am Ishmael," or even, "My name is Ishmael," but rather, "Call me Ishmael." Thus, there is no way of knowing whether the narrator is really named Ishmael or not. All we know is that he wishes to be called Ishmael. All of this illustrates the point that a discrepancy exists between an individual and his name. He may
20 or may not be named Ishmael, and even if he is, at the essential core of his existence, he is more than just his name.

So, you are you. Beyond that you have your name, and then beyond that you have your title. In the case of *Billy Budd*, he is a sailor or a foretopman. Because "foretopman" is a more specific
25 title than "sailor," *Billy Budd, Foretopman* goes even further than *Billy Budd, Sailor* to illustrate the tensions inevitably elicited by an individual consciousness placed in a specific societal role. As a "sailor," Billy may still be known as "Billy" more or less, but as a "foretopman," a more specific societal role with more specific
30 duties and responsibilities, Billy will have a harder time resisting the infringements of his office on his person.

Example: As "James Corolla," I may have my own impressions and opinions about *Billy Budd, Foretopman*. And these may change over time. But, once I decide to become "James Corolla,
35 Writer," my impressions and opinions about *Billy Budd, Foretopman* take on a greater weight and assume a larger air of finality. Furthermore, if I presume to be "James Corolla, Professor," my impressions and opinions about *Billy Budd, Foretopman* become even more weighty. What I choose to say
40 about *Billy Budd, Foretopman* can never again be simply something that I say as "James Corolla," since I've already said it

as "Professor," backed by all of the expectations and responsibilities associated with such a position. In this way, I exist as a "Professor" above and beyond my existence simply as
45 "James Corolla," and my place as "Professor," in some sense, eclipses my place as "James Corolla," at least with reference to *Billy Budd* and the other novels I choose to write about.

The moment that an individual enters into a society—and enter he must—he in some sense forfeits his rights to individual
50 autonomy, whether as a sailor, a writer, or whatever he may be. However, the sense of individuality remains and chafes against the constraints of the institution and its attendant laws. The clash between the individual and his society is one of the great themes of world literature, and, in *Billy Budd*, we have one of the
55 finest modern explorations of man caught between his own specific conscience and his broader sense of obligations to a just society.

As a self-described "Inside Narrative," *Billy Budd* places special emphasis on the interior consciousness of an individual, in
60 an attempt to explore the private selves of men thrust into a social world. Melville's true concern in *Billy Budd* is with this world behind a world. In each reader's attempt to get inside Melville's mind on the questions of morality, religion, and society, he or she will be sure to grapple fiercely with the interior narrative of his or
65 her own ideas and values.

13. According to lines 1–3, why have scholars been unable to agree about the correct title of the novel?

(A) They have misread clues provided in the novel's text.
(B) Political disagreements have led to conflicting factions.
(C) Scholars never agree about anything.
(D) Melville purposely never indicated the correct title.
(E) The novel was not published in Melville's lifetime, so a final title was never settled on.

14. The author primarily lists all the subtitles associated with *Billy Budd* (lines 5–9) in order to

(A) provide historical background information
(B) give an early example of the way in which titles indicate social position
(C) illustrate Melville's curious love of subtitles
(D) explain why bookstores have such a hard time selling Melville's works
(E) explain the differences between *Billy Budd* and *Moby-Dick*

GO ON TO THE NEXT PAGE

Section 2

15. The overall tone of this passage is

    (A) condescending
    (B) outraged
    (C) explanatory and objective
    (D) disengaged
    (E) excited and effusive

16. According to lines 14–21, what is unusual about the way Melville introduces his narrator in *Moby-Dick*?

    (A) He does not tell the reader whether "Ishmael" is the character's real name or not.
    (B) He does not give a physical description of the character.
    (C) He gives the narrator a highly unusual name.
    (D) He seems to imply that the narrator has a mysterious past.
    (E) He does not place the character in a social context, and therefore makes his name seem ambiguous.

17. The "discrepancy between an individual and his name" (line 17–19) is best understood as

    (A) the difference between a person's name and his social position
    (B) the way some people's names do not suit them
    (C) the impossibility of knowing whether the name someone gives is his real name
    (D) the difference between a person's name and his or her inner identity
    (E) the psychological difficulty inherent in any attempt to label another human being

18. The word "foretopman" (line 24) refers to

    (A) the foreman of a factory or mill
    (B) a particular kind of sailor
    (C) the winner of a wrestling match
    (D) the sailor who keeps watch from the crow's nest
    (E) the assistant to a factory foreman

19. In lines 27–31, the author says that calling Billy a "sailor" would be different from calling him a "foretopman," because

    (A) being a foretopman involves a different kind of work
    (B) a sailor is expected to travel on the open sea, while a foretopman only deals with ships in port
    (C) sailors in general are considered socially undesirable, but foretopmen are an exception
    (D) being a foretopman implies having military expertise that the average sailor does not possess
    (E) the position of foretopman comes with a specific set of responsibilities and expectations, which will limit the social identity of anyone who is given the title

20. How does the author make use of his own name in the fourth paragraph of the passage?

    (A) as an example of the various specializations available within a given field
    (B) as an example of the discrepancy between a given name and a person's inner identity
    (C) as an example of the constraints titles can place on an individual's social identity
    (D) to make *Billy Budd* seem less intimidating by providing a personal account of reading it
    (E) to indicate the importance of names in the way we think about other people

21. What is the meaning of the word "autonomy" in line 50?

    (A) freedom from the constraints of social expectation
    (B) the ability to choose one's own profession
    (C) freedom from religious or cultural oppression
    (D) a degree of choice in the amount of work one is expected to perform
    (E) the ability to go wherever one wishes to go

22. What is the meaning of the word "chafes" in line 51?

    (A) grows irritated
    (B) frays
    (C) limits
    (D) resists a limitation
    (E) breaks free

GO ON TO THE NEXT PAGE

Section 2

23. What does it mean that *Billy Budd* is an "Inside Narrative" (line 58)?

   (A) It portrays the "inside world" of a ship at sea.
   (B) The narrative focuses on the inner experience of the main character.
   (C) The novel is mostly concerned with social experiences that happen indoors, leaving the wilder outdoor world out of the story.
   (D) The novel is framed as a story-within-a-story, with the main plot functioning as an "inside" flashback within the "outer" plot.
   (E) The narrative openly talks about things such as storytelling technique and narrative devices, considerations that are usually left "outside" the words on the page.

24. What examples from *Billy Budd* itself does the author employ to justify his claim that the book contrasts the main character's "specific conscience" with his "broader sense of obligation" to society?

   (A) the novel's title and subtitles
   (B) the novel's title and several incidents from the narrative
   (C) the novel's title and several quotes from important characters
   (D) the novel's title and the personality of its main character
   (E) the opening and closing lines of the book

S T O P

IF YOU FINISH BEFORE TIME IS CALLED, YOU MAY CHECK YOUR WORK ON THIS TEST ONLY.
DO NOT TURN TO ANY OTHER SECTION IN THIS TEST.

Section 3

Time—25 Minutes
20 Questions

In this section solve each problem, using any available space on the page for scratchwork. Then decide which is the best of the choices given and fill in the corresponding oval on the answer sheet.

Notes:

1.   The use of a calculator is permitted. All numbers used are real numbers.

2.   Figures that accompany problems in this test are intended to provide information useful in solving the problems. They are drawn as accurately as possible EXCEPT when it is stated in a specific problem that the figure is not drawn to scale. All figures lie in a plane unless otherwise indicated.

3.   Unless otherwise specified, the domain of any function f is assumed to be the set of all real numbers x for which $f(x)$ is a real number.

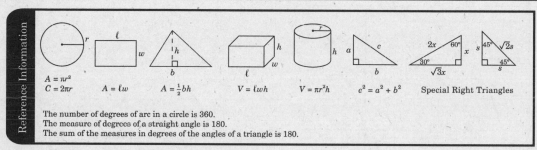

Reference Information

$A = \pi r^2$
$C = 2\pi r$
$A = \ell w$
$A = \frac{1}{2}bh$
$V = \ell wh$
$V = \pi r^2 h$
$c^2 = a^2 + b^2$
Special Right Triangles

The number of degrees of arc in a circle is 360.
The measure of degrees of a straight angle is 180.
The sum of the measures in degrees of the angles of a triangle is 180.

1. $19T$ is a number in which T represents a digit in the ones place. $T7$ is a number in which T is a digit in the tens place. If $19T - T7 = 1N6$, what digit does N represent?

(A) 4
(B) 5
(C) 6
(D) 7
(E) 8

2.   If $\frac{x}{2}$ is an integer, then which of the following values could be equal to x?

(A) −2
(B) 1
(C) 3
(D) 4.5
(E) 5

3.   John buys x boxes of apples that contain d apples each. If John spends a total of m dollars, then which of the following gives the price of one apple?

(A) xdm

(B) $\dfrac{dm}{x}$

(C) $\dfrac{xd}{m}$

(D) $\dfrac{m}{xd}$

(E) $\dfrac{d}{xm}$

GO ON TO THE NEXT PAGE

Section 3

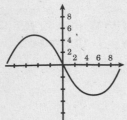

4. The function $f(x)$ produces the graph pictured above. Which of the following most closely resembles the graph of $f(x + 5)$?

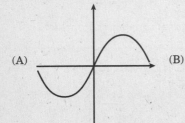

(A)

(B)

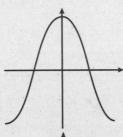

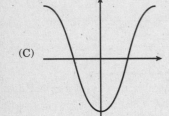

(C)

(D)

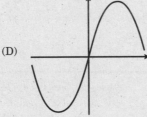

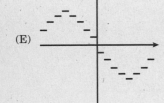

(E)

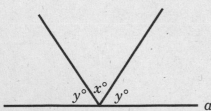

5. In the figure above, if a is a straight line, and the measure of angle x is 64°, what is the value of y in degrees?

(A) 52
(B) 58
(C) 63
(D) 116
(E) 180

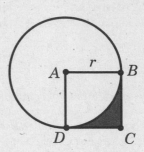

6. A is the center of circle A. B and D are points on the circle. $ABCD$ is a square. What is the area of the shaded region in terms of radius r?

(A) $\pi r^2 - r^2$

(B) $\dfrac{3\pi r^2}{4}$

(C) $r^2 - \dfrac{\pi r^2}{4}$

(D) $\dfrac{\pi r^2}{4}$

(E) $r^2 - \pi r^2$

7. Suppose there is a barrel filled with balls that are one of three colors: blue, red, or green. All blue balls have at least one star on them. All red balls have at least one dot on them. All balls with squares on them also have dots on them. No green balls have stars or dots on them. Given only this information, which of the following statements cannot be true?

(A) Some blue balls have dots on them.
(B) All red balls have three dots on them.
(C) All balls with dots on them are red.
(D) All blue balls have squares on them.
(E) Some green balls have squares on them.

8. If w is a prime number in which $q > w > 2$, which of the following CANNOT be a factor of $4wq$?

(A) w

(B) $\dfrac{q}{2}$

(C) wq

(D) $2w$

(E) w^2

GO ON TO THE NEXT PAGE

Section 3

9. If $4x - y = 10$, and $2x = 6$, what is $2y$?

   (A) 0
   (B) 2
   (C) 4
   (D) 6
   (E) 8

10. A cube has a volume of 64. What is the area of a circle whose radius is equal to the length of one of the edges of the cube?

    (A) 64π
    (B) 27π
    (C) 16π
    (D) 6π
    (E) $.75\pi$

11. A stack of cards contains three hearts and six clubs, and nothing else. A card is randomly selected from the jar and returned to the stack. Then a second card is randomly selected. What is the probability that both cards selected are clubs?

    (A) $\frac{1}{3}$
    (B) $\frac{4}{9}$
    (C) $\frac{1}{2}$
    (D) $\frac{2}{3}$
    (E) $\frac{4}{3}$

12. It takes Bonnie two hours, moving at a constant rate, to run 12 miles. If Floyd runs at half Bonnie's rate, how many <u>minutes</u> would it take Floyd to run 6 miles?

    (A) 2
    (B) 60
    (C) 75
    (D) 120
    (E) 240

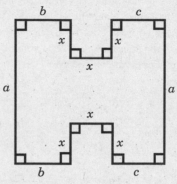

13. What is the perimeter of the figure above?

    (A) $2(a + b + c + 3x)$
    (B) $2(a + b + c) - 6x$
    (C) $2(a + b + c) - 3x$
    (D) $2a + b + c + 6x$
    (E) $2(a + b + c + x)$

14. If $a = bc$, which of the following must be equivalent to $\frac{b}{2}$?

    (A) $\frac{2a}{c}$
    (B) $\frac{a}{2c}$
    (C) $2ac$
    (D) $\frac{ac}{2}$
    (E) $\frac{c}{2a}$

15. Let $\boxed{z} = z^2 + 1$. What is $\boxed{x+y} - \boxed{x-y}$?

    (A) $2x$
    (B) $4xy$
    (C) $4y^2$
    (D) x^2y^2
    (E) $8xy$

16. In a certain sequence, each term is equal to -3 times the previous term. If the fifth term of the sequence is 27, what was the first term?

    (A) -18
    (B) $-\frac{1}{9}$
    (C) $\frac{1}{3}$
    (D) 9
    (E) 81

GO ON TO THE NEXT PAGE

Section 3

17. Joseph drove from his house to the football game at an average rate of 50 miles per hour. Because of traffic jams, he drove home from the football game along the same route at an average rate of only 35 miles per hour. If his total driving time to the game and back from the game equaled 3 hours and 24 minutes, then how many total miles did he drive?

(A) 35
(B) 50
(C) 70
(D) 85
(E) 140

18. For what values of x is the expression $\dfrac{3x^2 + x - 2}{6x^2 - x - 2}$ undefined?

(A) 0

(B) $-\dfrac{1}{2}$

(C) 0 and $\dfrac{1}{2}$

(D) -3 and 2

(E) $\dfrac{2}{3}$ and $-\dfrac{1}{2}$

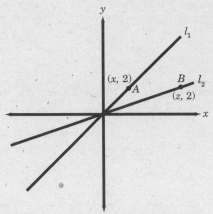

19. The slope of the line l_1 is $\dfrac{3}{2}$, and the slope of the line l_2 is $\dfrac{2}{3}$. What is the distance between points A and B?

(A) 1

(B) $\dfrac{4}{3}$

(C) $\dfrac{3}{2}$

(D) $\dfrac{5}{3}$

(E) 4

20. $\sqrt{\dfrac{x+2}{y+2}} = 2\sqrt{\dfrac{1}{4}}$. Solve for x in terms of y.

(A) $x = y + 2$
(B) $x = 2y$
(C) $x = y$
(D) $x = y^2$
(E) $x = 2\sqrt{y}$

S T O P

IF YOU FINISH BEFORE TIME IS CALLED, YOU MAY CHECK YOUR WORK ON THIS TEST ONLY.
DO NOT TURN TO ANY OTHER SECTION IN THIS TEST.

Section 4

Turn to Section 4 of your answer sheet to answer the questions in this section.

Time—25 Minutes
24 Questions

For each question in this section, select the best answer from among the choices given and fill in the corresponding oval on the answer sheet.

Each sentence below has one or two blanks, each blank indicating that something has been omitted. Beneath the sentence are five words or sets of words labeled A through E. Choose the word or set of words that, when inserted in the sentence, <u>best</u> fits the meaning of the sentence as a whole.

Example:

Medieval kingdoms did not become constitutional republics overnight; on the contrary, the change was ----.

(A) unpopular
(B) unexpected
(C) advantageous
(D) sufficient
(E) gradual

1. Antonio protested that he could not be ---- for a crime that he did not ----.

(A) condemned..commit
(B) regaled..pertain
(C) lauded..condone
(D) convincted..commiserate
(E) responsible..cauterize

2. Although many people found him to be physically ----, Pee Wee Russell's clarinet playing was widely regarded as ----.

(A) ugly..foul
(B) pristine..dramatic
(C) grotesque..beautiful
(D) handsome..gentle
(E) expressive..unique

3. Built on wooden stilts that had gradually rotted away over the years, the condition of Wayne's seaside home became more ---- with every passing storm.

(A) precarious
(B) adventurous
(C) absurd
(D) seasonal
(E) fruitful

4. By mixing horror with farce, Alfred Hitchcock made films at once ---- and hilarious.

(A) gruesome
(B) funny
(C) staid
(D) informational
(E) moving

5. All of the costumes were ----, proving that the designer knew virtually nothing about the historical setting of the play.

(A) empirical
(B) archetypal
(C) scrupulous
(D) plausible
(E) anachronistic

GO ON TO THE NEXT PAGE

Section 4

The two short passages below are followed by questions based on their content. Answer the questions based on what is <u>stated</u> or <u>implied</u> in each passage.

Passage 1

To argue that Shakespeare was not the author of the plays commonly attributed to him is to contemplate a conspiracy of unimaginable proportions. In this proposed scenario, Shakespeare agreed to act as a frontman for the Earl of Oxford,
5 the true author, because playwriting was beneath noblemen of the time. For this fraud to have worked, Shakespeare's theatrical company, friends, fellow writers, acquaintances, and rivals would all have had to have been either duped by the conspiracy, or in on it. Put together all the variables needed to maintain a hoax of
10 such magnitude, and it becomes clear that it simply could not have been done.

Passage 2

The reasons for doubting Shakespeare's authorship of the plays attributed to him are numerous. The breadth of reference and historical knowledge demonstrated in the plays simply does not match up with Shakespeare's personal history. The man had
5 neither the education nor travel experience to write so convincingly of distant countries and historical events. Those who argue that Shakespeare must have written the plays point to the immensity of the cover-up necessary to hide the true writer. In response, I can only say that while such cover up might have
10 required extreme effort, for Shakespeare himself to have written the plays would have required a miracle.

6. The author of the first passage lists Shakespeare's friends, fellow writers, and other contemporaries in order to

(A) illustrate the extent of the proposed conspiracy
(B) highlight Shakespeare's genius
(C) better describe Shakespeare's England
(D) provide context for understanding Shakespeare's actions
(E) support the argument that Shakespeare was a frontman

7. The author of the second passage brings up the immensity of the conspiracy that would have been needed to hide the true author of the plays in order to

(A) support Shakespeare's claim to authorship
(B) admit a change in beliefs
(C) preempt possible criticisms
(D) argue for a more open-minded view
(E) call for further inquiry

8. The fact that the Earl of Oxford died in 1604, before some of Shakespeare's plays were first publicly performed, weakens whose argument most?

(A) The information weakens neither argument.
(B) The information weakens both arguments equally.
(C) The information weakens the argument of passage 1.
(D) The information weakens the argument of passage 2.
(E) The Earl of Oxford's death has nothing to do with Shakespeare.

9. The authors of the first and second passage would disagree on all of the following EXCEPT

(A) Shakespeare was the author of all the plays attributed to him
(B) the Earl of Oxford is the most likely author of the "Shakespeare" plays
(C) Shakespeare's education was meager and insufficient
(D) Shakespeare was a better playwright than the Earl of Oxford
(E) the issue of who wrote the "Shakespeare" plays is important

GO ON TO THE NEXT PAGE

Section 4

The passage below is followed by questions based on its content. Answer the questions on the basis of what is <u>stated</u> or <u>implied</u> in the passage and in any introductory material that may be provided.

Questions 10–15 are based on the following passage. In the following passage, the American writer Mark Twain discusses literature and art and the ways in which the two are perceived.

I wonder why some things are? For instance, Art is allowed as much indecent license today as in earlier times—but the privileges of Literature in this respect have been sharply curtailed within the past eighty or ninety years. Early Eighteenth
5 century novelists such as Fielding and Smollett could portray the beastliness of their day in the beastliest language; we have plenty of foul subjects to deal with in our day, but we are not allowed to approach them very near, even with nice and guarded forms of speech. But not so with Art. The brush may still deal freely with
10 any subject, however revolting or indelicate. It makes a body ooze sarcasm at every pore, to go about Rome and Florence and see what this last generation has been doing with the statues. These works, which had stood in innocent nakedness for ages, are all fig-leaved now. Yes, every one of them. Nobody noticed their
15 nakedness before, perhaps; nobody can help noticing it now, the fig-leaf makes it so conspicuous. But the comical thing about it all, is that the fig leaf is confined to cold and pallid marble, which would be still cold and unsuggestive without this sham and ostentatious symbol of modesty, whereas warm-blooded paintings
20 have in no case been furnished with it.

At the door of the Uffizi, in Florence, one is confronted by statues of a man and a woman, noseless, battered, black with accumulated grime—they hardly suggest human beings—yet these ridiculous creatures have been thoughtfully and
25 conscientiously fig-leafed by this fastidious generation. You enter, and proceed to that most-visited little gallery that exists in the world—the Tribune—and there, against the wall, without obstructing rag or leaf, you may look your fill upon the foulest, the vilest, the obscenest picture the world possesses—Titian's Venus.
30 It isn't that she is naked and stretched out on a bed—no, it is the attitude of one of her arms and hand. If I ventured to describe that attitude, there would be a fine howl—but there the Venus lies, for anybody to gloat over that wants to—and there she has a right to lie, for she is a work of art, and Art has its privileges.
35 I saw young girls stealing furtive glances at her; I saw young men gaze long and absorbedly at her; I saw aged, infirm men hang upon her charms with a pathetic interest. How I should like to describe her--just to see what a holy indignation I could stir up in the world--just to hear the unreflecting average man deliver
40 himself about my grossness and coarseness, and all that. The world says that no worded description of a moving spectacle is a hundredth part as moving as the same spectacle seen with one's own eyes—yet the world is willing to let its son and its daughter
45 and itself look at Titian's beast, but won't stand a description of it in words. Which shows that the world is not as consistent as it might be.

10. In line 2, the word "license" is used to mean

(A) a document granting permission to perform a task
(B) immoral excess
(C) freedom from public objection or disapproval
(D) the badge of a bureaucrat
(E) censorship

11. When he describes the era of Fielding and Smollett (lines 4–6), what does Twain imply about the earlier attitude toward Literature?

(A) It was immoral; the earlier age had too much tolerance for literature about sin and vice.
(B) It was less advanced than the modern attitude, which protects impressionable children.
(C) It was a product of its time that could not be reproduced in the era in which Twain lived.
(D) It was better; Literature should be allowed to deal with the "foul subjects" of the day.
(E) In the past, people did not think much about morality when they thought about literature.

12. In the first and second paragraphs, Twain uses the example of the fig leaves to illustrate

(A) modern society's limited understanding of ancient standards of dress
(B) a possible method for improving the appearance of ancient sculpture when it begins
(C) foods nomads are easily able to find in the desert
(D) different cultural standards with regard to morality and decency in art
(E) the absurd lengths to which people are willing to go to censor "indecent" sculpture

13. In line 23, Twain writes that the statues in front of the Uffizi "hardly suggest human beings" because

(A) they are so abstract
(B) they have deteriorated
(C) they are so poorly sculpted
(D) they are made of stone
(E) they are so gigantic

GO ON TO THE NEXT PAGE

14. In line 25, the word "fastidious" most nearly means

   (A) prim
   (B) quick
   (C) hungry
   (D) fundamental
   (E) ancient

15. Why does Twain argue that the world's attitude toward Titian's painting of Venus is not "consistent"?

   (A) The world pretends that nudity is immoral, but then gazes on Titian's painting with unabashed interest.
   (B) The world objects to art that it should embrace.
   (C) People who pretend to understand the painting are really quite ignorant about art.
   (D) The world censors written descriptions that it allows paintings to display openly, even though most people say that a picture is more powerful than a written description.
   (E) Classical learning, for all its accomplishments, has failed to produce an adequate description of Venus's beauty.

GO ON TO THE NEXT PAGE

Section 4

The passage below is followed by questions based on its content. Answer the questions on the basis of what is <u>stated</u> or <u>implied</u> in the passage and in any introductory material that may be provided.

Questions 16–24 are based on the following passage.

In the following passage, the author describes Wing Biddlebaum, a mysterious loner who lives near the town of Winesburg, Ohio.

Upon the half-decayed veranda of a small frame house that stood near the edge of a ravine near the town of Winesburg, Ohio, a fat little old man walked nervously up and down. Across a long field that had been seeded for clover but that had produced only a
5 dense crop of yellow mustard weeds, he could see the public highway along which went a wagon filled with berry pickers returning from the fields. The berry pickers, youths and maidens, laughed and shouted boisterously. A boy clad in a blue shirt leaped from the wagon and attempted to drag after him one of the
10 maidens, who screamed and protested shrilly. The feet of the boy in the road kicked up a cloud of dust that floated across the face of the departing sun.

Wing Biddlebaum, forever frightened and beset by a ghostly band of doubts, did not think of himself as in any way a part of the
15 life of the town where he had lived for twenty years. Among all the people of Winesburg but one had come close to him. With George Willard, son of Tom Willard, the proprietor of the New Willard House, he had formed something like a friendship. George Willard was the reporter on the Winesburg Eagle and sometimes in the
20 evenings he walked out along the highway to Wing Biddlebaum's house. Now as the old man walked up and down on the veranda, his hands moving nervously about, he was hoping that George Willard would come and spend the evening with him. After the wagon containing the berry pickers had passed, he went across
25 the field through the tall mustard weeds and climbing a rail fence peered anxiously along the road to the town. For a moment he stood thus, rubbing his hands together and looking up and down the road, and then, fear overcoming him, ran back to walk again upon the porch on his own house.

30 Wing Biddlebaum talked much with his hands. The slender expressive fingers, forever active, striving to conceal themselves in his pockets or behind his back, came forth and became the piston rods of his machinery of expression.

The story of Wing Biddlebaum is a story of hands. Their
35 restless activity, like unto the beating of the wings of an imprisoned bird, had given him his name. Some obscure poet of the town had thought of it. The hands alarmed their owner. He wanted to keep them hidden away and looked with at the quiet inexpressive hands of other men who worked beside him in the
40 fields, or passed, driving sleepy teams on country roads.

The story of Wing Biddlebaum's hands is worth a book in itself. Sympathetically set forth it would tap many strange, beautiful qualities in obscure men. It is a job for a poet. In Winesburg the

hands had attracted attention merely because of their activity.
45 With them Wing Biddlebaum had picked as high as a hundred and forty quarts of strawberries in a day. They became his distinguishing feature, the source of his fame. Also they made more grotesque a grotesque and elusive individuality. The town was proud of the hands of Wing Biddlebaum in the same spirit in
50 which it was proud of Banker White's new stone house and Wesley Moyer's bay stallion, Tony Tip, that had won the two-fifteen trot at the fall races in Cleveland.

16. The first sentence of the passage introduces a sense of

(A) foreboding
(B) loneliness
(C) anger
(D) gaiety
(E) innocence

17. The effect of the description of the berry pickers in their cart is to

(A) highlight a contrast
(B) foreshadow an event
(C) illustrate a similarlity
(D) provide abstract analysiss
(E) build an allegory

18. The word "beset" (line 13) most nearly means

(A) plagued
(B) developed
(C) constructed
(D) coerce
(E) becalmed

19. The phrase "something like a friendship" in line 18 indicates that

(A) George Willard doesn't actually like Wing.
(B) Wing is befriending George as a way to try to become popular in Winesburg.
(C) Wing is so awkward and nervous he cannot form deep friendships even with people he likes.
(D) George's father Tom forbade him to be friends with Wing.
(E) Wing is mainly trying to convince George to give him a job as a reporter.

GO ON TO THE NEXT PAGE

Section 4

20. Why might Wing have waited for the berry pickers to pass before going out to look for George Willard?

   (A) He wanted to avoid being noticed.
   (B) He thought he might be forced to pick berries too.
   (C) He had recently argued with the berry pickers about how much noise they make.
   (D) He knew that George disliked the berry pickers.
   (E) He was more interested in pacing his porch than in looking for George.

21. Wing's name is a product of

   (A) his penchant for launching into never-ending stories
   (B) an allusion to his past as a pilot
   (C) a metaphor about the way his hands move
   (D) a reference to his grace and speed
   (E) a comment on Wing's love of birds

22. The comparison of Wing Biddlebaum to Banker White's stone house and Wesley Moyer's stallion

   (A) illustrates that Wing is a beloved figure of Winesburg
   (B) shows how mysterious and odd Wing is
   (C) demonstrates Wing's strength, speed, and fortitude
   (D) reinforces Wing's status in the town as a curiosity less than human
   (E) contrasts with earlier descriptions of Wing

23. The first two sentences of the last paragraph imply that

   (A) previous stories of Wing's hands have not been sympathetic
   (B) the story of Wing's hands has meaning and significance beyond Wing himself
   (C) the narrator feels unable to tell Wing's story
   (D) Wing has used his hands to build a hidden fortune
   (E) Wing is not the only person in the world with hands like his

24. Which of the following would be the best title for the short story of which this story is the opening?

   (A) Wing Takes Flight
   (B) George Willard's Friend
   (C) Hands
   (D) Winesburg Joy
   (E) Loving Life

S T O P

IF YOU FINISH BEFORE TIME IS CALLED, YOU MAY CHECK YOUR WORK ON THIS TEST ONLY.
DO NOT TURN TO ANY OTHER SECTION IN THIS TEST.

Section 5

Time—25 Minutes
18 Questions

In this section solve each problem, using any available space on the page for scratchwork. Then decide which is the best of the choices given and fill in the corresponding oval on the answer sheet.

Notes:

1.   The use of a calculator is permitted. All numbers used are real numbers.

2.   Figures that accompany problems in this test are intended to provide information useful in solving the problems. They are drawn as accurately as possible EXCEPT when it is stated in a specific problem that the figure is not drawn to scale. All figures lie in a plane unless otherwise indicated.

3.   Unless otherwise specified, the domain of any function f is assumed to be the set of all real numbers x for which $f(x)$ is a real number.

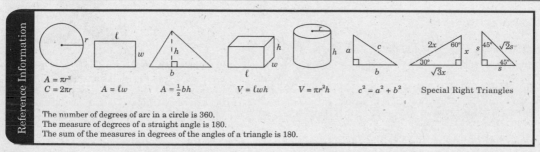

$A = \pi r^2$
$C = 2\pi r$ $A = \ell w$ $A = \frac{1}{2}bh$ $V = \ell wh$ $V = \pi r^2 h$ $c^2 = a^2 + b^2$ Special Right Triangles

The number of degrees of arc in a circle is 360.
The measure of degrees of a straight angle is 180.
The sum of the measures in degrees of the angles of a triangle is 180.

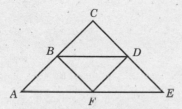

Figure Not Drawn to Scale

1.   Triangle $ABF \cong BCD \cong DEF \cong BDF$. By what factor does the ratio of the perimeter of triangle ACE exceed the perimeter of triangle ABF?

(A) 2
(B) 4
(C) 8
(D) 16
(E) 32

2.   If $\dfrac{x}{y+2} \geq 16$ and $y \geq 3$, what is the least possible value of x?

(A) 3

(B) $\dfrac{16}{5}$

(C) 16

(D) 48

(E) 80

3.   The speed at which a ball hits the ground is proportional to the height to which the ball rebounds. If the ball hits the ground at a speed of 20 miles per hour and rebounds to a height of 10 feet, then how fast must it be traveling (in miles per hour) to rebound to a height of 15 feet?

(A) 5
(B) 25
(C) 30
(D) 35
(E) 40

4.   What is the slope of the line that connects the midpoints of one line segment with endpoints at (–2,–4) and (–4,–4) and another line segment that has endpoints at (–2,4) and (2,8)?

(A) 0

(B) $\dfrac{3}{10}$

(C) $\dfrac{1}{2}$

(D) 1

(E) $\dfrac{10}{3}$

GO ON TO THE NEXT PAGE

Section 5

5. A bag if marbles contains x total marbles, where $10 < x < 20$ and m of the marbles are blue, while n of the marbles are yellow. If the probability of picking a blue marble at random from the bag is $\frac{5}{8}$, then what is the value of mn?

   (A) 5
   (B) 15
   (C) 16
   (D) 40
   (E) 60

6. Two trains leave the same station at the same time and travel for 2 hours. Train A travels due north at the rate of 28 kilometers per hour, while Train B travels due west at a rate of 21 kilometers per hour. At the end of 2 hours, what is the straight line distance, in kilometers, between the trains?

   (A) 14
   (B) 17
   (C) 42
   (D) 56
   (E) 70

7. Set A contains all the even integers between and including −50 and −2. Set B contains all the even integers between and including 0 and 52. What is the mean of the union of sets A and B?

   (A) −1
   (B) 1
   (C) 2
   (D) 26
   (E) 52

8. In square $ABCD$, $AB = 12$, $AH = GF = BE$, $AC \parallel HF$, and $BD \parallel EG$. What is the area of the shaded region of the square?

   (A) 16
   (B) 36
   (C) 72
   (D) 108
   (E) 144

GO ON TO THE NEXT PAGE

Section 5

Directions: for Student-Produced Response Questions 9-18, use the grids at the bottom of the answer sheet page on which you have answered questions 1-8.

Each of the remaining 10 questions requires you to solve the problem and enter your answer by marking the ovals in the special grid, as shown in the examples below.

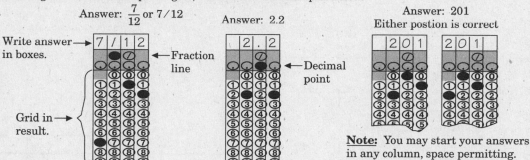

Answer: $\frac{7}{12}$ or 7/12

Write answer in boxes. → Fraction line

Grid in result. →

Answer: 2.2

← Decimal point

Answer: 201
Either postion is correct

Note: You may start your answers in any column, space permitting. Columns not needed should be left blank.

- Mark no more than one oval in any column.

- Because the answer sheet will be machine-scored, **you will receive credit only if the ovals are filled in completely.**

- Although not required, it is suggested that you write your answer in the boxes at the top of the columns to help you fill in the ovals accurately.

- Some problems may have more than one correct answer. In such cases, grid only one answer

- No question has a negative answer.

- **Mixed numbers** such as $2\frac{1}{2}$ must be gridded as 2.5 or 5/2. If 2 1 / 2 is gridded, it will be interpreted as $\frac{21}{2}$, not $2\frac{1}{2}$.)

- **Decimal Accuracy:** If you obtain a decimal answer, **enter the most accurate value the grid will accommodate.** For example, if you obtain an answer such as 0.6666 . . . , you should record the result as .666 or .667. **Less accurate values such as .66 or .67 are not acceptable.** Acceptable ways to grid $\frac{2}{3}$ = .666 . . .

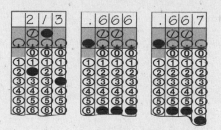

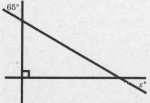

9. In the figure above, what is the value of x (in degrees)?

10. Seven apple trees in a grove are flowering. If there are 12 trees in total, what is the ratio of flowering to non-flowering trees? (Grid your ratio as a fraction.)

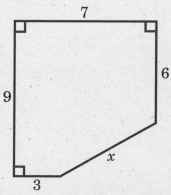

11. What is the perimeter of the polygon shown above?

GO ON TO THE NEXT PAGE

Section 5

12. If $(4x + y)^2 = 49$, $2y^2 = 18$, and $x, y > 0$, what is x?

_____

13. If $3x^{\frac{1}{2}}y^{-3} = \dfrac{x}{y^3}$, and x and y are nonzero real numbers, what is the value of x?

_____

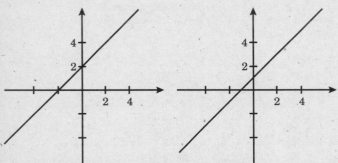

14. If the figure above and to the left represents the function $f(x)$, and the figure above and to the right represents $f(x + k)$, what is the value of k?

_____

15. If $f(x) = 2x^2 + x - 6$, $g(x) = \dfrac{x}{2}$, and $h(x) = 2x + 4$, what is the value of $\dfrac{f(3)}{g(h(3))}$?

16. A bag contains marbles and dice. There are three times as many marbles in the bag as there are dice. The marbles are either blue or red, and there are twice as many blue marbles than red marbles. If one item is to be drawn at random from the bag, what is the probability that the item will be a blue marble?

_____

17. Sequence A's first term is –6, and each term thereafter is 3 greater than the previous term. The nth term of sequence B is given by the formula $-5n + 25$. Note that the first term of sequence A is less than the first term of sequence B. What is the value of the term of sequence A that first exceeds the value of its corresponding term in sequence B?

_____

18. The conversion function between the units of length Kirkland (K) and Mather (M) is given by $K = \dfrac{r}{M^2}$, where r is a constant. If $4K = 12M$, then how many Kirklands long is a string of 8 Mathers?

S T O P

IF YOU FINISH BEFORE TIME IS CALLED, YOU MAY CHECK YOUR WORK ON THIS TEST ONLY.
DO NOT TURN TO ANY OTHER SECTION IN THIS TEST.

Section 6

Directions: The following sentences test correctness and effectiveness of expression. In choosing answers, follow the requirements of standard written English; that is, pay attention to grammar, choice of words, sentence construction, and punctuation.

In each of the following sentences, part of the sentence or the entire sentence is underlined. Beneath each sentence you will find five ways of phrasing the underlined part. Choice A repeats the original; the other four are different.

Choose the answer that best expresses the meaning of the original sentence. If you think the original is better than any of the alternatives, choose it; otherwise choose one of the others. Your choice should produce the most effective sentence—clear and precise, without awkwardness or ambiguity.

EXAMPLE:

SAMPLE ANSWER:

Laura Ingalls Wilder published her first book and she was sixty-five years old then.

(A) and she was sixty-five years old then
(B) when she was sixty-five
(C) at age sixty-five years old
(D) upon the reaching of sixty-five years
(E) at the time when she was sixty-five

1. In difficult economic times, people try to spend less, plan ahead, and relying on family support is oftentimes helpful.

   (A) plan ahead, and relying on family support
   (B) planning ahead, and relying on family support is oftentimes helpful
   (C) planning ahead and rely on family support is oftentimes helpful
   (D) and it's oftentimes helpful, planning ahead and to rely on family support
   (E) plan ahead, and rely on family support

2. The prisoner expressed no repentance, the judge was angered and imposed a heavy sentence.

   (A) repentance, the judge was angered
   (B) repentance, so the judge was angered
   (C) repentance; so the judge was angered
   (D) repentance that angered the judge
   (E) repentance angering the judge

3. In the past, quarreling men were accompanied to their duels by men called "seconds," a practice that is strange to us now.

   (A) a practice that is strange to us now
   (B) and since they did that practice, it is strange to us now
   (C) which is strange to us and it was a practice
   (D) a practice that is strange to them then
   (E) this is strange to us in practice

4. Initially, Frannie was unwilling to start jogging, and she tried it anyway and soon it became an enjoyable part of her morning routine.

   (A) and she tried it anyway
   (B) even though she tried it anyway
   (C) she tried it anyway
   (D) but she tried it anyway
   (E) thus she tried it anyway

GO ON TO THE NEXT PAGE

5. By telling rueful, funny, and cerebral stories set in New York City, <u>the popular conception of Manhattan has been changed by Woody Allen</u>.

   (A) the popular conception of Manhattan has been changed by Woody Allen
   (B) Manhattan as it is popularly conceived has been changed by Woody Allen
   (C) Woody Allen's popular conception of Manhattan has been changed
   (D) the popular conception of Manhattan were changed for Woody Allen
   (E) Woody Allen changed the popular conception of Manhattan

6. With admirable resolve, many young people have flocked to New York City in search of fame or <u>a new life, in the process they cause a glut in the real estate market</u>.

   (A) a new life, in the process they cause a glut in the real estate market
   (B) a new life, a glut in the real estate market being the result
   (C) a new life and in the process have caused a glut in the real estate market
   (D) a new life: and in the process, they are causing a glut in the real estate market
   (E) a new life, the real estate market has been glutted by this

7. <u>An urban legend, much repeated and embellished, that</u> enormous crocodiles prowl the sewers of Manhattan.

   (A) An urban legend, much repeated and embellished, that
   (B) That much repeated and embellished urban legend
   (C) An urban legend, much repeated and embellished, says that
   (D) Repeating and embellishing the urban legend, that
   (E) That urban legend was much repeated and embellished

8. <u>Although they were revered by the Egyptians, cats were feared in the Middle Ages, when they were often burned as witches</u>.

   (A) Although they were revered by the Egyptians, cats were feared in the Middle Ages, when they were often burned as witches.
   (B) Cats were feared in the Middle Ages, although they were revered by the Egyptians, when they were often burned as witches.
   (C) Although they were often burned as witches, cats were revered by the Egyptians, although they were feared in the Middle Ages.
   (D) Cats were revered by the Egyptians and feared in the Middle Ages, although they were often burned as witches.
   (E) Although they were revered by the Egyptians, fearing them in the Middle Ages, people often burned cats as witches.

9. When casting a musical, directors consider not only voice and acting ability, <u>but does the person look good</u>.

   (A) but does the person look good
   (B) but also looks
   (C) but whether or not the person looks good
   (D) and if the person looks good
   (E) however good the person looks

10. Benjamin Franklin wrote an accomplished autobiography, owned and edited a newspaper, and invented <u>bifocals; he is most widely known, however</u>, for his work as a diplomat and statesmen.

    (A) bifocals; he is most widely known, however,
    (B) bifocals, but is most widely known, however,
    (C) bifocals, having been most widely known
    (D) bifocals: however, known most widely
    (E) bifocals, since he is most widely known

11. Poets Elizabeth Barrett and Robert Browning had a <u>dramatic courtship, being that they had to</u> keep their love secret from Barrett's domineering father.

    (A) dramatic courtship, being that they had to
    (B) dramatic courtship although they had to
    (C) dramatic courtship: they had to
    (D) dramatic courtship; since they had to
    (E) dramatic courtship: part of which was that they had to

GO ON TO THE NEXT PAGE

Section 6

12. The teachers did not expect a complete victory, but they had
        A   B
    counted on the university granting at least some of his or her
                    C   D
    main requests. No error
                      E

13. The mayor issued a statement declaring that increased taxation is
        A   B
    not hardly an acceptable solution to the problems of the city.
      C   D
    No error
      E

14. Peter swum ten laps in record time, and won first prize
            A   B   C
    in the competition. No error
          D   E

15. More devotedly as any nun in the church, Mother Teresa worked
            A   B
    long hours to restore the health of her patients in the hospital.
      C   D
    No error
      E

16. The appeal of new technology lies in its ability to perform new
                    A
    functions; new machines are faster, more efficient, and cheap
                              B   C   D
    than ever before. No error
                        E

17. The Tao te Ching, an ancient Chinese text that advises
                      A   B
    simplicity and lack of desire, has had a profound influence on
                      C   D
    Chinese art and literature. No error
                                  E

18. To everyone's astonishment, the chairperson of the PTA was
                                                            A
    arrested to be drunk and disorderly on the streets of the town.
      B   C   D
    No error
      E

19. Strewn around his playpen was the toddler's favorite toys,
        A   B   C
    including a miniature car and a set of alphabet blocks. No error
                                  D   E

20. The unconscious, according to Freud, is divided into the id, which
                      A   B   C
    consists of instincts and desires, and the superego, which
                                                          D
    controls the id. No error
                      E

21. At the school assembly, one candidate for student council made
    a speech where he proposed holding a blood drive in the fall.
              A   B   C   D
    No error
      E

22. The typical American high school student has to take out several
                                                      A
    loans in order to attend college because in the last thirty years
            B   C
    they have grown extremely expensive. No error
      D   E

23. Despite several heavy-handed illusions to the lateness of the
      A   B   C
    hour, Ms. Wong's date didn't realize that she wanted to leave.
            D
    No error
      E

24. The professor asserted he could not scarcely imagine a better
                                    A
    role model for Sarah Lawrence students than Alice Walker,
      B   C
    herself a Sarah Lawrence alumna. No error
      D   E

GO ON TO THE NEXT PAGE

25. The month of July <u>has</u> so often <u>been associated</u> with vacations
              A   B
    that <u>the very mention</u> of the month conjures up visions of
              C
    barbecues, fireworks, and <u>the beach</u>. <u>No error</u>
                         D   E

26. The guest lecturer <u>strode up</u> to the podium, put down his papers,
                      A
    <u>and without</u> introduction <u>began</u> to read from <u>it</u>. <u>No error</u>
      B   C   D   E

27. If you are going to Beijing in December, <u>it is</u> essential to bring
                                 A
    along clothing <u>that works in</u> layers, as the sudden changes of
                  B
    temperature there <u>can</u> <u>catch one</u> off guard. <u>No error</u>
               C   D   E

28. The governor, as well as all fifty members <u>of his staff</u>, <u>have been</u>
                                  A   B
    working <u>nonstop</u> on the <u>reelection</u> campaign. <u>No error</u>
          C   D   E

29. After <u>drinking</u> glasses of pink lemonade, yellow lemonade, and
          A
    limeade, <u>the taste-tester</u> could not decide <u>which</u> drink tasted
          B   C
    <u>sweeter</u>. <u>No error</u>
     D   E

GO ON TO THE NEXT PAGE

Section 6

Directions: Each of the following passages is an early draft of an essay. Some parts of the passages need to be rewritten.

Read each passage and answer the questions that follow. Some questions are about particular sentences or parts of sentences and ask you to improve sentence structure and word choice. Other questions refer to parts of the essay or the entire essay and ask you to consider organization and development. In making your decisions, follow the conventions of standard written English. After you have chosen your answer, fill in the corresponding oval on your answer sheet.

<u>Questions 30–35</u> are based on the following passage.

(1) People frequently associate rap with violence, misogyny, and materialism. (2) Some rap music glorifies all three. (3) Not all rap music does. (4) Jay-Z is a hip-hop artist whose music frequently demeans women. (5) In his song "Anything," he praises his mother. (6) He raps, "As a man, I apologize for my dad," and "the most important lesson in life was when you said 'Strive for what you believe in, set goals and you can achieve them.'" (7) With the first lyric, he takes on the role of protector, apologizing for the bad behavior of his father. (8) With this lyric he implies that he will do better in his own adult personal life. (9) With the second lyric, he credited his mother for his success in life.

(10) DMX is another well-known rapper. (11) He often raps about the violence of life on the streets. (12) He raps about inflicting violence. (13) Some of his songs, however, bristle with nonviolent political commentary. (14) His song "Who We Be" addresses the misunderstanding from which the black community suffers. (15) Lyrics like, "the suffering young mothers—it happens too often" express an understanding of the toll taken on wives and mothers when their husbands and sons face prison.

(16) Even rappers whose songs reflect and sometimes glorify the violence that they knew in their lives often write songs that reveal the real respect they feel for women, and the revulsion they feel for violence. (17) It is a common misperception that hip-hop turns its back on what some call family values.

30. In the context of the first paragraph, which of the following best revises and combines sentences 2 and 3, which are reprinted below?

    Some rap music glorifies all three. Not all rap music does.

    (A) Some rap music glorifies all three, however not all rap music does.
    (B) It is true that some rap music glorifies all three, and some rap music doesn't.
    (C) While some rap music glorifies all three, not all rap music does.
    (D) In point of fact, some rap music glorifies all three, some rap music does not.
    (E) While some rap music glorifies all three and not all rap music does.

31. Which of the following sentences, added after sentence 3, is the best topic sentence for the second paragraph?

    (A) Let me tell you about a personal encounter I had with a rapper.
    (B) One such rapper is Jay-Z.
    (C) Even some music-industry executives secretly think this way.
    (D) This misguided perception is held by most people.
    (E) Many well-known rappers occasionally speak up for surprisingly traditional values.

32. Which of the following is the best way to revise and combine sentences 4 and 5, which are reprinted below?

    Jay-Z is a hip-hop artist whose music frequently demeans women. In his song "Anything," he praises his mother.

    (A) In his song "Anything," Jay-Z, a hip-hop artist whose music frequently demeans women, praises his mother.
    (B) Jay-Z is a hip-hop artist whose music frequently demeans women, and in his song "Anything," he praises his mother.
    (C) Although Jay-Z is a hip-hop artist whose music frequently demeans women, in his song "Anything," he praises his mother.
    (D) Praising his mother in his song "Anything," Jay-Z is a hip-hop artist whose music frequently demeans women.
    (E) Jay-Z is a hip-hop artist who frequently demeans women and creates a song like "Anything," which praises his mother.

GO ON TO THE NEXT PAGE

Section 6

33. In context, which of the following best revises the underlined part of sentence 9, which is reprinted here?

    With the second lyric, he credited his mother for his success in life.

    (A) (as it is)
    (B) he is crediting his mother
    (C) he credits his mother
    (D) his mother, who is to be credited
    (E) his mother got the credit

34. In order to change the repetitive nature of sentences 11 and 12 (reprinted here), which of the following is the best revision and combination of the underlined parts of the sentence?

    He often raps about the violence of life on the streets. He raps about inflicting violence.

    (A) life on the streets and about
    (B) street life, however he discusses
    (C) life on the streets but he raps about
    (D) life on the streets thus about
    (E) street life, moreover he raps about

35. The writer uses all of the following techniques EXCEPT

    (A) telling a personal story
    (B) debunking a commonly held belief
    (C) concluding with a summary
    (D) citing specific examples
    (E) analyzing lyrics

S T O P

IF YOU FINISH BEFORE TIME IS CALLED, YOU MAY CHECK YOUR WORK ON THIS TEST ONLY.
DO NOT TURN TO ANY OTHER SECTION IN THIS TEST.

Section 7

Turn to Section 7 of your answer sheet to answer the questions in this section.

Time—20 Minutes   For each question in this section, select the best answer
19 Questions   from among the choices given and fill in the corresponding
oval on the answer sheet.

Each sentence below has one or two blanks, each blank indicating that something has been omitted. Beneath the sentence are five words or sets of words labeled A through E. Choose the word or set of words that, when inserted in the sentence, <u>best</u> fits the meaning of the sentence as a whole.

Example:

Medieval kingdoms did not become constitutional republics overnight; on the contrary, the change was ----.

(A) unpopular
(B) unexpected
(C) advantageous
(D) sufficient
(E) gradual

---

1. While her stepsisters set a new mark for grumpiness, Marcy was ---- and lovely.

   (A) frosty
   (B) impeachable
   (C) endearing
   (D) tart
   (E) uncouth

2. Because she was easily annoyed and constantly cutting people off, Sarah was not known for her ----.

   (A) abruptness
   (B) devotion
   (C) patience
   (D) hindsight
   (E) charity

3. T. S. Eliot's most famous poem, *The Waste Land*, is a verbal ----; images from many levels of language and experience jumble jarringly together in it.

   (A) symphony
   (B) hodgepodge
   (C) portrait
   (D) gesture
   (E) epilogue

4. The idea that Shakespearean plays are only serious, high-minded, and tragic is false; many scenes from them are filled with ----.

   (A) malevolence
   (B) rhetoric
   (C) calamity
   (D) buffoonery
   (E) bliss

5. The use of high-tech metal detectors to ---- airport security is most effective when ---- thorough training of the security staff in how to use the new technology.

   (A) enhance . . accompanied by
   (B) amplify . . demoralized by
   (C) therapy . . cooperating with
   (D) belittle . . disparaged with
   (E) cultivate . . restrained by

6. Though Byron's work "The Prisoner of Chillon" was intended to depict the ---- reality of life behind bars, the author himself was a(n) ---- aristocrat with no firsthand experience of his subject.

   (A) brutal..criminal
   (B) unjust..fair-handed
   (C) chilling..common
   (D) harsh..privileged
   (E) luxurious..pampered

GO ON TO THE NEXT PAGE

Section 7

The passages below are followed by questions based on their content. Answer the questions on the basis of what is <u>stated</u> or <u>implied</u> in the passages and in any introductory material that may be provided.

<u>Questions 7–19</u> are based on the following passages.

In the mid-nineteenth century, the United States began to shift from an agrarian nation whose population lived mostly on farms and in small towns to a nation of major cities and industry. The following two passages, adapted from works written by the nineteenth-century American writers Henry David Thoreau and Walt Whitman, display two different views of the rise of cities and its effect on America.

Passage 1

When we walk, we naturally go to the fields and woods: what would become of us, if we walked only in a garden or a mall? Some philosophers have even felt the necessity of importing the woods to themselves, since they did not go to the woods. Of course it is of
5 no use to direct our steps to the woods, if they do not carry us there. I am alarmed when it happens that I have walked a mile into the woods bodily, without getting there in spirit. In my afternoon walk I would gladly forget all my morning occupations and my obligations to Society. But it sometimes happens that I
10 cannot easily shake off the village. The thought of some work will run in my head and I am not where my body is—I am out of my senses. In my walks I would like to return to my senses. What business have I in the woods, if I am thinking of something out of the woods? I suspect myself, and cannot help a shudder when I
15 find myself so implicated even in what are called good works.

My vicinity affords many good walks; and though for so many years I have walked almost every day, and sometimes for several days together, I have not yet exhausted them. An absolutely new prospect is a great happiness, and I can still get this any
20 afternoon. Two or three hours' walking will carry me to as strange a country as I expect ever to see. There is in fact a sort of harmony between the capabilities of the landscape within a circle of ten miles' radius, or the limits of an afternoon walk, and the threescore years and ten of human life. Neither will ever become
25 quite familiar to you.

Nowadays, almost all of man's improvements, so called, such as the building of houses and the cutting down of the forest and of all large trees, simply deform the landscape, and make it more and more tame and cheap.
30 From my rural house I can easily walk ten, fifteen, twenty, any number of miles, commencing at my own door, without going by any house, without crossing a road except where the fox and the mink do: first along by the river, and then the brook, and then the meadow and the woodside. There are square miles in my vicinity
35 which have no inhabitant. From many a hill I can see civilization and the abodes of man afar. The farmers and their works are scarcely more obvious than woodchucks and their burrows.

Man and his affairs, church and state and school, trade and commerce, and manufactures and agriculture—even politics, the
40 most alarming of them all—I am pleased to see how little space they occupy in the landscape.

Passage 2

The general subjective view of New York and Brooklyn, these great seething oceanic populations, as I see them in this visit, are to me best of all. After an absence of many years (I went away at
45 the outbreak of the Civil War, and have never been back to stay since), again I resume with curiosity an interaction with the crowds and streets I knew so well. In Broadway, the ferries, the west side of the city, along the wharves, and in the perpetual travel of the horse-cars, or the crowded excursion steamers, or in
50 Wall and Nassau streets by day and in the places of amusement at night, there is a bubbling and whirling and moving. I have taken all this in for the last three weeks.

There is no need to specify minutely. It is enough to say that (making all allowances for the shadows and side-streaks of a
55 massive city) the brief total of the impressions, the human qualities, of these vast cities, is to me comforting, even heroic, and beyond statement.

Alertness, generally fine physique, clear eyes that look straight at you, a singular combination of reticence and self-
60 possession mark the cities' inhabitants. Good nature and friendliness, and a prevailing range of according manners, taste, and intellect, surely beyond any other place upon earth, are not only constantly visible here in these mighty channels of men, but they form the rule and average. In this city I find a palpable
65 outcropping of the personal comradeship I look forward to as the subtlest, strongest future hold of this United States.

Today, defiant of cynics and pessimists, and with a full knowledge of all their arguments and exceptions, I state my belief that an appreciative and perceptive study of the current
70 humanity of New York gives the most direct proof yet of successful Democracy. For in old age, lame and sick, and having pondered for years on doubts and danger for this Republic of ours, I find in this visit to New York, and the daily contact and rapport with its myriad people, the best, most effective medicine my soul has yet
75 partaken. Manhattan Island and Brooklyn, the grandest physical habitat and surroundings of land and water the globe affords, are cities of the most superb democracy, amid superb surroundings.

GO ON TO THE NEXT PAGE

7. The first sentence of passage 1 is an example of

    (A) a rhetorical question
    (B) hyperbole
    (C) metaphor
    (D) alliteration
    (E) personification

8. What does Thoreau mean by saying he would "like to return to [his] senses" (line 12 of passage 1)?

    (A) He wants to become fully aware and fully a part of his surroundings.
    (B) He wants to write more poetry.
    (C) He wants to get his daily tasks done so that he can relax.
    (D) He wants to listen more carefully for wildlife.
    (E) He wants to think more deeply.

9. The term "exhausted" in line 18 of passage 1 refers to

    (A) tired
    (B) bored
    (C) found
    (D) completed
    (E) breathed

10. According to the final paragraph of passage 1, what does Thoreau appreciate most in human beings?

    (A) rural values
    (B) democratic thought
    (C) outdoor skills
    (D) social organizations such as villages
    (E) their absence

11. Whitman's tone in passage 2 can be best described as

    (A) curious and enthusiastic
    (B) bitter and nostalgic
    (C) confused and frightened
    (D) relieved and excited
    (E) wry and optimistic

12. What does Whitman mean by the term "oceanic" (line 43)?

    (A) The population is mostly made up of immigrants.
    (B) His thoughts on the subject are deep and profound.
    (C) Most of the people of the city are sailors.
    (D) The population is spread out over a vast area of land.
    (E) The population is large and enduring, yet always changing.

13. What aspect of cities most interests the author of passage 2?

    (A) their geographical organization
    (B) their inhabitants
    (C) their transportation systems
    (D) the distribution of wealth
    (E) their businesses

14. Lines 67–71 suggest that Whitman thinks that his argument will be

    (A) the subject of disagreement
    (B) received with enthusiasm
    (C) seen as a reflection of popular sentiment
    (D) largely ignored
    (E) dismissed as petty

15. How would Whitman react to Thoreau's assertion (line 40) that politics are the "most alarming" of man's activities?

    (A) He would disagree and point to rural communities as examples of good political structures.
    (B) He would agree completely.
    (C) He would agree, but only where rural communities are concerned.
    (D) He wouldn't care; he doesn't seem to be interested in politics.
    (E) He would strongly disagree and would point to the city as democracy embodied.

16. How would Thoreau be most likely to react to Whitman's claim that the city can be medicine for the soul (line 74)?

    (A) He would wholeheartedly agree.
    (B) He would agree that a person's environment can affect his soul, but would disagree with Whitman's choice of the city.
    (C) He would argue that one's environment has nothing to do with the soul, and that one should lose oneself in deep thought.
    (D) He would agree, but only if one can avoid the city's politics.
    (E) He would argue that this is only the case for an older man like Whitman who is unable to walk in the woods.

17. Which of the following describes a primary distinction between the two authors?

    (A) Thoreau is interested in politics; Whitman is interested in philosophy.
    (B) Thoreau is interested in people; Whitman is interested in his surroundings.
    (C) Thoreau is interested in nature; Whitman is interested in people.
    (D) Thoreau is interested in the city; Whitman is interested in the country.
    (E) Thoreau is interested in thoughts; Whitman is interested in emotions.

GO ON TO THE NEXT PAGE

18. The main point of both passages is to

   (A) examine and comment upon a particular location and its effect on man
   (B) argue the aesthetic qualities of the country versus the city
   (C) look at what environments are best for democracy
   (D) prove the supremacy of the city as a method of social organization
   (E) describe the effects of old age on perception

19. How would Whitman most likely react if he were set down in the middle of Thoreau's woods?

   (A) He would explore enthusiastically.
   (B) He would take a nap, grateful for the quiet.
   (C) He would set to work building a house.
   (D) He would seek out the few settlements visible.
   (E) He would change his mind about cities.

S T O P

IF YOU FINISH BEFORE TIME IS CALLED, YOU MAY CHECK YOUR WORK ON THIS TEST ONLY.
DO NOT TURN TO ANY OTHER SECTION IN THIS TEST.

Section 8

Time—20 Minutes
16 Questions

In this section solve each problem, using any available space on the page for scratchwork. Then decide which is the best of the choices given and fill in the corresponding oval on the answer sheet.

Notes:
1. The use of a calculator is permitted. All numbers used are real numbers.

2. Figures that accompany problems in this test are intended to provide information useful in solving the problems. They are drawn as accurately as possible EXCEPT when it is stated in a specific problem that the figure is not drawn to scale. All figures lie in a plane unless otherwise indicated.

3. Unless otherwise specified, the domain of any function f is assumed to be the set of all real numbers x for which $f(x)$ is a real number.

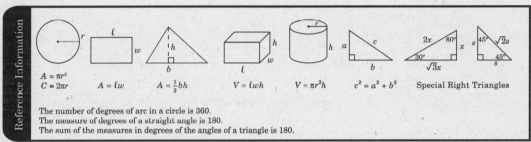

$A = \pi r^2$
$C = 2\pi r$ $A = \ell w$ $A = \frac{1}{2} bh$ $V = \ell wh$ $V = \pi r^2 h$ $c^2 = a^2 + b^2$ Special Right Triangles

The number of degrees of arc in a circle is 360.
The measure of degrees of a straight angle is 180.
The sum of the measures in degrees of the angles of a triangle is 180.

1. If the linear functions $f(x) = 2x + 7$, and $g(x) = kx + 2$ produce parallel lines, then what is the value of k?
   have same slope

   $f(x) = 2x+7 = g(x) = kx+2$

   (A) $-\frac{1}{2}$

   (B) $\frac{1}{2}$

   (C) 2

   (D) 4

   (E) 7

2. In a bag of candies, the ratio of red to green to blue candies is 4:3:6 respectively. If there are a total of 65 candies in a bag, how many are green?

   3 green

   (A) 3
   (B) 4
   (C) 5
   (D) 13
   (E) 15

3. If the mean of 11 consecutive numbers in a set is 200, and each number in the set is multiplied by 2, what is the new mean of the numbers in the set?

   (A) 50
   (B) 100
   (C) 200
   (D) 400
   (E) 800

4. If $y = x^2$, $x = \frac{z}{2}$, and $z = \frac{k}{2}$, what will happen to y if k doubles in value?

   (A) y will halve
   (B) y will double
   (C) y will triple
   (D) y will quadruple
   (E) y will square

5. If $f(x) = \dfrac{x}{\sqrt{x-3}}$ for all $x > 3$, then $f(12) =$

   (A) 3
   (B) 4
   (C) 5
   (D) 9
   (E) 12

GO ON TO THE NEXT PAGE

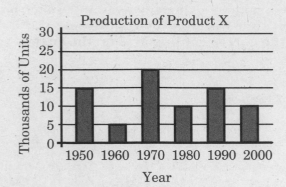

Production of Product X

6. According to the graph above, in which 10-year period was the percentage decrease in production of Product X the greatest?

(A) 1950–1960
(B) 1960–1970
(C) 1970–1980
(D) 1980–1990
(E) 1990–2000

7. What is the distance, rounded to the nearest hundredth, between the points (−1,6) and (7,−14)?

(A) 5.29
(B) 10.00
(C) 11.31
(D) 21.54
(E) 28.00

8. At what values of x is $\left|\frac{x}{4} + 4\right| < 8$?

(A) $-\infty < x < 0$
(B) $0 < x < \infty$
(C) $-48 < x < 16$
(D) $-\infty < x < -16$, $48 < x < \infty$
(E) $-16 < x < 48$

9. If $f(x) = x^2 - 1 + 2x$ and $g(x) = 1 - x$, then what is the graph of $f(g(x))$?

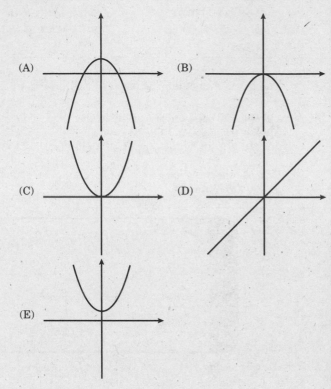

(A)

(B)

(C)

(D)

(E)

10. Let $x = y$. For what value of a is $(x + y)^2 = ax^2$?

(A) x
(B) y
(C) 1
(D) 2
(E) 4

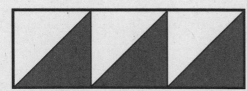

11. The figure above is composed of three adjacent squares with diagonals of length $\sqrt{2}$. What is the area of the shaded regions?

(A) 0.5
(B) 1
(C) 1.5
(D) 3
(E) 12

GO ON TO THE NEXT PAGE

Section 8

12. What is the range of the function h, where $h(x) = 2 + (x-2)^2$ is defined for $-1 \le x \le 3$?

    (A) $3 \le h(x) \le 11$
    (B) $2 \le h(x) \le 6$
    (C) $3 \le h(x) \le 6$
    (D) $6 \le h(x) \le 11$
    (E) $2 \le h(x) \le 11$

13. There are 300 people in the senior class at Carver High. Forty percent of them went to the prom with another senior from the class, paying a joint price of $60 per couple. Another 40% of the class brought a date from outside of the class; they were not allowed to buy the $60 tickets for couples, so they had to pay separately for their tickets. Ten percent of the students came alone, and 10% did not attend at all. All tickets sold individually were $35 for class members and $40 for nonmembers. How much money did the senior class bring in?

    (A) $57
    (B) $4,550
    (C) $8,850
    (D) $13,650
    (E) $20,850

14. The linear function $h(x)$ has a slope of $-\frac{1}{3}$. What is the slope of the line $h^{-1}(x)$?

    (A) -3
    (B) $-\frac{1}{3}$
    (C) 0
    (D) $\frac{1}{3}$
    (E) 3

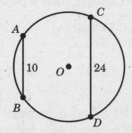

Figure Not Drawn to Scale

15. In the figure above, chord AB is parallel to chord CD, and the radius of circle O is 13. If the length of chord AB is 10 and the length of chord CD is 24, then what is the distance between the two chords?

    (A) 7
    (B) $7\sqrt{3}$
    (C) 17
    (D) $17\sqrt{2}$
    (E) $17\sqrt{3}$

16. If x and y are positive integers and $8x^1y^3 = 64y^2$, what is y^{-1} in terms of x?

    (A) $8x$
    (B) $\dfrac{x}{8}$
    (C) $\dfrac{x}{56}$
    (D) $\dfrac{1}{8x}$
    (E) $\dfrac{1}{56x}$

S T O P

Section 9

Turn to Section 9 of your answer sheet to answer the questions in this section.

Time—10 Minutes
14 Questions

For each question in this section, select the best answer from among the choices given and fill in the corresponding oval on the answer sheet.

<u>Directions:</u>   The following sentences test correctness and effectiveness of expression. In choosing answers, follow the requirements of standard written English; that is, pay attention to grammar, choice of words, sentence construction, and punctuation.

In each of the following sentences, part of the sentence or the entire sentence is underlined. Beneath each sentence you will find five ways of phrasing the underlined part. Choice A repeats the original; the other four are different.

Choose the answer that best expresses the meaning of the original sentence. If you think the original is better than any of the alternatives, choose it; otherwise choose one of the others. Your choice should produce the most effective sentence—clear and precise, without awkwardness or ambiguity.

EXAMPLE:

Laura Ingalls Wilder published her first book <u>and she was sixty-five years old then.</u>

(A) and she was sixty-five years old then
(B) when she was sixty-five
(C) at age sixty-five years old
(D) upon the reaching of sixty-five years
(E) at the time when she was sixty-five

SAMPLE ANSWER:

1. Though it appears colorless, <u>white light actually contain every color of the rainbow</u>.

   (A) white light actually contain every color of the rainbow
   (B) white light is actually containing every color of the rainbow
   (C) white light is containing every color of the rainbow, actually
   (D) white light actually contains every color of the rainbow
   (E) the colors of the rainbow contain white light

2. Solids turn to gasses in a process that <u>goes in the name of "sublimation."</u>

   (A) that goes in the name of "sublimation"
   (B) that would be called "sublimation"
   (C) that goes by the name of "sublimation"
   (D) that was known as "sublimation"
   (E) whose name is called "sublimation"

3. Rather than migrate south to escape the winter cold, <u>well insulated nests are used by some species</u> to guard against the harsh winter weather.

   (A) well insulated nests are used by some species
   (B) well insulated nests are what some species use
   (C) some species use well insulated nests
   (D) well insulated nests, some species use,
   (E) well insulated nests are being used by some species

GO ON TO THE NEXT PAGE

Section 9

4. After receiving the Nobel Prize for literature, <u>Seamus Heaney who is from Ireland returned to his native country and gave a speech</u>.

   (A) Seamus Heaney who is from Ireland returned to his native country and gave a speech
   (B) Seamus Heaney returned to his native country which is Ireland to give a speech
   (C) Seamus Heaney returned to the native country of his, Ireland, to speak
   (D) Seamus Heaney had returned to Ireland, his native country, to give a speech
   (E) Seamus Heaney returned to Ireland, his native country, to give a speech

5. Since Jason has a passion for eastern Europe, <u>he was often visiting</u> Hungary and Slovakia.

   (A) he was visiting
   (B) he often visited
   (C) he took a visit often to
   (D) often he visits
   (E) he often visits

6. Everyone <u>with a good sense of balance and not afraid of heights</u> can swing on a trapeze.

   (A) with a good sense of balance and not afraid of heights
   (B) with a good sense of balance and having no fear of heights
   (C) having a good sense of balance and without having a fear of heights
   (D) with a good sense of balance and without a fear of heights
   (E) with a good sense of balance and no fear of heights

7. <u>Having Mozart as their primary influence, the young composers set out to compose an opera that had the style of The Marriage of Figaro.</u>

   (A) Having Mozart as their primary influence, the young composers set out to compose an opera that had the style of The Marriage of Figaro.
   (B) With Mozart as their primary influence, the young composers set out to compose an opera in the style of The Marriage of Figaro.
   (C) With Mozart as their primary influence, the young composers have set out to compose an opera having the style of The Marriage of Figaro.
   (D) With the style of The Marriage of Figaro, the young composers set out to compose an opera with Mozart as their primary influence.
   (E) The young composers set out to compose an opera with Mozart as their primary influence, having the style of The Marriage of Figaro.

8. Anna's parents called the police <u>to investigate their daughter's sudden disappearance</u>.

   (A) to investigate their daughter's sudden disappearance
   (B) for investigating their daughter's sudden disappearance
   (C) to investigate the disappearance of their daughter all of the sudden
   (D) when investigating the disappearance of their sudden daughter
   (E) to suddenly investigate their daughter's disappearance

9. Several state agencies have begun to set up checkpoints along major highways <u>for the intention of stopping drunk driving</u>.

   (A) for the intention of stopping drunk driving
   (B) with the intention it will stop drunk driving
   (C) with the intention of stopping drunk driving
   (D) with the intention that it will stop drunk driving
   (E) with the intention to stop drunk driving

10. Robert's teammates say he cost them the game <u>he was neglecting</u> his responsibilities on the ballfield.

    (A) he was neglecting
    (B) with the reason that he was neglecting
    (C) by neglecting
    (D) because he had to be neglecting
    (E) in the neglect of

11. Some critics described Stravinsky's *Rite of Spring* as an unlistenable cacophony of sounds that <u>has been revised or toning it down</u> before its first public performance.

    (A) has been revised or toning it down
    (B) should have been revised or toned down
    (C) would have been revised or toned down
    (D) has revisions or toning down
    (E) was revised or toned down

GO ON TO THE NEXT PAGE

Section 9

12. The most sprawling information database in human history, many people who use the Internet these days take it for granted.

   (A) The most sprawling information database in human history, many people who use the Internet these days take it for granted

   (B) The Internet, the most sprawling information database in human history, is to be taken for granted by many people who use it these days.

   (C) These days many people who use the Internet, the most sprawling information database in human history, take it for granted.

   (D) The most sprawling information database in human history, the Internet, is these days taken for granted by many people who use it.

   (E) Taking the Internet for granted, many people use the most sprawling information database in human history these days.

13. Of every nation involved in the conflict, only the leadership of Great Britain proposed a solution that would stop the fighting.

   (A) only the Prime Minister of Great Britain proposed

   (B) Great Britain was the only one whose leadership proposed

   (C) only the leadership of Great Britain proposed

   (D) only Great Britain's leadership proposed

   (E) Great Britain's leadership only proposed

14. Although AIDS has spread most rapidly in Africa, other continents may soon experience similarly vast outbreaks of this deadly disease.

   (A) other continents may soon experience similarly vast outbreaks of this deadly disease

   (B) similar diseases may soon spread to the experience of other continents

   (C) other continents may soon have experienced similarly vast outbreaks of this deadly disease

   (D) similarly vast outbreaks of this deadly disease may soon be experienced by other continents

   (E) other continents may soon be experiencing similarly vast outbreaks of this deadly disease

S T O P

IF YOU FINISH BEFORE TIME IS CALLED, YOU MAY CHECK YOUR WORK ON THIS TEST ONLY.
DO NOT TURN TO ANY OTHER SECTION IN THIS TEST.

PRACTICE TEST 3
EXPLANATIONS

TEST 3 ANSWERS

Question Number	Answer	Right	Wrong	Question Number	Answer	Right	Wrong
	Section 2				Section 4, continued		
1	C	___	___	8	D	___	___
2	C	___	___	9	E	___	___
3	D	___	___	10	C	___	___
4	C	___	___	11	D	___	___
5	B	___	___	12	E	___	___
6	D	___	___	13	B	___	___
7	C	___	___	14	A	___	___
8	B	___	___	15	D	___	___
9	E	___	___	16	B	___	___
10	B	___	___	17	A	___	___
11	E	___	___	18	A	___	___
12	B	___	___	19	C	___	___
13	E	___	___	20	A	___	___
14	B	___	___	21	C	___	___
15	C	___	___	22	D	___	___
16	A	___	___	23	B	___	___
17	D	___	___	24	C	___	___
18	B	___	___		Section 5		
19	E	___	___	1	A	___	___
20	C	___	___	2	E	___	___
21	A	___	___	3	C	___	___
22	D	___	___	4	E	___	___
23	B	___	___	5	E	___	___
24	A	___	___	6	E	___	___
	Section 3			7	B	___	___
1	B	___	___	8	E	___	___
2	A	___	___	9	25	___	___
3	D	___	___	10	7/5	___	___
4	C	___	___	11	30	___	___
5	B	___	___	12	1	___	___
6	C	___	___	13	9	___	___
7	E	___	___	14	1	___	___
8	E	___	___	15	3	___	___
9	C	___	___	16	1/2	___	___
10	C	___	___	17	6	___	___
11	B	___	___	18	9	___	___
12	D	___	___		Section 6		
13	A	___	___	1	E	___	___
14	B	___	___	2	B	___	___
15	B	___	___	3	A	___	___
16	C	___	___	4	D	___	___
17	E	___	___	5	E	___	___
18	E	___	___	6	C	___	___
19	D	___	___	7	C	___	___
20	C	___	___	8	A	___	___
	Section 4			9	B	___	___
1	A	___	___	10	A	___	___
2	C	___	___	11	C	___	___
3	A	___	___	12	D	___	___
4	A	___	___	13	C	___	___
5	E	___	___	14	A	___	___
6	A	___	___	15	B	___	___
7	C	___	___	16	D	___	___

Question Number	Answer	Right	Wrong	Question Number	Answer	Right	Wrong
Section 6, continued				Section 7, continued			
17	E	___	___	17	C	___	___
18	B	___	___	18	A	___	___
19	B	___	___	19	D	___	___
20	E	___	___	Section 8			
21	A	___	___	1	C	___	___
22	D	___	___	2	E	___	___
23	B	___	___	3	D	___	___
24	A	___	___	4	D	___	___
25	E	___	___	5	B	___	___
26	D	___	___	6	A	___	___
27	D	___	___	7	D	___	___
28	B	___	___	8	C	___	___
29	D	___	___	9	D	___	___
30	C	___	___	10	E	___	___
31	E	___	___	11	C	___	___
32	C	___	___	12	E	___	___
33	C	___	___	13	D	___	___
34	A	___	___	14	A	___	___
35	A	___	___	15	C	___	___
Section 7				16	D	___	___
1	C	___	___	Section 9			
2	C	___	___	1	D	___	___
3	B	___	___	2	C	___	___
4	D	___	___	3	C	___	___
5	A	___	___	4	E	___	___
6	D	___	___	5	E	___	___
7	A	___	___	6	D	___	___
8	A	___	___	7	B	___	___
9	D	___	___	8	A	___	___
10	E	___	___	9	C	___	___
11	A	___	___	10	C	___	___
12	E	___	___	11	B	___	___
13	B	___	___	12	C	___	___
14	A	___	___	13	B	___	___
15	E	___	___	14	A	___	___
16	B	___	___				

CALCULATING YOUR SCORE

Writing Section Raw Score

A. Essay Score (from 1–6)

_____
A

B. Section 6 Multiple-Choice:

_____ – (_____ ÷ 4) =   _____
no. correct   no. incorrect   B

C. Section 9 Multiple-Choice:

_____ – (_____ ÷ 4) =   _____
no. correct   no. incorrect   C

D. Unrounded Multiple-Choice Score (B + C)

_____
D

E. Total Rounded Multiple- Choice Raw Score
(Rounded to the nearest whole number)

_____
E

F. Total Scaled Score
(See the Writing conversion table on the following pages)

_____
SAT Writing
Score

G. Writing Multiple-Choice Subscore
(See the Writing Multiple-Choice conversion table on the following pages)

_____
Writing MC
Score

Math Section Raw Score

A. Section 3 Raw Score:

_____ – (_____ ÷ 4) =   _____
no. correct   no. incorrect   Subtotal A

B. Section 5 Raw Score:

_____   _____
no. correct   Subtotal B

C. Section 8 Raw Score:

_____ – (_____ ÷ 4) =   _____
no. correct   no. incorrect   Subtotal C

D. Total Unrounded Raw Score
(Total A + B + C)

_____
D

E. Total Rounded Raw Score (Rounded to the nearest whole number)

_____
E

F. Scaled Score
(See the conversion table on the following pages)

_____
SAT Math
Score

Critical Reading Section Raw Score

A. Section 2 Raw Score: − (÷ 4) =

                  no. correct   no. incorrect   A

B. Section 4 Raw Score: − (÷ 4) =

                  no. correct   no. incorrect   B

C. Section 7 Raw Score: − (÷ 4) =

                  no. correct   no. incorrect   C

D. Total Unrounded Raw Score
(Total A + B + C)

                                               D

E. Total Rounded Raw Score
(Rounded to the nearest whole number)

                                               E

F. Scaled Score
(See the conversion table on the next page)

                                 SAT Critical
                                 Reading
                                 Score

CONVERTING YOUR RAW SCORES

Raw Score	Critical Reading Scaled Score	Math Scaled Score
67	800	
66	790	
65	770	
64	760	
63	750	
62	740	
61	720	
60	710	
59	700	
58	690	
57	680	
56	670	
55	670	
54	660	800
53	650	780
52	640	760
51	640	740
50	630	730
49	620	710
48	610	700
47	610	690
46	600	670
45	590	660
44	590	650
43	580	650
42	580	640
41	570	630
40	560	620
39	560	610
38	550	600
37	540	590
36	540	590
35	530	580
34	530	570
33	520	560
32	510	560
31	510	550
30	500	540
29	500	530
28	490	520
27	480	520
26	480	510
25	470	500
24	470	490
23	460	490
22	450	480
21	450	470
20	440	460
19	430	460

Raw Score	Critical Reading Scaled Score	Math Scaled Score
18	430	450
17	420	440
16	410	430
15	410	430
14	400	420
13	390	410
12	380	400
11	380	390
10	370	380
9	360	380
8	350	370
7	340	360
6	330	340
5	320	330
4	310	320
3	300	310
2	280	290
1	270	280
0	250	260
-1	250	250
-2	240	240
-3	230	230
-4	220	220
5	210	210
-6	200	200

Writing Subscores

- **Essay Subscore:** Subtotal A from Writing Score (page 560)
- **Multiple-Choice Subscore:** Calculate by plugging in Subtotal E from your writing score (page 560) into the score conversion table below

Raw Score	Multiple Choice Subscore	Raw Score	Multiple Choice Subscore
49	80	30	59
48	79	29	58
47	77	28	57
46	76	27	56
45	75	26	55
44	74	25	54
43	72	24	53
42	71	23	52
41	70	22	51
40	69	21	51
39	68	20	50
38	67	19	49
37	66	18	48
36	65	17	47
35	64	16	46
34	63	15	45
33	62	14	44
32	61	13	43
31	60	12	42

Raw Score	Multiple Choice Subscore	Raw Score	Multiple Choice Subscore
11	41	2	32
10	40	1	30
9	39	0	29
8	38	-1	27
7	37	-2	25
6	36	-3	24
5	35	-4	23
4	34	-5	22
3	33	-6	21

Writing Scaled Score

MC raw score	Essay Score					
	6	5	4	3	2	1
49	800	790	780	470	720	700
48	790	780	760	730	700	680
47	780	770	750	720	690	670
46	770	760	740	710	680	660
45	770	750	740	700	670	650
44	760	750	730	690	660	640
43	750	740	710	680	650	630
42	750	730	700	670	640	620
41	740	730	690	660	630	610
40	740	720	690	650	620	600
39	740	710	680	640	610	590
38	730	700	670	630	610	590
37	720	690	660	630	600	580
36	710	680	650	620	590	570
35	710	680	640	610	580	560
34	700	670	640	600	570	550
33	690	660	630	590	560	540
32	680	650	620	580	560	540
31	670	640	610	580	550	530
30	660	630	600	570	540	520
29	650	630	590	560	530	510
28	640	620	590	550	520	510
27	640	610	580	540	510	490
26	630	600	570	530	500	490
25	620	590	560	520	500	480
24	610	580	550	510	490	470
23	600	570	540	510	480	460
22	590	570	530	500	470	450
21	590	570	530	500	470	450
20	580	560	520	490	460	440
19	570	550	520	480	450	430
18	570	540	520	470	440	420
17	560	530	510	460	430	420
16	550	520	500	450	430	410
15	540	510	490	450	420	400
14	530	500	480	440	410	390
13	520	500	470	430	400	380
12	510	490	460	420	390	370

Writing Scaled Score

MC raw score	Essay Score					
	6	5	4	3	2	1
11	510	480	450	410	380	360
10	500	470	450	400	370	350
9	490	460	440	390	360	350
8	480	450	430	390	360	340
7	470	440	420	380	350	330
6	460	430	410	370	340	320
5	450	430	400	360	330	310
4	450	420	390	350	320	300
3	440	410	390	340	310	290
2	430	400	380	330	300	280
1	420	380	370	320	290	270
0	400	370	350	310	280	260
-1	380	360	340	290	270	260
-2	370	340	320	270	260	250
-3	360	330	310	260	250	240
-4	350	320	290	250	240	230
-5	340	310	280	240	230	220
-6	340	310	280	240	220	210

ESSAY

A 6 Essay

Several examples from science, technology, and the arts demonstrate that imagination is more powerful than knowledge. When Bill Gates and his partner founded Microsoft, they used their imagination to dream up a concept that they did not even know how to implement. Friederich Kekule developed an important chemistry model in a dream, rather than a classroom or lab. And finally, Bob Dylan became the voice of a generation and the foremost songwriter on earth without ever learning how to read music.

Bill Gates's success proves that imagination is more powerful than knowledge. When Gates founded Microsoft in the mid-1980s, he and his partner had the idea of creating an operating system or "shell" that would simplify using a personal computer. When IBM contracted Gates to create such a product, he and his partners did not admit that they had no idea how to write the software for operating system. Instead, they used their creativity to license parts of the software from other companies and then combined it into a program that led to the development of the now ubiquituss Microsoft Windows software.

Friederich Kekule's discovery of the ring theory shows how imagination can be more powerful than knowledge. Most chemists do their best work in the classroom or the lab, but Kekule created his ring theory of molecular structure in a dream. Kekule dreamed an image of snakes biting one another's tails, and when he awoke he applied the pattern he imagined to the molecular pattern of the carbon compound called benzene. His imagination rather than his everyday practical knowledge made the discovery possible.

Bob Dylan has remained at the top of the music charts for over four decades even though he can't read a note of music. Dylan's formidable imagination fueled his crafting of over five hundred songs, many of which have become timeless classics, but his knowledge of music fundamentals always remained basic. Rather than depend on a formal education or musical training, Dylan channeled the power of his ideas into his lyrics, making his imagination the primary engine behind his songs and his enormous popularity.

The examples of Gates, Kekule, and Dylan show how powerful creative thought can be—more powerful than even the finest education. Students today remain steadfastly focused on success in high school and gaining acceptance to top universities, but the most powerful surefire way to success doesn't lie between the covers of books—it lies in the imagination people harness between their ears. Gates didn't need a Harvard degree; Dylan didn't even need to read music—to succeed on a grand scale, people should focus more on developing their creativity and imaginations than pad their resumes.

Discussion

Below is a quick checklist of how this essay matches up to our Universal SAT Essay Template. Notice that it gets a YES in every box.

OUR UNIVERSAL SAT ESSAY TEMPLATE CRITERIA	YES OR NO?
Thesis statement in first sentence of paragraph 1	YES
Three examples listed in paragraph 1 in order from best to worst	YES
Topic sentence for example in paragraph 2	YES
3–4 development sentences to support paragraph 2's example	YES
Topic sentence for example in paragraph 3	YES
3–4 development sentences to support paragraph 3's example	YES
Topic sentence for example in paragraph 4	YES
3–4 development sentences to support paragraph 4's example	YES
Conclusion paragraph contains rephrased thesis statement	YES
About 15 sentences total	YES

Let's take a closer look at the essay based on our four key SAT essay ingredients: positioning, organization, examples, and command of language.

POSITIONING

The writer takes a strong and clear stance on the essay topic right from the start. The writer also uses the thesis statement to set the grader up for the examples that he or she will use to prove the position: Several examples from science, technology, and the arts demonstrate that imagination is more powerful than knowledge. After just the first sentence, the grader knows the writer's stance on the topic and that he or she will use examples from science, technology, and the arts to back it up. The remainder of the introduction spells out each example: Gates, Kekule, and Dylan. A perfect start to a "6" SAT Essay. The writer's conclusion expands upon the initial position by suggesting that everybody follow the example set by Gates, Kekule, and Dylan—people should harness the power of imagination and forget about building their resumes.

ORGANIZATION

The writer organizes this essay based exactly on the structure we suggest in our Universal SAT Essay Template. It contains five paragraphs of at least three sentences each. The paragraphs are organized into an introduction, three example paragraphs starting with the strongest example (Gates), and a conclusion that sums up and broadens the argument.

EXAMPLES

The writer spells out the three examples he or she will use to prove the position on the topic. In this case, the writer agrees with the topic's argument that *Imagination is more powerful than knowledge*. To prove it, the writer uses three diverse examples: one from technology (Bill Gates's success despite his company's lack of programming code), one from science (Friederich Kekule's dream of benzene's molecular structure), and one from the the arts (Bob Dylan's success as a songwriter despite his lack of knowledge about the basics of music theory). The writer's examples come from a wide array of fields, which conveys his or her breadth of knowledge. The variety of examples also strengthens the support for the writer's argument.

COMMAND OF LANGUAGE

SAT essay-graders should expect at least a few errors in *every* SAT essay. This essay contains a few minor slips regarding the writer's command of language, but nothing major enough to lower its score from a 6. These are some examples of the few minor errors it contains: The phrase for *operating system* omits the word *the*. The word *ubiquituss* should be spelled *ubiquitous*. The final sentence misspells *developing* and contains a parallelism error: *people should focus more on developping their creativity and imaginations than pad their resumes* should instead read, *people should focus on developing their creativity and imaginations rather than on padding their resumes*. Overall, the errors in this essay are minor and few, nothing substantial enough to cause a grader to lower this writer's score.

This essay definitely pours on the Special Sauce. The essay's impressive vocabulary (*implement*, *steadfastly*, *ubiquitous*) combined with appropriate and effective word choice convey the writer's strong command of language. The writer also varies the sentence structure quite a bit, which helps keep the essay interesting.

A 4 Essay

Imagination is more powerful than knowledge, in my opinion. I can think of two examples that prove the point. First: Bill Gates and Microsoft. Second: Einstein and the theory of relativeness.

Bill Gates's current wealth proves that imagination is more powerful than knowledge. When Gates founded Microsoft in the mid-1980s, he and his partner barely knew what they were doing in terms of programming software. But they had a great idea—to make the personal computer ease to use via new software. They were supposed to make software for IBM to do this but then had to take it from somewhere else! Quite a clever solution, which shows their imagination counted for more than their ability.

Albert Einstein is pretty much always thought of as a genius, but few consider the role imagination played in his inventions, namely that of relativeness. I can't explain to you this concept entirely, but I can tell you this: Nobody in the history of the human race ever questioned whether the experience of time passing could be relative before Einstein. Einstein's knowledge of physics mattered for discovery, but what mattered most was his capacity to imagine an experience of time different from the one people had contemplated for ages before him.

So as you can see, imagination is more powerful than knowledge. Had Gates and Einstein only had knowledge, they would likely be working in a lab somewhere today. Their imagination made their success possible.

Discussion

This essay fails to follow our Universal SAT Template from start to finish. Below is a quick checklist of the criteria for our Universal SAT Essay Template. Note the NOs to see exactly where this essay's key deficiencies lie.

OUR UNIVERSAL SAT ESSAY TEMPLATE CRITERIA	YES OR NO?
Thesis statement in first sentence of paragraph 1	YES
Three examples listed in paragraph 1 in order from best to worst	NO
Topic sentence for example in paragraph 2	YES
3–4 development sentences to support paragraph 2's example	YES
Topic sentence for example in paragraph 3	YES
3–4 development sentences to support paragraph 3's example	YES
Topic sentence for example in paragraph 4	NO
3–4 development sentences to support paragraph 4's example	NO
Conclusion paragraph contains rephrased thesis statement	NO
About 15 sentences total	YES

Let's take a closer look at the essay based on our four key SAT essay ingredients: positioning, organization, examples, and command of language.

POSITIONING

The writer takes a clear stance on the topic right from the start by agreeing that imagination is more powerful than knowledge. He or she uses only two examples to back up his or her position, but they're solid: one from science (Einstein) and one from technology (Gates). The conclusion paragraph restates the thesis statement but does not expand upon it. These kinds of weaknesses differentiate "4" essays like this one from "6" essays.

ORGANIZATION

According to our Universal SAT Essay Template, an ideal SAT essay should contain five paragraphs, each with at least three sentences. The five paragraphs should be broken down into an introduction, three example paragraphs, and a conclusion. This essay comes close. It contains four paragraphs: an introduction, two example paragraphs, and a conclusion. The introduction and conclusion are somewhat short and abrupt, and the third example paragraph is missing entirely. The writer does pay attention to internal paragraph structure, but overall the paragraphs lack the cohesiveness of "6" essays. The paragraphs include topic sentences and transitions, but the ideas are somewhat jumbled and often lack a sensible flow. These kinds of deficiencies make this essay a 4.

EXAMPLES

The writer's examples are solid, but they're not presented with confidence and authority. It feels like the writer is on the right track, but doesn't really have enough certainty about the examples to develop them thoroughly and keep them tied closely to proving the position. The phrase that states that Bill Gates and his partners barely knew what they were doing is an example of how this writer fails to present the examples with certainty and clarity. Remember that the SAT graders are looking for specificity in your examples. Vague phrases show the grader that you don't have a firm enough grasp on your subject to link it directly and specifically to the point you're trying to prove. Be specific!

COMMAND OF LANGUAGE

Essays that merit a 4 have competent command of language with at least a few notable errors. This essay contains only a few spelling mistakes (*knoledge* should be *knowledge*), but the writer reveals a broader weakness in command of language by writing in an inappropriate tone and flubbing the term *relativity* (the writer calls it *relativeness*). The tone issue centers around the writer's use of the first person *I* throughout the essay. First person is not an absolute no-no on SAT essays, but in this case, it's unnecessary and makes the essay feel amateurish. Phrases like *in my opinion* are implied, since the entire essay is intended to express the opinion of the writer on the topic presented. The writer also writes too casually for an SAT essay, as shown by his or her use of exclamations and phrases like *pretty much* , and by addressing the grader directly (*I can't explain to you*). Mistakes like these sour the Special Sauce of the essay and make the grader doubt the writer's command of language.

SECTION 2

Sentence Completions

1. C One-Blank/One-Way *Easy*

The sentence contains no switch and no comparison over time: It's one-way. The blank, which describes how physicists viewed string theory, must fit with the fact that string theory "presented so many unproven theories and research opportunities." String theory must be a pretty good field to be involved in, since it offers so much chance for research. To fill in the blank, you're looking for a word that is positive and fits with the idea of "lots of research opportunities." You can knock out *disappointing, turbulent,* and *dubious* because those are negative. Of the remaining choices, the only one that fits with the idea of having "lots of research opportunities" is *promising.*

2. C One-Blank/Two-Way *Easy*

The switch *though* indicates that the sentence is two-way. The blank describes what the chemist hopes for, and this must contrast with the chemist's former "disappointment." What's a word that is the opposite of disappointed? How about plain old "not disappointed"? So, you're looking for a positive word that fills in the blank and conveys the idea of "not disappointed." You can cut *collapse* and *flaws,* since those are negative words. Of the remaining choices, *hypothesis* is a trap. It feels correct for a second because it's associated with scientific experiments, but it doesn't make sense when plugged in to the blank. No experiment can "bring hypothesis"—hypothesis, unlike disappointment, is not a state of being. That leaves *renewal* and *success.* Both words are positive. *Renewal* implies a comeback of some sort, but is a bit vague about what sort of comeback it would be. *Success* is much more specific and the best answer. The chemist hopes his experiment is a success; he hopes it provides the data or result he's looking for.

3. D Two-Blank/Two-Way *Medium*

The sentence contains the two-way switch *although,* which indicates that this sentence will contrast. Spartacus wanted to do one thing, but his men wanted another thing. The first blank describes what Spartacus wanted, and the second what the men wanted: These two blanks must contrast. Cut *reward . . affluent* right away, since they don't contrast. From the sentence, you can get more information for what should fill the blanks. The men, according to the sentence, wanted to "continue to fight," so Spartacus must have wanted them to stop fighting. If Spartacus wanted to stop fighting, he'd want his army to stop being an army: He'd want to dissolve it. The men wanted to continue to fight, though, so they'd want to "stay an army." If Spartacus wanted to stop fighting, he wouldn't want to *execute* his army, since that would cause more violence, nor would he want to *outfit* ("supply") or *encourage* his army. What he'd want to do is *disband* it, while the men, in contrast, would want to stay *together*.

4.   **C**   One-Blank/One-Way   *Easy*

The sentence contains the one-way switch *because*. The blank in the sentence will agree with the other facts and ideas presented. The blank describes how Parliament treated Prince Albert, and the rest of the sentence explains that the British saw him as a meddler because Albert wasn't British. Since they saw him as a meddler, it follows that they'd treat him "badly and with hate." You can eliminate *ecstasy* and *interest* just because they're positive words. Among the other answer choices, only *contempt* captures the real anger that Parliament would feel for a meddler in British affairs.

5.   **B**   One-Blank/One-Way   *Medium*

The one-way switch *since* tells you that this sentence flows one way. What happens in the second half of the sentence will describe how the Battle of Hastings fit into English history. The blank describes what kind of event the Battle of Hastings was, and the rest of the sentence says that the outcome of the battle changed the future of the nation. So, it must be an important event. You're looking for a positive word that means "important." You can toss *petty, disastrous,* and *disputable* because all three are negative terms. That leaves you with *seminal* and *glorious*. *Glorious* means "wonderful and full of glory." While that's a positive word, it doesn't match with the meaning of important because it makes a judgment about the aftermath of the battle that the rest of the sentence does not make. The sentence is not saying that it's a good thing the Normans beat the Saxons; it's saying it's an important thing. *Seminal* means pivotal, crucial, or very important. Now that's more like it. *Seminal* it is.

6.   **D**   Two-Blank/One-Way   *Medium*

The sentence contains no switch and does not make a comparison over time: It's one-way. The first blank in the sentence describe how the paper must be "factually." The second blank states rules of good paper-writing that the students must conform to. You're looking for words that means something like "true" for the first blank, and "good writing" for the second. *Correct..grammar* fits both needs perfectly. If you didn't see that, you could have always cut answers with negative first words, since that blank describing how a good paper must be would not be negative.

7.   **C**   Two-Blank/Two-Way   *Medium*

The sentence contains the switch *though*, indicating that it contrasts. The reindeer are perceived one way by Americans, and in a very different way by the Sami. The first blank describes how Americans see reindeer, and the second explains the relationship of reindeer to the Sami. The sentence also links reindeer with the Sami's survival, so it's clear that the reindeer are important to them. You can eliminate **A, D,** and **E** because none of those pairs has a second word that matches with the idea of "important." That leaves *critical..instrumental* and *fanciful..crucial*. The first pair fails to contrast, so *fanciful..crucial* is the best choice.

8. B Two-Blank/Two-Way   *Difficult*

The two-way switch *despite* tells you this sentence will contrast. The citizens of Zambonia have endured such harsh rule that you might think they'd give up. But no, they refuse to forget their ancestors and will fight on! The first blank describes the rule the Zambonians suffered under. The second blank describes the traditions of their ancestors, and these traditions contrast to the rule they are currently suffering under. In other words, the current rule is "bad and oppressive," while the old traditions are "good and free." You can throw out *benevolent..idiosyncratic*, *idyllic..despicable*, and *legislative..acrimonious* because the first words of those pairs is not negative. Of the remaining two answer choices, you can cut *destructive..despicable* because the second word is not positive. That leaves *autocratic..egalitarian* as the right answer. Autocratic means "tyrannous," while egalitarian means "equal."

Short Reading Passage

9. E Words in Context   *Medium*

Words-in-Context questions can be especially tough when you have no clue what the word means in or out of context. Assuming you have no idea what the verb *to reel* means, how can you go about answering the question? The key is the context. Approach the question as you would a Sentence Completion question. Which word when subsituted for reeled would make the resulting sentence make sense? "I ---- on the pavement trying to catch my footing." Picture this author slipping and sliding on the street in an attempt to keep his or her balance. What would the author have done before needing to regain his balance? *Decoyed*? No. *Ensnared*? No. *Quavered*? No. *Swiveled* is closer because it means "turned around." The author very well may have turned around before trying to regain his or her balance. However, an even better verb is *staggered*, which means to lose one's balance. **E** is the correct answer.

10. B Specific Information   *Easy*

The author says that when the ground first shook, he or she thought there was definitely a "fight in that house." That makes the best answer to this question *family argument*. Answer **D** is a trap, since the author hears a "rattle" from within the house. But he doesn't a hear a literal rattle. He hears a fight.

11. E Main Idea   *Difficult*

The author of this passages seems pretty psyched about dry ice, right? That just about sums up the author's purpose for writing the passage, and that's what this Themes and Arguments question wants to know. The sense of being psyched about dry ice makes it easy to cut some of the answer choices based simply on their negativity. **B**'s "warn" and **C**'s "ridicule" are no-gos. **A** and **D** start off much better. They're positive statements about some of the main subjects of the passage: sublimation and dry ice. But the passage is about dry ice more than it is about sublimation, so **D** doesn't work. And while the author definitely passes along interesting facts about dry ice in this passage, is that his or her *purpose*? No. The purpose or reason for writing this passage is to show readers that dry ice is safe, convenient, and good to use. He or she wants to *convince* people to use dry ice.

12. **B**   Themes and Arguments   *Medium*

Why does the author start right off by mentioning that dry ice comes from a "normal part of the atmosphere"? The reason goes along with the author's purpose for writing the passage: to convince readers that dry ice is a safe, convenient alternative to everyday ice. The author adds the detail that dry ice comes from carbon dioxide, which humans exhale, to prove the same point that dry ice is a "normal" solid that nobody should *fear*. Which answer choice conveys that intention of easing fear? Only **B**. The verb *allay* may have confused you a bit, but it just means "to ease." Think of allay as "to lay aside." That's just what the author wants people to do with their fears of dry ice—give them a rest.

Long Reading Passage (Billy Budd)

13. **E**   Specific Information   *Medium*

If you hadn't read the passage or looked back at lines 1–3, each of the answer choices could conceivably be true of the general question, *Why have scholars been unable to agree about the correct title of the novel?* But if you did go back to the specified lines, you'd have read, "Because it went unpublished during Melville's lifetime, there has never been a clear consensus on the proper title for the work most commonly and concisely known as *Billy Budd*."

14. **B**   Technique   *Medium*

To answer this question, you have to think about the indicated lines in the context of the passage as a whole. After the author describes all the subtitles *Billy Budd* has had, he explains how those subtitles indicate the novel's view of the conflict between the individual and society. He then describes how that conflict can be represented by the idea of personal titles, such as writer, sailor, professor, and foretopman. Because the main subtitles in *Billy Budd* ascribe various personal titles to the main character, the main function of the subtitles in this passage is to illustrate the author's idea about personal titles and the way they indicate social position.

15. **C**   Attitude or Tone   *Medium*

The way to answer a question such as this is to think about your general impression of the author's attitude in this passage, and then give your impression a word. In this case, the author seems calm and instructive. His main goal seems to be to teach his readers about his subject; he does not advocate any particular argument and does not use rhetoric to persuade other people that his position is correct. He is certainly not *condescending* or *outraged*. Because of his calm demeanor, he cannot be said to be *excited and effusive*. But because of his obvious interest in his topic, it would be just as hard to label him as *disengaged*. *Explanatory and objective* is a much better fit: He is explaining his idea about *Billy Budd* in a comprehensive way.

16. **A**   Specific Information   *Easy*

In the specified lines, the author states that Melville's introduction of Ishmael, using the words "Call me Ishmael," is "curious" because the statement does not tell us whether Ishmael is the narrator's real name. So, **A** is the correct answer choice.

The most likely confusion presented by the other possible choices is that some of them also refer to the ambiguity of the character's name. But the author never says that Ishmael is an unusual name, as **C** implies, or that the name is ambiguous because of social context, as **E** implies.

17.   **D**   Themes and Arguments   *Difficult*
This question is pretty difficult—each answer choice indicates a fairly sophisticated and complex way of interpreting the question. To answer the question correctly, you have to find not just a plausible definition for "the discrepancy between an individual and his name," but also the definition that best describes the author's idea of the discrepancy. To find this definition, you have to look at the passage as a whole, both for specific clues and for a general sense of how the author thinks about identity.

The passage in general is concerned with the conflict between exterior labels, such as names and titles, and a person's inner conception of himself or herself. There are specific places where the passage says things like "at the essential core of his existence, he is more than just his name," and "you are you. Beyond that you have your name...." Both these passages seem to indicate that a person's name is not the essence of a person's inner identity. As a result, **D** is the right choice.

18.   **B**   Words in Context   *Medium*
The passage doesn't provide a specific definition of foretopman, but it does give a general definition, stating that a foretopman is a particular kind of sailor (*"Billy Budd, Foretopman* goes even further than *Billy Budd, Sailor"*). Once you see this, you can throw out answer choices, **A**, **C**, and **E**, since they contradict the notion of a foretopman as a sailor. **D** does define the foretopman as a specific kind of sailor, but it makes the definition *too* specific—the text never indicates that a foretopman keeps watch from the crow's nest. For that reason, **B** is the correct answer choice.

19.   **E**   Specific Information   *Difficult*
The lines referenced in the question say that being a sailor is different from being a foretopman, because "sailor" is a general category, while "foretopman" comes with specific duties and responsibilities. The question then becomes whether the passage describes what those duties and responsibilities are—if it says that a foretopman is a military sailor, then the correct answer is **D**; if it says that a foretopman is a port inspector, then the correct answer is **B**. But, in fact, the passage doesn't specifically define the role of a foretopman. It only implies that a foretopman is a particular kind of sailor.

With that in mind, you can limit the possible answer choices to **A** and **E**. **A** is on the right track, but it is an incomplete answer—being a foretopman does not exactly imply a different kind of work, only a specific set of duties within the general work of being a sailor. In addition, **A** fails to take into account the thematic importance of the idea that having a more specific role necessarily limits a your social identity, even if your inner identity is unchanged. So, **E** is the answer.

20.   **C**   Themes and Arguments   *Difficult*
Generally speaking, the author uses his own name, James Corolla, to illustrate his point about the ways in which titles can limit social identity. He does this by attaching various titles ("writer," "professor") to his name, and then describing how his arguments about *Billy Budd* take on different implications depending on his title. If he is a professor, for instance, his arguments are more weighty and authoritative

than if he is a writer, but he has less freedom to change his mind. So, the correct answer choice is **C**—he uses his own name as an example of the constraints titles can place on social identity.

21.   **A**   Words in Context   *Medium*

Each answer choice represents a plausible possible meaning for the word *autonomy*. The passage as a whole involves the theme of the constraints of social expectation: Once a person "enters society," he or she receives a label such as "writer" or "sailor," and is then expected to perform a set of actions based on that label. As a result, the meaning of autonomy in this passage is best represented by **A**. The other answer choices could define autonomy in a different context, but they don't have much to do with the context established by this passage.

22.   **D**   Words in Context   *Easy*

The line in question describes the way a person's individuality "chafes against" exterior social limitations. Society attempts to limit a person's role, and the person's sense of individuality resists the limitation, **D**. If answer **A** seemed right to you, that's because it's a trap—a literal meaning of *chafe* is the way one's skin grows irritated or sore from rubbing against something. But this passage uses chafe in a metaphorical sense rather than a literal sense.

23.   **B**   Specific Information   *Medium*

As the passage says in the indicated lines, an "inside narrative ... places special emphasis on the interior consciousness of an individual, in an attempt to explore the private selves of men thrust into a social world." So, **B** is the best choice: An inside narrative takes you inside the mind of a character to show how his inner experience compares with his outside experience of human society.

24.   **A**   Specific Information   *Medium*

This passage draws some very detailed conclusions based only on the novel's titles (*Billy Budd, Sailor* or *Billy Budd, Foretopman*) and subtitles ("An Inside Narrative"), which are laid out in the first paragraph. The other examples used to develop the argument—the opening of *Moby-Dick*, the author's own name and personal titles— are taken from outside the book itself. The best, and perhaps only, way to answer this question is to look through the passage and see what examples it uses. Once you've looked back through the passage and see that the narrative, characters, and text of *Billy Budd* are not discussed, **A** emerges as the clear choice.

SECTION 3

1.   **B**   Numbers and Operations: Basic Operations   *Easy*

The best way to solve is to pretend you're in elementary school and set it up this way:

$$
\begin{array}{r}
1\ 9\ T \\
-\ T\ 7 \\
\hline
1\ N\ 6
\end{array}
$$

Now ask yourself, if $T - 7 = 6$, what must T equal? 13. That means that $T = 3$ (since the 13 comes from carrying a 1 over from the tens place). Now that you know that $T = 3$, you can complete the equation: $193 - 37 = 1N6$. Since $193 - 37 = 156$, $N = 5$.

2.   **A**   Numbers and Operations: Basic Operations   *Easy*

Because $x/2$ is an integer, x must be a multiple of 2. In other words, it must be an even number. The only even number answer choice is –2. If you didn't see this right away, you could have also solved this problem by plugging in all five answers and testing them.

3.   **D**   Algebra: Solving Equations   *Easy*

To find the cost of an individual apple, you have to divide the total amount John spent by the total number of apples. The question tells you the total spent: m. Now, you have to figure out the total number of apples. You know that each box contains d apples and that John bought x boxes. Therefore, the number of apples equals the number of apples in each box multiplied the number of boxes: xd. So the answer is m divided by xd, **D**.

4.   **C**   Geometry: Coordinate Geometry   *Medium*

Don't get thrown off by this question because you don't know the function. All you have to know is what the graph of the function *looks* like. The graph of $f(x + 5)$ will look exactly the same as the graph of $f(x)$ with one major difference: The graph of $f(x + 5)$ will be pushed five places to the right along the x-axis. Think about it this way: $f(x)$, where $x = 1$ is $f(1)$, while $f(x + 5)$, where $x = 1$ is $f(6)$. So, the value of $f(x)$, where $x - 6$, is equal to the value of $f(x + 5)$, where $x = 1$. Among the answer choices, the graph pushed five spaces to the right along the x-axis is graph **C**.

5.   **B**   Geometry: Angles and Lines   *Easy*

Because a is a straight line, you know that it measures 180°. So, $x + y + y = 180$. The question tells you that $x = 64°$. Substitute that value into the equation: $64 + 2y = 180$. Solving for y, you get $2y = 116$, which means that $y = 58$. Note that if you had accidentally made $y = 64$ instead of x, **C** was an SAT trap waiting to punish you for the mistake.

6.   **C**   Geometry: Circles   *Easy*

The area of the shaded region is equal to the area of the square minus the area of a quarter-circle. (You know you're dealing with exactly a quarter circle because the angle that describes it is part of the square, meaning it's 90°.) Also, since r is both the length of the side of the square and the radius of the circle, the area of the square is r^2, and the area of the quarter-circle is $\frac{1}{4}\pi r^2$. So the area of the shaded region is equal to $r^2 - \frac{1}{4}\pi r^2$.

7.   **E**   Data Analysis, Statistics, Probability: Logic   *Medium*

You pretty much have to slog through each answer choice to solve this logic problem. You're looking for the one false answer, so you need to find and eliminate the scenarios in which the statement could be true. The first choice is "some blue balls have dots on them." The problem tells you that all blue balls have at least one star on them, but it doesn't specify what other markings blue balls have. In other words, some blue balls could have dots in addition to stars, so **A** could be true. The second choice is "all red balls have three dots on them." You know that all red balls have at least one dot on them, so it's entirely possible that all red balls could have three dots on them. Since this statement could be true, eliminate **B**. The third choice is "all balls with dots on them are red." Again, you know that all red balls must have at least one dot on them, and it is entirely possible that no other colored balls have dots on them. Eliminate **C**. The fourth choice is "all blue balls have squares on them." You know that all blue balls have at least one star on them and that all balls with squares on them also have dots on them. However, this information does not rule out the possibility that all blue balls have squares on them. Eliminate **D**. This leaves choice **E**, "some green balls have squares on them." This statement is always false because all balls with squares on them also have dots on them, and you know from the question that no green balls have stars or dots on them. **E**'s the answer.

8.   **E**   Numbers and Operations: Factors and Multiples   *Medium*

You should be able to solve this problem simply by elimination. Look at the answer choices to see which could be factors of $4wq$. Don't waste time assigning values to w and q. Since a factor is a number that divides cleanly into another number, you should be able to see that w would divide cleanly into $4wq$, as would wq and $2wq$. It may take a little thought, but you should see that $\frac{q}{2}$ will also divide cleanly into $4wq$ for the simple reason that it will divide cleanly into q. That leaves you with w^2, which won't divide cleanly.

9.   **C**   Algebra: Substitution   *Easy*

Here you can just substitute 6 for $2x$ into the equation $4x - y = 10$. Just remember to multiply that 6 by two, since $4x$ is twice as much as $2x$: $2(6) - y = 10$, so $-y = -2$, and $y = 2$. Of course, the question adds that tricky final step and asks you to find $2y$, which is 4. Always be careful of those final steps: they exist to get you to fall into SAT traps.

10.   **C**   Geometry: Solids   *Medium*

The volume of a cube is equal to s^3, where s is the length of each edge. So, to determine the length of an edge given the volume of a cube, just take the cube root of the volume. The cube root of 64 is 4, so that's the radius of the circle whose area you need to find. Substitute that 4 into the equation for the area of a circle ($A = \pi r^2$), and you get $A = (4^2)\pi = 16\pi$.

11.   **B**   Data Analysis, Statistics, Probability: Probability   *Medium*

The tricky part of this question is realizing that the first card was returned to the stack. That means that for both the first and second draws of the cards, the stack contains six clubs out of a total of nine cards. The probability of selecting a club in a single drawing is therefore $\frac{2}{3}$, and the probability of selecting clubs on both draws is the product of their individual probabilities, which is $\frac{2}{3} \times \frac{2}{3} = \frac{4}{9}$.

Even if you had no clue how to solve this problem, you should have been able to eliminate $\frac{4}{9}$ and then guess. The probability of an event is always 0, 1, or some value between 0 and 1, so $\frac{4}{9}$ must be wrong.

12.   **D**   Algebra: Solving Equations   *Medium*

Since you can calculate Floyd's rate only if you know Bonnie's rate, the first step is to figure out how fast Bonnie runs. To find out, just divide distance by time: $12 \div 2 = 6$ miles per hour. Floyd runs at half Bonnie's rate, so he must run 3 miles an hour. For a man running 3 miles an hour to run 6 miles, divide distance by rate: $6 \div 3 = 2$ hours. And finally, don't fall for the SAT trap. Remember to change units: the question asks how many *minutes* it will take Floyd to run 6 miles. Since there are 60 minutes in an hour, in 2 hours there are 120 minutes.

13. **A**   Geometry: Polygons   *Difficult*

Because all of the angles in the figure are right angles, you know that corresponding sides of the polygon are identical, so you can label each side in the follwing way:

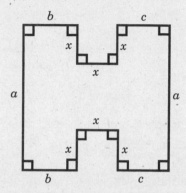

Now, you can solve for the perimeter, p, by adding the values of the lengths of the sides and simplifying:

$$p = a + b + x + x + x + c + a + c + x + x + x + b$$
$$p = 2a + 2b + 2c + 6x$$
$$p = 2(a + b + c + 3x)$$

14. **B**   Algebra: Substitution   *Difficult*

The best way to solve this problem is to solve for b directly and then divide that expression by 2. To solve for b, just move some variables around:

$$a = bc$$
$$\frac{a}{c} = b$$

Now, you can divide both sides of this equation by 2:

$$\frac{a}{2c} = \frac{b}{2}$$

15. **B**   Algebra: Functions   *Medium*

A weird symbol problem. In other words, a glorified function problem. In still other words, a substitution problem in disguise. From the question, you can see that the little square $\square$ means that you square whatever is inside it and then add one. So, $\boxed{x+y} - \boxed{x-y} = ((x + y)^2 + 1) - ((x - y)^2 + 1)$. Now you have to multiply out the binomials and simplify (remember to correctly distribute that negative sign outside the second group of parentheses).

$$x^2 + 2xy + y^2 + 1 - (x^2 - 2xy + y^2 + 1)$$

$$x^2 + 2xy + y^2 + 1 - x^2 + 2xy - y^2 - 1$$

the new SAT

16. **C**   Numbers and Operations: Sequences   *Medium*

Here's a standard sequence question with a twist. The question explains how the sequence works, but instead of giving you the first term and asking you to figure out a term somewhere along the sequence, the question does just the opposite. The question gives you the fifth term and asks you to find the first. You have the sequence $a, b, c, d, 27$, and you know that each term is equal to -3 times the term before, so just work backwards: $-3d = 27$, so $d = -9$, and so on. Keep on working backwards until you get to a, which is equal to $\frac{1}{3}$.

17. **E**   Algebra: Solving Equations   *Difficult*

The key to solving this problem is correctly translating the word problem into an equation. Often, when you face complicated word problems, the best thing to do is define all the variables. This will help you focus on what you're looking for and set up the equation. The question gives you two rates, one for Joseph's speed to the game and one returning home. We'll get crazy and call these rates $r_1 = 50$ and $r_2 = 35$. The question also tells you how long it took Joseph to get to and from the game: 3 hours and 24 minutes. This sort of mixed unit number is always difficult to deal with, so pick either hours or minutes and convert the number. We suggest picking hours, since the rates you're given are in $\frac{\text{miles}}{\text{hour}}$: 3 hours 24 minutes $= 3\frac{24}{60} = 3\frac{2}{5} = \frac{17}{5}$ hours. The question asks you to find distance, d. Now that you've got all the variables defined, set them up in the equation. The rate formula tells you that $r = d \times t$. Since this word problem tells you the total time, while giving different "to" and "from" rates and a variable for distance, it's smart to use the formula in a different form: $t = \frac{d}{r}$.

But it's not that simple. The problem contains two twists. First, since the question gives you two different rates and one total time, you actually have to add together the "to" and "from" to get the total time. Second, since you have to deal with the to and from trips separately, and the distance, d, covers both trips, you have to use $\frac{d}{2}$ for each half of the trip. Okay, now you can set up the proper equation using the variables we defined: $T = \frac{\frac{d}{2}}{r_1} + \frac{\frac{d}{2}}{r_2}$, which means that $\frac{17}{5} = \frac{\frac{d}{2}}{50} + \frac{\frac{d}{2}}{35}$. After that, it's just working out the math. First, get common denominators on the right of the equation so you can add the fractions: $\frac{17}{5} = \frac{\frac{7d}{2}}{350} + \frac{\frac{10d}{2}}{350}$, which means that $\frac{17}{5} = \frac{\frac{17d}{2}}{350}$. Multiply the fraction on the right by 2 to simplify down to $\frac{17}{5} = \frac{17d}{700}$ and then cross-multiply it out: $11{,}900 = 85d$. Then solve: $d = 140$ miles.

18. E   Algebra: Binomials and Quadratics   *Difficult*

To answer this question, you have to know two things: what makes a fraction undefined and how to factor polynomials. First things first: A fraction is undefined when its denominator equals 0. So, you're looking for the values of x at which $6x^2 - x - 2 = 0$. The numerator actually doesn't matter at all in this question—when looking for an undefined fraction, ignore the numerator. (Answer **B** is actually a trap waiting for you to factor the numerator and cancel out). When you factor the denominator, you end up with $(3x - 2)(2x + 1) = 0$. This means that for the values of x, where $3x - 2 = 0$ and $2x + 1 = 0$, the fraction is undefined. Work out those two equations and you come up with **E**.

19. D   Geometry: Coordinate Geometry   *Difficult*

You can't find the distance between the points until you know their x-coordinates, and you can't figure out the x-coordinates until you know the equations of the lines. The first step is to write the equations of the two lines. Since both lines pass through $(0,0)$, you can use the slope-intercept form of the equation of the line without the y-intercept (since it's 0): $y = mx$. The equation of l_1 is $y_1 = \frac{3}{2}x_1$ and l_s is $y_2 = \frac{2}{3}x_2$. Both points A and B have $y = 2$, which means the distance between the two points is just the difference in the x-coordinate. Substituting $y = 2$ into the first equation, you get $x = \frac{4}{3}$. Substituting $y = 2$ into the second equation, you get $x = 3$. So, the distance between the two points is $3 - \frac{4}{3} = \frac{5}{3}$.

20. C   Algebra: AbsoluteValue and Exponents   *Difficult*

The question asks you to solve for x in terms of y. That means you have to eventually get x on one side of the equal sign and y on the other. The first step in this problem is to get rid of those square root signs: Square both sides of the equation to make it happen:

$$\frac{x+2}{y+2} = 4\left(\frac{1}{4}\right)$$

You can then simplify this equation to get:

$$\frac{x+2}{y+2} = 1$$

Multiply both sides by $(y + 2)$ to get the y out of the denominator and to the other side of the equal sign. Then, just simplify from there.

$$x + 2 = y + 2$$

$$x = y$$

SECTION 4

Sentence Completions

1. A   Two-Blank/One-Way   *Easy*

The sentence contains no switch and does not make a comparison over time: It's one-way. The first blank describes what Antonio protests against, and the second blank describes why he is protesting this way. If Antonio is protesting against the word in the first blank, then that blank is probably negative. Who would protest against something good? So, you can drop **B**, **C**, and **E**, since the first words of each of those pairs is positive. That leaves **A**, *condemned..commit*, and **D**, *convicted..commiserate*. If you plug these two answers into the question, **A** is revealed as the better choice. "A crime he did not commiserate" doesn't make much sense because commiserate means "to express pity." Meanwhile "a crime he did not commit" makes perfect sense.

SAT traps are all over the answer choices in this question. Several of the choices sound quite similar to one another and are related to the subject of crime and punishment, especially *condone*, *convicted*, and *responsible*. But if you analyze the sentence, they won't trip you up.

2.   **C**   Two-Blank/Two-Way   *Medium*

The switch *although* tells you that the sentence is two-way. The first blank describes Pee Wee Russell's physical looks, while the second describes the music he makes. These two blanks have to contrast. One's good, one's bad. Cut *ugly..foul* immediately, since those words don't contrast. *Pristine..dramatic* could describe clarinet playing, but neither of them can really describe a face. They also don't contrast strongly enough to satisfy the switch word. Same goes for *handsome..gentle* and *expressive..unique*. No strong contrasts there. Only *grotesque..beautiful* works. Despite his grotesque (ugly) face, Pee Wee Russell played the clarinet beautifully. You've got contrast, and you've got a great description of the difference between Russell's face and his musicianship.

3.   **A**   One-Blank/One-Way   *Medium*

The sentence contains no switch and does not make a comparison over time. The blank, which describes how Wayne's house becomes "with every passing storm," will agree with the other facts in the sentence. The rest of the sentence describes the stilts on which the house is built as rotting away. If those stilts fall, the whole house will fall! You're looking for a negative word that expresses the danger of the situation. The only negative words in the answer choices are *precarious* and *absurd*. *Precarious*, which means "unstable," captures that meaning of danger exactly and is the best answer.

4.   **A**   One-Blank/One-Way   *Medium*

The sentence contains no switch and does not make a comparison over time: it's one-way. The blank describes how Hitchcock's films are (in addition to being "hilarious"), and the the rest of the sentence says that Hitchcock mixed horror with farce in his films. A mixture of horror and farce will therefore be something like "scary and hilarious." You're looking for a word that is negative and is similar to "scary" and "horror." The only negative words among the answer choices are *gruesome* and *staid*. Of those two, *staid* means "boring," while *gruesome* means "awful." Gruesome is a much better word for a horror film.

5.   **E**   One-Blank/One-Way   *Difficult*

The sentence contains no switch and does not make a comparison across time: It's one-way. So, the blank, which describes the costumes, will fit with the other facts presented in the sentence. According to the sentence, the costumes did not match with the historical setting of the play. To put it vaguely, the costumes were "bad." To put it more specifically, the costumes were "from the wrong time period." If you know the word *anachronistic*, the answer is clear, since the word means "out of chronological order." A perfect fit.

If you didn't know the definition of *anachronistic*, you could still have used the fact that you're looking for a negative word to cut as many answer choices as possible.

Dual Short Reading Passage

6. **A**   Technique   *Easy*

Technique questions like this one require you to evaluate why authors choose to include certain words, phrases, references, and so on. This question asks you to explain why the author of this passage includes a long list of everybody in Shakespeare's life who would have had to be involved in the great Shakespeare cover-up. The author's conclusion that such a hoax "simply could not have been done" suggests that he or she includes the list to show how vast and difficult it would have been to carry out. That makes **A** the correct answer.

7. **C**   Technique   *Difficult*

This Technique question asks why the author of passage 2, who argues against Shakespeare's authorship, brings up the argument made in passage 1, the author of which argues *for* Shakespeare's argument. Why would the author of passage 2 reference an argument that might undermine his own argument?

Take a look at the answers and find the ones that could make sense. **A** does not make sense because the passage 2 author strictly refutes the claim that Shakespeare wrote all of the plays attributed to him. The author is consistent throughout in his or her convictions, so **B** is also incorrect. Neither of these passages has an open-minded perspective on the issue; they're both very opinionated and conclusive, so cut **D** and **E**. That leaves only **C**, *preempt possible criticisms*. If the verb *preempt* confused you, consider its defintion: "to take or use for oneself." The author of passage 2 seizes passage 1's critique of the anti-Shakespeare argument and actually uses it to help defend the anti-Shakespeare argument: Even if the Shakespeare hoax required a massive effort, it pales in comparison to the miraculous effort that writing Shakespeare's plays solo would have required.

8. **D**   Relating Two Passages   *Medium*

To answer this question correctly, you have to apply information from passage 1 to assess the argument in passage 2. Passage 1 tells you that the Earl of Oxford is the leading candidate behind who actually wrote Shakespeare's plays. You have to then make the leap of logic that the author of passage 2, who definitely believes that someone other than Shakespeare wrote the plays, subscribes to the theory that the Earl of Oxford was the real playwright. The fact that the ol' Earl kicked the bucket years before some of the plays were even performed weakens the argument that the Earl helped write the plays, because he was already dead. That means the fact of his death weakens the argument in passage 2, so **D** is the correct answer.

9. **E**   Relating Two Passages   *Medium*

Here you've got a question that throws in a "disagree" and an EXCEPT. Whoa. All of that breaks down to this question: Which answer choice would the authors of passage 1 and passage 2 consider true? That makes it easy to cut choices that carry strong views for or against the idea of Shakespeare authoring all his plays. **A** is out. So is **B**, since the author of passage 1 thinks that Shakespeare is the most likely person to have written the plays. Passage 1 does not mention Shakespeare's education, so **C** cannot be correct. Authorship is the only issue here, not quality of playwriting, so the comparison contemplated in **D** is not the best answer. The authors could only agree on **E**, which states that the issue of Shakespeare's authorship is important. Neither author would have written these passages if they didn't consider the issue important. **E** it is.

Long Reading Passage (Art)

10. **C**   Words in Context   *Medium*

Remember that words in context questions are about context: check the passage around the word. In this question, except for **E**, each of the answer choices could represent a possible meaning for the word. Now for the context: in the passage, Twain says that Art is allowed as much license today as in the past, while literature is now censored. "License" is used in the sentence as a contrasting word to "curtail" or "censor." You can therefore discard **A** (this is obviously not the driver's license version of the word) and **D** (it is also not the bureaucratic version of the word). Because of the term *indecent* used before *license* in the text, **B** may seem to be a tempting answer. But a close reading of the passage will indicate that indecent refers to the freedom of art to portray indecent subjects, rather than to behave with "immoral excess." As a result, **C** is the only answer choice that fits: when it comes to portraying the indecent, Twain says, Art enjoys a freedom from public objection that is not granted to Literature.

11. **D**   Themes and Arguments   *Medium*

Because Twain uses words like "beastliness" and "foul", it may seem at first that he is critical of the era of Fielding and Smollett; this would make **A** and **B** seem like attractive answer choices. But a closer reading reveals that Twain seems to respect the openness of the earlier era: there were beastly subjects, and writers had the freedom and the power to tackle them with the beastly language that they required. In the current era, by contrast, Twain says that there are foul subjects, but writers have lost the ability to tackle them with the same forcefulness. In order to gain this understanding of the passage, think about Twain's tone: he is consistently critical of attempts to censor art.

12. **E**   Themes and Arguments   *Medium*

The passage never mentions ancient standards of dress or nomads in the desert, so you can throw out **A** and **C**. The best way to choose among the remaining answer choices is to look at the passage and see how the fig-leaf example is developed. Twain describes several times the pointlessness of using fig leaves to cover the private parts of sculptures, most of which are crumbling, and which are cold and unfeeling in any case, so the answer cannot be **B**. Choice **D** might appear tempting, as it involves questions of morality and decency in art, which is the main subject of the passage, but Twain never mentions different cultural standards with regard to this subject; in fact, he presents the case as a universal condition, one shared by "the world." Therefore, **E** is the correct answer: Twain uses the fig leaf example to criticize the ridiculous decisions people will make in order to keep "indecent" sculpture from being scrutinized by the public.

13. **B**   Implied Information   *Easy*

Twain writes that the figures before the Uffizi are "noseless, battered, black with accumulated grime." This indicates that they do not seem human because they have deteriorated with the passage of time (their noses have crumbled off, grime has accumulated, etc.). They are not *abstract*, *poorly sculpted*, or *gigantic*. They're simply ancient and crumbling.

14. **A**   Words in Context   *Medium*

The passage around the word in question describes a society that covers even the nakedness of sculptures that are falling apart. Twain describes this as a ridiculous act, and implies that anyone who wants to cover up stone sculptures that are falling apart anyway is excessively proper and formal. The only word that captures this meaning among the answer choices is **A**. Answers **B** and **C** try to trick you by forming a spurious association with first half of the word fastidious, "fast." Answer **D** doesn't fit the sentence at all, while answer **E** describes the sculptures themselves, not the act of covering those sculptures up.

15. **D**   Themes and Arguments   *Difficult*

Each of the answer choices except **E** describes an "inconsistency" that would be highly possible with respect to Titian's painting. However, if you return to the passage and look at the argument being made rather just look for key words, like *erotic* or *immoral*, you should be able to resist any traps in the answer choices. In the passage, Twain criticizes the world's inconsistency for pretending that pictures are more powerful than words, but then censoring writing while allowing pictures to hang openly on display. Specifically, Twain says that if he were to describe Titian's painting of Venus, his description would outrage people, even though no one is outraged by the painting itself. Once you've paraphrased the passage in this way, you can see that the correct answer is **D**.

Long Reading Passage (Fiction)

16. **B**   Attitude or Tone   *Easy*

The first sentence of the passage describes a "half-decayed veranda" that is outside of town, "near a ravine," and then tells of a fat little man who walks nervously back and forth. The image of this solitary, decaying house and its nervous inhabitant is one of sadness, of *loneliness*.

17. **A**   Technique   *Medium*

The laughing group of berry pickers creates a dramatic contrast to Wing, standing solitary on his stoop. The berry pickers illustrate the joys of youth and community, and show all that Wing is missing and does not feel a part of.

18. **A**   Words in Context   *Medium*

Treat this question as a Sentence Completion: "Wing Biddlebaum, forever frightened and ---- by a ghostly band of doubts, did not think of himself as in any way a part of the life of the town where he had lived for twenty years." What are the ghostly band

the new SAT

of doubts doing to him? They're bothering him, gnawing at him, and they won't leave him alone. *Developed*, *constructed*, *coerce*, and *becalm* (which means, to make calm) do not fit this idea of bothering. *Plague*, which means to endlessly bother, does.

19. C Implied Information   *Easy*

In the two sentences after the phrase "something like a friendship," the passage says that George sometimes walks out to visit Wing's house, and that on this particular night Wing is hoping that George will come and spend the evening with him. It's evident, then, that Wing truly does like George (see ya **B** and **E**). That George comes to visit Wing implies also that George also has friendly feelings for Wing, and that George's father Tom didn't forbade the two men from being friends. At the same time, as Wing waits and hopes George will show up, he is nervous, his hands flying about. This implies that the relationship between Wing and George is "something like a friendship" because Wing is such a nervous loner.

20. A Themes and Arguments   *Difficult*

Wing is a man beset with doubts who lives in a ramshackle house away from town and paces nervously. He feels apart from the town and is abashed at the way his hands flutter about when he speaks. He tries not to be noticed, so **A** is the best answer.

None of the other answers have any basis in the question. There's no indication that Wing might get "drafted" into helping to pick berries or that he's had any direct confrontation with the berry pickers at all. Neither is there any indication that George has any nasty past history with the berry pickers. Finally, from the fact that Wing hopes that George will come visit him, it makes no sense that he would rather pace his porch than look for George.

21. C Specific Information   *Medium*

The passage answers this question directly, if you remember where to look for it: "The story of Wing Biddlebaum is a story of hands. Their restless activity, like unto the beating of the wings of an imprisoned bird, had given him his name. Some obscure poet of the town had thought of it." So the name Wing is a metaphor for the way his hands move.

22. D Themes and Arguments   *Difficult*

The passage says that the town is proud of Wing the way that it is proud of Banker White's house and Wesley Moyer's prize stallion. While having a town's pride is a good thing, it isn't good to have the type of pride usually given to a house or a horse. In essence, the town sees Wing as an object, as a thing, as just another curiosity.

23. B Implied Information   *Difficult*

The first two sentences of the last paragraph state, "The story of Wing Biddlebaum's hands is worth a book in itself. Sympathetically set forth it would tap many strange, beautiful qualities in obscure men." The narrator is saying that telling a story about Wing's hands would "tap" (meaning tap into) the qualities of other obscure men. The story of Wing, the narrator is saying, is a kind of metaphor for the stories of all obscure men. Wing's story suddenly takes on a much broader significance, beyond just Wing himself: **B**.

24.　**C**　Main Idea　　　　　　　　　　　　　　　　　　　　　*Medium*

The story is about Wing, not George Willard, so title **B** would put the focus on the wrong character. The titles of **D** and **E** are much too happy for a story about a fat little nervous guy living alone in a decaying house. That leaves **A** and **C**. While **A** takes the name Wing and makes a nice little game out of it, in the story Wing doesn't seem to be doing much flying at all. He doesn't fly in fear or in joy; he just stays where he is. But **C**: For a story that focuses very closely on a man's hands, *Hands* makes a lot of sense.

SECTION 5

Multiple Choice Questions

1.　**A**　Geometry: Triangles　　　　　　　　　　　　　　　　*Easy*

The question states that all the little triangles that make up the big triangle are congruent. This means they all have the same side lengths. Since every side of the big triangle contains congruent sides from two small triangles, the entire perimeter of the triangle is twice the perimeter of one of the small triangles, so the factor by which the perimeter of *ACE* exceeds the perimeter of *ABE* is 2.

2.　**E**　Algebra: Inequalities　　　　　　　　　　　　　　　*Easy*

To find the least possible value of x, you have to isolate x on one side of the inequality. To do this, you have to multiply both sides of the equation by $y + 2$. But wait! According to the rules of inequalities, if $y + 2$ is a negative number, you'll have to reverse the inequality sign. So, first check to see if $y + 2$ is negative: Because $y \geq 3$, you know that it's positive. Whew. Since $y + 2$ is guaranteed to be a positive number, you can multiply away without fear: $x \geq 16(y + 2)$ or $x \geq 16y + 32$. From this inequality, you can see that the smallest value of x will occur when y is equal to its smallest possible value, 3. Therefore, $x \geq 16(3) + 32$, which reduces to $x \geq 80$.

3.　**C**　Numbers and Operations: Ratios　　　　　　　　　　*Easy*

This is a fancy word problem disguising a rather simple question. You may read this question and think: "oh boy, it's about physics!" and psych yourself out. It isn't about physics. It's about proportions. The speed at which the ball hits the ground is proportional to how high it bounces. You know when it hits at 20 mph it bounces 10 ft, and have to find out how fast it must be moving if it bounces 15 ft. So set up the proportion:

$$\frac{20}{10} = \frac{x}{15}$$

Now cross-multiply and then work out the equation:

$$10x = 300$$

$$x = 30$$

4.   **E**   Geometry: Coordinate Geometry   *Medium*

To find the slope of a line that connects two midpoints, you first have to find the midpoints. You could use the midpoint formula, but there's a faster way. The first midpoint you want to find lies between the points $(-2,-4)$ and $(-4,-4)$. Since the two points have the same y-coordinates, you can get the midpoint by keeping the y-coordinate, -4, and taking the number halfway between -2 and -4, which is -3. The first midpoint is $(-3,-4)$. The second midpoint is a little harder to visualize, so this time it's a good idea to use the midpoint formula: $M = \left(\frac{x_1+x_2}{2}, \frac{y_1+y_2}{2}\right)$. Plugging in the endpoints, $M_1 = \left(\frac{-2+2}{2}, \frac{4+8}{2}\right) = \left(\frac{0}{2}, \frac{12}{2}\right) = (0,6)$. Since slope equals the "rise over the run," you can use the two points to find the slope of the line that connects them:

$slope = \frac{y_2 - y_1}{x_2 - x_1} = \frac{6-(-4)}{0-(-3)} = \frac{10}{3}$.

5.   **E**   Data Analysis, Statistics, Probability: Probability   *Medium*

Since the probability of picking a blue marble from the bag is $\frac{5}{8}$, that means that for every 8 total marbles, there must be 5 blue marbles and 3 yellow marbles. But don't just go and multiply 5 and 3 to get the answer. That's an SAT Trap. Remember that the question tells you that the bag contains somewhere between 10 and 20 marbles. If that's the case, and the bag has to contain a ratio of 5 blue to 3 yellow marbles, then how many total marbles must it contain? If it contained exactly 5 blue and 3 yellow then it would contain just 8 marbles, which is too few. If it contained 10 blue and 6 yellow then it would hold 16. Ah, perfect. So the bag must contain 10 blue and 6 yellow marbles, and $10(6) = 60$.

6.   **E**   Geometry: Triangles   *Medium*

This is actually a triangle question, as you'll see if you sketch out the scenario described in the word problem:

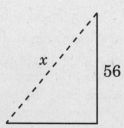

Once you've sketched the image, there are two ways to solve the problem. The quicker way is to realize that the sides of this triangle follow the 3:4:5 Pythagorean triple ratio. If you realized that, then you can figure out that the number that fits into the ration along with $42:56:x$ is 70. The other way to solve the problem is just to work out the Pythagorean theorem:

$$c^2 = 42^2 + 56^2$$

$$c^2 = 1764 + 3136$$

$$c^2 = 4900$$

7.   **B**   Numbers and Operations: Sets   *Difficult*

Any question that asks you to add together some immense group of numbers probably contains a shortcut. In this question, almost every positive term has a corresponding negative term, leaving only the 0 and 52 terms unaccounted for. All
corresponding negative and positive terms will sum to 0, so the sum of all 52 terms is
52, yielding a mean of 1.

8.   **E**   Geometry: Polygons   *Difficult*

To find the area of the shaded region, you need to find the area of all four unshaded
triangles in the question. The big triangle's area is the easiest to find. The question
tells you that it has a base length of 12, and if you know the rules of how a square
works, you'll know that the intersection of diagonals drawn from the corners are
right bisectors of each other, meaning that the triangle is a right isosceles triangle
(45-45-90). Since the sides of a 45-45-90 triangle follow the ratio of $1:1:\sqrt{2}$, the sides
of this triangle must be $6\sqrt{2}$. The two $6\sqrt{2}$ sides are the base and the height, since
they share a right angle, so the area of that triangle is $A = \frac{1}{2}(6\sqrt{2})(6\sqrt{2}) = 36$. Onto the
little triangle: Since EG is parallel to BD, HF is parallel to AC, and AC and BD are perpendicular, you know that EG and HF are perpendicular and that EG and HF will both
form 45° angles with DC. You've got another 45-45-90 triangle on your hands. The
hypotenuse of that triangle must equal 4, since $GF = AH = BE$, which means that GF
also equals DG and FC. Since $DG = GF = FC$ and $DC = 12$, GF must equal $12 \div 3 = 4$.
The sides of this 45-45-90 triangle are $2\sqrt{2}$, and the area is $A = \frac{1}{2}(2\sqrt{2})(2\sqrt{2}) = 4$. On to
the medium sized triangles! Since you now know that BE and AH are equal to 4, you
know that the hypotenuse of each of the medium triangles is $12 - 4 = 8$. You also
know that EG is perpendicular to AC and that HF is perpendicular to BD, so you're
once more dealing with 45-45-90 triangles. The legs of these triangles are $4\sqrt{2}$, so the
area is $A = \frac{1}{2}(4\sqrt{2})(4\sqrt{2}) = 16$. The unshaded areas = 36 + 4 + 16 + 16 = 72. And
the area of the shaded region is the area of the whole square minus the area of the
unshaded region. Shaded area = $(12 \times 12) - (72) = 144 - 72 = 72$. Sheesh. Finally.

Grid-Ins

9.   **25**   Geometry: Coordinate Geometry   *Easy*

When two lines intersect, opposite angles will always be equal. This means that you
know that the top angle in the triangle is 65° and that x is equal to the angle on the
bottom right of the triangle. The right angle, of course, is 90°. Since the sum of the

interior angles of a triangle is 180°, finding the third angle (and x) is simple: $x + 65 + 90 = 180$, so $x = 25$.

10. **7/5**   Numbers and Operations: Ratios   *Easy*

Since there are seven flowering trees, you know that there are $12 - 7 = 5$ non-flowering trees. This makes the ratio of flowering to non-flowering trees 7:5. Gridding your ratio as a fraction means your answer should be 7/5.

11. **30**   Geometry: Polygons   *Easy*

The perimeter of the figure is $7 + 6 + 9 + 3 + x = 25 + x$. The easiest way to find x is to create a right triangle in which x is the hypotenuse. Imagine extending the sides of lengths 6 and 3 to form a larger rectangle with a right triangle in the corner. The legs of this triangle have lengths $9 - 6 = 3$ and $7 - 3 = 4$. The Pythagorean theorem does the rest: $\sqrt{3^2 + 4^2} = \sqrt{9 + 16} = \sqrt{25} = 5$. The perimeter of the figure is 25 + 5 = 30.

12. **1**   Algebra: Solving Equations   *Easy*

To solve for x, you first have to solve for y, which means you need to approach the equation $2y^2 = 18$ first.

$$2y^2 = 18$$
$$y^2 = 9$$
$$y = 3$$

Now, take on the equation $(4x + y)^2 = 49$, but instead of diving right in and squaring that binomial by itself, pause for a second. Is there a better way? Yes! Take the square root of both sides. The square roots of 49 are 7 and –7. According to the question, x and $y > 0$, so you can ignore that –7. By taking the square root of each side, you get $4x + y = 7$. Plug in 3 for y, and you get $4x = 4$, so $x = 1$.

13. **9**   Numbers and Operations: Exponents   *Medium*

To conquer the new SAT Math, you have to know three kinds of exponents: regular old-fashioned exponents, negative exponents, and fractional exponents. Fractional exponents are just another way of writing roots: For instance, $x^{\frac{1}{2}} = \sqrt{x}$. Numbers or variables with negative exponents are equal to the reciprocal of the number of variables with a positive exponent: $x^{-4} = \frac{1}{x^4}$. So, if you see fractional or negative exponents in a problem, the first thing to do is simplify, then solve.

In this problem, you're given $3x^{\frac{1}{2}}y^{-3} = \frac{x}{y^3}$. If you simplify the expression on the left according to the rules we just discussed, you get $\frac{3\sqrt{x}}{y^3} = \frac{x}{y^3}$. Now, you can cancel out: $3\sqrt{x} = x$. If you square both sides, you get rid of the radical and have $9x = x^2$. Divide both sides by x, and you have $x = 9$.

14. 1   Geometry: Coordinate Geometry   *Medium*

The graph of $f(x)$ is a line that passes through the points $(-2,0)$ and $(0,2)$. The graph of $f(x + k)$ passes through points $(-1,0)$ and $(0,1)$. This difference of just 1 in both x- and y-intercept means that for every value of x in $f(x)$, $f(x + k)$ is one greater. In other words, $k = 1$.

15. 3   Algebra: Functions   *Medium*

Functions attack! Have no fear. Problems like this one are just glorified substitution questions. For the numerator, just plug 3 in for x in $f(x)$. In the denominator, you have to substitute one function into the other, then substitute the 3 in for x. Deal with the denominator first: $g(h(x)) = \frac{2x+4}{2} = x+2$. Now this sucker is ripe for the picking: $\frac{f(3)}{g(h(3))} = \frac{2(3)^2+3-6}{3+2} = \frac{18+3-6}{5} = \frac{15}{5} = 3$.

16. 1/2   Data Analysis, Statistics, Probability: Probability   *Difficult*

To figure out the probability of pulling a blue marble from the bag, you need to figure out the total number of items in the bag and the number of blue marbles. To do that efficiently, assign values that fit the criteria stated in the problem. For instance, since the question says that there are three times as many marbles in the bag as there are dice, say that there are 3 marbles in the bag and 1 die. Out of the 3 marbles in the bag, the question says twice as many will be blue as will be red. In other words, 2 will be blue and 1 will be red. Now you know that you have 2 blue marbles in a bag out of a total of 3 marbles and 1 die, so the chances of pulling a blue marble from the bag are $\frac{2}{4} = \frac{1}{2}$.

17. 6   Numbers and Operations: Sequences   *Difficult*

First things first. List the first few terms of each sequence to familiarize yourself with them. Look at these few terms and decide if you can arrive at a solution by continuing to list terms or if you must try to find some pattern or shortcut to solve the problem: $A = \{-6, -3, 0, 3 \ldots\}$ and $B = \{20, 15, 10, 5 \ldots\}$. By looking at the first four terms, you should see that soon after the fourth term, the value of a given term in A should exceed the value of the corresponding term in B, since they are converging so quickly. When you calculate just one more term in each sequence, you see that the fifth term of A, 6, is greater than the fifth term of B, 0. Therefore, the value of the term in sequence A that first exceeds the value of the corresponding term in sequence B is 6.

It's usually a safe bet to list three or four terms in a sequence if you don't know how to start solving a given problem involving sequences. This will often allow you to perceive more about the sequence than you can at first glance.

18. 9   Algebra: Functions as Models   *Difficult*

The conversion function between the mythical units of Kirklands and Mathers is just like any other function. But there's a mystery constant, r, in the function that you don't know. The first thing you have to do is find its value. Since you know that $4K = 12M$, you can plug those values in to find r:

$$4 = \frac{r}{12^2}$$

$$4(144) = r$$

$$r = 576$$

Now use $r = 576$ and the function to solve for how many Kirklands there are in 8 Mathers:

$$K = \frac{576}{8^2}$$

$$K = 9$$

SECTION 6

Improving Sentences

1. **E** Parallelism *Easy*

In order to fix the error of parallelism in the original sentence, you need to describe all of the actions using infinitives, as **E** does. Getting rid of that phrase *oftentimes helpful* is fine, since the phrase doesn't add much to the sentence anyway. Even if you worried about ditching that phrase, though, the two answer choices that include it, **B** and **C**, both have big grammatical problems that make them wrong. **B** uses two gerunds, which makes that first infinitive *to spend* the odd man out. **C** uses one infinitive, *rely*, but it still has that problematic gerund *planning*.

2. **B** Run-Ons *Easy*

The original sentence is a run-on. The correct answer, **B**, adds the conjunction *so*, which turns the second half of the sentence into a dependent clause and fixes the problem. The semicolon in **C** might have tempted you, but because that choice also adds a *so*, the second half of the sentence is dependent on the first and is no longer a complete sentence on its own.

3. **A** No Error *Medium*

4. **D** Coordination and Subordination *Medium*

Here we have a case of faulty coordination. The word *and* does a bad job of expressing the relationship between *Frannie was unwilling to start jogging* and *she tried it anyway*. Whatever word connects the two clauses should suggest that Frannie had to overcome her own unwillingness before she started jogging. **D** does that. The phrase *Frannie was unwilling to start jogging, but she tried it anyway* makes her triumph over her unwillingness clear.

B inverts the cause and effect of the sentence. Frannie wasn't unwilling despite the fact that she tried jogging; Frannie tried running despite the fact that she tried jogging. **C** leaves out a coordinating word altogether. This is no solution. **E** sets up precisely the wrong relationship between the two clauses; it essentially says that Frannie tried jogging because she didn't want to jog.

5.   **E**   Passive Voice   *Medium*

There's no heinous error in this sentence, but there is indeed an SAT error: passive voice. The second half of the sentence wastes time getting to the point, which is that Woody Allen is the guy changing the conception of New York City. The original sentence doesn't identify Woody as the performer of the action until the very end of the sentence. The right answer, **E**, tells the reader right away that Allen is the performer.

6.   **C**   Run-Ons   *Medium*

Here we have a run-on sentence. Since there's no semicolon to be found among the answer choices, all you need do is implement that popular run-on fixing technique of inserting a coordinating conjunction such as *and*. There it is in **C**.

    D adds the needed *and*, but it also adds a colon, which creates new grammatical problems of its own.

7.   **C**   Fragments   *Medium*

This sentence suffers from vanishing verbs, which makes it a fragment. Sure, *rumors* are getting *repeated* and *embellished*, but there's no verb explaining what the *urban legends* are doing. According to the right answer, **C**, the urban legend is *saying*. That's enough. Fixing fragments doesn't mean you have to change the meaning of the sentence entirely—you just need a verb in there to clear things up.

8.   **A**   No Error   *Difficult*

9.   **B**   Parallelism   *Difficult*

This is a slightly deceptive one; you know to look for parallelism errors in lists, and this is a list, but it's not an obvious list because it's broken into two parts. However, a list it is—a list with a parallelism problem. The sentence says that directors consider *voice* and *acting ability* and *does the person look good*. That third consideration is wrong because, unlike the first two members of the list, it isn't a noun. The right answer choice, **B**, makes *does the person look good* into a noun: *looks*. **B** might sound a little abrupt to you as you're reading through the answer choices, but if you read it back into the sentence, you'll see that it sounds right.

10. **A**   No Error   *Difficult*

11. **C**   Passive Voice   *Difficult*

The phrase *being that they had to keep their love secret* is extremely wordy. **C** provides the same information in far fewer words, always a good thing.

    B is wrong, since the relationship wasn't dramatic *although* the father disapproved, but *because* he disapproved. The sentiment behind **D** is correct, but the use of the semicolon is not. If a comma replaced the semicolon, **D** would make the cut. You can eliminate **E** not only because it uses the colon incorrectly, but because it is just too darn wordy.

Identifying Sentence Errors

12. D   Pronouns   *Easy*

Pay close attention whenever you see the phrase *his or her* in an Identifying Sentence Errors question. Just as you'll see some sentences with an incorrect use of the plural "their" (*everybody put on their shoes*), you'll also see a few incorrectly singular "his or her" possessives. *The teachers* is a plural subject, and therefore should be replaced with the plural pronoun *their*.

13. C   Double Negative   *Easy*

Words like *hardly* are dead giveaways of double negative errors. *Hardly* is one of those words that's negative even though it doesn't sound negative. Remember: It's never a good idea to put a negative word next to another negative word. Got it? This means that **C** is the answer. A corrected version of the sentence would read either *taxation is not an acceptable solution* or *taxation is hardly an acceptable solution*.

   A involves the correct form of the verb *to declare*. Problems with verbs in this section of the SAT will mostly involve tense and subject-verb agreement, and *declaring* involves neither.

14. A   Tense   *Easy*

Swim is a classic Annoying Verb. You should familiarize yourself with all of the verbs on our Annoying Verbs list—many of these appear again and again on the SAT. In this sentence, *swum* should be *swam*.

15. B   Idioms   *Easy*

In English, the phrase *more devotedly as* is a violation of the rules of idiom. You have to say *more devotedly than*.

16. D   Parallelism   *Easy*

The list in this sentence, which explains the appeal of new technology, starts with the comparison words *faster* and *more efficient*. Both imply that new technology is faster and more efficient than something (most likely, old technology). Even though the subject of comparison isn't named, it is implied. The third item on the list, however, poses a problem. The word *cheap* does not imply a comparison. Instead of *cheap*, the third item in the list should be *cheaper*.

   Although this is technically a parallelism problem, you can also figure out the right answer by using your technique for identifying faulty comparisons. By extending the implied comparison, you get *new machines are faster than old machines, more efficient than old machines, and cheap than old machines*. In that extended form, it becomes even clearer that **D** is the right answer.

17. E   No Error   *Easy*

18. B   Gerunds   *Medium*

When one verb follows another, as *arrested* and *be* follow each other in this sentence, the second verb has to be a gerund. So *arrested to be* should be *arrested for being*.

19. B Subject-Verb Agreement *Medium*

This sentence is awkward and confusing because its verb, *strewn*, precedes its subject, *toys*. Whenever this subject-verb inversion happens, be on the lookout for subject-verb agreement issues. The SAT inverts subject and verb because it knows that this makes it easier to miss hearing an error in number. *Strewn around the playpen was . . . the toys* may not sound funny to you, but flip things around so that the subject precedes the verb: Now you get *The toys was strewn around the playpen*. That construction makes it easier to see that the verb form *was* should actually be in the plural form *were*, to match the plural word *toys*. The answer is **B**.

Strewn may look odd, but that really is the correct past tense of the verb *to strew*. You may be hung up on strange-sounding, past-tense verb forms on the SAT; the best way to avoid this problem is to go over the list of Annoying Verbs in the Identifying Sentence Errors section of this book.

20. E No Error *Medium*

21. A Other *Medium*

The word *where* refers to a physical location. A speech isn't a location. In corrected form, this part of the sentence would read *one candidate for student council made a speech in which he proposed holding a blood drive*.

22. D Pronouns *Medium*

As you examine the pronouns in the sentence, you might notice that in the phrase *they have grown extremely expensive*, the plural word *they* refers not to *loans*, another plural word, but to *college*, a singular word. Plural pronouns like *they* cannot be used to refer to singular subjects. **D** is the answer. Always be especially cautious when checking pronoun agreement—if you rush, it's easy to assume that *they* refers to loans and decide that the sentence is error-free.

23. B Wrong Word *Medium*

Illusions are "tricks" or "false images." *Allusions* are "references." Ms. Wong was making allusions, not illusions, to the late hour. This is a straightforward case of wrong word usage. In order to nail these questions, it's important to read over our list of commonly confused SAT words.

24. A Double Negative *Medium*

Always be alert to the possible presence of a double negative when you encounter a word that is negative but doesn't sound it, like *scarcely*. In this question, **A** is the answer because it is incorrect to place the negative word *not* directly beside the negative word *scarcely*. To solve the problem, the phrase would have to be rewritten as *he could not imagine* or *he could scarcely imagine*.

25. E No Error *Medium*

Don't be misled into thinking *the beach* creates a parellelism or agreement error because it doesn't match *barbecues* and *fireworks* exactly. Sure, those first two words don't have the word *the* preceding them, but the list is still correct. A definite article before a noun in a list will never affect parallelism. Would you prefer *visions of barbecues, fireworks, and beach*? **E** is the best answer.

26. **D**   Pronouns   *Medium*

Take heed whenever you see a pronoun separated from the noun it replaces, as in answer choice **D**. What does *it* refer to? *His papers*. Because this guy has more than one paper, the pronoun that refers to those plural papers should be plural (*them*) not singular (*it*).

   Strode up, although it certainly sounds strange, is actually the correct past-tense form of the verb *to stride*. If you missed this one, check out our list of Annoying Verbs.

27. **D**   Pronouns   *Difficult*

This is an especially tricky case of pronoun shift because the two pronouns involved—*you* and *one*—are placed so far apart. Sentences that have long intervening clauses, as this sentence does, should be checked carefully for problems with both subject-verb agreement and pronoun agreement. Here, the writer begins by talking about *you* (*if you are going to Beijing*) but shifts to *one* at the end of the sentence (*catch one off guard*).

28. **B**   Subject-Verb Agreement   *Difficult*

The important thing to spot right away is the use of the construction *as well as*. This is one of those terrible, tricky phrases, like "along with" and "in addition to," that sound as if they make their subject plural but in fact *do not*. No matter who else is working *as well as* the governor, the governor is still the sentence's subject—and so it's the governor who determines the sentence's verb form. And since *the governor* is a singular subject, the verb should be singular as well. The correct answer is **B**. The most effective way to deal with these tricky phrases is to memorize them.

29. **D**   Abverbs and Adjectives   *Difficult*

When comparing two items, you have to use a word like *uglier*, *shorter*, or *sweeter*, and when comparing three or more items you must use a word like *ugliest*, *shortest*, or *sweetest*. Since this sentence compares three items, the word *sweeter* should be *sweetest*. **D** it is.

Improving Paragraphs

30. **C**   Sentence Combination   *Medium*

All of the answer choices here express the same basic meaning: Even though some rap glorifies all three, some rap does not. Since all the answer choices have the same content, you have to eliminate answers based on grammar. Only **C** is grammatically correct. **A** and **D** are run-on sentences. The *and* in **B** doesn't correctly reflect the relationship of contrast between rap that does and does not glorify violence. **E** also uses *and* in an illogical way.

31. **E**   Sentence Addition   *Medium*

Before you answer this question, it's important to go back and remind yourself of the main idea of the second paragraph. The correct answer, **E**, is the one that provides the most appropriate introduction to the second paragraph by talking about well-known rappers and traditional values.

A few of the other answers are easy to cut: **A** is out in left field, since no *personal encounters with rappers* are discussed anywhere in the essay. **C** is easy to ditch, since industry executives aren't mentioned in the second paragraph or elsewhere.

B mentions Jay-Z, but it's vague and gives the reader no idea of what the paragraph is truly about. **D** is a fine sentence on its own, but it refers to the first paragraph more than it does to the second, so **E** is the better answer.

---

32. C   Sentence Combination   *Difficult*

Before looking at the answer choices, figure out the problem with the two sentences as they stand—they present two seemingly contradictory ideas, with no explanation of the contradiction. How can Jay-Z simultaneously demean women and praise his mother? Look for the answer choice that resolves this conundrum.

Only **C** makes the paradox clear by using the word *although*. All of the other answer choices combine the two sentences but don't clear up the confusing combination of a sometimes-misogynist rapper giving props to his mom.

---

33. C   Sentence Revision   *Easy*

Context matters on this one. So does tense. If you don't go back and reread a few sentences before, after, and including the problem sentence, you might be tempted to choose **A**. Out of context, that sentence is grammatically perfect. If you go back and reread, however, you'll see that *credited* should not be in the past tense because the rest of the paragraph is in the present tense. Therefore, **C** is the answer.

---

34. A   Sentence Combination   *Difficult*

Once you decide how these two sentences relate to each other, it's your job to figure out which of the connecting words given by the answer choices is the right one. It's not *however* or *but*; those imply that rapping about violence and rapping about violent death are somehow opposed to one another. *Thus* or *moreover* make more sense, but both **D** and **E** have grammar problems. **A**, the right answer, uses the simple but serviceable word *and*, and it is grammatically correct.

---

35. A   Essay Analysis   *Difficult*

This is an EXCEPT question, so you're looking for the technique NOT used in the essay. In this essay, the one thing the writer does not do is tell a personal story. This is a fairly formal essay on rap, and the writer does not introduce favorite songs or give personal anecdotes about rap appreciation. **B** is incorrect because the entire essay is meant to debunk the myth that rappers are violent misogynists. **C** can be eliminated because the last paragraph is a summary. Cut **D** since the writer does talk about specific rappers and lyrics. **E** is wrong because the bulk of the essay is spent analyzing lyrics.

SECTION 7

Sentence Completions

1. C   One-Blank/Two-Way   *Easy*

The switch *while* tells you that the sentence is two-way. The blank, which describes how Marcy is, must contrast with her stepsister's *grumpiness*. So, the word you're looking for is a positive word that's something like "friendly." You can knock out *frosty, tart, uncouth,* and *impeachable,* because those four words are all negative, meaning cold, sour, dirty, and condemnable respectively. That leaves *endearing,* which means "charming" and provides a perfect contrast to grumpiness.

2. C One-Blank/One-Way *Easy*

The sentence contains the one-way switch *because.* So the word that fills in the blank will create agreement with the rest of the facts in the sentence. But this sentence has a trick. The blank is what Sarah is *not* known for, so it describes how Sarah isn't, and the rest of the sentence describes Sarah as "easily annoyed and constantly cutting people off." In other words, she isn't very *nice* or *patient.* Go through the answer choices, and there's *patience* at **C**.

Note that *abruptness* is a trap waiting to get speedy test-takers who miss the twist in the sentence that makes the blank describe the opposite of abrupt, annoying behavior.

3. B One-Blank/One-Way *Medium*

The sentence contains no switch and does not make a comparison over time: It's one-way. The blank, which describes *The Waste Land,* will agree with the information in the rest of the sentence, which describes the poem as full of "many levels of language" that are "jumbled jarringly together." So, the blank must read something like "mixture." The answer choices contain two answers that fit the bill: *symphony* and *hodgepodge.* To decide between these two, you need to take a second look at that word *jarringly.* A symphony is a mixture of voices and instruments, but it's beautiful and smooth, not jarring. A *hodgepodge* is a somewhat messier mixture, and it better fits the description of the poem as jarring.

4. D One-Blank/One-Way *Medium*

The sentence contains no switch or comparison over time. That means it's one-way. The word that fills in the blank has to fit with the idea that Shakespeare's plays are *not* only serious, high-minded, and tragic. So, the blank word must say that the plays are filled with unserious, silly, funny stuff. The word that fits this idea of silliness is *buffoonery.*

5. A Two-Blank/One-Way *Medium*

The sentence contains no switch and no comparison over time: it's one-way. The two halves of the sentence must match, either positive to positive or negative to negative. Since no one is going to install new metal detectors to make airport security *worse,* the first word must be positive. That cuts out *belittle* as a possible answer. You can also cut *corroborate .. demoralized by* and *cultivate .. restrained by,* because while first choice is positive, the second makes the last half of the sentence distinctly negative. That leaves *enhance .. accompanied by* and *therapy .. cooperating* with. The first of those two choices is much better, because you can't really *therapy* airport security, but you can *enhance* it.

6. D Two-Blank/Two-Way *Difficult*

The switch *though* lets you know right away that this is a two-way sentence. You need to find words that establish a contrast between what Byron intended to convey about prison life in his poem and his actual experience. The first blank describes the "reality of life behind bars." A life behind bars is not likely to be pleasant, so you're looking for a negative word: You can cut out *luxurious..pampered*, because life behind bars will not be luxurious. The second blank describes Byron's aristocratic life and must contrast with the unpleasant life behind bars. So, you're looking for a positive word like *pleasant*. That lets you cut **A**, **B**, and **C**, leaving *harsh..privileged*, which gives you just the *negative..positive* contrast you're looking for.

Long Reading Passage (Cities)

7. A   Technique   *Easy*

The first line of passage 1 is a question asked not to get an answer but to create interest and momentum in an essay. That's the very definition of a rhetorical question, which is the right answer.

8. A   Implied Information   *Medium*

As Thoreau describes it in this passage, the problem with civilized life is that man often ends up outside of himself, lost in thought and concentrating on the tasks of the day. The benefit of being in the woods is that a man can become reintegrated into the surrounding world by becoming more fully conscious of it. **A** best fits with this idea of reintegration.

9. D   Words in Context   *Easy*

Tired is the most common meaning of *exhausted*, but this is a words-in-context question, and the context can't be overlooked. Thoreau states that he has been walking on the paths near his home for many years, but he still finds new walks and vistas. This clues you in to what the meaning of exhausted could be. If he has been walking on the paths for many years, you might expect that he would have taken all the walks, but his comments make it clear that he hasn't taken, or *completed*, every possible walk.

10. E   Implied Information   *Medium*

This is a bit of a trick question. The final paragraph actually indicates that Thoreau doesn't think much of people at all. He is most happy when the things of mankind—politics, church, state, trade, agriculture, industry—seem small and far away. In other words, what he most values in human beings is *their absence*.

11. A   Attitude or Tone   *Medium*

A number of these answer choices are half right. You, of course, need one that's entirely right. He is excited but not relieved (throw out **D**), and optimistic but not wry (see ya **E**). Answers **B** and (**C**) don't really capture Whitman's excited tone at all. But **A**, yeah, **A** does the trick.

12. E   Words-in-Context   *Difficult*

This is a fairly difficult question, particularly since Whitman, the author of the passage, uses *oceanic* in an obscure and idiosyncratic way. The key to answering this question is, of course, to look at the context. The two adjectives that accompany the word oceanic are *great* and *seething*, suggesting something that is large and in tumult (like an ocean, which is huge and unchanging, yet constantly moved by waves). So, the correct answer is **E**.

13. **B**   Implied Information   *Easy*

In passage 2, Whitman refers at different times to the "population," the "crowds," the "human qualities," of New York in particular and of cities in general. In other words, Whitman is moved and excited by the cities' *inhabitants*.

14. **A**   Implied Information   *Medium*

In the specified lines, Whitman says, "Today, defiant of cynics and pessimists, and with a full knowledge of all their arguments and exceptions...." Whitman understands that not everyone agrees with his high opinion of cities and the people in them. He expects disagreement.

15. **E**   Relating Two Passages   *Medium*

This question first requires that you decide whether Whitman thinks politics are a good thing or not. Whitman is clearly excited by cities and thinks of them as physical democracies. So, if he loves cities and thinks of cities as democracies, then his feelings about politics, and especially American politics, must be equally positive. You can eliminate the answers that have him either agreeing with or indifferent to Thoreau's claim. The two remaining answers offer a choice of either the city or rural areas as a political ideal for Whitman. Choosing between these two should be easy; he admires the city as "the most direct proof yet of successful Democracy," so the correct answer must be **E**.

16. **B**   Relating Two Passages   *Difficult*

Thoreau's passage 1 is all about how the woods can return a man to his senses, free his deadened spirits, in essence, give a man back his soul. So, Thoreau would agree with Whitman that an individual's environment can have a huge influence on the state of that individual's soul. However, Thoreau sees the city and human society as the cause of sickness in a person's soul, not as a medicine. Thoreau loves the woods, not the city.

17. **C**   Relating Two Passages   *Medium*

You can go through these answer choices crossing out the ones that do not accurately describe Thoreau, and then see what's left to choose from. Thoreau states a preference for the woods and solitary life, and seems happy only when politics, people, and cities are far away. So throw out **A**, **B**, and **D**. The remaining two choices describe Whitman as interested in either people or emotions. While Whitman is himself quite emotional, his passage is focused entirely on the people of New York, so **C** is the best answer.

18. **A**   Relating Two Passages   *Difficult*

Although the two passages make very different arguments and come to almost opposite conclusions, both share a very basic core idea. Each passage focuses on the effect of environment and surroundings on an individual. Thoreau chooses the forest and Whitman the city, but each is examining the effect of a particular place on men.

19. **D**   Relating Two Passages   *Difficult*

This question requires that you have a good sense of the second passage as a whole. Whitman is marked by his enthusiasm and his curiosity about human institutions. Therefore, of these alternatives, Whitman would most likely seek out rural settlements to meet the people who live there

SECTION 8

1. **C**   Geometry: Coordinate Geometry   *Easy*

Parallel lines have equal slopes. The formula for a line is $y = mx + b$, where m is the slope. The slope of $f(x) = 2x + 7$ is therefore 2. So k must also equal 2.

2. **E**   Numbers and Operations: Ratios   *Easy*

The question gives you a ratio that is part:part:part. But in order to solve the problem, you need to know how many green candies there would be in a bag with a *total* of 65 candies in it. To make this calculation, you first have to turn that part:part:part ratio into a part:whole ratio. Since, for every three green candies in the bag there are 4 red ones and 6 blue ones, $\frac{3}{13}$ of the candies are green. To find the total number of green candies in a bag that contains 65 candies, calculate $\frac{3}{13} \times 65 = 15$.

3. **D**   Data Analysis Statistics Probability: Statistical Analysis   *Easy*

To answer this question, you *could* figure out the value of each number in the set, multiply each by 2, and then recalculate the mean. But don't waste your time. Instead, learn this key fact: When you double the value of every member of a set of numbers, the mean of that set will double as well. So, since the mean was 200, it must now be 400.

4. **D**   Algebra: Variation   *Easy*

For variation questions like this one, assign simple values to the variables and then work out the math to see how the change stated in the question affects the result. If $k = 1$, then $z = \frac{1}{2}$, and $y = \frac{1}{4}$. If $k = 2$, then $z = 1$ and $y = 1$. So, y will quadruple if k doubles.

5. **B**   Algebra: Functions   *Easy*

The question is a basic substitution problem involving functions. It defines $f(x)$ and then asks you to calculate $f(12)$. Just plug 12 in for x in the function and do the math:
$f(12) = \frac{12}{\sqrt{12-3}} = \frac{12}{\sqrt{9}} = \frac{12}{3} = 4$.

6. **A**   Data Analysis Statistics Probability: Graphs, Charts, and Tables   *Easy*

There are only three 10-year periods in which the production of Product X decreased at all: 1950–1960, 1970–1980, and 1990–2000, so you can immediately eliminate **B** and **D**. Now you just have to calculate which of the three 10-year periods saw the greatest percentage decrease. Note that there's a difference between total decrease and percentage decrease. The percentage decrease is calculated by taking the decrease in production and dividing it by the initial production. So, for the 10-year period from 1950–1960, production dropped from 15,000 units to 5,000 units. The percentage decrease is therefore $\frac{15000 - 5000}{15000} = \frac{10000}{15000} = 0.67$, or 67%. While the total decrease in dollars for the period of 1970–1980 was also 10,000, the percentage decrease was smaller: $\frac{20000 - 10000}{20000} = \frac{10000}{20000} = 0.5$, or 50%. The percentage decrease for 1990–2000 was even smaller, just 33%, so 1950–1960 is the answer.

7.   **D**   Geometry: Coordinate Geometry   *Medium*

This distance formula question is straightforward. To solve it, plug the points into the distance formula: $d = \sqrt{(x_2 - x_1)^2 + (y_2 - y_1)^2} = \sqrt{(7 - (-1))^2 + (-14 - 6)^2}$. Now work out the math, round it to the nearest hundredth, and you're set: $d = \sqrt{8^2 + 20^2} = \sqrt{464} = 21.54$.

8.   **C**   Algebra: Inequalities   *Medium*

Since absolute value eliminates negative signs, you have to make sure that you take into account negative values of x. You can do exactly that by taking the absolute value out of the inequality by "splitting" the equation: Set the expression against both the positive and negative of the number on the other side of the inequality. In this question, take the $\frac{x}{4} + 4$ and set it against both 8 and –8 (and remember to turn around that inequality when you're dealing with the negative number). Okay, so $\frac{x}{4} + 4 < 8$ and $\frac{x}{4} + 4 > -8$. First, work out $\frac{x}{4} + 4 < 8$. Subtract 4 from both sides to get $\frac{x}{4} < 4$, then multiply each side by 4 to get x < 16. Now, for $\frac{x}{4} + 4 > -8$. Subtract 4 from each side, $\frac{x}{4} > -12$, then multiply by 4: $x > -48$. So x has to be larger than –48 and smaller than 16.

9.   **D**   Algebra: Functions   *Difficult*

Before you can even begin to think about what the graph of $f(g(x))$ looks like, you have to figure out what the function $f(g(x))$ looks like. As with all compound functions, plug $g(x)$ into $f(x)$ and then work it out: $f(g(x)) = (1 - x)^2 - 1 + 2x = (1 - x)(1 - x) - 1 + 2x$. You're probably not used to using FOIL on binomials that have the variable second, but just follow the standard First Outside, Inside Last pattern, and you'll see that $f(g(x))1 = 1 - 2x + x^2 - 1 + 2x = x^2$. So, after all that, $f(g(x)) = x^2$, which means that the graph of the function looks like a parabola with its vertex at the origin and its bowl facing up, just like the graph in answer **C**.

10.   **E**   Algebra: Absolute Value and Exponents   *Difficult*

Since $x = y$, you can rewrite the left side of the equation as $(2x)^2$. Distribute out that exponent, and you get $4x^2$, so $4x^2 = ax^2$, which means that $a = 4$.

11.   **C**   Geometry: Polygons   *Medium*

Diagonals cut squares into two congruent 45-45-90 triangles. Since you already know that the long side of each of these triangles is $\sqrt{2}$, you can use the handy 45-45-90 side length ratio to figure out the other two sides. The ratio is 1: 1: $\sqrt{2}$, so the side lengths of the triangles in this problem are 1. Don't go picking **E** as your answer, though: that's a trap. You have to find the combined area of the shaded regions. Each square has an area of 1 (since $1 \times 1 = 1$). The diagonals split those squares in half, so each triangle is equal to 0.5, and the entire shaded area is 1.5.

12. **E** Algebra: Domain and Range   *Medium*

Plug the equation into your graphing calculator and you'll see that in the domain $-1 \le x \le 3$, the parabola reaches its highest point at $x = -1$ and its lowest point at $x = 2$. Plug -1 into the equation: $h(x) = 2 + (x - 2)^2 = 2 + (-1 - 2)^2 = 11$. Plug 2 into the equation: $h(x) = 2 + (x - 2)^2 = 2 + (2 - 2)^2 = 2$. So, the range of $h(x)$ for the given domain is $2 \le h(x) \le 11$.

13. **D** Numbers and Operations: Percents   *Difficult*

The best way to solve this problem is to calculate how much the class made off of each separate group of students and then add up the results. The senior-senior couples make up 40% of the class of 300: $40\% \times 300 = 120$ people. But here's the first trick of the question: Since couples pay *per couple* rather than per person, 60 couples bought their tickets to the prom for $60 per couple, which adds up to $60 \times \$60 = \$3600$. There were also $40\% \times 300 = 120$ students who took dates from outside the class. For those students and their dates to attend prom, they had to purchase one $40 ticket and one $35 ticket, a total of $75. So, there were 120 couples who paid $75 for their tickets, for a total of $120 \times \$75 = \$9000$. Finally, 10% of the class came to the prom by themselves, meaning that 30 people purchased individual tickets. Their tickets generated $30 \times \$35 = \$1050$. All these amounts added together come to $13,650.

14. **A** Geometry: Coordinate Geometry   *Difficult*

Don't be horrified that this problem asks you about the slope of a function but doesn't even tell you what the function is! It doesn't matter. All you need to know is that the negative exponent creates an inverse function and that the slope of two inverse linear functions are reciprocals of each other. The reciprocal of $-\frac{1}{3}$ is -3, so **A** is the correct answer.

15. **C** Geometry: Circles   *Difficult*

To solve this problem, you have to first remember the fact that two radii extended to the endpoints of a chord form an isosceles triangle. Then you have to know that the heights of these two triangles equals the distance between them.

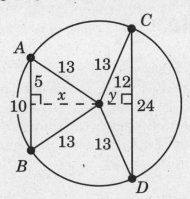

Since you're dealing with isosceles triangles, these heights are easy to figure out: They're perpendicular bisectors of their respective triangle bases. You're now dealing with one right triangle that has sides of length 5, x, and 13, and another with sides 12, 13, and y. If you know your Pythagorean triples (learn them!), you'll see that both triangles belong to the triple 5, 12, 13, so the heights of the two triangles are 5 and 12 and the distance between chords AB and CD is 17. You can still get the answer using the plain old Pythagorean formula, but it will take a little longer.

16.   **D**   Numbers and Operations: Exponents   *Difficult*

To solve this problem you have to know how negative exponents work. To be even more specific, you have to know that $x^{-1} = \dfrac{1}{x}$. If you know that, the rest is simplifying. First, you can divide 8 out from both sides of the equation:

$$x^{-1}y^3 = 8y^2$$

Then you can substitute for x^{-1} to get:

$$\frac{1}{x}$$

$$\frac{y^3}{x} = 8y^2$$

Divide y^2 out from both sides:

$$\frac{y}{x} = 8$$

The question asks you to figure out the value of y^{-1}, so the first thing you have to do is isolate that y:

$$y = 8x$$

Then solve for y^{-1}:

$$y^{-1} = \frac{1}{8x}$$

SECTION 9

Improving Sentences

1.   **D**   Subject-VerbAgreement   *Easy*

The subject of this sentence, *white light*, is a singular noun that requires a singular verb. The sentence has a plural verb, however, and therein lies the error: *contain* should be *contains*. That means you can cut any answer choice with contain. So **A** and **E** are out. **B** and **C** use the incorrect verb form *is containing*. Only **D** deliver the singular verb the sentence needs.

2.   **C**   Idioms   *Easy*

This sentence requires you to know the idiom *goes by the name of*. The original sentence uses *in* instead of *of* (so cut **A**), but choice **C** corrects the problem. The other choices either use incorrect vocabulary or faulty verb tenses.

3. **C** Misplaced Modifiers   *Easy*

As it's written, this sentence describes *nests* that don't fly south for the winter. Nests never fly anywhere. When you see sentences that imply bizarre situations like this one, that's usually a strong tipoff that you're up against a misplaced modifier. Here you need to put the subject of the sentence (*some species*) in the right place, the spot currently occupied by those flying *nests*. The only answer choice that swaps *species* with *nests* is **C**, and that's your answer.

4. **E** Run-Ons   *Easy*

This sentence runs a bunch of ideas together with no conjunction. It's also redundant and wordy. The best answer will clean up the run-on problem and clear up exactly what the sentence is trying to convey: that Seamus Heaney is from Ireland and that he went back there to give a speech after winning the Nobel Prize. **A** is definitely out since the original sentence reads like a train wreck. **D** uses the incorrect tense (*had returned*). **C** uses a clunky possessive phrase (*the native country of his*) to convey that Heaney is Irish. **B** is close, but it uses *which* with improper punctuation. That leaves **E**, the correct answer.

5. **E** Tenses   *Easy*

The first and second clauses of this sentence must have the same tense. Right now the first clause is in the present tense; the second is in the past. You can cut **A**, **B**, and **C** since they all contain past tense verbs. **D** and **E** are similar, but **E** gets the order of *he* and *often* correct, so it's the better choice.

6. **D** Parallelism   *Medium*

Two phrases in this sentence don't match up: *with a good sense of balance* and *not afraid of heights*. **A**, **B**, and **E** all suffer from this same problem, actually, so you should cut them. **C** attempts to make things parallel, but in an awkward incorrect way (by using *having*). Only **D** really sets things straight by aligning *with a good sense of balance* with its parallel match *without a fear of heights*.

7. **B** Tenses   *Medium*

This sentence has mismatched tenses in several places. First, it's wrong to use the past tense *had* in the final clause when the previous clauses are in the present. **E** makes the same mistake, but in different places: it puts the past in the first clause, the present in the last clause. **C** has a misplaced modifier, which makes the composers sound like they're in the style of Mozart's opera. **D** introduces a new unnecessary tense (*have set*) and uses the phrase *having the style* to mean in the style. **B** gets the tense and the phrase *in the style of* right on, and it's the correct answer.

8. **A** No Error   *Medium*

9. **C** Idioms   *Medium*

To answer this question correctly, you must be familiar with the idiomatic expression *with the intention of*. Knowing that idiom makes spotting the error in this sentence a breeze. Answer choices **B**, **D**, and **E** come close, but none of those choices contains the "with...of" construction necessary to complete the idiomatic phrase *with the intention of*. Only **C** does the job.

10. C   Run-Ons   *Medium*

This sentence reads like two sentences that crashed into one another. The challenge is finding the answer choice that best solves the problem. A few of the answer choices appear to do the trick at first glance, but **C** does the best job. The phrase *by neglecting* links the two disjointed parts of the sentence and makes the sentence make sense. A phrase such as *because he was neglecting* could have worked too, but that choice isn't available. **D** comes close, but the verb *to be* has no place in that phrase and makes **D** not the best choice. The other two choices, *in the neglect of* and *with the reason that he* was neglecting are not grammatically correct.

11. B   Tenses   *Medium*

The key to answering this question is to notice that its action happened in the past. Once you realize that, you can eliminate **A** and **E** as possible choices. Now think about the critics complaints: they thought *Rites of Spring* was terrible and felt that it *should* have been revised. Only answer **B** catches this sense of *should*.

12. C   Misplaced Modifiers   *Medium*

Here the misplaced modifier makes the people who use the Internet sound like they're the database. The people are not the database—the Internet is. That means the sentence must be reorganized to clear up the misplaced modifier. **E** solves the misplaced modifier problem, but the separation of the Internet and its definition (*the most sprawling…*) introduces unnecessary ambiguity. So **A** and **E** are now out. **D** and **B** address the misplaced modifier problem, but they do so using the passive voice. Only **C** solves the misplaced modifier problem without using the passive voice.

13. B   Misplaced Modifiers   *Difficult*

It's easy to overlook the problem here, so pay very close attention when you reread this sentence. The subject of the first clause is *nation*, so the subject of the clause after the comma should be a nation, not that nation's leadership. In other words, there's a misplaced modifier on the loose. **D** and **E** seem to make the nation of Great Britain the subject of the clause after the comma, but they actually just shroud leadership behind a possessive Great Britain. So **D** and **E** are out. **C** clearly makes leadership the subject, not the nation of Great Britain. Only answer choice **B** puts the nation of Great Britain in its proper place within the sentence, which fixes the misplaced modifier problem and makes the sentence make sense.

14. A   No Error   *Difficult*

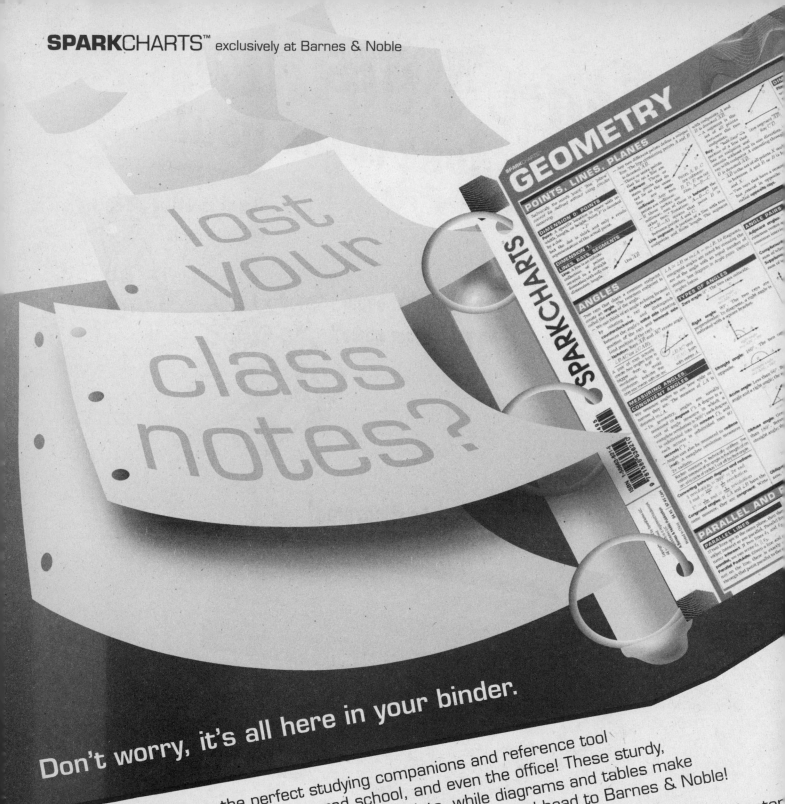